BUSINESS MATH Practical Applications

SECOND EDITION

Cheryl Cleaves
Margie Hobbs
Paul Dudenhefer

State Technical Institute at Memphis

PRENTICE HALL, *Englewood Cliffs, New Jersey* 07632

Library of Congress Cataloging-in-Publication Data

Cleaves, Cheryl S.
Business math : practical applications / Cheryl Cleaves, Margie Hobbs, Paul Dudenhefer.—2nd ed.
p. cm.
ISBN 0-13-104944-5 :
1. Business mathematics. I. Hobbs, Margie J. II. Dudenhefer, Paul. III. Title.
HF5691.C53 1990
650'.01'513--dc20 89-37551
CIP

Editorial/production supervision: *Eleanor Ode Walter*
Interior design and page layout: *Andy Zutis*
Cover design: *Bruce Kenselaar*
Manufacturing buyers: *Ed O'Dougherty, Mary Ann Gloriande*
Photo research: *Ilene Cherna*
Development editors: *Karen Dean, Susanna Lesan*

Cover photograph: Tom Tracy/The Stock Shop

Chapter opening photograph credits:

Chapter 1 Randy Matusow
Chapter 2 IBM
Chapter 3 Barbara Alper/Stock, Boston
Chapter 4 George Gardner/The Image Works
Chapter 5 Mohawk Data Sciences Corp.
Chapter 6 Hewlett Packard
Chapter 7 Alvis Upitis/The Image Bank
Chapter 8 Dan McCoy/Rainbow
Chapter 9 Texas Instruments
Chapter 11 Michael Grecco/Stock, Boston
Chapter 12 Jon Feingersh/Stock, Boston
Chapter 13 Charles Feil/Stock, Boston
Chapter 14 Sepp Seitz/Woodfin Camp & Associates
Chapter 15 Larry Dale Gordon/The Image Bank
Chapter 16 George Hall/Woodfin Camp & Associates
Chapter 17 Arlene Collins/Monkmeyer Press
Chapter 18 Nubar Alexanian/Woodfin Camp & Associates
Chapter 19 IBM

Chapter 14 Real World Application Box:
Norand Data Systems; MSI Data Corp.; NCR.

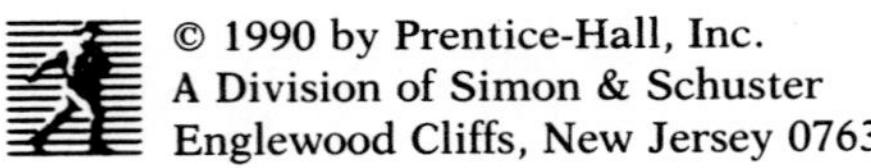

Printed in the United States of America
10 9 8 7 6 5 4 3

ISBN 0-13-104944-5

Prentice-Hall International (UK) Limited, *London*
Prentice-Hall of Australia Pty. Limited, *Sydney*
Prentice-Hall Canada, Inc., *Toronto*
Prentice-Hall Hispanoamericana, S.A., *Mexico*
Prentice-Hall of India Private Limited, *New Delhi*
Prentice-Hall of Japan, Inc., *Tokyo*
Simon & Schuster Asia Pte. Ltd., *Singapore*
Editora Prentice-Hall do Brasil, Ltda., *Rio de Janeiro*

Contents

Preface

To the Student

In almost any career you pursue, the business math you learn in this book will serve you well and help you get ahead. Anyone can learn to deal with a certain amount of math, even those who have avoided the formal study of mathematics. We have given much thought to the best way to teach business math. If you will follow the course of the book as we have laid it out, making use of the special features we have put in the text, you will get the most out of this book and out of this course. The following features are meant to help you learn business math procedures.

Learning Objectives. The chapter begins with a statement of learning objectives, which lay out for you what you should look for and learn in that chapter. If you read and think about these before you begin the chapter, you will know what to look for as you go through the chapter.

Key Terms Defined in the Margins. Part of learning business math is learning the basic vocabulary of business. This vocabulary is introduced in the text, and in the margin the terms are repeated with definitions. Each key term is **boldfaced** in the index. The terms in the margin offer you a good opportunity to review for a test.

Self-Checks. These short quizzes appear throughout the chapter; they are a signal to you to check yourself to make sure that you understand what you have just read or worked out before you go on to the next topic. The solutions are at the end of each chapter, so that you can get immediate feedback on whether you have understood the material.

Section Reviews. These are exercises that appear at the end of each of the major sections of the chapter (often two or three times a chapter). Your instructor may assign certain of these exercises as homework, or you may want to do them on your own to polish the skills you have learned in the section. Answers to odd-numbered exercises appear at the end of the book.

Step-by-Step Boxes. These boxes appear throughout the text to help introduce a new procedure. In order to make these procedures as clear as possible, we break them down for you into step-by-step instructions. Each box is then followed by an example.

Calculator Sequences and Calculator Solution Boxes. The use of a calculator is basic in all types of math, and especially business math, which is why we provided you with a calculator to go with this book. In most chapters we have a calculator solution box that deals with a key procedure from that chapter. The box shows how to analyze the procedure and set up a problem for a calculator solution, then shows the keystrokes involved in the solution. Calculator sequences showing keystrokes are also provided throughout the chapter as part of the examples.

Tips and Traps Boxes. These boxes point up helpful hints or pitfalls involved in business math procedures. Often, looking at the wrong and right way of doing something can save you from a costly or time-consuming error down the line. We do not always have to learn from our own mistakes—sometimes we can learn from other people's experience and not make the same mistakes ourselves.

Real World Application Boxes. Just when you were wondering what all this has to do with the real world, along comes a Real World Application box to tell you! These boxes present a problem from the business world and show how the procedures learned in the chapter are used to solve the problem. Examples include banking, apartment rental, excise taxes and the hotel business, buying property and paying taxes on it, figuring tips for food service, and many more. The boxes also contain extra exercises if you want to pursue the subject further and try your skills.

Summary Chart. At the end of the chapter there is a handy summary, in the form of a chart. This chart summarizes the Step-by-Step boxes from that chapter, with new examples. The chart also contains the page numbers where each topic is covered in the chapter, so you can go back and check it if you have questions. This chart is an excellent tool to use to review a chapter.

Chapter Review Exercises. These are exercises that occur at the end of the chapter and review all of the procedures and topics covered in the chapter. These exercises may be assigned by your instructor as homework, or you may want to work them on your own for extra practice. The answers to odd-numbered exercises are at the end of the book.

Trial Test. Take this to test yourself before you face the real one in class. Again, answers to odd-numbered exercises appear at the end of the book; your professor has the worked-out solutions to the entire test.

If you use all of the features in this book, you will be learning business math in a most efficient and effective way. But we also have some supplements besides the text that will help you even more.

Calculator. The use of a calculator is basic in all types of math, especially business math, which is why we have provided a calculator for your textbook. Instructions for using this calculator are on the back inside cover of your book. Calculator solutions to examples appear throughout the book.

Student Solutions Manual with Review Problems. This manual can be purchased at your bookstore. It will give you extra "learning insurance" to help you master this course. The manual contains worked-out solutions to the odd-numbered exercises in the section reviews, chapter review, and trial test from each chapter of the text. (Answers to these exercises appear in the back of your text, but here in the manual you can study the full worked-out solutions.) For additional practice, there is also a whole new set of exercises to parallel the section and chapter reviews in your text. These new exercises have worked-out solutions at the end of the book.

How to Study Business Math. Your professor can get free copies of this booklet, which goes over the various learning techniques you can use in class and in preparation for class to make learning business math much more efficient.

Student Tutorial Software. This unique learning program is both interactive and diagnostic. Whether students are reviewing, practicing, or taking a quiz, all their responses are analyzed and incorrect ones elicit explanations and page references for further study. Further, all problems have detailed step-by-step solutions available! The program is user-friendly and designed both for students to use independently for self-review of any unit and for instructors to give quizzes, chapter tests, midterms, or finals.

Business Simulation Practice Set. This practice set covers three months of business transactions of Matthew Hardware and Appliances. In the practice set you perform many of the transactions yourself, such as buying merchandise, paying the payroll, and pricing the merchandise. It is a good way to put into practice the procedures you have learned in the text.

Stock Market and Investment Practice Set. This practice set gives basic information on how to make decisions about investing money.

To the Instructor

We have tried to provide a text that your students will enjoy using and that you will find easy and helpful to teach from. In addition to the text, we have provided a complete supplements package to make your teaching life easier.

The most important supplement is the Annotated Instructor's Edition, which contains the complete student text with worked-out solutions to all exercises as well as teaching aids in the margins and lecture notes with points to stress in the front of the book. The rest of the supplements are described in full in the Annotated Instructor's Edition; for your convenience a short list is given here:

• Annotated Instructor's Edition • Test Item File and Computerized Test Item File • Testing Resource Library • Transparency Acetates • Overhead Calculator • Classroom Presentation Software • Lotus 1-2-3®/Twin™ Templates for Selected Exercises • Lecture Outlines on Disk and Hard Copy • Student Solutions Manual with Review Problems • Student Tutorial Software • How to Study Math Booklet • Numbering Systems and Programming in BASIC Booklet • Business Simulation Practice Set • Stock Market and Investment Practice Set • Student Notebook for Classroom Presentation Software

Acknowledgments

Comments and suggestions from a broad cross-section of business math instructors are always crucial in a project of this size, and we thank our reviewers for their interest and help. They were invaluable in pointing out any inaccuracies or errors that slipped in and in making valuable suggestions in various stages of the manuscript.

Camille Anthony, Bay State Junior College
Bernadette Antkoviak, Harrisburg Area Community College
Fay Armstrong, Houston Community College
Corine Baker, S. Seattle Community College
Jerome Baness, Illinois Valley Community College
Rex Bishop, Charles County Community College
Marg Y. Blyth, Detroit College of Business
James Carey, Onondaga Community College
Charles Cheetham, County College of Morris
Janet Ciccarelli, Herkimer County Community College
Dick Clark, Portland Community College
Rita Cross, Northland Community College
John Cuniffe, Northland Pioneer College
James F. Dowis, Des Moines Area Community College
Norm Dreisen, Essex Community College
William L. Drezdzon, Oakton Community College
Nell Edmundson, Miami Dade Community College
Margaret Ferguson, Houston Community College
Clark Ford, Middle Tennessee State University
Joseph F. Gallo, Cuyahoga Community College District
Frank Goulard, Portland Community College
Cecil Green, Riverside Community College
Stephen Griffin, Tarrant County Junior College
Jackie Hedgpeth, Antelope Valley College
Joseph Hinsburg, Pima County Community College
Kanta K. Idnani, Phillips College
Barbara Jackson, Skagit Valley College
Frederick Janke, Tompkins-Cortland Community College
John Johnson, Seattle Central Community College
Carolyn Karnes, Macomb Community College
Kenneth Ketelhohn, Milwaukee Area Technical College
Ed Laughbaum, Columbus State Community College
S. Lee, Heald Business College
Nolan Lickey, Westark Community College
Jane Loprest, Bucks County Community College
D. Maas, Lansing Community College
Lynn Mack, Piedmont Technical College
Paul Martin, Aims Community College
Roberta Miller, Indian River Community College
Linda Mogren, DeKalb Technical Institute
Mary Pretti, State Technical Institute at Memphis
Dave Randall, Oakland Community College
Joan Ryan, Lane Community College
Lona P. Scala, Roberts-Walsh Business School
Gerald W. Shields, Austin Community College
Beverly Sisk, Gwinnett Technical Institute
Debiruth Stanford, DeVry Institute of Technology
Herbert Stein, Merritt College
Alice Steljes, Illinois Valley Community College
Louise Stevens, Golden West College
Kitty Tabers, Oakton Community College
Keith Wilson, Oklahoma City Community College
Chuck Wiseman, Oakland Community College

We also want to thank Roberta Lewis, who contributed to the Stocks and Bonds chapter of the text; Lynn Mack, who helped write the Annotated Instructor's Edition margin notes; and Shirley Lawrence, who contributed Real World Application boxes and wrote the lecture outlines for the Annotated Instructor's Edition.

Accuracy is always a concern in mathematics, and we were fortunate to have the help of several colleagues who worked with us to produce the level of accuracy needed in a college textbook. The reviewers mentioned above were of course our first source of corrections and queries. We also had the help of Elizabeth Bliss of Trident Technical College, who checked every example, exercise, trial test, and worked-out solution in the text, the Student Solutions Manual, and the Annotated Instructor's Edition.

The manuscripts of the text and the Test Item File were also class-tested by Kathleen Murphrey of San Antonio College and Mike Armstrong of Highline Community College, so that any remaining errors found in the class setting could be corrected.

We also reviewed all of this work and then rechecked it in all stages of production. Further, we looked at every page of every supplement to ensure the most accurate package that we could produce. Finally, the first printing of the text was class tested in its entirety at several schools. The results of these extensive efforts are before you: this is the fully checked and corrected second printing.

The staff at Prentice Hall has been overwhelmingly supportive of this project. Although the list of persons working on this text and supplements package is extensive, we would like to single out a few key persons. We acknowledge first Robert Kern, our acquisitions editor, for his enthusiasm for the project and his careful attention to the text and its supplements as they developed. We thank Karen Dean and Susanna Lesan, who assisted in the development of the original manuscript, for their expert contributions. Eleanor Walter, the production editor, did an excellent job of keeping us on schedule and ensuring that the text would meet her high standards. Linda Thompson, the copy editor, is a former math teacher, and her work was outstanding in helping us maintain accuracy and consistency. Jenny Sheehan, the supplements editor, ably coordinated the extensive supplements package that accompanies the text. Sophie Papanikolaou, managing editor of supplements production, led her team of editors in the difficult task of getting the supplements out on schedule. Michele Jay, marketing manager, coordinated the massive marketing and sales effort for the project. Andy Zutis and Sue Behnke provided the book design and page layout, and Rita Ropes proofread the galley and page proofs.

We appreciate the contribution of those who provided technical information on business procedures and forms, especially Betty Johnson. We also acknowledge the reviewers and users of the first edition, who made comments and suggestions for improvement.

Finally, we express our deepest gratitude to our families: Charles Cleaves; Allen and Holly Hobbs; Gaynell, Paul, Paulette, David, and Diane Dudenhefer. Their support and encouragement were vital to the completion of this project.

Cheryl Cleaves
Margie Hobbs
Paul Dudenhefer

BUSINESS MATH

Whole Numbers 1

Learning Objectives

1. Read and round whole numbers to a specified place or digit. (pp. 3–6)
2. Add and subtract whole numbers. (pp. 7–9)
3. Estimate and check sums and differences. (pp. 7–9)
4. Multiply and divide whole numbers. (pp. 13–18)
5. Estimate and check products and quotients. (pp. 13–18)

The business world runs on numbers and calculations. We see and use numbers every day in school, at the store, at work, even in the video arcade. We go to the store that advertises the sale, take out a CD at the bank with the highest interest rates, apply for mortgages at the bank with the best terms, and grumble about lower take-home pay when social security withholding goes up.

This course will prepare you to enter the business world with the mathematical survival tools needed to blaze a successful career path. The chapters on business topics build on your knowledge of basic mathematics, so it is important to begin the course with a review of the basic mathematics skills you will need in the chapters to come.

In most businesses, arithmetic computations are done on a machine. Even so, the businessperson needs a thorough understanding of basic mathematics in order to make the best use of a calculator. A machine will only do what we tell it to do. Pressing a wrong key or performing the wrong operations on a calculator will result in an incorrect answer. If you understand the mathematics and know how to make reasonable estimates, you can catch and correct these errors.

Reading and Rounding Whole Numbers

Reading Numbers

In many business situations, it is necessary to say or write the name of a number in words. Telephone conversations and face-to-face meetings often involve discussion of quantities of goods or dollar amounts. When you write a check, you enter the amount of the check not only as a number but also as a word name. In most formal business contracts, amounts of money are usually written as both numbers and words in order to state the terms as clearly as possible.

Our number system is called the decimal number system, and it is made up of ten digits:

0, 1, 2, 3, 4, 5, 6, 7, 8, 9

Trillions			Billions			Millions			Thousands			Units		
Hundred trillions (100,000,000,000,000)	Ten trillions (10,000,000,000,000)	Trillions (1,000,000,000,000)	Hundred billions (100,000,000,000)	Ten billions (10,000,000,000)	Billions (1,000,000,000)	Hundred millions (100,000,000)	Ten millions (10,000,000)	Millions (1,000,000)	Hundred thousands (100,000)	Ten thousands (10,000)	Thousands (1,000)	Hundreds (100)	Tens (10)	Ones (1)
3	8	1	3	4	5	2	8	7	3	6	9	0	2	1

Figure 1-1 Place-Value Chart for Whole Numbers

place-value system: a system in which a digit has a value according to its place, or position, in a number.

We use these digits in a **place-value system,** which gives a digit a value according to its place, or position, in a number. Let's use the number 381,345,287,369,021 as an example. Figure 1-1 shows the value of each place up through trillions. Note that the value of each place is *ten* times the value place to the right.

When you read a number, you name the digits and the groups, from left to right, without using the word *and.* The exact steps for reading a number are given in the procedure box. Throughout this book, procedure boxes give

Real World Application

Many times very large whole numbers cannot be shown on a graph because of the space these numbers require. In the graph below, the numbers used on the vertical axis appear to show rather small amounts for sales of security systems. Actually, the numbers give the amounts in millions of dollars, as indicated on the graph. The \$600 is really $\$600 \times 1{,}000{,}000 = \$600{,}000{,}000$, which is read six hundred million dollars. Can you see how much more space would be required for a number this large to be placed on the graph?

Application Questions

1. What is the actual estimated amount of sales in 1989? How is this number read?

2. Find the actual estimated amount of sales in 1987.

3. What is the actual value of 2.5 million dollars?

By Shelley Arps, USA TODAY

you a clear, simple, step-by-step summary of how to perform operations or solve problems. A procedure box is followed by an example, which shows how to apply the ideas in the box.

Step by Step

Reading a Whole Number

Step 1. Beginning at the right end of the number, use commas to separate the number into groups of 3 digits.

Step 2. Name the groups (*units, thousands, millions,* and so on).

Step 3. Starting at the left end of the number, read the numerals in each group and indicate the group name.
- **a.** If a group has all zeros, it does not have to be read.
- **b.** The group name *units* does not have to be read.

EXAMPLE 1

Read the number 3007047203.

3,007,047,203	Start at the right end of the number and use commas to separate the number into groups of 3 digits.
billions, millions, thousands, units	Name the groups.
three billion, seven million, forty-seven thousand, two hundred three.	Read the numbers and the name for each group of digits.

Rounding Numbers

Most business transactions are based on precise and accurate calculations done on a calculator or computer. In the everyday business world, however, it is often necessary to make a quick estimate of some quantity or total. In such situations, you **round** numbers to check a calculation or to find an approximate answer to a question. Finding approximate answers can help make quick decisions and let us detect possible errors in precise calculations. You usually round a number to a specified place or to the first or second digit from the left in a number, following the rules given in the procedure box.

round, rounding: a way to find an estimated or approximate answer.

Step by Step

Rounding a Whole Number to a Specified Place or Digit

Step 1. Find the digit in the place to which you are rounding.

Step 2. Look at the next digit to the right.
- **a.** If this digit is less than 5, replace it and any other digits to the right with zeros.
- **b.** If this digit is 5 or more, add 1 to the digit in the place to which you are rounding, and replace all digits to the right of the place to which you are rounding with zeros.

EXAMPLE 2

Round 2,758 to the nearest hundred and to the first digit.

Rounding to the nearest hundred

2,758	The digit in the hundreds place is 7.
2,758	The digit to the right of 7 is 5, so Step 2b applies.
2,800	Add 1 to 7 and replace all digits to the right of the 8 with zeros.

2,758 rounded to the nearest hundred is 2,800.

Rounding to the first digit

2,758	The digit to the right of the first digit is 7, so Step 2b applies.
3,000	Add 1 to 2 and replace all digits to the right of the 3 with zeros.

2,758 rounded to the first digit is 3,000.

Source: USA TODAY research, Treasury Dept.
By Aaron Hightower, USA TODAY

You will find Self-Check questions throughout each chapter. These questions give you a chance to review the material you have just read. After you have done the exercises, check your answers against the solutions provided at the end of the chapter on pp. 28–29. This should give you a good idea of how well you have understood the chapter so far.

Self-Check

1. Read the number 4,204,049,201.
2. Round 3,685 to the nearest hundred, and round 3,685 to the first digit.

Section Review

Show how these numbers are read by writing the word name of each number.

1. 4,209
2. 97,168
3. 301,000,009
4. 5,200,000

Round to the indicated place.

5. 378 (nearest hundred)
6. 8,248 (nearest hundred)

7. 9,374 (nearest thousand)

8. 348,218 (nearest ten thousand)

9. 834 (nearest ten)

10. 29,712 (nearest thousand)

11. 29,712 (nearest ten thousand)

12. 275,398,484 (nearest million)

13. 27,500,000,078 (nearest billion)

14. 897,284,017 (nearest ten million)

Round to the third digit.

15. 3,784,809 **16.** 2,063,948 **17.** 5,178

18. 17,295,183,109 **19.** 10,097,437

Round to the first digit.

20. 5,475 **21.** 396 **22.** 18,924

23. 685,294 **24.** 7,098,764

Adding and Subtracting Whole Numbers and Estimating Results

Adding Whole Numbers and Estimating Sums

In an addition problem, the numbers being added are called **addends.** The answer, or result of the addition, is called the **sum,** or **total.**

addends: numbers being added.

sum, or **total:** answer or result in addition.

$$\begin{array}{r} 2 \\ 3 \\ +\ 4 \\ \hline 9 \end{array}$$

2, 3, 4 ← addends

9 ← sum or total

You can check your total by adding the numbers twice, once from the top of the list to the bottom and once from the bottom to the top. One way to speed up your calculations is to group numbers into groups of 10, as shown in the next example.

EXAMPLE 3

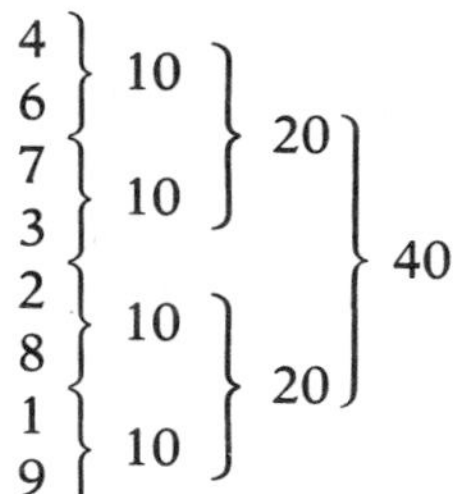

Add each pair of numbers that equals ten and then add the groups.

In many situations, it is helpful to estimate the answer to a problem *before* finding the exact answer. For example, why waste time adding a long column of numbers if all you need to know is whether the total is more than 10,000? Also, estimation can be used to see if an answer is reasonable. To estimate a sum, round each addend to the first digit and add the *rounded* amounts.

EXAMPLE 4

22 885	rounds to	900
569	rounds to	600
343	rounds to	300
231	rounds to	200
+ 562	rounds to	+ 600
2,590		2,600

Note that in this case, the total, 2,590, rounds to 2,600.

Subtracting Whole Numbers and Estimating Differences

subtrahend: the amount being subtracted.

minuend: the original amount from which something is subtracted.

difference: the answer or result of subtraction.

In a subtraction problem, the number being subtracted (the amount being taken away) is called the **subtrahend.** The number from which the subtrahend is being taken (the original amount) is the **minuend.** The answer or result (the amount of the original quantity that remains) is called the **difference.** The fact that the difference plus the subtrahend equals the minuend gives you a way to check the answers to subtraction problems.

7 ⟵	minuend	5	(difference)
− 2 ⟵	subtrahend	+ 2	(subtrahend)
5 ⟵	difference	7	(minuend)

When you are trying to find the difference between two whole numbers, it is often necessary to subtract one digit from a smaller digit. When this happens, you must "borrow," or regroup the digits in the minuend. Example 5 shows how you regroup in the minuend and then how you check the answer.

EXAMPLE 5

Subtract 27 from 64.

$$\begin{array}{r} 64 \\ -\ 27 \\ \hline \end{array}$$

Arrange the numbers so that the digits in the ones place line up.

$\overset{5}{\cancel{6}}\ \overset{14}{\cancel{4}}$ $-\ 2\ 7$ $3\ 7$	7 is larger than 4, so you must regroup. Borrow one 10 from the tens place (thus 6 becomes 5), and add 10 ones to the ones place. Subtract ones; then subtract tens.

Check:

37 + 27 64	The sum of the subtrahend and difference equals the minuend. The difference is correct.

As was also true for addition, you can use rounding as a check to minimize careless mistakes in subtraction and to find an estimated answer to a subtraction problem. To estimate, round the minuend and subtrahend to the first digit and then subtract to find the rounded difference.

EXAMPLE 6

Estimate the difference between 3,704,847 and 1,170,074 by rounding each term to the first digit. Then subtract to find the exact answer.

3,704,847	rounds to	4,000,000	Note that in this case, the exact solution rounded to the first digit is the same as the estimate. The estimate is used to see if the exact answer is a reasonable one.
− 1,170,074	rounds to	− 1,000,000	
2,534,773		3,000,000	

Self-Check

3. Add the following numbers and check the sum.

  328
  583
+ 726

4. Estimate the sum by rounding each term to the first digit.

  473
  342
  233
  478
+ 903

5. Subtract 36 from 55 and check your answer.

6. Estimate the difference between 4,615,958 and 2,398,609 by rounding each number to the first digit.

Section Review

Add. Check each sum.

1.	**2.**	**3.**	**4.**	**5.**	**6.**
6	1	6	7	4	8
3	9	9	2	5	8
4	5	4	7	6	1
+ 7	8	9	7	1	2
	+ 2	6	7	3	4
		+ 1	+ 8	+ 9	+ 9

Add. Check each sum.

7.
```
  8,152
  3,363
  4,529
  8,327
+ 6,416
```

8.
```
  9,892
  7,433
  4,090
  5,282
+ 1,987
```

Write in columns and add.

9. 47 + 385 + 87 + 439 + 874

10. 32,948 + 6,804 + 15,695 + 415 + 7,739

Add.

11.
```
  734
  643
  688
  656
  928
  197
  785
  527
  337
+ 278
```

12.
```
  683
  252
  867
  867
  325
  274
  835
  713
  118
+ 627
```

13.
```
  1,661
  9,342
  2,994
  5,778
  1,770
  5,445
  1,770
  2,656
  3,874
+ 8,724
```

14.
```
  44,349
  71,486
  67,565
  57,971
+ 48,699
```

Estimate by rounding each number to the first digit. Then find the exact sum.

15.
```
  74,374
  82,849
  72,494
+ 89,219
```

16.
```
  374
  847
  521
  873
+ 482
```

17.
```
  3,748
  9,409
  3,577
+ 4,601
```

Estimate by rounding each number to the nearest hundred. Then find the exact answer.

18.
```
  3,470
    843
  3,872
+   574
```

19.
```
  747
  854
  324
+ 687
```

20.
```
  4,274
    643
  1,274
+    97
```

Solve.

21. Mary Luciana bought 48 pencils, 96 pens, 36 diskettes, and 50 bottles of correction fluid. How many items did she buy?

22. Jorge Englade has 57 baseball cards from 1978, 43 cards from 1979, 104 cards from 1980, 210 cards from 1983, and 309 cards from 1987. How many cards does he have in all?

23. Linda Cagle collects dolls. She has 12 antique dolls, 135 Barbie dolls, 35 Shirley Temple dolls and 287 other dolls. How many dolls are there in all?

24. A furniture-manufacturing plant had the following labor-hours in one week: Monday, 483; Tuesday, 472; Wednesday, 497; Thursday, 486; Friday, 464; Saturday, 146; Sunday, 87. Find the total labor-hours worked during the week.

25. A student had the following test scores: 92, 87, 96, 85, 72, 84, 57, 98. What is the student's total number of points?

Subtract. Check your answer.

26. $\begin{array}{r} 75{,}184 \\ -\ 65{,}428 \\ \hline \end{array}$ **27.** $\begin{array}{r} 937{,}452 \\ -\ 395{,}773 \\ \hline \end{array}$ **28.** $\begin{array}{r} 2{,}090{,}684 \\ -\ 224{,}943 \\ \hline \end{array}$ **29.** $\begin{array}{r} 3{,}000{,}000 \\ -\ 291{,}438 \\ \hline \end{array}$

30. $\begin{array}{r} 19{,}000{,}000 \\ -\ 14{,}284{,}394 \\ \hline \end{array}$ **31.** $\begin{array}{r} 7{,}007{,}000 \\ -\ 3{,}018{,}094 \\ \hline \end{array}$ **32.** $\begin{array}{r} 9{,}010{,}000 \\ -\ 3{,}687{,}429 \\ \hline \end{array}$ **33.** $\begin{array}{r} 29{,}007{,}400 \\ -\ 18{,}457{,}396 \\ \hline \end{array}$

Estimate by rounding each number to the first digit. Then find the exact answer.

34. $\begin{array}{r} 9{,}748 \\ -\ 5{,}676 \\ \hline \end{array}$

35. $\begin{array}{r} 370{,}408 \\ -\ 187{,}506 \\ \hline \end{array}$

36. $\begin{array}{r} 83{,}748{,}194 \\ -\ 27{,}209{,}104 \\ \hline \end{array}$

Estimate by rounding each number to the nearest thousand. Then subtract to get an exact answer.

37.
$$\begin{array}{r} 12{,}748 \\ -\ \ 5{,}438 \\ \hline \end{array}$$

38.
$$\begin{array}{r} 84{,}378 \\ -\ 28{,}746 \\ \hline \end{array}$$

39.
$$\begin{array}{r} 109{,}849 \\ -\ \ 35{,}464 \\ \hline \end{array}$$

Solve.

40. Sam Andrews has 42 packages of hamburger buns on hand but expects to use 130 packages. How many must he order?

41. Frieda Salla had 148 tickets to sell for a baseball show. If she has sold 75 tickets, how many does she still have to sell?

42. An inventory shows 596 fan belts on hand. If the normal in-stock count is 840, how many should be ordered?

Multiplying and Dividing Whole Numbers

Multiplication and division work together much the same way that addition and subtraction do. Division gives us a way of understanding how the parts fit together to make a whole and how the whole can be broken up or divided into parts. Multiplication and division are the basis of many of the important calculations made in the business world, and a good understanding of these operations is essential.

Multiplying Whole Numbers and Estimating Products

Before we review the techniques and shortcuts of multiplication, let's look at the names given to the parts of a multiplication problem.

multiplicand: the number that is being multiplied; the upper number in a multiplication problem.

multiplier: the number that is used to multiply by; the lower number in a multiplication problem.

product: the answer, or result, in multiplication. Partial products are the in-between numbers that come from the multiplication of each separate digit of the multiplier; they are added together to get the product.

```
   127 ⟵ multiplicand (or factor)
×   13 ⟵ multiplier (or factor)
   381 ⟵ first partial product
  1 27 ⟵ second partial product
 1,651 ⟵ product
```

When you multiply numbers that contain two or more digits, the most important thing to remember is to *place the partial products* properly. The right-hand digit of each partial product is written directly below the multiplier digit. This lines up the partial products correctly so that tens are added to tens, hundreds to hundreds, and so forth.

Step by Step

Multiplying Whole Numbers by Two or More Digits

Step 1. Write the problem so that the ones, tens, hundreds, and all following places of the multiplicand (top number) and multiplier (bottom number) line up.

Step 2. Write the first number of each partial product directly below the corresponding number in the multiplier.

```
   127
×   53
   381     3 × 127 = 381     The 1 in 381 lines up with the 3 in 53.
  6 35     5 × 127 = 635     The 5 in 635 lines up with the 5 in 53.
 6,731
```

EXAMPLE 7

```
                    1,223     Line up the ones, tens, and hundreds
                 ×    144     places of the two numbers.
                      |||
(4 × 1,223) =       4 892     Note how each partial product lines up
                       ||     under the product above it.
(4 × 1,223) =       48 92
                        |
(1 × 1,223) =       122 3
                  176,112
```

TIPS & TRAPS

A common mistake in multiplying is to forget to indent the partial products. Remember, always write the first number of each partial product directly below the corresponding number in the multiplier.

```
   265                                                        265
×   23                                                     ×   23
   795    We get the second partial product, 530, by mul-     795
   530    tiplying 2 × 265. Therefore, the 0 in 530 should   5 30
 1,325    be directly below the 2 in 23.                     6,095

WRONG                                                      CORRECT
```

Zeros, used correctly, are a part of some of the most helpful shortcuts in multiplying and dividing numbers. Used incorrectly, they can give you your worst headaches. You must pay careful attention to the position of zeros in partial products. When one of the numbers being multiplied is 10, 100, or 1,000 (a power of 10), you can use a very simple shortcut to find the product.

Step by Step

A Shortcut for Multiplying Any Number by Powers of 10 (10, 100, 1,000, etc.)

To multiply a number by 10, 100, 1,000, 10,000, or similar numbers, simply count the number of zeros in 10, 100, 1,000, or 10,000, and add that number of zeros to the number which you are multiplying.

178 × 10 = 1,780	10 has 1 zero. Add 1 zero to 178.
178 × 100 = 17,800	100 has 2 zeros. Add 2 zeros to 178.
178 × 1,000 = 178,000	1,000 has 3 zeros. Add 3 zeros to 178.
178 × 10,000 = 1,780,000	10,000 has 4 zeros. Add 4 zeros to 178.

Another shortcut to multiplication can be taken if one or more of the numbers being multiplied ends in zeros.

Step by Step

A Shortcut for Multiplying Numbers That End in Zero

Step 1. Separate the zeros at the end of each number.

Step 2. Multiply the nonzero numbers.

Step 3. Attach to the end of the product the same number of zeros you separated in Step 1.

270	becomes	27	0	A total of 2 zeros are separated from
× 80		× 8	0	the numbers being multiplied.
		216	00	A total of 2 zeros are reattached to the product.

EXAMPLE 8

Multiply 20,700 by 860.

207	00	*Three* zeros are separated here.	Separate 3 zeros at the end of 20,700 and 860. Line up the first nonzero numbers to the left of the zeros. Find the product of the nonzero numbers.
× 86	0		
1 242			
16 56			
17,802	000	*Three* zeros are reattached here.	Reattach the zeros that were separated in the first step.

20,700 × 860 = 17,802,000

If the multiplier has a zero in the middle (such as 102, 507, or 1,306, for example), you can use another shortcut to multiplication.

Step by Step

A Shortcut for Multiplying by a Number with Zero in the Middle

When a multiplier has a zero in the middle, it is not necessary to write a partial product consisting only of zeros. Instead, write a partial product of zero directly below the zero in the multiplier and then write the first number of the next partial product on the same line, directly below the appropriate number in the multiplier.

EXAMPLE 9

Multiply 144 by 203.

```
   144
 × 203
   432
 28 80
29,232
```

The partial product 0 lines up with the 0 in 203.

The 8 in the partial product of 2 × 144 lines up with the 2 of 203.

To estimate a product, round each number being multiplied to the first digit and then multiply the rounded numbers. Since a rounded number ends in one or more zeros, you can use the multiplication shortcuts involving zeros when you multiply rounded numbers. Estimated products are used in the business world to calculate approximate prices and expenses, to compare two or more offers or prices quickly, and to project future costs and needs.

EXAMPLE 10

Estimate the product of 474 and 46 by rounding each number to the first digit. Find the exact product.

```
   474  rounds to    500  which      5 | 00
 ×  46  rounds to  ×  50  becomes  × 5 | 0
 2 844                              25 | 000
 18 96
21,804                             = 25,000
```

Note that the exact solution, 21,804, rounded to the first digit is not the same as the estimate rounded to the first digit. However, the estimate is close enough to verify that the number of digits in the exact answer is correct and the exact answer is reasonable.

Self-Check

7. Multiply 6,823 by 634.
8. Multiply 730 by 60.
9. Multiply 904 by 24.
10. Estimate the product of 385 and 42 by rounding each number to the first digit.

Dividing Whole Numbers and Estimating Quotients

Knowing the names of the parts of a division problem will make it easier to understand and follow the rules and shortcuts for division. The number being divided (the whole) is called the **dividend.** The number doing the dividing is called the **divisor,** and the answer, or the number of times the divisor goes into the dividend, is the **quotient.** If the divisor does not divide the dividend into an equal number of parts, the answer consists of a quotient and a **remainder.** There are several ways to describe a division problem in words. We might say here, "Three divides into seventeen five times with a remainder of two," or "Seventeen divided by three equals five, remainder two."

dividend: number being divided.

divisor: number doing the dividing.

quotient: the answer, or result, of division.

remainder: what is left over if division does not come out even.

```
quotient  →      5 R2 ← remainder
divisor   →   3)17
dividend  →     15
                 2
```

Two other ways of indicating a division problem are as follows:

dividend → 250, divisor → 5: $\frac{250}{5} = 50$ ← quotient and $250 \div 5 = 50$ ← quotient (250 = dividend, 5 = divisor)

Source: College of Financial Planning, Denver
By LeRoy Lottmann, USA TODAY

Lining up numbers correctly is as important in division as it is in multiplication. Example 11 shows how the parts of a division problem should line up with one another.

EXAMPLE 11

Find the quotient of $84 \div 4$.

```
  21
4)84    4 divides into 8 twice.
  8     4 × 2 = 8
   4    8 − 8 = 0; bring down the 4.
   4    4 divides into 4 once.
   0    4 − 4 = 0
```

Each number in the quotient is directly above the number in the dividend that was divided by the divisor.
4 divides into 84 exactly 21 times. There is no remainder.

If 84 divided by 4 equals 21, then 4 times 21 equals 84. Remember, in a division problem that has no remainder, the dividend always equals the divisor times the quotient. You can use this fact to check the quotient.

EXAMPLE 12

Check the quotient in Example 11.

If $84 \div 4 = 21$, then 4×21 should equal 84.

```
  21
×  4
  84,   so the quotient is
        correct.
```

If the quotient of a division problem is correct, then the product of the divisor and the quotient should equal the dividend.

When you check the answer to a division problem with a remainder, you multiply the divisor times the quotient and then add the remainder. If the quotient and remainder are correct, then the dividend should equal the divisor times the quotient plus the remainder.

EXAMPLE 13

Find the quotient of 78 divided by 5. Check the answer.

```
  15 R3
5)78
  5
  28
  25
   3
```

If the answer is correct, then (5 × 15) + 3 should equal 78.

If the quotient and remainder are correct, then the divisor times the quotient, plus the remainder, should equal the dividend.

Check:

```
  15      75
×  5    +  3
  75      78
```

The answer is correct.

Zeros in Division. You must pay close attention to zeros in division, just as you did in multiplication. If the divisor in a problem does not divide into a number in the quotient at least one time, you write a zero in the quotient above the number. This is a very important step and cannot be skipped.

EXAMPLE 14

Find the quotient of $\frac{2,535}{5}$, paying close attention to the zero in the quotient.

```
    507
5)2,535
  2 5
    3
    0
    35
    35
     0
```

5 does not divide into 3, so zero is written in the quotient above the 3. The answer is 507.

You find an estimated quotient by rounding the divisor and dividend to the first digit and then dividing to find the quotient. Since rounded numbers end in one or more zeros, you can make use of some helpful shortcuts in dividing rounded numbers. When both the divisor and dividend end in one or more zeros, you can drop the *same number* of zeros from both divisor and dividend. The quotient remains the same.

EXAMPLE 15

Estimate the quotient in this problem by rounding the divisor and dividend to the first digit, dropping the same number of zeros from the divisor and dividend, and then doing the division.

270)34,814 rounds to 300)30,000 — The divisor, 270, rounds to 300. The dividend, 34,814, rounds to 30,000.

300)30,000 becomes 3)300 — Drop two zeros from the divisor and dividend.

```
  100
3)300
```

300 divided by 3 is 100. The estimated quotient is 100.

TIPS & TRAPS

A common mistake in division is lining up the digits in the quotient incorrectly.

```
      150
23)34,500
   23
   11 5
   11 5
      0
```

WRONG

The 1 in the quotient should begin over the 4 in the 34,500.

```
      1,500
23)34,500
   23
   11 5
   11 5
      0
```

CORRECT

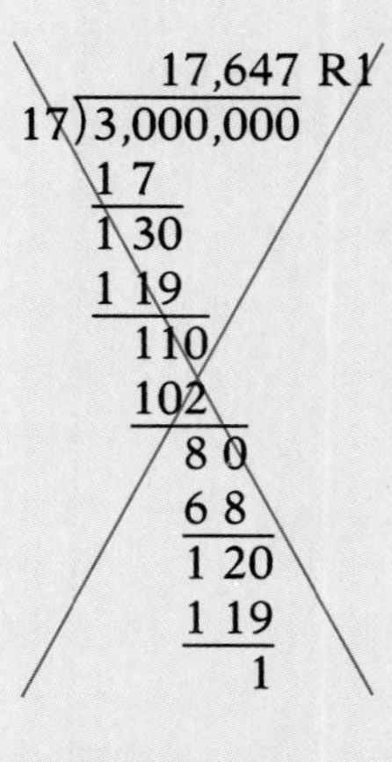

WRONG

The 1 in the quotient should begin over the first 0 in the 3,000,000.

```
   176,470 R10
17)3,000,000
   1 7
   1 30
   1 19
     110
     102
       8 0
       6 8
       1 20
       1 19
         10
```

CORRECT

Self-Check

11. Find the quotient of 96 ÷ 6.

12. Check the quotient in Question 1.

13. Find the quotient of 71 ÷ 4.

14. Check the quotient in Question 13.

15. Find the quotient of $\frac{5{,}226}{4}$.

16. Estimate the quotient of 78,688 divided by 48 by rounding the divisor and dividend to the first digit.

Section Review

Multiply. Check each product.

1. 5,931 × 835 **2.** 5,565 × 839 **3.** 1,987 × 394 **4.** 78,626 × 87 **5.** 708 × 59

6. 2,105 × 64 **7.** 70,803 × 98 **8.** 2,174 × 308 **9.** 1,700 × 507 **10.** 3,987 × 1,033

Multiply:

11. 33×500 **12.** $283 \times 3{,}000$ **13.** 160×300 **14.** 405×400

15. 50×600 **16.** $25 \times 10{,}000$ **17.** $7{,}870 \times 6{,}000$ **18.** $974 \times 7{,}000$

19. 270×600 **20.** $560 \times 9{,}000$

Estimate by rounding each number to the first digit. Then find the exact answer.

21. $\begin{array}{r} 7{,}489 \\ \times \quad 34 \\ \hline \end{array}$

22. $\begin{array}{r} 378 \\ \times \ 72 \\ \hline \end{array}$

Estimate by rounding each number to the nearest hundred. Then find the exact answer.

23. $\begin{array}{r} 3{,}128 \\ \times \quad 478 \\ \hline \end{array}$

24. $\begin{array}{r} 378 \\ \times \ 546 \\ \hline \end{array}$

Solve.

25. An office has 15 printers. The supply coordinator is expected to keep 8 ribbons for each printer. How many ribbons should be kept on hand?

26. A florist has 152 orders for 12 red roses. How many roses are required to fill the orders?

27. A day care center has 28 children. If each child eats one piece of fruit each day, how many pieces of fruit are required for a week (5 days)?

Divide.

28. $7\overline{)315}$ **29.** $5\overline{)213}$ **30.** $9\overline{)216}$

31. $6\overline{)314}$

Divide.

32. $1{,}232 \div 4$ **33.** $4{,}020 \div 5$ **34.** $6\overline{)1{,}247}$

35. $8\overline{)3{,}362}$

Estimate each quotient. Then find the exact quotient.

36. $85\overline{)748{,}431}$ **37.** $346\overline{)174{,}891}$

Solve.

38. A parts dealer has 2,988 washers. The washers are packaged with 12 (1 dozen) in each package. How many packages can be made?

39. A stack of countertops measures 238 inches. If each countertop is 2 inches thick, how many are in the stack?

40. If 127 employees earn $1,524 in one hour, what is the average hourly wage per employee?

Summary

Topic	Page	What to Remember	Examples
Reading whole numbers	5	Use commas to separate the number into groups of three digits and name the groups (units, millions, billions, and so on). Read the number from left to right, naming the numerals in each group and the group name. If a group has all zeros, it does not have to be read. Do not read the group name units or use the word *and* in reading a number.	574 is read "five hundred seventy-four." 3,804,321 is read "three million, eight hundred four thousand, three hundred twenty-one."
Rounding numbers	5	Find the digit in the place to which you are rounding. Look at the digit to the right. If it is less than 5, replace it and any other digits to the right with zeros. If the digit is 5 or more, add 1 to the digit to which you are rounding, and replace all the digits to the right with zeros.	4,860 rounded to the nearest hundred is 4,900. 7,439 rounded to the nearest thousand is 7,000. 8,392,471 rounded to the second digit is 8,400,000. 4,095 rounded to the first digit is 4,000.
Adding	7–8	Finding the sum of several numbers can be done faster if you group the numbers, find the group sums, and then find the sum of the group sums.	3, 5 } 10; 5, 7 } 10; 10 + 10 } 20; + 8 → 8; 20 + 8 } 28
Adding in columns	7–8	When you add numbers that have more than one digit, write the numbers in a column, find the sum of the numbers in the units column, and write the sum directly below the units column. If the sum is more than 10, write the number of units in the sum in the units column, and carry the number of tens in the sum over into the tens column. Continue this process until you have added all the columns.	carry 1; 364 + 473 = 837
Subtracting	8–9	When you must subtract a large digit from a smaller one, you must regroup the digits and borrow from the column to the left of the column you are subtracting. When you borrow 1 group of ten from a column and add it to the column to the right, remember to subtract 1 from the digit in the column from which you are borrowing and add 10 to the column in which you are subtracting.	7 ~~5~~ ~~4~~ (regrouped 4 14); − 3 2 9 = 4 2 5
Multiplying	14	The multiplicand and multiplier are the numbers being multiplied. They are also called factors. The product (answer) is obtained by adding the partial products of the factors. It is important to line up the partial products correctly before you add them.	543 × 32; partial products 1 086 and 16 29; product 17,376

Topic	Page	What to Remember	Example
Multiplication shortcut: when one or both numbers end in zeros	15	When one or both numbers end in zeros, separate the zeros, multiply the nonzero digits, and attach to the end of the product the same number of zeros you separated in the first step.	3,650 × 5,300 *Rewrite:* 365 0 × 53 00 1 095 18 25 19,345 000 = 19,345,000
Multiplication shortcut: when the multiplier has a zero in the middle	16	When one of the digits within a multiplier is zero, there is no need to write a row of zeros as a middle partial product. Simply enter a zero in the column under the zero and then enter the next partial product to the left of the zero. Be very careful to line up the partial products correctly.	732 × 205 3 660 146 40 150,060
Division	17–18	The number you are dividing is the dividend, the number by which you are dividing is the divisor, and the answer is the quotient. If the dividend is not a multiple of the divisor, the answer will have a remainder. Remember to line up the digits correctly when you divide.	287 R1 3)862 6 26 24 22 21 1
Estimating	18	You can quickly estimate the answer to any problem by rounding the numbers to the first digit or to a specified place value and solving the problem.	Estimate the product of 499 × 32 by rounding the numbers to the first digit. 499 rounds to 500; 32 rounds to 30. 500 × 30 = 1500. Estimate the quotient of 53,789 ÷ 47 by rounding the divisor and dividend to the first digit. 47 rounds to 50 and 53,789 rounds to 50,000. Drop one zero from each rounded number and divide. The estimated quotient is 1,000.

Chapter Review

Perform the following rounding operations.

1. Show how 34,304 is read by writing the word name.

2. Show how 2,000,400 is read by writing the word name.

3. Round 8,529 to the nearest hundred.

4. Round 34,984 to the nearest thousand.

5. Round 2,498,204 to the third digit.

6. Round 16,304 to the first digit.

Perform the following operations.

7. 4 + 3 + 7 + 9 + 8 + 1

8. 23 + 31 + 46 + 87

9.
$$\begin{array}{r} 483 \\ 296 \\ 583 \\ +\ 320 \\ \hline \end{array}$$

10.
$$\begin{array}{r} 607 \\ 523 \\ 849 \\ +\ 1{,}238 \\ \hline \end{array}$$

11. 863 − 22

12. 957 − 145

13. 398 − 286

14. 923 − 586

15. 8,023 − 5,876

16. 4,230 − 3,079

17. 84 × 32

18. 67 × 93

19. 907 × 36

20. 8,040 × 30

21. 392 ÷ 7

22. $8\overline{)4{,}072}$

23. $52\overline{)837}$

24. $77\overline{)83{,}216}$

25. The sales for each of 5 days were $9,183, $8,214, $6,834, $7,023, and $8,916. Find the total sales.

26. Better Serve Store had 4,896 gallons of gasoline on hand and sold 1,083 gallons. How many gallons were still on hand?

27. The Wallpaper Shop purchased 2,304 rolls of wallpaper for $4 per roll. Find the total price of the wallpaper.

28. Mrs. Bryan has $82,000 and plans to divide it equally among her 16 grandchildren. How much will each grandchild receive?

Trial Test

Perform the indicated operations.

1. 483 + 291 + 468

2. 8,042 − 3,587

3. 523 × 86

4. 870 × 90

5. $32\overline{)25{,}120}$

6. $48\overline{)5{,}040}$

7. 558 ÷ 9

8. $8\overline{)409}$

Write the following numbers in words.

9. 503

10. 12,056,039

Round the following to the indicated place.

11. 84,321 (nearest hundred)

12. 58,967 (nearest thousand)

13. 80,235 (second digit)

14. 587,213 (first digit)

Estimate the following by rounding to hundreds.

15. 863 + 983 + 271

16. 987 − 346

Estimate the following by rounding to the first digit.

17. 892 × 46

18. $53\overline{)4{,}021}$

19. An inventory clerk counted the following items: 438 rings, 72 watches, and 643 pen and pencil sets. How many items were counted?

20. A warehouse is 31 feet high. Boxes that are each 2 feet high are to be stacked in the warehouse. How many boxes may be stacked one on top of the other in this warehouse?

Self-Check Solutions

1. Four billion, two hundred four million, forty-nine thousand, two hundred one

2. 3,700; 4,000

3.
```
   11
  328
  583
+ 726
-----
1,637
```

4.
```
   21
  473  rounds to    500
  342  rounds to    300
  233  rounds to    200
  478  rounds to    500
+ 903  rounds to  + 900
-----             -----
2,429             2,400
```

5.
```
 415
  55      36
- 36    + 19
----    ----
  19      55
```

6.
```
  4,615,958  rounds to    5,000,000
- 2,398,609  rounds to  - 2,000,000
                        -----------
                          3,000,000
```

7.
```
                    6,823                          634
                 ×    634                      × 6,823
(6823 × 4) =       27 292     (634 × 3) =        1 902
(6823 × 3) =      204 69      (634 × 2) =       12 68
(6823 × 6) =    4 093 8       (634 × 8) =      507 2
                4,325,782     (634 × 6) =    3 804
                                             4,325,782
```

8.
```
   73 | 0      730 × 60 = 43,800
 ×  6 | 0
  438 | 00
```

9.
```
                   904
                 ×  24
(904 × 4) =      3 616
(904 × 2) =     18 08
                21,696
```

10.

$$\begin{array}{r} 385 \\ \times\ \ 42 \\ \hline 770 \\ 15\,40 \\ \hline 16{,}170 \end{array} \quad \begin{array}{l} \text{rounds to} \\ \text{rounds to} \end{array} \quad \begin{array}{r} 400 \\ \times\ \ 40 \\ \hline \end{array} \qquad \text{Rewrite:} \quad \begin{array}{r|l} 4 & 00 \\ \times\ 4 & 0 \\ \hline 16 & 000 \end{array}$$

11.

$$\begin{array}{r} 16 \\ 6\overline{)96} \\ \underline{6}\ \ \\ 36 \\ \underline{36} \\ 0 \end{array}$$

12.

$$\begin{array}{r} 16 \\ \times\ \ 6 \\ \hline 96 \end{array}$$

13.

$$\begin{array}{r} 17 \text{ R3} \\ 4\overline{)71}\phantom{\text{ R3}} \\ \underline{4}\ \ \phantom{\text{ R3}} \\ 31\phantom{\text{ R3}} \\ \underline{28}\phantom{\text{ R3}} \\ 3\phantom{\text{ R3}} \end{array}$$

14.

$$\begin{array}{r} 17 \\ \times\ \ 4 \\ \hline 68 \\ +\ \ 3 \\ \hline 71 \end{array}$$

15.

$$\begin{array}{r} 1{,}306 \text{ R2} \\ 4\overline{)5{,}226}\phantom{\text{ R2}} \\ \underline{4}\phantom{\text{ R2}} \\ 1\,2\phantom{\text{ R2}} \\ \underline{1\,2}\phantom{\text{ R2}} \\ 02\phantom{\text{ R2}} \\ \underline{0}\phantom{\text{ R2}} \\ 26\phantom{\text{ R2}} \\ \underline{24}\phantom{\text{ R2}} \\ 2\phantom{\text{ R2}} \end{array}$$

16. 78,688 rounds to 80,000
48 rounds to 50

$$\begin{array}{r} 1{,}600 \\ 50\overline{)80{,}000} \\ \underline{50} \\ 30\,0 \\ \underline{30\,0} \\ 0 \end{array}$$

Fractions 2

Learning Objectives

1. Recognize types of fractions and convert between improper fractions and mixed numbers. (pp. 31–33)
2. Reduce fractions to lowest terms. (pp. 33–36)
3. Write fractions in higher terms. (p. 36)
4. Find the least common denominator of fractions. (pp. 40–41)
5. Add and subtract fractions and mixed numbers. (pp. 39–44)
6. Multiply and divide fractions and mixed numbers. (pp. 50–54)
7. Find and use reciprocals. (pp. 53–54)

Fractions, in their many forms, are used in the business world every day: "All Winter Coats $\frac{1}{3}$ Off!" "Four Out of Five Doctors Recommend. . .". "$\frac{1}{3}$ the Calories of Butter." "Half-Price Sale Today!" Let's first review the meanings of some important terms before we begin to work with fractions.

Numerator: The top term in a fraction. This is the *dividend,* or number *being divided.*

numerator: the top term of a fraction or the number being divided.

Denominator: The bottom term in a fraction. This is the *divisor,* or the number that *divides into* the numerator.

denominator: the bottom term of a fraction, or the number that divides into the numerator.

Fraction line: The horizontal line separating the numerator and denominator; $\frac{2}{4}$ means $2 \div 4$.

fraction line: the horizontal line separating the numerator and denominator of a fraction; the division symbol.

$$\frac{2}{4} \quad \begin{array}{l} \longleftarrow \text{numerator} \\ \longleftarrow \text{fraction line} \\ \longleftarrow \text{denominator} \end{array}$$

Proper fraction: A fraction with numerator smaller than its denominator. A proper fraction has a value less than 1.

proper fraction: a fraction with a numerator smaller than its denominator.

$$\frac{3}{4}, \frac{1}{2}, \frac{9}{10}, \frac{4}{7}$$

Improper fraction: A fraction with numerator equal to or greater than its denominator. An improper fraction has a value equal to or greater than 1.

improper fraction: a fraction with a numerator equal to or larger than its denominator.

$$\frac{7}{7}, \frac{8}{3}, \frac{10}{2}, \frac{15}{13}$$

Mixed number: A number composed of both a whole number and a fraction.

mixed number: a number composed of both a whole number and a fraction.

$$3\frac{7}{8}, 1\frac{2}{5}$$

Converting Fractions

Since fractions have so many different forms, it is often necessary to convert or change a fraction to a different type of fraction before you can solve a problem. When you add or subtract fractions, you must first rewrite the fractions so that they have the same denominator. After fractions have been rewritten or converted, and then added, subtracted, multiplied, or divided, you reduce the fraction in the answer to its lowest terms.

Converting Improper Fractions to Whole or Mixed Numbers

equivalent: equal to, or the same numerical value.

To convert or change an improper fraction into a whole or mixed number, you simply divide the numerator by the denominator. The quotient and remainder are used to write an equivalent whole or mixed number. An **equivalent** number is one that has the same numerical value as the original improper fraction.

Step by Step

Changing Improper Fractions to Whole or Mixed Numbers

Step 1. Divide the numerator of the improper fraction by the denominator.

Step 2. a. If there is no remainder, the quotient is the *whole number* equivalent to the improper fraction.

b. If there is a remainder, the improper fraction is a mixed number. The fraction in the mixed number is the remainder of the division over the original denominator.

EXAMPLE 1

Change $\frac{139}{8}$ to a whole or mixed number.

$$\begin{array}{r} 17 \text{ R3, or } 17\frac{3}{8} \\ 8\overline{)139} \\ \underline{8} \\ 59 \\ \underline{56} \\ 3 \end{array}$$

Divide 139 by 8. The quotient is 17 R3, which equals $17\frac{3}{8}$.

$$\frac{139}{8} = 17\frac{3}{8}$$

Converting Mixed Numbers to Improper Fractions

Sometimes you need to convert a mixed number to an improper fraction. The denominator of the improper fraction is always the same as the denominator of the fractional part of the mixed number.

Step by Step

Changing Mixed Numbers to Improper Fractions

Step 1. Multiply the denominator by the whole number.

Step 2. Add the result from Step 1 to the numerator.

Step 3. Write the result from Step 2 over the original denominator.

EXAMPLE 2

Change $2\frac{3}{4}$ to an improper fraction.

$$2\frac{3}{4} = \frac{(4 \times 2) + 3}{4} = \frac{11}{4}$$

Find the new numerator: Multiply the whole number times the denominator of the fraction and add the product to the original numerator. The new denominator is the same as the original denominator.

TIPS & TRAPS
To help remember this procedure, visualize the steps as forming a circle. Start at the denominator of the fractional part, move clockwise, and end with the denominator.

plus 3 times

$$\frac{2}{5} \longleftarrow \frac{(5 \times 3) + 2}{5} = \frac{17}{5} \quad \begin{matrix}\text{(numerator of the improper fraction)} \\ \text{(denominator of the improper fraction)}\end{matrix}$$

$$3\frac{2}{5} = \frac{17}{5}$$

Reducing Fractions to Lowest Terms

If you multiply or divide both the numerator and the denominator of a fraction by the same number, the value of the fraction remains the same. A fraction is said to be in lowest terms when there is no number (other than 1) that can divide evenly into both the numerator and the denominator.

Step by Step

Reducing a Fraction to Lowest Terms

Step 1. Inspect the numerator and denominator to find any whole number that can divide evenly into both numbers.

Step 2. Divide both the numerator and denominator by that number, and inspect the new fraction to find any other number that can divide evenly into both parts of the fraction.

Step 3. Repeat Steps 1 and 2 until there are no more numbers that will divide evenly into both numerator and denominator.

EXAMPLE 3

Reduce $\frac{30}{36}$ to lowest terms.

$\frac{30}{36} = \frac{30 \div 2}{36 \div 2} = \frac{15}{18}$ Both the numerator and denominator can be divided evenly by 2.

$\frac{15}{18} = \frac{15 \div 3}{18 \div 3} = \frac{5}{6}$ Both numerator and denominator of the new fraction can be divided evenly by 3.

$\frac{30}{36} = \frac{5}{6}$ No more numbers can divide evenly into both numerator and denominator. The fraction is now in lowest terms.

divisibility: whether a number can be divided by another number.

Sometimes the numerator and denominator of a fraction are so large that you must divide both parts many times before you find the lowest terms. When this happens, it is helpful to know some shortcuts for recognizing **divisibility,** whether some number can be divided by another number.

Step by Step

Shortcuts for Determining Divisibility

A number can be divided by:	If:	For example:	
2	The number ends in an even digit (0, 2, 4, 6, or 8).	154	154 ends in 4, which is even. Therefore, 154 is divisible by 2. $154 \div 2 = 77$
3	The sum of its digits is divisible by 3.	1,761	$1 + 7 + 6 + 1 = 15$, which is divisible by 3. Therefore, 1,761 is divisible by 3. $1{,}761 \div 3 = 587$
4	The last two digits are divisible by 4.	2,352	52 is divisible by 4 ($52 = 4 \times 13$). Therefore, 2,352 is divisible by 4. $2{,}352 \div 4 = 588$
5	The last digit is either 5 or 0.	3,645	3,645 ends in 5. Therefore, it is divisible by 5. $3{,}645 \div 5 = 729$
6	The number is divisible by both 2 and 3, or the number is even and the sum of the digits is divisible by 3.	72	72 ends in an even digit and therefore is divisible by 2; the sum of the digits ($7 + 2$) equals 9, which is divisible by 3. Therefore, 72 is divisible by 6. $72 \div 6 = 12$

8	The last three digits are divisible by 8.	7,272	272, the last three digits of 7,272, is divisible by 8 ($8 \times 34 = 272$). Therefore, 7,272 is divisible by 8. $7{,}272 \div 8 = 909$
9	The sum of the digits is divisible by 9.	5,877	$5 + 8 + 7 + 7 = 27$, which is divisible by 9. Therefore, 5,877 is divisible by 9. $5{,}877 \div 9 = 653$
10	The last digit is 0.	6,790	The last digit is 0. Therefore, 6,790 is divisible by 10. $6{,}790 \div 10 = 679$

EXAMPLE 4

Use the divisibility shortcuts to reduce $\frac{108}{180}$ to lowest terms.

$$\frac{108}{180} = \frac{108 \div 4}{180 \div 4} = \frac{27}{45}$$

108 and 180 are divisible by 4 (the last two digits in both numbers are divisible by 4).

$$\frac{27}{45} = \frac{27 \div 9}{45 \div 9} = \frac{3}{5}$$

27 and 45 are divisible by 9 (the sums of the digits are divisible by 9).

There is no number that can divide evenly into 3 and 5. Therefore, the fraction is written in lowest terms.

The divisibility rules can help us reduce fractions, but there will still be a certain amount of trial and error involved, particularly when the numerator and denominator are both large numbers. The fastest way to reduce a fraction to lowest terms is to divide the numerator and denominator by the **greatest common divisor (GCD),** which is the greatest number that divides evenly into both parts of a fraction. Let's look at a helpful shortcut to finding the GCD.

greatest common divisor (GCD): the greatest or largest number that will divide into a group of two or more numbers.

Step by Step

A Shortcut for Finding the Greatest Common Divisor of Two Numbers

Step 1. Divide the larger number by the smaller number.

Step 2. Divide the remainder from Step 1 into the divisor from Step 1.

Step 3. Divide the remainder from Step 2 into the divisor from Step 2.

Step 4. Continue this division process until the division has no remainder. The divisor that produced no remainder is the greatest common divisor.

EXAMPLE 5

Use the GCD shortcut to write $\frac{168}{198}$ in lowest terms.

$168\overline{)198}$ = 1 R30	Divide the larger number by the smaller number.
$30\overline{)168}$ = 5 R18	Divide the original divisor by the remainder of the first division.
$18\overline{)30}$ = 1 R12	Divide the divisor of each previous division by the remainder of that division.
$12\overline{)18}$ = 1 R6	
$6\overline{)12}$ = 2	The divisor that does not yield a remainder is the greatest common divisor.
$\frac{168}{198} = \frac{168 \div 6}{198 \div 6} = \frac{28}{33}$	Divide the numerator and denominator by the GCD to reduce the fraction to lowest terms.

Rewriting Fractions in Higher Terms

Just as you can reduce a fraction to lowest terms by dividing the numerator and denominator by the same number, you rewrite a fraction in *higher* terms by *multiplying* the numerator and denominator by the same number. This is important in addition and subtraction of fractions, as you shall see later in this chapter. You write a fraction as a new fraction with a greater denominator by multiplying both the numerator and denominator by the number that gives the new denominator from the original one.

Changing a Fraction to a New Fraction with a Greater Denominator

Step 1. Divide the *new* denominator by the *old* denominator. The result of this division tells you by what number you must multiply the old denominator to get the new denominator.

Step 2. Multiply *both* the original numerator and denominator by the number you found in Step 1. This gives you the new fraction.

EXAMPLE 6

Rewrite $\frac{5}{8}$ as a fraction with a denominator of 72.

$\frac{5}{8} = \frac{?}{72}$	State the problem clearly.
$8\overline{)72}$ = 9	Divide the new denominator (72) by the old denominator (8) to find the number by which the numerator and denominator must be multiplied. That number is 9.

$$\frac{5}{8} = \frac{5 \times 9}{8 \times 9} = \frac{45}{72}$$

Multiply the numerator and denominator by 9 to get the new fraction with a denominator of 72.

Self-Check

1. Convert $\frac{388}{16}$ to a whole or mixed number.

2. Change $6\frac{2}{3}$ to an improper fraction.

Reduce each fraction to lowest terms.

3. $\frac{7}{28}$

4. $\frac{48}{78}$

5. $\frac{315}{360}$

6. Convert $\frac{3}{8}$ to an equivalent fraction with a denominator of 152.

Section Review

Change to whole or mixed numbers.

1. $\frac{124}{6}$

2. $\frac{52}{15}$

3. $\frac{84}{12}$

4. $\frac{83}{4}$

5. $\frac{17}{2}$

6. $\frac{77}{11}$

7. $\frac{62}{5}$

8. $\frac{19}{10}$

9. $\frac{372}{25}$

10. $\frac{904}{9}$

Change to improper fractions.

11. $5\frac{5}{6}$

12. $7\frac{3}{8}$

13. $4\frac{1}{3}$

14. $10\frac{1}{5}$

15. $33\frac{1}{3}$

16. $66\frac{2}{3}$

Reduce each fraction to lowest terms. Try to use the greatest common divisor.

17. $\frac{25}{40}$

18. $\frac{18}{20}$

19. $\frac{15}{18}$

20. $\frac{20}{30}$

21. $\frac{21}{24}$

22. $\frac{30}{48}$

23. $\frac{21}{56}$

24. $\frac{27}{36}$

25. $\frac{48}{64}$

26. $\frac{16}{48}$

27. $\frac{24}{60}$

28. $\frac{18}{63}$

Reduce to lowest terms.

29. $\frac{56}{72}$

30. $\frac{54}{84}$

31. $\frac{120}{144}$

32. $\frac{78}{104}$

33. $\frac{75}{125}$

34. $\frac{78}{96}$

35. $\frac{32}{48}$

36. $\frac{220}{242}$

37. $\frac{65}{120}$

38. $\frac{30}{140}$

Rewrite as a fraction with the indicated denominator.

39. $\frac{3}{4} = \frac{\quad}{72}$

40. $\frac{7}{9} = \frac{\quad}{81}$

41. $\frac{5}{6} = \frac{\quad}{12}$

42. $\frac{5}{8} = \frac{\quad}{32}$

43. $\frac{2}{3} = \frac{\quad}{15}$

44. $\frac{4}{7} = \frac{\quad}{49}$

45. $\frac{9}{11} = \frac{}{77}$

46. $\frac{3}{14} = \frac{}{56}$

47. $\frac{9}{11} = \frac{}{143}$

48. $\frac{4}{15} = \frac{}{105}$

49. A company employed 105 people. If 15 of the employees left the company in a 3-month period, what fractional part of the employees left?

50. If 8 students in a class of 30 earned grades of A, what fractional part of the class earned A's?

Adding and Subtracting Fractions

You may often be asked to add or subtract fractions, operations that are not readily performed on most calculators. Before you can add or subtract fractions, you must make sure that all the fractions being added or subtracted have the same denominator. This means that it is often necessary to rewrite one or more fractions in higher terms before solving a problem.

Adding Fractions with the Same Denominator

If you are adding several fractions with the same denominator, you simply add the numerators to find the numerator of the sum and then write that number over the original denominator. You then reduce the sum to lowest terms. Convert improper fractions to whole or mixed numbers.

EXAMPLE 7

Find the sum of $\frac{1}{4} + \frac{3}{4} + \frac{4}{4}$.

$\frac{1}{4} + \frac{3}{4} + \frac{4}{4} = \frac{8}{4}$ The sum of the numerators is the numerator of the sum. The original denominator is the denominator of the sum.

$\frac{8}{4} = 2$ Convert the improper fraction to a whole number.

Adding Fractions with Different Denominators

Before we can add fractions with different denominators, we must find their **least common denominator (LCD),** which is the smallest number that can be divided evenly by each original denominator.

least common denominator (LCD): the least or smallest number into which each of two or more denominators divides evenly.

Step by Step

Adding Fractions

Step 1. If the denominators are not the same, find the least common denominator.

Step 2. Change each fraction to an equivalent fraction having the least common denominator.

Step 3. Add the numerators.

Step 4. The least common denominator is the denominator of the sum.

Step 5. Reduce the fraction to lowest terms. Change any improper fractions to whole or mixed numbers.

Sometimes simple inspection of the numbers being added tells you the LCD.

EXAMPLE 8

Find the sum of $\frac{1}{2} + \frac{3}{4}$.

$$\frac{1}{2} + \frac{3}{4} = \frac{1 \times 2}{2 \times 2} + \frac{3}{4} = \frac{2}{4} + \frac{3}{4}$$

You know that $2 \times 2 = 4$, so simple inspection tells you that 4 is the LCD. Multiply $\frac{1}{2}$ by $\frac{2}{2}$ to get $\frac{2}{4}$, which can be added to $\frac{3}{4}$.

$$= \frac{5}{4} = 1\frac{1}{4}$$

The sum of the numerators is the numerator of the sum. The LCD of the addends is the denominator of the sum. Write the answer as a mixed number.

Often, however, you must add several fractions with different denominators, and simple inspection does not tell you the least common denominator. When this happens, you use a special method of finding the LCD.

Finding the Least Common Denominator. Before we can use the most efficient way of finding the lowest common denominator of two or more fractions, we need to look at prime numbers.

prime number: a whole number larger than one that is divisible only by itself and 1.

A **prime number** is a whole number larger than 1 that is divisible only by itself and 1. The first ten prime numbers are

2, 3, 5, 7, 11, 13, 17, 19, 23, and 29

Prime numbers are used to help find quickly and accurately the least common denominator of two or more fractions.

Step by Step

Finding the Least Common Denominator of Two or More Fractions

Step 1. Write the denominators in a horizontal row and divide each one by the smallest prime number that can divide evenly into any of the numbers.

Step 2. Write a new row of numbers using the quotients of the division in Step 1 and bringing down any numbers that are not divisible by the first prime number.

Step 3. Continue this process until the only number in the row is 1.

Step 4. Multiply all the prime numbers along the left side to find the lowest common denominator.

EXAMPLE 9

Add $\frac{5}{6} + \frac{5}{8} + \frac{1}{12}$.

$$\begin{array}{r|rrr} 2 & 6 & 8 & 12 \\ 2 & 3 & 4 & 6 \\ 2 & 3 & 2 & 3 \\ 3 & 3 & 1 & 3 \\ & 1 & 1 & 1 \end{array}$$

Find the LCD: Write the denominators in a row and divide by 2, which is the smallest prime number.

Repeat the division with 2. 2 does not divide evenly into 3, so we bring the 3 down to the next line.

The LCD equals the product of all the prime numbers on the left: $2 \times 2 \times 2 \times 3 = 24$. The LCD is 24.

Now that you have found the LCD, you have to write $\frac{5}{6}, \frac{5}{8}$, and $\frac{1}{12}$ as equivalent fractions with a denominator of 24. We saw how to do this in Example 6.

$$\frac{5}{6} = \frac{?}{24} \qquad 6\overline{)24}^{\,4} \qquad \frac{5}{6} = \frac{5 \times 4}{6 \times 4} = \frac{20}{24}$$

When we change each fraction, we get

$$\frac{20}{24} + \frac{15}{24} + \frac{2}{24} = \frac{37}{24} = 1\frac{13}{24}$$

Write the sum as a mixed number in lowest terms.

ADDING MIXED NUMBERS. You add mixed numbers in several steps: First, you find the LCD of the fractional parts and change the fractions to equivalent fractions with the LCD; then you add the whole numbers and the fractions.

Step by Step

Adding Mixed Numbers

Step 1. If the fractions have different denominators, find the LCD.

Step 2. Change each fraction to an equivalent fraction with the LCD as the denominator.

Step 3. Add the whole numbers and the fractions. If the sum of the fractions is an improper fraction, convert it to a whole or mixed number, and add it to the sum of the whole numbers.

EXAMPLE 10

Add $3\frac{2}{5} + 10\frac{3}{10} + 4\frac{4}{15}$.

{1}

Find the LCD.

$$\begin{array}{r|rrr} 2 & 5 & 10 & 15 \\ 3 & 5 & 5 & 15 \\ 5 & 5 & 5 & 5 \\ & 1 & 1 & 1 \end{array}$$

LCD =
$2 \times 3 \times 5 = 30$

{2}

Change the fractions to equivalent fractions with the LCD as denominator.

$$\frac{2}{5} = \frac{?}{30} \quad 5\overline{)30}^{\,6} \quad \frac{2}{5} = \frac{2 \times 6}{5 \times 6} = \frac{12}{30}$$

$$\frac{3}{10} = \frac{?}{30} \quad 10\overline{)30}^{\,3} \quad \frac{3}{10} = \frac{3 \times 3}{10 \times 3} = \frac{9}{30}$$

$$\frac{4}{15} = \frac{?}{30} \quad 15\overline{)30}^{\,2} \quad \frac{4}{15} = \frac{4 \times 2}{15 \times 2} = \frac{8}{30}$$

{3}

Add whole numbers and the fractions.

$$\begin{array}{rcr} 3\frac{2}{5} & = & 3\frac{12}{30} \\ 10\frac{3}{10} & = & 10\frac{9}{30} \\ + \quad 4\frac{4}{15} & = & 4\frac{8}{30} \\ \hline & & 17\frac{29}{30} \end{array}$$

Self-Check

Add the following numbers.

7. $\frac{1}{9} + \frac{2}{9} + \frac{3}{9}$ **8.** $\frac{2}{3} + \frac{1}{6}$ **9.** $\frac{3}{5} + \frac{7}{8} + \frac{2}{10}$ **10.** $4\frac{5}{6} + 7\frac{1}{2}$

Subtracting Fractions

You subtract fractions much the same way you add them: You find the least common denominator, change the fractions to equivalent fractions with the LCD, and subtract the fractions.

Step by Step

Subtracting Fractions

Step 1. If the fractions have different denominators, find the LCD.

Step 2. Change each fraction to an equivalent fraction with the LCD as the denominator.

Step 3. Subtract the whole numbers and the fractions. Reduce the answer to lowest terms.

EXAMPLE 11

Subtract $\frac{24}{25} - \frac{9}{25}$.

$$\frac{24}{25} - \frac{9}{25} = \frac{15}{25}$$

The difference between the numerators is the numerator of the difference. The denominator is the denominator of the numbers being subtracted.

$$\frac{15 \div 5}{25 \div 5} = \frac{3}{5}$$

Write the difference in lowest terms.

EXAMPLE 12

Subtract $\frac{5}{12} - \frac{4}{15}$.

{1} Find the LCD.

$$\begin{array}{r|rr} 2 & 12 & 15 \\ 2 & 6 & 15 \\ 3 & 3 & 15 \\ 5 & 1 & 5 \\ & 1 & 1 \end{array}$$

$2 \times 2 \times 3 \times 5 = 60$

{2} Change the fractions to equivalent fractions that have the LCD as denominator.

$\frac{5}{12} = \frac{?}{60}$ $\quad 12\overline{)60}$ gives 5

$$\frac{5}{12} = \frac{5 \times 5}{12 \times 5} = \frac{25}{60}$$

$\frac{4}{15} = \frac{?}{60}$ $\quad 15\overline{)60}$ gives 4

$$\frac{4}{15} = \frac{4 \times 4}{15 \times 4} = \frac{16}{60}$$

{3} Subtract. Reduce the answer to lowest terms.

$$\frac{25}{60} - \frac{16}{60} = \frac{9}{60} = \frac{3}{20}$$

You subtract mixed numbers in much the same way you add mixed numbers: First, you find the LCD if one is needed; then you change the fractions to equivalent fractions with that LCD. You subtract the fractions and then the whole numbers. Finally, you change the answer into a whole or mixed number with the fraction in lowest terms.

EXAMPLE 13

Subtract $8\frac{7}{10} - 1\frac{1}{2}$.

$$\begin{array}{rcr} 8\frac{7}{10} & = & 8\frac{7}{10} \\ -\;1\frac{1}{2} & = & 1\frac{5}{10} \\ \hline & & 7\frac{2}{10} = 7\frac{1}{5} \end{array}$$

Simple inspection tells you that 10 is the LCD, so you convert both fractions to equivalent fractions with 10 as denominators.

Subtract the whole numbers and the fractions. Write the answer as a mixed number.

In the subtraction of mixed numbers, it is sometimes necessary to subtract a larger fraction from a smaller fraction. When this happens, you must borrow 1 from the whole number part of the minuend (the top number) and add it to the fraction in the form of a fraction with the LCD as numerator and denominator. You then subtract the fractions and the whole numbers and reduce the answer to lowest terms.

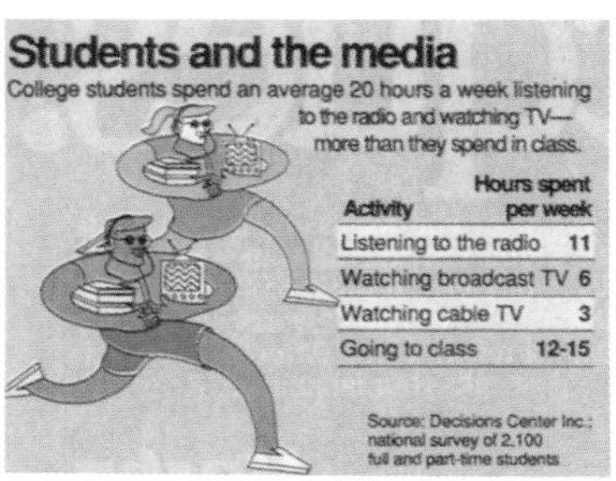

"Students and the Media"
By Shelley Arps, USA TODAY

Step by Step

Borrowing in the Subtraction of Mixed Numbers

Step 1. If the fractions have different denominators, find the LCD and change the fractions to equivalent forms with the LCD as denominator.

Step 2. If necessary, borrow 1 from the whole number in the minuend; subtract 1 from the whole number and add 1, in the form of the LCD over the LCD, to the fraction.

Step 3. Subtract the fractions and the whole numbers and then reduce the fraction to lowest terms.

EXAMPLE 14

Subtract $10\frac{1}{3} - 7\frac{3}{5}$.

$$\begin{array}{rcr} 10\frac{1}{3} & = & 10\frac{5}{15} \\ -\ 7\frac{3}{5} & = & 7\frac{9}{15} \\ \hline \end{array}$$

Convert both fractions to equivalent fractions with denominators of 15. We cannot subtract $\frac{9}{15}$ from $\frac{5}{15}$, so we borrow 1 from 10, write the 1 as $\frac{15}{15}$, and add it to $\frac{5}{15}$.

$$\begin{array}{rcr} 10\frac{5}{15} & = & 9\frac{20}{15} \\ -\ 7\frac{9}{15} & = & 7\frac{9}{15} \\ \hline & & 2\frac{11}{15} \end{array}$$

Rewrite the problem to show the borrowing, and then subtract the whole numbers and the fractions. The fraction is already in lowest terms, so you do not have to reduce it.

Self-Check

Subtract.

11. $\frac{8}{9} - \frac{2}{9}$ **12.** $\frac{3}{4} - \frac{5}{7}$ **13.** $5\frac{3}{4} - 2\frac{1}{2}$ **14.** $9\frac{1}{2} - 6\frac{2}{3}$

Section Review

Find the least common denominator for these fractions.

1. $\frac{1}{4}, \frac{1}{12}, \frac{11}{16}$ **2.** $\frac{7}{8}, \frac{1}{14}, \frac{13}{16}$

3. $\frac{2}{3}, \frac{1}{5}, \frac{1}{7}, \frac{10}{12}$

4. $\frac{1}{8}, \frac{5}{9}, \frac{7}{12}, \frac{9}{17}$

5. $\frac{5}{72}, \frac{7}{48}, \frac{7}{36}, \frac{5}{42}$

Add.

6. $\frac{3}{4} + \frac{4}{5}$

7. $\frac{7}{8} + \frac{1}{2}$

8. $\frac{2}{5} + \frac{2}{3}$

9. $\frac{3}{4} + \frac{7}{8}$

10. $\frac{5}{6} + \frac{17}{18}$

11. $\frac{1}{4} + \frac{11}{12} + \frac{7}{16}$

12. $\frac{1}{6} + \frac{7}{8} + \frac{5}{12}$

13. $\frac{7}{9} + \frac{13}{16} + \frac{2}{3}$

14. $\frac{5}{6} + \frac{1}{12} + \frac{4}{9}$

15. $\frac{3}{4} + \frac{7}{15} + \frac{5}{6} + \frac{3}{5} + \frac{3}{20}$

16. $7\frac{1}{2} + 4\frac{3}{8}$

17. $11\frac{5}{6} + 8\frac{2}{3}$

18. $15\frac{1}{2} + 9\frac{3}{4}$

19. $7\frac{2}{3} + 3\frac{5}{6} + 4\frac{1}{2}$

20. $8\frac{7}{10} + 9\frac{1}{5} + 5\frac{1}{2}$

21. $3\frac{1}{4} + 2\frac{1}{3} + 3\frac{5}{6}$

22. $73\frac{1}{2} + 18\frac{1}{3}$

23. $36\frac{2}{3} + 28\frac{1}{2}$

24. $96\frac{5}{6} + 57\frac{4}{7}$

25. $20\frac{7}{12} + 27\frac{5}{8} + 7\frac{5}{6}$

26. $54\frac{1}{2} + 37\frac{2}{3} + 15\frac{5}{6}$

27. $11\frac{2}{3} + 68\frac{1}{5} + 57\frac{5}{8}$

28. Two types of fabric are needed for curtains. The lining requires $12\frac{3}{8}$ yards and the curtain fabric needed is $16\frac{5}{8}$ yards. How many yards of fabric are needed?

29. Three pieces of lumber measure $5\frac{3}{8}$ feet, $7\frac{1}{2}$ feet, and $9\frac{3}{4}$ feet. What is the total length of the lumber?

Subtract.

30. $\frac{5}{12} - \frac{1}{4}$

31. $\frac{2}{3} - \frac{1}{6}$

32. $\frac{1}{2} - \frac{1}{3}$

33. $\frac{6}{7} - \frac{5}{14}$

34. $\frac{13}{16} - \frac{2}{3}$

35. $\frac{11}{15} - \frac{1}{6}$

Subtract. *Remember:* Fractions must have a *common denominator.* Borrow when necessary. Reduce the answer to lowest terms.

36. $7\frac{4}{5} - 4\frac{1}{2}$

37. $4\frac{1}{2} - 3\frac{6}{7}$

38. $4\frac{5}{6} - 3\frac{1}{3}$

39. $8\frac{2}{3} - 2\frac{1}{2}$

40. $4\frac{5}{12} - 1\frac{1}{3}$

41. $3\frac{1}{2} - 1\frac{1}{4}$

42. $7\frac{5}{9} - 5\frac{1}{2}$

43. $564\frac{5}{9} - 317\frac{5}{6}$

44. $232\frac{2}{15} - 189\frac{2}{5}$

45. $83\frac{1}{9} - 46\frac{1}{3}$

46. $9\frac{3}{7} - 7\frac{3}{5}$

47. $106\frac{1}{4} - 37\frac{9}{24}$

48. $38\frac{1}{2} - 26\frac{1}{3}$

49. $182\frac{9}{12} - 90\frac{5}{6}$

50. $317\frac{3}{4} - 196\frac{2}{3}$

Solve.

51. A board $3\frac{5}{8}$ feet long must be sawed from a 6-foot board. How long is the remaining piece?

52. Cindy Vaughn worked the following hours during a week: $7\frac{3}{4}$, $5\frac{1}{2}$, $6\frac{1}{4}$, $9\frac{1}{4}$, and $8\frac{3}{4}$. Louise Vaughn worked 40 hours. Who worked the most hours? How many more?

Multiplying and Dividing Fractions

When you multiply and divide fractions, you do *not* have to use common denominators.

Multiplying Fractions

Step by Step

Multiplying Fractions

Step 1. Multiply the numerators to find the numerator of the product.

Step 2. Multiply the denominators to find the denominator of the product.

Step 3. Reduce the answer to lowest terms.

EXAMPLE 15

Multiply $\frac{3}{5} \times \frac{5}{7}$.

$\frac{3}{5} \times \frac{5}{7} = \frac{15}{35} = \frac{3}{7}$

Multiply the numerators and the denominators to find the product. Reduce the answer to lowest terms.

TIPS & TRAPS
You can shorten your written steps when you multiply a whole number and a fraction if you *mentally* see the whole number as an improper fraction.

(mentally)

$$5 \times \frac{2}{3} = \frac{5}{1} \times \frac{2}{3} = \frac{10}{3}$$

The whole number is in the numerator, so it is multiplied by the numerator in the fraction.

Reducing Fractions Before Multiplying. When you multiply fractions, you can save time by reducing fractions *before* you multiply them. In a multiplication problem, if *any* numerator and *any* denominator can be divided by the same number, you can reduce the fractions before you multiply them. You can then multiply the reduced numbers faster and with greater accuracy than you could multiply the larger numbers.

EXAMPLE 16

Multiply $\frac{3}{4} \times \frac{2}{9}$. Reduce the terms before multiplying.

$\frac{\overset{1}{\cancel{3}}}{\underset{2}{\cancel{4}}} \times \frac{\overset{1}{\cancel{2}}}{\underset{3}{\cancel{9}}} = \frac{1}{2} \times \frac{1}{3}$

Reduce the 3 and 9 to 1 and 3.
Reduce the 2 and 4 to 1 and 2.

$\frac{1}{2} \times \frac{1}{3} = \frac{1}{6}$

Multiply the reduced numerators and denominators to find the product.

Multiplying Mixed Numbers. Multiplying mixed numbers can be done by changing the mixed numbers to fractions.

Step by Step

Multiplying Mixed Numbers

Step 1. Change the mixed numbers to improper fractions.

Step 2. Multiply the numerators and the denominators.

Step 3. Reduce the answer to lowest terms.

Real World Application

If you are renting or leasing a house or an apartment at the present time, or plan to do so in the future, you are a customer of a property manager. The handling of rental real estate is the business of a property management office, and the owner of the property is the client of this business. There are laws, which vary from state to state, that protect the rights of the tenant and the owner. When a rental agreement is signed, it specifies the dates of the agreement, and when rents are due. If your first payment is due on the first day of the month and your move-in date is the fifteenth of the month, then you must pro-rate the rent for the time that you occupy the apartment during that first month.

To find the pro-rated rent, you must first find the amount of rent you will pay for an entire year, 12 months. You will not find the rent per day during a month because the number of days in a month varies. You now know how much rent you will pay for the 365 days in the year. With this information you can find how much rent you must pay for any part of a year.

Example: Your rental agreement states that your rent of $395 is due on the first day of March, but you actually move in on the fifteenth of March. How much rent must you pay for the month of March?

$\$395 \times 12 \text{ months} = \$4{,}740$ per year or 365 days

$\$4{,}740 \times \frac{17}{365} = \$220.77$ rent due for the 17 days you occupied the apartment in March

Application Questions

1. How much rent must you pay for the month of June if your rent is due on the first of the month and you move in on June 21? The monthly rent is $325.

2. a. Pro-rate your rent on an apartment which rents for $455 if the rental agreement requires you to make the first payment on January 1, and you actually move in on January 16.

b. How much rent will you pay for February?

EXAMPLE 17

Multiply $2\frac{1}{3} \times 3\frac{3}{4}$.

$2\frac{1}{3} \times 3\frac{3}{4} = \frac{(3 \times 2) + 1}{3} \times \frac{(4 \times 3) + 3}{4} =$ Change the mixed numbers to improper fractions.

$\frac{7}{\overset{}{\underset{1}{\cancel{3}}}} \times \frac{\overset{5}{\cancel{15}}}{4} = \frac{35}{4}$ Reduce 3 and 15 to 1 and 5. Multiply the numerators and denominators.

$\frac{35}{4} = 8\frac{3}{4}$ Change the answer to a mixed number.

Self-Check

Multiply and reduce to lowest terms. Reduce before multiplying whenever possible.

15. $\frac{5}{7} \times \frac{1}{6}$ **16.** $\frac{5}{6} \times \frac{3}{4} \times \frac{4}{5}$ **17.** $5\frac{3}{4} \times 3\frac{8}{9}$

Dividing Fractions

Division of fractions is very similar to multiplication of fractions. Multiplication and division work together for fractions just as they do for whole numbers.

FINDING RECIPROCALS. Before we discuss the division of fractions, we need to look at **reciprocals.** Two numbers are reciprocals if their product is 1. Thus, $\frac{2}{3}$ and $\frac{3}{2}$ are reciprocals ($\frac{2}{3} \times \frac{3}{2} = 1$) and $\frac{7}{8}$ and $\frac{8}{7}$ are reciprocals ($\frac{7}{8} \times \frac{8}{7} = 1$). You find the reciprocal of any fraction by turning the fraction upside down or switching the numerator and the denominator. The reciprocal of any whole number is a fraction with that number as the denominator and a numerator of 1. For example, the reciprocal of 2 is $\frac{1}{2}$.

reciprocals: two numbers that give a product of 1 when multiplied by each other. $\frac{7}{8}$ and $\frac{8}{7}$ are reciprocals.

Step by Step

Finding the Reciprocal of a Number

Step 1. Write the number as a fraction. If the number is a whole number, write it as a fraction with a denominator of 1.

Step 2. Turn the fraction upside down: Let the numerator become the denominator and the denominator become the numerator.

EXAMPLE 18

Study the following list of numbers and their reciprocals.

The reciprocal of $\frac{3}{4}$ is $\frac{4}{3}$.

The reciprocal of $\frac{2}{9}$ is $\frac{9}{2}$.

The reciprocal of $\frac{1}{2}$ is $\frac{2}{1}$ or 2.

The reciprocal of 7 is $\frac{1}{7}$. $\left(\text{Remember, } 7 = \frac{7}{1}.\right)$

The reciprocal of $3\frac{1}{8}$ is $\frac{8}{25}$. $\left(\text{Remember, } 3\frac{1}{8} = \frac{25}{8}.\right)$

USING RECIPROCALS TO DIVIDE FRACTIONS. To divide when at least one of the numbers is a fraction, *multiply* the dividend (the number being divided) by the *reciprocal* of the divisor. It does not matter whether the dividend or divisor is a whole number, a fraction, or a mixed number.

Step by Step

Using Reciprocals to Divide Fractions

Step 1. Find the reciprocal of the divisor. If the dividend is a mixed number, change it to an improper fraction.

Step 2. *Multiply* the dividend by the *reciprocal* of the divisor.

Step 3. Express the answer as a whole or mixed number.

EXAMPLE 19

Find the quotient of $\frac{3}{4} \div \frac{1}{6}$.

$\frac{3}{4} \div \frac{1}{6} = \frac{3}{4} \times \frac{6}{1}$

Multiply the dividend by the reciprocal of the divisor. The reciprocal of $\frac{1}{6}$ is $\frac{6}{1}$.

$\frac{3}{\cancel{4}_2} \times \frac{\cancel{6}^3}{1} = \frac{9}{2}$

Reduce 6 and 4 to 3 and 2.

$\frac{9}{2} = 4\frac{1}{2}$

Express the answer as a mixed number.

EXAMPLE 20

Find the quotient of $5\frac{1}{2} \div 7\frac{1}{3}$.

$5\frac{1}{2} \div 7\frac{1}{3} = \frac{(5 \times 2) + 1}{2} \div \frac{(7 \times 3) + 1}{3} = \frac{11}{2} \div \frac{22}{3}$

Change the mixed numbers to improper fractions.

$\frac{11}{2} \div \frac{22}{3} = \frac{\cancel{11}^1}{2} \times \frac{3}{\cancel{22}_2} = \frac{3}{4}$

Multiply the dividend by the reciprocal of the divisor. Reduce 11 and 22 to 1 and 2 before multiplying.

Self-Check

18. Find the reciprocals of the following numbers:

a. $\frac{3}{5}$ **b.** 9 **c.** $3\frac{3}{8}$

Find the following quotients.

19. $\frac{5}{8} \div \frac{3}{4}$ **20.** $5\frac{1}{4} \div 2\frac{2}{3}$

Section Review

Multiply.

1. $\frac{1}{4} \times \frac{7}{8}$ **2.** $\frac{9}{10} \times \frac{3}{4}$ **3.** $\frac{5}{6} \times \frac{1}{3}$

4. $\frac{1}{8} \times \frac{7}{8}$ **5.** $\frac{3}{5} \times \frac{3}{4}$ **6.** $\frac{1}{2} \times \frac{1}{2}$

Multiply and change answers that are improper fractions to mixed numbers.

7. $5 \times \frac{2}{3}$ **8.** $\frac{3}{7} \times 8$

9. $\frac{7}{8} \times 3$

10. $6 \times \frac{4}{5}$

Multiply and reduce to lowest terms. Reduce before multiplying whenever possible.

11. $\frac{5}{6} \times \frac{2}{3}$

12. $\frac{3}{4} \times \frac{4}{5}$

13. $\frac{3}{4} \times \frac{8}{9} \times \frac{7}{12}$

14. $\frac{2}{5} \times \frac{5}{6} \times \frac{7}{8}$

15. $\frac{9}{10} \times \frac{8}{5} \times \frac{7}{15}$

16. $\frac{9}{10} \times \frac{2}{5} \times \frac{5}{9} \times \frac{3}{7}$

17. $\frac{5}{9} \times \frac{8}{21} \times \frac{9}{10} \times \frac{6}{7}$

18. $\frac{15}{25} \times \frac{13}{20} \times \frac{14}{30}$

19. $\frac{1}{8} \times \frac{3}{5} \times \frac{40}{41}$

Multiply.

20. $3\frac{1}{3} \times 4\frac{1}{4}$

21. $4\frac{1}{5} \times 8\frac{5}{6}$

22. $6\frac{2}{9} \times 4\frac{1}{2}$

23. $7\frac{5}{8} \times 9\frac{5}{6}$

24. $8\frac{2}{5} \times 9\frac{4}{9}$

25. $9\frac{1}{6} \times 10\frac{2}{7}$

26. $10\frac{1}{2} \times 1\frac{5}{7}$

Solve.

27. Suzanna Kale received $\frac{3}{4}$ of a regular day's pay as a tribute to her birthday. If she regularly earns \$64 a day, how much birthday pay did she receive?

28. A recipe for pecan pralines calls for the following.

$\frac{3}{4}$ cup brown sugar

$\frac{3}{4}$ cup white sugar

$\frac{1}{2}$ cup evaporated milk

$\frac{1}{4}$ teaspoon vanilla

2 tablespoons margarine

1 cup pecans

Helen Brewer is making treats for her second-grade class, so she must make $2\frac{1}{2}$ times as many pralines as this recipe yields. How much of each ingredient is needed?

29. The price of computers has fallen by $\frac{2}{5}$. If the original price of a computer was \$10,275, by how much has the price fallen?

30. After a family reunion, $10\frac{2}{3}$ cakes were left. If Janie Womble took $\frac{3}{8}$ of these cakes, how many did she take?

Find the reciprocal of each of the following numbers.

31. $\frac{5}{8}$ **32.** $\frac{2}{3}$ **33.** $\frac{1}{4}$ **34.** 8 **35.** $3\frac{1}{4}$

36. $2\frac{3}{8}$ **37.** $1\frac{3}{5}$ **38.** $2\frac{5}{9}$

Perform each division and reduce the answer to lowest terms.

39. $\frac{3}{4} \div \frac{1}{4}$

40. $\frac{5}{6} \div \frac{1}{8}$

41. $\frac{15}{36} \div \frac{7}{8}$

42. $\frac{3}{8} \div 3$

43. $\frac{3}{10} \div 6$

44. $15 \div \frac{3}{4}$

45. $7\frac{1}{2} \div 2$

46. $7\frac{1}{2} \div 1\frac{2}{3}$

47. $3\frac{1}{7} \div 5\frac{1}{2}$

48. $6\frac{4}{5} \div 8\frac{5}{6}$

Solve.

49. A board 244 inches long is cut into pieces that are each $7\frac{5}{8}$ inches. How many pieces can be cut?

50. A stack of $1\frac{5}{8}$-inch plywood measures 91 inches. How many pieces of plywood are in the stack?

Summary

Topic	Page	What to Remember	Examples
Types of fractions	31	Proper fraction: Numerator is smaller than denominator.	$\frac{5}{8}, \frac{55}{73}, \frac{356}{893}$
		Improper fraction: Numerator is equal to or larger than denominator.	$\frac{8}{8}, \frac{36}{19}, \frac{488}{301}$
		Mixed number: A number made up of a whole number and a fraction.	$5\frac{2}{9}, 33\frac{1}{3}, 45\frac{54}{73}$
Changing an improper fraction to a whole or mixed number	32	Divide the numerator by the denominator. If there is no remainder, then the improper fraction is equivalent to a whole number. If there is a remainder, write it over the original denominator to find the fraction in the mixed number.	$\frac{150}{3} \rightarrow 3\overline{)150}$ = 50 $\rightarrow 50$ $\frac{153}{3} \rightarrow 3\overline{)153}$ = 50 R3 (150, 3) $\rightarrow 50\frac{3}{153}$
Changing a mixed number to an improper fraction	33	Multiply the whole number by the denominator of the fraction and add the product to the original numerator of the fraction. This is the new numerator. The new denominator is the same as the original denominator in the fraction.	$5\frac{5}{8} = \frac{(5 \times 8) + 5}{8} = \frac{45}{8}$
Reducing a fraction to lowest terms	33	See if the numerator and denominator can both be divided evenly by the same number. Divide and see if the new numerator and denominator can both be divided by some number. Continue until there are no more numbers that can divide both terms.	$\frac{12}{36} = \frac{12 \div 2}{36 \div 2} = \frac{6}{18}$ $= \frac{6 \div 2}{18 \div 2} = \frac{3}{9}$ $= \frac{3 \div 3}{9 \div 3} = \frac{1}{3}$ No more divisors. $\frac{1}{3}$ is in lowest terms.
GCD shortcut	35	To find the GCD of two numbers, divide the larger number by the smaller number. Divide the remainder of the first division into the divisor from the first division. Divide the remainder of the second division into the divisor from the second division. Continue dividing until the answer to the division has no remainder. The last divisor that produced no remainder is the GCD.	Find the GCD of 27 and 36. $27\overline{)36}$ = 1 R9 (27, 9) $9\overline{)27}$ = 3 (27) The GCD is 9.
Changing a fraction to a new fraction with a greater denominator	36	Divide the *new* denominator by the *old* denominator. Multiply the quotient times the numerator and denominator of the old fraction to find the new fraction.	Write $\frac{3}{4}$ as an equivalent fraction with denominator of 20. $4\overline{)20}$ = 5 $\frac{3 \times 5}{4 \times 5} = \frac{15}{20}$

Topic	Page	What to Remember	Examples
Adding fractions with like denominators	39	The sum of the numerators is the numerator of the sum. The denominator is the same denominator as in the fractions being added. Write the new fraction in lowest terms.	$\frac{3}{5} + \frac{7}{5} + \frac{5}{5} = \frac{15}{5} = 3$
Prime numbers	40	A prime number is a whole number greater than 1 that is divisible only by itself and 1.	The first ten prime numbers are 2, 3, 5, 7, 11, 13, 17, 19, 23, and 29.
Finding the LCD of two or more fractions	40	Write the denominators in a horizontal row and divide each one by the smallest prime number that can divide evenly into two or more of the numbers. Write a new row of numbers using the quotients of the division in the first step, bringing down any numbers that are not divisible by this prime number. Continue this process until the only number in the row is 1. Multiply all the prime numbers to find the least common denominator.	Find the least common denominator of $\frac{5}{6}, \frac{6}{15},$ and $\frac{7}{20}$. $\begin{array}{r\|rrr} 2 & 6 & 15 & 20 \\ 2 & 3 & 15 & 10 \\ 3 & 3 & 15 & 5 \\ 5 & 1 & 5 & 5 \\ \hline & 1 & 1 & 1 \end{array}$ LCD = 2 × 2 × 3 × 5 = 60
Adding fractions with unlike denominators	41	Find the LCD of all the fractions and change each fraction to an equivalent fraction with that denominator. The sum of the numerators is the numerator of the sum. The LCD is the denominator of the sum. Reduce to lowest terms. Change improper fractions to whole or mixed numbers.	Add $\frac{5}{6} + \frac{6}{15} + \frac{7}{20}$. Find the LCD (see preceding example) and change fractions to equivalent fractions with the LCD. $\frac{5 \times 10}{6 \times 10} = \frac{50}{60}$ $\frac{6 \times 4}{15 \times 4} = \frac{24}{60}$ $\frac{7 \times 3}{20 \times 3} = \frac{21}{60}$ Add the fractions and reduce the sum to lowest terms. $\frac{5}{6} + \frac{6}{15} + \frac{7}{20} = \frac{50}{60} + \frac{24}{60} + \frac{21}{60}$ $= \frac{95}{60} = \frac{19}{12} = 1\frac{7}{12}$
Adding mixed numbers	41	Find the LCD if necessary and change the fractions to equivalent fractions with that denominator. Add the fractions and the whole numbers. Write the sum as a whole or mixed number.	$5\frac{3}{4} = 5\frac{9}{12}$ $+\ 6\frac{2}{3} = 6\frac{8}{12}$ $11\frac{17}{12} = 12\frac{5}{12}$

Topic	Page	What to Remember	Examples
Subtracting fractions	42	Find the LCD if necessary and change the fractions to equivalent fractions with that denominator. Subtract the numerators and reduce the difference to lowest terms.	$\frac{7}{8} - \frac{1}{3} = \frac{21}{24} - \frac{8}{24} = \frac{13}{24}$
Borrowing in the subtraction of mixed numbers	44	Find the LCD if necessary and change the fractions to equivalent fractions with that denominator. If necessary, borrow a 1 from the whole number in the minuend and add it to the fraction in the minuend. Subtract the fractions and reduce the difference to lowest terms.	$24\frac{1}{2} = 24\frac{2}{4} = 23\frac{6}{4}$ $-\ 11\frac{3}{4} = 11\frac{3}{4} = 11\frac{3}{4}$ $12\frac{3}{4}$
Multiplying fractions	50	Multiply the numerators to find the numerator of the product. Multiply the denominators to find the denominator of the product. Write the answer in lowest terms.	$\frac{3}{2} \times \frac{12}{17} = \frac{36}{34} = 1\frac{2}{34} = 1\frac{1}{17}$
Reducing terms before multiplying	51	When a numerator and denominator have one or more common divisors, you can reduce them before you multiply.	$\frac{\overset{2}{\cancel{16}}}{\underset{5}{\cancel{25}}} \times \frac{\overset{1}{\cancel{5}}}{\underset{3}{\cancel{24}}} = \frac{2}{5} \times \frac{1}{3} = \frac{2}{15}$
Multiplying mixed numbers	51	Change the mixed numbers to improper fractions. Multiply the numerators and denominators. Reduce the product fraction to lowest terms.	$3\frac{3}{4} \times 3\frac{2}{3} = \frac{15}{4} \times \frac{11}{3} = \frac{165}{12}$ $= \frac{55}{4} = 13\frac{3}{4}$
Finding the reciprocal of a number	53	Write the number as a fraction. If the number is a whole number, write it as a fraction with a denominator of 1. Turn the fraction upside down: Let the numerator become the denominator and the denominator become the numerator.	The reciprocal of 6 is $\frac{1}{6}$. The reciprocal of $\frac{2}{3}$ is $\frac{3}{2}$.
Using reciprocals to divide fractions	53	Find the reciprocal of the divisor. If the dividend or divisor is a mixed number, change it to an improper fraction. *Multiply* the dividend by the *reciprocal* of the divisor. Write the answer in lowest terms.	To divide $\frac{55}{68}$ by $\frac{11}{17}$, multiply $\frac{55}{68} \times \frac{17}{11}$. $\frac{\overset{5}{\cancel{55}}}{\underset{4}{\cancel{68}}} \times \frac{\overset{1}{\cancel{17}}}{\underset{1}{\cancel{11}}} = \frac{5}{4} = 1\frac{1}{4}$

Chapter Review

Change to a whole or mixed number.

1. $\frac{692}{12}$

Change to an improper fraction.

2. $17\frac{3}{4}$

Find the greatest common divisor (GCD) and then reduce to lowest terms.

3. $\frac{14}{42}$

4. $\frac{36}{45}$

5. $\frac{88}{242}$

Change to the indicated denominator.

6. $\frac{5}{8} = \frac{\quad}{64}$

Find the lowest common denominator (LCD).

7. $\frac{3}{8}, \frac{4}{9}, \frac{11}{15}, \frac{5}{12}$

8. $\frac{11}{12}, \frac{35}{72}, \frac{7}{8}$

Add. Reduce answers to lowest terms.

9. $\frac{13}{30} + \frac{7}{15} + \frac{1}{3}$

10. $\frac{3}{7} + \frac{9}{14} + \frac{1}{2}$

11. $\frac{1}{2} + \frac{5}{8} + \frac{7}{12}$

12. $4\frac{5}{6} + 7\frac{1}{2} + 9\frac{1}{3} + 7\frac{4}{9}$

13. $82\frac{3}{4} + 19\frac{4}{5} + 91\frac{1}{3}$

14. $140\frac{5}{8} + 98\frac{5}{6} + 88\frac{3}{5}$

Subtract. Reduce answers to lowest terms.

15. $\frac{2}{3} - \frac{3}{8}$

16. $\frac{7}{16} - \frac{5}{12}$

17. $\frac{5}{8} - \frac{2}{7}$

18. $2\frac{3}{4} - 1\frac{7}{8}$

19. $8\frac{1}{6} - 7\frac{7}{12}$

20. $104\frac{1}{5} - 59\frac{3}{4}$

Add or subtract as indicated:

21. $434\frac{3}{4} - 315$

22. $146\frac{7}{8} - 142$

23. $375 - 286\frac{2}{3}$

Multiply.

24. $\frac{7}{9} \times \frac{2}{11}$

25. $\frac{2}{5} \times \frac{4}{9} \times \frac{1}{4}$

26. $\frac{5}{8} \times 3$

27. $\frac{1}{8} \times \frac{4}{5} \times \frac{8}{9}$

28. $4\frac{2}{3} \times 15$

29. $8\frac{2}{3} \times 4\frac{11}{12}$

30. $6\frac{7}{8} \times 7\frac{1}{2}$

Find the reciprocal of each of the following.

31. $\frac{3}{11}$ **32.** 5 **33.** $2\frac{1}{4}$

Divide.

34. $\frac{1}{4} \div \frac{7}{8}$ **35.** $16 \div \frac{4}{5}$

36. $\frac{17}{42} \div 8$

37. $3\frac{2}{3} \div 2\frac{1}{2}$

38. $3\frac{4}{5} \div 7\frac{5}{6}$

39. $7\frac{5}{7} \div 6\frac{11}{14}$

Solve.

40. Templeton stock closed at $15\frac{1}{8}$ after opening at $13\frac{7}{8}$. What was the net increase in the price of the stock?

41. Glenda Chaille processes 850 tax returns in a normal day. If she only works $\frac{3}{4}$ day, how many returns should she be able to process?

42. An institutional recipe for raisin cookies follow. It makes $3\frac{1}{2}$ times the servings one would use in the home.

$5\frac{1}{4}$ cups sugar

$2\frac{1}{3}$ cups margarine

14 eggs

$5\frac{1}{4}$ cups chopped raisins

$8\frac{3}{4}$ cups flour

$3\frac{1}{2}$ teaspoons soda

$3\frac{1}{2}$ teaspoons cloves

$3\frac{1}{2}$ teaspoons cinnamon

The recipe can be used in the home if it is divided by $3\frac{1}{2}$. How much of each ingredient is needed?

43. Fabric that is $26\frac{1}{4}$ yards long is cut into $3\frac{3}{4}$ yard lengths. How many lengths are there?

Trial Test

Perform the indicated operation. Reduce all answers to lowest terms.

1. $\frac{5}{6} - \frac{4}{6}$

2. $\frac{5}{8} + \frac{9}{10}$

3. $\frac{5}{8} \times \frac{7}{10}$

4. $\frac{5}{6} \div \frac{3}{4}$

5. $10\frac{1}{2} \div 5\frac{3}{4}$

6. $56 \times 32\frac{6}{7}$

7. $98\frac{2}{3} - 53\frac{4}{5}$

8. $2\frac{1}{2} + 3\frac{1}{3}$

9. $6\frac{4}{7} \times 5\frac{1}{4}$

10. $35\frac{3}{4} + 57\frac{5}{6} + 38\frac{5}{9}$

11. $5\frac{3}{4} - 2\frac{7}{8}$

12. $\frac{4}{7} \times \frac{10}{11}$

13. $257 + 53\frac{5}{6}$

14. $\frac{4}{5} - \frac{1}{3}$

15. $137 - 89\frac{4}{5}$

16. $\frac{24}{35} \times \frac{5}{32}$

17. $324\frac{3}{4} - 115$

Solve.

18. Dale Burton ordered $\frac{3}{4}$ truckload of merchandise. If approximately $\frac{1}{3}$ of the $\frac{3}{4}$ truckload of merchandise has been unloaded, how much remains to be unloaded?

19. A chicken grower orders 860 baby chicks but expects to lose $\frac{1}{8}$ of them. How many does the grower expect to lose?

20. A company that employs 580 people expects to lay off 87 workers. What fractional part of the workers are expected to be laid off?

1. $16\overline{)388}$ = 24 R4, or $24\frac{4}{16} = 24\frac{1}{4}$

$$\begin{array}{r} 24 \\ 16\overline{)388} \\ \underline{32} \\ 68 \\ \underline{64} \\ 4 \end{array}$$

2. $6\frac{2}{3} = \frac{(3 \times 6) + 2}{3} = \frac{20}{3}$

3. $\frac{7}{28} = \frac{7 \div 7}{28 \div 7} = \frac{1}{4}$

4. $\frac{48}{78} = \frac{48 \div 6}{78 \div 6} = \frac{8}{13}$

5. $\frac{315}{360} = \frac{315 \div 45}{360 \div 45} = \frac{7}{8}$

6. $\frac{3}{8} = \frac{?}{152}$

$$\begin{array}{r} 19 \\ 8\overline{)152} \end{array}$$

$\frac{3}{8} = \frac{3 \times 19}{8 \times 19} = \frac{57}{152}$

7. $\frac{1}{9} + \frac{2}{9} + \frac{3}{9} = \frac{6}{9} = \frac{2}{3}$

8. $$\begin{array}{rcl} \frac{2}{3} & = & \frac{4}{6} \\ + \ \frac{1}{6} & = & \frac{1}{6} \\ \hline & & \frac{5}{6} \end{array}$$

9. $$\begin{array}{rcl} \frac{3}{5} & = & \frac{24}{40} \\ \frac{7}{8} & = & \frac{35}{40} \\ + \ \frac{2}{10} & = & \frac{8}{40} \\ \hline & & \frac{67}{40} = 1\frac{27}{40} \end{array}$$

10. $$\begin{array}{rcl} 4\frac{5}{6} & = & 4\frac{5}{6} \\ + \ 7\frac{1}{2} & = & 7\frac{3}{6} \\ \hline & & 11\frac{8}{6} = 11\frac{4}{3} = 12\frac{1}{3} \end{array}$$

11. $\frac{8}{9} - \frac{2}{9} = \frac{6}{9} = \frac{2}{3}$

12. $$\begin{array}{rcl} \frac{3}{4} & = & \frac{21}{28} \\ - \ \frac{5}{7} & = & \frac{20}{28} \\ \hline & & \frac{1}{28} \end{array}$$

13. $$\begin{array}{rcl} 5\frac{3}{4} & = & 5\frac{3}{4} \\ - \ 2\frac{1}{2} & = & 2\frac{2}{4} \\ \hline & & 3\frac{1}{4} \end{array}$$

14. $$\begin{array}{rcccl} 9\frac{1}{2} & = & 9\frac{3}{6} & = & 8\frac{9}{6} \\ - \ 6\frac{2}{3} & = & 6\frac{4}{6} & = & 6\frac{4}{6} \\ \hline & & & & 2\frac{5}{6} \end{array}$$

15. $\frac{5}{7} \times \frac{1}{6} = \frac{5}{42}$

16. $\frac{\overset{1}{\cancel{5}}}{\underset{2}{\cancel{6}}} \times \frac{\overset{1}{\cancel{3}}}{\underset{1}{\cancel{4}}} \times \frac{\overset{1}{\cancel{4}}}{\underset{1}{\cancel{5}}} = \frac{1}{2}$

17. $5\frac{3}{4} \times 3\frac{8}{9} = \frac{(4 \times 5) + 3}{4} \times \frac{(9 \times 3) + 8}{9}$

$= \frac{23}{4} \times \frac{35}{9} = \frac{805}{36} = 22\frac{13}{36}$

18. **a.** $\frac{5}{3}$ **b.** $\frac{1}{9}$ **c.** $3\frac{3}{8} = \frac{27}{8}$, so the reciprocal is $\frac{8}{27}$

19. $\frac{5}{8} \div \frac{3}{4} = \frac{5}{\underset{2}{\cancel{8}}} \times \frac{\overset{1}{\cancel{4}}}{3} = \frac{5}{6}$

20. $5\frac{1}{4} \div 2\frac{2}{3} = \frac{21}{4} \div \frac{8}{3} = \frac{21}{4} \times \frac{3}{8} = \frac{63}{32} = 1\frac{31}{32}$

Decimals 3

Learning Objectives

1. Recognize and read pure, mixed, and complex decimals. (pp. 71–72)
2. Round decimals to nearest digit. (pp. 72–73)
3. Add and subtract decimals. (pp. 74–76)
4. Multiply and divide decimals. (pp. 78–82)
5. Convert decimals to fractions and fractions to decimals (pp. 85–88)

Decimal numbers, like fractions, give us a way of writing amounts that are less than one, or part of a whole. We use decimals in some form or another every day—even our money system is based on decimals. Calculators utilize decimals, and decimals are the basis of percent, interest, markup and markdown calculations.

Reading and Rounding Decimals

Reading Decimals

A **decimal fraction** is a fraction with a denominator of 10, 100, 1,000, 10,000, 100,000 (or any power of 10). Examples of decimal fractions are numbers such as $\frac{3}{10}$ or $\frac{288}{100}$. You can write these fractions in decimal form, 0.3, or 2.88, by extending the place-value chart used in Chapter 1. This is shown in Figure 3-1.

decimal fraction: a fraction with a denominator of 10, 100, 1,000, and the like.

Thousands	Hundreds	Tens	Ones	Decimal point	Tenths	Hundredths	Thousandths	Ten-thousandths	Hundred-thousandths	Millionths
2	3	1	5	.	6	2	7	4	3	2

Figure 3-1
Place-Value Chart for Decimals

There are three different types of decimals:

A **pure decimal** has a value less than 1 (0.3 or 0.78).

A **mixed decimal** is composed of a whole number and a pure decimal (7.71 or 23.409).

A **complex decimal** is composed of a pure or mixed decimal and a fraction ($15.12\frac{3}{7}$).

pure decimal: a decimal with a value of less than 1.

mixed decimal: a decimal composed of a whole number and a pure decimal.

complex decimal: a decimal composed of a pure or mixed decimal and a fraction.

When you read a pure decimal, you read it as a whole number, but at the end of the number you say the name of the place value of the last digit in the number. You read 0.209 as "two hundred nine thousandths." (Note that the last digit of the decimal, 9, is in the thousandths place.)

When you read a mixed or complex decimal, you read the decimal point as *and*. Thus you read 5.03 as "five *and* three hundredths." The fraction in a complex decimal is understood as being a fraction of the *last* place in the decimal number. Thus $0.33\frac{1}{3}$ is read "thirty-three and one-third hundredths," not "thirty-three hundredths and one-third."

EXAMPLE 1

Examine the following decimals, their fraction equivalents, and names.

Decimal	Number of places to the right of the decimal point (equals the number of zeros in the denominator of the decimal fraction)	Fraction equivalent of decimal	Word name of decimal
0.7	1 place (denominator = 10)	$\frac{7}{10}$	Seven tenths
2.56	2 places (denominator = 100)	$2\frac{56}{100}$	Two and fifty-six hundredths
5.836	3 places (denominator = 1,000)	$5\frac{836}{1{,}000}$	Five and eight hundred thirty-six thousandths
0.4003	4 places (denominator = 10,000)	$\frac{4{,}003}{10{,}000}$	Four thousand three ten-thousandths

You read the number in Figure 3-1 as "two thousand, three hundred fifteen and six hundred twenty-seven thousand, four hundred thirty-two millionths."

Rounding Decimals

You round decimals for the same reasons and in the same way that you round whole numbers.

Step by Step

Rounding a Decimal to a Specified Place or Digit

Step 1. Find the digit in the place to which you are rounding.

Step 2. Look at the next digit to the right.

- **a.** If the digit is less than 5, drop it and any other digits to the right.
- **b.** If the digit is 5 or more, add 1 to the place to which you are rounding and drop all digits to the right of that place.

EXAMPLE 2

Round 17.3754 to the nearest hundredth.

17.3754 The digit in the hundredths place is 7.

17.3754	The digit to the right of 7 is 5, so we add 1 to 7 and drop all digits to the right of
17.38	the 8.

17.3754 rounded to the nearest hundredth is 17.38.

EXAMPLE 3

Round $193.48 to the nearest dollar.

$193.48	Rounding to the nearest dollar also means rounding to the nearest whole number.
$193.48	The digit in the ones place is 3.
$193	The digit to the right of 3 is 4, so we drop the 4 and all digits to the right of the decimal point.

$193.48 rounded to the nearest dollar is $193.

EXAMPLE 4

Round $17.375 to the nearest cent.

$17.375	Since one cent is one hundredth of a dollar, rounding to the nearest cent means rounding to the nearest hundredth. The digit in the hundredths place is 7.
$17.375	The digit to the right of 7 is 5, so we round the 7 to 8 and drop all digits to the
$17.38	right of 8.

$17.375 rounded to the nearest cent is $17.38.

Self-Check

1. Write the word names of each decimal.

a. 7.3 **b.** 33.07 **c.** 0.582 **d.** 1.0009 **e.** 0.63

Round the following decimals to the indicated place.

2. 0.3128 (nearest thousandth)

3. $493.91 (nearest dollar)

4. $34.528 (nearest cent)

Section Review

Write the words used to read these decimals.

1. 0.5

2. 0.27

3. 0.108

4. 0.013

5. 0.00275

6. 0.120704

Write the word name of each decimal.

7. 17.8

8. 3.04

9. 128.23

10. 3,000.003

11. 500.0007

12. 184.271

13. $0.08\frac{1}{3}$

14. $0.016\frac{2}{3}$

15. $0.83\frac{1}{3}$

16. $5.37\frac{1}{2}$

Round to the indicated place.

17. 0.1345 (nearest thousandth)

18. 384.72 (nearest tenth)

19. 384.73 (nearest ten)

20. 1,745.376 (nearest hundredth)

21. 1,745.376 (nearest hundred)

22. 32.57 (nearest whole number)

23. $175.24 (nearest dollar)

24. $5.333 (nearest cent)

Adding and Subtracting Decimals

Adding and subtracting decimals is very similar to adding and subtracting whole numbers. You need to pay close attention to how the numbers line up with each other in a problem, and you use the same regrouping techniques as you do with whole numbers.

Real World Application

Many students wait on tables while attending college. Often the restaurant requires these employees to keep all of their customers' receipts and money until the end of a shift. At this time, each employee is to subtract the total of the receipts from the total money collected to pay the restaurant owner. The remainder is the amount of tips or gratuities the waiter or waitress has received.

Total amount collected
− Total of receipts
Total of tips

Example: On a particular day, a waitress collects a total of $165.98. Below are copies of her receipts. How much did she receive in tips?

Total amount collected	=	$165.98
− Total of receipts	=	128.25
Total of tips	=	37.73

Application Questions

1. A total of $169.73 was collected during the dinner shift of a restaurant. The receipts were for the following amounts: $38.21, $21.53, $15.45, and $25.78. What was the amount of tips?

2. If you receive $38.45 in tips during lunch, and your total amount collected was $142.78, what was the total of your receipts?

Adding Decimals

When you add decimals, the most important thing is lining up the decimal points in all the numbers being added. Decimals, like whole numbers, are based on a place-value system, so the position of a digit in a decimal or whole number determines the digit's numerical value. This is why all the numbers in the ones column are added together, all the numbers in the tens column are added together, and so on. Remember, a whole number is understood to have a decimal point at the end, so that writing 2. or 2.0 is the same as writing 2, although you generally use either 2 or 2.0.

EXAMPLE 5

Add 32 + 2.55 + 8.85 + 0.625.

```
32
 2.55
 8.85
 0.625
------
44.025
```

A decimal point is understood to follow the 32.
All decimal points are lined up with one another. Add the numbers as you would add whole numbers.

TIPS & TRAPS
A common mistake in adding decimals is not to align the decimal points.

```
  15 <—— not lined up          1 5   <—— not lined up      15        All digits and
 4.28    correctly             4.28      correctly          4.28     decimal points are
 3.04                          3.04                         3.04     lined up correctly.
0.7 35 <—— not lined up        0.735                        0.735
1.4 82     correctly           9.555                       23.055

WRONG                          WRONG                       CORRECT
```

Subtracting Decimals

The procedure for subtracting decimals is similar to the procedure for adding decimals. The decimal points must line up with one another. A blank in any place is interpreted as a zero.

EXAMPLE 6

Subtract: 26.3 − 15.84.

```
    5 12 10
  2 6 .3  0
− 1 5 .8  4
-----------
  1 0 .4  6
```

Write the numbers so that the decimal points line up. Subtract the numbers, borrowing as you would in whole-number subtraction.

Self-Check

5. Add 6.005 + 0.03 + 924 + 3.9.

6. Subtract 407.96 − 298.39.

Section Review

Add.

1. 0.3 + 0.05 + 0.266 + 0.63

2. 31.005 + 5.36 + 0.708 + 4.16

3. 78.87 + 54 + 32.9569 + 0.0043

4. 9.004 + 0.07 + 723 + 8.7

Solve.

5. A shopper purchased a cake pan for $8.95, a bath mat for $9.59, and a bottle of shampoo for $2.39. Find the total cost of the purchases.

6. Robert McNab ordered 18.3 square meters of carpet for his halls, 123.5 square meters of carpet for bedrooms, 28.7 square meters of carpet for the family room, and 12.9 square meters of carpet for the play room. Find the total number of square meters of carpet he ordered.

Subtract.

7. 500.05 − 123.31

8. 815.01 − 335.6

9. 125.35 − 67.8975

10. 404.04 − 135.8716

11. 423 − 287.4

12. 807.38 − 529.79

13. 482.073 − 62.97

14. 5,003.02 − 689.93

15.
$$\begin{array}{r} 486.57 \\ -\ 160.83 \\ \hline \end{array}$$

16.
$$\begin{array}{r} 1{,}423.97 \\ -\ \ 802.89 \\ \hline \end{array}$$

17.
$$\begin{array}{r} 21.0357 \\ -\ 18.7289 \\ \hline \end{array}$$

18.
$$\begin{array}{r} 5.8376 \\ -\ 2.9608 \\ \hline \end{array}$$

19.
$$\begin{array}{r} 0.02135 \\ -\ 0.019876 \\ \hline \end{array}$$

20.
$$\begin{array}{r} 6.213502 \\ -\ 3.098107 \\ \hline \end{array}$$

Solve.

21. Four tires that retailed for $486.95 are on sale for $397.99. By how much are the tires reduced?

22. If two lengths of metal sheeting measuring 12.5 inches and 15.36 inches are cut from a roll of metal measuring 96 inches, how much remains on the roll?

23. Leon Treadwell's checkbook had a balance of $196.82 before he wrote checks for $21.75 and $82.46. What was his balance after he wrote the checks?

24. Janet Morris weighed 149.3 pounds before she began a weight-loss program. After 8 weeks she weighed 129.7 pounds. How much did she lose?

Multiplying and Dividing Decimals

When you multiply and divide fractions, you do not have to find a common denominator. Likewise, when you multiply decimals, it is not necessary to line up the decimal points. It is important, however, to keep track of the number of decimal places in the numbers being multiplied.

Multiplying Decimals

When you multiply decimal numbers, you count the number of places to the right of the decimal point in both the numbers being multiplied. The product must have as many places to the right of the decimal point as there are *total* digits to the right of the decimal points in the numbers being multiplied.

Step by Step

Multiplying Decimals

Step 1. First multiply the numbers, ignoring the decimal points.

Step 2. Count and add the number of digits to the right of the decimal points in the numbers being multiplied.

Step 3. Start at the *right* end of the product and count *back* as many places to the left as the total number of places you found in Step 2.

Step 4. If there are more digits to the right of the decimal points than there are places in the product, insert zeros in front of the product.

EXAMPLE 7

Multiply 3.5 × 3.

3.5	There is 1 digit to the right of the decimal point.
× 3	
10.5	The product has 1 digit to the right of the decimal point.

TIPS & TRAPS

A common mistake is to drop unnecessary zeros *before* placing the decimal point in the product.

WRONG (crossed out)	CORRECT	
2.5	2.5	There is 1 digit to the right of the decimal point.
× 0.14	× 0.14	There are 2 digits to the right of the decimal point.
10 0	100	
25	25	
0.0350	0.350	Count 3 places to the left of the last digit in the product.

EXAMPLE 8

Multiply 2.35 × 0.015

2.35	There are 2 digits to the right of the decimal point.
× 0.015	There are 3 digits to the right of the decimal point.
1175	
235	
0.03525	There are 5 places to the right of the decimal point in the product.

Note that the zero to the left of the decimal product in Example 8 is not necessary, but it helps to point out the decimal. Because of this, we always use the zero to the left of the decimal point.

Self-Check

Multiply.

7. $\begin{array}{r} 19.7 \\ \times \quad 4 \\ \hline \end{array}$ **8.** $\begin{array}{r} 1.382 \\ \times \ 1.26 \\ \hline \end{array}$ **9.** 0.0321 × 10 **10.** 0.71936 × 10,000

Dividing Decimals

In the division of decimals, you must pay careful attention to lining up digits and decimal points and follow the same procedures you used in the division of whole numbers.

Dividing a Decimal by a Whole Number. When you divide a decimal by a whole number, you must make sure that the decimal point in the quotient is directly above the decimal point in the dividend, and you divide as you would divide two whole numbers. If the division does not come out even, you can carry it out as far as you want simply by adding more zeros to the dividend. If you are planning to round an answer to a specific place, you carry the division out to one place *beyond* the specified place and then round the answer.

Step by Step

Dividing a Decimal by a Whole Number

Step 1. Place the decimal point in the quotient directly above the decimal point in the dividend.

Step 2. Divide as you would divide whole numbers.

EXAMPLE 11

Divide: 5.95 ÷ 17.

$$\begin{array}{r} 0.35 \\ 17\overline{)5.95} \\ \underline{5\,1} \\ 85 \\ \underline{85} \end{array}$$

TIPS & TRAPS

A common mistake is to add zeros to the dividend without inserting a decimal first.

Divide: 12 ÷ 8.

WRONG (crossed out):

$$\begin{array}{r} 1\,5 \\ 8\overline{)12\,0} \\ \underline{8} \\ 4\,0 \\ \underline{4\,0} \end{array}$$

← The zero was added, but the decimal point was left out.

CORRECT:

$$\begin{array}{r} 1.5 \\ 8\overline{)12.0} \\ \underline{8} \\ 4\,0 \\ \underline{4\,0} \end{array}$$

← The zero and decimal point are placed correctly in the dividend, and the decimal point in the quotient is in the correct place.

States Spending Most on Higher Education
By Juan Thomassie, USA TODAY

EXAMPLE 12

Find the quotient of 37.4 ÷ 24 to the nearest hundredth.

```
     1.558   rounds to 1.56
24)37.400
   24
   13 4
   12 0
    1 40
    1 20
      200
      192
        2
```

We are rounding the answer to the nearest hundredth, so we carry the division out to the thousandths place and then round.

DIVIDING DECIMALS AND WHOLE NUMBERS BY DECIMALS. When you divide any number by a decimal, you must first change the divisor into a whole number. You can move the decimal point in a divisor as many places to the right as necessary to make it a whole number, as long as you move the decimal point in the dividend the *same* number of places to the right. Add zeros to the dividend, if necessary. Then divide as usual, lining up the decimal points in the quotient and the dividend.

EXAMPLE 13

Find the quotient of 59.9 ÷ 0.39 to the nearest hundredth.

```
0.39)59.9 ⟶ 39)5,990
```

Move both decimal points two places to the right.

```
      153.589   rounds to 153.59
39)5,990.000
   3 9
   2 09
   1 95
     140
     117
      23 0
      19 5
       3 50
       3 12
         380
         351
```

Divide, carrying the division out to the thousandths place. Round the answer.

DIVIDING BY POWERS OF 10 (10, 100, 1, 000 10,000, . . .) Just as there is a shortcut for *multiplying* by 10, 100, 1,000, and so forth, there is a shortcut for *dividing* by these numbers. For division, you move the decimal point to the *left* the same number of spaces as there are zeros in the *divisor*.

Step by Step

Rule for Dividing Any Number by a Power of 10 (10, 100, 1,000, 10,000, and so on)

To divide a number by 10, 100, 1,000, 10,000, and so on, move the decimal point to the left as many places as the divisor has zeros.

If the divisor is:	Move the decimal point to the left:
10	1 place
100	2 places
1,000	3 places
10,000	4 places
100,000	5 places
1,000,000	6 places

Insert zeros on the left when necessary.

EXAMPLE 14

218.74 ÷ 100 = 2 18.74 = 2.1874

There are 2 zeros in the divisor, so you move the decimal point 2 places to the left.

EXAMPLE 15

Divide 49.72 by 1,000.

49.72 ÷ 1,000 = 0 049.72 = 0.04972

There are 3 zeros in the divisor, so you move the decimal point 3 places to the left, adding a zero to the left of the 4.

Self-Check

Divide. Round to the nearest hundredth if division does not terminate.

11. 123.72 ÷ 12

12. $35\overline{)589.06}$

13. $0.35\overline{)0.0084}$

14. 9,845.3 ÷ 1,000

15. 68,790 ÷ 100

Section Review

Multiply.

1. 27.63 × 7

2. 384 × 3.51

3. 6.42 × 7.8

4. 0.0015 × 6.003

5. 75.84 × 0.28

6. 73.41 × 15

7. 27.58 × 10

8. 1.394 × 100

9. 0.19874 × 1000 **10.** 54 × 100 **11.** 27.3 × 1000 **12.** 38.17 × 10,000

13. 1745.4 × 10 **14.** 0.1754 × 1,000,000 **15.** 37 × 10,000 **16.** 0.004 × 10

Solve.

17. Find the cost of 1,000 gallons of paint if 1 gallon costs $12.85.

18. Ernie Jones worked 37.5 hours at the rate of $5.97 per hour. Calculate his earnings.

Divide. Round to the nearest hundredth if division does not terminate.

19. 1.65 ÷ 11 **20.** 0.105 ÷ 15 **21.** $25\overline{)54.68}$ **22.** $27\overline{)365.04}$

23. $34\overline{)291.48}$ **24.** $74\overline{)85.486}$ **25.** $2.8\overline{)94.546}$

26. $0.041\overline{)8.897}$

27. $296.36 \div 0.19$

28. $0.0056\overline{)0.4576}$

29. $0.68\overline{)41{,}285}$

30. $923.19 \div 0.541$

31. 85.72 ÷ 10 **32.** 4.139 ÷ 100 **33.** 19.874 ÷ 1000 **34.** 39 ÷ 10

35. 0.18 ÷ 100 **36.** 274.85 ÷ 10,000 **37.** 3,749,298 ÷ 100,000

38. 574 ÷ 10,000 **39.** 0.178 ÷ 10 **40.** 3,741.29 ÷ 100

Solve.

41. If 100 gallons of gasoline cost $98.90, what is the cost per gallon?

42. If Dynamo Sugar costs $2.87 for 80 ounces, what is the cost per ounce?

Converting Between Decimals and Fractions

Converting Decimals to Fractions

Sometimes you need to change or convert a number from decimal form into fractional form. Remember, decimals are simply another way of writing fractions with denominators of 10, 100, 1,000, 10,000, and so on.

Step by Step

Converting a Decimal to a Fraction

Step 1. Write the decimal number, without the decimal point, as the numerator.

Step 2. The denominator is 1 followed by as many zeros as there are places to the right of the decimal point.

Step 3. Reduce the resulting fraction to lowest terms.

EXAMPLE 16

Change 0.38 to a fraction.

$\frac{38}{100}$ The decimal number, without the decimal point, is the numerator of the fraction. There are 2 places to the right of the decimal point, so the denominator has 2 zeros after the 1.

$\frac{38}{100} = \frac{19}{50}$ Reduce the fraction to lowest terms.

EXAMPLE 17

Change 2.017 to a mixed number and an improper fraction.

Changing to a mixed number:

$2.017 = 2\frac{17}{1,000}$ — The decimal part, without the decimal point, is the numerator of the fraction.

There are 3 places to the right of the decimal point, so the denominator has 3 zeros after the 1.

$2\frac{17}{1000}$ — The fraction in the mixed number is in lowest terms.

Changing to an improper fraction:

$\frac{2,017}{1,000}$ — The decimal number, without the decimal point, is the numerator of the fraction.

There are 3 places to the right of the decimal point, so the denominator has 3 zeros after the 1.

$2.017 = \frac{2,017}{1,000}$ — The improper fraction cannot be reduced to lower terms.

Self-Check

Change the following decimals to fractions.

16. 0.68 **17.** 4.106

Converting Fractions to Decimals

Remember that fractions indicate division; therefore, you can rewrite the fraction as a division problem. When you multiply or divide a decimal, you can continue adding zeros to the *right* of the decimal point without changing the value of the number. This lets you carry out a division as far as you want to.

Step by Step

Converting a Fraction to a Decimal

Step 1. Write the numerator as a number with a decimal point and a zero after it.

Step 2. Divide the numerator by the denominator, taking the division out as many places as necessary to complete the division. Continue adding zeros to the right of the decimal point.

EXAMPLE 18

Change $\frac{1}{4}$ to a decimal number.

$$\begin{array}{r} 0.25 \\ 4\overline{)1.00} \\ \underline{8} \\ 20 \\ \underline{20} \end{array}$$

Write the numerator as a decimal number. Divide the numerator by the denominator, adding as many zeros to the right of the decimal point as you need to complete the division.

$\frac{1}{4} = 0.25$

When the division comes out even (that is, there is no remainder), we say that the division terminates, and the quotient is called a **terminating decimal.** If, however, the division *never* comes out even (there is always a remainder), we call the number a **nonterminating,** or **repeating, decimal.** There are three ways of showing a nonterminating decimal quotient.

terminating decimal: the quotient of a division of a fraction that comes out even, with no remainder.

nonterminating, or repeating, decimal: the quotient of a division that does not come out even, no matter how many decimal places it is carried to.

EXAMPLE 19

Change $\frac{2}{3}$ to a decimal number.

$$\begin{array}{r} 0.66\frac{2}{3} \\ 3\overline{)2.00} \\ \underline{1\,8} \\ 20 \\ \underline{18} \\ 2 \end{array}$$

Divide the numerator by the denominator and write the answer as a complex decimal with a decimal part and fractional part.

$$\begin{array}{r} 0.66 \longrightarrow 0.\overline{6} \\ 3\overline{)2.00} \\ \underline{1\,8} \\ 20 \\ \underline{18} \\ 2 \end{array}$$

A second way to write a repeating decimal is to place a short bar over the number that repeats.

$$\begin{array}{r} 0.666 \text{ rounds to } 0.67 \\ 3\overline{)2.000} \\ \underline{1\,8} \\ 20 \\ \underline{18} \\ 20 \\ \underline{18} \\ 2 \end{array}$$

In the business world, we often round off a repeating decimal.

There are two methods for converting a mixed number to a mixed decimal. In the first method, you change the fractional part to a decimal and then add it to the whole number part of the mixed number. In the second method, you change the mixed number to an improper fraction, which we then convert to a mixed decimal.

EXAMPLE 20

Convert $2\frac{1}{4}$ to a decimal. There are two methods of doing this.

Method 1: Change the fractional part to a decimal and add it to the whole-number part.

$$\begin{array}{r} 0.25 \\ 4\overline{)1.00} \\ \underline{1\,0} \\ 20 \\ \underline{20} \end{array}$$

Convert the fractional part of the mixed number into a decimal.

$2 + 0.25 = 2.25$

Add the whole number part and the decimal part.

$2\frac{1}{4} = 2.25$

Method 2: Change the mixed number to an improper fraction and then change the improper fraction to a mixed decimal.

$2\frac{1}{4} = \frac{9}{4}$

Change the mixed number to an improper fraction.

$$\begin{array}{r} 2.25 \\ 4\overline{)9.00} \\ \underline{8} \\ 1\,0 \\ \underline{8} \\ 20 \\ \underline{20} \end{array}$$

Divide the numerator by the denominator to find the mixed decimal.

$2\frac{1}{4} = 2.25$

Self-Check

Convert the following fractions to decimals.

18. $\frac{1}{15}$ **19.** $\frac{3}{7}$ **20.** $4\frac{1}{5}$

Section Review

Change to a fraction in lowest terms.

1. 0.75 **2.** 0.6 **3.** 0.64

4. 3.075 **5.** 5.5 **6.** 17.05

Change to decimals. Divide to hundredths and make a fraction of the remainder.

7. $\frac{3}{5}$

8. $\frac{2}{7}$

9. $\frac{1}{8}$

10. $\frac{5}{6}$

11. $\frac{4}{9}$

12. $\frac{3}{11}$

Perform the indicated operations.

13. $2\frac{3}{4} + 5.83$

14. $3.9 \div 1\frac{1}{5}$

15. $5\frac{1}{7} \times 4.2$

16. $12.8 \div 3\frac{1}{3}$

17. $\frac{1}{2} \times 0.278$

18. $325\frac{1}{4} \times 0.13$

19. $37\frac{4}{5} \div 3.78$

20. $\dfrac{3.7}{1\frac{1}{2}}$

Summary

Topic	Page	What to Remember	Examples
Reading pure decimals	71	Ignore the decimal point and read the number as an ordinary whole number. Name the place value of the last digit.	0.3869 is read "three thousand, eight-hundred sixty-nine ten-thousandths."
Reading mixed decimals	72	Read the whole number part, insert the word *and* for the decimal, and read the decimal as an ordinary whole number, naming the place value of the last digit.	5.745 is read "five and seven hundred forty-five thousandths."
Reading complex decimals	72	Read as a pure or mixed decimal and then name the place value of the last *whole* digit.	$47.26\frac{1}{3}$ is read "forty-seven and twenty-six and one-third hundredths."
Rounding a decimal to a specified place or digit	72	Find the digit to which you are rounding. Look at the next digit to the right. If the digit is less than 5, drop it and any other digits to the right. If the digit is 5 or more, add 1 to the place to which you are rounding, and drop all digits to the right.	37.357 rounded to the nearest tenth is 37.4. 3.4819 rounded to the third digit is 3.48.
Adding decimal numbers	76	Write the numbers in a column with the decimal points lined up. A decimal point is understood to follow the final digit in whole number. Add the numbers as you add whole numbers. Place the decimal point in the answer under the decimal points in the addends.	$\begin{array}{r} 32.68 \\ 3.31 \\ +\ 49 \\ \hline 84.99 \end{array}$
Subtracting decimal numbers	76	Write the minuend and subtrahend so that the decimal points line up. If the minuend has fewer digits than the subtrahend, add as many zeros as you need to the right of the decimal so every digit in the subtrahend has a zero above each digit in the minuend. Subtract as you subtract whole numbers. Place the decimal point in the answer under the decimal points of the subtrahend and minuend.	$\begin{array}{r} 568.91 \\ -\ 376.75 \\ \hline 192.16 \end{array}$ $\begin{array}{r} 24.70 \\ -\ 18.25 \\ \hline 6.45 \end{array}$
Multiplying decimals	79	Multiply the numbers, ignoring the decimal points. Write the decimal point so that the product of the decimal numbers has the number of decimal places that multiplicand and multiplier have together.	$\begin{array}{rl} 36.48 & \text{2 decimal places} \\ \times\ 2.52 & \text{2 decimal places} \\ \hline 7296 & \\ 18\ 240\ \ & \\ 72\ 96\ \ \ \ & \\ \hline 91.9296 & \text{4 decimal places} \end{array}$ (4 places total)
Multiplying any number by 10, 100, 1,000, 10,000, and so on.	79	Move the decimal point to the right as many places as the multiplier (10, 100, 1,000, 10,000, . . .) has zeros.	$32.9841 \times 100 = 3{,}298.41$ $0.000307 \times 1{,}000 = 0.307$ $1.436 \times 10 = 14.36$

Topic	Page	What to Remember	Example
Dividing a decimal by a whole number	80	Place the decimal point in the quotient directly above the decimal point in the dividend. Divide as you would with whole numbers.	$45\overline{)58.5}$ = 1.3; 45; 13 5; 13 5
Dividing any number by a decimal	81	Convert the divisor to a whole number by multiplying it and the dividend by 10, 100, or 1,000, as needed. Do this by moving the decimal points in the divisor and dividend the same number of places to the right.	$3.5\overline{)0.770}$ is changed to $35\overline{)7.70}$. Solve: $35\overline{)7.70}$ = 0.22; 7 0; 70; 70
Dividing any number by 10, 100, 1000, 10,000, and so on.	81	Move the decimal point to the left as many places as the divisor has zeros. Add zeros on the left if necessary.	$769 \div 10 = 76.9$ $3.048 \div 100 = 0.03048$
Changing a decimal into a fraction	85	Write the decimal number without the decimal point as the numerator. The denominator is 1 followed by as many zeros as there are places to the right of the decimal point. Reduce the fraction to lowest terms.	$0.584 = \frac{584}{1,000} = \frac{73}{125}$
Changing a fraction into a decimal number	86	Divide the numerator by the denominator. Add zeros to the right of the decimal point, carrying the division out as far as necessary to complete the division.	$\frac{57}{76} = 76\overline{)57.00}$ = 0.75; 53 2; 3 80; 3 80
Changing a mixed number into a decimal number	87	There are two methods of doing this: Change the fraction to a decimal and add it to the whole number part. *Or* Change the mixed number to an improper fraction and divide to convert the improper fraction to a decimal.	$3\frac{3}{5} = 3 + 5\overline{)3.0}$ = 0.6 = 3.6; 3 0 $3\frac{3}{5} = \frac{(5 \times 3) + 3}{5} = \frac{18}{5}$ $= 5\overline{)18.0}$ = 3.6; 15; 3 0; 3 0

Chapter Review

Write the word name.

1. 274.1759

2. 200.02

Round to the specified place.

3. 175.37489 (nearest thousandth)

4. 1.0478 (the third digit)

Add.

5. $28.84 + 86 + 391.7$

6. $1275.381 + 394 + 8 + 12.0075 + 315$

Subtract.

7. $74 - 3.715$

8. $83.189 - 27.9$

Multiply.

9. $\begin{array}{r} 127.5 \\ \times \quad 7.8 \\ \hline \end{array}$

10. 0.174×0.19

11. $\begin{array}{r} 0.0075 \\ \times \quad 0.047 \\ \hline \end{array}$

12. 39.273×7.15

13. $\begin{array}{r} 287 \\ \times \ 0.12 \\ \hline \end{array}$

14. $\begin{array}{r} 318.5 \\ \times \quad 0.03 \\ \hline \end{array}$

15. $\begin{array}{r} 17{,}439.8 \\ \times \qquad 100 \\ \hline \end{array}$

16. $\begin{array}{r} 34.5 \\ \times \ 1000 \\ \hline \end{array}$

Divide. Round to hundredths if division does not terminate.

17. $76.057 \div 34$

18. $0.0025\overline{)75.895}$

19. $2.4\overline{)419.75}$

20. $293.06 \div 9.6$

21. $3749.28 \div 10$

22. $0.075 \div 100$

23. $3{,}578{,}423 \div 10{,}000$

Change the following decimals to common fractions or mixed numbers in lowest terms.

24. 0.55

25. 0.4

26. 0.375

27. 5.125

28. 17.25

29. 3.82

Change the following fractions to decimals. Carry out to hundredths, and make a fraction of the remainder.

30. $\frac{1}{4}$

31. $\frac{3}{7}$

32. $\frac{1}{6}$

33. $\frac{4}{5}$

34. $\frac{5}{9}$

35. $\frac{6}{11}$

Perform the indicated operation.

36. $2\frac{7}{8} + 3.98$

37. $3\frac{1}{9} \times 3\frac{2}{5}$

38. $5.7 - 1\frac{3}{5}$ **39.** $53\frac{3}{5} \div 5.36$ **40.** $\frac{21}{0.3}$ **41.** $\frac{9.8}{0.14}$

Compute each sum or difference, and round to the third digit.

42. $17.28 + 31.3$ **43.** $3.1814 - 0.148$

Compute each product or quotient, and round to the second digit.

44. 0.127×3.5 **45.** $57{,}000 \div 1.4$

46. Five bolts of fabric, having the following number of meters left on them, were to be reduced in price: 32.5 m, 46.3 m, 18.7 m, 10.8 m, 15 m. Find the total number of meters of fabric to be reduced in price.

47. What is the cost to the nearest dollar of computer paper that sells for $36.87 a box?

48. The lengths of two medical implants measure 43.7 centimeters and 7.38 centimeters. What is the difference in their lengths?

49. An employee who earns $5.86 per hour works a 40-hour week. What are the employee's wages for a week?

Trial Test

1. Round 30.5375 to the third digit.

2. Write the word name of 24.1307.

Perform the indicated operation.

3. $39.17 - 15.078$

4. 27.418×100

5. $0.387 + 3.17 + 17 + 204.3$

6. $28.34 \div 50$ (nearest hundredth)

7. $\begin{array}{r} 324 \\ \times\ 1.38 \\ \hline \end{array}$

8. $0.138 \div 10$

9. $128 - 38.18$

10. $\begin{array}{r} 17.75 \\ \times\ 0.325 \\ \hline \end{array}$

11. $2{,}347 + 0.178 + 3.5 + 28.341$

12. $91.25 \div 12.5$

13. $317.24 - 138$

14. $374.17 \div 100$

15. $2\frac{5}{8} - 1.015$

16. Change $\frac{5}{7}$ to a decimal (nearest hundredth).

17. Change 0.34 to a fraction reduced to lowest terms.

18. What is the cost of $5\frac{1}{2}$ dozen doughnuts if they cost \$2.49 a dozen?

19. A patient's chart showed a temperature reading of 101.23 degrees Fahrenheit at 3 P.M. and 99.47 degrees Fahrenheit at 10 P.M. What was the drop in temperature?

20. A surveyor took the following measurements on a four-sided lot: 87.9 feet, 104.3 feet, 123.8 feet, and 96.2 feet. How much fencing is required to surround the property?

Self-Check Solutions

1. a. Seven and three-tenths
b. Thirty-three and seven hundredths
c. Five hundred eighty-two thousandths
d. One and nine ten-thousandths
e. Sixty-three hundredths

2. 0.313

3. \$494

4. \$34.53

5.
$$\begin{array}{r} 6.005 \\ 0.03 \\ 924 \\ +\quad 3.9 \\ \hline 933.935 \end{array}$$

6.
$$\begin{array}{r} 407.96 \\ -\ 298.39 \\ \hline 109.57 \end{array}$$

7.
$$\begin{array}{r} 19.7 \\ \times\quad 4 \\ \hline 78.8 \end{array}$$

8.
$$\begin{array}{r} 1.382 \\ \times\ 1.26 \\ \hline 8292 \\ 2764 \\ 1\,382 \\ \hline 1.74132 \end{array}$$

9. $0.0321 \times 10 = 0.321$

10. $0.71936 \times 10{,}000 = 7{,}193.6$

11. $12\overline{)123.72}$ = 10.31

$$\begin{array}{r} 10.31 \\ 12\overline{)123.72} \\ \underline{12} \\ 03 \\ \underline{0} \\ 3\,7 \\ \underline{3\,6} \\ 12 \\ \underline{12} \end{array}$$

12. $35\overline{)589.060}$ = 16.830, or 16.83

$$\begin{array}{r} 16.830 \\ 35\overline{)589.060} \\ \underline{35} \\ 239 \\ \underline{210} \\ 29\,0 \\ \underline{28\,0} \\ 1\,06 \\ \underline{1\,05} \\ 10 \\ \underline{0} \end{array}$$

13. $0.35\overline{)0.00\,840}$ = 0.024, or 0.02

$$\begin{array}{r} 0.024 \\ 0.35\overline{)0.00\,840} \\ \underline{70} \\ 140 \\ \underline{140} \end{array}$$

14. $9{,}845.3 \div 1{,}000 = 9.8453$

15. $68{,}790 \div 100 = 687.9$

16. $0.68 = \dfrac{68}{100} = \dfrac{17}{25}$

17. $4.106 = 4\dfrac{106}{1{,}000} = 4\dfrac{53}{500}$

18. $15\overline{)1.0000}$ = 0.0666 ⟶ $.0\overline{6}$, or 0.067

$$\begin{array}{r} 0.0666 \\ 15\overline{)1.0000} \\ \underline{90} \\ 100 \\ \underline{90} \\ 100 \\ \underline{90} \\ 10 \end{array}$$

19. $7\overline{)3.0000000}$ = 0.4285714, or 0.43 (rounded)

$$\begin{array}{r} 0.4285714 \\ 7\overline{)3.0000000} \\ \underline{2\,8} \\ 20 \\ \underline{14} \\ 60 \\ \underline{56} \\ 40 \\ \underline{35} \\ 50 \\ \underline{49} \\ 10 \\ \underline{7} \\ 30 \\ \underline{28} \\ 2 \end{array}$$

20. $4\dfrac{1}{5} = \dfrac{21}{5} = 4.2$

$$\begin{array}{r} 4.2 \\ 5\overline{)21.0} \\ \underline{20} \\ 10 \\ \underline{10} \end{array}$$

Bank Records 4

Learning Objectives

1. Understand types of documents and how they are used in banking. (pp. 99–102, 106–110)
2. Write and endorse checks. (pp. 99–102)
3. Correctly fill out and use deposit slips and check registers. (pp. 101–102)
4. Understand the information provided on a bank statement. (pp. 106–107)
5. Reconcile the information on the bank statement with the information in the checkbook. (pp. 106–108)

Most of us are familiar with the banking records that go with a personal or business checking account. The specific forms, policies, and procedures for checking accounts may vary from bank to bank, but once you know the reasoning behind these banking procedures, it is easy enough to understand the minor variations that occur. For business purposes and for personal use, it is important to use banking forms correctly, keep accurate records, and keep track of financial transactions.

Checking Account Forms

The Bank Check

The main form used in a checking account is a **check,** a piece of paper ordering the bank to pay someone an amount of money from a particular account. The basic features of a check are shown in Figure 4-1.

check: a piece of paper ordering the bank to pay someone an amount of money from a particular account.

payee: the person or company to whom a check is made out—the one who gets the money.

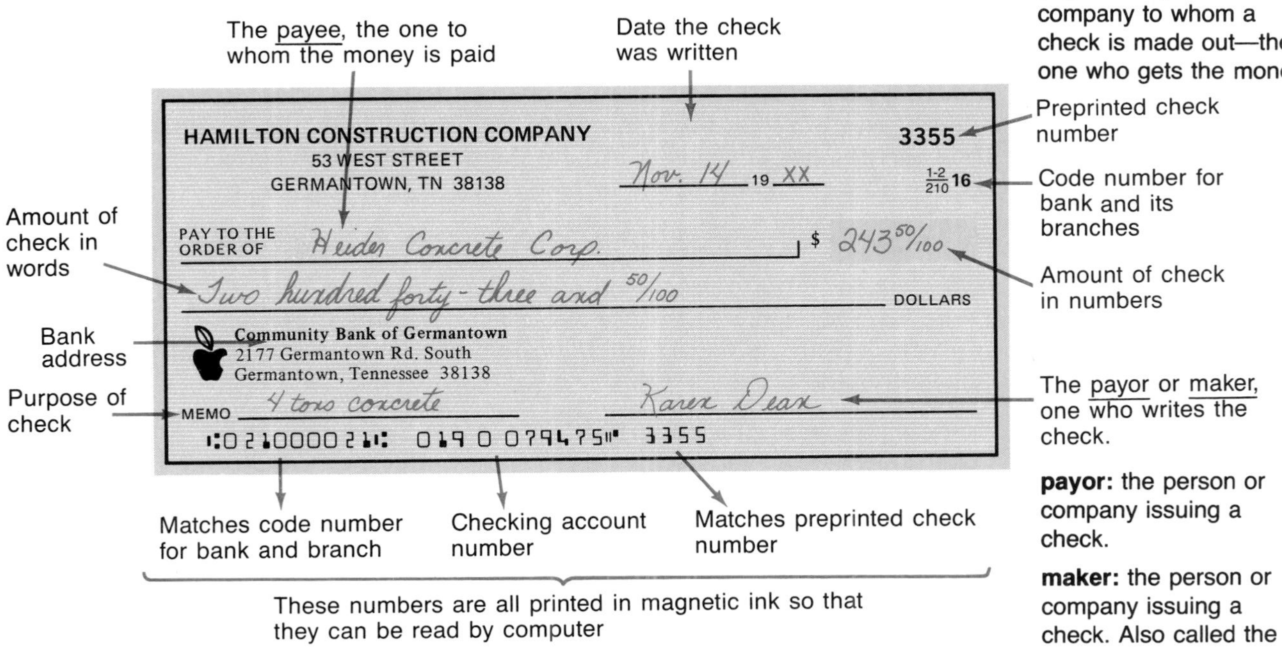

The payee, the one to whom the money is paid

Date the check was written

Preprinted check number

Code number for bank and its branches

Amount of check in words

Amount of check in numbers

Bank address

Purpose of check

The payor or maker, one who writes the check.

HAMILTON CONSTRUCTION COMPANY
53 WEST STREET
GERMANTOWN, TN 38138

3355

Nov. 14 19 XX

$\frac{1-2}{210}$ 16

PAY TO THE ORDER OF Heider Concrete Corp. $ 243 50/100

Two hundred forty-three and 50/100 DOLLARS

Community Bank of Germantown
2177 Germantown Rd. South
Germantown, Tennessee 38138

MEMO 4 tons concrete

Karen Dean

⑆0210000 21⑆ 019 0 079475⑈ 3355

Matches code number for bank and branch

Checking account number

Matches preprinted check number

These numbers are all printed in magnetic ink so that they can be read by computer

Figure 4-1 A Sample Check

payor: the person or company issuing a check.

maker: the person or company issuing a check. Also called the *payor.*

When a checking account is opened, the person or members of the company who will be writing checks on the account sign a signature card, which is kept on record at the bank. Whenever there is a question about a signature or whether or not a person is authorized to write checks on an account, the bank refers to the signature card to resolve the question.

EXAMPLE 1

Write a check dated April 6, 19XX, to Ruben Espinoza in the amount of $98.79, for computer diskettes.

XYZ COMPANY 123
1234 B Boulevard
Somewhere, USA 4/6 19 XX 87-278/840
PAY TO THE ORDER OF Ruben Espinoza $ 98.79
Ninety-eight and 79/100 DOLLARS
Community Bank of Germantown
2177 Germantown Rd. South
Germantown, Tennessee 38138
MEMO computer diskettes Your Name
:08400 2781: 10 5634 3" 123

Enter the date, 4/6/XX.

Write the name of the payee, Ruben Espinoza.

Enter the amount of the check in numbers.

Enter the amount of the check in words. Note the fraction $\frac{79}{100}$ showing cents, or hundredths of dollars.

Write the purpose of the check on the memo line.

Sign your name.

check stub: a blank form attached to a check and used to record all checks, deposits, and interest, and to keep a running balance

The Check Stub

Most businesses and individuals who have checking accounts use either a check stub or a check register to record all the checks they write and all the deposits they make. Check stubs are provided by the bank, usually in a bound book with the perforated check attached to its stub.

A **check stub** has a place to list the check number (if it is not preprinted), the date, the amount of the check, the person to whom the check is made, and what the check is written for. Below that there is a place to record the balance brought forward from the last check, the amount deposited since the last check was written, the amount of the check, and the new balance.

When filling out the check stub, you simply add any deposits and subtract the amount of the check to get the new balance. It's a good idea to fill out the check stub *before* writing the check so that you won't forget to do it.

EXAMPLE 2

Complete the stub for check number 150, written on April 9, 19XX, to Sigmund Larson in the amount of $45.68 for packing materials. The amount brought forward is $3,842.90. Deposits of $325, $694.30, and $28.35 were made after the previous check was written.

150 Date 4/9 19 XX
Amount $45.68
To Sigmund Larson Co.
For packing materials

Balance	3,842	90
Deposits	1,047	65
Total	4,890	55
Amount This Check	45	68
Balance	4,844	87

Enter the check number, 150.

Enter the date, 4/9/XX.

Enter the amount, $45.68.

Enter the payee, Sigmund Larson.

Enter the purpose, packing materials.

Enter the balance, $3,842.90.

Enter the total deposit, $1,047.65.

Enter the amount of the check, $45.68.

Add deposit and subtract amount of the check to find new balance.

Figure 4-2 A Check Register

RECORD ALL CHARGES OR CREDITS THAT AFFECT YOUR ACCOUNT							
NUMBER	DATE	DESCRIPTION OF TRANSACTION	AMOUNT OF CHECK	√	FEE	AMOUNT OF DEPOSIT	BALANCE
							$ 6,843 00
543	8/9	Golden Wheat Dist	$ 685 56		$	$	6,157 44
544	8/9	Consolidated Berry Farms	89 78				6,067 66
	8/9	Cash withdrawal	250 00				5,817 66
	8/10	Deposit				1,525 61	7,343 27

The Check Register

Some business firms and most individuals use a **check register** to maintain a record of all checks they have written and deposits they have made. The check register is a bound set of forms supplied by the bank and kept with the checks. The check register provides space to enter the check number, date, description of transaction (payee and purpose of check), and amount of each check, the date and amount of each deposit, and the balance after the transaction. A sample check register page is shown in Figure 4-2.

check register: a bound set of blank forms supplied by a bank and kept with the checks; used to record all checks, deposits, and interest and to keep a running balance.

The register has a place to enter the check number, the date, the payee, and the purpose of the check. On the right side of the register at the top is BALANCE, or the balance brought forward—the balance before the next check is written or before the next deposit is made. There are columns to enter the amount of a check or the amount of a deposit, to enter the amount of a check fee (some banks charge a fee for each check written), and a √ column. This column is used to check off each check at the end of the month, when you're figuring your bank balance, which we describe later in the chapter.

The Deposit Slip

The **deposit slip** is filled out when money (either checks or cash) is to be added to an account. A sample deposit slip is shown in Figure 4-3. Deposit slips are given to the person opening an account along with a set of preprinted checks. The bank account number is written at the bottom of the slip in magnetic ink.

deposit slip: blank form provided by the bank; used to record cash or checks that are being deposited in an account.

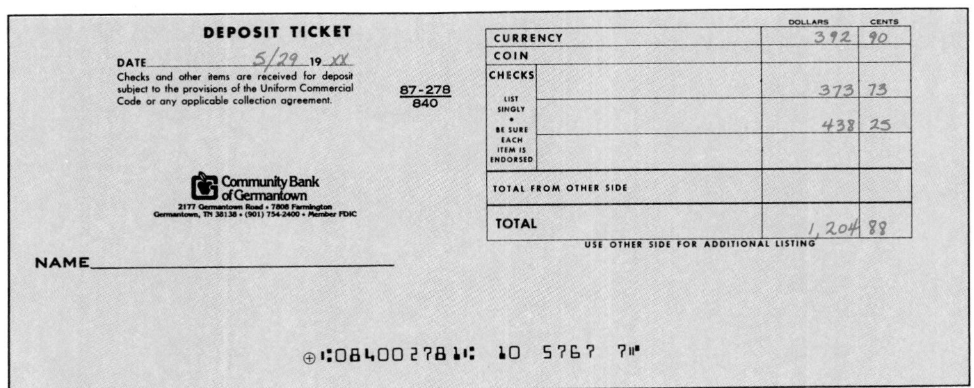
DEPOSIT TICKET

DATE 5/29 19 XX

Checks and other items are received for deposit subject to the provisions of the Uniform Commercial Code or any applicable collection agreement.

87-278
840

Community Bank of Germantown
2177 Germantown Road • 7808 Farmington
Germantown, TN 38138 • (901) 754-2400 • Member FDIC

NAME ____________

	DOLLARS	CENTS
CURRENCY	392	90
COIN		
CHECKS LIST SINGLY • BE SURE EACH ITEM IS ENDORSED	373	73
	438	25
TOTAL FROM OTHER SIDE		
TOTAL	1,204	88

USE OTHER SIDE FOR ADDITIONAL LISTING

⑆084002781⑆ 10 5767 7⑈

Figure 4-3 A Deposit Slip

A deposit slip has a place for the date and for listing the checks and cash to be deposited. Usually cash and checks are listed separately, and each check is also listed separately. The deposits are then added and the sum is written in the place marked "Total Deposit" at the bottom of the slip. The rest of the markings on this deposit slip are for bank use only and are not of interest to us.

Check Endorsements

endorse: signing or stamping the back of a check by the payee. See also *restricted endorsement.*

restricted endorsement: occurs when the payee signs a check on the back and adds "for deposit only" and the account number. This means that the check can *only* be deposited to that account; it cannot be cashed.

Before a check can be cashed or deposited, it must be **endorsed.** This means that the payee, the person or company to whom the check is made out, signs the check on the back. There are several different types of check endorsement. The simplest type, which you would use if you wanted to cash the check, is just your signature on the back of the check. If you want to deposit the check instead, you sign your name and write under it "for deposit only" and your checking account number. This is called a **restricted endorsement,** since it says that the money can only be deposited in your account, not paid out. There are other types of restricted endorsement that businesses use in order to safeguard the process of paying out money; in general these involve an exact identification of the person to whom money can be paid.

Figure 4-4 Rules for Placement of Check Endorsements

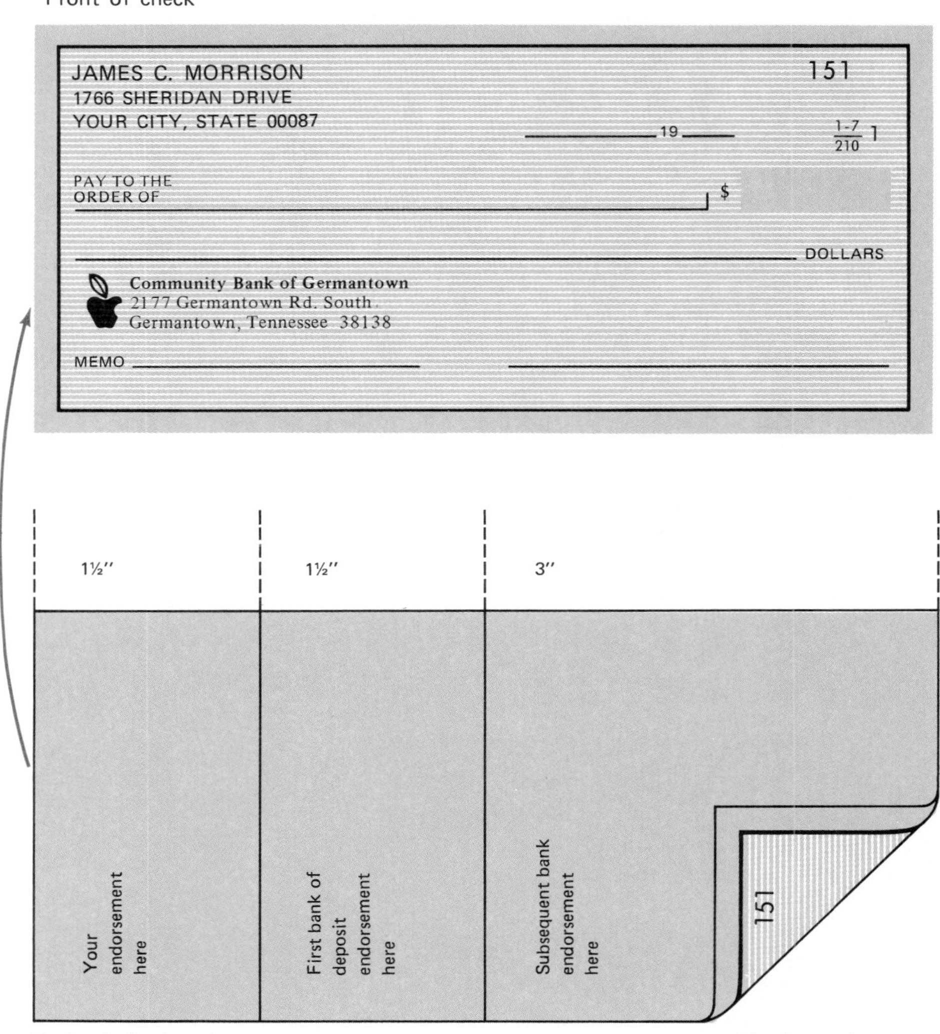

In 1988 the Federal Reserve Board issued regulations concerning the way that endorsements can be placed on checks. As shown in Figure 4-4, the endorsement must be placed within $1\frac{1}{2}$ inches from the top of the check. The rest of the back of the check is reserved for bank endorsements. Many check-printing companies now mark this space and provide lines for endorsements.

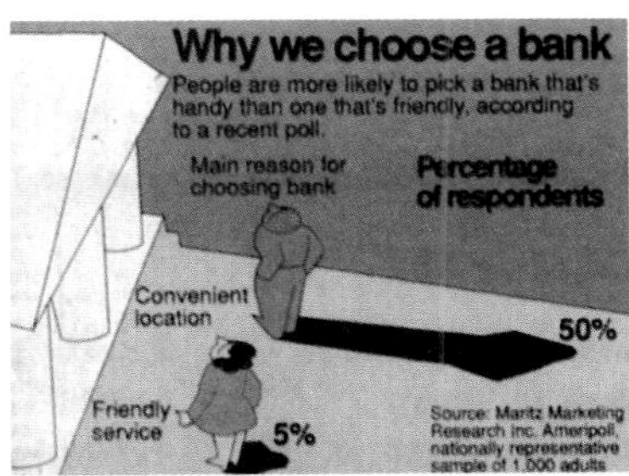

By Elys McLean-Ibrahim, USA TODAY

Self-Check

Enter the following transactions in the bank records for Park's Oriental Grocery Store with the account number 63-1579-5. On April 29, 19XX, with an account balance brought forward of $7,869.40. Mr. Man Park added $858.63 in cash and two checks in the amounts of $157.38 and $32.49. Later that day, he wrote a check in the amount of $155.30 to Green Harvest for fresh vegetables.

1. Fill out the deposit slip for April 29, 19XX.

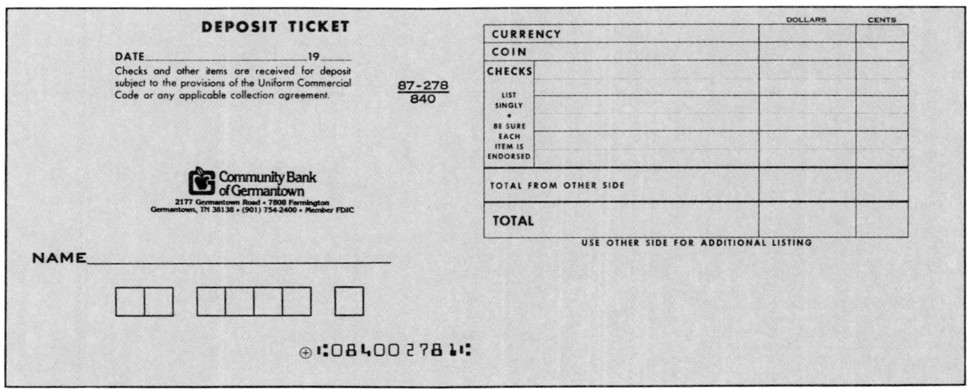

DEPOSIT TICKET

DATE ____________ 19____

Checks and other items are received for deposit subject to the provisions of the Uniform Commercial Code or any applicable collection agreement.

87-278/840

Community Bank of Germantown
2177 Germantown Road • 7808 Farmington
Germantown, TN 38138 • (901) 754-2400 • Member FDIC

NAME ____________

⑆084002781⑆

	DOLLARS	CENTS
CURRENCY		
COIN		
CHECKS		
LIST SINGLY • BE SURE EACH ITEM IS ENDORSED		
TOTAL FROM OTHER SIDE		
TOTAL		

USE OTHER SIDE FOR ADDITIONAL LISTING

2. Write a check dated April 29, 19XX, to Green Harvest in the amount of $155.30, for fresh vegetables. Fill out the check stub for this check.

456 Date ______ 19____
Amount ____________
To ____________
For ____________

Balance		
Deposits		
Total		
Amount This Check		
Balance		

Park's Oriental Grocery
1428 Central Ave.
Germantown, TN 38138

456

____________ 19____ 87-278/840

PAY TO THE ORDER OF ____________ $

____________ DOLLARS

Community Bank of Germantown
2177 Germantown Rd. South
Germantown, Tennessee 38138

MEMO ____________

⑆084002781⑆ 63 1579 5⑈ 456

3. Enter all the transactions described in the check register. Show the new balance brought forward of Park's Oriental Grocery Store.

RECORD ALL CHARGES OR CREDITS THAT AFFECT YOUR ACCOUNT

NUMBER	DATE	DESCRIPTION OF TRANSACTION	AMOUNT OF CHECK		√	FEE	AMOUNT OF DEPOSIT		BALANCE	
			$			$	$		$	

Section Review

1. Write a check dated June 13, 19XX, to Byron Johnson in the amount of $296.83 for a washing machine.

456

______________ 19____ 87-278/840

PAY TO THE ORDER OF ______________________________ $

______________________________ DOLLARS

Community Bank of Germantown
2177 Germantown Rd. South
Germantown, Tennessee 38138

MEMO ______________ ______________

⑆08400 278 1⑆

2. Write a check dated August 18, 19XX, to Valley Electric Coop in the amount of $189.32 for utilities.

789

______________ 19____ 87-278/840

PAY TO THE ORDER OF ______________________________ $

______________________________ DOLLARS

Community Bank of Germantown
2177 Germantown Rd. South
Germantown, Tennessee 38138

MEMO ______________ ______________

⑆08400 278 1⑆

3. Complete a deposit slip to add checks in the amounts of $136.00 and $278.96 and $480 cash to account 12-2803-5 on May 8, 19XX.

DEPOSIT TICKET

DATE______________ 19____

Checks and other items are received for deposit subject to the provisions of the Uniform Commercial Code or any applicable collection agreement.

87-278/840

Community Bank of Germantown
2177 Germantown Road • 7808 Farmington
Germantown, TN 38138 • (901) 754-2400 • Member FDIC

NAME______________________

		DOLLARS	CENTS
CURRENCY			
COIN			
CHECKS			
LIST SINGLY • BE SURE EACH ITEM IS ENDORSED			
TOTAL FROM OTHER SIDE			
TOTAL			

USE OTHER SIDE FOR ADDITIONAL LISTING

⑆08400 278 1⑆

4. Complete a deposit slip on November 11, 19XX, to show the deposit of $100 in cash, checks in the amounts of $87.83, $42.97, and $106.32, with a $472.13 total from the other side of the deposit slip. Your account number is 8021346.

DEPOSIT TICKET

DATE ______________ 19____

Checks and other items are received for deposit subject to the provisions of the Uniform Commercial Code or any applicable collection agreement.

87-278/840

Community Bank of Germantown
2177 Germantown Road • 7808 Farmington
Germantown, TN 38138 • (901) 754-2400 • Member FDIC

	DOLLARS	CENTS
CURRENCY		
COIN		
CHECKS		
LIST SINGLY		
•		
BE SURE EACH ITEM IS ENDORSED		
TOTAL FROM OTHER SIDE		
TOTAL		

USE OTHER SIDE FOR ADDITIONAL LISTING

NAME ______________________________

⊕ ⑆08400 2781⑆

5. Complete the stub for check 786, written on May 10, 19XX, to Jacqueline Voss in the amount of $28.97 for office supplies. The amount brought forward is $4,307.21.

786 Date __________ 19 XX

Amount ______________________

To ______________________

For ______________________

Balance		
Deposits		
Total		
Amount This Check		
Balance		

6. Complete the stub for check 1021, written on September 30, 19XX, to Louis Jenkins for plumbing repairs. The amount brought forward is $1,021.03 and the amount of the check is $65. Deposits of $146.00 and $297.83 were made before the check was written.

1021 Date __________ 19 XX

Amount ______________________

To ______________________

For ______________________

Balance		
Deposits		
Total		
Amount This Check		
Balance		

7. Enter the following information and transactions in the check register for Happy Center Day Care. On July 10, 19XX, with an account balance of $983.47, check 1213 was written to Linens Inc. for $220.00 for laundry services, and check 1214 was written to Bugs Away for $65.00 for extermination services. On July 11, $80 was withdrawn from an automatic

teller machine and on July 12, checks in the amount of $123.86, $123.86, and $67.52 were deposited. Show the balance after these transactions.

RECORD ALL CHARGES OR CREDITS THAT AFFECT YOUR ACCOUNT							
NUMBER	DATE	DESCRIPTION OF TRANSACTION	AMOUNT OF CHECK	√	FEE	AMOUNT OF DEPOSIT	BALANCE $
			$		$	$	

The Bank Reconciliation Process

In this section we discuss the monthly bank statement sent out by the bank to checking account customers and show how to reconcile any differences between that statement and the customer's own check stubs or check register. (To make things simple, we refer to a customer's check stubs or check register as the *checkbook.*)

bank statement: monthly statement sent by the bank to an account holder listing all transactions in the account for that month.

service charge: a fee the bank charges for operating a checking account.

returned check fee: a fee charged to your account when someone writes you a check without the funds to cover it and you deposit it in your account. When *you* write a check without the funds to cover it, you are charged an *NSF* fee.

nonsufficient funds (NSF) fee: a fee charged to your account when you write a check and do not have enough money in your account to cover it.

automatic teller machine (ATM): computerized banking service offered by many banks; account holder can perform many banking functions using a bank card and bank computer, without the help of a bank teller.

The Bank Statement

Every month the bank sends out a **bank statement,** a listing of all transactions that took place in the customer's account during the past month. It includes all checks cashed, all deposits made, all service charges, and the like. A sample bank statement is shown in Figure 4-5.

Most bank statements have a section explaining the various letter codes and symbols contained in the statement. One of the first steps to take when you receive a bank statement is to check this explanatory section for any terms that you do not understand in the statement.

One of the items that may appear on a bank statement is a **service charge.** This is a fee the bank charges for operating the checking account; it may be a standard monthly fee or a charge for each check.

Another type of bank charge appearing on the bank statement is for the **nonsufficient funds (NSF) check.** If someone writes you a check but does not have enough money in the bank to cover it, your bank will return the check to the bank it was drawn on and may charge your account for handling it and sending it back. This is called a **returned check fee.** If *you* write an NSF check, your bank will charge you an **NSF charge.**

Another important transaction entered on the bank statement comes from using an **automatic teller machine (ATM).** If you withdraw cash or make a deposit using this machine, you should make a record of it in your checkbook. You will receive a record from the machine at the time you use it, and the transaction will appear on your bank statement.

Many banks allow customers to pay bills automatically with automatic transfers. For example, loan payments, credit-card payments, and other

Figure 4-5 A Bank Statement

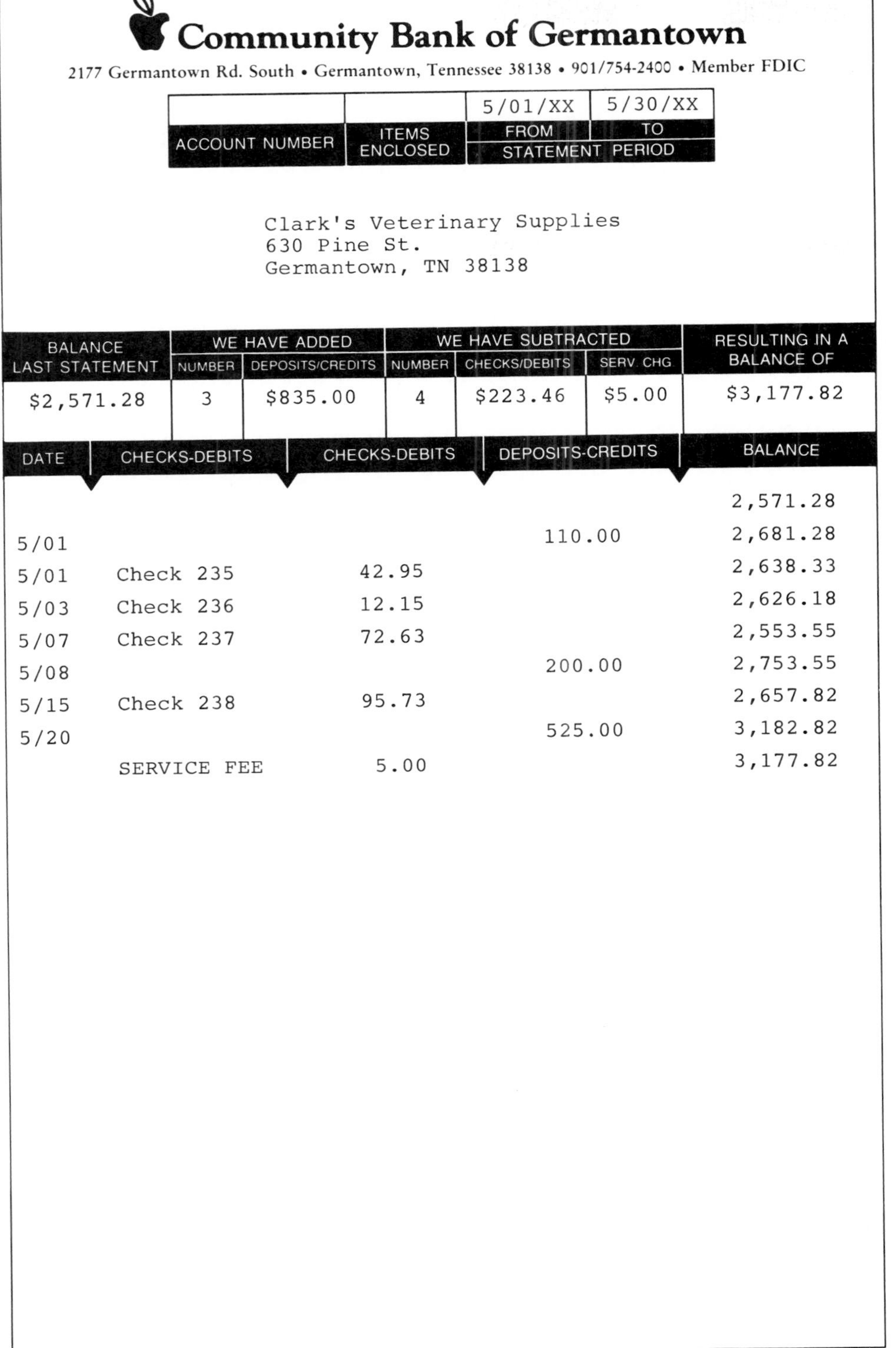

Community Bank of Germantown

2177 Germantown Rd. South • Germantown, Tennessee 38138 • 901/754-2400 • Member FDIC

ACCOUNT NUMBER	ITEMS ENCLOSED	STATEMENT PERIOD FROM	STATEMENT PERIOD TO
		5/01/XX	5/30/XX

Clark's Veterinary Supplies
630 Pine St.
Germantown, TN 38138

BALANCE LAST STATEMENT	WE HAVE ADDED NUMBER	WE HAVE ADDED DEPOSITS/CREDITS	WE HAVE SUBTRACTED NUMBER	WE HAVE SUBTRACTED CHECKS/DEBITS	WE HAVE SUBTRACTED SERV. CHG	RESULTING IN A BALANCE OF
$2,571.28	3	$835.00	4	$223.46	$5.00	$3,177.82

DATE	CHECKS-DEBITS	CHECKS-DEBITS	DEPOSITS-CREDITS	BALANCE
				2,571.28
5/01			110.00	2,681.28
5/01	Check 235	42.95		2,638.33
5/03	Check 236	12.15		2,626.18
5/07	Check 237	72.63		2,553.55
5/08			200.00	2,753.55
5/15	Check 238	95.73		2,657.82
5/20			525.00	3,182.82
	SERVICE FEE	5.00		3,177.82

bills are paid by the bank on a certain day of the month. These transfers also appear on the bank statement.

What does *not* appear on the bank statement is any check you wrote or deposit you made near the end of the month, too late for it to reach the bank in time to be included in this month's statement. For this reason and others, your bank statement and your checkbook may not agree. We discuss this in the next section.

Reconciling the Bank Statement and the Checkbook

The first thing to do when you receive a bank statement is to go over it and check its contents against your checkbook. You can check off all the checks and deposits listed on the statement by using the √ column we showed earlier in the check register or by marking the check stub.

outstanding checks: checks that do not reach the bank in time to appear on the monthly statement.

As we just noted, you will probably find that some checks recorded in your checkbook are not listed on the bank statement. These are called **outstanding checks.** Because it may take several days between the time you write a check and the time it is presented at your bank for payment, there may be a number of checks written near the end of the month that do not appear on the bank statement for that month.

TIPS & TRAPS
When you are reconciling the bank statement with the checkbook in actual practice, it is helpful to mark in your checkbook the checks and deposits that have cleared the bank and are included with the statement. After you have made this notation, you can quickly see that the *unmarked* checks and deposits have *not* been included in the bank statement. These should be used as outstanding checks and deposits. When checks have cleared the bank, they should be arranged in numerical sequence and placed in a safe storage place in case they are needed at a later date as proof of payment.

deposits in transit: deposits made by mail or after regular banking hours that do not clear the bank in time to appear on the monthly bank statement. Also called *outstanding deposits.*

Just as you might have outstanding checks, so you might also have deposits in your records that do not appear on your bank statement. These are called **deposits in transit.** They are deposits made by mail or after regular banking hours that do not clear the bank in time to appear on a given month's statement.

A *returned check* is a check that is made out to you and deposited in your account but is not honored by the maker's bank, usually because there is not enough money in the maker's account to pay it. When this occurs the amount of the check will then be deducted by your bank from your account. Depending on when this happens, it might be a reason for your checkbook and the bank statement not to be in agreement.

bank reconciliation: a process in which the bank statement and the account holder's checkbook are brought into agreement.

When the bank statement and the checkbook do not agree, certain steps should be taken to reconcile the two. The process of making the bank statement agree with the checkbook balance is called *reconciling a bank statement,* or **bank reconciliation.**

Step by Step

Reconciling a Bank Statement

Step 1. Add the amount of deposits in transit to the ending bank statement balance.

Step 2. Subtract the amount of outstanding checks from the sum of the bank statement balance plus the deposits in transit.

Step 3. Add to the checkbook balance the amount of any deposits appearing on the bank statement but not in the checkbook.

Step 4. Subtract any charges appearing on the bank statement from the checkbook balance resulting from Step 3.

Step 5. Compare the amounts in Steps 2 and 4.

These steps can be boiled down to two rules:

- **Adjusted bank statement balance** = ending balance on statement + outstanding deposits − outstanding checks
- **Adjusted checkbook balance** = checkbook balance + unrecorded deposits − service fees − returned checks

adjusted bank statement balance: consists of the balance on the bank statement plus any outstanding deposits minus any outstanding checks.

adjusted checkbook balance: consists of the checkbook balance minus any service fees and minus any returned items.

A sample check register and bank statement are shown in Figure 4-6 (p. 110). The figures from these two items are used in the following example of reconciling a bank statement.

EXAMPLE 3

Use the bank statement and check register in Figure 4-6 and prepare a bank reconciliation.

List the information you have and see how each piece of information fits into the formulas for finding the adjusted statement and adjusted checkbook balances.

Information on bank statement:

Balance = \$2,973.24	Balance on statement
Service charge = \$3.21	Service fee
Returned check = \$42.75	Returned item

Information in check register:

Balance = \$2,891.30	Checkbook balance
Deposits = \$243.27 + \$175.00	Total outstanding deposits = \$418.27
Checks outstanding = \$142.53 + \$12.75 + \$297.38 + \$93.51	Total outstanding checks = \$546.17

To reconcile the bank statement and the checkbook balance, you must calculate the adjusted statement balance and the adjusted checkbook balance by using the formulas and the numbers you have available.

Adjusted statement balance = statement balance + outstanding deposits − outstanding checks

\$2,973.24	Balance on statement
+ 418.27	Add deposits not shown on statement.
\$3,391.51	Subtract all the checks not shown on the statement to find the adjusted statement balance.
− 546.17	
\$2,845.34	

Adjusted checkbook balance = checkbook balance + unrecorded deposits − service fees − returned items

\$2,891.30	Balance in checkbook
− 3.21	Subtract the service fee.
\$2,888.09	Subtract the returned item to find the adjusted checkbook balance.
− 42.75	
\$2,845.34	

The adjusted statement balance and the adjusted checkbook balance are the same, so the statement and check register are reconciled. This adjusted balance should be indicated in the check register.

Figure 4-6 Bank Reconciliation Example

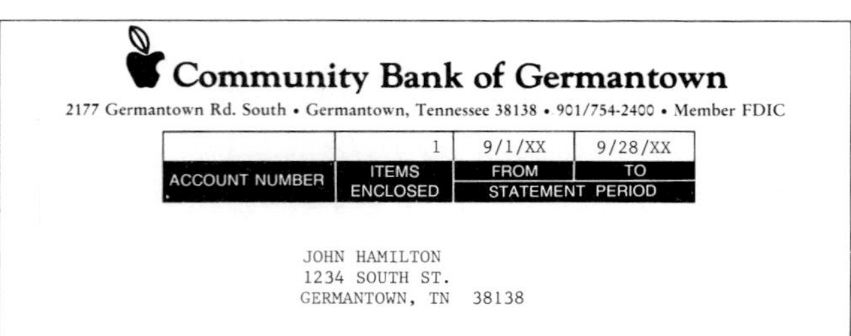
Community Bank of Germantown
2177 Germantown Rd. South • Germantown, Tennessee 38138 • 901/754-2400 • Member FDIC

ACCOUNT NUMBER	ITEMS ENCLOSED	FROM (STATEMENT PERIOD)	TO (STATEMENT PERIOD)
	1	9/1/XX	9/28/XX

JOHN HAMILTON
1234 SOUTH ST.
GERMANTOWN, TN 38138

BALANCE LAST STATEMENT	WE HAVE ADDED: NUMBER	WE HAVE ADDED: DEPOSITS/CREDITS	WE HAVE SUBTRACTED: NUMBER	WE HAVE SUBTRACTED: CHECKS/DEBITS	WE HAVE SUBTRACTED: SERV CHG	RESULTING IN A BALANCE OF
$2,772.86	2	$942.18	17	$741.80	$3.21	$2,973.24

DATE	CHECKS-DEBITS	CHECKS-DEBITS	DEPOSITS-CREDITS	BALANCE
9/1	12.18	6.24		2,754.44
9/3	28.76	42.75 (returned item)		2,682.93
9/7	146.17			2,536.76
9/10	43.68	17.32		2,475.76
9/15	62.19		500.00	2,913.57
9/17	12.88	32.16		2,868.53
9/20	68.00			2,800.53
9/23	42.37	12.96		2,745.20
9/23	36.01			2,709.19
9/24			400.00	3,109.19
9/25	178.13			2,931.06
9/27			42.18	2,973.24

RECORD ALL CHARGES OR CREDITS THAT AFFECT YOUR ACCOUNT

NUMBER	DATE	DESCRIPTION OF TRANSACTION	AMOUNT OF CHECK	✓	FEE	AMOUNT OF DEPOSIT	BALANCE
							$2346 39
1094	9/23	Andy's Shoe Shop	$42 37	✓			2304 02
1095	9/23	Lucky's Super Market	12 96	✓			2791 16
1096	9/23	Lou's Fabric Store	36 01	✓			2755 15
1097	9/24	Lifetime I. Co.	142 53				2612 62
Dep	9/24	Payroll Salary		✓		400 00	3012 62
1098	9/25	Modern Hardware Inc	12 75				2999 87
1099	9/25	Luca's Tire Store	178 13	✓			2821 74
Dep	9/27	From Sale of Trailer				243 27	3065 01
Dep	9/27	Southern Telephone (Ref)		✓		42 18	3107 19
1100	9/27	Lucky's Super Market	297 38				2809 81
Dep	9/29	From Lucille Young				175 00	2984 81
1101	9/30	Shoreline Gas Company	93 51				2891 30
	9/30	Adjusted Balance					2845 34

REMEMBER TO RECORD AUTOMATIC PAYMENTS / DEPOSITS ON DATE AUTHORIZED.

$2,973 24	BALANCE AS SHOWN ON BANK STATEMENT	BALANCE AS SHOWN IN YOUR CHECKBOOK	$2,891 30
418 27	ADD DEPOSITS NOT SHOWN ON STATEMENT	SUBTRACT AMOUNT OF SERVICE CHARGE	3 21
3,391 51	NEW TOTAL	NEW TOTAL	2888 09
546 17	*SUBTRACT TOTAL OF OUTSTANDING CHECKS	ADJUSTMENTS IF ANY	42 75
2845 34	YOUR ADJUSTED STATEMENT BALANCE ← SHOULD EQUAL →	YOUR ADJUSTED CHECKBOOK BALANCE	2845 34

* OUTSTANDING CHECKS

CHECK NUMBER	DATE	AMOUNT
1097	9/24	$ 142 53
1098	9/25	12 75
1100	9/27	297 38
1101	9/30	93 51
	TOTAL............	$

Calculators are very helpful in reconciling bank records. The work in Example 3 can be done on a calculator in the following steps:

Calculator Solution

To Find the Adjusted Statement Balance:

[AC] 2973.24 [+] 243.27 [+] 175	Begin with the statement balance; add the outstanding deposits.
[−] 142.53 [−] 12.75 [−] 297.38	Subtract the outstanding checks.
[−] 93.51	
[=] ⇒ 2845.34	

To Find the Adjusted Checkbook Balance:

[AC] 2891.30 [−] 3.21 [−] 42.75	Begin with the checkbook balance; subtract the service fees and returned items.
[=] ⇒ 2845.34	

Self-Check

4. A bank statement shows a balance of $12.32. The service charge for this statement period was $2.95. The checkbook showed deposits of $300.00, $100, and $250.00 that did not appear on the statement. Outstanding checks were in the amounts of $36.52, $205.16, $18.92, $25.93, and $200.00. The checkbook balance was $178.74. Reconcile the bank statement with the checkbook balance.

		SHOULD EQUAL		
$	BALANCE AS SHOWN ON BANK STATEMENT		BALANCE AS SHOWN IN YOUR CHECKBOOK	$
	ADD DEPOSITS NOT SHOWN ON STATEMENT		SUBTRACT AMOUNT OF SERVICE CHARGE	
	NEW TOTAL		NEW TOTAL	
	*SUBTRACT TOTAL OF OUTSTANDING CHECKS		ADJUSTMENTS IF ANY	
	YOUR ADJUSTED STATEMENT BALANCE	←→	YOUR ADJUSTED CHECKBOOK BALANCE	

* OUTSTANDING CHECKS

CHECK NUMBER	DATE	AMOUNT
		$
	TOTAL........	$

Real World Application

HOW LONG CAN THEY HOLD YOUR MONEY?

As of September 1, 1988, there are new limits on how long banks can hold deposits. (When we say *hold,* we mean the time the bank takes to process a check, the amount of time between when you deposit cash or a check and the money is recorded by the bank as being in your account.) There are a number of things that affect this time period, as you can see from the chart below; one of the most important is whether the check being deposited is from a local bank or a bank in another city or state.

No one likes to have checks bounce, and we all try to avoid having an overdrawn account. This chart shows one more reason why it is a good idea not to overdraw your account—the bank can take twice as long to hold deposits in accounts that are frequently overdrawn. That means that you may have to wait 7 to 11 working days before you can use the money from a check you deposit.

Application Questions

1. You live in one city and work in another and your employer's bank is not the same bank or in the same town as your bank. You deposit your paycheck for $493.70 on Thursday morning, July 3. According to your checkbook, your balance before you make this deposit is $281.50. You have a doctor's bill for $500 that was due July 1. When will it be safe to write the check?

2. You deposit a check in an ATM on Friday afternoon, January 5, in another town from where you bank. The ATM is not in the bank where you have an account, but it accepts cards and deposits from other banks in the same state. When you get your bank statement at the end of the month, you are dismayed to see that a check you wrote bounced because the January 5 deposit did not clear the bank until January 15. Why did it take so long?

How Long Can They Hold Your Money?

The number of business days that banks, savings and loan associations, and credit unions can hold deposits, as of September 1, 1988.

Deposits	Days
AT TELLER WINDOWS	
Cash	1
Checks:	
Up to $100	1
Remainder over $100	3 local*; 7 nonlocal
Government checks	1
Cashier's check	1
Electronic transfer	1
AT A.T.M. BEFORE NOON**	
Cash	2
Check	3 local; 7 nonlocal
Government check (U.S.)	1
Government check (state, local)	2
Cashier's check, certified check	2

Deposits	Days
INTO A NEW ACCOUNT	
Cash	1
Checks	Institutions may set policy
Government and cashiers' checks:	
Up to $5,000	1
Remainder over $5,000	9
FOR FREQUENTLY OVERDRAWN ACCOUNTS	
Checks	7 local; 11 nonlocal

* Local means drawn on banks in the same city.

** For deposits after noon, add a day; deposits made at automatic teller machines maintained by banks where depositor has no account may be held seven days.

Source: American Bankers Association

Section Review

1. Answer the following questions about William White's bank statement.
   a. How many deposits were made during the month?
   b. What amount of service charge was paid?
   c. What was the amount of the largest check written?
   d. How many checks appear on the bank statement?
   e. Give the balance at the beginning of the statement period.
   f. Give the balance at the end of the statement period.
   g. What is the amount of check 718?
   h. On what date did check 717 clear the bank?

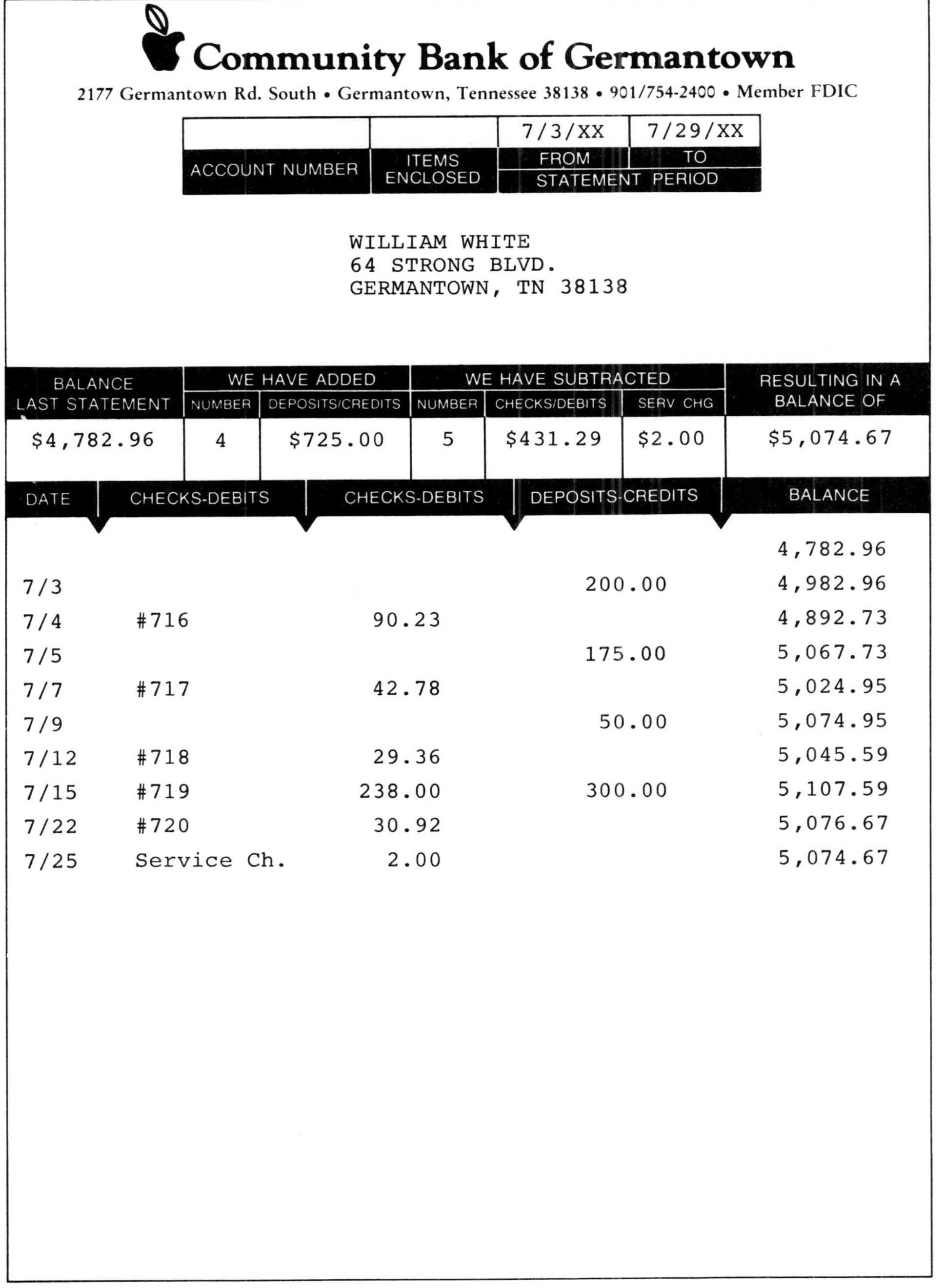

Community Bank of Germantown

2177 Germantown Rd. South • Germantown, Tennessee 38138 • 901/754-2400 • Member FDIC

ACCOUNT NUMBER	ITEMS ENCLOSED	FROM	TO
		7/3/XX	7/29/XX
		STATEMENT PERIOD	

WILLIAM WHITE
64 STRONG BLVD.
GERMANTOWN, TN 38138

BALANCE LAST STATEMENT	WE HAVE ADDED		WE HAVE SUBTRACTED			RESULTING IN A BALANCE OF
	NUMBER	DEPOSITS/CREDITS	NUMBER	CHECKS/DEBITS	SERV CHG	
$4,782.96	4	$725.00	5	$431.29	$2.00	$5,074.67

DATE	CHECKS-DEBITS	CHECKS-DEBITS	DEPOSITS-CREDITS	BALANCE
				4,782.96
7/3			200.00	4,982.96
7/4	#716	90.23		4,892.73
7/5			175.00	5,067.73
7/7	#717	42.78		5,024.95
7/9			50.00	5,074.95
7/12	#718	29.36		5,045.59
7/15	#719	238.00	300.00	5,107.59
7/22	#720	30.92		5,076.67
7/25	Service Ch.	2.00		5,074.67

2. Use the blank reconciliation form to reconcile the accompanying checkbook register and statement. Checks and deposits that have cleared the bank but are not shown on the pages of the check register are listed on a previous page of the check register.

RECORD ALL CHARGES OR CREDITS THAT AFFECT YOUR ACCOUNT

NUMBER	DATE	DESCRIPTION OF TRANSACTION	AMOUNT OF CHECK	✓	FEE	AMOUNT OF DEPOSIT	BALANCE
							$ 6413 24
783	3/16		96 03	✓			6317 21
784	3/16		58 17				6259 04
785	3/16		73 27				6185 77
786	3/18		142 38	✓			6043 39
787	3/20		487 93	✓			5555 46
788	3/25		38 47	✓			5516 99
789	3/27		72 83				5444 16
790	3/28		146 17				5297 99
791	3/29		152 03				5145 96
Dep	3/31	Salary		✓		1600 00	6745 96
792	3/31		182 13				6563 83
793	3/31		16 18				6547 65

REMEMBER TO RECORD AUTOMATIC PAYMENTS / DEPOSITS ON DATE AUTHORIZED.

Community Bank of Germantown

2177 Germantown Rd. South • Germantown, Tennessee 38138 • 901/754-2400 • Member FDIC

ACCOUNT NUMBER	ITEMS ENCLOSED	FROM	TO
		3/1/XX	3/31/XX

STATEMENT PERIOD

David Hernandez
25 Santa Rosa Dr.
Germantown, TN 38138

BALANCE LAST STATEMENT	WE HAVE ADDED: NUMBER	DEPOSITS-CREDITS	WE HAVE SUBTRACTED: NUMBER	CHECKS-DEBITS	SERV CHG	RESULTING IN A BALANCE OF
$5,283.17	2	$3,200.00	16	$1,234.74	$16.00	$7,232.43

DATE	CHECKS-DEBITS	CHECKS-DEBITS	DEPOSITS-CREDITS	BALANCE
3/4	42.83	5.86		5,234.48
3/5	42.97			5,191.51
3/6	12.15	3.72		5,175.64
	46.83			5,128.81
3/7	81.36			5,047.45
3/10	47.93			4,999.52
3/12	63.87			4,935.65
3/14	15.83	92.57		4,827.25
3/15	14.01		1,600.00	6,413.24
3/17	96.03			6,317.21
3/20	142.38			6,174.83
3/25	487.93			5,686.90
3/29	38.47			5,648.43
3/31	Service Charge	16.00	1,600.00	7,232.43

$	BALANCE AS SHOWN ON BANK STATEMENT		BALANCE AS SHOWN IN YOUR CHECKBOOK	$
	ADD DEPOSITS NOT SHOWN ON STATEMENT		SUBTRACT AMOUNT OF SERVICE CHARGE	
	NEW TOTAL		NEW TOTAL	
	*SUBTRACT TOTAL OF OUTSTANDING CHECKS		ADJUSTMENTS IF ANY	
	YOUR ADJUSTED STATEMENT BALANCE	SHOULD ⟷ EQUAL	YOUR ADJUSTED CHECKBOOK BALANCE	

* OUTSTANDING CHECKS

CHECK NUMBER	DATE	AMOUNT
		$
	TOTAL........	$

Summary

Topic	Page	What to Remember	Example
Imprinted check	99	A check is a piece of paper ordering the bank to pay someone an amount of money from a particular account. An imprinted check carries the name of the account holder, who must fill in the name of the person or company to whom the money is to be paid.	ABC Yarns 1234 Main St. Germantown, TN 38138 468 April 28 19 XX 87-278/840 PAY TO THE ORDER OF Arachne Mills $ 1,578.00 One Thousand five hundred seventy-eight and no/100 DOLLARS Community Bank of Germantown 2177 Germantown Rd. South Germantown, Tennessee 38138 MEMO wool skeins Mary Bishop ⑆08400 278⑆ 10 54 28 3⑈ 468
Check stub	100	A check stub is a form that comes with most business checking accounts and provides spaces to record information about every check that is written. It also has spaces to record deposit and balance information.	Date March 11 19 XX Amount #346.28 To A-1 Stationery Supplies For Office Supplies Balance 5298 76 Deposits 298 96 Total 5597 72 Amount This Check 346 28 Balance 5251 44
Deposit slip	101–102	A deposit slip is a form that tells the bank which account should receive money (cash or checks) that is being deposited. Imprinted deposit slips are provided with the checks for an account and, like the checks, they carry the name of the account holder. For every deposit, a deposit slip must be filled out to describe each check and all the cash being deposited.	DEPOSIT TICKET DATE 9/12 19 XX Checks and other items are received for deposit subject to the provisions of the Uniform Commercial Code or any applicable collection agreement 87-278/840 Community Bank of Germantown CURRENCY 357 00 COIN CHECKS 34 56; 43 89; 24 01 TOTAL FROM OTHER SIDE TOTAL 519 46 USE OTHER SIDE FOR ADDITIONAL LISTING NAME ABC Yarns 1 2 3 4 5 6 7 ⑆08400 278⑆
Check register	101	A check register is a bound set of forms on which the account holder records every transaction made in an account. The register indicates the current balance brought forward and lists all checks, withdrawals, and deposits.	RECORD ALL CHARGES OR CREDITS THAT AFFECT YOUR ACCOUNT NUMBER / DATE / DESCRIPTION OF TRANSACTION / AMOUNT OF CHECK / √ / FEE / AMOUNT OF DEPOSIT / BALANCE Balance $4561 09 145 3/3 B. J. Smith 130 45 — 4430 64 146 9/4 Black Sheep Inc 151 38 — 3979 26 Deposit 1030 48 — 5009 74

Topic	Page	What to Remember	Examples
Bank statement	106–107	A bank statement is a monthly record that most banks send to each account holder. The statement shows all deposits, withdrawals, and service charges and summarizes all other activity in the account. The account holder must compare the bank statement with his or her check register to make sure both records are complete and accurate and to reconcile the bank statement.	See statement below

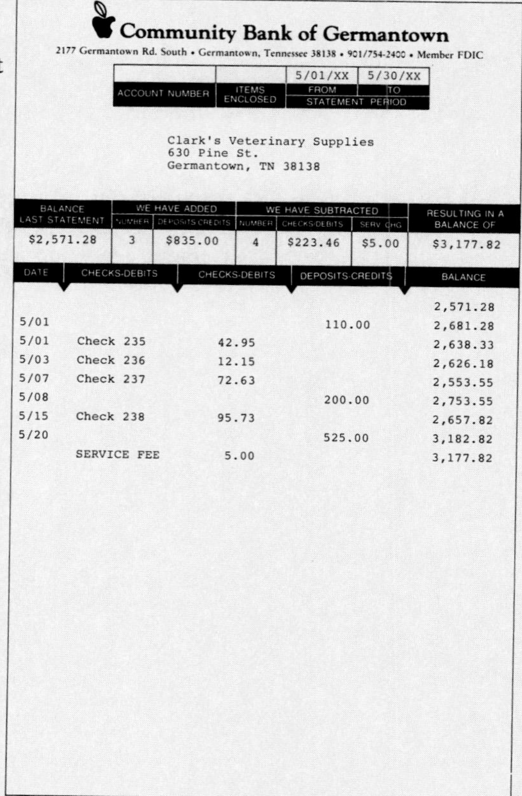

Community Bank of Germantown
2177 Germantown Rd. South • Germantown, Tennessee 38138 • 901/754-2400 • Member FDIC

ACCOUNT NUMBER	ITEMS ENCLOSED	STATEMENT PERIOD FROM	TO
		5/01/XX	5/30/XX

Clark's Veterinary Supplies
630 Pine St.
Germantown, TN 38138

BALANCE LAST STATEMENT	WE HAVE ADDED NUMBER	DEPOSITS-CREDITS	WE HAVE SUBTRACTED NUMBER	CHECKS-DEBITS	SERV CHG	RESULTING IN A BALANCE OF
$2,571.28	3	$835.00	4	$223.46	$5.00	$3,177.82

DATE	CHECKS-DEBITS	CHECKS-DEBITS	DEPOSITS-CREDITS	BALANCE
				2,571.28
5/01			110.00	2,681.28
5/01	Check 235	42.95		2,638.33
5/03	Check 236	12.15		2,626.18
5/07	Check 237	72.63		2,553.55
5/08			200.00	2,753.55
5/15	Check 238	95.73		2,657.82
5/20			525.00	3,182.82
	SERVICE FEE	5.00		3,177.82

Topic	Page	What to Remember	Examples
Bank reconciliation	108–109	Bank reconciliation is the process of comparing the transactions recorded in the check register with those listed on the bank statement. Adjusted statement balance = balance on statement + outstanding deposits − outstanding checks Adjusted checkbook balance = checkbook balance − service fees − returned items	See form below

$		$
316.56	BALANCE AS SHOWN ON BANK STATEMENT	
2000.00	ADD DEPOSITS NOT SHOWN ON STATEMENT	
2316.56	NEW TOTAL	
1487.69	*SUBTRACT TOTAL OF OUTSTANDING CHECKS	
828.87	YOUR ADJUSTED STATEMENT BALANCE	

SHOULD EQUAL

	$
BALANCE AS SHOWN IN YOUR CHECKBOOK	842.87
SUBTRACT AMOUNT OF SERVICE CHARGE	14.00
NEW TOTAL	828.87
ADJUSTMENTS IF ANY	
YOUR ADJUSTED CHECKBOOK BALANCE	828.87

* OUTSTANDING CHECKS

CHECK NUMBER	DATE	AMOUNT
3105	8/15	$ 17.83
3106	8/15	19.27
3112	8/16	126.83
3114	8/17	42.00
3117	8/18	16.17
ATM	8/20	50.00
ATM	8/21	80.00
3118	8/22	325.14
3119	8/23	683.32
3120	8/24	127.13
	TOTAL	1487.69 $

1. Fill out the check, check register, and deposit slip provided to show the following transactions: on May 5, a check in the amount of $695.55 to Ali Baba Brass; on May 8, a deposit of two checks in the amounts of $1,945.00 and $22.96 into an account with a balance brought forward of $4,562.70.

123

__________ 19____ 87-278/840

PAY TO THE ORDER OF ____________________ $

____________________ DOLLARS

Community Bank of Germantown
2177 Germantown Rd. South
Germantown, Tennessee 38138

MEMO __________

⑆08400278⑆ 6345219⑈

RECORD ALL CHARGES OR CREDITS THAT AFFECT YOUR ACCOUNT

NUMBER	DATE	DESCRIPTION OF TRANSACTION	AMOUNT OF CHECK		✓	FEE	AMOUNT OF DEPOSIT		BALANCE $	
			$			$	$			

DEPOSIT TICKET

DATE__________ 19____

Checks and other items are received for deposit subject to the provisions of the Uniform Commercial Code or any applicable collection agreement.

87-278 / 840

		DOLLARS	CENTS
CURRENCY			
COIN			
CHECKS			
LIST SINGLY • BE SURE EACH ITEM IS ENDORSED			
TOTAL FROM OTHER SIDE			
TOTAL			

USE OTHER SIDE FOR ADDITIONAL LISTING

Community Bank of Germantown
2177 Germantown Road • 7808 Farmington
Germantown, TN 38138 • (901) 754-2400 • Member FDIC

NAME____________________

⑆08400278⑆

2. Answer the following questions about Charles Bryant's bank statement.
   a. How many deposits were made during the month?
   b. What amount of service charge was paid?
   c. What was the largest amount for which a check was written?

   d. How many checks cleared the bank?
   e. Give the balance at the beginning of the statement period.
   f. Give the balance at the end of the statement period.
   g. What is the amount of check 433?
   h. On what day did Charles use a money machine for a withdrawal?

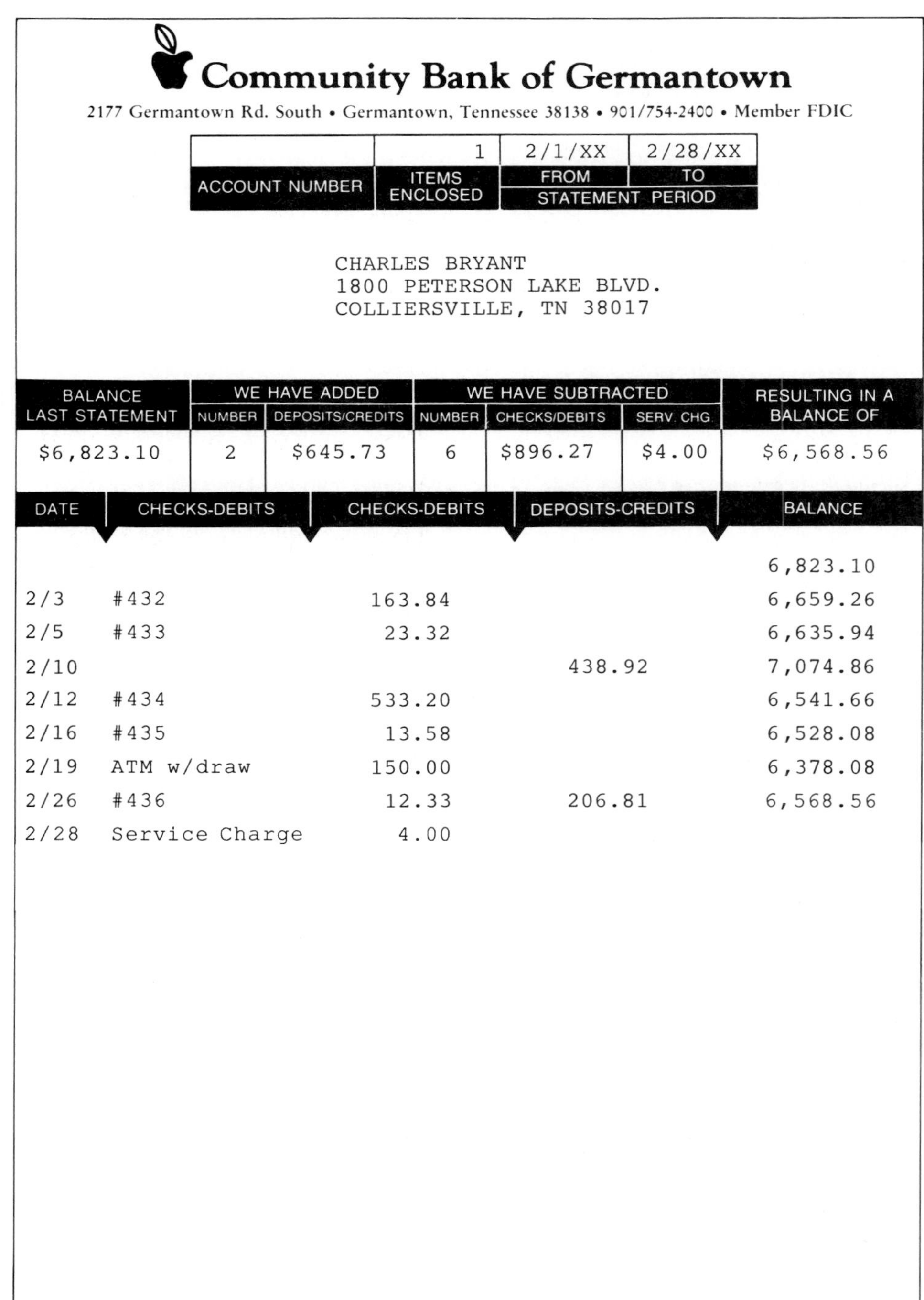

Community Bank of Germantown

2177 Germantown Rd. South • Germantown, Tennessee 38138 • 901/754-2400 • Member FDIC

ACCOUNT NUMBER	ITEMS ENCLOSED	FROM	TO
		STATEMENT PERIOD	
	1	2/1/XX	2/28/XX

CHARLES BRYANT
1800 PETERSON LAKE BLVD.
COLLIERSVILLE, TN 38017

BALANCE LAST STATEMENT	WE HAVE ADDED		WE HAVE SUBTRACTED			RESULTING IN A BALANCE OF
	NUMBER	DEPOSITS/CREDITS	NUMBER	CHECKS/DEBITS	SERV. CHG.	
$6,823.10	2	$645.73	6	$896.27	$4.00	$6,568.56

DATE	CHECKS-DEBITS	CHECKS-DEBITS	DEPOSITS-CREDITS	BALANCE
				6,823.10
2/3	#432	163.84		6,659.26
2/5	#433	23.32		6,635.94
2/10			438.92	7,074.86
2/12	#434	533.20		6,541.66
2/16	#435	13.58		6,528.08
2/19	ATM w/draw	150.00		6,378.08
2/26	#436	12.33	206.81	6,568.56
2/28	Service Charge	4.00		

3. A bank statement shows a balance of $432.34. The service charge for this statement period was $3. The checkbook register showed deposits of $350.50 and $75.68 that did not appear on the statement. Outstanding checks were in the amounts of $356.20, $12.32, and $28.43. The checkbook balance was $464.57. Use the accompanying blank reconciliation form to reconcile the bank statement with the checkbook balance.

$		BALANCE AS SHOWN ON BANK STATEMENT		BALANCE AS SHOWN IN YOUR CHECKBOOK	$	
		ADD DEPOSITS NOT SHOWN ON STATEMENT		SUBTRACT AMOUNT OF SERVICE CHARGE		
		NEW TOTAL		NEW TOTAL		
		*SUBTRACT TOTAL OF OUTSTANDING CHECKS		ADJUSTMENTS IF ANY		
		YOUR ADJUSTED STATEMENT BALANCE	SHOULD ↔ EQUAL	YOUR ADJUSTED CHECKBOOK BALANCE		

* OUTSTANDING CHECKS

CHECK NUMBER	DATE	AMOUNT	
		$	
		TOTAL..........	$

1. Fill out the check register and check stub provided. The balance brought forward is $2,301.42, deposits were made for $200 on May 12 and $83.17 on May 20, and check 195 was written on May 25 to Lon Associates for $152.50 for supplies.

RECORD ALL CHARGES OR CREDITS THAT AFFECT YOUR ACCOUNT

NUMBER	DATE	DESCRIPTION OF TRANSACTION	AMOUNT OF CHECK	√	FEE	AMOUNT OF DEPOSIT	BALANCE
							$
			$		$	$	

Date ________ 19____

Amount ________________

To ________________

For ________________

Balance	
Deposits	
Total	
Amount This Check	
Balance	

2. Answer the following questions about Steve Woods' bank statement.

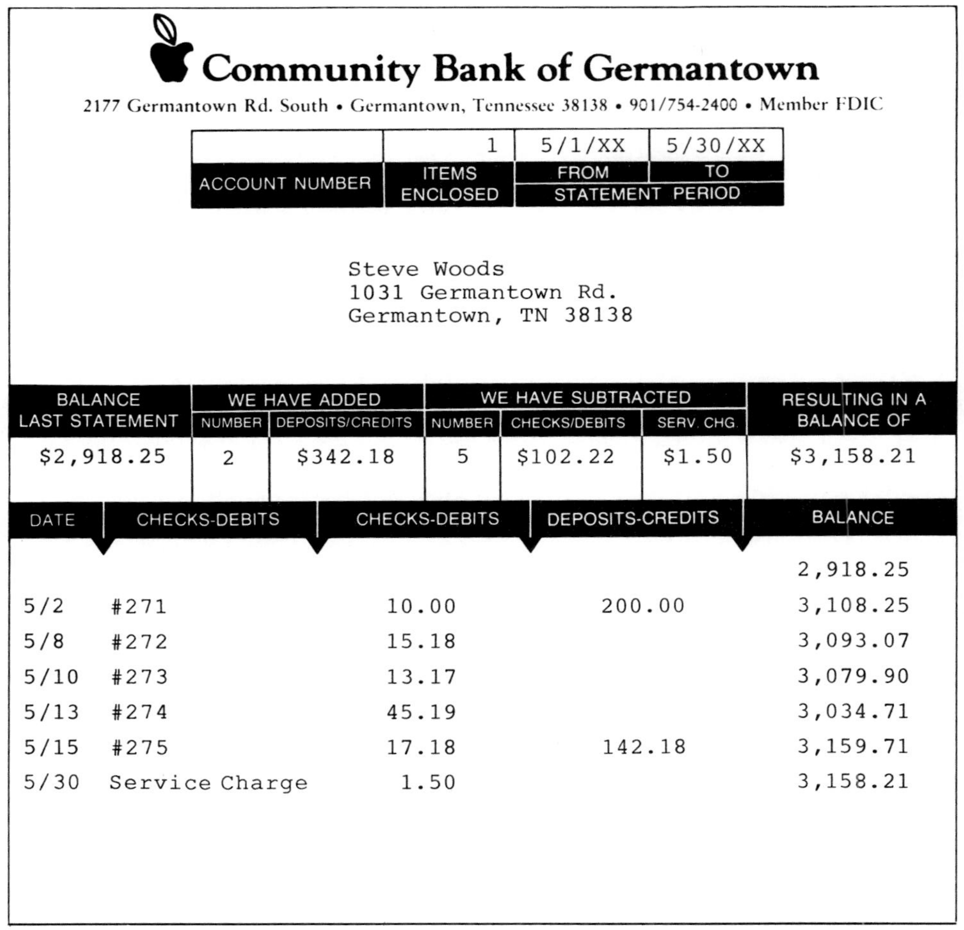

Community Bank of Germantown

2177 Germantown Rd. South • Germantown, Tennessee 38138 • 901/754-2400 • Member FDIC

ACCOUNT NUMBER	ITEMS ENCLOSED	STATEMENT PERIOD FROM	STATEMENT PERIOD TO
	1	5/1/XX	5/30/XX

Steve Woods
1031 Germantown Rd.
Germantown, TN 38138

BALANCE LAST STATEMENT	WE HAVE ADDED NUMBER	WE HAVE ADDED DEPOSITS/CREDITS	WE HAVE SUBTRACTED NUMBER	WE HAVE SUBTRACTED CHECKS/DEBITS	SERV. CHG.	RESULTING IN A BALANCE OF
$2,918.25	2	$342.18	5	$102.22	$1.50	$3,158.21

DATE	CHECKS-DEBITS	CHECKS-DEBITS	DEPOSITS-CREDITS	BALANCE
				2,918.25
5/2	#271	10.00	200.00	3,108.25
5/8	#272	15.18		3,093.07
5/10	#273	13.17		3,079.90
5/13	#274	45.19		3,034.71
5/15	#275	17.18	142.18	3,159.71
5/30	Service Charge	1.50		3,158.21

a. What is the balance at the beginning of the statement period?
b. How many checks cleared the bank during the statement period?

c. What was the service charge for the statement period?
d. Check 272 was written for what amount?
e. On what date was check 275 accounted?
f. What was the total of the deposits?
g. What was the balance at the end of the statement period?
h. What was the total amount for all checks written during the period?

3. Reconcile the checkbook balance of $1,817.93 with the bank statement balance of $860.21. A service fee of $15.00 and one returned item of $213.83 were charged against the account. Outstanding deposits were in the amounts of $800.00 and $412.13. Outstanding checks were written for $243.17, $167.18, $13.97, $42.12, and $16.80. Find each of the following.
a. Bank statement balance
b. Outstanding deposits
c. Outstanding checks
d. Adjusted bank statement balance
e. Checkbook balance
f. Service fee
g. Returned items
h. Adjusted checkbook balance

$		BALANCE AS SHOWN ON BANK STATEMENT		BALANCE AS SHOWN IN YOUR CHECKBOOK	$	
		ADD DEPOSITS NOT SHOWN ON STATEMENT		SUBTRACT AMOUNT OF SERVICE CHARGE		
		NEW TOTAL		NEW TOTAL		
		*SUBTRACT TOTAL OF OUTSTANDING CHECKS		ADJUSTMENTS IF ANY RETURNED ITEM		
		YOUR ADJUSTED STATEMENT BALANCE	SHOULD ↔ EQUAL	YOUR ADJUSTED CHECKBOOK BALANCE		

* OUTSTANDING CHECKS

CHECK NUMBER	DATE	AMOUNT		
		$		
		TOTAL..........		$

1.

DEPOSIT TICKET

DATE 4/29 19 XX

Checks and other items are received for deposit subject to the provisions of the Uniform Commercial Code or any applicable collection agreement.

87-278
840

Community Bank of Germantown
2177 Germantown Road • 7808 Farmington
Germantown, TN 38138 • (901) 754-2400 • Member FDIC

NAME Park's Oriental Grocery

6 3 | 1 5 7 9 | 5

⑆08400278⑆

	DOLLARS	CENTS
CURRENCY	858	63
COIN		
CHECKS (LIST SINGLY • BE SURE EACH ITEM IS ENDORSED)	157	38
	32	49
TOTAL FROM OTHER SIDE		
TOTAL	1,048	50

USE OTHER SIDE FOR ADDITIONAL LISTING

2.

456 Date 4/29 19 XX

Amount $155.30

To Green Harvest

For fresh vegetables

Balance	7,869	40
Deposits	1,048	50
Total	8,917	90
Amount This Check	155	30
Balance	8,762	60

456

April 29 19 XX 87-278/840

PAY TO THE ORDER OF Green Harvest $ 155.30

One hundred fifty-five and 30/100 DOLLARS

Community Bank of Germantown
2177 Germantown Rd. South
Germantown, Tennessee 38138

MEMO fresh vegetables Man Park

⑆08400278⑆

3.

RECORD ALL CHARGES OR CREDITS THAT AFFECT YOUR ACCOUNT

NUMBER	DATE	DESCRIPTION OF TRANSACTION	AMOUNT OF CHECK		√	FEE	AMOUNT OF DEPOSIT		BALANCE	
									7869	40
	4/29	Deposit					1048	50	8917	90
	4/29	Green Harvest	155	30					8762	60

4.

$ 12	32	BALANCE AS SHOWN ON BANK STATEMENT		BALANCE AS SHOWN IN YOUR CHECKBOOK	$ 178	74
650	00	ADD DEPOSITS NOT SHOWN ON STATEMENT		SUBTRACT AMOUNT OF SERVICE CHARGE	2	95
662	32	NEW TOTAL		NEW TOTAL	175	79
486	53	*SUBTRACT TOTAL OF OUTSTANDING CHECKS		ADJUSTMENTS IF ANY		
175	79	YOUR ADJUSTED STATEMENT BALANCE	SHOULD ⟷ EQUAL	YOUR ADJUSTED CHECKBOOK BALANCE	175	79

* OUTSTANDING CHECKS

CHECK NUMBER	DATE	AMOUNT	
		$ 36	52
		205	16
		18	92
		25	93
		200	00
		TOTAL 486	53

$

Using Equations to Solve Problems 5

Learning Objectives

1. Use basic math skills to solve equations and check the answers. (pp. 125–130)
2. Use the key word approach to analyze and solve word problems and check the answers. (pp. 131–135)

equation: a symbolic statement that the numbers and symbols on each side of the equal sign have the same value.

unknown: the quantity in a problem or an equation that is not given or known; usually represented by a letter in an equation. Also called *variable.*

variable: the quantity in a problem or an equation that is not given or known; usually represented by a letter in an equation. Also called *unknown.*

solving an equation: finding the numerical value of the unknown quantity in an equation.

In the business applications of mathematics, statements are often written in a simple, short, symbolic form called an equation. An **equation** is any statement that uses an equals sign. In an equation, **unknown** quantities, called **variables,** are often represented by letters. The familiar symbols +, −, ×, and ÷ are used along with parentheses and fraction bars to show relationships among variables and numbers in the equation.

Solving an equation means finding the missing or unknown amount. To do this, you isolate the unknown on the left side of the equation, with numbers and mathematical symbols all on the right. The rest of this chapter shows how to rewrite and simplify equations so that you can find the value of an unknown variable.

Writing Statements in Symbolic Form

The first step in solving any problem is to identify what is known and what is unknown. Next, letters are assigned to the unknown quantities. Finally, an equation is set up to solve for the unknown. Suppose that 15 of the 25 people who work at Pandora Carton Manufacturers work on the day shift and you want to know how many people work there in the evening. You know that 15 people work there during the day, that 25 people work there in all, and that some unknown quantity work there in the evening. Assign the letter N to the unknown number of night-shift workers. The information from the problem can then be written in words as "the night-shift workers plus the day-shift workers equal 25" and in symbols: $N + 15 = 25$.

In order to solve this equation, you do the opposite of whatever operation (addition, subtraction, multiplication, division) is used in the equation, and you do it on *both* sides of the equation.

Step by Step

Solving a Simple Equation

Step 1. Do the opposite of the operation that is used in the equation. If a number is added, you subtract the number; if a number is subtracted, you add the number, and so on.

Step 2. Do this on *both* sides of the equation.

EXAMPLE 1

Solve the equation $N + 15 = 25$.

$$\begin{array}{rcr} N + 15 & = & 25 \\ -15 & & -15 \\ \hline N & = & 10 \end{array}$$

$$N = 10$$

In this equation, 15 is added, so you do the opposite: You subtract 15 from both sides of the equation. This leaves you with $N = 10$.

Check:

$$N + 15 = 25$$
$$10 + 15 \stackrel{?}{=} 25$$
$$25 = 25$$

To check, put the number into the original equation in place of the letter and see if both sides of the equation represent the same number.

The following examples show these two steps applied to equations involving a number of different operations.

EXAMPLE 2

Solve the equation $A + 3 = 24$. (A number increased by 3 is 24.)

$$\begin{array}{rcr} A + 3 & = & 24 \\ -3 & & -3 \\ \hline A & = & 21 \end{array}$$

The equation shows that 3 is added, so you do the opposite: You subtract 3 from both sides of the equation.

Check:

$$A + 3 = 24$$
$$21 + 3 \stackrel{?}{=} 24$$
$$24 = 24$$

To check, substitute the number for the letter in the equation and see if both sides are equal.

EXAMPLE 3

Find the value of A if $A - 5 = 8$. (A number decreased by 5 is 8.)

$$\begin{array}{rcr} A - 5 & = & 8 \\ +5 & & +5 \\ \hline A & = & 13 \end{array}$$

The equation shows 5 is subtracted, so you do the opposite: You add 5 to both sides of the equation.

Check:

$$A - 5 = 8$$
$$13 - 5 \stackrel{?}{=} 8$$
$$8 = 8$$

To check, substitute the number for the letter in the equation and see if both sides yield the same number.

EXAMPLE 4

Solve the equation $2A = 18$. (A number multiplied by 2 is 18.)

$$2A = 18$$
$$\frac{\not{2}A}{\not{2}} = \frac{18}{2}$$
$$A = 9$$

The equation shows multiplication by 2; so you do the opposite: You divide both sides of the equation by 2.

Check:

$$2A = 18$$
$$2(9) \stackrel{?}{=} 18$$
$$18 = 18$$

To check, substitute the number for the letter in the equation and see if both sides are equal.

EXAMPLE 5

Find the value of A if $\frac{A}{4} = 5$. (A number divided by 4 is 5.)

$$\frac{A}{4} = 5$$

$$4\left(\frac{A}{4}\right) = 5(4)$$

$$A = 20$$

The equation shows division by 4, so you do the opposite: You multiply both sides of the equation by 4.

Check:

$$\frac{A}{4} = 5$$

$$\frac{20}{4} \stackrel{?}{=} 5$$

$$5 = 5$$

To check, substitute the number for the letter in the equation and see if both sides are equal.

Most equations used in the business world are more complex than the ones we showed in Examples 1–5, and they require several more solution steps. When you solve an equation, you follow certain rules concerning the order in which you do the steps.

Step by Step

The Steps for Solving an Equation

Step 1. To solve an equation with more than one operation involved, *first* do additions and subtractions.

Step 2. Next, do multiplications and divisions.

EXAMPLE 6

Find A if $2A + 1 = 15$. (Two times a number increased by 1 is 15.)

The equation uses both addition and multiplication; handle addition first and then multiplication.

$$\begin{array}{rcr} 2A + 1 & = & 15 \\ -1 & & -\ 1 \\ \hline 2A & = & 14 \end{array}$$

The equation shows addition of 1, so do the opposite: Subtract 1 from both sides of the equation.

$$2A = 14$$

$$\frac{2A}{2} = \frac{14}{2}$$

$$A = 7$$

The equation shows multiplication by 2, so do the opposite: Divide both sides of the equation by 2.

Check:

$$2A + 1 = 15$$

$$2(7) + 1 \stackrel{?}{=} 15$$

$$14 + 1 \stackrel{?}{=} 15$$

$$15 = 15$$

To check you substitute the number for the letter in the equation and see if both sides are equal.

EXAMPLE 7

Solve the equation $\frac{A}{5} - 3 = 1$. (A number divided by 5 and decreased by 3 is 1.)

The equation uses both subtraction and division; you handle subtraction first and then division.

$$\begin{array}{rcr} \dfrac{A}{5} - 3 & = & 1 \\ +3 & & +3 \\ \hline \dfrac{A}{5} & = & 4 \end{array}$$

The equation shows subtraction of 3, so do the opposite: Add 3 to both sides of the equation.

$$\frac{A}{5} = 4$$

$$\cancel{5}\left(\frac{A}{\cancel{5}}\right) = 4(5)$$

$$A = 20$$

The equation shows division by 5, so multiply both sides by 5.

Check:

$$\frac{A}{5} - 3 = 1$$

$$\frac{20}{5} - 3 \stackrel{?}{=} 1$$

$$4 - 3 \stackrel{?}{=} 1$$

$$1 = 1$$

To check, substitute the number for the letter in the equation and see if both sides are equal.

The next example shows what to do when parentheses are involved in an equation. Recall that parentheses must be removed before going ahead with the rest of the equation.

Step by Step

Solving Equations Containing Parentheses

Step 1. Remove parentheses by multiplying the number just before the parentheses by each quantity inside the parentheses.

Step 2. Next, do additions and subtractions.

Step 3. Then, do multiplications and divisions.

EXAMPLE 8

Solve the equation $5(A + 3) = 25$.

$$5(A + 3) = 25$$

$$5A + 15 = 25$$

The parentheses must be removed first, so you perform the operation that will do that—multiplication. (You are *not* doing the opposite of what is shown in the equation, and you do *not* do it on both sides of the equation, just where the parentheses occur.)

$$\begin{array}{rcr} 5A + 15 & = & 25 \\ -15 & & -15 \\ \hline 5A & = & 10 \end{array}$$

Now the equation shows addition of 15, so you do the opposite: Subtract 15 from both sides of the equation.

$$\frac{\cancel{5}A}{\cancel{5}} = \frac{10}{5}$$

$$A = 2$$

The equation shows multiplication, so do the opposite: Divide both sides of the equation by 5.

Check:

$$5(A + 3) = 25$$

$$5(2 + 3) \stackrel{?}{=} 25$$

$$10 + 15 \stackrel{?}{=} 25$$

$$25 = 25$$

To check, substitute the number for the letter in the equation and see if both sides are equal.

TIPS & TRAPS

Parentheses in an equation should grab your attention, because they say DO ME FIRST; you need to perform the operations to remove the parentheses before you do anything else in the equation. Trying to deal with an equation *without* removing parentheses can lead to wrong answers, as shown here.

Find X if $5(X - 2) = 45$.

$$5(X - 2) = 45$$

$$\begin{array}{rcr} 5X - 10 & = & 45 \\ +\ 10 & & +\ 10 \\ \hline 5X & = & 55 \end{array}$$

$$\frac{\not{5}X}{\not{5}} = \frac{55}{5}$$

$$X = 11$$

CORRECT

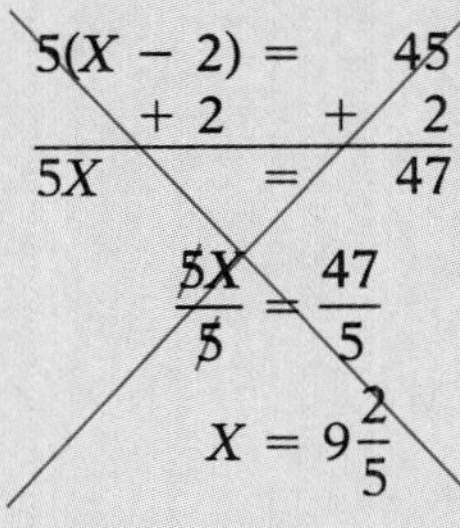

WRONG

Some problems involve the use of the unknown more than once in an equation; in this case you simply combine the unknowns and then follow the usual steps for solving an equation.

Step by Step

Combining Unknowns in an Equation

Step 1. Combine the unknowns by adding or subtracting the numbers in front of the letters. If no number is written in front of a letter, it is understood to be a 1. Thus, $X = 1X$.

Step 2. Next, do additions and subtractions.

Step 3. Then, do multiplications and divisions.

EXAMPLE 9

Find A if $A + 3A - 2 = 14$.

$$A + 3A - 2 = 14$$

First combine the unknowns. Remember that A is the same as $1A$, so $A + 3A = 4A$.

$$\begin{array}{rcr} 4A - 2 & = & 14 \\ +\ 2 & & +\ 2 \\ \hline 4A & = & 16 \end{array}$$

The equation uses both subtraction and multiplication; handle subtraction first. Do this by *adding* 2 to both sides of the equation.

$$\frac{\not{4}A}{\not{4}} = \frac{16}{4}$$

$$A = 4$$

The equation shows multiplication by 4, so do the opposite: Divide both sides of the equation by 4.

Check:

$$A + 3A - 2 = 14$$
$$4 + 3(4) - 2 \stackrel{?}{=} 14$$
$$4 + 12 - 2 \stackrel{?}{=} 14$$
$$16 - 2 \stackrel{?}{=} 14$$
$$14 = 14$$

To check, substitute the number for the letter in the equation, and see both sides are the same.

Self-Check

Identify the operation illustrated in each equation.

1. $P + I = A$ 2. $R = \frac{M}{N}$ 3. $AS = T$ 4. $S = R - T$

Find the value of N.

5. $N + 3 = 12$ 6. $N - 5 = 44$ 7. $4N = 36$ 8. $\frac{N}{7} = 3$

9. $3N + 5 = 17$ 10. $\frac{N}{3} - 1 = 10$ 11. $2(N + 6) = 18$

12. $N - 9 + 3N = 19$

Section Review

Identify the operation or operations illustrated in the following equations.

1. $M - N = P$ 2. $AB = R$ 3. $D = \frac{P}{Q}$

4. $F = G + H$ 5. $C = AM - J$

6. $\frac{A}{P} + R = S$

Find the value of the variable.

7. $N - 5 = 12$ 8. $N + 8 = 20$

9. $5N = 35$ 10. $3N = 27$

11. $\frac{A}{6} = 2$ 12. $\frac{A}{2} = 3$

13. $2N + 4 = 12$ 14. $3N - 5 = 10$

15. $\frac{A}{3} + 4 = 12$

16. $2(X - 3) = 8$

17. $4X - X = 21$

18. $3X - 4 + 2X = 11$

Solving Word Problems

The methods used to solve equations are also used to solve word problems. Solving word problems, however, requires additional analysis before we can apply the techniques just discussed. When you first read a word problem, you must ask: What are we supposed to find? What facts are given? What facts are implied? You must choose a symbol to stand for the unknown quantity and use that symbol to write the mathematical information about the unknown quantity. After you have stated the problem in symbols, you are ready to follow the procedures discussed earlier in this chapter.

Certain key words in a word problem give you clues as to whether a certain quantity is added to, subtracted from, or multiplied or divided by another quantity. For example, if a word problem tells you that Carol's salary in 1990 *exceeds* her 1989 salary by $2,500, you know that you should *add* $2,500 to her 1989 salary to find her 1990 salary. Many times, when you see the word *of* in a problem, you can assume that the problem involves multiplication. The verb in a problem, whether it is a form of *is* or some other verb, connects the unknown quantity and the known amounts. The verb generally stands for the equals sign. Table 5-1 summarizes important key words and

Table 5-1 Key Words and What They Mean in Word Problems

Addition	Subtraction	Multiplication	Division	Equality
The sum of	Less than	Times	Divide(s)	Equals
Plus/total	Decreased by	Multiplied by	Divided by	Is/was/are
Increased by	Subtracted from	Of	Divided into	Is equal to
More/more than	Difference between	The product of	Half of (divided by two)	The result is
Added to	Diminished by	Twice (two times)	Per	What is left
Exceeds	Take away	Double (two times)		What remains
Expands	Reduced by	Triple (three times)		The same as
Greater than	Less/minus	Half ($\frac{1}{2}$ times)		Gives/giving
Gain/profit	Loss			Makes
Longer	Lower			Leaves
Older	Shrinks			
Heavier	Smaller than			
Wider	Younger			
Taller	Slower			

what they mean when they are used in a word problem. This list should help you analyze the information in word problems and write it in symbols.

EXAMPLE 10

The difference between a number and 6 is 4. Find the number.

The word *difference* in the problem tells you to use subtraction to find the unknown number.

Unknown	Facts	Plan	Solution
Number $= n$	Other number $= 6$ Difference $= 4$	If 6 is subtracted from a number, the result is 4. $n - 6 = 4$	$n - 6 = 4$ $+6 \quad +6$ $n = 10$

The number is 10.

Check
$10 - 6 \stackrel{?}{=} 4$ $4 = 4$

EXAMPLE 11

Wanda plans to save $\frac{1}{10}$ of her salary each week. If her weekly salary is \$350, find the amount she will save each week.

The word *of* in the problem tells you to use multiplication to find the unknown number.

Unknown	Facts	Plan	Solution
Amount to be saved $= S$	Total salary $= \$350$ Portion to be saved $= \frac{1}{10}$	$\frac{1}{10}$ of salary will be saved $\frac{1}{10}(350) = S$	$S = \frac{1}{\cancel{10}_1} \cdot \frac{\cancel{350}^{35}}{1}$ $S = 35$

Wanda will save \$35 each week.

Check
$\frac{1}{10}(350) \stackrel{?}{=} 35$ $35 = 35$

> **TIPS & TRAPS**
> It's a good idea to read a word problem several times. With each reading a different aspect of the problem is analyzed.
> 1. Read for a general understanding of the problem.
> 2. Read to determine what you want to find.
> 3. Read to locate the given and implied facts.
> 4. Read to relate the known and unknown facts (write the equation).
> 5. After solving the equation, read to see if the solution satisfies the conditions of the problem.

EXAMPLE 12

At Alexander's Cafe last Wednesday, there were twice as many requests for seats in the nonsmoking section as there were requests for seats in the smoking section. If a total of 342 customers came through the cafe that day, how many were smokers? How many were nonsmokers?

Study the key words: In "twice as many" requests for the nonsmoking section, the word *twice* indicates that you should let S equal the number of smokers and let $2S$ equal the number of nonsmokers. The expression "a total of 342 customers" tells us that the *sum* of the number of smokers and the number of nonsmokers will equal the number of customers.

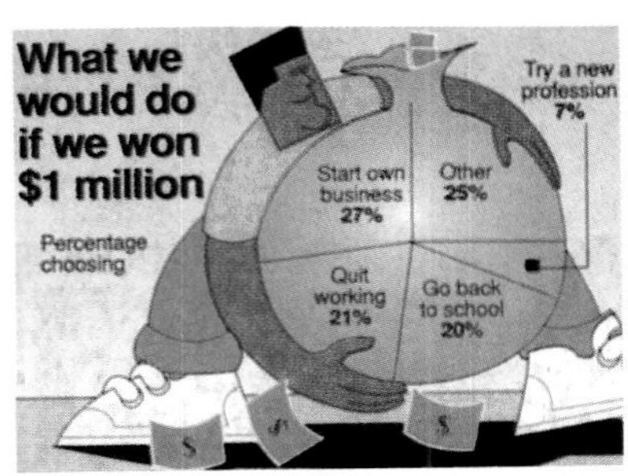

Source: Chex Cereals survey of 500 adults
By Rod Little, USA TODAY

Unknown	Facts	Plan	Solution
Number of smokers = S Number of non-smokers = $2S$	Total number of customers = 342	Number of smokers + number of nonsmokers = total number of customers.	$S + 2S = 342$
		Combine terms.	$3S = 342$
		Divide both sides of the equation by 3.	$S = 114$
		Multiply 114 by 2 to find $2S$.	$2S = 228$

Check
Does $114 + 2(114) = 342?$
$342 = 342$

There were 114 smokers and 228 nonsmokers.

EXAMPLE 13

Juana supervises six times as many data entry clerks as Millie. There are ten fewer clerks working for Millie than working for Juana. How many people are working for each supervisor?

Study the key words: In "six times as many," the words *six times* indicates that you should let M equal the number of clerks working for Millie and let $6M$ equal the number of clerks working for Juana. The expression "ten fewer clerks" tells us that the *difference between* $6M$ and M is ten.

Unknown	Facts	Plan	Solution
Number of Millie's employees = M Number of Juana's employees = $6M$ (six times as many)	The difference between the number of clerks working for Juana and the number working for Millie is 10.	Subtract the number of Millie's clerks from the number of Juana's clerks and get a difference of 10.	$6M - M = 10$
		Combine terms.	$5M = 10$
		Divide both sides of the equation by 5.	$M = 2$
		Multiply 2 by 6 to find $6M$.	$6M = 12$

Check
Does $6(2) - 2 = 10?$ $12 - 2 \stackrel{?}{=} 10$ $10 = 10$

Millie supervises 2 clerks; Juana supervises 12 clerks.

Real World Application

HOW TO SOLVE ANOTHER TRICKY WORD PROBLEM

Many problems encountered daily can be solved by using proportions. Most problems that involve a relationship between two sets of numbers can be solved by this technique, but you must be careful to be consistent in setting up the equation.

Proportions contain two equal ratios (fractions) used to compare two quantities; for example, 2 ounces in 4 gallons is equivalent to 4 ounces in 8 gallons. Expressed as a proportion, this example would be:

$$\frac{2 \text{ ozs.}}{4 \text{ gals.}} = \frac{4 \text{ ozs.}}{8 \text{ gals.}}$$

If one of the four numbers in the proportion is missing, you can find it by using cross-multiplication:

$$\frac{3}{x} \times \frac{7}{5}$$

$$7 \cdot x = 3 \cdot 5$$

$$7x = 15$$

$$x = 15 \div 7$$

$$x = 2\frac{1}{7}$$

In solving a word problem by this method, it is helpful to write in words the units being compared. There are usually 3 known values and 2 different units. Write a comparison of the two units first; then solve the problem.

Example: Your car gets 23 miles to a gallon of gas. How far can you go on 16 gallons of gas?

$$\frac{\text{miles}}{\text{gallons}} \longrightarrow \frac{23 \text{ miles}}{1 \text{ gal.}} = \frac{x \text{ miles}}{16 \text{ gals.}}$$

$$1x = 23 \cdot 16$$

$$1x = 368$$

$$x = 368 \text{ miles on 16 gallons}$$

Example: The label on a container of weed killer gives directions for mixing 3 ounces to 2 gallons of water. If your sprayer holds 5 gallons, how many ounces of the weed killer must you use?

$$\frac{\text{ounces}}{\text{gallons}} \longrightarrow \frac{3 \text{ ozs.}}{2 \text{ gals.}} = \frac{x \text{ ozs.}}{5 \text{ gals.}}$$

$$2x = 15$$

$$x = 7\frac{1}{2} \text{ ounces}$$

Application Questions

1. A scale drawing of an office building is not labeled, but indicates $\frac{1}{4}'' = 5'$. On the drawing, one wall measures 2 inches. How long is the wall?

2. A recipe uses 3 cups of flour to $1\frac{1}{4}$ cups of milk. If you have 2 cups of flour, how much milk should you use?

3. For 32 hours of work, you are paid \$241.60. How much would you receive for 37 hours?

Many problems give a *total* number of two types of items. You want to know the number of each of the two types of items. The next example illustrates this type of problem.

EXAMPLE 14

A card-shop owner spent a total of \$950 ordering 600 cards from one company. The humorous cards cost \$1.75 each and the nature cards cost \$1.50 each. How many of each style card did she order? How much did she spend on each type of card?

Study the problem: You know the total cost ($950) and the total number of cards ordered (600). You also know how much each type of card costs. The number of humorous cards added to the number of nature cards totals 600. The amount of money spent on both types of cards totals $950. In this type of problem, you may use the most expensive item as the variable, H, or the number of humorous cards. Then, the nature cards can be represented as $600 - H$, the total number of cards minus the humorous cards.

Unknown	Facts	Plan	Solution
Number of humorous cards = H Number of nature cards = $600 - H$	Total number of cards = 600 Cost of humorous cards = $1.75H Cost of nature cards = $1.50(600 − H) Total sale = $950	The sum of the costs of both types of cards equals the total sale.	$1.75H + 1.50(600 - H) = 950$
		Remove the parentheses.	$1.75H + 900 - 1.50H = 950$
		Combine terms.	$0.25H + 900 = 950$
		Subtract 900 from both sides of the equation.	$0.25H = 50$
		Divide both sides of the equation by 0.25.	$H = 200$
		Subtract 200 from 600 to find $600 - H$.	$600 - H = 400$

200 humorous cards were bought and 400 nature cards were bought.

Check
Does $1.75(200) + 1.5(600 - 200) = 950$?
$350 + 900 - 300 \stackrel{?}{=} 950$
$950 = 950$

Self-Check

13. The difference between a number and 7 is 8. Find the number.

14. Manny plans to save $\frac{1}{12}$ of his salary each week. If his weekly salary is $372, find the amount he will save each week.

15. Last week at the Sunshine Valley Rock Festival, Joel sold three times as many tie-dyed T-shirts as silk-screened shirts. He sold 176 shirts altogether. How many tie-dyed shirts did he sell?

16. Elaine sold three times as many magazine subscriptions as Ron did. Ron sold 16 fewer subscriptions than Elaine did. How many subscriptions did each one sell?

17. Will ordered two times as many boxes of ballpoint pens as boxes of felt-tip pens. Ballpoint pens cost $3.50 per box, and felt-tip pens cost $4.50. If Will's order of pens totaled $46, how many boxes of each type of pen did he buy?

18. A real-estate salesperson bought promotional calendars and date books to give to her customers at the end of the year. The calendars cost $0.75 each and the date books cost $0.50 each. She ordered a total of 500 promotional items and spent $300. How many of each item did she order?

Section Review

1. The sum of a number and 6 is 15. Find the number.

Unknown	Facts	Plan	Solution

Check

2. The difference between a number and 6 is 12. Find the number.

Unknown	Facts	Plan	Solution

Check

3. The product of a number and 12 is 60. Find the number.

Unknown	Facts	Plan	Solution

Check

4. Nine is the quotient of a number divided by 7. Find the number.

Unknown	Facts	Plan	Solution

Check

5. An electrician pays $\frac{2}{5}$ of the money he earns for supplies. If he earned $240 for a certain job, how much did he spend on supplies?

Unknown	Facts	Plan	Solution

Check

6. Liz Bliss spends 18 hours on a project and estimates that she has completed $\frac{1}{3}$ of the project. How many hours does she expect the project to take?

Unknown	Facts	Plan	Solution

Check

7. An inventory clerk is expected to have 2,000 fan belts in stock. If the current count is 1,584 fan belts, how many more should be ordered?

Unknown	Facts	Plan	Solution

Check

8. A personal computer costs $4,000, and a printer costs $1,500. What is the total cost of the equipment?

Unknown	Facts	Plan	Solution

Check

9. Carrie McConnel spends $\frac{1}{6}$ of her weekly earnings on groceries. How much does she spend on groceries if her weekly earnings are $345?

Unknown	Facts	Plan	Solution

Check

10. A purse that sells for $68.99 is reduced by $25.50. What is the price of the purse after the reduction?

Unknown	Facts	Plan	Solution

Check

11. Shaquita Davis earns $350 for working 40 hours. How much does she make for each hour of work?

Unknown	Facts	Plan	Solution

Check

12. Wilson's Auto, Inc., has 37 employees and a weekly payroll of $10,878. If each employee makes the same amount, how much does each make?

Unknown	Facts	Plan	Solution

Check

13. Molly McWherter earns $7.36 per hour. How much would she make for 37 hours of work?

Unknown	Facts	Plan	Solution

Check

14. An imprint machine makes 1,897 imprints per hour. How many imprints can be made in 12 hours?

Unknown	Facts	Plan	Solution

Check

15. Wallpaper costs $12.97 per roll and a kitchen requires 9 rolls. What is the cost of the wallpaper needed to paper the kitchen?

Unknown	Facts	Plan	Solution

Check

16. Mack Construction Co. was billed for plasterboard installation. If the job required 3,582 square feet of plasterboard and cost $2,435.76, what was the cost per square foot?

Unknown	Facts	Plan	Solution

Check

17. Allen Brent purchased 250 pounds of tomatoes, 400 pounds of potatoes, 50 pounds of broccoli, and 130 pounds of birdseed for his chain stores. If all items are placed on the same shipment, what is the total weight of the shipment?

Unknown	Facts	Plan	Solution

Check

18. Harks Manufacturer is negotiating a waste-removal contract. A study indicates that, in general, 304 pounds of waste are produced on Monday, 450 pounds are produced on Tuesday, 483 pounds are produced on Wednesday, 387 pounds are produced on Thursday, and 293 pounds are produced on Friday. The plant is closed on Saturday and Sunday. How many pounds of waste are produced per week?

Unknown	Facts	Plan	Solution

Check

19. Cecil Hastings was overstocked with men's shirts and reduced the price from $18.99 to $15.97. How much was each shirt reduced?

Unknown	Facts	Plan	Solution

Check

20. Cecil (Problem 19) counted 216 shirts to be reduced. What was the total amount of reduction for 216 shirts?

Unknown	Facts	Plan	Solution

Check

21. The wholesale cost of an executive desk is $375, and the wholesale cost of a secretarial desk is $300. Allen Furniture Company filled an order for 40 desks, costing a total of $12,825. How many desks of each type had been ordered?

Unknown	Facts	Plan	Solution

Check

22. A computer store sold 144 cases of two grades of computer paper. Microperforated paper cost $15.97 per case, and standard perforated paper cost $9.75 per case. If the store had paper sales totaling $1,715, how many cases of each type were sold? What was the dollar value of each type sold?

Unknown	Facts	Plan	Solution

Check

23. A retailer purchased 1,000 light bulbs. Headlight bulbs cost $13.95 each, and taillight bulbs cost $7.55 each. If the retailer spent $9,342 on headlight stock, how many headlights and how many taillights were sold? What was the dollar value of the headlights ordered? What was the dollar value of the taillights ordered?

Unknown	Facts	Plan	Solution

Check

Summary

Topic	Page	What to Remember	Examples
Solving an equation	125–126	Do the *opposite* of the operation that is shown in the equation, and do it on *both sides* of the equation:	
		If the equation shows addition, subtract the same number from both sides of the equation.	$A + 11 = 19$. Find the value of A. $A + 11 = 19$ $\quad - 11 \quad - 11$ $A = 8$
		If the equation shows subtraction, add the same number to both sides of the equation.	$A - 7 = 12$. Find the value of A. $A - 7 = 12$ $\quad + 7 \quad + 7$ $A = 19$
		If the equation shows multiplication, divide both sides of the equation by the same number.	$4A = 36$. Find the value of A. $\frac{4A}{4} = \frac{36}{4}$ $A = 9$
		If the equation shows division, multiply both sides of the equation by the same number.	$\frac{A}{7} = 6$. Find the value of A. $\frac{A}{7} \times 7 = 6 \times 7$ $A = 42$
Equations with more than one operation	127–128	Do the additions and subtractions first; then do the multiplications and divisions.	$4A + 4 = 20$ Find the value of A. $4A + 4 = 20$ Undo addition first. $\quad - 4 \quad - 4$ $4A = 16$ $\frac{4A}{4} = \frac{16}{4}$ Then undo division. $A = 4$
Removing parentheses	128–129	Remove parentheses by multiplying everything within the parentheses by the number to the left of the parentheses.	$3(A + 4) = 27$ $3A + 12 = 27$ $\quad - 12 \quad - 12$ $3A = 15$ $\frac{3A}{3} = \frac{15}{3}$ $A = 5$
Combining unknowns	129–130	Combine all possible numbers and variables before taking other steps to solve the equation.	$A - 5 + 5A = 25$ $6A - 5 = 25$ $\quad + 5 \quad + 5$ $6A = 30$ $\frac{6A}{6} = \frac{30}{6}$ $A = 5$

<table>
<tr><th>Topic</th><th>Page</th><th>What to Remember</th><th>Example</th></tr>
<tr><td>Using key words</td><td>131–135</td><td>Use key words in a problem to convert the facts of a word problem to mathematical symbols.</td><td>See Table 5-1 for key words.</td></tr>
<tr><td>Difference problems</td><td>132</td><td>The word “difference” in the problem tells you to use subtraction to write the equation.</td><td>The difference between a number and 3 is 12. Find the number.
<table>
<tr><th>Unknown</th><th>Facts</th><th>Solution</th></tr>
<tr><td>Number = n</td><td>Other number = 3
Difference = 12
$n - 3 = 12$</td><td>$n - 3 = 12$
$+3 \quad +3$
$n = 15$</td></tr>
</table></td></tr>
<tr><td>Finding a part</td><td>132</td><td>Of in the problem usually tells you to use multiplication to find the unknown number.</td><td>Gabriella spends $\frac{2}{5}$ of her workday typing. If she works 40 hours a week, how many hours does she type each week?
<table>
<tr><th>Unknown</th><th>Facts</th><th>Solution</th></tr>
<tr><td>Number of hours typing = T</td><td>Total hours at work = 40</td><td>$T = 40 \times \frac{2}{5}$</td></tr>
<tr><td></td><td>Part of day spent typing = $\frac{2}{5}$</td><td>$T = 16$ hours</td></tr>
</table></td></tr>
<tr><td>Finding parts of a whole</td><td>133</td><td>Twice as many tells you that one part of the whole is two times the size of the other part, and total tells you to add the two parts.</td><td>There are twice as many students in the daytime aerobics class as there are in the night class.
If there are 48 students total, how many students are in each class?
<table>
<tr><th>Unknown</th><th>Facts</th><th>Solution</th></tr>
<tr><td>Number of night students = S
Number of day students = $2S$</td><td>Total number of students = 48</td><td>$S + 2S = 48$
$3S = 48$
$\frac{\cancel{3}S}{\cancel{3}} = \frac{48}{3}$
$S = 16$</td></tr>
</table></td></tr>
<tr><td>Finding parts of a whole</td><td>133</td><td>Three times as many tells you to use multiplication, and four fewer than tells you to use subtraction when you write the problem in symbols.</td><td>Last week Beth sold three times as many fax machines as Leon did. Leon sold 4 fewer machines than Beth did. How many fax machines did each one sell?
<table>
<tr><th>Unknown</th><th>Facts</th><th>Solution</th></tr>
<tr><td>Number of Leon's sales = L
Number of Beth's sales = $3L$</td><td>The difference between Beth's and Leon's sales is 4.</td><td>$3L - L = 4$
$\frac{\cancel{2}L}{\cancel{2}} = \frac{4}{2}$
$L = 2$</td></tr>
</table></td></tr>
</table>

Topic	Page	What to Remember	Examples
Finding parts given a total	134–135	The total minus one part equals the other part.	Charles sold 20 sets of baseball cards for a total of \$525. Fleer sets sell for \$30 and Tops sets sell for \$25. How many sets of each type were sold?

Unknown	Facts	Solution
Number of Fleer sets sold = F	Total number of sets sold = 20	$30F + 25(20 - F) = 525$
Number of Tops sets sold = $20 - F$	Value of Fleer sets = $30F$ Value of Tops sets = $25(20 - F)$ Total value = \$525 $30F + 25(20 - F) = 525$	$30F + 500 - 25F = 525$ $5F + 500 = 525$ $5F = 525 - 500$ $5F = 25$ $F = 5$ (Fleer sets) $20 - F = 15$ (Tops sets)

There are 5 Fleer sets and 15 Tops sets.

Identify the operation illustrated in the following formulas:

1. $C = S - M$

2. $B = \frac{P}{R}$

3. $W = RT$

4. $P + T = S$

Solve the following.

5. $R + 3 = 8$

6. $A - 5 = 7$

7. $3M = 45$

8. $4N = 48$

9. $\frac{B}{12} = 3$

10. $\frac{A}{4} = 17$

11. $\frac{A}{4} - 3 = 5$

12. $\frac{A}{3} + 2 = 6$

13. The sum of a number and 12 is 48. What is the number?

Unknown	Facts	Plan	Solution

Check

14. The difference between a number and 15 is 23. What is the number?

Unknown	Facts	Plan	Solution

Check

15. The product of a number and 7 is 56. What is the number?

Unknown	Facts	Plan	Solution

Check

16. Five more than 3 times a number is 17. What is the number?

Unknown	Facts	Plan	Solution

Check

17. Milton's adjusted checkbook balance was $482.52 and his adjusted bank balance was $458.91. By how much did the two balances differ?

Unknown	Facts	Plan	Solution

Check

18. A widget maker has made 482 widgets. This is two-thirds of the total number needed. How many widgets are needed?

Unknown	Facts	Plan	Solution

Check

19. An office desk costs 3 times as much as an office chair. Together, they cost $440. How much does each piece of furniture cost?

Unknown	Facts	Plan	Solution

Check

20. A purchasing agent ordered twice as many regular light bulbs costing $6 per dozen as she ordered long-life bulbs at $8 per dozen. If the order came to a total of $600, how many of each type of bulb did she order?

Unknown	Facts	Plan	Solution

Check

21. A payroll clerk wrote 18 checks totaling $6,750. Half of the checks were each for $20 more than the other half. What was the amount of each check?

Unknown	Facts	Plan	Solution

Check

22. An employee who had a paycheck of $418 paid the following bills: $104.18 for utilities, $29.89 for groceries, $50 for credit card payment, and $18.97 for insurance. What was the amount left after paying these bills?

Unknown	Facts	Plan	Solution

Check

23. If a secretary earning $204.80 per week got a raise equal to one-fifth of his earnings, what was his new salary?

Unknown	Facts	Plan	Solution

Check

24. Elmo sold twice as many shirts as Garry, who sold 4 fewer shirts than Jim. If the three together sold 16 shirts, how many shirts did each one sell?

Unknown	Facts	Plan	Solution

Check

25. How many cases of cereal can be stacked on top of one another in a 24-foot-high warehouse if each case of cereal measures 1.2 feet high?

Unknown	Facts	Plan	Solution

Check

26. One employee earns 1.3 times as much as another employee, who earns $318 per week. How much does the first employee earn?

Unknown	Facts	Plan	Solution

Check

27. A consultant earned a total of \$53,456 in one year. What was her weekly income?

Unknown	Facts	Plan	Solution

Check

28. If the price of airline tickets increased by 5¢ per dollar, how much would Sal pay for a ticket that had cost \$485 before the rate increase?

Unknown	Facts	Plan	Solution

Check

29. Unicorn Bakery took in \$444 for 36 orders for cheesecakes on Wednesday. The small cheesecakes sell for \$8, and the large cheesecakes cost \$14. How many small cheesecakes were ordered? How many large cheesecakes were ordered? What was the total amount taken in for each of the sizes of cheesecake?

Unknown	Facts	Plan	Solution

Check

30. Athletic concessions sold roasted peanuts ($1), soft drinks ($1.75), and hot dogs ($2) at football games. If the total sales for the fourth game totaled $1,694 and people bought twice as many peanuts as hot dogs and four times as many soft drinks as hot dogs, how many of each item were purchased?

Unknown	Facts	Plan	Solution

Check

Trial Test

Identify the operation illustrated in the following formulas.

1. $P + I = A$

2. $S - M = C$

3. $F = PA$

4. $R = \frac{P}{B}$

Solve.

5. $N + 7 = 18$

6. $5N = 45$

7. $\frac{A}{3} = 6$

8. $B - 8 = 7$

9. $3A - 5 = 10$

10. $5A + 8 = 33$

11. $2(N + 1) = 14$

12. $5A + A = 30$

13. The sum of a number and 12 is 38. Find the number.

Unknown	Facts	Plan	Solution

Check

14. The product of a number and 6 is 42. What is the number?

Unknown	Facts	Plan	Solution

Check

15. An employee who was earning $249 weekly received a raise of $36. How much is the new salary?

Unknown	Facts	Plan	Solution

Check

16. An inventory clerk is expected to keep 600 filters on hand. A physical count shows there are 298 filters in stock. How many filters should be ordered?

Unknown	Facts	Plan	Solution

Check

17. A container of oil holds 585 gallons. How many containers each holding 4.5 gallons will be needed if all the oil is to be transferred to the smaller containers?

Unknown	Facts	Plan	Solution

Check

18. The buyer for a specialty gift store purchased an equal number of two types of designer telephones for a total cost of $7,200. The top-quality phones cost $80 each, and the neon and plastic phones cost $120 each. How many of each type of phone were purchased and what was the total dollar value of each type?

Unknown	Facts	Plan	Solution

Check

19. A five-and-ten store sold plastic cups for $3.50 each and ceramic cups for $4 each. If 400 cups were sold for a total of $1,458, how many cups of each type were sold? What was the dollar value of each type of cup sold?

Unknown	Facts	Plan	Solution

Check

20. An appliance dealer sold 9 more washing machines than dryers. Washing machines sell for $480 and dryers sell for $350. If total dollar sales were $21,750, how many of each appliance were sold? What was the dollar value of washing machines sold and the dollar value of dryers sold?

Unknown	Facts	Plan	Solution

Check

Self-Check Solutions

1. Addition **2.** Division **3.** Multiplication **4.** Subtraction

5.
$$\begin{array}{rcr} N + 3 = & & 12 \\ -3 & & -3 \\ \hline N & = & 9 \end{array}$$

6.
$$\begin{array}{rcr} N - 5 = & & 44 \\ +5 & & +5 \\ \hline N & = & 49 \end{array}$$

7.
$$4N = 36$$
$$\frac{\cancel{4}N}{\cancel{4}} = \frac{36}{4}$$
$$N = 9$$

8.
$$\frac{N}{7} = 3$$
$$\cancel{7}\left(\frac{N}{\cancel{7}}\right) = 3(7)$$
$$N = 21$$

9.
$$\begin{array}{rcr} 3N + 5 = & & 17 \\ -5 & & -5 \\ \hline 3N & = & 12 \end{array}$$
$$\frac{\cancel{3}N}{\cancel{3}} = \frac{12}{3}$$
$$N = 4$$

10.
$$\begin{array}{rcr} \frac{N}{3} - 1 = & & 10 \\ +1 & & +1 \\ \hline \frac{N}{3} & = & 11 \end{array}$$
$$\cancel{3}\left(\frac{N}{\cancel{3}}\right) = 11(3)$$
$$N = 33$$

11.
$$\begin{array}{rcr} 2(N + 6) = & & 18 \\ 2N + 12 = & & 18 \\ -12 & & -12 \\ \hline 2N & = & 6 \end{array}$$
$$\frac{\cancel{2}N}{\cancel{2}} = \frac{6}{2}$$
$$N = 3$$

12.
$$\begin{array}{rcr} N - 9 + 3N = & & 19 \\ 4N - 9 = & & 19 \\ +9 & & +9 \\ \hline 4N & = & 28 \end{array}$$
$$\frac{\cancel{4}N}{\cancel{4}} = \frac{28}{4}$$
$$N = 7$$

13.

Unknown	Facts	Plan	Solution
Number = N	Other number = 7 Difference = 8	If 7 is subtracted from a number, the result is 8. Add 7 to both sides.	$\begin{array}{rcr} N - 7 = & & 8 \\ +7 & & +7 \\ \hline N & = & 15 \end{array}$

The number is 15.

Check
$15 - 7 \stackrel{?}{=} 8$ $8 = 8$

14.

Unknown	Facts	Plan	Solution
Amount to be saved = S	Total salary = \$372 Portion to be saved = $\frac{1}{12}$	$\frac{1}{12}$ of salary will be saved. Multiply.	$\frac{1}{12}(372) = S$ $\frac{1}{\cancel{12}_{1}} \cdot \frac{\cancel{372}^{31}}{1} = S$ $31 = S$

Manny will save \$31 each week.

Check
$\frac{1}{\cancel{12}_{1}} \cdot \frac{\cancel{372}^{31}}{1} \stackrel{?}{=} 31$ $31 = 31$

15.

Unknown	Facts	Plan	Solution
Number of silk-screen shirts sold = N Number of tie-dyed shirts sold = $3N$ (three times as many)	Total number of shirts sold = 176	Number of silk screen shirts sold + number of tie-dyed shirts sold = 176 Combine terms. Divide both sides of the equation by 4. Find the number of tie-dyed shirts by multiplying 44 by 3.	$N + 3N = 176$ $4N = 176$ $\frac{4N}{4} = \frac{176}{4}$ $N = 44$ $3N = 132$

There were 44 silk screen and 132 tie-dyed shirts sold.

Check
Does $44 + 3(44) \stackrel{?}{=} 176$ $44 + 132 \stackrel{?}{=} 176$ $176 = 176$

16.

Unknown	Facts	Plan	Solution
Number of subscriptions sold by Ron = M Number of subscriptions sold by Elaine = $3M$ (three times as many)	The difference between the number of Elaine's and Ron's subscriptions = 16.	Subtract the number of Ron's from the number of Elaine's and get a difference of 16. Combine terms. Divide both sides by 2. Multiply 8 by 3.	$3M - M = 16$ $2M = 16$ $\frac{2M}{2} = \frac{16}{2}$ $M = 8$ $3M = 24$

Ron sold 8 magazine subscriptions and Elaine sold 24.

Check
$3(8) - 8 \stackrel{?}{=} 16$ $24 - 8 \stackrel{?}{=} 16$ $16 = 16$

17.

Unknown	Facts	Plan	Solution
Number of boxes of felt-tip pens = N Number of boxes of ballpoint pens = $2N$	Total value of felt-tip pens = \$4.50N Total value of ballpoint pens = \$3.50 × $2N$ Total order = \$46	Total value of felt-tip pens plus total value of ballpoint pens = total order. Multiply. Combine the numbers. Divide both side of the equation by 11.50. Multiply 4 by 2.	$4.50N + (3.50 \times 2N) = 46$ $4.50N + 7.00N = 46$ $11.50N = 46$ $\frac{11.50N}{11.50} = \frac{46}{11.50}$ $N = 4$ $2N = 8$

Will ordered 4 boxes of felt-tip pens and 8 boxes of ballpoint pens.

Check
$4.50(4) + (3.50 \times 8) \stackrel{?}{=} 46$ $18 + 28 \stackrel{?}{=} 46$ $46 = 46$

18.

Unknown	Facts	Plan	Solution
Number of calendars = C	Total number of calendars and datebooks = 500	The cost of calendars plus the cost of the datebooks = the total order.	$0.75C + 0.50(500 - C) = 300$
Number of datebooks = $500 - C$	Cost of calendars = \$0.75C	Remove parentheses.	$0.75C + 250 - 0.50C = 300$
	Cost of datebooks = \$0.50(500 − C)	Combine terms.	$0.25C + 250 = 300$
		Subtract 250 from both sides.	$\begin{array}{r} - 250 \quad - 250 \\ \hline 0.25C = 50 \end{array}$
	Total order = \$300	Divide both sides by 0.25.	$\frac{\not{0.25}C}{\not{0.25}} = \frac{50}{0.25}$
			$C = 200$
		Subtract 200 from 500.	$500 - C = 300$

Check

$0.75(200) + 0.50(500 - 200) \stackrel{?}{=} 300$

$150 + 0.50(300) \stackrel{?}{=} 300$

$300 = 300$

200 calendars and 300 datebooks were ordered.

Percents 6

Learning Objectives

1. Change decimals and fractions to percents. (pp. 161–163)
2. Change percents to decimals and fractions. (pp. 165–167)
3. Understand and use the percentage formula. (pp. 170–173)
4. Understand how to solve percentage problems. (pp. 175–179)

Percents are one of the most important arithmetic processes used in business. Percents give us a special way of writing fractions that lets us compare parts with wholes and with one another. Because percents are used throughout the business world, it is essential to gain a thorough understanding of this mathematical concept, which is used throughout this text.

percent: a hundredth of a whole amount; a fraction with a denominator of 100. *Percent* means *per hundred.*

The word **percent** means *hundredths,* or *per hundred,* or *over* 100 (in a fraction). That is, 44 percent equals 44 hundredths, or 44 per hundred, or $\frac{44}{100}$. Remember, $\frac{44}{100}$ can be written as 0.44. If you find that 44 percent of the students in the class watch a certain television program, you are saying that the number of students who watch that show divided by the total number of students can be expressed as the fraction $\frac{44}{100}$ or as the decimal 0.44. It does not mean that there are 100 students in the class; rather, it means that the fraction showing the number of watchers divided by the total number of students can be converted to a fraction with a numerator of 44 and denominator of 100. If we find that 22% of the students in another class watch that show, we are saying that the number of students who watch that show divided by the total number of students can be expressed as the fraction $\frac{22}{100}$ or as the decimal 0.22. Again, this does not mean that 22 students in the second class watch the show in question; instead, the number of students who watch the show divided by the total number of students can be expressed as a fraction with numerator of 22 and denominator of 100. This allows us to compare the popularity of the show in the two classes, even though the classes have different total numbers of students.

The symbol for *percent* is %; you can write 35 percent symbolically as 35%, or as the common fraction $\frac{35}{100}$, or as the decimal fraction 0.35.

$$35 \text{ percent} = 35 \text{ hundredths} = 35\% = \frac{35}{100} = 0.35$$

Just as there are mixed fractions and decimals, so there are mixed percents. Examples of mixed percents would include such numbers as $25\frac{1}{7}\%$ or $66\frac{2}{9}\%$.

Converting Decimals and Fractions to Percents

The businessperson must be able to handle percents in whatever form they appear, even if they are written as fractions or as decimals. A person who cannot convert fractions and decimals to their percent equivalents will have difficulty managing a business.

In this section we will examine how to write both fractions and decimals as percents.

Converting Decimals to Percents

We know that hundredths and percent have the same meaning. That is, 0.01 (1 hundredth) = 1%.

Also,

$$
\begin{aligned}
0.02 &= 2\% \\
0.03 &= 3\% \\
&\vdots \\
0.10 &= 10\% \\
0.11 &= 11\% \\
&\vdots
\end{aligned}
$$

You can convert a decimal into a percent by multiplying the decimal by 100 and adding a percent sign:

$$0.11 \times 100 = 11\%$$

Step by Step

Converting a Decimal to a Percent

Multiply the decimal by 100 by moving the decimal point two places to the right and add a % sign.

EXAMPLE 1

Look at how the following decimals are converted to percents.

$0.27 \times 100 = 0.27. = 27\%$	Multiply 0.27 by 100 (move the decimal point two places to the right). Write a % sign after the number.
$0.875 \times 100 = 0.87.5 = 87.5\%$	Multiply 0.875 by 100 (move the decimal point two places to the right). Write a % sign after the number.
$1.73 \times 100 = 1.73. = 173\%$	Multiply 1.73 by 100 (move the decimal point two places to right). Write a % sign after the number.
$0.004 \times 100 = 0.00.4 = 0.4\%$	Multiply 0.004 by 100 (move the decimal point two places to the right). Write a % sign after the number.

In Example 1, we changed several types of decimals to percents. The procedure is the same regardless of the number of decimal places in the number and regardless of whether the number is more than, equal to, or less than 1.

Converting Fractions to Percents

As we have noted, hundredths means percent. This makes it quite easy to convert any fraction with a denominator of 100 to a percent. Fractions that do not have a denominator of 100 can be changed to a percent by first changing the fraction to a decimal equivalent and then multiplying it by 100.

Step by Step

Converting a Fraction to a Percent

Step 1. Write the fraction as a decimal by dividing the numerator by the denominator.

Step 2. Move the decimal point two places to the right (multiply by 100), and write the % sign.

EXAMPLE 2

Look at how the following are converted. You always divide the numerator by the denominator and multiply the decimal result by 100 to find the percent.

$\frac{67}{100} \times 100 = 0.67 \times 100 = 0.67. = 67\%$

$\frac{1}{4}$ $\quad 4\overline{)1.00} = 0.25$; 8, 20, 20 $\quad 0.25 \times 100 = 0.25. = 25\%$

$3\frac{1}{2}$ $\quad 2\overline{)1.0} = 0.5$; 1 0 $\quad 3 + 0.5 = 3.5;\ 3.5 \times 100 = 3.50. = 350\%$

$\frac{7}{4}$ $\quad 4\overline{)7.00} = 1.75$; 4, 3 0, 2 8, 20, 20 $\quad 1.75 \times 100 = 1.75. = 175\%$

$\frac{2}{3}$ $\quad 3\overline{)2.000} = 0.666$; 1 8, 20, 18, 2 $\quad$ 0.666 rounds to 0.67. $\quad 0.67 \times 100 = 0.67. = 67\%$

Self-Check

1. Change the following decimals to percents.
   a. 0.39 **b.** 0.693 **c.** 2.92 **d.** 0.0007

2. Change the following fractions to percents.

a. $\frac{39}{100}$ **b.** $5\frac{1}{4}$ **c.** $\frac{9}{4}$

Section Review

Change the following decimals to percents.

1. 0.23

2. 0.675

3. 0.82

4. 2.63

5. 0.03

6. 0.007

7. 0.34

8. 3.741

9. 0.601

10. 0.0004

11. 1

12. 0.6

13. 3

Convert the following fractions or mixed numbers to percents.

14. $\frac{17}{100}$

15. $\frac{99}{100}$

16. $\frac{6}{100}$

17. $\frac{20}{100}$

18. $\frac{52}{100}$

19. $\frac{13}{20}$

20. $\frac{1}{10}$

21. $3\frac{2}{5}$

22. $\frac{5}{4}$

23. $7\frac{1}{2}$

Change each decimal or whole number to a percent.

24. 0.37

25. 0.811

26. 0.2

27. 2.54

28. 4

Change each fraction or mixed number to a percent. Round to the nearest hundredth percent if necessary.

29. $\frac{39}{100}$

30. $\frac{2}{5}$

31. $\frac{1}{3}$

32. $1\frac{5}{8}$

33. $\frac{3}{100}$

Converting Percents to Decimals and Fractions

There are many occasions when you must convert percents to decimals or fractions. A sign tells you that all the shoes on the table are 25% off marked price, but the shoes have different prices and the sign does not tell you the actual amount of money subtracted from the price of each pair of shoes. Similar situations are common in business. Normally, percents tell you only about the relationship between two things, and they cannot be used in percent form for doing calculations. Percents must be written in decimal or fractional equivalents before they can be used in calculations: You must convert 25% to a decimal, 0.25, or to a fraction, $\frac{1}{4}$, before you can use the information to solve a problem. In this section, we see how to make these changes.

Converting Percents to Decimals

To write percents as decimals, you reverse the procedure for converting decimals to percents. That is, you divide by 100 and drop the percent (%) sign. Remember, to divide a decimal number by 100, you move the decimal point two places to the left.

Step by Step

Converting a Percent to a Decimal

Step 1. Divide the percent by 100 by moving the decimal point two places to the left.

Step 2. Drop the % sign from the number.

EXAMPLE 3

To change a percent to a decimal, move the decimal point two places to the left (which is the same as dividing the number by 100) and drop the percent sign.

37% = .37. = 0.37

26.5% = .26.5 = 0.265

127% = 1.27. = 1.27

7% = .07. = 0.07

0.9% = .00.9 = 0.009

Converting Mixed Percents to Decimals

When you change a mixed percent to a decimal, you first write the fractional part as a decimal. If the fraction converts to a terminating decimal (that is, the division of the numerator by the denominator comes out even), you convert the fraction to its equivalent decimal before you change the percent to a decimal. If the fraction converts to a repeating decimal, you convert the fraction to a decimal and round to some appropriate decimal place, usually hundredths. Then you change the percent to a decimal number. The basic procedure is the same, whether the percent is more than 100%, less than 1%, or a mixed-number percent.

Step by Step

Converting a Mixed or Fractional Percent to a Decimal

Step 1. Change the fraction to a decimal by dividing the numerator by the denominator. If the division does not terminate, round to the desired place.

Step 2. Write the whole number part and the fraction part together as a mixed decimal number.

Step 3. Move the decimal point two places to the left and drop the % sign.

EXAMPLE 4

Look at the following examples of how you change a mixed or fractional percent to a decimal number.

$27\frac{1}{2}\% = 27\% + 0.5\% = 27.5\% = .275 \div 100 = 0.27.5 = 0.275$

$$\begin{array}{r} 0.5 \\ 2\overline{)1.0} \\ \underline{1\,0} \end{array}$$

$\frac{1}{4}\% = 0.25\% = 0.25 \div 100 = 0.00.25 = 0.0025$

$$\begin{array}{r} 0.25 \\ 4\overline{)1.00} \\ \underline{8} \\ 20 \\ \underline{20} \end{array}$$

$167\frac{1}{3}\% = 167\% + 0.33\% = 167.33\% = 167.33 \div 100$

$= 1.67.33$

$= 1.6733$

$$\begin{array}{r} 0.33\overline{3}\text{, or } 0.33 \\ 3\overline{)1.000} \\ \underline{9} \\ 10 \\ \underline{9} \\ 10 \end{array}$$

Converting Percents to Fractions

You use the same procedure whether the percent is more than 100%, less than 1%, or a mixed-number percent.

Step by Step

Changing a Percent to a Fraction

Step 1. Divide the number in the percent by 100 either by writing the percent as a fraction with the denominator of 100 or by multiplying the number by $\frac{1}{100}$.

Step 2. Reduce the fraction to lowest terms, writing it as a mixed number if it is more than 1.

EXAMPLE 5

Look at these examples of how to change a percent to a fraction.

$175\% = \frac{175}{100} = 1\frac{75}{100} = 1\frac{3}{4}$ $\qquad 66\frac{2}{3}\% = \frac{66\frac{2}{3}}{100} = \frac{200}{3} \div \frac{100}{1} = \frac{200}{3} \times \frac{1}{100} = \frac{2}{3}$

TIPS & TRAPS

In converting decimals, percents, and fractions from one form to another, it is helpful to know certain equivalent forms. It is especially helpful to know:

$\frac{1}{3} = 0.33\overline{3} = 0.33 \text{ (rounded)} = 0.33\frac{1}{3} = 33\frac{1}{3}\%$

$\frac{2}{3} = 0.66\overline{6} = 0.67 \text{ (rounded)} = 0.66\frac{2}{3} = 66\frac{2}{3}\%$

Real World Application

If you own a business which occupies space in a shopping center or mall, your lease may require you to pay a percent of the common area maintenance (CAM). This fee pays for parking lot maintenance, grounds contracts, taxes, sign maintenance, and other expenses that are part of the operating expenses of such a project. The amount each business pays depends on the size of the building. Each percent is based on the square footage per building and the total square footage of the mall or shopping center.

If your building is 8,640 square feet and the shopping center has a total of 69,590 square feet, then you occupy 12.42% of the space and must pay 12.42% of the CAM.

$$\frac{8{,}640}{69{,}590} = .1242 = 12.42\%$$

The total common area maintenance is $9,519.34; your share of the CAM is 12.42% of this total, or $1,182.30.

$$12.42\% \times \$9{,}519.34 = .1242 \times \$9{,}519.34$$
$$= \$1{,}182.30$$

Application Questions

1. If your business occupies 1,400 square feet in a mall containing 88,260 square feet, what percent of the mall do you occupy? If the total common area maintenance is $15,621.88, what is your share?

2. A lease requires the owner of a business occupying 2,000 square feet of a 78,900 square foot shopping center to pay a percent of the yearly taxes based on space occupied. If the taxes for the year were $18,789, how much must the owner pay?

Self-Check

3. Change the following percents to decimals.

a. $15\frac{1}{2}\%$ **b.** $\frac{1}{8}\%$ **c.** $125\frac{1}{3}\%$ **d.** $\frac{3}{7}\%$

Convert the following percents to fractions.

4. a. 45% **b.** 180%

5. a. $\frac{3}{4}\%$ **b.** $33\frac{1}{3}\%$

Section Review

Change the following percents to decimals.

1. 98% **2.** 84.6%

3. 256% **4.** 52%

5. 91.7% **6.** 3%

7. 0.5%

8. 0.02%

9. 6%

10. 9%

Convert each percent to a whole number, mixed number, or fraction, reduced to lowest terms.

11. 10%

12. 20%

13. 6%

14. 170%

15. 89%

16. 361%

17. 250%

Write each percent as a decimal.

18. 36%

19. 274%

20. 6%

21. 30%

22. 0.4%

Convert each percent to a whole number, mixed number, or fraction, reduced to lowest terms.

23. 45%

24. 25%

25. 225%

26. 300%

27. $12\frac{1}{2}\%$

Fill in the missing blanks.

	Percent	Fraction	Decimal
28.	$33\frac{1}{3}\%$	(a)	(b)

	Percent	Fraction	Decimal
29.	(a) ____	$\frac{2}{5}$	(b) ____
30.	(a) ____	(b) ____	0.125
31.	50%	(a) ____	(b) ____
32.	(a) ____	(b) ____	0.8
33.	$87\frac{1}{2}\%$	(a) ____	(b) ____
34.	(a) ____	$\frac{5}{8}$	(b) ____

The Percentage Formula

Many problems in business are solved by using percents, and many of the business problems that involve percents are solved by using the formula

$$\text{Portion} = \text{rate} \times \text{base},$$

or

$$P = R \times B$$

in which the **base** (B) is the original number or entire quantity, the **portion** (P) is the part of the base, and the **rate** (R) is a percent that tells us how the base and the portion are related. In the statement "50 is 20% of 250," 250 is the base, or the entire quantity, 50 is the portion, and 20% is the rate.

You may often need to use the percentage formula in a different form.

base: an original number, entire amount, or whole quantity

portion: a part of a whole amount.

rate: a percent indicating how the portion (or part) relates to the base (or whole).

You can *rearrange* the basic percentage formula, $P = R \times B$, to solve for R or B by dividing both sides of the formula by either R or B.

To solve the percentage formula for rate (R), divide both sides of the formula by base (B):

$$P = R \times B \qquad \frac{P}{B} = \frac{R \times \overset{1}{\cancel{B}}}{\underset{1}{\cancel{B}}} \qquad \frac{P}{B} = R, \quad \text{or} \quad R = \frac{P}{B}$$

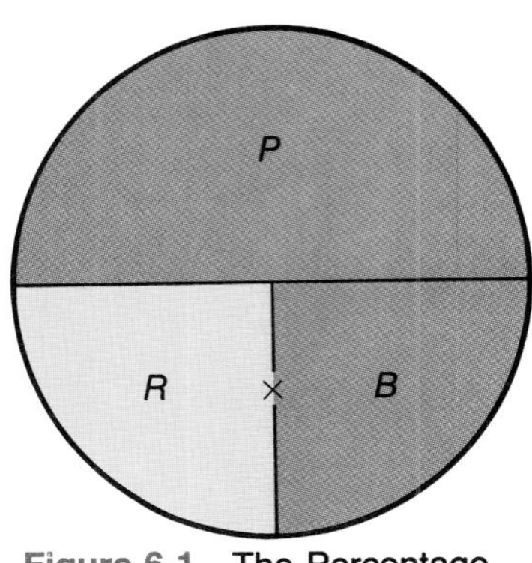

Figure 6-1 The Percentage Formula Diagram

To solve the percentage formula for base (B), divide both sides of the formula by rate (R):

$$P = R \times B \qquad \frac{P}{R} = \frac{\overset{1}{\cancel{R}} \times B}{\underset{1}{\cancel{R}}} \qquad \frac{P}{R} = B, \quad \text{or} \quad B = \frac{P}{R}$$

Figure 6-1 shows an easy way to remember how to find any one of the three terms in the percentage formula. Simply put your finger over the missing term and look at the diagram to see the relationship between the other two terms. The diagram tells you whether to multiply or divide the numbers you know.

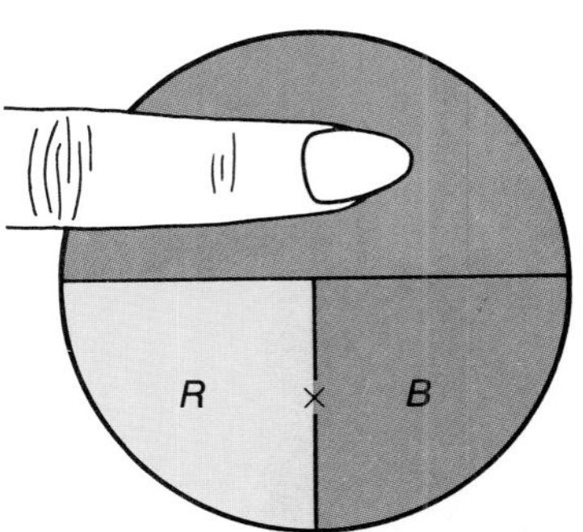

Figure 6-2 Using the Percentage Formula Diagram to Solve for Portion

Solving for Portion

Figure 6-2 shows the percentage formula diagram in solving for portion. Put your finger over the P and note that the diagram shows $R \times B$. Remember, whenever you substitute a known amount for rate, you must change the amount of the rate from percent form to decimal form or to fractional form.

Step by Step

The Percentage Formula: Solving for Portion

Portion = rate × base

or

$$P = R \times B$$

Base is the original number or quantity.
Rate is a percent.
Portion is the number that is a part of the base.

EXAMPLE 6

Find P if $R = 6\%$ and $B = \$20$. In this problem, you are looking for P, so you use the original formula, $P = R \times B$.

$P = ?$	The portion of the base is unknown.
$R = 6\% = 0.06. = 0.06$	The rate is 6%. Change the percent to a decimal before using it to solve the problem.
$B = \$20$	The entire quantity is $20.
$P = R \times B$ $= 0.06 \times \$20 = \$1.20$ $P = \$1.20$	Substitute the known amounts into the formula and find the value of P.

TIPS & TRAPS

It is important to change the rate (percent) to a decimal or a fraction *before* you make any calculations. Look at what happens in Example 6 if you do not change the rate to a decimal number:

$$\cancel{P = 6\% \times \$20 = \$120}$$

WRONG

We must express the percent as a decimal, as we did in Example 6, to find the correct answer:

$$P = 0.06 \times \$20 = \$1.20$$

CORRECT

Solving for Base

Figure 6-3 shows the percentage formula diagram for solving for base. Put your finger over the B and note that the diagram shows $\frac{P}{R}$.

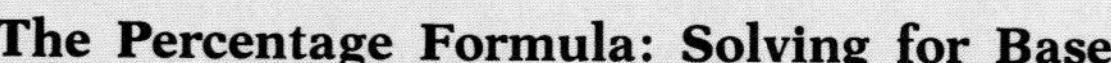

The Percentage Formula: Solving for Base

$$\text{Base} = \frac{\text{portion}}{\text{rate}}, \quad \text{or} \quad B = \frac{P}{R}$$

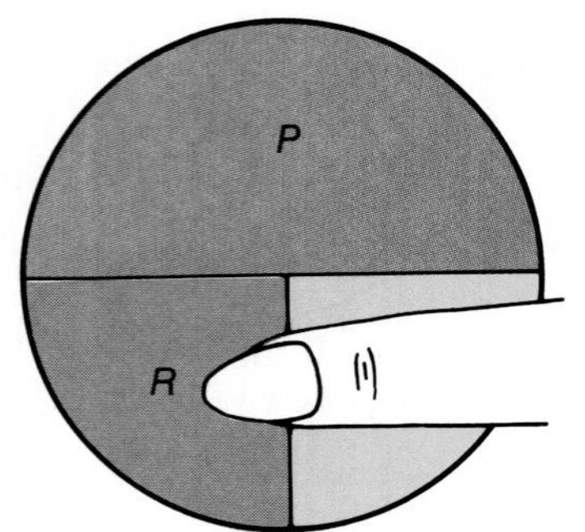

Figure 6-3 Using the Percentage Formula Diagram to Solve for Base

EXAMPLE 7

Find B if $P = 42$ and $R = 33\frac{1}{3}\%$. In this problem you are looking for B, so you use the rearranged formula, $B = \frac{P}{R}$.

$B = ?$ — The base, or entire quantity, is unknown.

$P = 42$ — The portion of the entire quantity is 42.

$R = 33\frac{1}{3}\% = \frac{1}{3}$

$B = \frac{42}{\frac{1}{3}}$ — The rate, $33\frac{1}{3}\%$, must be changed to a fraction or decimal before it can be used in the formula. ($33\frac{1}{3}\%$ gives a nonterminating decimal.)

$42 \div \frac{1}{3} = \frac{42}{1} \times \frac{3}{1} = 126$ — Substitute the known amounts in the formula and find the value of B.

The base equals 126.

Calculator Sequence

In Example 7, we can change the percent to a decimal and solve the problem in one continuous calculator sequence.

[AC] 1 [÷] 3 [=] [M+] [CE/C] 42 [÷] [MRC] [=] ⇒ 126.001

Solving For Rate

Figure 6-4 shows the percentage formula diagram for solving for rate. Put your finger over the R and note that the diagram shows $\frac{P}{B}$. When we have used the formula $R = \frac{P}{B}$ to solve for a missing rate, the result of the calculation is the decimal or fractional equivalent of the rate, which must be written in percent form. Remember that you multiply the decimal times 100 by moving the decimal point two places to the right and write a % sign after the number to convert the rate to a percent.

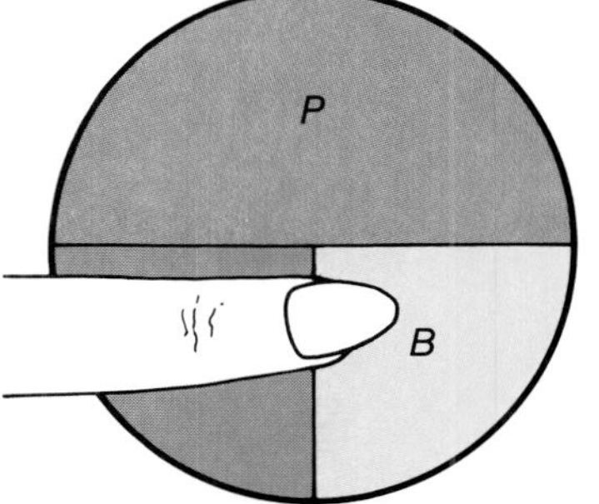

Figure 6-4 Using the Percentage Formula Diagram to Solve for Rate

The Percentage Formula: Solving for Rate

$$\text{Rate} = \frac{\text{portion}}{\text{base}}, \quad \text{or} \quad R = \frac{P}{B}$$

EXAMPLE 8

Find R if $P = 20$ and $B = 200$.

In this problem, you are looking for R, so you use the rearranged formula $R = \frac{P}{B}$

$R = ?$	The rate, or percent, is unknown.
$P = 20$	The portion of the entire quantity is 20.
$B = 200$	The entire quantity is 200.
$R = \frac{P}{B} = \frac{20}{200} = 0.1$	Substitute the known values into the formula and do the arithmetic.
$R = 0.1 = 0.10.\% = 10\%$	The answer is a decimal and must be changed to percent form.

By Elys McLean-Ibrahim, USA TODAY

Self-Check

6. Find P if $R = 25\%$ and $B = 300$.

7. Find B if $P = 36$ and $R = 66\frac{2}{3}\%$.

8. Find R if $P = 70$ and $B = 280$.

Section Review

Find P, R, or B using the basic percentage formula or one of its forms.

1. $B = 300$, $R = 27\%$

2. $B = \$1,900$, $R = 106\%$

3. $B = 1,000$, $R = 2\frac{1}{2}\%$

4. $B = \$500$, $R = 7.25\%$

5. $P = 25$, $B = 100$

6. $P = 170$, $B = 85$

7. $P = 2$, $B = 6$

8. $P = 18$, $B = 300$

9. $P = \$600$, $R = 5\%$

10. $P = 26$, $R = 6\frac{1}{2}\%$

11. $P = 15.5$, $R = 7.75\%$

12. $P = 6$, $R = 120\%$

Round numbers to the nearest hundredth and percents to the nearest whole-number percent.

13. $B = 36$, $R = 42\%$

14. $P = 68$, $B = 85$

15. $P = \$835$, $R = 3.2\%$

16. $R = 72\%$, $B = 16$

17. $R = 136\%$, $B = 834$

18. $P = 397$, $B = 200$

19. $B = 52$, $R = 17\%$

20. $P = 512$, $B = 128$

21. $P = 125$, $B = 50$

22. $B = 892$, $R = 63\%$

23. $B = 643$, $R = 8\%$

24. $P = 803$, $B = 4{,}015$

Solving Percentage Problems

The percentage formula in its different forms has many applications in the business world. In the chapters to come, we explore the use of percentages in calculating sales and property taxes, trade and cash discounts, markup, markdown, and turnover; percentages are also used in working with interest, depreciation and overhead, and income taxes. Before you can apply percentages in these business settings, you must understand how to analyze and solve a percentage problem.

Very few percentage problems that you encounter in business tell you the values of P, R, and B directly. Percentage problems are usually written in words that must be analyzed before you can tell which form of the percentage formula you should use or which term of the formula corresponds to which number in the problem. In this section, we analyze and solve some typical problems using the percentage formula.

Step by Step

Solving a Percentage Problem

Step 1. Examine the words carefully to identify each term correctly.

- **a.** Rate is always expressed as a percent.
- **b.** The number that immediately follows the word *of* is usually the base or entire quantity.
- **c.** The number that is not a percent and does not follow the word *of* is usually the portion.

Step 2. Always remember to change the rate, which is expressed as a percent, to a decimal or fraction before you solve the equation.

Step 3. When you solve for rate, remember to change the answer, which will be in the form of a decimal, to a percent.

Real World Application

If you have considered renting or buying a home you may want to think about the following rule of thumb used in many real estate offices: Your rent or house payment should be about 25% of your monthly gross pay.

If your gross pay is $1,000 a month, then your rent payment should not be more than $250 a month.

$$\$1{,}000 \times 25\% = \$1{,}000 \times .25 = \$250$$

Example: You are interested in renting an apartment for $325 a month. Your monthly gross pay is $1,050. Should you be able to make this payment, based on this rule of thumb?

$$\frac{\$325}{\$1{,}050} = .3095 = 31\%$$

Since $325 is about 31% of your monthly salary, you may find this apartment too expensive.

Application Questions

1. In looking for an apartment, you see an advertisement for an apartment which rents for $405 a month. If your monthly salary is $1,625, is this apartment affordable for you?

2. If your gross pay is $1,250 a month, what is the approximate rent you should be able to pay?

3. If your house payment is $375 a month and your monthly gross pay is $1,115, what percent of your pay is your house payment?

Solving for Portion

EXAMPLE 9

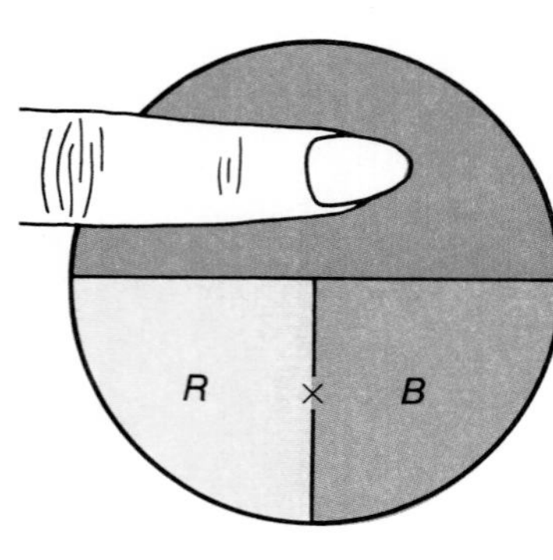

During a special 1-day sale, 20% of the customers making purchases in the morning used store coupons. If 600 customers passed through the cash registers that morning, how many coupons were turned in?

First, identify the terms. The rate is the percent, and the base is the total number *of* customers, 600. You use the original formula, $P = R \times B$, to find the portion.

$P = ?$	The portion is unknown.
$R = 20\% = .20. = 0.20$ or 0.2	The rate is 20%. Change the percent to a decimal before using it to solve the problem.
$B = 600$	The base is 600. Note that 600 is the number that immediately follows *of* in the statement.
$P = R \times B$ $= 0.2 \times 600 = 120$	Substitute the known amounts and do the arithmetic. 120 people used coupons.
Does $P = R \times B$? $120 = 0.2 \times 600$ $120 = 120$	Check your answer by substituting all the known amounts into the equation and doing the arithmetic. The amounts are equal, and the answer is correct.

EXAMPLE 10

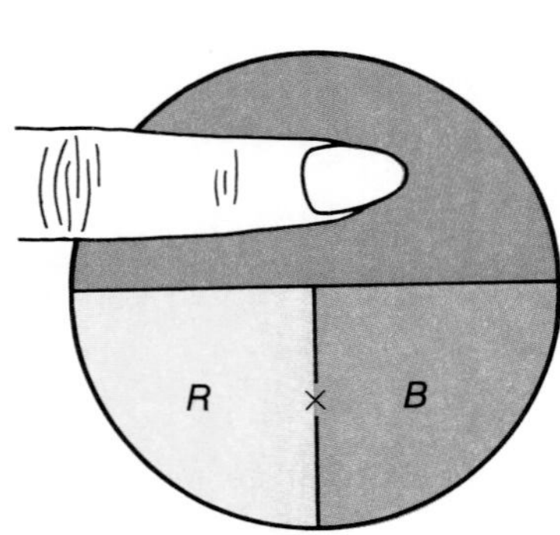

If $66\frac{2}{3}\%$ of the 900 employees in a company choose a particular health insurance plan, how many people from that company are enrolled in the plan?

First, identify the terms. The rate is the percent, and the base is the number that follows the word *of*. You use the original formula, $P = R \times B$, to find the portion.

$P = ?$	The portion is unknown.
$R = 66\frac{2}{3}\% = \frac{2}{3}$	The rate is $66\frac{2}{3}\%$. The percent must be changed to a fraction before it can be used to solve the problem.
$B = 900$	The base is 900. Note that 900 is the number that immediately follows the word *of*.
$P = R \times B$ $= \frac{2}{\cancel{3}_1} \times \frac{\cancel{900}^{300}}{1} = 600$	Substitute the known values into the formula and do the arithmetic. 600 of the company's employees are enrolled in the plan.
Does $P = R \times B$? $600 = \frac{2}{3} \times 900$ $600 = 600$	Check your answer by substituting all the known amounts into the equation and doing the arithmetic. The amounts are equal, and the answer is correct.

TIPS & TRAPS

The following key words may help you recognize the rate, base, or portion more quickly:

Rate is always written as a percent.

Base is called total amount, original amount, entire amount, and so on; it usually follows the word *of*. Sometimes there is no number with the word that follows *of*, but that word appears in another sentence with an amount. This amount is the base.

Portion is called part, partial amount, percentage, amount of increase or decrease, amount of change, and so on; it is often associated with the word *is*.

EXAMPLE 11

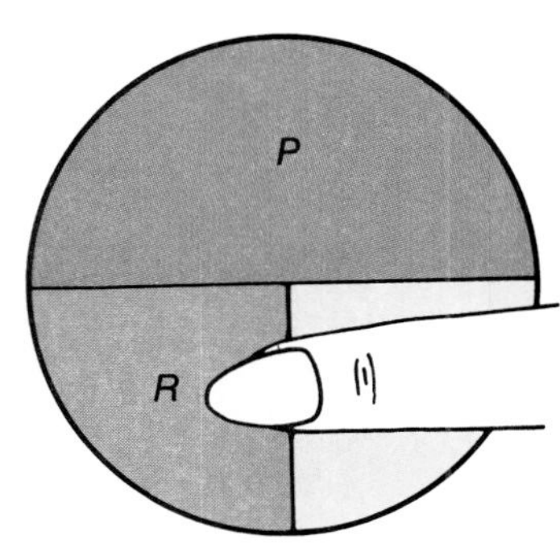

Stan sets aside 25% of his weekly income for rent. If he sets aside \$50 each week, what is his weekly income?

Identify the terms: The rate is the number written as a percent. The portion is given, \$50. Notice that the unknown quantity weekly income follows the word *of*. This is a clue that you are looking for the base.

$P = \$50$	The portion is \$50.
$R = 25\% = .25. = 0.25$	The rate is 25%. Change the percent to a decimal before doing the arithmetic.
$B = ?$	The base is unknown.
$B = \frac{P}{R}$	Use a rearranged form of the percentage formula to find the base.
$B = \frac{\$50}{0.25} = \$200$	Substitute the known values into the formula and do the arithmetic.

\$50 is 25% of 200. Stan earns \$200 each week.

EXAMPLE 12

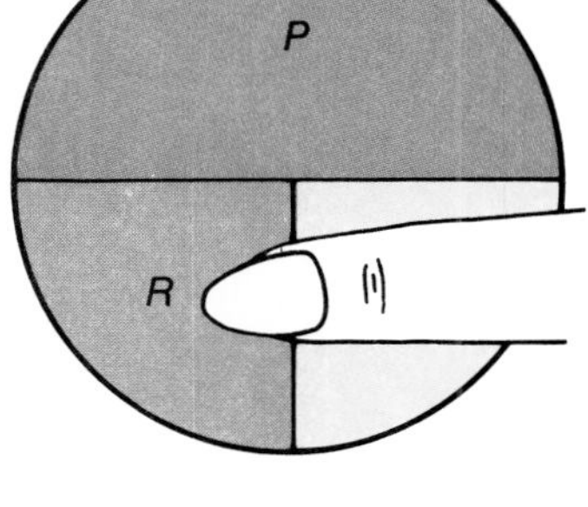

Thirty percent of Hill Community College's graduates continued their education at some 4-year college. If 60 people continued their education, how many Hill Community College graduates were there?

Identify the terms: You might not recognize the rate immediately because it is written in words, thirty percent. The base is the total number of graduates, so 60 is the portion of the graduates who continue their education.

$B = ?$	The base, or the total number, is unknown.
$P = 60$	The portion of the base is 60.
$R = 30\% = .30. = 0.30$ or 0.3	The rate is 30%. Express the percent as a decimal.
$B = \frac{P}{R}$	Since the base is unknown, use the rearranged percentage formula.

$B = \frac{60}{0.3} = 200$ — Substitute the known values into the formula and do the arithmetic.

There were 200 graduates of Hill Community College.

Solving for Rate

EXAMPLE 13

If 20 out of 50 automobiles on sale were sold, what percent of the sale cars were purchased?

When you identify the terms in a percent problem, look for the rate, or the number written as a percent, first. Then look for the base, which usually follows the word *of*. In this problem, you can see that the rate is unknown, so you use the rearranged percentage formula $R = \frac{P}{B}$.

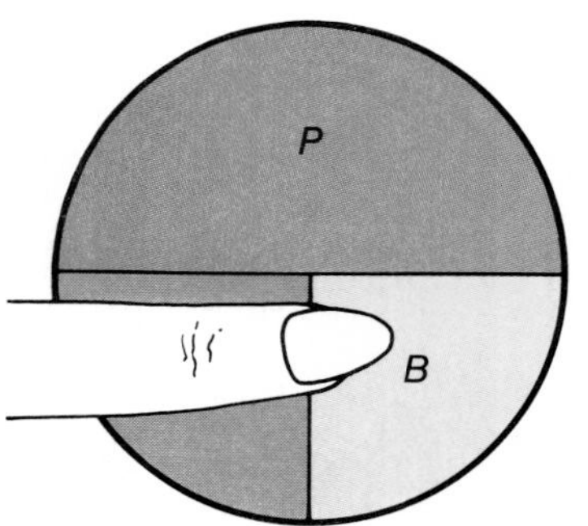

$P = 20$	The portion is 20.
$B = 50$	The base is 50.
$R = ?$	The rate is unknown.
$R = \frac{P}{B}$	Use the rearranged percentage formula to solve for rate.
$R = \frac{20}{50} = 0.40. = 40\%$	Substitute the known values into the formula and do the arithmetic. The solution for the rate is a decimal number, 0.4, which must be written as a percent.

Finding Percent of Increase or Decrease

Change is often expressed in terms of a percent difference between two amounts. An announcement that transit fares will increase by 10% on January 1 means that the base is the original, lower fare; the portion is the amount of change; and the rate is 10%.

Step by Step

Finding Percent of Increase or Decrease

Step 1. Find the difference between the original amount and the increased or decreased amount. The difference is the portion.

Step 2. Divide the portion by the original amounts using the following version of the percentage formula:

$$R = \frac{P}{B}$$

Step 3. Rewrite the decimal as a percent.

Hottest business areas

These five business categories grew the most last year, based on Yellow Pages listings:

Category	1988 pct. change
Facsimile communication equipment	+119.0%
Money order service	+47.5%
Exercise & physical fitness programs	+42.6%
Bed & Breakfast accommodations	+40.1%
Collectibles	+37.3%

Source: American Business Information
By Marcia Staimer, USA TODAY

EXAMPLE 14

Ellis was earning \$375 per week until he received a raise. Now he earns \$397.50 per week. What was the percent of increase of his raise?

$$\begin{array}{r} \$397.50 \\ -\ 375.00 \\ \hline \$\ 22.50 \end{array}$$

Find the difference between the old and new amounts. The difference, $22.50, is the portion.

$P = \$22.50$ The portion is $22.50.

$B = \$375$ The base is $375, the original salary.

$R = ?$ The rate (percent of increase) is unknown.

$R = \dfrac{P}{B}$ Use the rearranged percentage formula to solve for rate.

$R = \dfrac{\$22.50}{\$375} = 0.06 = 6\%$ Rewrite the decimal, 0.06, as a percent, 6%.

His salary increased by 6%.

EXAMPLE 15

A computer printer cost $980 last year. Now the same printer costs $882. What was the percent of decrease in price from last year?

$$\begin{array}{r} \$980 \\ -\ 882 \\ \hline \$\ 98 \end{array}$$

Subtract the new (lower) price from the original (higher) price. The difference, $98, is the portion.

$P = \$98$ The portion is $98.

$B = \$980$ The base is $980, the original cost.

$R = ?$ The rate (percent of decrease) is unknown.

$R = \dfrac{P}{B}$ Use the rearranged percentage formula to solve for rate.

$R = \dfrac{98}{980} = 0.1 = 10\%$ Rewrite the decimal, 0.1, as a percent, 10%.

The cost of the printer decreased by 10%.

Self-Check

9. Find 40% of 160.

10. What number is $33\frac{1}{3}\%$ of 150?

11. What number is 154% of 30?

12. Jenny sold 80% of the tie-dyed T-shirts she took to the Green Valley Music Festival. If she sold 42 shirts, how many shirts did she bring?

13. Ali gave correct answers to 23 of the 25 questions on the driving test. What percent of the questions did he get correct?

14. Mathilda just started a new job where she earns $450 per week. At her previous job, she was earning $400 per week. What was her percent raise when she began her new job?

15. The number of sixth-grade students at Spring Valley Elementary School fell from 78 in 1989 to 68 in 1990. What was the percent decrease in sixth-grade students?

Real World Application

MIDDLE-CLASS NECESSITIES: ON THE INCREASE?

The table from *Fortune* (October 10, 1988) shows the increase or decrease in some basic costs and salaries from 1981 to 1987. The original table showed these figures and also supplied the percent increase or decrease. But we removed the figures from the percent column so that you can figure them out yourself. Fill in the "% Change" column on the far right side of the table.

Middle-Class Necessities

Are They More Expensive?	**1981[a]**	**1987**	**% Change**
House Price	$84,965	$88,624	
Mortgage Payments	$666	$594	
Four-Year College Costs[b]			
Public Average Annual	$3,436	$4,130	
Private Average Annual	$7,569	$10,050	
Appendectomy[c]	$636	$714	
Can People More Easily Afford Them?			
Family Income	$28,483	$30,853	
Per Capita Income	$10,784	$12,287	
Saving Rate	7.5%	3.2%	
What's the Trade-Off?			
Leisure Hours (Weekly)[d]	19.2 hrs.	16.6 hrs.	
Working Mothers (Percent of Women with Preschool Children)	48.9%	56.7%	

[a] In 1987 dollars.

[b] The College Board.

[c] *Medical Economics* magazine

[d] Louis Harris & Associates.

Source: *Fortune,* October 10, 1988, p. 40. Used with permission.

Section Review

Use the percentage formula or a variation to solve the following problems.

1. Find 30% of 80.

2. Find 150% of 20.

3. 30% of 27 equals what number?

4. What number is 70% of 300?

5. 90% of what number is 27?

6. 82% of what number is 94.3?

7. $33\frac{1}{3}$% of what number is 60?

8. 112 is 14% of what number?

9. 97 is what percent of 100?

10. What percent of 54 is 36?

11. 51.52 is what percent of 2,576?

12. What percent of 180 is 60?

13. 42 is what percent of 21?

14. 27 is what percent of 9?

15. Eighty percent of one store's customers paid with credit cards. Forty customers came in that day. How many customers paid for their purchases with credit cards?

16. If a picture frame costs $30 and the tax on the frame is 6% of the cost, how much is the tax on the picture frame?

17. Seventy percent of the town's population voted in an election. If 1,589 people voted, what is the population of the town?

18. Five percent of a batch of fuses were found to be faulty during an inspection. If 27 fuses were faulty, how many fuses were inspected?

19. Thirty-seven of the 50 shareholders attended the meeting. What percent of the shareholders attended the meeting?

20. In Memphis the sales tax is $7\frac{3}{4}$%. How much tax is paid on a purchase of $20.60? (Round to the nearest cent.)

21. A business math student answered 60 questions correctly on a 75-question test. What percent of the questions were answered correctly?

22. A football stadium has a capacity of 53,983. If 47,892 fans attended a game, what percent of the seats were filled?

23. A large university campus has 197 restrooms. If 38 of these are designed to accommodate disabled persons, what percent can accommodate the disabled?

24. The United Way expects to raise $63 million in the current drive. The chairperson projects that 60% of the funds will be raised in the first 12 weeks. How many dollars are expected to be raised in the first 12 weeks?

25. The financial officer for an accounting firm allows $3,400 for supplies in the annual budget. After 3 months, $898.32 has been spent on supplies. Is this figure within 25% of the annual budget?

26. An accountant who is currently earning $42,380 annually expects a 6.5% raise. What is the amount of the expected raise?

27. A single family property increased in value from $85,900 to $94,060.50. What was the percent of the increase?

28. The price of a personal computer fell from $3,400 to $2,890. Find the percent of decrease.

29. Larry Gates' salary increased from $14,804 to $16,062.34. What was the percent raise?

30. Karl Atkins is a member of a union that contracted to take a temporary wage decrease of 6%. If Karl was earning $7.50 per hour, how much was his wage cut? What is his new hourly rate?

Summary

Topic	Page	What to Remember	Example
Changing a decimal to a percent	162	Multiply the decimal by 100 by moving the decimal point two places to the right and add a % sign.	$0.15 = 15\%$
Changing a fraction with a denominator of 100 to a percent	163	Write the numerator with a % sign after it.	$\frac{37}{100} = 37\%$
Changing any fraction to a percent	163	Divide the numerator by the denominator. Move the decimal point two places to the right and write the % sign.	$\frac{3}{5} = 0.60 = 60\%$
Changing a percent to a decimal	166	Move the decimal point two places to the left and drop the % sign from the number.	$48\% = 0.48$ $157\% = 1.57$
Changing a percent that contains a fraction to a decimal	166	Divide the numerator of the fraction by the denominator. Write the whole number part and fractional part as a decimal number. Move the decimal point two places to the left and drop the % sign.	$33\frac{1}{3}\% = 33.33\% = 0.3333$ or $33\frac{1}{3}\% = 0.33\frac{1}{3}$
Changing a percent to a fraction	167	Write the percent as a fraction with 100 in the denominator. Write the fraction in lowest terms.	$75\% = 0.75 = \frac{75}{100} = \frac{3}{4}$
Solving for portion	171	$P = R \times B$. Always remember to change the rate from percent form to decimal or fractional form before you do the arithmetic.	$B = 20$ and $R = 15\%$. Find P. $P = R \times B = 0.15 \times 20 = 3$
Solving for base	172	$B = \frac{P}{R}$. Always remember to change the rate from percent form to decimal or fractional form before you do the arithmetic.	$P = 36$ and $R = 9\%$. Find B. $B = \frac{P}{R} = \frac{36}{0.09} = 400$
Solving for rate	173	$R = \frac{P}{B}$. Remember to convert the answer from decimal form to percent form.	$P = 4$ and $B = 5$. Find R. $R = \frac{P}{B} = \frac{4}{5} = 0.80 = 80\%$
Solving a percentage problem	176–178	Identify each term. Rate is always written as a percent and must be rewritten as a decimal or fraction. The number after the word *of* is usually the base, or entire quantity. The number that is not a percent and does not follow the word *of* is usually the percentage. If you are solving for rate, remember to change the answer from decimal form to percent form.	What number is 30% of 150? $R = 30\% = 0.3$, $B = 150$ $P = R \times B = 0.3 \times 150 = 45$

Chapter Review

1. Write the symbol for percent.

Convert each decimal to a percent.

2. 0.64

3. 0.7

4. 0.0072

5. 0.813

6. 3

Convert each fraction or mixed number to a percent.

7. $\frac{3}{9}$

8. $\frac{3}{100}$

9. $\frac{5}{8}$

10. $\frac{37}{100}$

11. $7\frac{1}{2}$

Change each percent to a decimal.

12. 0.03%

13. $\frac{2}{3}\%$

14. 30%

15. 8%

16. 336%

17. 0.8%

18. $\frac{3}{8}\%$

19. Convert 225% to a mixed number.

20. Convert 500% to a whole number.

Convert each percent to a fraction.

21. $66\frac{2}{3}\%$

22. 85%

Solve.

23. Find 130% of \$48.

24. 40 is what percent of 10?

25. What percent of 8 is 3?

26. Find 100% of 73.

27. What number is $66\frac{2}{3}\%$ of 33?

28. 1% of 2,100 equals what number?

29. Twelve classrooms are being used for lab sessions. If there are 60 rooms, what percent of the classrooms are being used for lab sessions?

30. Three percent of the transistors being tested were defective. If 600 transistors were tested, how many were defective?

31. State sales tax is 6%. If the tax on an item amounts to \$5.94, how much did the item cost?

32. If 96% of the people in a room are high-school graduates, what percent of the people are not high-school graduates?

33. If 100% of the 80 invited guests attended the party, how many people attended the party?

34. The number of automobile accidents for a medium-sized city decreased from 135 to 128. What was the percent of decrease?

35. John Zapel's salary increased from \$34,200 to \$36,520. What was the rate of increase?

Change each percent to a decimal.

1. 24%

2. 68.7%

3. 9%

4. 20%

5. $27\frac{1}{2}\%$

6. 276%

7. 0.5%

8. $156\frac{2}{3}\%$

9. $\frac{1}{8}\%$

10. 0.04%

Convert each decimal to a percent.

11. 0.24

12. 0.925

13. 0.6

14. 3.64

15. $0.37\frac{1}{2}$

Convert each percent to a fraction or mixed number.

16. 35%

17. $87\frac{1}{2}\%$

18. $\frac{1}{4}\%$

19. $33\frac{1}{3}\%$

20. 375%

Change each fraction or mixed number to a percent.

21. $\frac{21}{100}$

22. $\frac{1}{5}$

23. $\frac{3}{8}$

24. 1

25. $\frac{7}{9}$

Solve.

26. Find 30% of $240.

27. Find 1% of 26.

28. What number is $33\frac{1}{3}$% of 96?

29. 25% of 452 equals what number?

30. What number is 10% of 478?

31. 50 is what percent of 20?

32. What percent of 8 is 7?

33. 100% of 32 is how much?

34. 120% of $36 is how much?

35. 0.3% of what number is 6.39?

36. What number is $\frac{1}{2}$% of 500?

37. 22% of what number is 24.86?

38. Find the interest on a loan of $500 if the simple interest rate is $10\frac{3}{4}$% of the amount borrowed.

39. What is the sales tax on an item that costs $42 if the tax rate is 6%?

40. If 100% of 22 rooms are full, how many rooms are full?

41. Twelve employees at a meat packing plant were sick on Monday. If the plant employs 360 people, what percent of the employees were sick on Monday?

42. A department store had 15% turnover in personnel last year. If the store employs 600 people, how many employees were replaced last year?

43. One hundred seventeen of the 150 students in a class received passing grades. What percent of the class passed?

44. The Dawson family left a 15% tip for a restaurant check. If the check totaled $19.47, find the amount of the tip. What was the total cost of the meal, including the tip?

45. In a class of 29 students, 3 are color-blind. Find the percent of the class that is color-blind. Round to the nearest whole percent.

46. The Corner Gas Station sold 52,600 gallons of gasoline. Of this amount, 19,400 gallons were premium unleaded. What percent of the gas sold was premium unleaded? Round to the nearest whole percent.

47. If a 40-question test has 24 questions that are multiple choice, what percent of the questions are multiple choice?

48. A certain make and model of automobile was projected to have a 3% rate of defective autos. If the number of defective automobiles was projected to be 1,698, how many automobiles were to be produced?

49. A family's income increased by $2,300, which was a 15% increase. What was the family's original income?

50. Of the 52 questions on this trial test, 15 are word problems. What percent of the problems are word problems? (Round to the nearest whole number percent.)

51. Karen Denny, a management trainee, earns $21,560. When she completes the training program she will earn $24,794. What percent increase does she expect?

52. Alan Wise paid $24,840 for a new van. Because he found he was unable to make the payments, he had to sell the van. A buyer agreed to pay him $19,623.60 for the van. What was his rate of loss?

Self-Check Solutions

1. a. 0.39 × 100 = 0.39.; 39% **b.** 0.693 × 100 = 0.69.3; 69.3%
c. 2.92 × 100 = 2.92.; 292% **d.** 0.0007 × 100 = 0.00.07; 0.07%

2. a. $\frac{39}{100} = 39\%$

b. $5\frac{1}{4} = \frac{21}{4}$; $4\overline{)21.00}$ = 5.25; $5.25 \times 100 = 5.25.$; 525%

$$\begin{array}{r} 5.25 \\ 4\overline{)21.00} \\ \underline{20} \\ 1\,0 \\ \underline{8} \\ 20 \\ \underline{20} \end{array}$$

c. $\frac{9}{4}$; $4\overline{)9.00}$ = 2.25; $2.25 \times 100 = 2.25.$; 225%

$$\begin{array}{r} 2.25 \\ 4\overline{)9.00} \\ \underline{8} \\ 1\,0 \\ \underline{8} \\ 20 \\ \underline{20} \end{array}$$

3. a. $15\frac{1}{2}\% = 15.5\% = 15.5 \div 100 = 0.155$

b. $\frac{1}{8}\% = 0.125\% = 0.125 \div 100 = 0.00125$

$$\begin{array}{r} 0.125 \\ 8\overline{)1.000} \\ \underline{8} \\ 20 \\ \underline{16} \\ 40 \\ \underline{40} \end{array}$$

c. $125\frac{1}{3}\% = 125.3\% = 125.3 \div 100 = 1.253$

d. $\frac{3}{7}\% = 0.428 = 0.004$ (rounded)

$$\begin{array}{r} 0.\overline{4285714} \\ 7\overline{)3.0000000} \\ \underline{2\,8} \\ 20 \\ \underline{14} \\ 60 \\ \underline{56} \\ 40 \\ \underline{35} \\ 50 \\ \underline{49} \\ 10 \\ \underline{7} \\ 30 \\ \underline{28} \\ 2 \end{array}$$

4. a. $45\% = \frac{45}{100} = \frac{9}{20}$ **b.** $180\% = \frac{180}{100} = \frac{18}{10} = \frac{9}{5} = 1\frac{4}{5}$

5. a. $\frac{3}{4}\% = \frac{3}{4} \times \frac{1}{100} = \frac{3}{400}$ **b.** $33\frac{1}{3}\% = 33\frac{1}{3} \times \frac{1}{100} = \frac{\cancel{100}^{1}}{3} \times \frac{1}{\cancel{100}_{1}} = \frac{1}{3}$

6. $R = 25\% = .25. = 0.25$; $B = 300$

$P = R \times B$

$P = 0.25 \times 300$

$= 75$

7. $P = 36$; $R = 66\frac{2}{3}\% = \frac{2}{3}$

$$B = \frac{P}{R}$$

$$B = \frac{36}{\frac{2}{3}}, \text{ or } 36 \div \frac{2}{3}$$

$$= \frac{\overset{18}{\cancel{36}}}{1} \times \frac{3}{\underset{1}{\cancel{2}}}$$

$$= 54$$

8. $P = 70$; $B = 280$

$$R = \frac{P}{B} = \frac{70}{280} = 0.25$$
$$= 25\%$$

9. $R = 40\% = 0.40$; $B = 160$
$P = R \times B = 0.4 \times 160 = 64$

10. $R = 33\frac{1}{3}\% = \frac{1}{3}$
$B = 150$

$$P = R \times B = \frac{1}{\underset{1}{\cancel{3}}} \times \frac{\overset{50}{\cancel{150}}}{1} = 50$$

11. $R = 154\% = 1.54$; $B = 30$
$P = R \times B = 1.54 \times 30 = 46.2$,
which rounds to 46

12. $R = 80\% = 0.80$ or 0.8; $P = 42$

$$B = \frac{P}{R}$$

$$B = \frac{42}{0.8}$$
$= 52.5$, or approximately 53 shirts

13. $P = 23$; $B = 25$

$$R = \frac{P}{B}$$

$$R = \frac{23}{25} = 0.92 = 92\%$$

14. $450 - 400 = \$50$ (increase)
$P = \$50$; $B = 400$ (original salary)

$$R = \frac{P}{B}$$

$$R = \frac{50}{400} = 0.125 = 12.5\%$$

15. $78 - 68 = 10$ (decrease)
$P = 10$; $B = 78$ (original count)

$$R = \frac{P}{B}$$

$$R = \frac{10}{78} = 0.128 \quad \text{(rounded)}$$
$= 12.8\%$

Payroll 7

Learning Objectives

1. Calculate gross pay for employees receiving a salary, a wage, a piecework or production rate, a commission, or a salary plus commission. (pp. 195–199)
2. Calculate the amounts of regular and special overtime paychecks. (pp. 196–197)
3. Understand and calculate federal income tax and FICA tax using tables or other appropriate methods of computation. (pp. 203–212)
4. Understand and calculate the unemployment taxes that employers must pay for employees, and understand the tax forms employers must submit to the federal government. (pp. 212–214)

As employees you earn your paychecks; as employers you pay wages and salaries to your employees. If you have worked and received a paycheck, you know that a large part is taken out of your paycheck before you ever see it. Your employer *withholds* (deducts) taxes, union dues, medical insurance payments, unemployment insurance, and so on. Thus there is a difference between **gross earnings** (or **gross pay**), the amount earned before deductions, and **net earnings** (or **net pay**), or *take-home pay*, the amount in the paycheck.

gross earnings or **gross pay:** total amount of earnings before any deductions are made.

net earnings or **net pay:** amount of pay left after deductions are made (also called *take-home pay*).

This chapter considers payroll issues from the point of view of the employee and the employer. The chapter begins by discussing how people are paid—in salary or in wages, by the year or by the hour—and how often they are paid. The employer's responsibility for withholding taxes and paying them to the government is discussed. The math used in figuring deductions and taxes and the bookkeeping the employer must do to meet the federal, state, and local tax regulations are also covered.

Calculating Gross Pay

Employees can be paid a wage or a salary, and some employees are paid solely or partially by a commission. Companies differ in how often they pay employees, which determines how many paychecks an employee receives in a year. If employees are paid *weekly*, they receive 52 paychecks a year; if they are paid **biweekly** (every other week), they receive 26 paychecks a year. **Semimonthly** (twice a month) paychecks are issued 24 times a year, and *monthly* paychecks come 12 times a year. This section shows what all these possibilities mean to the person who is collecting the paycheck.

biweekly: every other week, 26 pay periods per year.

semimonthly: twice a month, 24 pay periods in a year.

Salaries

Salary is usually stated as a certain amount of money paid each year to an employee for his or her services. A salaried employee is paid the same, whether he or she works fewer or more than the usual number of hours. We can find the amount of a salaried employee's paycheck before deductions by dividing the amount of the salary by the number of paychecks he or she will receive in the course of a year.

salary: an amount of money paid to an employee for work done.

EXAMPLE 1

If Mary Ward earns a salary of $30,000 a year and is paid biweekly, how much is her paycheck before taxes are taken out? If Mary were paid semimonthly (twice a month), how much would her paycheck be before taxes?

$30,000 ÷ 26 = $1,153.85 — Biweekly paychecks are issued 26 times a year, so divide Mary's salary by 26.

Mary's biweekly paycheck is $1,153.85.

$30,000 ÷ 24 = $1,250 — Semimonthly paychecks are issued 24 times a year, so divide Mary's salary by 24.

Mary's semimonthly paycheck is $1,250.

Hourly Wages

hourly rate or **hourly wage:** rate of pay for each hour worked.

Fair Labor Standards Act: a federal law that sets the standard work week at 40 hours. An employee must be paid at least 1.5 times the regular hourly rate for time worked over 40 hours.

overtime rate: rate of pay for hours worked beyond 40 hours in a week (sometimes given for work on holidays).

time and a half: 1.5 times the regular pay rate. This is the minimum rate required for more than 40 hours of work in a week.

Some jobs pay according to the number of hours an employee has worked since the last paycheck. The **hourly rate,** or **hourly wage,** is the amount of money paid for each hour the employee works. The **Fair Labor Standards Act** of 1938 set a standard work week of 40 hours. An hourly employee's pay is made up of a regular hourly rate and an **overtime rate.** An employee who works 40 hours in a week gets the regular rate. An employee who works more than 40 hours is paid the regular rate for the 40 hours and the overtime rate for the hours over 40 worked. An employee must be paid at least 1.5 times his or her regular hourly rate for any time worked after 40 hours. The overtime rate is often called **time and a half,** because 1.5 is one and one-half times the regular rate.

In order to figure how much an hourly employee has earned since the last paycheck, you multiply the number of hours worked (up to 40 hours) times the hourly rate of pay. If the employee has worked overtime, you use the following method to figure gross earnings.

Step by Step

Calculating Gross Earnings with Overtime

Step 1. Multiply 40 hours times the regular rate of pay.

Step 2. Multiply the number of overtime hours worked times the regular rate times 1.5.

Step 3. Add the two amounts from Steps 1 and 2 for the total pay.

EXAMPLE 2

Marcia Scott, whose regular rate of pay is $7.25 per hour, worked 46 hours last week. Find her gross pay for last week.

40 × $7.25 = $290 — Find the amount earned for 40 hours of work at the regular rate of pay.

6 × $7.25 × 1.5 = $65.25 — Find the overtime earnings by multiplying the number of overtime hours times the regular rate times 1.5. Round to the nearest cent.

$290 + $65.25 = $355.25 — Add the regular-rate earnings and the overtime-rate earnings to find Marcia's total gross earnings.

double time: pay rate that is twice the regular pay rate.

Marcia's gross pay was $355.25.

Special Overtime Rates

Overtime can be calculated at a rate other than 1.5 times the regular hourly rate. Sometimes overtime is paid for all hours worked *per day* in excess of eight or for work on the weekend. Some employers pay twice the regular-pay rate (often called **double time**) for holidays. Occasionally overtime is calculated at three times the regular hourly rate. A combination of rates is often used in determining an employee's total amount of pay.

EXAMPLE 3

An employee for a national motel chain worked at the rate of $8 per hour. If the employee worked 48 hours one week and then worked 4 hours on a holiday during the same week, for which he was paid double time, find his gross earnings for the 52-hour week.

40 × $8 = $320	Find his regular pay for 40 hours.
8 × 1.5 × $8 = $96	Multiply his 8 regular overtime hours by 1.5 times his regular pay.
4 × 2 × $8 = $64	Multiply his 4 hours at double time by twice his regular rate.
$320 + 96 + 64 = $480	Add the three amounts to find his gross earnings.

The employee's gross earnings were $480.

Self-Check

1. If Melvin Smith earns a salary of $19,000 a year and is paid weekly, how much is his weekly paycheck before taxes are taken out?
2. Doris Ilardis worked 47 hours one week. Her regular pay was $7.60 per hour. Find her gross earnings for the week.
3. Louisa Adamson, whose regular rate of pay is $8.25 per hour, worked 44 hours last week. Find her gross pay for last week.
4. A switchboard operator worked at the rate of $6.80 per hour. If he worked 48 hours and then worked 4 hours on a holiday, during the same week, for which he was paid double time, find his gross earnings for the week.

Piecework Wages

Some employers offer employees incentives to higher production by paying according to the amount of acceptable work done. This type of wage is called a **piecework,** or *production,* **rate** and is typically offered in production or manufacturing jobs. Garment makers and some other types of factory workers, agricultural workers, and employees who perform repetitive tasks such as stuffing envelopes or packaging parts may be paid by this method. The gross earnings are calculated by multiplying the number of items produced by the pay per item.

piecework rate: pay rate based on the amount of acceptable work done (also called *production rate*).

EXAMPLE 4

A shirt manufacturer pays a worker $0.12 for each acceptable shirt completed under the prescribed job description. If the worker had the following work record, find the gross earnings for the week: Monday, 250 shirts; Tuesday, 300 shirts; Wednesday, 178 shirts; Thursday, 326 shirts; Friday, 296 shirts.

250 + 300 + 178 + 326 + 296 = 1,350 shirts	Find the total number of shirts made.
1,350 × $0.12 = $162	Multiply the number of shirts by the piece rate to find the gross pay.

Gross earnings for the week are $162.

differential piece rate: pay rate based on the number of items produced; increases as the items produced per time period increases (also called *escalating piece rate*).

Sometimes employees earn wages at a **differential piece rate,** which may also be called an *escalating piece rate*. This method of paying wages offers employees an even greater incentive to complete more pieces of work in a given period of time. As the number of items produced by the worker increases, so does the pay per item.

EXAMPLE 5

Last week, Jorge Sanchez assembled 317 microchip boards. Find Jorge's gross earnings if the manufacturer pays at the following differential piece rate:

Microchip boards	*Rate per board*
1–100	$1.32
101–300	$1.42
301 and over	$1.58

First 100 items:	1.32 × 100 = $132.00	Find how many boards were completed at each pay rate, multiply the number of boards by the rate, and add the amounts.
Next 200 items:	1.42 × 200 = $284.00	
Last 17 items:	1.58 × 17 = $ 26.86	
	$442.86	

Jorge's gross earnings last week were $442.86.

Commission

commission: earnings based on a percent of total sales.

straight commission: salary based entirely on a percent of total sales.

salary plus commission: a certain basic salary that is earned in addition to a commission on sales.

Many salespeople earn a salary based on a percent of their total sales. This way of paying salary is called **commission.** There are several ways that gross earnings can be figured if commission is involved. A person whose entire salary is a percent of total sales is working on **straight commission.** A person who receives a basic sum in addition to a commission on sales is working on a **salary plus commission** basis.

A commission can be an amount of money earned per article sold, a percent of the value of each article sold, or an amount or percent over a specified quota. In the latter case, the salesperson has to sell a specified number of items before he or she starts earning commission.

The following examples show how to figure gross earnings when people are paid commissions.

EXAMPLE 6

A restaurant-supplies salesperson receives 5% of his total sales as commission. His sales totaled $5,000 during a given week. Find his gross earnings.

Use the percentage formula, $P = R \times B$.

$P = 0.05 \times \$5{,}000 = \$250$	Change the rate of 5% to a decimal and multiply it times the base of \$5,000.

The salesperson's gross earnings are \$250.

EXAMPLE 7

Ms. Jones is paid by the salary-plus-commission method. She receives \$150 weekly in salary and 3% of all sales over \$2,000. If she sold \$6,000 worth of goods, find her gross earnings.

\$6,000 − \$2,000 = \$4,000	Find the amount on which commission is paid.
$P = R \times B$ $= 0.03 \times 4{,}000$	Change the rate of 3% to a decimal. Multiply the rate times the base of \$4,000.
= \$120 (commission)	Ms. Jones' commission is \$120.
\$120 + \$150 = \$270	Add the commission and salary to find gross earnings.

Ms. Jones's gross earnings are \$270.

Self-Check

5. A belt manufacturer pays a worker \$0.75 for each buckle attached under the prescribed job description. If Franklin had the following work record, find the gross earnings for the week: Monday, 32 buckles, Tuesday, 34 buckles, Wednesday, 38 buckles, Thursday, 35 buckles, Friday, 30 buckles.
6. Last week, Melissa packaged 180 boxes of Holiday Cheese Assortment. Find her gross earnings if she is paid at the following differential piece rate:

Cheese packages	*Rate per package*
1–100	\$1.32
101–300	\$1.42
301 and over	\$1.58

7. A paper mill sales representative receives 6% of his total sales as commission. His sales last week totaled \$5,000. Find his gross earnings.
8. Ms. Ferris is paid by the salary-plus-commission method. She receives \$175 weekly in salary and 4% of all sales over \$2,000. If she sold \$6,000 in merchandise, find her gross earnings.

Section Review

1. James Knowles has a salaried job. He earns \$425 a week. One week, he worked 46 hours. Find his gross earnings for the week.

2. Ms. Chaille worked 27 hours in one week at \$5.25 per hour. Find her gross earnings.

3. Mr. Stout worked 40 hours at $12 per hour. Find his gross earnings for the week.

4. Ms. Wood worked 52 hours in a week. She was paid at the hourly rate of $6.50 with time and a half for overtime. Find her gross earnings.

5. Mr. Jinkins worked a total of 58 hours in one week. Of these hours, he was paid for 8 at the regular overtime rate of 1.5 times his hourly wage, and for 10 at the holiday rate of 2 times his hourly wage. Find his gross earnings for the week if his hourly pay is $14.95.

6. Mr. James is paid 1.5 times his regular pay for all hours worked in a week exceeding 40. He worked 52 hours and earns $8.50 per hour. Calculate his gross pay.

7. Find the gross earnings of each employee.

			Hours Worked					Total	Hourly	Regular	Overtime	Overtime	Gross
Employee	**M**	**T**	**W**	**T**	**F**	**S**	**S**	**Hours**	**Rate**	**Pay**	**Rate × Hours**	**Pay**	**Pay**
Allen, H.	8	9	8	7	10	4	0	____	$9.86	____	____	____	____
Brown, J.	4	6	8	9	9	5	0	____	$4.97	____	____	____	____
Pick, J.	8	8	8	8	8	4	0	____	$6.87	____	____	____	____
Sayer, C.	9	10	8	9	11	9	0	____	$5.82	____	____	____	____
Lovet, L.	8	8	8	8	0	0	0	____	$7.15	____	____	____	____

8. Complete the following payroll records for employees who earn time and a half for more than 40 hours on Monday through Saturday and double time for any work on Sunday.

Employee	Hours Worked M	T	W	T	F	S	S	Total Hours	Hourly Rate	Regular Pay	$1\frac{1}{2}$ Overtime Pay	Double Time Pay	Gross Earnings
Mitze, A.	8	8	4	3	8	2	4	_____	$8.00	_____	_____	_____	_____
James, Q.	8	8	8	8	8	0	4	_____	$4.70	_____	_____	_____	_____
Adams, A.	5	5	8	11	10	9	5	_____	$6.75	_____	_____	_____	_____
Smith, M.	8	8	8	8	8	8	8	_____	$4.55	_____	_____	_____	_____

9. For sewing buttons on shirts, employees are paid $0.08 a shirt. Marty Hughes completes an average of 500 shirts a day. Find her average gross weekly earnings for a 5-day week.

10. Employees are paid $3.50 per piece for a certain job. In a week's time, Scott Marvel produced a total of 78 pieces. Find his gross earnings for the week.

Widgets International pays widget twisters at the following escalating piece rate for properly twisted widgets.

Items per week	*Piece rate*
1–150	$1.85
151–300	$1.95
301 and over	$2.08

Find the gross weekly earnings for employees who twisted the following number of widgets in a week.

11. 117 widgets

12. 158 widgets

13. 257 widgets

14. 325 widgets

15. A salesperson is paid 5% commission on sales of $18,200. Find his gross salary.

16. A computer salesperson is paid 1% commission for all sales. If she needs a monthly income of $1,500, find the monthly sales volume she must meet.

17. A produce salesperson earns 5% commission on $8,000 in produce sales. Find his gross pay on this sale.

18. Find the gross pay of a yarn company sales representative who earns 5% of her total sales of $6,000.

19. Find the gross pay of a salesperson who receives a 10% commission on $8,000 in sales.

20. A salesperson is paid a salary of $200 plus 3% of all sales. Find her gross income if new sales are $8,000.

21. A real estate salesperson receives a 6% commission on the sale of a piece of property for $130,000. Find his gross pay for this sale.

22. A salesperson sells $250,000 in equipment. At a 7% straight commission, calculate the gross earnings.

23. A salesperson is paid a salary of $400 plus 8% of sales. Calculate the gross income if new sales are $9,890.

24. A salesperson earns $150 plus 7% commission on all sales over $2,000. What are the gross earnings if sales for a week are $3,276?

25. Find the gross earnings if a salesperson earns $275 plus 2% of all sales over $3,000 and the sales for a week are $5,982.

26. A salesperson is paid $2,000 plus 5% of the total sales volume. If the salesperson sold $3,000 in merchandise, find the gross earnings.

Payroll Deductions

This section considers the payroll deductions that cause the net pay to be less than the gross pay. These deductions include federal, state, and local taxes, FICA (social security) taxes, union dues, medical insurance, credit union payments, and so on.

As an employee you should be concerned with what taxes you pay on your income and how those taxes are figured. If you work in the payroll department of a company or manage a company, you are concerned with other people's taxes as well. Employers have to pay taxes, and they are responsible for the withholding and paying of their employees' taxes. In fact, the bookkeeping involved in payroll provides a major source of employment for many people in the business world.

Federal Withholding Tax

federal withholding tax (FWT): a federal tax based on income, marital status, and exemptions that is paid by all persons earning a certain amount of money in the United States. An estimated amount is usually withheld from a person's paycheck.

The largest deduction from an employee's paycheck usually comes in the form of *income tax*, which is the same as **federal withholding tax (FWT).** The amount of tax withheld is based on three things: the employee's gross earnings, the employee's marital status, and number of withholding exemp-

Figure 7-1 A W-4 Form

------------ Cut here and give the certificate to your employer. Keep the top portion for your records. ------------

Form **W-4**
Department of the Treasury
Internal Revenue Service

Employee's Withholding Allowance Certificate

▶ **For Privacy Act and Paperwork Reduction Act Notice, see reverse.**

OMB No. 1545-0010

1 Type or print your first name and middle initial: Steven A. | Last name: Katz | 2 Your social security number: 128 - 82 - 5556

Home address (number and street or rural route): 1312 Loch Ave.

City or town, state, and ZIP code: Johntown, NJ 07781

3 Marital Status: ☒ Single ☐ Married ☐ Married, but withhold at higher Single rate.
Note: *If married, but legally separated, or spouse is a nonresident alien, check the Single box.*

4 Total number of allowances you are claiming (from line G above or from the Worksheets on back if they apply) . . . **4** 1

5 Additional amount, if any, you want deducted from each pay . . . . **5** $

6 I claim exemption from withholding and I certify that I meet **ALL** of the following conditions for exemption:

- Last year I had a right to a refund of **ALL** Federal income tax withheld because I had **NO** tax liability; **AND**
- This year I expect a refund of **ALL** Federal income tax withheld because I expect to have **NO** tax liability; **AND**
- This year if my income exceeds $500 and includes nonwage income, another person cannot claim me as a dependent.

If you meet all of the above conditions, enter the year effective and "EXEMPT" here . . . . . ▶ **6** 19

7 Are you a full-time student? (**Note:** *Full-time students are not automatically exempt.*) . . . . **7** ☐ **Yes** ☒ **No**

Under penalties of perjury, I certify that I am entitled to the number of withholding allowances claimed on this certificate or entitled to claim exempt status.

Employee's signature ▶ Steven A. Katz **Date ▶** October 18, 19XX

8 Employer's name and address (**Employer:** Complete 8 and 10 **only if sending to IRS**): Herbert Fare Hospital | **9** Office code (optional) | **10** Employer identification number: 203 - 146

withholding allowance: an allowance that reduces the amount of federal withholding tax owed or withheld. One allowance each is allowed for the taxpayer, the taxpayer's spouse, and each of the taxpayer's children and elderly dependents. Also called an *exemption*.

Circular E: IRS publication called *The Employer's Tax Guide.*

tions the person can claim. A **withholding allowance,** also called an **exemption,** is an amount of gross earnings that is not subject to tax; each employee is allowed one withholding allowance for himself or herself, one for his or her spouse if the spouse does not work, and one for each dependent (such as a child or elderly parent who lives with the taxpayer but does not work). Every employee fills out a W-4 form showing how many withholding allowances or exemptions he or she claims. The employer uses this information to figure how much to deduct from the employee's paycheck for withholding tax. A sample W-4 form is shown in Figure 7-1.

There are two ways to figure the amount of withholding tax for an employee, by the table or by the percentage method.

Finding Tax by the Table Method

The table method uses one of a number of tables provided in a pamplet published by the Internal Revenue Service and called *The Employer's Tax Guide* **(Circular E).** Tables 7-1 and 7-2 show portions of these tables: Table 7-1 is for Single Persons—Semimonthly Payroll Period, and Table 7-2 (p. 206) is for Married Persons—Weekly Payroll Period. In order to use these tables, you must know the person's salary, whether it is a weekly or semimonthly salary, whether the person is single or married, and how many withholding allowances are claimed.

Step by Step

Using a Tax Table

Step 1. Read down the columns at the left that are labeled "At least" and "But less than" until you come to the range that includes the person's salary. In Table 7-1, if the salary is $750, you would find the range that says "At least 740/But less than 760."

Step 2. Look across the table until you find the correct number of withholding allowances.

Step 3. The number shown where the two columns intersect is the amount of tax that the person owes either weekly or semimonthly, depending on which table you use.

Table 7-1

SINGLE Persons–SEMIMONTHLY Payroll Period

(For Wages Paid After December 1988)

And the wages are–		And the number of withholding allowances claimed is–										
At least	But less than	0	1	2	3	4	5	6	7	8	9	10
		The amount of income tax to be withheld shall be–										
$580	$600	$82	$69	$57	$44	$32	$19	$7	$0	$0	$0	$0
600	620	85	72	60	47	35	22	10	0	0	0	0
620	640	88	75	63	50	38	25	13	0	0	0	0
640	660	91	78	66	53	41	28	16	3	0	0	0
660	680	94	81	69	56	44	31	19	6	0	0	0
680	700	97	84	72	59	47	34	22	9	0	0	0
700	720	100	87	75	62	50	37	25	12	0	0	0
720	740	103	90	78	65	53	40	28	15	3	0	0
740	760	106	93	81	68	56	43	31	18	6	0	0
760	780	109	96	84	71	59	46	34	21	9	0	0
780	800	112	99	87	74	62	49	37	24	12	0	0
800	820	115	102	90	77	65	52	40	27	15	2	0
820	840	119	105	93	80	68	55	43	30	18	5	0
840	860	125	108	96	83	71	58	46	33	21	8	0
860	880	130	111	99	86	74	61	49	36	24	11	0
880	900	136	114	102	89	77	64	52	39	27	14	2
900	920	141	118	105	92	80	67	55	42	30	17	5
920	940	147	124	108	95	83	70	58	45	33	20	8
940	960	153	129	111	98	86	73	61	48	36	23	11
960	980	158	135	114	101	89	76	64	51	39	26	14
980	1,000	164	141	117	104	92	79	67	54	42	29	17
1,000	1,020	169	146	123	107	95	82	70	57	45	32	20
1,020	1,040	175	152	128	110	98	85	73	60	48	35	23
1,040	1,060	181	157	134	113	101	88	76	63	51	38	26
1,060	1,080	186	163	140	116	104	91	79	66	54	41	29
1,080	1,100	192	169	145	122	107	94	82	69	57	44	32
1,100	1,120	197	174	151	127	110	97	85	72	60	47	35
1,120	1,140	203	180	156	133	113	100	88	75	63	50	38
1,140	1,160	209	185	162	139	116	103	91	78	66	53	41
1,160	1,180	214	191	168	144	121	106	94	81	69	56	44
1,180	1,200	220	197	173	150	127	109	97	84	72	59	47
1,200	1,220	225	202	179	155	132	112	100	87	75	62	50
1,220	1,240	231	208	184	161	138	115	103	90	78	65	53
1,240	1,260	237	213	190	167	143	120	106	93	81	68	56
1,260	1,280	242	219	196	172	149	126	109	96	84	71	59
1,280	1,300	248	225	201	178	155	131	112	99	87	74	62
1,300	1,320	253	230	207	183	160	137	115	102	90	77	65
1,320	1,340	259	236	212	189	166	142	119	105	93	80	68
1,340	1,360	265	241	218	195	171	148	125	108	96	83	71
1,360	1,380	270	247	224	200	177	154	130	111	99	86	74
1,380	1,400	276	253	229	206	183	159	136	114	102	89	77
1,400	1,420	281	258	235	211	188	165	141	118	105	92	80
1,420	1,440	287	264	240	217	194	170	147	124	108	95	83
1,440	1,460	293	269	246	223	199	176	153	129	111	98	86
1,460	1,480	298	275	252	228	205	182	158	135	114	101	89
1,480	1,500	304	281	257	234	211	187	164	141	117	104	92
1,500	1,520	309	286	263	239	216	193	169	146	123	107	95
1,520	1,540	315	292	268	245	222	198	175	152	128	110	98
1,540	1,560	321	297	274	251	227	204	181	157	134	113	101
1,560	1,580	326	303	280	256	233	210	186	163	140	116	104
1,580	1,600	332	309	285	262	239	215	192	169	145	122	107
1,600	1,620	337	314	291	267	244	221	197	174	151	127	110
1,620	1,640	343	320	296	273	250	226	203	180	156	133	113
1,640	1,660	349	325	302	279	255	232	209	185	162	139	116
1,660	1,680	354	331	308	284	261	238	214	191	168	144	121
1,680	1,700	360	337	313	290	267	243	220	197	173	150	127
1,700	1,720	365	342	319	295	272	249	225	202	179	155	132
1,720	1,740	371	348	324	301	278	254	231	208	184	161	138
1,740	1,760	377	353	330	307	283	260	237	213	190	167	143
1,760	1,780	382	359	336	312	289	266	242	219	196	172	149
1,780	1,800	388	365	341	318	295	271	248	225	201	178	155
1,800	1,820	393	370	347	323	300	277	253	230	207	183	160
1,820	1,840	399	376	352	329	306	282	259	236	212	189	166
1,840	1,860	405	381	358	335	311	288	265	241	218	195	171
1,860	1,880	410	387	364	340	317	294	270	247	224	200	177
$1,880 and over		Use Table 3(a) for a **SINGLE person** on page 22. Also see the instructions on page 20.										

Page 33

EXAMPLE 8

Toni Liss has a gross semimonthly income of $840, is single, and claims three withholding allowances. Find the amount of withholding tax to be deducted from her gross earnings. Look in Table 7-1. The amount $840 is seen in *both* the "At least" and "But less than" columns. Since $840 is not in the range "At least $820 but less than $840," choose the withholding given in the row "At least $840 but less than $860" under the column for three withholding allowances. The withholding tax is $83.

Table 7-2

MARRIED Persons–**WEEKLY** Payroll Period

(For Wages Paid After December 1988)

And the wages are–		And the number of withholding allowances claimed is–										
At least	But less than	0	1	2	3	4	5	6	7	8	9	10
		The amount of income tax to be withheld shall be–										
$0	$65	$0	$0	$0	$0	$0	$0	$0	$0	$0	$0	$0
65	70	1	0	0	0	0	0	0	0	0	0	0
70	75	2	0	0	0	0	0	0	0	0	0	0
75	80	2	0	0	0	0	0	0	0	0	0	0
80	85	3	0	0	0	0	0	0	0	0	0	0
85	90	4	0	0	0	0	0	0	0	0	0	0
90	95	5	0	0	0	0	0	0	0	0	0	0
95	100	5	0	0	0	0	0	0	0	0	0	0
100	105	6	0	0	0	0	0	0	0	0	0	0
105	110	7	1	0	0	0	0	0	0	0	0	0
110	115	8	2	0	0	0	0	0	0	0	0	0
115	120	8	3	0	0	0	0	0	0	0	0	0
120	125	9	3	0	0	0	0	0	0	0	0	0
125	130	10	4	0	0	0	0	0	0	0	0	0
130	135	11	5	0	0	0	0	0	0	0	0	0
135	140	11	6	0	0	0	0	0	0	0	0	0
140	145	12	6	1	0	0	0	0	0	0	0	0
145	150	13	7	1	0	0	0	0	0	0	0	0
150	155	14	8	2	0	0	0	0	0	0	0	0
155	160	14	9	3	0	0	0	0	0	0	0	0
160	165	15	9	4	0	0	0	0	0	0	0	0
165	170	16	10	4	0	0	0	0	0	0	0	0
170	175	17	11	5	0	0	0	0	0	0	0	0
175	180	17	12	6	0	0	0	0	0	0	0	0
180	185	18	12	7	1	0	0	0	0	0	0	0
185	190	19	13	7	2	0	0	0	0	0	0	0
190	195	20	14	8	2	0	0	0	0	0	0	0
195	200	20	15	9	3	0	0	0	0	0	0	0
200	210	22	16	10	4	0	0	0	0	0	0	0
210	220	23	17	11	6	0	0	0	0	0	0	0
220	230	25	19	13	7	1	0	0	0	0	0	0
230	240	26	20	14	9	3	0	0	0	0	0	0
240	250	28	22	16	10	4	0	0	0	0	0	0
250	260	29	23	17	12	6	0	0	0	0	0	0
260	270	31	25	19	13	7	2	0	0	0	0	0
270	280	32	26	20	15	9	3	0	0	0	0	0
280	290	34	28	22	16	10	5	0	0	0	0	0
290	300	35	29	23	18	12	6	0	0	0	0	0
300	310	37	31	25	19	13	8	2	0	0	0	0
310	320	38	32	26	21	15	9	3	0	0	0	0
320	330	40	34	28	22	16	11	5	0	0	0	0
330	340	41	35	29	24	18	12	6	1	0	0	0
340	350	43	37	31	25	19	14	8	2	0	0	0
350	360	44	38	32	27	21	15	9	4	0	0	0
360	370	46	40	34	28	22	17	11	5	0	0	0
370	380	47	41	35	30	24	18	12	7	1	0	0
380	390	49	43	37	31	25	20	14	8	2	0	0
390	400	50	44	38	33	27	21	15	10	4	0	0
400	410	52	46	40	34	28	23	17	11	5	0	0
410	420	53	47	41	36	30	24	18	13	7	1	0
420	430	55	49	43	37	31	26	20	14	8	3	0
430	440	56	50	44	39	33	27	21	16	10	4	0
440	450	58	52	46	40	34	29	23	17	11	6	0
450	460	59	53	47	42	36	30	24	19	13	7	1
460	470	61	55	49	43	37	32	26	20	14	9	3
470	480	62	56	50	45	39	33	27	22	16	10	4
480	490	64	58	52	46	40	35	29	23	17	12	6
490	500	65	59	53	48	42	36	30	25	19	13	7
500	510	67	61	55	49	43	38	32	26	20	15	9
510	520	68	62	56	51	45	39	33	28	22	16	10
520	530	70	64	58	52	46	41	35	29	23	18	12
530	540	71	65	59	54	48	42	36	31	25	19	13
540	550	73	67	61	55	49	44	38	32	26	21	15
550	560	74	68	62	57	51	45	39	34	28	22	16
560	570	76	70	64	58	52	47	41	35	29	24	18
570	580	77	71	65	60	54	48	42	37	31	25	19
580	590	79	73	67	61	55	50	44	38	32	27	21
590	600	80	74	68	63	57	51	45	40	34	28	22
600	610	82	76	70	64	58	53	47	41	35	30	24
610	620	83	77	71	66	60	54	48	43	37	31	25

Page 26

(Continued on next page)

EXAMPLE 9

Bill Johnson is married, has a gross weekly salary of $515, and claims two withholding allowances. Find the amount of withholding tax to be deducted from his gross salary. Look in the first two columns of Table 7-2 to find the range for $515. Then move across to the column for two withholding allowances. The amount of withholding tax is $56.

Finding Tax by the Percentage Method

Many companies calculate withholding tax and prepare payrolls by computer. Computerized payrolls generally do not depend on tax tables;

instead they use percentage calculations. The federal government publishes Form Y, which shows the percentage of the income that should be withheld from the salary of an individual in a certain income bracket. You cannot use a simple percentage calculation to find the amount of tax owed because the tax rate increases as the income increases.

We show two tables here that are issued by the federal government for calculating income tax. Table 7-3, Income Tax Withholding—Percentage Method, shows how much to subtract from gross pay for each withholding allowance claimed. After this is done, you turn to Table 7-4, Tables for Percentage Method of Withholding, which shows the amount of tax to be withheld.

Table 7-3

Income Tax Withholding—Percentage Method

If you do not want to use the wage bracket tables to figure how much income tax to withhold, you can use a percentage computation based on the table below and the appropriate rate table. This method works for any number of withholding allowances the employee claims.

Percentage Method Income Tax Withholding Table

Payroll Period	One withholding allowance
Weekly	$38.46
Biweekly	76.92
Semimonthly	83.33
Monthly	166.67
Quarterly	500.00
Semiannually	1,000.00
Annually	2,000.00
Daily or miscellaneous (each day of the payroll period)	7.69

Table 7-4

Tables for Percentage Method of Withholding

(For Wages Paid After December 1988)

TABLE 1—If the Payroll Period With Respect to an Employee Is Weekly

(a) SINGLE person—including head of household:

If the amount of wages (after subtracting withholding allowances) is: / *The amount of income tax to be withheld shall be:*

Not over $21 0

Over—	But not over—		of excess over—
$21	—$378	15%	—$21
$378	—$885	$53.55 plus 28%	—$378
$885	—$2,028	$195.51 plus 33%	—$885
$2,028		$572.70 plus 28%	—$2,028

(b) MARRIED person—

If the amount of wages (after subtracting withholding allowances) is: / *The amount of income tax to be withheld shall be:*

Not over $62 0

Over—	But not over—		of excess over—
$62	—$657	15%	—$62
$657	—$1,501	$89.25 plus 28%	—$657
$1,501	—$3,695	$325.57 plus 33%	—$1,501
$3,695		$1,049.59 plus 28%	—$3,695

TABLE 2—If the Payroll Period With Respect to an Employee Is Biweekly

(a) SINGLE person—including head of household:

If the amount of wages (after subtracting withholding allowances) is: / *The amount of income tax to be withheld shall be:*

Not over $42 0

Over—	But not over—		of excess over—
$42	—$756	15%	—$42
$756	—$1,769	$107.10 plus 28%	—$756
$1,769	—$4,055	$390.74 plus 33%	—$1,769
$4,055		$1,145.12 plus 28%	—$4,055

(b) MARRIED person—

If the amount of wages (after subtracting withholding allowances) is: / *The amount of income tax to be withheld shall be:*

Not over $123 0

Over—	But not over—		of excess over—
$123	—$1,313	15%	—$123
$1,313	—$3,002	$178.50 plus 28%	—$1,313
$3,002	—$7,389	$651.42 plus 33%	—$3,002
$7,389		$2,099.13 plus 28%	—$7,389

TABLE 3—If the Payroll Period With Respect to an Employee Is Semimonthly

(a) SINGLE person—including head of household:

If the amount of wages (after subtracting withholding allowances) is: / *The amount of income tax to be withheld shall be:*

Not over $46 0

Over—	But not over—		of excess over—
$46	—$819	15%	—$46
$819	—$1,917	$115.95 plus 28%	—$819
$1,917	—$4,393	$423.39 plus 33%	—$1,917
$4,393		$1,240.47 plus 28%	—$4,393

(b) MARRIED person—

If the amount of wages (after subtracting withholding allowances) is: / *The amount of income tax to be withheld shall be:*

Not over $133 0

Over—	But not over—		of excess over—
$133	—$1,423	15%	—$133
$1,423	—$3,252	$193.50 plus 28%	—$1,423
$3,252	—$8,005	$705.62 plus 33%	—$3,252
$8,005		$2,274.11 plus 28%	—$8,005

TABLE 4—If the Payroll Period With Respect to an Employee Is Monthly

(a) SINGLE person—including head of household:

If the amount of wages (after subtracting withholding allowances) is: / *The amount of income tax to be withheld shall be:*

Not over $92 0

Over—	But not over—		of excess over—
$92	—$1,638	15%	—$92
$1,638	—$3,833	$231.90 plus 28%	—$1,638
$3,833	—$8,786	$846.50 plus 33%	—$3,833
$8,786		$2,480.99 plus 28%	—$8,786

(b) MARRIED person—

If the amount of wages (after subtracting withholding allowances) is: / *The amount of income tax to be withheld shall be:*

Not over $267 0

Over—	But not over—		of excess over—
$267	—$2,846	15%	—$267
$2,846	—$6,504	$386.85 plus 28%	—$2,846
$6,504	—$16,010	$1,411.09 plus 33%	—$6,504
$16,010		$4,548.07 plus 28%	—$16,010

Step by Step

Calculating Tax by the Percentage Method

Step 1. Use Table 7-3. Multiply the number of withholding allowances times the amount shown in the right column, depending on whether wages are weekly, semimonthly, and so on.

Step 2. Subtract the product found in Step 1 from gross pay; the result is the taxable income.

Step 3. Use Table 7-4 and the taxable income figured in Step 2. Follow the directions in the table to calculate the correct amount of tax to withhold.

EXAMPLE 10

Find the tax on Yaz Elliot's semimonthly gross earnings of $1,150. He is single and claims two withholding allowances.

2 × $83.33 = $166.66	Use Table 7-3. Multiply the number of withholding allowances claimed times the amount of a withholding allowance for a semimonthly payroll period.
$1,150 − $166.66 = $983.34	Subtract the withholding allowance from gross income to find taxable income.
$983.34 is in the $819–$1,917 bracket	Turn to Table 7-4 and find taxable income range in the left column for a semimonthly employee.

The schedule in Table 7-4 tells us that the tax in that bracket is $115.95 + 28% of income in excess of $819.

$983.34 − $819 = $164.34	Subtract $819 from the taxable income in order to find the amount of income in excess of $819.
$164.34 × 0.28 = $46.02	Find 28% of the amount of income in excess of $819.
$115.95 + $46.02 = $161.97	Add $46.02 to $115.95 to find the amount of tax to be withheld.

$161.97 is the amount of tax to be withheld.

When the amount of tax is calculated by the percentage method, the result may differ slightly from the result obtained in the tax table, but the amounts will be close enough to be acceptable.

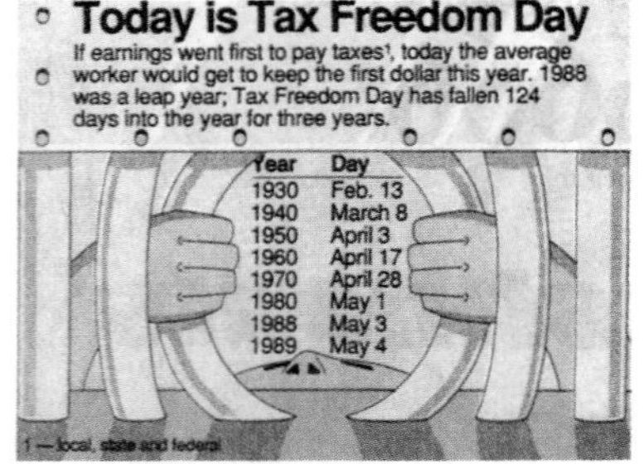
Today is Tax Freedom Day

If earnings went first to pay taxes[1], today the average worker would get to keep the first dollar this year. 1988 was a leap year; Tax Freedom Day has fallen 124 days into the year for three years.

Year	Day
1930	Feb. 13
1940	March 8
1950	April 3
1960	April 17
1970	April 28
1980	May 1
1988	May 3
1989	May 4

1 — local, state and federal

Source: Tax Foundation Inc.
By Elys McLean-Ibrahim, USA TODAY

Self-Check

9. B. J. Mullin is married, has a gross weekly salary of $486, and claims three withholding allowances. Use the table method to find the amount of withholding tax to be deducted from his weekly salary.
10. Maddy Waxman has a gross weekly income of $380, is single, and claims one withholding allowance. Find the amount of withholding tax to be deducted from her weekly paycheck using the percentage method.

FICA Tax

The second-largest amount withheld from an employee's paycheck is usually the deduction for FICA tax. **FICA (Federal Insurance Contributions Act) tax** is also referred to as **social security (SS) tax.** It comes from an emergency measure passed by Congress during the depression of the 1930s. The money from this tax goes into a fund that pays monthly benefits to retired and disabled workers.

FICA (Federal Insurance Contributions Act) tax: a federal tax that goes into a fund that pays monthly benefits to retired and disabled workers. It is also called *social security (SS) tax.*

The amount of tax and the amount of salary that is taxed change periodically as the Congress passes new legislation. In a recent year, the FICA tax rate was 7.51% (0.0751) of the first $48,000 gross earnings. This means that after a person has earned $48,000 in a year, no FICA tax will be withheld on any additional money he or she earns. A person who earns $48,000 in a year pays exactly the same FICA tax as a person who earns $100,000.

Employers also pay a share of FICA tax: The employer contributes the same amount as the employee contributes to an employee's social security account. Employers can figure FICA tax for employees and themselves by using a FICA table, part of which is shown in Table 7-5 (p. 210), or by using the percent method, multiplying the salary times 7.51%.

The FICA tax table is somewhat like the federal income tax tables discussed earlier in the chapter, in that it also has "Wages at least" and "But less than" columns. If the gross weekly earnings are more than $100, you have to look at the lower right-hand side of the chart. Here you find gross weekly earnings in amounts up to $1,000. If the gross earnings are $675, you take the amount for $600 given in the lower right corner, $45.06, and then you look up the rest of the gross earnings figure, $75, and find that the tax on that is $5.63. Add the two tax amounts together to find the total FICA tax owed: $45.06 + $5.63 = $50.69.

EXAMPLE 11

An employee has a gross weekly income of $275. Use Table 7-5 to find how much FICA tax should be withheld.

$275 = $200 + $75		
Social security tax on $200 =	$15.02	Look in Table 7-5 to find the amount of tax to be withheld on $200 and on $75.
Social security tax on $75 =	$ 5.63	Add the two amounts.
	$20.65	Total FICA tax to be withheld.

EXAMPLE 12

Lisa Perez, vice president of marketing for Golden Sun Enterprises, earns $49,400 annually, or $950 per week. Find the amount of FICA tax that should be withheld for the 51st week.

At the end of the 51st week, Lisa will have earned a total gross salary of $48,450 . Since FICA tax is withheld on only the first $48,000, she does not pay FICA on $450 of her 51st week's earnings. We subtract $450 from her weekly gross of $950 to find that she pays FICA on only $500 of her earnings that week.

$500 × 0.0751 = $37.55 — Multiply her taxable income by the 7.51% tax rate to find how much FICA tax should be withheld in the 51st week. No additional FICA tax would be withheld for the year.

Table 7-5

Social Security Employee Tax Table for 1989

7.51% employee tax deductions

Wages at least	But less than	Tax to be withheld	Wages at least	But less than	Tax to be withheld	Wages at least	But less than	Tax to be withheld	Wages at least	But less than	Tax to be withheld
51.07	51.20	3.84	63.72	63.85	4.79	76.37	76.50	5.74	89.02	89.15	6.69
51.20	51.34	3.85	63.85	63.99	4.80	76.50	76.64	5.75	89.15	89.29	6.70
51.34	51.47	3.86	63.99	64.12	4.81	76.64	76.77	5.76	89.29	89.42	6.71
51.47	51.60	3.87	64.12	64.25	4.82	76.77	76.90	5.77	89.42	89.55	6.72
51.60	51.74	3.88	64.25	64.39	4.83	76.90	77.04	5.78	89.55	89.69	6.73
51.74	51.87	3.89	64.39	64.52	4.84	77.04	77.17	5.79	89.69	89.82	6.74
51.87	52.00	3.90	64.52	64.65	4.85	77.17	77.30	5.80	89.82	89.95	6.75
52.00	52.14	3.91	64.65	64.79	4.86	77.30	77.44	5.81	89.95	90.08	6.76
52.14	52.27	3.92	64.79	64.92	4.87	77.44	77.57	5.82	90.08	90.22	6.77
52.27	52.40	3.93	64.92	65.05	4.88	77.57	77.70	5.83	90.22	90.35	6.78
52.40	52.53	3.94	65.05	65.18	4.89	77.70	77.83	5.84	90.35	90.48	6.79
52.53	52.67	3.95	65.18	65.32	4.90	77.83	77.97	5.85	90.48	90.62	6.80
52.67	52.80	3.96	65.32	65.45	4.91	77.97	78.10	5.86	90.62	90.75	6.81
52.80	52.93	3.97	65.45	65.58	4.92	78.10	78.23	5.87	90.75	90.88	6.82
52.93	53.07	3.98	65.58	65.72	4.93	78.23	78.37	5.88	90.88	91.02	6.83
53.07	53.20	3.99	65.72	65.85	4.94	78.37	78.50	5.89	91.02	91.15	6.84
53.20	53.33	4.00	65.85	65.98	4.95	78.50	78.63	5.90	91.15	91.28	6.85
53.33	53.47	4.01	65.98	66.12	4.96	78.63	78.77	5.91	91.28	91.42	6.86
53.47	53.60	4.02	66.12	66.25	4.97	78.77	78.90	5.92	91.42	91.55	6.87
53.60	53.73	4.03	66.25	66.38	4.98	78.90	79.03	5.93	91.55	91.68	6.88
53.73	53.87	4.04	66.38	66.52	4.99	79.03	79.17	5.94	91.68	91.82	6.89
53.87	54.00	4.05	66.52	66.65	5.00	79.17	79.30	5.95	91.82	91.95	6.90
54.00	54.13	4.06	66.65	66.78	5.01	79.30	79.43	5.96	91.95	92.08	6.91
54.13	54.27	4.07	66.78	66.92	5.02	79.43	79.57	5.97	92.08	92.22	6.92
54.27	54.40	4.08	66.92	67.05	5.03	79.57	79.70	5.98	92.22	92.35	6.93
54.40	54.53	4.09	67.05	67.18	5.04	79.70	79.83	5.99	92.35	92.48	6.94
54.53	54.67	4.10	67.18	67.32	5.05	79.83	79.97	6.00	92.48	92.61	6.95
54.67	54.80	4.11	67.32	67.45	5.06	79.97	80.10	6.01	92.61	92.75	6.96
54.80	54.93	4.12	67.45	67.58	5.07	80.10	80.23	6.02	92.75	92.88	6.97
54.93	55.06	4.13	67.58	67.71	5.08	80.23	80.36	6.03	92.88	93.01	6.98
55.06	55.20	4.14	67.71	67.85	5.09	80.36	80.50	6.04	93.01	93.15	6.99
55.20	55.33	4.15	67.85	67.98	5.10	80.50	80.63	6.05	93.15	93.28	7.00
55.33	55.46	4.16	67.98	68.11	5.11	80.63	80.76	6.06	93.28	93.41	7.01
55.46	55.60	4.17	68.11	68.25	5.12	80.76	80.90	6.07	93.41	93.55	7.02
55.60	55.73	4.18	68.25	68.38	5.13	80.90	81.03	6.08	93.55	93.68	7.03
55.73	55.86	4.19	68.38	68.51	5.14	81.03	81.16	6.09	93.68	93.81	7.04
55.86	56.00	4.20	68.51	68.65	5.15	81.16	81.30	6.10	93.81	93.95	7.05
56.00	56.13	4.21	68.65	68.78	5.16	81.30	81.43	6.11	93.95	94.08	7.06
56.13	56.26	4.22	68.78	68.91	5.17	81.43	81.56	6.12	94.08	94.21	7.07
56.26	56.40	4.23	68.91	69.05	5.18	81.56	81.70	6.13	94.21	94.35	7.08
56.40	56.53	4.24	69.05	69.18	5.19	81.70	81.83	6.14	94.35	94.48	7.09
56.53	56.66	4.25	69.18	69.31	5.20	81.83	81.96	6.15	94.48	94.61	7.10
56.66	56.80	4.26	69.31	69.45	5.21	81.96	82.10	6.16	94.61	94.75	7.11
56.80	56.93	4.27	69.45	69.58	5.22	82.10	82.23	6.17	94.75	94.88	7.12
56.93	57.06	4.28	69.58	69.71	5.23	82.23	82.36	6.18	94.88	95.01	7.13
57.06	57.20	4.29	69.71	69.85	5.24	82.36	82.50	6.19	95.01	95.14	7.14
57.20	57.33	4.30	69.85	69.98	5.25	82.50	82.63	6.20	95.14	95.28	7.15
57.33	57.46	4.31	69.98	70.11	5.26	82.63	82.76	6.21	95.28	95.41	7.16
57.46	57.59	4.32	70.11	70.24	5.27	82.76	82.89	6.22	95.41	95.54	7.17
57.59	57.73	4.33	70.24	70.38	5.28	82.89	83.03	6.23	95.54	95.68	7.18
57.73	57.86	4.34	70.38	70.51	5.29	83.03	83.16	6.24	95.68	95.81	7.19
57.86	57.99	4.35	70.51	70.64	5.30	83.16	83.29	6.25	95.81	95.94	7.20
57.99	58.13	4.36	70.64	70.78	5.31	83.29	83.43	6.26	95.94	96.08	7.21
58.13	58.26	4.37	70.78	70.91	5.32	83.43	83.56	6.27	96.08	96.21	7.22
58.26	58.39	4.38	70.91	71.04	5.33	83.56	83.69	6.28	96.21	96.34	7.23
58.39	58.53	4.39	71.04	71.18	5.34	83.69	83.83	6.29	96.34	96.48	7.24
58.53	58.66	4.40	71.18	71.31	5.35	83.83	83.96	6.30	96.48	96.61	7.25
58.66	58.79	4.41	71.31	71.44	5.36	83.96	84.09	6.31	96.61	96.74	7.26
58.79	58.93	4.42	71.44	71.58	5.37	84.09	84.23	6.32	96.74	96.88	7.27
58.93	59.06	4.43	71.58	71.71	5.38	84.23	84.36	6.33	96.88	97.01	7.28
59.06	59.19	4.44	71.71	71.84	5.39	84.36	84.49	6.34	97.01	97.14	7.29
59.19	59.33	4.45	71.84	71.98	5.40	84.49	84.63	6.35	97.14	97.28	7.30
59.33	59.46	4.46	71.98	72.11	5.41	84.63	84.76	6.36	97.28	97.41	7.31
59.46	59.59	4.47	72.11	72.24	5.42	84.76	84.89	6.37	97.41	97.54	7.32
59.59	59.73	4.48	72.24	72.38	5.43	84.89	85.02	6.38	97.54	97.67	7.33
59.73	59.86	4.49	72.38	72.51	5.44	85.02	85.16	6.39	97.67	97.81	7.34
59.86	59.99	4.50	72.51	72.64	5.45	85.16	85.29	6.40	97.81	97.94	7.35
59.99	60.12	4.51	72.64	72.77	5.46	85.29	85.42	6.41	97.94	98.07	7.36
60.12	60.26	4.52	72.77	72.91	5.47	85.42	85.56	6.42	98.07	98.21	7.37
60.26	60.39	4.53	72.91	73.04	5.48	85.56	85.69	6.43	98.21	98.34	7.38
60.39	60.52	4.54	73.04	73.17	5.49	85.69	85.82	6.44	98.34	98.47	7.39
60.52	60.66	4.55	73.17	73.31	5.50	85.82	85.96	6.45	98.47	98.61	7.40
60.66	60.79	4.56	73.31	73.44	5.51	85.96	86.09	6.46	98.61	98.74	7.41
60.79	60.92	4.57	73.44	73.57	5.52	86.09	86.22	6.47	98.74	98.87	7.42
60.92	61.06	4.58	73.57	73.71	5.53	86.22	86.36	6.48	98.87	99.01	7.43
61.06	61.19	4.59	73.71	73.84	5.54	86.36	86.49	6.49	99.01	99.14	7.44
61.19	61.32	4.60	73.84	73.97	5.55	86.49	86.62	6.50	99.14	99.27	7.45
61.32	61.46	4.61	73.97	74.11	5.56	86.62	86.76	6.51	99.27	99.41	7.46
61.46	61.59	4.62	74.11	74.24	5.57	86.76	86.89	6.52	99.41	99.54	7.47
61.59	61.72	4.63	74.24	74.37	5.58	86.89	87.02	6.53	99.54	99.67	7.48
61.72	61.86	4.64	74.37	74.51	5.59	87.02	87.16	6.54	99.67	99.81	7.49
61.86	61.99	4.65	74.51	74.64	5.60	87.16	87.29	6.55	99.81	99.94	7.50
61.99	62.12	4.66	74.64	74.77	5.61	87.29	87.42	6.56	99.94	100.00	7.51
62.12	62.26	4.67	74.77	74.91	5.62	87.42	87.55	6.57			
62.26	62.39	4.68	74.91	75.04	5.63	87.55	87.69	6.58			
62.39	62.52	4.69	75.04	75.17	5.64	87.69	87.82	6.59			
62.52	62.65	4.70	75.17	75.30	5.65	87.82	87.95	6.60			
62.65	62.79	4.71	75.30	75.44	5.66	87.95	88.09	6.61			
62.79	62.92	4.72	75.44	75.57	5.67	88.09	88.22	6.62			
62.92	63.05	4.73	75.57	75.70	5.68	88.22	88.35	6.63			
63.05	63.19	4.74	75.70	75.84	5.69	88.35	88.49	6.64			
63.19	63.32	4.75	75.84	75.97	5.70	88.49	88.62	6.65			
63.32	63.45	4.76	75.97	76.10	5.71	88.62	88.75	6.66			
63.45	63.59	4.77	76.10	76.24	5.72	88.75	88.89	6.67			
63.59	63.72	4.78	76.24	76.37	5.73	88.89	89.02	6.68			

Wages	Taxes
100	$7.51
200	15.02
300	22.53
400	30.04
500	37.55
600	45.06
700	52.57
800	60.08
900	67.59
1,000	75.10

Page 45

Real World Application

HOW TO READ YOUR PAY STUB

With all the various ways of being paid and figuring gross earnings, not to mention the many deductions that are made and the ways of figuring net earnings, some people may feel that they need a separate course in how to figure out their pay stubs! The accompanying figure shows a sample pay stub and explains the various categories of payments and deductions contained on it. Your pay stub may not look exactly like this, but it will probably contain many of these entries, so it pays to get the hang of how to read it. Companies can make mistakes, and in this case they'll be making a mistake with *your* money!

Application Questions

1. What is the gross pay for this pay period?

2. Find the total amount deducted from the check. What percent of the gross pay is the total deducted?

3. Based on the amount of federal withholding tax listed on the pay stub, use Table 7-2 to find the number of withholding allowances claimed.

4. What amount will appear on the paycheck that goes with this pay stub?

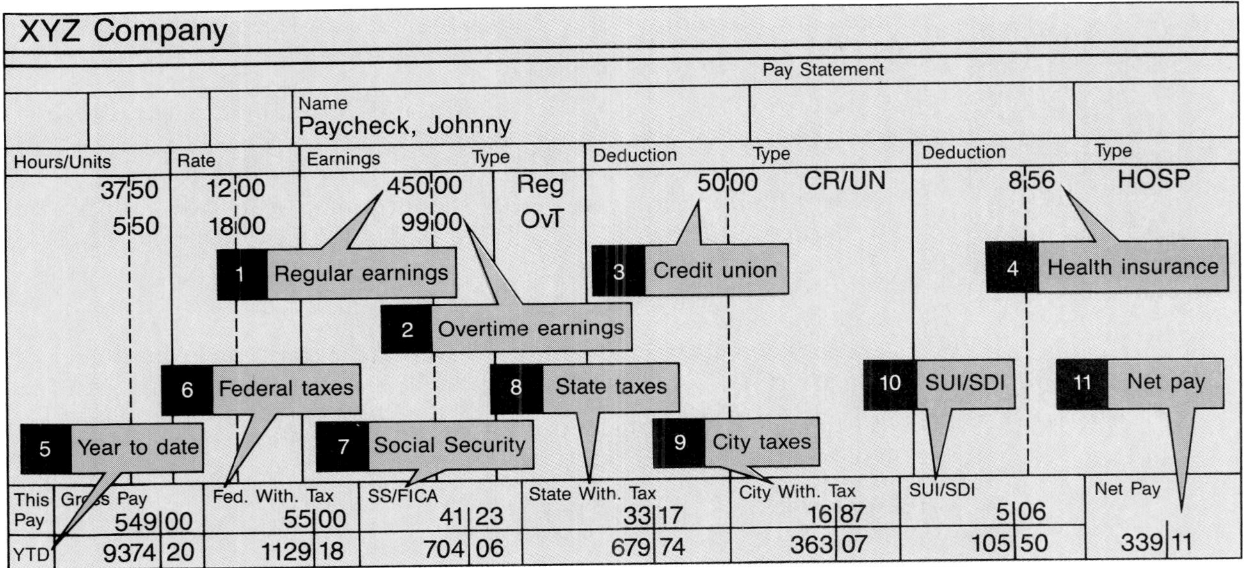

1. Regular weekly earnings ($450.00)
2. Overtime earnings ($99.00): $12.00 × 1.5 = $18.00 an hour for hours over 37.5 per week. 5.5 hrs. × $18 = $99.00
3. Credit union ($50.00): Here's a $50 automatic deduction for a contribution to a credit union savings plan.
4. Health insurance ($8.56): Other insurance premiums that could be deducted automatically include life and dental insurance.
5. YTD ($9374.20): Year-to-date running totals let you know how much you've been paid so far this year.
6. Federal withholding tax ($55.00): If you are paid weekly, multiply this number by 52 to find out how much you will pay in federal taxes by year's end.
7. Social Security/FICA ($41.23): Contact the Social Security Administration to make sure your account is being and has been properly credited.
8. State withholding tax ($33.17): The amount of state tax varies from state to state.
9. City withholding taxes ($16.87): Many cities do not require a city income tax.
10. SUI/SDI ($5.06): Often the state and federal unemployment insurance and disability tax is paid by the employer. When the employee is responsible for these taxes, he will pay up to a certain amount each year.
11. Net pay ($339.11): This is the amount you take home for this particular week.

Figuring Net Earnings

In addition to taxes, there are a number of other deductions that can be made from an employee's paycheck. Many of these are made at the employee's request, such as insurance or union dues. There are often state and local income taxes that must also be withheld by the employer in addition to the federal income tax and FICA tax. When all these deductions have been made, the amount left is called *net earnings,* or *take-home* pay. The following examples show how to figure net earnings.

EXAMPLE 13

Hillary Sinclair's gross weekly earnings are $206. Five percent of her gross earnings is deducted for her retirement fund and $5.83 is deducted for insurance. Find her net earnings if Hillary is married and claims three withholding allowances.

Source: Laurdan Associates Inc.
By Rod Little, USA TODAY

Income tax withholding:
$4.00

In Table 7-2, find the amount of income tax to be withheld.

FICA tax withholding:
$\$206 \times 0.0751 = \$15.47$

Find the FICA tax by the percentage method: 7.51% of $206 = $\$206 \times 0.0751$.

Retirement fund withholding:
$0.05 \times \$206 = \$10.30$

Use the formula $P = R \times B$. Multiply rate (5% = 0.05) by base (gross pay of $206).

Add all deductions:
Total deductions

$$= \text{income tax} + \text{FICA tax} + \text{insurance} + \text{retirement fund}$$
$$= \$4 + \$15.47 + \$5.83 + \$10.30 = \$35.60$$

$$\text{Gross earnings} - \text{total deductions} = \text{net earnings}$$
$$\$206 - \$35.60 = \$170.40$$

Hillary's weekly take-home pay is $170.40.

The Employer's Taxes

federal unemployment tax (FUTA): a federal tax that is paid by the employer for each employee.

state unemployment tax (SUTA): a state tax that is paid by the employer.

The major taxes paid by the employer are the employer's share of the FICA tax, which we have already discussed, and federal and state unemployment taxes. The federal and state unemployment taxes do not affect the paycheck of the employee; they are paid entirely by the employer. **Federal unemployment tax (FUTA)** is currently 6.2% of the first $7,000 earned by an employee in a year *minus* any amount that the employer has paid in **state unemployment tax (SUTA),** up to a limit of 5.4% of the first $7,000. SUTA varies in different states, according to the employment record of the company in question. A company with a good employment record is one that does not fire employees frequently, a practice that places heavier demands on the state's unemployment benefit funds. An employer with a good employment record might pay much less than 5.4%, but such an employer would be given credit by the federal goverment for having paid at the 5.4% rate. To calculate FUTA, an employer pays the SUTA and subtracts that amount from the 6.2% owed to the federal government for the FUTA. Examples 14 and 15 illustrate this process.

EXAMPLE 14

Melanie McFarren earned $15,300 last year. If the state unemployment tax (SUTA) is 5.4% of the first $7,000 earned in a year, how much SUTA must Melanie's employer pay for her?

$P = R \times B$ $= 5.4\% \times \$7{,}000$ $= .054 \times \$7{,}000 = \$378$	Use the percentage formula. The base is $7,000 because SUTA is paid only on the first $7,000 earned in a given year.

The employer owes $378 in SUTA for Melanie.

EXAMPLE 15

Find the amount of federal unemployment tax (FUTA) the company must pay for Melanie (Example 14). Remember, the FUTA rate is 6.2% of the first $7,000 earned in a year minus the amount that has been paid to the SUTA.

$P = R \times B$ $= 6.2\% \times \$7{,}000$ $= 0.062 \times \$7{,}000 = \$434$	Use the percentage formula. The base is $7,000 because SUTA and FUTA are paid only on the first $7,000 earned in a given year. This is the *total amount* of unemployment tax to be paid to *both* SUTA and FUTA.
FUTA = total unemployment tax − SUTA $= \$434 - \$378 = \$56$	Subtract the SUTA amount (calculated in Example 14) from the total amount to find the FUTA amount due.

The employer owes $56 in FUTA for Melanie.

The Employer's Payroll Record Keeping

The employer has to pay taxes, withhold employees' taxes, and keep detailed records of these transactions. The payroll department of many companies contains a good percentage of the company's employees, even if most of the calculating is done on computer. Many entry-level jobs are available in payroll departments, so it pays to learn about the responsibilities of the employer.

To track how much money is withheld from each paycheck, how much is paid, and when it is paid for each tax and each employee, the employer has to keep several records up to date. The first of these is the payroll register, which lists each employee each week and shows how much he or she earned, how much of that amount is taxable, which taxes were withheld, and what the net earnings were.

The second type of record that is often kept is the employee's earnings record, which is an individual record for each employee showing how much he or she has earned and how much tax was paid each paycheck. This second type of record is cumulative, so that at any point the employer can see how much an employee has earned in the year to date. This is helpful in figuring FICA tax, which is no longer deducted after an employee has earned $48,000 in gross pay.

When money withheld from employees' paychecks is paid to the government, which is done on a regular basis, various forms must be filled out and sent to the government with the payments. The first of these is **Form 941,** which covers the quarterly payment of three taxes: the employees' share of FICA taxes, the employer's share of the FICA tax, and the employees' federal income taxes. An example of Form 941 is shown in Figure 7-2 (p. 214).

Form 941: A form that employers submit quarterly to indicate the employee's share of FICA taxes, the employer's share of FICA taxes, and the employee's federal withholding taxes that have been withheld.

Figure 7-2 Form 941

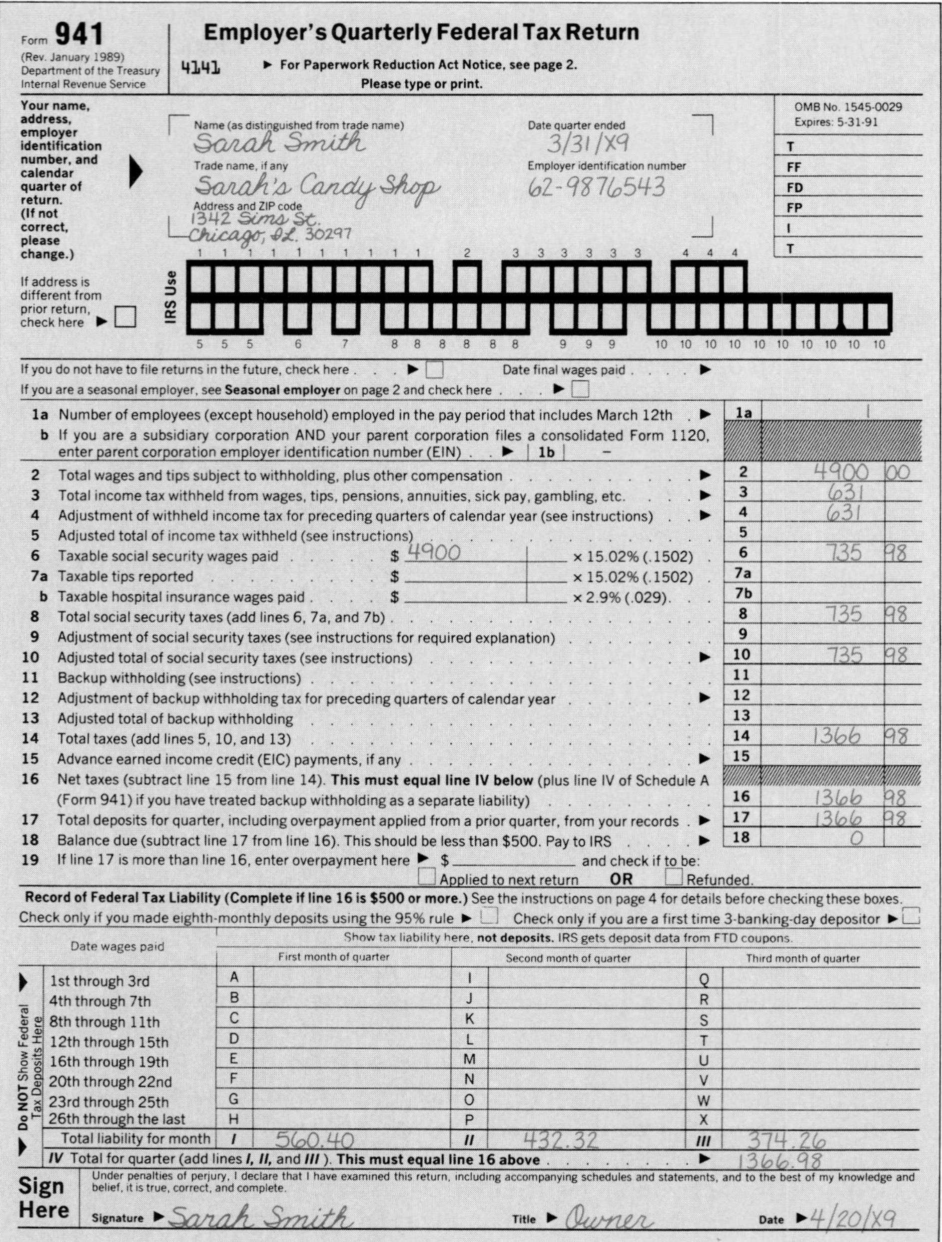

Form **941** (Rev. January 1989) Department of the Treasury Internal Revenue Service

Employer's Quarterly Federal Tax Return

4141 ► For Paperwork Reduction Act Notice, see page 2.

Please type or print.

Your name, address, employer identification number, and calendar quarter of return. (If not correct, please change.)

Name (as distinguished from trade name): Sarah Smith

Date quarter ended: 3/31/X9

Trade name, if any: Sarah's Candy Shop

Employer identification number: 62-9876543

Address and ZIP code: 1342 Sims St. Chicago, IL. 30297

OMB No. 1545-0029 Expires: 5-31-91

T / FF / FD / FP / I / T

If address is different from prior return, check here ► ☐

IRS Use

If you do not have to file returns in the future, check here . . . ► ☐ Date final wages paid . . . . ►

If you are a seasonal employer, see **Seasonal employer** on page 2 and check here . . . . ► ☐

		Line	Amount
1a	Number of employees (except household) employed in the pay period that includes March 12th ►	1a	
b	If you are a subsidiary corporation AND your parent corporation files a consolidated Form 1120, enter parent corporation employer identification number (EIN) . . ► 1b –		
2	Total wages and tips subject to withholding, plus other compensation ►	2	4900 00
3	Total income tax withheld from wages, tips, pensions, annuities, sick pay, gambling, etc. ►	3	631
4	Adjustment of withheld income tax for preceding quarters of calendar year (see instructions) ►	4	631
5	Adjusted total of income tax withheld (see instructions)	5	
6	Taxable social security wages paid . . . . . $ 4900 × 15.02% (.1502)	6	735 98
7a	Taxable tips reported . . . . . $ ____ × 15.02% (.1502)	7a	
b	Taxable hospital insurance wages paid . . . . $ ____ × 2.9% (.029)	7b	
8	Total social security taxes (add lines 6, 7a, and 7b)	8	735 98
9	Adjustment of social security taxes (see instructions for required explanation)	9	
10	Adjusted total of social security taxes (see instructions) ►	10	735 98
11	Backup withholding (see instructions)	11	
12	Adjustment of backup withholding tax for preceding quarters of calendar year ►	12	
13	Adjusted total of backup withholding	13	
14	Total taxes (add lines 5, 10, and 13)	14	1366 98
15	Advance earned income credit (EIC) payments, if any ►	15	
16	Net taxes (subtract line 15 from line 14). **This must equal line IV below** (plus line IV of Schedule A (Form 941) if you have treated backup withholding as a separate liability)	16	1366 98
17	Total deposits for quarter, including overpayment applied from a prior quarter, from your records ►	17	1366 98
18	Balance due (subtract line 17 from line 16). This should be less than $500. Pay to IRS ►	18	0
19	If line 17 is more than line 16, enter overpayment here ► $ ____ and check if to be: ☐ Applied to next return **OR** ☐ Refunded.		

Record of Federal Tax Liability (Complete if line 16 is $500 or more.) See the instructions on page 4 for details before checking these boxes.

Check only if you made eighth-monthly deposits using the 95% rule ► ☐ Check only if you are a first time 3-banking-day depositor ► ☐

Show tax liability here, **not deposits.** IRS gets deposit data from FTD coupons.

Do NOT Show Federal Tax Deposits Here

Date wages paid		First month of quarter		Second month of quarter		Third month of quarter
1st through 3rd	A		I		Q	
4th through 7th	B		J		R	
8th through 11th	C		K		S	
12th through 15th	D		L		T	
16th through 19th	E		M		U	
20th through 22nd	F		N		V	
23rd through 25th	G		O		W	
26th through the last	H		P		X	
Total liability for month	*I*	560.40	*II*	432.32	*III*	374.26
IV Total for quarter (add lines *I*, *II*, and *III*). **This must equal line 16 above** ►						1366.98

Sign Here Under penalties of perjury, I declare that I have examined this return, including accompanying schedules and statements, and to the best of my knowledge and belief, it is true, correct, and complete.

Signature ► Sarah Smith Title ► Owner Date ► 4/20/X9

Self-Check

11. Erica Echison earns a gross weekly income of $270. Use Table 7-5 to find how much FICA tax should be withheld.

12. Doug Bloch earns $48,100 annually, or $925 per week. Find the amount of FICA tax that should be withheld from his check during the 52nd week.

13. Misty Diehl's gross weekly earnings are $415. Three percent of her gross earnings is deducted for her retirement fund and $4.79 is deducted for insurance. Find the net earnings if Misty is married and claims two withholding allowances.

Section Review

Use Table 7-2 (weekly payroll period) to find the amount of withholding tax for the gross earnings of the following married persons with the indicated number of withholding allowances.

1. $225, 4 exemptions

2. $138.50, 3 exemptions

3. $295, 2 exemptions

4. $475, 0 exemptions

5. $395, 3 exemptions

Use Tables 7-3 and 7-4 and the percentage method to find the amount of tax to be withheld from the gross earnings of the following married persons who are paid weekly and have the indicated number of withholding allowances.

6. $273.96, 5 exemptions

7. $420, 8 exemptions

8. $875, 2 exemptions

9. $1,020, 3 exemptions

In Exercises 10–14, refer to Table 7-5 to determine the amount of FICA tax to be deducted from the gross weekly earnings.

10. $73

11. $89

12. $157

13. $368

14. $87.98

Use the percentage method to find the FICA tax for the following:

15. Weekly gross income of $157

16. Monthly gross income of $3,500

17. Yearly gross income of $24,000

18. Semimonthly gross income of $426

19. Yearly gross income of $18,225

20. Yearly gross income of $51,300

Complete the following payroll register. All employees are married and paid weekly and the number in parentheses is the number of withholding allowances that each person claims.

Employee & Withholding Allowances	Gross Earnings	With-holding Tax	FICA	Other Deductions	Total Deductions	Net Earnings
21. Abrams (3)	$145.00	_____	___	$21.94	_____	_____
22. Cowgill (0)	$139.25	_____	___	$15.21	_____	_____
23. Mason (4)	$165.00	_____	___	$ 0	_____	_____
24. Sachs (2)	$476.28	_____	___	$19.38	_____	_____

25. Deductions for an employee are as follows: withholding tax $47; FICA tax $27.83, retirement, $24.95, insurance, $8.45. Find the total deductions.

26. Vince Brimaldi earned $32,876 last year. If the state unemployment tax is 5.4% of the first $7,000 earned in a year, how much SUTA must Vince's employer pay for him if the employer pays at the 5.4% rate?

Summary

Topic	Page	What to Remember	Examples
Salary	195–196	A salaried employee's paycheck equals the annual salary divided by the number of paychecks issued during the year.	If Barbara earns $23,500 per year, how much is her weekly gross pay? $\frac{\$23,500}{52} = \$451.92$
Hourly pay	196	Hourly employees are paid an hourly rate for the number of hours worked since the last paycheck.	Aldo earns $6.25 per hour. He worked 40 hours last week and 38 hours this week. What is his gross pay for these two weeks? $40 + 38 = 78$ hours; $78 \times \$6.25 = \$487.50$.
Overtime pay	197	Multiply 40 hours times the regular rate, and multiply the number of overtime hours times 1.5 times the regular pay rate. Add the two numbers.	Belinda worked 44 hours one week. Her regular pay was $7.75 per hour. Find her gross earnings for the week. $40 \times \$7.75 = \$310$ $4 \times \$7.75 \times 1.5 = \$46.50$ $\$310 + \$46.50 = \$356.50$
Piecework, or production, pay	197–198	Piecework pay is based on the amount of acceptable work completed.	Willy earns $0.30 for each acceptable widget he twists. Last week Willy twisted 1,224 acceptable widgets. Find his gross earnings for the week. $1,224 \times \$0.30 = \$367.20$
Differential, or escalating, piece rate	198	The amount pay per item increases as the number of items produced increases.	Nadine does piecework for a jeweler and earns $0.25 per piece for finishing 1–25 pins, $0.50 per piece for finishing 26–50 pins, and $0.75 per piece for finishing any pins over 50. Yesterday she finished 70 pins. How much did she earn? $(25 \times \$.25) + (25 \times \$.50) + (20 \times \$.75) = \$33.75$
Straight commission	198–199	A person's salary is based on a percent of his or her total sales.	Bart earns a 4% commission on the appliances he sells. His sales last week totaled $8,000. Find his gross earnings. $0.04 \times \$8,000 = \$320$
Salary plus commission	198–199	A person receives a basic salary plus a percent of his or her sales.	Elaine earns $250 weekly plus 2% of all sales over $1,500. Last week she made $9,500 worth of sales. Find her gross earnings. $\$9,500 - \$1,500 = \$8,000$ Commission $= 0.02 \times \$8,000 = \$160$ $\$250 + \$160 = \$410$

Topic	Page	What to Remember	Example
Federal withholding tax (table method)	204–205	Find the correct table (single or married, number of withholding allowances) in Circular E to determine the amount of federal tax to be withheld.	Archy is married, has a gross weekly salary of $480, and claims two withholding allowances. Find the amount of tax to be deducted from his gross salary. Look in the first two columns of Table 7-2 to find the range for $480. Then move across to the column for two withholding allowances. The amount of federal tax to be withheld is $52.
Federal withholding tax (percentage method)	208	Many companies with computerized payrolls use the percentage method of calculating federal withholding tax. The percentages vary according to payroll period and whether a person is married or single and are given in Circular E.	Find the federal tax on Ruth's monthly income of $1,438. She is single and claims 2 exemptions. 2 exemptions × $166.67 = $333.34 $1,435 − $333.34 = $1,101.66 $1,101.66 is in the $92–$1,638 bracket (Table 7-4), so the amount of withholding tax is 15% of the amount over $92. $1,101.66 − $92 = $1,009.66 $1,009.66 × 0.15 = $151.45
FICA withholding (table method)	209–210	Find the correct salary range in the FICA withholding table to find the amount of FICA tax to be withheld for a given salary.	Wes earns $46,280 per year. If he earns $890 each week, what is his weekly FICA withholding? Look in the lower right-hand box and find the taxes for $800. This amount is $60.08. Next, locate the wages range containing $90. The amount of tax for $90 is $6.76. The total FICA for the week is $60.08 + $6.76 = $66.84.
FICA withholding (percentage method)	209	The FICA tax rate used in this text is 7.51 percent (0.0751) of the first $48,000 gross earnings. The employer pays the same amount of FICA tax for each employee as the employee pays.	Calculate the FICA for Wes using the percentage method. $890 × 0.0751 = $66.839, which rounds to $66.84.

Topic	Page	What to Remember	Example
Other deductions	210–212	An employer may withhold insurance payments, union dues, and state and local taxes from an employee's paycheck.	Beth's gross weekly earnings are \$388. Four percent of her gross earnings is deducted for her retirement fund and \$7.48 is deducted for insurance. Find her net earnings if Beth is married and claims three withholding allowances. Income tax withholding: In Table 7-2, find the amount of income tax to be withheld: \$31. FICA tax withholding: Find the FICA tax by the percentage method: \$388 × 0.0751 = \$29.14. Retirement fund withholding: 0.04 × \$388 = \$15.52. Add all deductions: Income tax + FICA tax+ insurance + retirement fund = \$31 + \$29.14 + \$7.48 + \$15.52 = \$83.14 Net earnings = \$304.86
SUTA (state unemployment tax)	212–213	The SUTA is currently 5.4% of the first \$7,000 earned by an employee in a year.	Joe earned \$19,800 last year. If the SUTA is 5.4% of the first \$7,000 earned in a year, how much SUTA must Joe's employer pay for him? 5.4% × \$7,000 = 0.054 × \$7,000 = \$378
FUTA (federal unemployment tax)	212–213	The FUTA is currently 6.2% of the first \$7,000 earned by an employee in a year *minus* any SUTA that the employer has paid, up to a limit of 5.4%.	How much FUTA must Joe's company pay for him? The FUTA rate is 6.2% of the first \$7,000 earned in a year, minus the amount that has been paid to the SUTA. 6.2% × \$7,000 = 0.062 × \$7,000 = \$434 (*total* unemployment tax) \$434 − \$378 = \$56 FUTA owed
Form 941	213–214	The employer must file federal Form 941, which covers the quarterly payment of FICA taxes (employer's and employee's shares)	See Figure 7-2.

Chapter Review

1. Louise Isaacson earns a salary of $18,524 a year and is paid semimonthly (twice a month). How much is her paycheck before taxes are taken out?

2. Lorenzo Long earns a salary of $17,382 a year and is paid biweekly (every two weeks). How much is his paycheck before taxes are taken out?

3. Thurl Ray worked 52 hours one week. His regular pay was $8.24 per hour. Find his gross earnings for one week.

4. Bob Wilson works for a national food chain at the rate of $5.26 per hour. Last week he worked 46 hours, plus an additional 4 hours on a holiday (earning double-time pay) during the same week. Find Bob's gross earnings for last week.

An employer pays at the following differential piece rate:

1–200 items	$1.28
201–300 items	$1.86
More than 300	$2.14

5. Find the gross earnings of an employee who produces 185 items.

6. Find the gross earnings of an employee who produces 237 items.

7. Find the gross earnings of an employee who produces 358 items.

8. A tire salesperson receives 6% of her total sales as commission. If her sales totaled $6,830 during a given week, find her gross earnings.

9. Rob Linder is paid by the salary-plus-commission method. His sales last week totaled $5,892. Find his gross earnings if he receives $150 weekly in salary and 5% of all sales over $3,000.

10. An employee has a gross weekly income of $260, is married, and claims 1 withholding allowance. Use the percentage method (Tables 7-3 and 7-4) to find the amount of withholding tax to be deducted from the gross earnings.

11. Use Table 7-5 to find how much FICA tax should be withheld for the employee in Problem 10.

12. An engineer earns $52,260 annually or $1,005 per week. Find the amount of FICA tax that should be withheld for the fifteenth week of the year.

13. Find the amount of FICA tax for the employee in Problem 12 that should be withheld for the forty-eighth week.

14. Find the amount of FICA tax for the employee in Problem 12 that should be withheld for the fifty-first week.

15. An employee has gross weekly earnings of $521. Four percent of her gross earnings is deducted for retirement and $8.39 is deducted for insurance. Find the total deductions if the employee is single and claims three withholding allowances.

16. Find the net earnings for the employee in Problem 15.

17. An employee earns $18,275 during a given year. If the state unemployment tax (SUTA) rate is 5.4% of the first $7,000 earned in a year, how much SUTA must the employer pay for the employee?

18. The federal unemployment tax (FUTA) rate is 6.2% of the first $7,000 earned in a year minus the state unemployment tax paid. Find the federal unemployment tax that must be paid for the employee.

Trial Test

1. An employee works 43 hours in a week for a salary of $354 per week. What are the employee's gross weekly earnings?

2. June Jackson earns $5.83 an hour. Find her gross earnings if she worked 46 hours (time and a half for overtime).

3. Willy Bell checks wrappers on cans in a cannery. He receives $0.07 for each case of cans. If he checks 750 cases on an average day, find his gross weekly salary. (A workweek is 5 days.)

4. An employee is paid on the following escalating piece rate.
   1–100 $1.58; 101–250 $1.72; 251–up $1.94
   Find her gross earnings for completing 475 pieces.

5. A restaurant-supplies salesperson works on 3% commission. If her sales for a week are $4,200, find her gross earnings.

6. A salesperson works on 5% commission. If he sells $7,500 in merchandise, find his gross earnings.

7. Find the gross earnings of a salesperson who receives a 9% commission and whose sales totaled $5,800.

8. Use the percentage method to find the FICA tax (at 7.51%) for an employee whose gross earnings are $213.86. Round to the nearest cent.

9. Use Table 7-5 to find the FICA tax for an employee whose gross earnings are $361.25.

10. How much income tax should be withheld for a married employee who earns $286 weekly and has two exemptions? (Use Table 7-2.)

11. Use Table 7-2 to find the income tax paid by a married employee with four exemptions if his weekly gross earnings are $276.

12. An employee has gross earnings of $157. The employee has a 3% retirement deduction and pays $21 for insurance. Find the sum of these deductions.

13. If an employee had net earnings of $177.58 and total deductions of $43.69, find her gross earnings.

14. An employee has a gross income of $258.21 and total deductions of $31.17. Find the net earnings.

Complete the weekly register for married employees. The number of each person's exemptions is listed after each name. Round to the nearest cent.

Employee (Exemptions)	Gross Earnings	FICA	Withholding Tax	Other Deductions	Net Earnings
15. Jackson (0)	$235.00	______	______	$25.12	______
16. Love (2)	173.80	______	______	12.87	______
17. Chow (1)	292.17	______	______	—	______
18. Ferrante (3)	77.15	______	______	4.88	______
19. Towns (4)	210.13	______	______	0	______

15.

16.

17.

18.

19.

20. How much SUTA tax must an employer pay to the state for a part-time employee who earns $5,290? The SUTA tax rate is 5.4% of the wages.

21. How much SUTA tax must an employer pay to the state for an employee who earns $38,200?

22. How much FUTA tax must an employer pay to the state for the employee in Problem 21? The FUTA tax rate is 6.2% of the first $7,000 minus the SUTA tax.

23. How much SUTA tax does the employee in Problem 21 pay?

Self-Check Solutions

1. $19,000 ÷ 52 = $365.38

2.
40 × $7.60 =	$304	(regular-rate pay)
7 × $7.60 × 1.5 =	+ $ 79.80	(additional overtime pay)
	$383.80	(gross earnings)

3.
40 × $8.25 =	$330
4 × $8.25 × 1.5 =	+ $ 49.50
	$379.50

4.
40 × $6.80 =	$272	
8 × $6.80 × 1.5 =	$ 81.60	
4 × $6.80 × 2 =	+ $ 54.40	(double overtime pay)
	$408.00	(gross earnings)

5. Total buckles = 32 + 34 + 38 + 35 + 30 = 169
   Gross earnings = 169 × $0.75 = $126.75

6.
First 100 boxes:	$1.32 × 100 =	$132	
Last 80 boxes:	$1.42 × 80 =	+ $113.60	
		$245.60	(gross earnings)

7. $P = RB$
   = 0.06 × $5,000
   = $300 (gross earnings)

8. $6,000 − $2,000 = $4,000 (amount on which commission is paid)
   $P = RB$
   = 0.04 × $4000
   = $160
   $160 + $175 = $335 (gross earnings)

9. Find the table for married persons. Move down the *at least* column to the amount $480. Then move across to the column marked 3 at the top. The amount is $46.

10. Using Table 7-3 for a weekly salary of a single person with one withholding allowance, we see that the amount is $38.46. We subtract $38.46 from gross pay, $380, and get $341.54; this is the taxable income. Look next at Table 7-4: the tax is 15% of the excess amount over $21, so you subtract $21 from $341.54 and get $320.54, and multiply that times 15%: $320.54 × 0.15 = $48.08.

11. $270 − $200 = $70. Look in the box in the lower right-hand corner of Table 7-5. Find $200 under *wages* and read $15.02 in the *taxes* column. Then look in the second *wages at least* column to find $26.98. $70 is in this range. The tax is $5.26. The total tax is $15.02 + $5.26 = $20.28.

12. $925 × 52 = $48,100
    FICA is not paid on $100 of the fifty-second week's earnings.
    $925 − $100 = $825
    FICA *is* paid on $825 of the earnings.
    $825 × 0.0751 = $61.96 (FICA tax paid on fifty-second week's earnings)

13. $0.03 \times \$415 = \$12.45$ (retirement deduction)

$\$4.79$ (insurance deduction)

$0.0751 \times \$415 = \$31.17$ (social security deduction)

$\$41$ (withholding tax deduction)

$\$89.41$ (total deductions)

Net earnings $= \$415 - \$89.41 = \$325.59$

8 Trade and Cash Discounts

Learning Objectives

1. Calculate the amount of discount and the net price using a single trade discount. (pp. 229–231)
2. Calculate the amount of discount and the net price using a trade discount series. (pp. 234–236)
3. Calculate due dates from different credit terms. (pp. 239–243)
4. Calculate discounts and discounted prices for different credit terms. (pp. 239–246)

A discount is an amount of money that is deducted or subtracted from an original price. In business, manufacturers and distributors give discounts as incentives for a sale or as a convenient way of pricing merchandise to retail merchants. Two common types of discounts used in business are *trade* and *cash discounts.*

Single Trade Discounts

Most products go from the manufacturer to the consumer by way of the retail merchant (retailer).

Manufacturer
↓
Retailer
↓
Consumer

The manufacturer normally describes each of its products in a book or catalog that is made available to retailers. In this catalog the manufacturer suggests a price at which each product should be sold to the consumer. This price is called the **suggested retail price**, the **catalog price**, or, most commonly, the **list price.**

When a manufacturer sells an item to a retailer, the manufacturer deducts a certain amount from the list price of the article. The amount deducted is called the **trade discount.** The retailer pays the **net price,** which is the difference between the list price and the trade discount.

The trade discount is not usually stated in the published catalog. Instead, the retailer calculates it from the list price and the **discount rate.** The discount rate is the *percent* of the list price that the manufacturer allows the retailer to deduct from the list price.

The manufacturer sends the retailer lists of discount rates for each article in the catalog. The discount rates vary considerably with such factors as the customer class, the season, the condition of the economy, whether a product is being discontinued, and the manufacturer's efforts to encourage larger purchases by the retailer. Each time the discount rate changes, the manufacturer sends the retailer a listing of the changes. Each new discount rate refers to the original list price in the catalog.

suggested retail price: the price at which a product should be sold to the consumer; this price is usually listed in a manufacturer's catalog, also called *catalog price* or *list price.*

trade discount: the amount deducted by the manufacturer from the list price of an article.

net price: the amount paid by the retailer for an article; this amount is the difference in the list price and the trade discount of the article.

discount rate: the percent of the list price which the manufacturer allows the retailer to deduct from the list price.

When one discount rate is quoted on the list price, this discount rate is known as a **single discount rate.**

Calculating Trade Discounts

To find the trade discount when the list price and a single discount rate are given, use the following formula.

> **Calculating the Amount of the Trade Discount**
>
> Trade discount = list price × single discount rate

Note that this formula is in fact a version of the basic percentage formula,

Portion (part) = rate (percent) × base (whole), or $P = R \times B$

and we use it the same way we used the percentage formula in Chapter 6.

Once we have found the amount of the trade discount, we can calculate the *net price,* or the discounted price, of an item.

> **Calculating the Net Price of a Discounted Item**
>
> Net price = list price − trade discount

EXAMPLE 1

The list price of a refrigerator is $600. The wholesaler can buy the refrigerator at the list price less 20%. Find the trade discount and the net price of the refrigerator.

Trade discount = list price × single discount rate

$600 × 20% = $600 × 0.20 $600 × 0.20 = $120	Change the percent discount to a decimal and multiply the list price times the decimal.

List price − trade discount = net price

$600 − $120 = $480	Subtract the trade discount from the list price to find the net price.

The Complements Method. There is another method for calculating the net price when you know the list price and the single discount rate. This method is often used when you do not need to know the actual amount of the trade discount, only the net price.

complement: the difference between 100% and the percent of discount.

The method uses the complements of percents. The **complement** of a percent is the difference between that percent and 100%. For example, the complement of 35% is 65%, since 100% − 35% = 65%. The complement of 20% is 80% because 100% − 20% = 80%.

If the single discount rate is the percentage of the list price that the retailer *does not* pay, then 100% minus the single discount rate, which equals the complement of the discount rate, is the portion of the list price the retailer *does* pay.

Step by Step

Using Complements to Find the Net Price

Step 1. Find the complement by subtracting the single discount rate from 100%.

Step 2. Multiply the complement (in decimal form) by the list price to get net price:

Net price = list price × (100% − single discount rate)

EXAMPLE 2

A retailer buys 300 pens at $0.30 each, 200 legal pads at $0.60 each, and 100 boxes of paper clips at $0.90 each. The discount rate for the order is 12%. Find the net price of the order.

300 × $0.30 = $ 90	Find the list price of the pens.
200 × $0.60 = $120	Find the list price of the legal pads.
100 × $0.90 = $ 90	Find the list price of the paper clips.
$300	Add to find the total list price.

Net price = list price × (100% − single discount rate)

$300 × (100% − 12%) = $300 × 88%	Subtract the discount rate from 100% to find the complement.
= $300 × 0.88 = $264	Multiply the total list price times the decimal equivalent of the complement to find the net price.

The net price of the order is $264.

Self-Check

1. Use the method of Example 1 to complete Invoice 2501. Use the method of Example 2 to check that your net price is correct.

			Invoice No. 2501 October 15, 19__
Quantity	**Description**	**Unit Price**	**Total Price**
15	Notebooks	$1.50	______
10	Looseleaf paper	$0.89	______
30	Ballpoint pens	$0.79	______
		Total list price	______
		40% trade discount	______
		Net price	______

Section Review

Complete the following table. Round all answers to the nearest cent.

	List Price	Single Discount Rate	Trade Discount
1.	$300	15%	________
2.	$48	10%	________
3.	$127.50	20%	________
4.	$100	12%	________
5.	$37.85	20%	________
6.	$425	15%	________

7. Find the trade discount on a piece of furniture listed at $1,025 less 10% (single discount rate).

8. The list price for velvet by Harris Fabrics is $6.25 per yard less 6%. What is the trade discount? Round to the nearest cent.

9. Find the trade discount on a suit listed at $165 less 12%.

10. Rocha Bros. offered a $12\frac{1}{2}$% discount on a tractor listed at $10,851. What was the trade discount? Round to the nearest cent.

11. Find the trade discount on an order of 30 lamps listed at $35 each less 9%.

12. The list price on skirts is $22, and the list price on corduroy jumpers is $37. If Petitt's Clothing Store orders 30 skirts and 40 jumpers at a discount rate of 11%, what is the trade discount on the purchase?

13. A stationery shop bought 10 boxes of writing paper that were listed at $1 each, and 200 greeting cards listed at $0.50 each. If the single discount rate for the purchase is 15%, find the trade discount.

Complete the following table. Round all answers to the nearest cent.

	List Price	Trade Discount	Net Price
14.	$1,480	$301	______
15.	$21	$3	______
16.	$24.62	$5.93	______
17.	$6.85	$0.72	______
18.	$0.89	$0.12	______
19.	$378.61	$42.58	______

20. The list price of carpeting from Marie's Mill Outlet is $19 per square yard. The trade discount is $2.50 per square yard. What is the net price per square yard?

Complete the following table.

	List Price	Single Discount Rate	Trade Discount	Net Price
21.	$25	5%	______	______
22.	$1,263	12%	______	______
23.	$0.89	2%	______	______
24.	$27.50	3%	______	______
25.	$2,100	17%	______	______

Complete the following table.

	List Price	Single Discount Rate	Complement	Net Price
26.	$15.97	4%	______	______
27.	$421	5%	______	______
28.	$138.54	6%	______	______
29.	$721.18	3%	______	______
30.	$16.97	11%	______	______

Trade Discount Series

trade discount series: trade discounts that are deducted successively from the list price by the manufacturer to promote a particular item or encourage additional business from a retailer.

Sometimes a manufacturer wants to promote a particular item or encourage additional business from a retailer. In such cases, the manufacturer may offer additional discounts that are deducted one after another from the list price. Such discounts are called a **trade discount series.** For example, a discount series would be written as \$400 (list price) with a discount of 20/10/5 (discount rates). This means that a discount of 20% is allowed off the list price, a discount of 10% is allowed off the amount that was left after the first discount, and a discount of 5% is allowed off the amount that was left after the second discount. This *does not* mean a total discount of 35% is allowed.

One way to calculate the net price is to make a series of calculations:

\$400 × 0.20 = \$80	\$400 − \$80 = \$320	The first discount is taken on the list price of \$400, which then leaves \$320.
\$320 × 0.10 = \$32	\$320 − \$32 = \$288	The second discount is taken on \$320, which leaves \$288.
\$288 × 0.05 = \$14.40	\$288 − \$14.40 = \$273.60	The third discount is taken on \$288, which leaves the net price of \$273.60.

Thus, the net price of a \$400 order with a discount of 20/10/5 is \$273.60. Always remember: In a trade discount series you *never* add the discount rates together—a discount series of 20/10/5 does *not* equal a single discount of 35%.

As you can see, it is very time-consuming to figure a trade discount series this way. The business world uses a faster way of calculating the net price of a purchase after a series discount has been taken.

net decimal equivalent: the decimal that results from multiplying the complement of each discount rate in a series discount.

USING THE NET DECIMAL EQUIVALENT TO FIND THE NET PRICE. To calculate the net price, find the complement of each discount rate, write these complements as equivalent decimals, and multiply the decimals. The result is called the **net decimal equivalent.** Then multiply the list price times the net decimal equivalent to get the net price.

Step by Step

Finding Net Price with the Net Decimal Equivalent

Step 1. Find the complement of each discount rate and write it as an equivalent decimal.

Step 2. Multiply the decimals in Step 1. The product is the net decimal equivalent.

Step 3. Multiply the list price times the net decimal equivalent. The product is the net price.

EXAMPLE 3

Find the net price of an order with a list price of \$600 and a trade discount series of 15/10/5. (*Remember:* To find the complement, you subtract the discount rate from 100%.)

100% − 15% = 85% = 0.85 100% − 10% = 90% = 0.90 100% − 5% = 95% = 0.95	Find the complement of each discount rate and write it as an equivalent decimal.

$0.85 \times 0.90 \times 0.95 = 0.72675$ Multiply the decimals times each other to find the net decimal equivalent.

Net price = list price × net decimal equivalent

$\$600 \times 0.72675 = \$436.05$ Multiply the list price times the net decimal equivalent to find the net price. Round to the nearest cent.

A purchase that costs $600 with a trade discount series of 15/10/5 has a net price of $436.05.

TIPS & TRAPS

We have said that the series discount rate of 20/10/5 is *not* equivalent to the single discount rate of 35% (which is the *sum* of 20%, 10%, and 5%). Let's look at what happens if you combine the series discount rates incorrectly, and then show the correct way.

Example: Find the net price of an article listed at $100 with a discount of 20/10/5.

~~Net price = list price × (100% − single discount rate)~~
~~$100 × (100% − 35%) = $100 × 0.65 = $65~~

WRONG

Net decimal equivalent = $0.8 \times 0.9 \times 0.95 = 0.684$
Net price = list price × net decimal equivalent
$\$100 \times 0.684 = \$68.40$

CORRECT

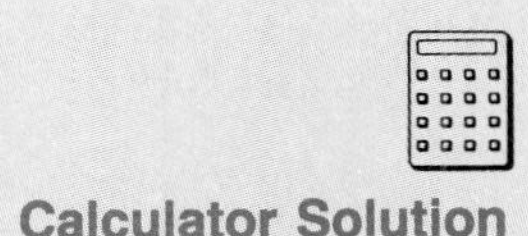

Calculator Solution

A common business application of this method is to compare prices and terms offered by competing manufacturers selling the same or similar items. The following example shows this application using a calculator.

One manufacturer lists a couch at $700 with a discount of 20/10/10. Another manufacturer lists the same couch at $650 with a discount of 10/10/10. Which is the better deal?

In calculating both net prices, use the formula

Net price = list price × net decimal equivalent

Find the net price of the first couch in one continuous series of calculations:

Net price = [AC] 700 [×] .8 [×] .9 [×] .9 [=] ⇒ 453.60

Find the net price of the second couch in another continuous series of calculations:

Net price = [AC] 650 [×] .9 [×] .9 [×] .9 [=] ⇒ 473.85

The better deal is the couch listed at $700 with a discount of 20/10/10 because the net price of this couch is $20.25 less than the net price of the other couch.

single discount equivalent: a percent that is the complement of the percent form of the net decimal equivalent.

Using the Single Discount Equivalent to Find the Amount of Discount. You know how much you have to pay for an item (the net decimal equivalent × list price), but what if you want to know how much you have *saved* by using a discount series? You can calculate the savings the long way, by finding the net price and then subtracting the net price from the list price. Or, you can again use the complements method to do this in fewer steps. There is a method for finding what the amount of the discount would be if the trade discount series were equated to a single discount. This discount is called the **single discount equivalent;** it is the complement of the percent form of the net decimal equivalent.

Finding the Amount of Discount with the Single Discount Equivalent

Single discount equivalent = 100% − net decimal equivalent (in percent form)

EXAMPLE 4

Use the single discount equivalent to calculate the amount of the discount on a $1,500 purchase with a discount series of 30/20/10.

100% − 30% = 70% = 0.7 100% − 20% = 80% = 0.8 100% − 10% = 90% = 0.9	Find the complement of each discount rate and write it as an equivalent decimal.
0.7(0.8)(0.9) = 0.504	Multiply the decimals times each other to find the net decimal equivalent.
1.000 − 0.504 = 0.496	Subtract the net decimal equivalent from 1 to find the single discount equivalent.

Thus, the single discount equivalent for the trade discount series 30/20/10 is 0.496 (which can also be written as 49.6%).

$1,500 × 0.496 = $744	Multiply the list price times the single-discount equivalent to find the amount of the discount.

Self-Check

2. Find the net price of an order with a list price of $800 and a trade discount series of 12/10/8. Use the net decimal equivalent.
3. Use the single-discount equivalent to calculate the amount of the discount on a $2,200 purchase with a discount series of 25/15/10.
4. One distributor lists a dot-matrix printer at $460 with a discount of 15/12/5. Another distributor lists the same printer at $380 with a discount of 10/10/50. Which is the better deal?

Section Review

Complete the following table.

	List Price	Discount Rates	Decimal Equivalents of Complements	Net Decimal Equivalent	Net Price
1.	$200	20/10	______	______	____

	List Price	Discount Rates	Decimal Equivalents of Complements	Net Decimal Equivalent	Net Price
2.	$50	10/7/5	________	________	______
3.	$1,500	20/15/10	________	________	______
4.	$35	20/15/5	________	________	______
5.	$400	15/5	________	________	______

6. Discount rates of 10% and 5% were allowed on ladies' scarves listed at $4. What was the net price of each scarf?

7. Find the net price of an item listed at $800 with a series discount of 25/10/5.

8. A trade discount series of 10/5/5 is offered on a typewriter, which is listed at $800. Also, a trade discount series of 5/10/5 is offered on a desk chair listed at $250. Find the total net price for the typewriter and the chair. Round to the nearest cent.

9. Five desks are listed at $400 each, with a trade discount of 20/10/10. Also, ten bookcases are listed at $200 each, discounted 10/20/10. Find the total net price for the desks and bookcases.

Complete the following table.

	Net Decimal Equivalent	Net Decimal Equivalent in Percent Form	Single Discount Equivalent in Percent Form
10.	0.765	________	________
11.	0.82	________	________
12.	0.6835	________	________
13.	0.6502	________	________
14.	0.7434	________	________

Find the *single discount equivalent* for the following series.

15. 20/10

16. 30/20/5

17. 10%, 5%, 2%

18. 10/5

19. 20/15

20. A television is listed at $400 less 20%. The same television is listed by another manufacturer for $425 less 21%. Which is the better deal?

21. A hutch is listed at $650 with a trade discount of $65. The same hutch is listed by another manufacturer for $595 with a trade discount of $25. Which is the better deal?

22. One manufacturer lists an aquarium for $58.95 with a trade discount of $5.90. Another manufacturer lists the same aquarium for $60 with a trade discount of $9.45. Which is the better deal?

23. One manufacturer lists a table at $200 less 12%. Another manufacturer lists the same table at $190 less 11%. Which is the better deal?

24. One manufacturer lists picture frames at $20 each, discounted 10/5/10. Another manufacturer lists the same picture frames at $19 with a series discount of 10/10/10. Which is the better deal?

25. A trunk is listed at $250 discounted 10/10/5. The same trunk is listed by another manufacturer for $260 discounted 10/10/10. Which is the better deal?

Cash Discounts

Many manufacturers and distributors allow customers to take a **cash discount,** which is a reduction of the amount due on an invoice, to encourage prompt payment of the bill. The cash discount is a specified percentage of the price of the goods. If the customer pays the bill within a certain amount of time, he or she will receive a cash discount. Many companies use computerized billing systems that compute the exact amount of a cash discount and show it on the invoice, so that the customer does not need to figure the discount and resulting net price. But the customer must still determine when the bill must be paid to receive the discount.

cash discount: a reduction of the amount due on an invoice allowed by manufacturers and distributors to encourage prompt payment of a bill.

Calculating Due Dates

Bills are often due within 30 days from the date of the invoice. To figure out the exact day of the month the payment is due, you have to know how many days are in a month, 30 or 31 (or 28 in the case of February). There are two ways to help remember which months have 30 days and which have 31. The first method is shown in Figure 8-1; it is called the *knuckle method.* Each knuckle represents a month with 31 days and each space between knuckles represents a month with 30 days (except February, which has 28 days unless it is a leap year, when it has 29).

Figure 8-1

The knuckle months (Jan., March, May, July, Aug., Oct., and Dec.) have 31 days. The other months have 30 or fewer days.

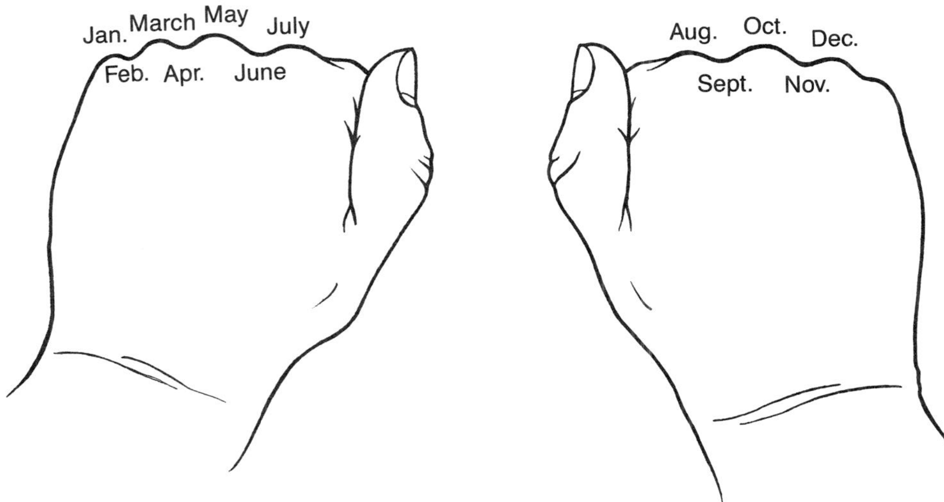

Another way to remember which months have 30 days and which have 31 is the following rhyme:

Thirty days hath September
April, June, and November;
February has 28 alone,
All the rest have 31;
Excepting leap year—that's the time
When February's days are 29.

With this in mind, let's look at one of the most common credit terms and dating methods.

Ordinary Dating Method Discount

credit terms: the percent of discount, the allowable time limit for discount, and information about shipping costs that are listed on an invoice; also called **sales terms**.

One of the most common **credit terms** is stated as 2/10, n/30. This is read "two ten, net thirty." The 2/10 means a 2% discount may be taken if the bill is paid within 10 days of the invoice date. The n/30 means the net amount of the bill is due if the bill is paid after 11 days but within 30 days of the date on the invoice. After the 30th day the bill is overdue, and the buyer may have to pay interest charges.

If an invoice is dated January 4 with credit terms of 2/10, n/30 and is paid on or before January 14, then a 2% discount is allowed. The net amount of the bill is due if it is paid on January 15 or any day up to and including February 3. If the bill is paid on February 4 or any day after February 4, it is subject to interest charges.

To find the amount of the cash discount, multiply the net amount on the invoice by the percent stated in the sales terms. To find the discounted amount (the amount to be paid), subtract the cash discount from the net amount on the invoice. Another way to find the amount due is to multiply the net amount times the complement of the discount rate, as you did for trade discounts in the first part of this chapter.

EXAMPLE 5

Find the discount date and the due date for an invoice dated July 27 with terms 2/10, n/30.

July is a "knuckle" month, so it has 31 days. To find the number of days from July 27 to the end of the month, subtract.

31	days in July
− 27	date on invoice
4	days remaining in July

Next, subtract the 4 from the number of days in the discount.

10	days in the discount period
− 4	days in July
6th	day in August, the last day to pay and claim a discount

The same procedure is used to determine the due date for the invoice. There are 4 days remaining in July, so subtract to find the number of days in August before the bill is due.

30	days in the period to pay the bill
− 4	days in July
26th	day in August, the last day to pay the bill before it is past due

Another common credit term is 2/10, 1/15, n/30. These terms are read "two ten, one fifteen, net thirty." A 2% discount is allowed if the bill is paid within 10 days of the invoice date; a 1% discount is allowed if the bill is paid during the 11th through 15th days; and the net amount is due if the bill is paid during the 16th through 30th days of the invoice date.

A bill dated September 2 with sales terms 2/10, 1/15, n/30 receives a 2% discount if paid on or before September 12. A 1% discount is allowed if the bill is paid on September 13 or any day up to and including September 17. The net amount of the bill is due if it is paid on September 18 or any day up to and including October 2. If the bill is paid on October 3 or any day after October 3, it is subject to interest charges.

EXAMPLE 6

Sycamore Enterprises received a $1,248 bill for computer supplies, dated September 2, with sales terms 2/10, 1/15, n/30. A 5% penalty is charged for payment after 30 days. Find the amount due if the bill is paid (a) on or before September 12; (b) on or between September 13 and September 17; (c) on or between September 18 and October 2; and (d) on or after October 3.

(a) If the bill is paid on or before September 12 (within 10 days), the 2% discount applies:

$$\text{Discount} = \$1{,}248 \times 2\% = \$1{,}248 \times 0.02 = \$24.96$$

$$\text{Amount due} = \$1{,}248 - \$24.96 = \$1{,}223.04$$

(b) If the bill is paid on or between September 13 and September 17 (within 15 days), the 1% discount applies:

$$\text{Discount} = \$1{,}248 \times 1\% = \$1{,}248 \times 0.01 = \$12.48$$

$$\text{Amount due} = \$1{,}248 - \$12.48 = \$1{,}235.52$$

(c) If the bill is paid on or between September 18 and October 2 (within 30 days), the net amount of $1,248 is due.

(d) If the bill is paid on or after October 3, a 5% penalty is added:

$$\text{Amount of penalty} = \$1{,}248 \times 5\% = \$1{,}248 \times 0.05 = \$62.40$$

$$\text{Amount due} = \$1{,}248 + \$62.40 = \$1{,}310.40$$

Self-Check

5. Ms. Alvarez received an invoice dated March 9, with terms 2/10, n/30, amounting to $540. She paid the bill on March 12. How much was the cash discount? How much should Ms. Alvarez have paid?

6. How much would have to be paid on an invoice for $450 with terms 4/10, 1/15, n/30 if the bill is paid: (a) 7 days after the invoice date; (b) 15 days after the invoice date; (c) 25 days after the invoice date?

7. Maddy's Muffins received a bill for $648, dated April 6, with sales terms 2/10, 1/15, n/30. A 3% penalty is charged for payment after 30 days. Find the amount due if the bill is paid (a) on or before April 16; (b) on or between April 17 and April 21; (c) on or between April 22 and May 6; (d) on or after May 7.

End of Month (EOM) Discount

end-of-month (EOM) discount: sales terms that allow a percent discount if the bill is paid during a specified period after the first day of the month after the month in the invoice.

Sometimes the sales terms read 2/10 *EOM*, where EOM stands for **end of month**. These terms mean that a 2% discount is allowed if the bill is paid during the first 10 days of the month *after* the month in the date of the invoice.

Thus, if a bill is dated November 9, a 2% discount is allowed as long as the bill is paid on or before December 10.

EXAMPLE 7

Newman, Inc., received a bill dated September 17 for $5,000 with terms 2/10 EOM. The invoice was paid on October 9. How much did Newman, Inc., pay?

Since the bill was paid within the first 10 days of the month after the month on the invoice, a 2% discount was allowed. The complement of 2% is 98%.

$$\text{Amount due} = \$5{,}000 \times 98\% = \$5{,}000 \times 0.98 = \$4{,}900$$

The amount due on November 4 is $4,900.

An exception to this rule occurs when the invoice is dated *on or after the 26th of the month*. When this happens, the discount is allowed if the bill is paid during the first ten days of the *second month after* the month in the date on the invoice. Thus, if an invoice is dated May 28 with terms 2/10 EOM, a 2% discount is allowed as long as the bill is paid on or before July 10. This allows retailers adequate time to pay the invoice when merchandise is billed.

EXAMPLE 8

Ms. Riddle received a bill for $200 dated April 27. The sales terms on the invoice were 3/10 EOM. She paid the bill on June 2. How much did Ms. Riddle pay?

Since the bill was paid within the first 10 days of the second month after the month on the invoice, a 3% discount was allowed. The complement of 3% is 97%.

$$\text{Amount due} = \$200 \times 97\% = \$200 \times 0.97 = \$194$$

The amount due on June 2 is $194.

Receipt of Goods (ROG) Discount

receipt of goods (ROG) discount: sales terms in which the discount is determined from the day the goods are received instead of the invoice date.

Sometimes the sales terms are determined from the day the *goods are received* instead of the invoice date. When this is the case, the sales terms are written 1/10 *ROG*, where ROG stands for **receipt of goods**. The sales terms mean that a 1% discount is allowed on the bill if it is paid within 10 days of the receipt of goods.

If an invoice is dated September 6 but the goods do not arrive until the 14th and the sales terms are 2/15 ROG, then a 2% discount is allowed if the bill is paid on any date up to and including September 29. If no net period is given in the sales terms, it is understood to be 30 days from the receipt of goods.

EXAMPLE 9

An invoice for $400 is dated November 9 and has sales terms 2/10 ROG. The merchandise arrives November 13. (a) If the bill is paid on November 21, what is the amount due? (b) If the bill is paid on December 2, what is the amount due?

(a) Since the bill is being paid within 10 days of the receipt of goods, a 2% discount is allowed. The complement of 2% is 98%.

Amount due = $400 × 98% = $400 × 0.98 = $392

The amount due on November 21 is $392.

(b) No discount is allowed, since the bill is not being paid within 10 days of the receipt of goods. Thus, $400 is due.

TIPS & TRAPS
It is important to be able to distinguish types of payment terms as they appear on an invoice. For example, an invoice for $200 is dated September 28 but the merchandise arrives on October 15. The sales terms are 2/10 ROG but the account manager thinks this means the bill can be paid within 10 days of the second month after the month in the date of the invoice (EOM) and pays the bill with a 2% discount on November 5. Does the discount apply? No, since the bill should have been paid within 10 days of the receipt of the goods. That date is the 25th of October.

Partial Payments

A company sometimes cannot pay the full amount due in time to take advantage of discount credit terms. Most sellers allow buyers to make partial payments and take advantage of the discount terms if the partial payment is made within the time specified in the credit terms. When this happens the discount terms apply only to the partial payment, or the portion of the entire bill that is actually paid. The remaining balance of the bill is expected to be paid within the time specified by the credit terms. Some sellers penalize buyers for payments made after the date specified in the terms. This penalty is usually a percent of the unpaid balance.

To find how much the bill is reduced by a partial payment, divide the partial payment by the complement of the discount rate in decimal form. This tells us how much credit exists toward paying the total bill. It might help to think of the discount on a partial payment as giving credit for paying more than actually was paid.

Step by Step

Finding the Amount of Outstanding Balance After a Partial Payment

Step 1. Find the complement of the discount rate.

Step 2. Divide the partial payment by the complement of the discount rate.

Step 3. Subtract this amount from the total bill to get the outstanding balance.

EXAMPLE 10

Luther Semmes received an invoice for $875 with terms of 3/10, n/30 but could not pay the entire bill within 10 days, so he sent a check for $500. What amount was credited to his account?

$$\frac{\text{Partial payment}}{1 - 0.03} = \frac{\$500}{0.97} = \$515.46$$

Divide the amount of the partial payment by the complement of the discount rate to find the amount of credit.

$\$875 - \$515.46 = \$359.54$ Subtract the amount of credit from the total invoice to find the outstanding balance.

TIPS & TRAPS

Remember to find the *complement* of the discount rate and then divide the partial payment by this complement. Students sometimes just multiply the discount rate times the partial payment, which is wrong.

WRONG (crossed out)	CORRECT
From Example 11,	From Example 11,
$\$500 \times 0.03 = \$15$	$\dfrac{\$500}{0.97} = \$515.46$
$\$500 - \$15 = \$485$	
$\$875 - \$485 = \$390$	$\$875 - \$515.46 = \$359.54$

Freight Terms

The distribution of manufactured goods is handled by carriers (truck, rail, ship, plane, and the like). The cost of shipping may be paid by the buyer

Real World Application

TRADE DISCOUNTS

An important part of owning a business is the purchasing of equipment and supplies to run the office. Before paying an invoice, all items must be checked and amounts refigured before writing the check for payment. At this time the terms of the invoice can be applied. Using the information on the invoice below, fill in the extended amount for each line, the merchandise total, the tax amount, and the total invoice amount. Locate the terms of the invoice and find how much you would write a check for to pay Harper on each of the following dates:

March 5, 1989
March 12, 1989
March 25, 1989

INVOICE DATE	TERMS	DATE OF ORDER	ORDERED BY	PHONE NO.	REMIT TO ►
02/27/XX	2/10, 1/15, n/30	02/27/XX		803-000-4488	HARPER General Accounting Office

LINE NO.	MANUFACTURER PRODUCT NUMBER	QTY. ORD.	QTY. B.O.	QTY. SHP.	U/M	DESCRIPTION	UNIT PRICE		EXTENDED AMOUNT
001	REMYY370/02253	3	0	3	EA	TONER, F/ROYAL TA210 COP I	11.90		
002	Sk 1230M402	5	0	3	EA	CORRECTABLE FILM RIBBON	10.95		
003	JRLM01023	10	0	10	EA	COVER-UP CORRECTION TAPE	9.90		
004	rTu123456	9	0	9	EA	PAPER, BOND, WHITE, 8½ x 11	58.23		

DATE REC'D.	OUR ORDER NO.	MDSE. TOTAL	TAX RATE	TAX AMOUNT	FREIGHT AMOUNT	TOTAL INVOICE AMOUNT ►	
	01460900001		5.00		0.00		

or seller. If the freight is paid by the buyer, the term **FOB shipping point** is used. The term FOB shipping point means free on board at the shipping point. For example, CCC Industries located in Tulsa purchased parts from Rawhide in Chicago and Rawhide ships FOB Chicago. Then CCC Industries must pay the freight from Chicago to Tulsa. The terms of freight shipment are indicated on a document called a *bill of lading* that is attached to each shipment. This document includes a description of the merchandise, the number of pieces, weight, name of consignee, destination, and method of payment of freight charges. If the buyer is to pay the freight charges, the bill of lading is marked *freight collect*. The freight company then collects freight charges upon delivery of the goods.

FOB shipping point: stands for free on board shipping point, and means that the buyer of the goods pays freight costs.

If the freight is paid by the seller, the term **FOB destination** is often used. If Rawhide paid the freight in the preceding example, the term FOB Tulsa could also have been used. Most manufacturers will pay the shipping charge for shipments above some minimum dollar value. Some shipments of very small items may be marked *prepay and add.* This means the seller pays the shipping charge and adds it to the invoice, so the buyer pays the shipping charge to the seller rather than to the freight company. Cash discounts do *not* apply to freight or shipping charges. When cash discounts are calculated on such invoices the shipping charges are subtracted from the total before the net price is calculated. The shipping charges are then added back to the net price to get the total amount to be paid to the seller.

FOB destination: stands for free on board destination, and means that the seller of the goods pays freight costs.

Freight payment terms are usually specified on the *manufacturer's price list* so that purchasers clearly understand who is responsible for freight charges and under what circumstances. The invoice is usually marked *freight prepaid* if the seller is paying the freight charges. It is marked *prepay and add* if the seller initially pays the freight charges and then they are added to the invoice total. If the buyer is paying the shipping charges directly to the shipping company, the invoice makes no mention of shipping charges.

EXAMPLE 11

Calculate the cash discount and net amount paid for an order for $800 with sales terms of 3/10, 1/15, n/30 if the cost of shipping was $40 (which is included in the $800). The invoice was dated June 13, marked *freight prepay and add*, and paid June 24.

Cost of merchandise
= Total invoice − shipping fee
= $800 − $40 = $760

We apply the discount rate to *only* the cost of the merchandise.

Cash discount = $760 × 0.01 = $7.60

Net amount = $800 − $7.60 = $792.40

The bill was paid within 15 days, so the 1% discount applies.

Self-Check

8. Ed Rosicky received a bill for $800 dated July 5th, with sales terms of 2/10 EOM. He paid the bill on August 8th. How much did Ed pay?
9. An invoice for $900 is dated October 15 and has sales terms 2/10 ROG. The merchandise arrives October 21. (a) If the bill is paid on October 27, what is the amount due? (b) If the bill is paid on November 3, what is the amount due?
10. Delois Johnson could not pay the entire amount of a bill for $730 within the discount period, so she made a payment of $400. If the terms of the transaction were 3/10, n/30, find the amount credited to the account and find the outstanding balance due within thirty days of the invoice date.

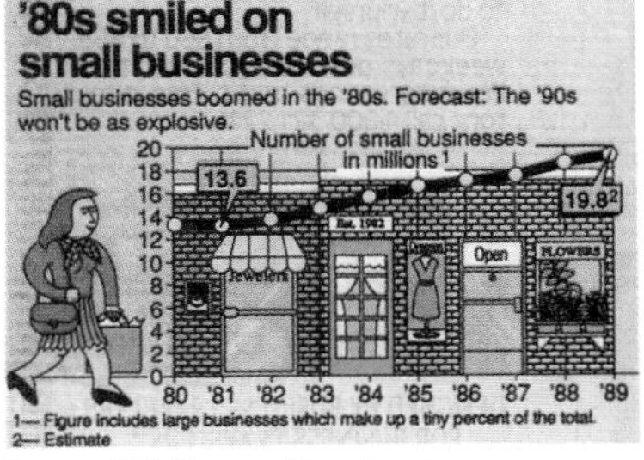

Source: U.S. Treasury Department
By Shelley Arps, USA TODAY

11. Lucy's Bicycle Shop received a shipment of bicycles from Wishh Company. The bill of lading was marked FOB destination. Who paid the freight?

Section Review

1. Mr. Matthews received a bill dated March 1 with sales terms 3/10, n/30. What percent discount will he receive if he pays the bill on March 5?

2. Ms. Wagner received a bill dated September 3 with sales terms 2/10, n/30. Did she receive a discount if she paid the bill on September 15?

3. An invoice dated February 13 had sales terms 2/10, n/30. The bill was paid February 19. Was a cash discount allowed?

4. Mr. Carruth received an invoice for $300 dated March 3 with sales terms 1/10, n/30. He paid the bill on March 6. What was his cash discount?

5. Find the cash discount on an invoice for $270 dated April 17 with terms 2/10, n/30 if the bill was paid April 22.

6. Find the cash discount on an invoice for $50 dated May 3 with terms 1/15, n/30 if the bill was paid May 14.

7. Mr. Collings received an invoice dated June 5 for $70 with terms 2/10, n/30. He paid the bill on June 9. What was his cash discount and how much did he pay?

8. Mrs. Randle received an invoice dated July 3 for $165 with terms 2/10, n/30. She paid the bill on July 7. How much did she pay?

9. How much would have to be paid on an invoice for $350 with terms 2/10, 1/15, n/30, if the bill is paid: (a) 7 days after the invoice date; (b) 15 days after the invoice date; (c) 25 days after the invoice date?

10. How much would have to be paid on an invoice for $28 with terms 3/10 EOM if the bill dated June 8 is paid: (a) July 2; (b) July 20?

11. Mr. Baldwin received an invoice for $650 dated January 26. The sales terms in the invoice were 2/10 EOM. He paid the bill on March 4. How much did Mr. Baldwin pay?

12. How much would have to be paid on an invoice for $328 with terms 2/10 ROG if the invoice is dated January 3, the merchandise arrives January 8, and the invoice is paid: (a) January 11; (b) January 15; (c) January 25?

13. Find the cash discount and net amount paid on an invoice dated August 19 if it is paid on August 25 and has terms 3/10, 1/15, n/30. The amount of the invoice is $826.

14. Leona Horne purchased a recliner for $624 with sales terms of 2/15, n/30. If she made a partial payment of $200 within 15 days, how much was credited to her account and what was her outstanding balance after the credit?

Summary

Topic	Page	What to Remember	Examples
Finding the amount of a single trade discount	230–231	Trade discount = list price × single discount rate	The list price is $76 and the trade discount is 25%. Find the amount of trade discount. $76 × 25% = $76 × 0.25 = $19
Finding the net price	230–231	Net price = list price − trade discount	Net price = $76 − $19 = $57

Topic	Page	What to Remember	Examples
Finding net price if list price and single discount rate are known	230–231	Use the *complement* of the decimal form of the discount rate. Net price = list price × (100% − single discount rate)	The list price is $480 and the trade discount is 15%. Find the net price. Net price = $480 × (1.00 − 0.15) = $480 × 0.85 = $408
Finding net price of an item with a series discount	234–236	Net price = list price × net decimal equivalent Multiply the complements of the decimal form of each discount to find the net decimal equivalent.	The list price is $960, and the discount series is 10/5/2. Find the net price. (1.00 − 0.1)(1.00 − 0.05)(1.00 − 0.02) = (0.9)(0.95)(0.98) = 0.8379 0.8379 × $960 = $804.38
Finding the amount of discount with the single discount equivalent	236	Amount of discount = list price × single discount equivalent Multiply the complements of the decimal forms of each discount to find the net decimal equivalent. Subtract the net decimal equivalent from 1 to find the decimal form of the single discount equivalent. Multiply the list price by the single discount equivalent to find the amount of discount.	The list price is $2,800 and the discount series is 25/15/10. Find the amount of discount. (1.00 − 0.25)(1.00 − 0.15)(1.00 − 0.1) = (0.75)(0.85)(0.9) = 0.57375 1 − 0.57375 = 0.42625 Amount of discount = $2,800 × 0.42625 = $1,193.50
Calculating due dates	239–240	Count from the *next day after* the date of the invoice, *or* add the number of days to the invoice date. If the invoice date and due date are in different months, subtract the number of days remaining in the first month from the total number of days to the due date. The number is the due date in the second month. Use the knuckle method to determine how many days are in each month: each knuckle represents a 31-day month, and each space between knuckles represents a 28-, 29-, or 30-day month.	By what date must an invoice dated July 10 be paid if it is due in 10 days? July 10 + 10 days = July 20. By what date must an invoice dated May 15 be paid if it is due in 30 days? May 31 − May 15 = 16 days remaining in the first month; 30 − 16 = 14. The due date is June 14.
Ordinary dating method discount	240	Sales terms 2/10, n/30, mean the buyer takes a 2% discount within 10 days of the invoice date but pays the net amount after 10 days and within 30 days of the invoice date.	What are the discount date and the due date of a $2,500 invoice dated July 17 with terms 2/10, n/30? How much money would be due on each date? *Discount date:* July 17 + 10 days = July 27 Amount due on or before discount date = $2,500 × (1.00 − 0.02) = $2,500 × 0.98 = $2,450 *Due date:* July 31 – July 17 = 14 days remaining in the first month 30 − 14 = 16, so the net amount, $2,500, is due on or before August 16.

Topic	Page	What to Remember	Example
End of month (EOM) discount	241–242	Sales terms 2/10 EOM mean that a 2% discount is allowed if the bill is paid during the first 10 days of the month *after* the month in the invoice date.	To take the discount, by what date would Smith, Inc. have to pay a bill for \$880 dated November 5 with terms 2/10 EOM? How much would Smith, Inc. pay? Discount date = December 10 Amount due on or before December 10 = \$880 × (1.00 − 0.02) = \$880 × 0.98 = \$862.40
Receipt of goods (ROG) discount	242–243	Sales terms 1/10 ROG mean that a 1% discount is allowed on the bill if it is paid within 10 days of the receipt of the goods.	How much would have to be paid on an invoice for \$500 with terms 1/10 ROG if the merchandise arrives April 2 and is paid on April 8? \$500 (0.01) = \$5 cash discount \$500 − \$5 = \$495 amount paid
Partial payments	243–244	Discount terms may be applied to partial payments made within the time specified. To find the amount of outstanding balance after a partial payment has been made with a discount: Divide the partial payment by the complement of the discount rate, then subtract this amount from the total bill.	Jaime Estrada purchased carpet for \$1,568 with sales terms of 3/10, n/30. He paid \$1,000 on the bill within the 10 days specified. How much was credited to his account and what was his outstanding balance after the payment? \$1,000 ÷ 0.97 = \$1,030.93 credited to account \$1,568 − \$1,030.93 = \$537.03 balance due
Freight terms: FOB shipping point FOB destination	244–245	FOB shipping point means the buyer pays freight costs. FOB destination means the seller pays freight costs.	A shipment is sent from a manufacturer in Boston to a wholesaler in Dallas and marked FOB destination. Who pays the freight cost? The manufacturer in Boston pays, since FOB destination means the seller pays freight costs.

Chapter Review

1. What do the initials ROG represent? EOM?

2. What is the complement of 20%?

3. The list price of a filing cabinet is $225. The trade discount is $36.50. What is the net price?

4. Find the single discount equivalent for the discount series 20/15/10.

5. Find the net decimal equivalent of the series 20/10/10.

6. The list price of a couch is $700. The retailer can buy the couch at the list price minus 20%. Find the trade discount.

7. An invoice for $500 dated March 7 has sales terms 2/10 ROG. The merchandise arrived March 11. If the bill was paid on March 18, what was the amount due?

8. In Problem 7, if the bill was paid on April 3, what was the amount due?

9. Megan Love purchased tires for $392 with terms of 2/10, n/30. She elected to pay $200 on the account during the first 10 days. How much was actually credited to her account? What was her outstanding balance after the payment?

10. A retailer buys 20 lamps at $40 each and 30 pictures at $50 each. Find the trade discount if the discount for the order is 15%.

11. A retailer can buy a card table listed for $25 for 20% less than the list price. How much does the retailer have to pay for the table?

12. Computalk, Inc., received a bill for $10,000 on May 27. The sales terms on the invoice were 2/10 EOM. If the bill was paid on June 3, how much was paid?

13. A manufacturer lists a lawn mower at $67.95 with a trade discount of $6.50. Another manufacturer lists the same lawn mower at $66.95 with a trade discount of $5.75. Which is the better deal?

14. Mr. Bryan received a bill dated May 1 with sales terms 3/10, 1/15, n/30. What percent discount will he receive if he pays the bill on May 6?

15. A trade discount series of 10/10 is offered on 20 digital watches that are listed at $110 each. Also, a trade discount series of 10/20 is offered on 10 signet rings that are listed at $40 each. Find the total net price for the watches and rings.

16. Mr. Jackson received an invoice for $400 dated June 6 with sales terms 2/10, n/30. He paid the bill on June 9. What was his cash discount?

17. One manufacturer lists a microwave oven for $600 less 20%. Another manufacturer lists the same microwave oven for $590 less 18%. Which manufacturer is offering the better deal?

18. Find the net price if a discount series of 10/10/5 is deducted from $80.

19. A retailer buys 30 blankets listed at $35 each for 10% less than the list price. How much does the retailer have to pay for the blankets?

20. One manufacturer lists smoke detectors at $50 less 10/10. Another manufacturer lists the same smoke detectors at $51 less 10/10/5. Which is the better deal?

Trial Test

1. The list price of a refrigerator is $550. The retailer can buy the refrigerator at the list price minus 20%. Find the trade discount.

2. The list price of a television is $560. The trade discount is $27.50. What is the net price?

3. A retailer can buy a lamp that is listed at $36.55 for 20% less than the list price. How much does the retailer have to pay for the lamp?

4. A manufacturer lists a dress at $39.75 with a trade discount of $3.60. Another manufacturer lists the same dress at $42 with a trade discount of $6.75. Which is the better deal?

5. One manufacturer lists a chair for $250 less 20%. Another manufacturer lists the same chair at $240 less 10%. Which manufacturer is offering the better deal?

6. Find the net price if a discount series of 20/10/5 is deducted from $70.

7. Find the net decimal equivalent of the series 20/10/5.

8. Find the single discount equivalent for the discount series 20/20/10.

9. What do the initials ROG represent?

10. A retailer buys 20 boxes of stationery at $4 each and 400 greeting cards at $0.50 each. The discount rate for the order is 15%. Find the trade discount.

11. A retailer buys 30 electric frying pans listed at $40 each, for 10% less than the list price. How much does the retailer have to pay for the frying pans?

12. What is the complement of 15%?

13. What do the initials EOM represent?

14. Ms. Ryan received a bill dated September 1 with sales terms 3/10, 1/15, n/30. What percent discount will she receive if she pays the bill on September 6?

15. Mr. Williams received an invoice for $200 dated March 6 with sales terms 1/10, n/30. He paid the bill on March 9. What was his cash discount?

16. Mrs. Montgomery received a bill for $300 dated April 7. The sales terms on the invoice were 2/10 EOM. If she paid the bill on May 2, how much did Mrs. Montgomery pay?

17. An invoice for $400 dated December 7 has sales terms 2/10 ROG. The merchandise arrived December 11. If the bill is paid on December 18, what is the amount due?

18. If the bill in Problem 17 is paid on January 2, what is the amount due?

19. A trade discount series of 10% and 20% is offered on 20 dartboards that are listed at $14 each. Also, a trade discount series of 20% and 10% is offered on 10 bowling balls that are listed at $40 each. Find the total net price for the dartboards and bowling balls.

20. One manufacturer lists artificial flower arrangements at $30 less 10% and 10%. Another manufacturer lists the same flower arrangements at $31 less 10%, 10%, and 5%. Which is the better deal?

21. The Dean Specialty Company purchased monogrammed items worth \$895 and made a partial payment of \$600 on day 12. If the sales terms were 3/15, n/30, how much was credited to the account? What was the outstanding balance?

Self-Check Solutions

1.

	Total Price
	\$22.50
	8.90
	23.70
Total list price	55.10
40% trade discount	−22.04
	\$33.06

Complements method

$1 - 0.4 = 0.6$

$0.6 \times \$55.10 = \$33.06$

2. $100\% - 12\% = 88\%$, and $88\% = 0.88$
$100\% - 10\% = 90\%$, and $90\% = 0.9$
$100\% - 8\% = 92\%$, and $92\% = 0.92$

$0.88(0.9)(0.92) = 0.72864$

$\$800 \times 0.72864 = \$582.91$ net price

3. $100\% - 25\% = 75\%$, and $75\% = 0.75$
$100\% - 15\% = 85\%$, and $85\% = 0.85$
$100\% - 10\% = 90\%$, and $90\% = 0.9$

$0.75(0.85)(0.9) = 0.57375$

$1 - 0.57375 = 0.42625$ single discount equivalent

$\$2{,}200 \times 0.42625 = \$937.75$ trade discount

4. $100\% - 15\% = 85\%$, and $85\% = 0.85$
$100\% - 12\% = 88\%$, and $88\% = 0.88$
$100\% - 5\% = 95\%$, and $95\% = 0.95$

$\$460 \times 0.85(0.88)(0.95) = 326.876 = \$326.88$ net price

$100\% - 10\% = 90\%$ and $90\% = 0.9$
$100\% - 10\% = 90\%$ and $90\% = 0.9$
$100\% - 50\% = 50\%$ and $50\% = 0.5$

$\$380 \times 0.9(0.9)(0.5) = \$153.90$ net price

The \$380 printer is a better deal.

5. $\$540(0.02) = \$10.80$ cash discount
$\$540 - \$10.80 = \$529.20$ amount to pay

6. a. $\$450(0.04) = \$18$ cash discount
$\$450 - \$18 = \$432$ amount to pay

b. $450(0.01) = $4.50 cash discount
$450 − $4.50 = $445.50 amount to pay
c. $450 due (no discount)

7. a. $648(0.02) = $12.96 cash discount
$648 − $12.96 = $635.04 amount due
b. $648(0.01) = $6.48 cash discount
$648 − $6.48 = $641.52 amount due
c. $648 due (no discount)
d. $648(0.03) = $19.44 penalty
$648 + $19.44 = $667.44 due

8. $800(0.02) = $16 cash discount
$800 − $16 = $784 amount paid

9. a. $900(0.02) = $18 cash discount
$900 − $18 = $882 amount due
b. $900 due (no discount)

10. $400 ÷ 0.97 = $412.37 amount credited
$730 − $412.37 = $317.63 outstanding balance due

11. Wishh Company paid the freight.

Markup and Markdown 9

Learning Objectives

1. Solve for cost, markup amount, markup percent, and selling price when markup is based on cost. (pp. 257–259)
2. Solve for cost, markup amount, markup percent, and selling price when markup is based on selling price. (pp. 259–262)
3. Compare two types of markup. (pp. 262–263)
4. Calculate amount and percent of markdown. (pp. 271–273)
5. Find the final selling price after an item has been marked up and marked down several times. (pp. 273–74)
6. Determine the price of perishable and seasonal merchandise. (p. 274–275)

Any successful business must keep prices low enough to attract customers, yet high enough to pay expenses and make a profit. A businessperson bases pricing decisions on a number of different factors. Let's look at some of these factors before examining the mathematics of the business of buying and selling.

Selling price The price of the merchandise on the retail market is the *selling price*.

Cost The price paid to the supplier of the merchandise is the *cost*.

Markup The difference between the cost and selling price is the *markup*. This must be enough to pay expenses and make a profit. Markup is sometimes called *gross profit*, or *margin*.

Operating expenses The cost of running a business operation makes up the *operating expenses*. Expenses such as wages, salaries, rent, utilities, advertising, and insurance are considered operating expenses.

Net profit The amount that remains after the cost of merchandise and operating expenses have been paid is *net profit*.

Net loss If the cost of merchandise and operating expenses together are more than the markup or gross profit for a given period, the difference is called the *net loss*.

Markdown The amount that merchandise has been reduced is the *markdown*.

Reduced price The price to which merchandise is reduced is called the *reduced price*.

Markup

Markup is most often shown as a percentage of either the cost or the selling price of an item. In calculating the percent of markup on merchandise, most manufacturers use the method of markup on *cost*, since they typically keep their records in terms of cost. Some wholesalers and a few retailers use this method. Most retailers, however, use the *selling price* as a base to compute percent of markup, since they keep most of their records in terms of selling price.

Markup Based on Cost

You can use a simple formula to describe the relationship between cost, markup, and selling price, regardless of whether the markup is based on cost or selling price.

Step by Step

Finding Selling Price, Cost, and Markup

1. To find selling price, we use this formula:

   Selling price = cost + markup $\quad S = C + M$

2. To find cost, we use a variation of the formula:

   Cost = selling price − markup $\quad C = S - M$

3. To find markup, we use another variation:

   Markup = selling price − cost $\quad M = S - C$

Source: U.S. Department of Labor
By LeRoy Lottmann, USA TODAY

You can use this formula and its variations to find the value of any one of the three elements if you know the values of the other two. Markup can be either a dollar amount or a percent. When it is expressed as a percent, it is expressed as a percent of cost or selling price.

Finding the Percent of Markup Based on Cost. Most markup problems give you two out of the three elements and ask you to find the third. There is a handy table you can draw to organize the information you have and determine what you need to find out. The table is set up with cost (*C*) and markup (*M*) on top and selling price (*S*) on the bottom, like this:

100%	C	\$
%	M	\$
%	S	\$

To complete the table, place percents on the left and dollar amounts on the right.

This section shows how to calculate the percent of markup based on cost. When markup is based on cost, cost is always 100%, as noted in the table. The rest of the numbers, both percents and dollars, can be filled in according to the problem, as shown in the first example.

EXAMPLE 1

Kim buys hats from a distributor for \$3 each and sells them for \$5 each. Find the amount of markup and the percent of markup based on cost.

First we find the amount of markup by using this formula: $M = S - C$. Use a table to set up the problem.

100%	C	\$3
	M	
	S	\$5

Remember, when doing a markup based on cost, cost is always 100%. Fill in the other two numbers you know from the problem: cost = \$3 and selling price = \$5.

Amount of markup = selling price − cost $\qquad$ The amount of markup is \$2.

Next use the percentage formula to find the *percent* of markup. Remember, Chapter 6 indicated that the percentage formula may be written $P = R \times B$, $R = \frac{P}{B}$, or $B = \frac{P}{R}$. When finding markup based on cost, use the cost as the *base*, the amount of markup as the *portion*, and the percent of markup as the *rate*. The percentage formula diagram is shown here in the margin.

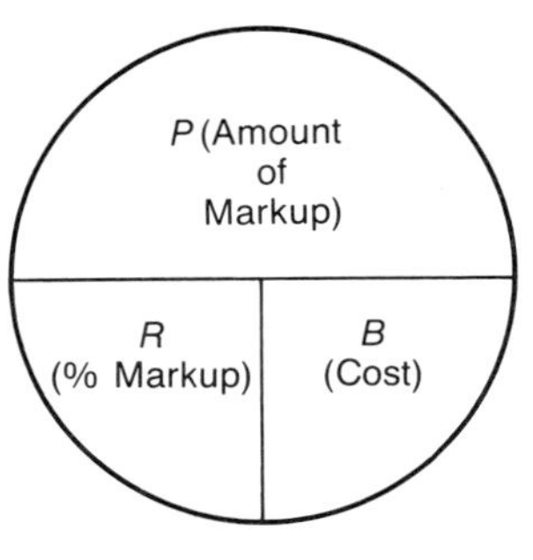

Use the form $R = \frac{P}{B}$ of the percentage formula to find the percent of markup based on the cost.

$R = \frac{P}{B} = \frac{2}{3}$ — Divide the amount of markup (portion) by the cost (the base) to find the percent of markup (the rate).

$= 0.6666$, or 67% (rounded) — The rate of markup based on cost is 67%.

Look back at the table: Cost plus markup equals selling price for both percents and dollar amounts.

100%	*C*	\$3
67%	*M*	\$2
167%	*S*	\$5

Check:
$167\% \times 3 = 1.67 \times 3$
$= \$5$ (rounded) — The answer is correct.

FINDING THE AMOUNT OF MARKUP AND SELLING PRICE BASED ON COST. In some instances you may know the cost and the markup percent based on cost and need to find the amount of markup and the selling price. You can compute these amounts more easily if you use the table format.

EXAMPLE 2

A boutique pays \$5 a pair for handmade earrings and sells them at a 50% markup based on cost. Find the amount of markup and the selling price of the earrings.

Selling price = cost + amount of markup

	100%	*C*	\$5 (base)
(rate) +	50%	*M*	(portion)
	150%	*S*	

The markup is based on cost, so we know the cost is the base, or 100%. We add the cost percent (100) and the markup percent (50) to find the selling price percent.

Use the percentage formula $P = R \times B$ to find the amount of markup:

$P = 0.50(5)$
$= 2.50$ — Multiply the markup percent (rate) times the cost (base) to find the amount of markup.

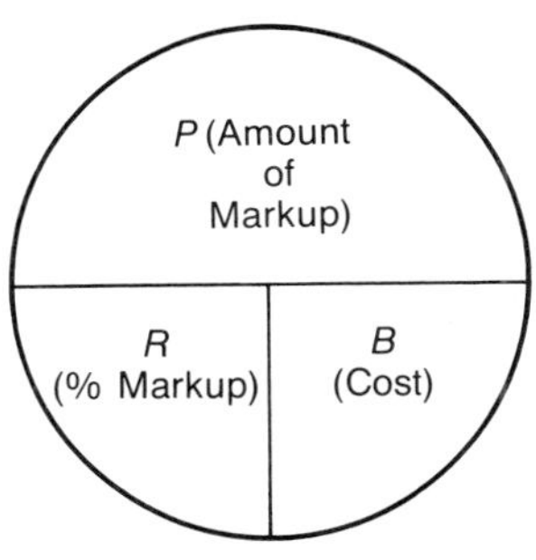

Now we can finish the calculation and complete the table:

	100%	*C*	\$5
+	50%	*M*	\$2.50
	150%	*S*	\$7.50

The selling price is \$7.50.

Check:
$150\% \times 5 = 1.5 \times 5 = \$7.50$ — The answer is correct.

EXAMPLE 3

A camera sells for \$20. The markup is 50% of the cost. Find the cost of the camera and the amount of markup.

Selling price = cost + amount of markup

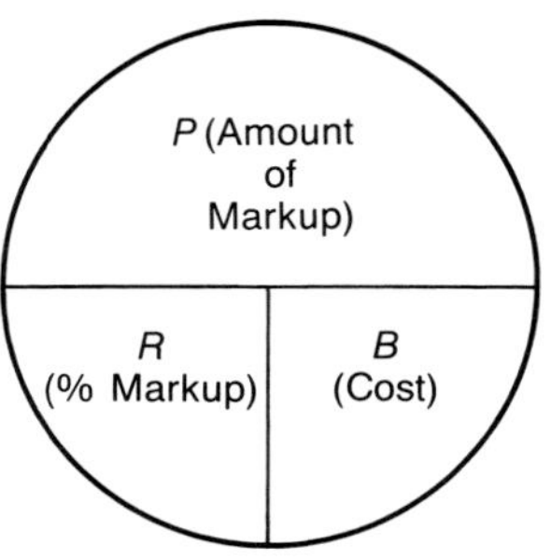

100%	C	
+ 50%	M	
150%	S	\$20

The markup is based on cost, so we know the cost is the base, or 100%. We add the cost percent (100) and the markup percent (50) to find the selling price percent.

In this example, you must use 150% and \$20 to find the cost (base). Thus, 150% of the cost equals \$20. Since you are looking for the base, you use the formula $B = \frac{P}{R}$.

$B = \frac{P}{R} = \frac{20}{1.5} =$ \$13.33, rounded to the nearest cent

Thus, the cost is \$13.33. To find the amount of markup, subtract: \$20 − 13.33 = \$6.67. Complete the table as a check:

100%	C	\$13.33
+ 50%	M	\$ 6.67
150%	S	\$20.00

Check:
150% × 13.33 = 1.5 × 13.33 = \$20 (rounded)

Self-Check

1. Bess buys mugs from a distributor for \$2 each and sells them for \$6 each. Find the amount of markup and the percent of markup based on the cost.
2. A boutique pays \$4 each for handmade belts and sells them at a 60% markup based on cost. Find the amount of markup and the selling price of the belts.
3. A compact disc player sells for \$300. The markup is 40% of the cost. Find the cost of the CD player and the markup.

Markup Based on Selling Price

As noted earlier, most retailers base markup on the selling price because this method works best with their other records. Each problem in this section will specify whether the markup is based on cost or selling price. Remember, if the markup is based on *cost*, then the *cost* is the *base* and represents 100%. If the markup is based on *selling price*, then the *selling price* is the *base* and represents 100%.

EXAMPLE 4

An item costs \$5 and sells for \$10. Find the percent of markup based on the selling price.

Amount of markup = selling price − cost

	C	\$ 5
+	M	
100%	S	\$10

The markup is based on selling price, so you know the selling price is the base, or 100%.

\$10
− \$ 5
\$ 5

Subtract the cost from the selling price to find the amount of markup.

The amount of markup, \$5, is the portion, and you know that the selling price, \$10, is the base. Use the formula $R = \frac{P}{B}$ to find the rate:

$R = \frac{P}{B} = \frac{5}{10} = 0.5 = 50\%$ — The percent of markup based on selling price is 50%.

Complete the table as a check of your work. To complete the table, you still need the percent that represents the cost.

	50%	C	\$ 5
+	50%	M	\$ 5
	100%	S	\$10

Subtract the markup percent from the selling price percent to find the cost percent (100% − 50% = 50%), completing the table.

Check:
50% × 10 = 0.5 × 10 = \$5 — The answer is correct.

EXAMPLE 5

Find the cost and selling price if an item is marked up \$5 with a 20% markup based on the selling price. (If the selling price percent is 100% and the markup is 20%, then the cost percent equals 100% − 20%, or 80%.)

Selling price = cost + amount of markup

80%	C	
20%	M	\$5
100%	S	

The markup is based on selling price, so the selling price is the base, or 100%.

Use the formula $B = \frac{P}{R}$ to find the base or selling price. The portion is \$5 and the rate is 20%, or 0.2.

$B = \frac{P}{R} = \frac{\$5}{0.2} = \$25$ — The base or selling price is \$25.

80%	C	\$20
20%	M	\$ 5
100%	S	\$25

Complete the table.

Check:
80% × 25 = 0.8 × 25 = \$20 — The answer is correct.

EXAMPLE 6

Find the markup and cost of an item that sells for \$2.99 and is marked up 25% of the selling price.

Selling price = cost + amount of markup

75%	C	
25%	M	
100%	S	\$2.99

The markup is based on selling price, so the selling price is the base, or 100%.

Since you are looking for the markup, or portion, use the basic formula $P = RB$. The selling price, or base, is \$2.99, and the rate is 25%.

$P = RB$
$= 0.25(2.99)$
$= \$0.75$ (rounded to the nearest cent)

Multiply the rate times the base (selling price) to find the portion (markup).

75%	C	\$2.24
25%	M	\$0.75
100%	S	\$2.99

Complete the table.

Check:

$75\% \times 2.99 = 0.75 \times 2.99$

$= \$2.24$ (rounded) The answer is correct.

EXAMPLE 7

Find the selling price and amount of markup if the item costs \$28 and is marked up 30% of the selling price.

$100\% - 30\% = 70\%$ Selling price percent minus markup percent equals cost percent.

Selling price = cost + amount of markup

70%	C	\$28
30%	M	
100%	S	

Markup is based on selling price, so the selling price is the base, or 100%.

You do not know the markup, so you cannot use the amount of markup to find the selling price. You do know the cost is \$28, which is 70% of the selling price. Use the formula $B = \frac{P}{R}$ to find the selling price, or base.

$B = \frac{P}{R} = \frac{\$28}{0.7} = \$40$ Divide the portion (cost) by the rate to find the base (selling price).

70%	C	\$28
30%	M	\$12
100%	S	\$40

(\$40 − \$28 = \$12)

Check:

$30\% \times 40 = 0.30 \times 40 = \$12$ The answer is correct.

All problems of this type are solved in basically the same way. The important thing to remember is that when the markup percent is based on the selling price, the selling price is the base and represents 100%; when the markup percent is based on the cost, the cost is the base and represents 100%. You can then use the percentage formula or one of its variations, substitute in the two known values, and solve for the third value.

Comparing Two Types of Markup

If you go into a store and are told that the markup percent is 25%, you don't know whether that means markup based on cost or on selling price. What's the difference? Let's use a new computer as an example. The store pays \$600 for it and sells it for \$800. Here is the difference in percent of markup:

$$\frac{\$200 \text{ markup}}{\$800 \text{ selling price}} = 25\% \text{ markup based on selling price}$$

$$\frac{\$200 \text{ markup}}{\$600 \text{ cost}} = 33\frac{1}{3}\% \text{ markup based on cost}$$

There may be times when you need to switch from a markup based on cost to a markup based on selling price, or vice versa. Here is how to do it.

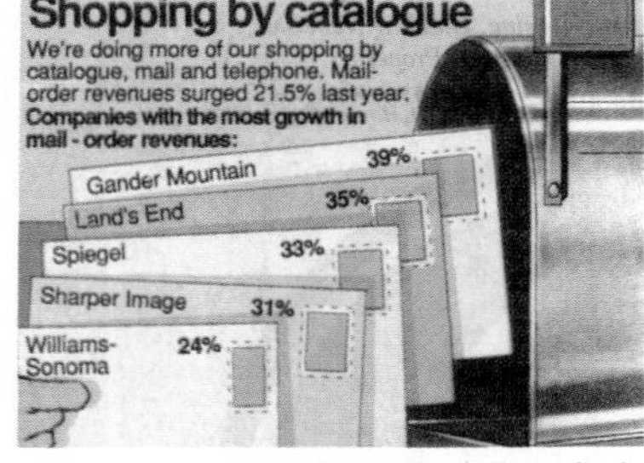

Source: Maxwell Sroge Co., mail-order consultant
By Suzy Parker, USA TODAY

Step by Step

Converting from Markup Percent Based on Selling Price to Markup Percent Based on Cost

Step 1. Find the percent of markup based on selling price.

Step 2. Use the following formula:

$$\frac{\text{Markup percent based on selling price (decimal form)}}{1 - \text{markup percent of selling price (decimal form)}}$$
$$= \text{markup percent (decimal form) based on cost}$$

EXAMPLE 8

A desk is marked up 50% based on selling price. What is the equivalent percent based on the cost?

$50\% = 0.5$ — Convert the percent to a decimal and put it in the formula.

$$\frac{\text{Markup percent based on selling price}}{1 - \text{markup percent of selling price}} = \text{markup percent based on cost}$$

$$\frac{0.5}{1 - 0.5} = \frac{0.5}{0.5} = 1, \text{ or } 100\%$$

The markup based on cost is 100%.

Step by Step

Converting from Markup Percent Based on Cost to Markup Percent Based on Selling Price

Step 1. Find the percent of markup based on cost.

Step 2. Use the following formula:

$$\frac{\text{Markup percent based on cost (decimal form)}}{1 + \text{markup percent based on cost (decimal form)}}$$
$$= \text{markup percent (decimal form) based on selling price}$$

EXAMPLE 9

A computer is marked up 40% based on cost. What is the markup percent based on selling price?

$40\% = 0.4$ — Convert the percent to a decimal and use the formula.

$$\frac{\text{Markup percent based on cost}}{1 + \text{markup percent based on cost}} = \text{markup percent based on selling price}$$

$$\frac{0.4}{1 + 0.4} = \frac{0.4}{1.4}$$
$$= 0.2857, \text{ or } 29\%$$

The markup based on selling price is 29%.

Self-Check

4. A box of cassette tapes costs \$4 and sells for \$12. Find the percent of markup based on the selling price.

5. Find the cost and selling price if an item is marked up $5 with a 40% markup based on the selling price.
6. Find the markup and cost of a magazine that sells for $3.50 and is marked up 50% of the selling price.
7. Find the selling price and amount of markup if a box of photocopier paper costs $40 and is marked up 60% of the selling price.
8. A chair is marked up 60% based on selling price. What is the percent of markup based on cost?
9. A lamp is marked up 120% based on cost. What is the percent of markup based on the selling price?

Section Review

In each of the following, find the missing numbers in the table if the markup is based on the cost.

1.

100%	C	$50
50%	M	$25
	S	

2.

	C	$4
25%	M	$1
	S	

3.

100%	C	$41
100%	M	
	S	

4.

	C	$25
	M	
	S	$30

In each of the following, find the missing numbers in the table if the markup is based on the selling price.

5.

42%	C	\$38
	M	
100%	S	

6.

	C	\$86
50%	M	
	S	

7.

	C	
15%	M	\$8
	S	

8.

42%	C	\$16
	M	
	S	

Solve the following problems. Be careful to notice whether markup is based on the cost or the selling price.

9. An item costs $15 and is marked up 40%. Find the markup and selling price based on the cost.

10. An item costs $3 and is marked up 40%. Find the markup and selling price based on the cost.

11. An item is marked up $9 and sells for $45. Find the cost and markup percent if the markup is based on the cost.

12. An item costs $12 and is marked up $7.20. Find the selling price and percent of markup based on the cost.

13. An item sells for $198.50 and costs $158.70. Find the markup and markup percent based on the cost. Round to the nearest tenth percent.

14. Find the cost and markup on an item if the selling price is $75 and this item is marked up 100% of the cost.

15. If an article is marked up $12, which is 50% of the cost, find the cost and selling price.

16. An item sells for $28.70 and has a markup of 50% based on the selling price. Find the amount of markup and the cost.

17. An item is marked up $15.30, which is 30% of the selling price. Find the cost and selling price of the item.

18. An item costs \$4.60 and is marked up \$3.07. Find the selling price and the percent of markup based on the selling price. Round percents to the nearest hundredth.

19. An item costs \$40 and sells for \$58.50. Find the percent of markup based on selling price and the amount of markup. Round percents to the nearest hundredth.

20. An item sells for \$15. Its cost is \$10. Find the percent of markup based on the selling price.

21. An item sells for \$35, which includes a markup of 60% of the selling price. Find the cost and amount of markup.

Fill in the blanks in Exercises 22–33. Round percents to the nearest hundredth percent.

	Cost	Markup	Selling Price	Markup Percent Based on Cost	Markup Percent Based on Selling Price
22.	$ 38	$ 20	_____	_____	_____
23.	___	$ 32	$ 89	_____	_____
24.	$486	_____	_____	_____	30%
25.	$ 1.56	_____	$ 2	_____	—
26.	_____	$ 5.89	_____	15%	_____
27.	_____	$ 27.38	_____	40%	_____
28.	$ 25	_____	_____	_____	48%
29.	_____	_____	$124	150%	—
30.	_____	$ 28	_____	_____	27%
31.	_____	_____	$ 18.95	_____	15%
32.	$ 16.28	$ 15.92	_____	_____	_____
33.	$ 8.99	_____	_____	21%	_____

Room has been left below and on the next page for your worked-out solutions to Exercises 22–33.

22.

23.

24.

25.

26.

27.

28.

29.

30.

31.

32.

33.

Markdown

Merchants often have to reduce the price of merchandise from the price at which it was originally marked. There are many reasons for this: Sometimes merchandise is marked too high to begin with; sometimes it gets worn or dirty or goes out of style; flowers, fruits, vegetables, and baked goods that have been around a day or two must be sold for less than fresh items; and competition from other stores may require that a retailer lower prices.

Calculating Markdowns

No matter what the reason for the reduction in price, you can determine the amount of markdown by subtracting the sale price from the original selling price. You can then figure the percent of markdown by using a variation of the percentage formula, $R = \frac{P}{B}$.

Step by Step

Calculating Amount of Markdown and Percent of Markdown

Step 1. Amount of markdown can be found with this formula:

Amount of markdown = original selling price − sale price

Step 2. Percent of markdown can then be found with the percentage formula:

$R = \frac{P}{B}$, where R = percent of markdown, B = original selling price, and P = amount of markdown

EXAMPLE 10

A lamp originally sold for $36 and was marked down to sell for $30. Find the *amount of markdown* and the *markdown percent.*

Markdown = original selling price − sale price

= $36 − $30 = $6 The amount of markdown was $6.

To find the markdown percent, use $36 (original price) as the base (B) and $6 (amount of markdown) as the portion (P). Use the formula $R = \frac{P}{B}$.

$$R = \frac{P}{B}$$

$$= \frac{\text{amount of markdown}}{\text{original selling price}}$$

$$= \frac{\$6}{\$36} = .1666$$

$$= 16.67\%$$

Divide the amount of markdown by the original selling price and change the decimal to a percent.

The lamp was marked down 16.67%.

If you know the original price of an item and the markdown percent, you can determine the amount of markdown and subtract this amount from the original price to get the sale price.

Sale price = original selling price − markdown

EXAMPLE 11

An item was originally priced at $12 and was reduced by 25%. Find the amount of markdown and the sale price.
Use the percentage formula $P = RB$ to find the amount of markdown. The original price is the base.

$P = 25\% \times \$12 = 0.25 \times \$12$ — The original price, $12, is the base, and the rate is 25%.

$= \$3$ — The amount of markdown is $3.

To find the sale price, use the markdown formula:

Sale price = original selling price − markdown

$\$12 - \$3 = \$9$
The sale price is $9.

Self-Check

10. A typewriter originally sold for $480 and was marked down to sell for $420. Find the amount of markdown and the markdown percent.

11. A calculator that was originally priced at $78 was reduced by 15%. Find the amount of markdown and the sale price (reduced price).

Markup and Markdown in the Marketplace

Calculating a Series of Markdowns and Markups

Every business expects to mark down the price of seasonal and slow-moving merchandise. Sometimes prices are marked down several times or marked up between markdowns before the merchandise is sold. The percent of each markdown is based on the *previous selling price.*

EXAMPLE 12

Stanley's China Shop paid a wholesale price of $600 for a set of imported china. Stanley marked up the china 50% on the selling price on August 8. On October 1, the china was marked down 25% for a special 10-day promotion. On October 11, the china was marked up 15%. The china was again marked down 30% for a preholiday sale. Because it still had not sold, it was marked down an additional 10% after the holidays. What was the final selling price of the china?

Original selling price

Selling price = cost + markup — Find the original selling price.
$C = \$600,\ M = 0.5S$ — Markup was 50% of the selling price.

$$\begin{aligned} S &= 600 + 0.5S \\ 1.0S &= 600 + 0.5S \\ -0.5S & \quad\quad - 0.5S \\ \hline 0.5S &= 600 \end{aligned}$$

Subtract 0.5S from each side of the equation.

$$\frac{0.5S}{0.5} = \frac{600}{0.5}$$

Divide each side of the equation by 0.5.

$$S = \frac{600}{0.5} = \$1{,}200$$

The original selling price was $1,200.

25% markdown on October 1

100% (original selling price) − 25% (markdown) = 75% (new selling price)

$1{,}200 \times 75\% = 1{,}200 \times 0.75 = \$900$ — The selling price from October 1 through October 10 is 75% of the original price.

15% markup on October 11

100% (previous selling price) + 15% (markup) = 115% (new selling price)

900 × 115% = 900 × 1.15 = \$1,035 — The selling price on October 11 is 115% of the previous price (October 1–10).

30% markdown for preholiday sale

100% (previous selling price) − 30% (markdown) = 70% (new selling price)

1,035 × 70% = 1,035 × 0.70 = \$724.50 — The selling price for the preholiday sale is 70% of the previous (October 11) price.

Final markdown

100% − 10% = 90%
724.50 × 90% = 724.50 × 0.90 = \$652.05. — The china was finally priced at \$652.05.

How Much Should Perishable or Seasonal Items Be Marked Up?

Most businesses anticipate that some merchandise will have to be marked down from the original selling price. Most retail stores mark down seasonal merchandise such as holiday items to 50% of the original price. Most of these markdowns are made the day after the holiday.

Stores that sell perishable or strictly seasonal items (fresh fruits, vegetables, swimsuits, or coats, for example) usually anticipate from past experience how much merchandise will have to be marked down or thrown out due to spoilage. The original markup of such an item is set to obtain the desired profit level based on the projected number of items sold at "full price" (the original selling price).

EXAMPLE 13

Fast Stop Grocery specializes in fresh fruits and vegetables. A portion of most merchandise must be reduced for quick sale, and some must be thrown out because of spoilage. Harry Tate, the manager, must mark the selling price of incoming produce high enough to make the desired amount of profit while taking expected markdowns and spoilage into account. Harry receives 400 pounds of bananas, for which he pays \$0.15 per pound. On the average, 8% of the bananas will spoil. Find the selling price per pound to obtain a 175% markup on cost.

400 × 0.15 = \$60 — Figure the cost of the bananas to Harry.
\$60 × 1.75 = \$105 — Figure the dollar amount of markup.
$S = C + M$ — Figure the total selling price.
= \$60 + \$105 = \$165 — Harry must receive \$165 on the bananas he expects to sell.

100% − 8% = 92%
400 × 0.92 = 368 — If 8% of the bananas are likely to spoil, he can expect to sell 92%. Find how many pounds he can expect to sell. He can expect to sell 368 pounds of bananas.

Find the selling price per pound.

$$\frac{\text{Total selling price}}{\text{Number of pounds expected to sell}} = \frac{\$165}{368} = \$0.448 \text{ or } \$0.45$$

Real World Application

SALE PRICES

From 9:00 AM until noon Saturday
TAKE AN ADDITIONAL 25% OFF
Already Reduced Prices

No. Donna's
STYLE #2684
SIZE Medium
PRICE $48.00

During "off times" of the season or slow times of day, some department stores offer an extra incentive for shoppers as shown in the headlines above. How do you determine if you can afford the items advertised?

If a shirt is originally priced $48, a 20% discount gives a sale price of $38.40.

$P = RB$ The original price, \$48, is the base; the rate is 20%.

$= 20\% \times \$48$

$= \$9.60$ The amount of markdown is \$9.60.

Sale price = original price − markdown

= \$48.00 − \$9.60

Sale price = \$38.40

The additional 25% is taken off the sale price, which gives a final sale price of \$28.80.

$P = RB$ The sale price, \$38.40, is the base. The rate is the additional 25%.

$= 25\% \times \$38.40$

$= \$9.60$ The amount of markdown is \$9.60.

Final sale price = sale price − markdown

= \$38.40 − \$9.60

Final sale price = \$28.80

Your answer will not be the same if you add 20% and 25% and then find the sale price.

$P = RB$

$P = 45\% \times \$48$

$P = \$21.60$

Sale price = \$48 − \$21.60

Sale price = \$26.40 NOT THE SALE PRICE!

Application Questions

1. What is the final sale price of an item originally priced \$110, if it is marked down 20% and an additional 10% is to be taken from this reduced price?

2. During a bonus sale at a local department store, you are given an additional 20% discount off the following ticketed items:

No. Donna's
STYLE # 7162
SIZE S
PRICE $31.99

No. Donna's
STYLE #3762
SIZE 8
PRICE $15.99

No. Donna's
STYLE #237
SIZE —
PRICE $10.99

What is your final total price to be paid?

3. From a sale rack marked 25% off, you select the following items:

Item	Original Price
dress	\$85
blouse	\$25
slacks	\$30
sweater	\$40

Because you are shopping during an anniversary sale, you are given an additional 10% off. What is the total amount you have spent?

Harry must sell the bananas for \$0.45 per pound to receive the profit he desires. If he sells more than 92% of the bananas, he will receive additional profit.

Self-Check

12. Anastasia paid a wholesale price of $24 each for Le Paris swimsuits. On May 5 she marked up the suits 50% of her cost. On June 15, she marked the swimsuits down 15% for a 2-day sale, and on June 17 she marked the suits up by 10%. On August 30, she sold all swimsuits remaining in the store for 40% off. What was the final selling price of the Le Paris swimsuit?

13. Farmer Brown's fruit stand sells fresh fruits and vegetables. Becky Brown, the manager, must mark the selling price of incoming produce high enough to make the desired amount of profit while taking expected markdowns and spoilage into account. Becky paid $0.35 per pound for 300 pounds of grapes. On the average, 12% of the grapes will spoil. Find the selling price per pound needed to obtain a 175% markup on cost.

Section Review

1. A fiberglass shower surround originally sold for $379.98 and was marked down to sell for $341.98. Find the amount of markdown and the markdown percent.

2. A three-speed fan originally sold for $29.88 and was reduced to sell for $25.40. Find the amount of markdown and the markdown percent.

3. An area rug originally sold for $89.99 and was reduced to sell for $65. Find the amount of markdown and the markdown percent.

4. A room air conditioner that originally sold for $509.99 was reduced to sell for $400. Find the amount of markdown and the markdown percent.

5. A portable CD player was originally priced at $249.99 and was reduced by 20%. Find the amount of markdown and the sale price (reduced price).

6. A set of bender rollers was originally priced at $39.99 and was reduced by 30%. Find the amount of markdown and the sale price.

7. A set of stainless cookware was originally priced at $79 and was reduced by 25%. Find the amount of markdown and the sale price.

8. A down comforter was originally priced at $280 and was reduced by 64%. Find the amount of markdown and the sale price.

9. Crystal stemware originally marked to sell for $31.25 was reduced 20% for a special promotion. The stemware was then reduced an additional 30% to turn inventory. What were the amount of markdown and the sale price for each of the reductions?

10. A camcorder that originally sold for $1,199 was reduced to sell for $999. It was then reduced an additional 40%. What were the amount of markdown and markdown percent for the first reduction, and what was the final selling price for the camcorder?

11. James McDonell operates a vegetable store. He purchases 800 pounds of potatoes at $0.18 per pound. If he anticipates a spoilage rate of 20% of the potatoes and wishes to make a profit of 140% of the purchase, how much must he mark the potatoes per pound?

12. Helen Jimenez received a shipment of oranges that were shipped after a severe frost, so she expected losses to be high. She paid \$0.26 per pound for the 500 pounds and expected to lose 35% of the oranges. If she wished to make a 125% markup on cost, find the selling price per pound.

Summary

Topic	Page	What to Remember	Examples
Markup based on cost	258–260	Selling price (S) = cost (C) + markup (M) Cost is the base, or 100%.	The next four examples show how to work with markup based on cost.
Finding markup	258–260	Markup amount = $S - C$	$C = \$2$, $S = \$4$. Find the markup amount and percent. $M = S - C = \$4 - \$2 = \$2$ The markup amount is \$2. $\frac{\$2}{\$2} = 1 = 100\%$ The markup percent is 100%.
Finding markup amount and selling price	258–260	The markup is based on cost, so C is the base, or 100%. Multiply the markup percent (rate) times the cost (base) to find the markup amount (portion).	$C = \$1.50$, $M = 40\%$. Find the markup amount and the selling price. Markup amount $= 0.40(1.50) = \$0.60$ $S = C +$ markup amount $= \$1.50 + \$0.60 = \$2.10$ The markup amount is \$0.60 and the selling price is \$2.10. *Check:* $S = C +$ markup amount $\$2.10 = \$1.50 + \$0.60$
Finding the cost and the amount of markup	258–260	The markup is based on cost, so C is the base, or 100%, S is the portion, and the markup percent is the rate. Add the markup percent to the cost percent to find the selling price percent.	$S = C +$ markup amount $S = \$45$; M percent $= 60\% = 0.6$. Find the cost and the markup amount and percent. Cost = selling price divided by the selling price percent: $C = \frac{S}{S\%} = \frac{45}{1.6} = \$28.13$ The cost is \$28.13. Markup amount $= S - C$ $= \$45 - \$28.13 = \$16.87$ *Check:* $S = C + M$ $\$28.13 + \$16.87 = \$45$
Markup based on selling price	260–262	Selling price (S) = cost (C) + markup amount (M) Selling price is the base, or 100%.	The next four examples show how to work with markup based on selling price.
Finding the markup percent based on selling price	260–262	S is the base, or 100%, the markup amount is the portion, and the percent of markup is the rate.	$S = \$80$, $C = \$60$. Find the markup percent. Markup amount $= S - C$ $= \$80 - \$60 = \$20$ $R = \frac{P}{B} = \frac{20}{80} = 0.25 = 25\%$ *Check:* $S = C + M$ $\$80 = \$60 + \$20$

Topic	Page	What to Remember	Example
Finding cost and selling price	260–262	S is the base, or 100%, the markup amount is the portion, and the percent of markup is the rate.	Markup amount = \$50, markup percent = 25% = 0.25. Find the cost and selling price. $B = \frac{P}{R} = \frac{50}{0.25} = \$200$ The selling price is \$200. $C = S - M$ $= \$200 - \$50 = \$150$ The cost is \$150. *Check:* $S = C + M$ $\$200 = \$150 + \$50$
Finding markup and cost	260–262	The selling price is the base, the markup amount is the portion, and the markup percent is the rate.	S = \$12.80 and markup percent = 20% = 0.2. Use $P = RB$ to find the markup, or portion. $P = RB = 0.2 \times 12.8 = 2.56$ The markup amount is \$2.56. $C = S - M$ $= \$12.80 - \$2.56 = \$10.24$ *Check:* $S = C + M$ $\$12.80 = \$10.24 + \$2.56.$
Finding selling price and amount of markup	260–262	S is the base, or 100%, the cost is the portion of the selling price, and the markup percent is the rate.	C = \$6.00, markup percent = 70% = 0.7 of the selling price. Cost = 30% = .3 $.3S = \$6.00$ $\frac{.3S}{.3} = \frac{6}{.3}$ $S = \$20$ $M = S - C$ $\$20 - \$6 = \$14$ The markup amount is \$14.
Markdown	271–273	Markdown = original price − sale price and Sale price = original price − markdown $\frac{\text{Markdown amount}}{\text{original price}}$ = markdown percent (decimal form)	The next three examples show how to solve problems involving markdown.
Finding the markdown amount and percent	271–273	The original price is the base, or 100%, the markdown amount is the portion, and the markdown percent is the rate. Use $R = \frac{P}{B}$ to find the markdown percent. Markdown percent (decimal form) $= \frac{\text{markdown amount}}{\text{original price}}$	Original price = \$4.50, sale price = \$3. Find the markdown amount and percent. Markdown = original price − sale price = \$4.50 − \$3.00 = \$1.50 The markdown amount is \$1.50. $\frac{1.50}{4.50}$ = 33% (rounded) The markdown percent is 33%.

Topic	Page	What to Remember	Example
Finding the amount of markdown and the sale price	271–273	The original price is the base, the markdown amount is the portion, and the markdown percent is the rate. Use the formula $P = RB$.	Original price = \$780, markdown percent = 20% = 0.2. Find the amount of markdown and the sale price. Markdown amount = markdown percent × original price = 0.2 × \$780 = \$156 The markdown amount is \$156. Sale price = original price − markdown = \$780 − \$156 = \$624 The sale price is \$624.
Calculating a series of markdowns and markups	273–274	Each markup or markdown is taken on the previous selling price. Multiply the previous selling price by the decimal complement of the markdown percent to find the new price after a markdown. Multiply the previous price by 1 plus the decimal form of the markup percent to find the new price after a markup.	Cost = \$7. Marked up 70% on cost, then marked down 20%, marked down an additional 10% then marked up 20%, and marked down a final 25%. What was the final price? 7 × 1.7 = \$11.90 11.90 × 0.8 = 9.52 9.52 × .9 = 8.57 8.57 × 1.2 = 10.28 10.28 × 0.75 = 7.71 The final price was \$7.71.
Setting the price of perishable items	274	Figure the total cost, the amount of markup needed, and the total selling price. Figure how much of the item is likely to be sold and divide that amount into the total selling price.	400 lemons cost \$25, and 25% are expected to rot before being sold. A 75% markup on cost is needed. Total selling price: \$25 × 1.75 = \$43.75 Number expected to sell = 400 × 0.75 = 300 Selling price per lemon $= \frac{\$43.75}{300} = \$0.15$ The lemons should be sold at \$0.15 each.

Chapter Review

1. If an item sells for $12 and costs $9, what is the markup?

2. An item sells for $73 and has a $26 markup. Find the cost.

3. A copy machine costs $397 and has a 25% markup based on cost. Find the selling price.

4. A restaurant charges $3.25 for a fish dinner. The cost of preparing the dinner is $2.50. What percent markup is there on cost?

5. What is the markup on an office deck that sells for $329, if the markup is 36% of the selling price?

6. A blender costs $95. What is the selling price if the markup is 30% of the selling price?

7. A commercial mixer has a 26% markup on cost. If the markup is $19.50, find the cost of the mixer.

8. Produce bought for a supermarket is marked up 75% of cost. If a truckload of potatoes costs $200, how much should they sell for?

9. A markup of 140% of cost is made by a jewelry store. If the item retails for \$1,000, how much did it cost? Round to the nearest cent.

10. An item that originally sold for \$21.50 was discounted 20%. What is the amount of discount? What is the sale price? (Round to nearest cent.)

11. An item originally sold for \$60 and has been reduced to sell for \$50. Find the percent of markdown. (Round to the nearest tenth percent.)

12. An item originally sold for \$10. The marked-down price is \$8. Find the percent of markdown based on the original price. (Round to the nearest tenth percent.)

13. Find the final selling price for a miter saw originally priced at \$239.99 if it underwent three markdowns of 15%, 20%, and 10% before selling.

14. Karen Marshall ordered 700 pounds of squash for her chain of vegetable shops. She paid \$0.12 per pound for the squash and expected 18% of the squash to rot. If she wished to make a markup on cost of 95% on the squash, what should be the per-pound price?

Trial Test

1. A calculator sells for $23.99 and cost $16.83. What is the markup?

2. A mixer sells for $109.98 and has a markup of $36.18. Find the cost.

3. A cookbook has a 34% markup on cost. If the markup is $5.27, find the cost of the cookbook.

4. A computer stand sells for $385. What is the amount of markup if it is 45% of the selling price?

5. A box of computer paper costs $16.80. Find the selling price if there is a 35% markup based on cost.

6. The reduced price of a dress is $54.99. Find the original price if a reduction of 40% is taken.

7. A daily organizer that originally sold for $86.90 was discounted 30%. What is the amount of discount?

8. What is the discount price of the organizer in Problem 7?

9. If a television cost $87.15 and was marked up $39.60, what is the selling price?

10. A refrigerator that sells for $387.99 was marked down $97. What is the sale price?

11. What was the percent of markdown for the refrigerator in Problem 10?

12. A wallet cost $16.05 to produce. The wallet sells for $25.68. What is the percent markup on cost?

13. A lamp costs $88. What is the selling price if the markup is 45% of the selling price?

14. A file cabinet originally sold for $215 but was damaged and had to be reduced. If the reduced cabinet sold for $129, what was the percent of markdown based on the original price?

15. A bookcase desk originally sold for $129.99 was marked down 25%. During the sale it was damaged and had to be reduced by 50% more. What was the final selling price of the desk?

16. Donald Byrd, the accountant for Quick Stop Shop, calculates the selling price for all produce. If 400 pounds of potatoes were purchased for $0.13 per pound and 18% of the potatoes were expected to rot before being sold, determine the price per pound that the potatoes must sell for if a profit of 120% of the purchase price is desired.

Self-Check Solutions

1.

100%	C	\$2
200%	M	\$4
300%	S	\$6

$$\text{Markup} = S - C = \$6 - \$2 = \$4$$

$$\text{Percent of markup based on cost} = \frac{P\text{ (markup)}}{B\text{ (cost)}} = \frac{\$4}{\$2} = 2 = 200\%$$

2.

100%	C	\$4.00
60%	M	\$2.40
160%	S	\$6.40

$$\text{Markup} = R\text{ (percent markup)} \times B\text{ (cost)}$$
$$= 0.60 \times \$4 = \$2.40$$
$$\text{Selling price} = C + M = \$4 + \$2.40 = \$6.40$$

3.

100%	C	\$214.29
40%	M	\$ 85.71
140%	S	\$300

$$C\% + M\% = S\%$$
$$100\% + 40\% = 140\%$$

$$\text{Cost} = \frac{P\text{ (selling price)}}{R\text{ (percent of selling price based on cost)}}$$
$$= \frac{\$300}{1.4} = \$214.29\text{ (rounded)}$$

$$\text{Markup} = S - C = \$300 - \$214.29 = \$85.71$$

4.

	C	\$ 4
66.67%	M	\$ 8
100%	S	\$12

Find amount of markup first.

$$M = S - C = \$12 - \$4 = \$8$$

$$\text{Percent of markup based on selling price} = \frac{P\text{ (markup)}}{B\text{ (selling price)}} = \frac{\$8}{\$12}$$
$$= 0.66667$$
$$= 66.67\%$$

5.

60%	C	\$ 7.50
40%	M	\$ 5.00
100%	S	\$12.50

$$S\% - M\% = C\%$$
$$100\% - 40\% = 60\%$$

$$\text{Selling price} = \frac{P\text{ (amount of markup)}}{R\text{ (percent of markup based on selling price)}} = \frac{\$5}{0.4} = \$12.50$$

$$C = S - M = \$12.50 - \$5 = \$7.50$$

6.

50%	C	\$1.75
50%	M	\$1.75
100%	S	\$3.50

$$S\% - M\% = C\%$$
$$100\% - 50\% = 50\%$$

$$\text{Markup} = B\text{ (selling price)} \times R\text{ (percent markup based on selling price)}$$
$$= \$3.50 \times 0.5 = \$1.75$$

Since the markup and cost are represented by the same percents, their dollar amounts will be equal.

7.

40%	C	$ 40
60%	M	$ 60
100%	S	$100

$$S\% - M\% = C\%$$

$$100\% - 60\% = 40\%$$

$$\text{Selling price} = \frac{P \text{ (cost)}}{R \text{ (percent of cost based on selling price)}} = \frac{\$40}{0.4} = \$100$$

$$M = S - C = \$100 - \$40 = \$60$$

8. $$\text{Markup percent based on cost} = \frac{\text{markup percent of selling price}}{1 - \text{markup percent of selling price}} = \frac{0.60}{1 - 0.60} = \frac{0.60}{0.40} = 1.5, \text{ or } 150\%$$

9. $$\text{Markup percent based on selling price} = \frac{\text{markup percent based on cost}}{1 + \text{markup percent on cost}} = \frac{1.20}{1 + 1.20} = \frac{1.20}{2.20} = 0.5455, \text{ or } 54.55\%$$

10. $$\text{Markdown} = \text{original selling price} - \text{sale price} = \$480 - \$420 = \$60$$

$$\%\text{ markdown} = \frac{P}{B} = \frac{\$60}{\$480} = 0.125 = 12.5\%$$

11. $\text{Markdown} = R \times B = 0.15 \times \$78 = \$11.70$

$\text{Sale price} = \text{original price} - \text{markdown} = \$78 - \$11.70 = \$66.30$

12. *May* 5 *markup:*

$\text{Markup} = R \times B = 0.5 \times \$24 = \$12$

$S = C + M = \$24 + \$12 = \$36$ (original selling price)

June 15 *markdown:*

$\text{Markdown} = R \times B = 0.15 \times \$36 = \$5.40$

$\text{Sale price} = \$36 - \$5.40 = \$30.60$

June 17 *markup:*

$\text{Markup} = R \times B = 0.10 \times \$30.60 = \$3.06$

$\text{New marked price} = \$30.60 + \$3.06 = \$33.66$

August 30 *markdown:*

$\text{Markdown} = R \times B = 0.40 \times \$33.66 = \$13.46$

$\text{Final sale price} = \$33.66 - \$13.46 = \$20.20$

13.

$\text{Cost} = 300 \times \$0.35 = \$105$

$\text{Amount of markup} = \$105 \times 1.75 = \$183.75$

$\text{Total selling price} = C + M = \$105 + \$183.75 = \$288.75$

$\%\text{ of grapes expected to sell} = 100\% - 12\% = 88\%$

$\text{Pounds of grapes expected to sell} = 300 \times 0.88 = 264 \text{ pounds}$

$$\text{Selling price per pound} = \frac{\$288.75}{264} = \$1.09 \text{ per pound}$$

10 Simple Interest and Simple Discount

Learning Objectives

1. Use the simple interest formula to calculate unknown interest, principal, rate, or time when three of the terms are known. (pp. 289–291)
2. Solve interest problems when time is expressed in months or fractional years (pp. 291–293)
3. Determine the ordinary time and exact time of loans made during a single calendar year and over portions of two calendar years. (pp. 300–304)
4. Calculate simple interest by table. (pp. 304–306)
5. Understand the difference between discounted and undiscounted notes. (pp. 306–308)
6. Use the simple interest formula to calculate proceeds and maturity value of promissory notes. (pp. 307–310)

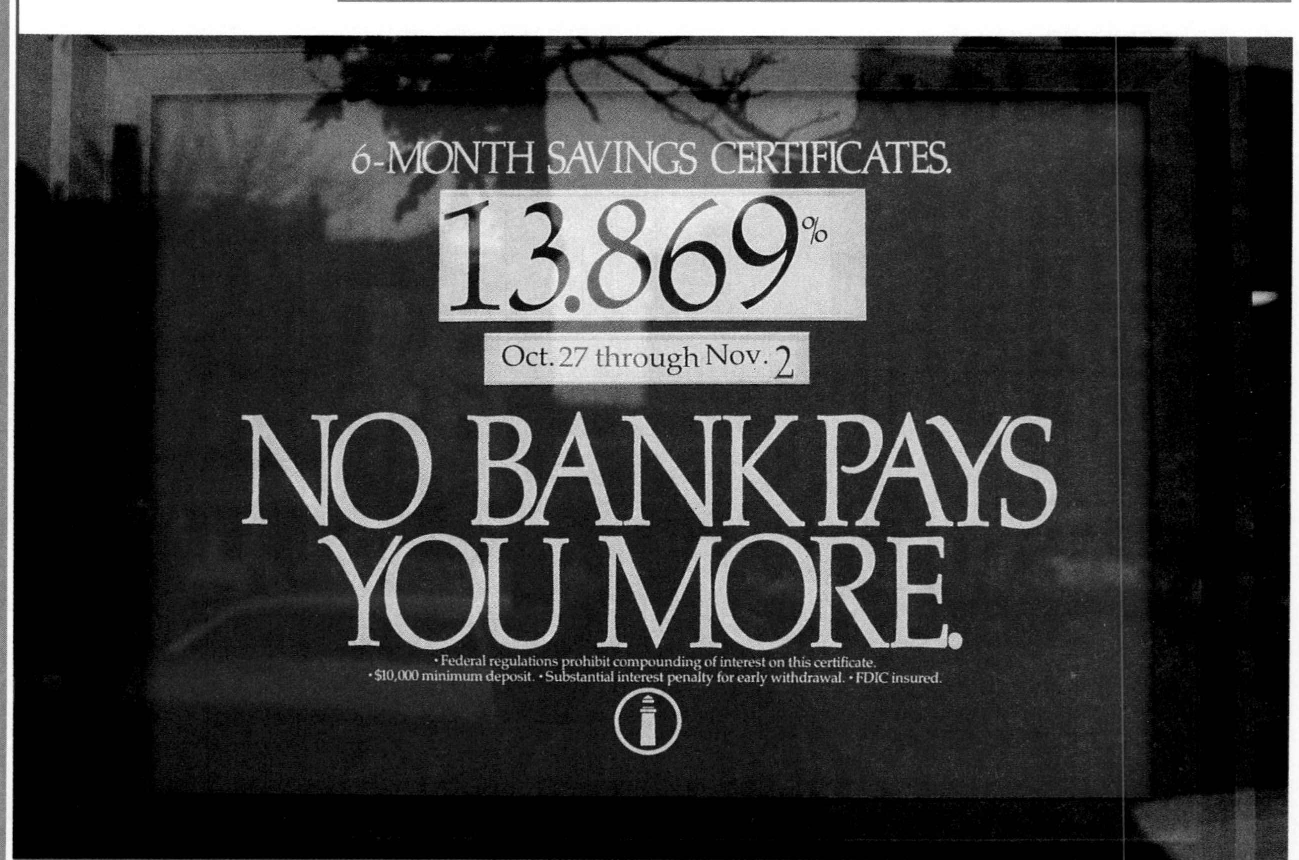

Every business and every person at some time borrows or invests money. A person (or business) who borrows money must pay for the use of the money. A person who invests money will be paid by the person or firm who uses the money. The price paid for using money is called **interest.**

In the business world, we encounter two basic kinds of interest, *simple* and *compound*. **Simple interest** is used when a loan or investment is repaid in a lump sum. The person using the money has use of the full amount of money for the entire time of the loan or investment. **Compound interest,** which is explained in Chapter 11, most often applies to installment loans and credit cards.

interest: the price or fee for using money.

simple interest: the amount of money paid or earned on a loan or investment of a lump sum for a specified period of time.

compound interest: a procedure for calculating interest at regular intervals, covered in Chapter 11.

Finding Simple Interest

As we mentioned in Chapter 6, interest is the amount of money paid for the use of money. **Principal** is the amount of money borrowed or invested. **Rate** is the percent of interest charged on the loan or earned on the investment each year. The rate, or percent, is always written as a decimal number or fraction when we solve simple interest problems. **Time** is the number of days, months, or years that the money is borrowed or invested. In solving problems, the time is usually written as a number of years or as a fraction of a year. The simple interest formula tells us how interest, principal, rate, and time are related and gives us a way of figuring one of these values if the other three values are known.

principal: the amount of money borrowed or invested.

rate: the percent or decimal or fractional equivalent of the percent that is charged or earned for the use of money.

time: the number of days, months, or years that money is loaned or invested.

Step by Step

The Simple Interest Formula

$$\text{Interest} = \text{Principal} \times \text{Rate} \times \text{Time}$$

$$I = PRT$$

I = amount of interest, P = amount of principal, R = percent of interest or rate, and T = time of loan

The next example shows how to use the formula to find the amount of interest paid on a loan of $1,500 for one year at a simple interest rate of 12%. Remember, in solving problems, rate must always be written in decimal or fraction form, and time is generally written as a number of years or a fraction of a year.

EXAMPLE 1

Find the interest paid on a loan of \$1,500 for 1 year at a simple interest rate of 12%.

$I = PRT$	Use the simple interest formula.
I is unknown.	
$P = \$1{,}500$	
$R = 12\% = 0.12$	Write the rate in decimal form.
$T = 1$ year	
$I = (\$1{,}500)(0.12)(1) = \$180$	Substitute numbers for letters in the equation and multiply.

The interest on the loan is \$180.

In a calculator solution, there is no need to multiply by 1 year, since this does not change the value of the equation.

Calculator Solution

To solve the equation on a calculator without a percent key, enter

[AC] 1500 [×] .12 [=] ⇒ 180

(Use decimal equivalent of 12% and equals key.)
To solve the equation on a calculator with a percent key, enter

[AC] 1500 [×] 12 [%] ⇒ 180

(Use 12 and percent key.)

EXAMPLE 2

Mrs. James borrowed \$500 at $12\frac{1}{2}\%$ simple interest for 2 years. How much interest did she pay?

$I = PRT$	Use the simple interest formula.
I is unknown.	
$P = \$500$	
$R = 12\frac{1}{2}\% = 0.125$	(Go to Chapter 6, Example 4, if you need to review changing a mixed percent to a decimal.)
$T = 2$ years	
$I = (\$500)(0.125)(2) = \$125$	Substitute numbers for letters and multiply.

Mrs. James will pay \$125 interest.

maturity value: the amount of principal plus the amount of interest.

The *total* amount of money due at the end of a loan period is called the **maturity value** of the loan.

Step by Step

Finding the Maturity Value of a Loan

Maturity value = amount of principal + amount of interest

EXAMPLE 3

How much money will Mrs. James (Example 2) pay at the end of 2 years?

Maturity value = principal + interest

= \$500 + \$125 = \$625

Mrs. James will pay \$625 at the end of her loan period.

Time in Fractional Parts of Years

Not all loans or investments are made for a whole number of years, but time *is* figured in years unless otherwise specified. To convert months to the decimal equivalent of a year, we *divide* the number of months by 12.

EXAMPLE 4

Convert 5 months and 15 months to years, expressed in decimal form.

5 months $= \frac{5}{12}$ year — 5 months equal $\frac{5}{12}$ year.

$12\overline{)5.0000000}$ = 0.4166666 year = 0.42 year — To write the fraction as a decimal, divide the number of months (the numerator) by the number of months in a year (the denominator).

5 months = 0.42 year (rounded)

15 months $= \frac{15}{12}$ years — 15 months equal $\frac{15}{12}$ years.

$12\overline{)15.00}$ = 1.25 years — To write the fraction as a decimal, divide the number of months (the numerator) by the number of months in a year (the denominator).

15 months = 1.25 years

EXAMPLE 5

A technician invested \$2,500 for 45 months at $12\frac{1}{2}\%$ interest. How much interest did the technician earn?

$I = PRT$ — Use the simple interest formula.

I is unknown.

$P = \$2,500$

$R = 12\frac{1}{2}\% = 0.125$ — Write the rate as a decimal number.

$T = 45 \text{ months} = \frac{45}{12} \text{ years}$ — Write the time in terms of years.

$I = \$2,500(0.125)\left(\frac{45}{12}\right)$ — Substitute numbers for letters, multiply, and round to the nearest cent.

$= \$1,171.88$

When time is expressed in months, the calculator sequence is the same as when time is expressed in years, except that we do not enter a whole number for the time. Instead, we enter the months, divide by 12, and then press the = key. All other steps are the same:

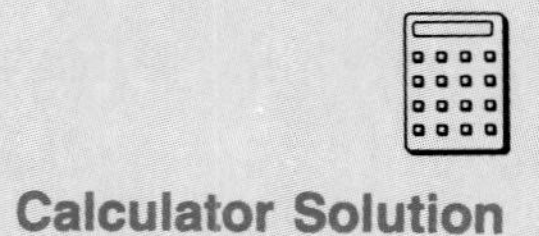

Calculator Solution

[AC] 2500 [×] .125 [×] 45 [÷] 12 [=] ⇒ 1171.875

Real World Application

BALLOON PAYMENT LOANS

Are you interested in buying a "new" used car or installing a pool? A simple interest loan with a low monthly payment sounds good, but be sure you understand what this monthly payment means.

A simple interest loan with a final "balloon payment" can be a good deal for both the consumer and the banker. For the banker, this loan reduces the rate risk, since the loan rate is actually locked in for a short period of time. For the consumer, this loan allows you to make lower monthly payments.

Example: You borrow $5,000 at 13% simple interest rate for a year.

For 12 monthly payments:

$$\$5{,}000 \times 13\% \times 1 = \$650 \text{ interest}$$

$$\frac{\$5{,}650}{12} = \$470.83 \text{ monthly payment}$$

Your banker will offer to make the loan as if it is to be extended over 5 years, or 60 monthly payments. This means a much lower monthly payment.

For 60 monthly payments:

$$\frac{\$5{,}650}{60} = \$94.17 \text{ monthly payment}$$

The lower monthly payment is tempting! The banker will expect you to make these lower payment for a year. You will actually make 11 payments of $94.17:

$$\$94.17 \times 11 = \$1{,}035.87 \text{ amount paid during the first 11 months}$$

The 12th and final payment, the "balloon payment," is the *remainder* of the loan:

$$\$5{,}650 - \$1{,}035.87 = \$4{,}614.13$$

At this time you are expected to pay the balance of the loan in the balloon payment shown above. Don't panic! Usually the loan is refinanced for another year. But beware—you may have to pay a higher interest rate for the next year.

Application Questions

1. What is the amount of the final balloon payment for a $1,000 loan at 10% interest for a year, extended over 5 years?

2. Find the monthly payment for a $2,500 loan at 12% interest for one year extended over a 3-year period.

3. a. You need a loan of $5,000 at 10% interest for one year. What is the amount of the monthly payment?

b. If your banker agrees to extend the monthly payments over 2 years, how much will your monthly payments be? How much will the final balloon payment be?

Self-Check

1. Find the interest paid on a loan of \$2,400 for 1 year at a simple interest rate of 11%.
2. Find the interest paid on a loan of \$800 at $8\frac{1}{2}\%$ simple interest for 2 years.
3. Find the total amount of money that the borrower will pay back on a loan (maturity value) of \$1,400 at $12\frac{1}{2}\%$ simple interest for 3 years.
4. Convert 8 months and 40 months to years, expressed in decimal form.

Using the Simple Interest Formula

The formula $I = PRT$ is used to find the simple interest on a loan. However, there are times when the principal or the rate or the time needs to be found instead of the interest. The different forms of this formula can easily be remembered with a circle diagram (see Figure 10-1) like the one used for percents. Cover the unknown term with your finger to see the correct form of the simple interest formula needed to find the missing value:

$$I = PRT \qquad P = \frac{I}{RT} \qquad R = \frac{I}{PT} \qquad T = \frac{I}{PR}$$

Figure 10-1 A diagram of the simple interest formula

EXAMPLE 6

Mr. Carneal borrowed \$800 for $3\frac{1}{2}$ years and paid \$348 simple interest on the loan. What rate of interest did he pay?

$R = \frac{I}{PT}$ — Find the correct form of the simple interest formula on the circle diagram.

R is unknown.
$I = \$348$
$P = \$800$
$I = 3.5$ years

$R = \frac{348}{(800)(3.5)} = 0.124$ — Substitute numbers for letters in the equation; then multiply, divide, and round.

$0.124 = 12.4\%$ — Change the rate from decimal form to percent form by moving the decimal point two places to the right.

He paid 12.4% interest.

Calculator Sequence

Multiply $P \times T$, store the result in memory, and divide I by the stored product:

[AC] 800 [×] 3.5 [=] [M+] [CE/C] 348 [÷] [MRC] [=] ⇒ 0.1242857

or

Divide I by P and divide the result by T:

[AC] 348 [÷] 800 [÷] 3.5 [=] ⇒ 0.1242857

EXAMPLE 7

Ms. Cox wished to borrow some money. She was told she could borrow a sum of money for 18 months at 18% simple interest and pay $540 in interest charges. How much money could she borrow?

$P = \frac{I}{RT}$ — Find the correct form of the simple interest formula on the circle diagram.

P is unknown
$I = \$540$
$R = 18\% = 0.18$
$T = 18 \text{ months} = \frac{18}{12} = 1.5 \text{ years}$

$P = \frac{540}{0.18(1.5)} = \$2{,}000$ — Substitute numbers for letters in the equation, multiply, and divide.

The principal is $2,000.

Calculator Sequence

Multiply $R \times T$, store the result in memory, and divide I by the stored product:

[AC] .18 [×] 1.5 [=] [M⁺] [CE/C] 540 [÷] [MRC] [=] ⇒ 2000, or

Divide I by R and divide the result by T.

[AC] 540 [÷] .18 [÷] 1.5 [=] ⇒ 2000

EXAMPLE 8

Mr. Lee borrowed $2,400 at 14% simple interest. If he paid $840 interest, what was the duration of the loan?

$T = \frac{I}{PR}$ — Find the correct form of the simple interest formula on the circle diagram.

T is unknown.
$I = \$840$
$P = \$2{,}400$
$R = 14\% = 0.14$

$T = \frac{840}{2{,}400(0.14)} = 2.5 \text{ years}$ — Substitute numbers for letters in the equation, multiply, and divide.

The duration of the loan is 2.5 years.

Source: USA TODAY research
By Julie Stacey, USA TODAY

Self-Check

5. Maddy borrowed $1,200 for 30 months and paid $360 simple interest on the loan. What interest rate did she pay?
6. Raul borrowed $500 for 7 months and paid $53.96 in interest. How much was the rate of interest?
7. Linda agreed to lend money to Alex at a special interest of 9%, on the condition that he borrow enough that he would pay her $500 in interest over a 2-year period. What was the minimum amount Alex could borrow?
8. Rob borrowed $6,000 at 12% simple interest. If he paid $360 interest, what was the duration of the loan?

The 6%, 60-Day Method

The simple interest on a 60-day loan of 6% can be calculated mentally. In this case, the rate multiplied by the time reduces to 0.01, or $\frac{1}{100}$.

$$\frac{\overset{1}{\cancel{6}}}{100} \times \frac{\overset{1}{\cancel{60}}}{\underset{\underset{1}{\cancel{60}}}{\cancel{360}}} = \frac{1}{100}, \quad \text{or} \quad \overset{0.01}{\cancel{0.06}} \times \frac{\overset{1}{\cancel{60}}}{\underset{\underset{1}{\cancel{60}}}{\cancel{360}}} = 0.01$$

EXAMPLE 9

Find the interest paid on a loan of \$2,500 for 60 days at a simple interest rate of 6%.

$$\frac{\overset{25}{\cancel{2{,}500}}}{1} \times \frac{1}{\underset{1}{\cancel{100}}} = \$25, \quad \text{or} \quad \$2{,}500 \times 0.01 = \$25.00. = \$25$$

The interest is \$25.

There are other pairs of rates and days that yield a multiplier of 0.01.

4% and 90 days: $\frac{\overset{0.01}{\cancel{0.04}}}{1} \times \frac{\overset{1}{\cancel{90}}}{\underset{\underset{1}{\cancel{90}}}{\cancel{360}}} = 0.01$

$4\frac{1}{2}$% and 80 days: $\frac{\overset{0.001}{\cancel{0.045}}}{1} \times \frac{\overset{10}{\cancel{80}}}{\underset{\underset{1}{\cancel{8}}}{\cancel{360}}} = 0.01$

8% and 45 days: $\frac{\overset{0.01}{\cancel{0.08}}}{1} \times \frac{\overset{1}{\cancel{45}}}{\underset{\underset{1}{\cancel{45}}}{\cancel{360}}} = 0.01$

10% and 36 days: $\frac{0.1}{1} \times \frac{\overset{1}{\cancel{36}}}{\underset{10}{\cancel{360}}} = \frac{0.1}{10} = 0.01$

12% and 30 days: $\frac{\overset{0.01}{\cancel{0.12}}}{1} \times \frac{\overset{1}{\cancel{30}}}{\underset{\underset{1}{\cancel{30}}}{\cancel{360}}} = 0.01$

EXAMPLE 10

Find the interest on a loan of \$3,725 for 45 days at 8% simple interest.

$I = PRT$

$P = \$3{,}725$

$RT = 0.01$

$I = (\$3{,}725)(0.01) = \$37.25$

The interest is \$37.25.

6% Rate, Days Different from 60. If the rate is 6% but the days are different from 60, the 6%, 60-day method may still be useful.

EXAMPLE 11

Find the interest at 6% for 30 days on a $1,200 loan.

$I = PRT$ 6% and 60 days = 0.01

$P = \$1{,}200$

$RT = (0.01)\left(\frac{1}{2}\right)$ 30 days $= \frac{1}{2}$(60 days) since $\frac{30}{60} = \frac{1}{2}$

6% and 30 days $= (0.01)\left(\frac{1}{2}\right)$

$I = \$1{,}200(0.01)\left(\frac{1}{2}\right)$

$I = 12\left(\frac{1}{2}\right)$

$I = \$6$

The interest is $6.

60 Days, Rate Different from 6%. If the loan is for 60 days but the rate is different from 6%, the 6%, 60-day method may still be useful.

EXAMPLE 12

Find the simple interest on a loan of $500 at 12% interest for 60 days.

$I = PRT$ 6% and 60 days = 0.01

$P = \$500$ 12% = 2(6%)

$RT = (0.01)(2)$ 12% and 60 days = (0.01)(2)

$$I = 500(0.01)(2) = 5(2) = \$10$$

The interest is $10.

Section Review

Find the simple interest in each of the following problems. Round to the nearest cent when necessary.

	Principal	Rate	Time	Interest
1.	$500	12%	2 years	_____
2.	$1,000	$9\frac{1}{2}$%	3 years	_____
3.	$3,575	21%	3 years	_____
4.	$2,975	$12\frac{1}{2}$%	2 years	_____
5.	$800	18%	1 year	_____

6. Capco, Inc., borrowed $4,275 for 3 years at 15% interest. How much simple interest did the company pay? How much would have to be repaid altogether?

7. Legan Company borrowed $15,280 at $16\frac{1}{2}\%$ for 12 years. How much simple interest did the company pay? What was the total amount paid back?

Find the rate of simple interest in each of the following problems.

	Principal	Interest	Time	Rate
8.	$300	$102	2 years	______
9.	$800	$124	1 year	______
10.	$1,280	$256	2 years	______
11.	$1,000	$375	3 years	______
12.	$40,000	$64,000	10 years	______
13.	$175	$52.50	2 years	______
14.	$423	$355.32	4 years	______

In each of the following problems, find the duration (time) of the loan using the formula for simple interest.

	Principal	Rate	Interest	Time
15.	$450	10%	$135	______
16.	$700	18%	$252	______
17.	$1,500	$21\frac{1}{2}\%$	$483.75	______
18.	$2,000	$16\frac{1}{2}\%$	$825	______
19.	$800	$15\frac{3}{4}\%$	$252	______

20. A loan of $7,500 at $16\frac{1}{2}\%$ was paid back with $618.75 simple interest. How long was the loan outstanding?

21. An investor received $1,440 on a loan of $12,000 at 16% simple interest. How long was the money invested?

22. Simple interest of $78.01 was paid on a loan of $269 with an interest rate of $14\frac{1}{2}\%$. What length of time was required to repay the loan?

In each of the following problems, find the principal, based on simple interest.

	Interest	Rate	Time	Principal
23.	$100	10%	2 years	______
24.	$281.25	$12\frac{1}{2}\%$	3 years	______
25.	$90	9%	1 year	______
26.	$180	11.25%	2 years	______
27.	$661.50	8.82%	5 years	______
28.	$304.64	$13\frac{3}{5}\%$	4 years	______

29. A loan for 3 years with an annual simple interest rate of 18% cost $486 interest. Find the principal.

30. An investor earned $1,530 interest on funds invested at $12\frac{3}{4}\%$ simple interest for 4 years. How much was invested?

Write a fraction expressing each amount of time as a part of a year (12 months = 1 year).

31. 7 months

32. 18 months

33. 16 months

34. 9 months

35. 3 months

36. Draw the circle showing the four parts of an interest problem, and write the formula for each part.

37. Robert Ellis made a car loan for $2,500 to be paid off in $3\frac{1}{2}$ years. The simple interest rate for the loan was 12%. How much interest did he pay?

38. Jill Jones bought a dining-room suite and paid for the furniture in full after 1 month, with a finance charge of $18.75. If she was charged 18% interest, how much did the suite cost?

39. Sue Jackson invested $500 at 8% for 6 months. How much interest did she receive?

40. Mark Hammer borrowed $500 for 3 months and paid $12.50 interest. What was the rate of interest?

Use the 6%, 60-day method.

41. Find the interest paid on a loan of $1,200 for 60 days at a simple interest rate of 6%.

42. Find the interest paid on a loan of \$2,100 for 90 days at a simple interest rate of 4%.

43. Find the interest paid on a loan of \$800 for 120 days at a simple interest rate of 6%.

Ordinary and Exact Time

ordinary time: 30 days per month regardless of the month of the year.

ordinary interest: interest that is calculated using 360 days as the denominator of the time fraction.

exact time: the exact number of days of a loan or investment.

exact interest: interest that is calculated using 365 days (or 366 days in a leap year) as the denominator of the time fraction.

Sometimes the time of a loan is indicated by the beginning and ending dates of the loan rather than by a specific number of months or days. If this is the case, the number of days to be counted in each month must be determined. If you count 30 days in each month, the time is **ordinary.** If you count the exact number of days in a month, this is **exact time.** The interest is called **ordinary interest** when 360 is used for the denominator of the time fraction. The interest is called **exact interest** when 365 (or 366 in a leap year) is used for the denominator of the time fraction.

Suppose you have a loan taken out on July 12 and due September 12. If you use ordinary time, you consider the time to be 2 months, or 2 × 30 days = 60 days. If you figure the exact time, you must add the 19 days remaining in July, the 31 days in August, and the 12 days in September, to get the total of 62 days. This calculation is much simpler if you use Table 10-1, which gives the number of each day in the year.

Finding Ordinary and Exact Time

To use Table 10-1 to find the exact time of the loan we just described, note that July 12 is the 193rd day of the year and September 12 is the 255th day. Subtract 193 from 255 to find the total number of days.

$$\begin{array}{r} 255 \\ \underline{193} \\ 62 \text{ days} \end{array}$$

If the period of a loan includes February, count it as 30 days for ordinary time but 28 days for exact time. In leap years, February has 29 days, so the exact time is determined by counting 28 days and adding 1 to the total number of days if February 29 is within the loan period.

It is easy to remember which years are leap years: They are the years whose numbers are divisible by 4. (Remember the rule for divisibility by 4: If the last *two* digits form a number that is divisible by 4, the entire number is divisible by 4.) The year 1992 is a leap year because 92 is divisible by 4; thus, 1992 is divisible by 4.

EXAMPLE 13

A loan made on September 5 is due July 5 of the *following year*. Find the ordinary time and exact time for the loan in a non–leap year and a leap year.

Table 10-1 The Number of Each Day of the Year (for Calculating Dates)

Days of month	Jan.	Feb.	Mar.	Apr.	May	Jun.	Jul.	Aug.	Sept.	Oct.	Nov.	Dec.
1	1	32	60	91	121	152	182	213	244	274	305	335
2	2	33	61	92	122	153	183	214	245	275	306	336
3	3	34	62	93	123	154	184	215	246	276	307	337
4	4	35	63	94	124	155	185	216	247	277	308	338
5	5	36	64	95	125	156	186	217	248	278	309	339
6	6	37	65	96	126	157	187	218	249	279	310	340
7	7	38	66	97	127	158	188	219	250	280	311	341
8	8	39	67	98	128	159	189	220	251	281	312	342
9	9	40	68	99	129	160	190	221	252	282	313	343
10	10	41	69	100	130	161	191	222	253	283	314	344
11	11	42	70	101	131	162	192	223	254	284	315	345
12	12	43	71	102	132	163	193	224	255	285	316	346
13	13	44	72	103	133	164	194	225	256	286	317	347
14	14	45	73	104	134	165	195	226	257	287	318	348
15	15	46	74	105	135	166	196	227	258	288	319	349
16	16	47	75	106	136	167	197	228	259	289	320	350
17	17	48	76	107	137	168	198	229	260	290	321	351
18	18	49	77	108	138	169	199	230	261	291	322	352
19	19	50	78	109	139	170	200	231	262	292	323	353
20	20	51	79	110	140	171	201	232	263	293	324	354
21	21	52	80	111	141	172	202	233	264	294	325	355
22	22	53	81	112	142	173	203	234	265	295	326	356
23	23	54	82	113	143	174	204	235	266	296	327	357
24	24	55	83	114	144	175	205	236	267	297	328	358
25	25	56	84	115	145	176	206	237	268	298	329	359
26	26	57	85	116	146	177	207	238	269	299	330	360
27	27	58	86	117	147	178	208	239	270	300	331	361
28	28	59	87	118	148	179	209	240	271	301	332	362
29	29	*	88	119	149	180	210	241	272	302	333	363
30	30		89	120	150	181	211	242	273	303	334	364
31	31		90		151		212	243		304		365

*See discussion on leap year. For centennial years (those at the turn of the century), leap years occur only when the number of the year is divisible by 400. Thus, 2000 will be a leap year (2000/400 divides exactly), but 1700, 1800, and 1900 were not leap years.

Ordinary time in a non–leap year or leap year

There are 10 months between September and July.
10 months × 30 days/month = 300 days

Exact time in a non–leap year

December 31 = day 365 September 5 = day 248 117 days	Look in Table 10-1 to find the exact time of the loan in the first year.
July 5 is the 186th day	Look in Table 10-1 to find the number of July 5.
117 + 186 = 303 days	Add the number of days in each year to find the exact time of the loan.

Exact time in a leap year

117 + 186 + 1 = 304 days	In a leap year, you add an extra day to get the correct answer.

Finding the Due Date

due date: the date that a loan matures or is due. It is a specific length of time from the beginning date of a loan.

Sometimes the beginning date of a loan and the number of days for which it is made are known, and the **due date** must be determined. If the beginning date and due date are in the same year, simply add the number of days of the loan to the number of the beginning date (from Table 10-1) and find the corresponding end date. If the beginning date and due date are in different years, a two-step solution is needed.

EXAMPLE 14

Figure the due date using ordinary time and exact time for a 90-day loan made on November 15.

Ordinary time

Count 3 months from November 15 to find a due date of February 15.

In ordinary time, there are 30 days in a month, and 90 days is the same as 3 months.

Exact time

November 15 = day 319
+ 90 days
409

Use Table 10-1 to find the number for November 15, and add 90 days to that number.

Since there are only 365 days in an exact year, the loan is due in the second year. Subtract the number of days in an exact year (365) from the number of days of the loan to find the number of the due date in the second year.

Day 409
− 365 days
44

The loan is due on day 44 in the second year.

Day 44 = February 13

Find day 44 in Table 10-1.

The loan is due February 13.

Using Time Fractions

Whenever you solve an interest problem, you need to know whether the time and interest are ordinary or exact, so that you can write the time fraction correctly. Remember, in interest problems time is usually expressed in terms of years. A month is always $\frac{1}{12}$ of a year. In exact time, a day is $\frac{1}{365}$ year; in ordinary time, where each month is considered to have 30 days, a day is $\frac{1}{360}$ year. There are three commonly used methods for determining the time fraction in interest problems.

1. Ordinary interest using ordinary time:

$$\frac{\text{Ordinary time (30 days per month)}}{360}$$

2. Exact interest using exact time:

$$\frac{\text{Exact time (exact days of loan)}}{365}$$

3. Ordinary interest using exact time:

$$\frac{\text{Exact time (exact days of loan)}}{360}$$

To make these fractions easy to recall, just remember that if you are calculating *ordinary interest*, the *denominator* of the time fraction is 360. If you are calculating *exact interest*, the denominator is 365. Ordinary and exact *time* tells you what to put in the *numerator* of the time fraction. For ordinary time, 30 days per month is used. For exact time, the exact number of days of the loan is used.

TIPS & TRAPS

Thinking of fractions like these might help you remember how to write the time fraction for any combination of ordinary and exact interest and time.

$$\begin{array}{ll} \text{Numerator} & \text{ordinary time: 30 days in a month} \\ \hline \text{Denominator} & \text{ordinary interest: 360 days in a year} \end{array}$$

$$\frac{\text{exact time: 28, 29, 30, or 31 days in a month}}{\text{exact interest: 365 days in a year}}$$

EXAMPLE 15

Use ordinary time to find the ordinary interest on a loan of \$500 at 17%. The loan was made on March 15 and was due on May 15.

$P = 500$
$R = 17\% = 0.17$
$T = \frac{60}{360}$

$$I = PRT = (\$500)(0.17)\left(\frac{60}{360}\right) = \$14.17 \quad \text{(to nearest cent)}$$

The interest is \$14.17.

Calculator Sequence

[AC] 500 [×] .17 [×] 60 [÷] 360 [=] ⇒ 14.166666

EXAMPLE 16

Find the exact interest using exact time on the loan in Example 15.

Here we are finding *exact interest*, so the denominator of the time fraction is 365. The numerator of the time fraction is the *exact* number of days from March 15 to May 15 because the problem calls for exact time.

To figure exact time:

May 5 =	135
March 15 =	74
	61 days

$I = PRT$
$P = \$500$
$R = 0.17$
$T = \frac{61}{365}$

$$I = \$(500)(0.17)\left(\frac{61}{365}\right) = \$14.21 \quad \text{(to nearest cent)}$$

The interest is \$14.21.

Calculator Sequence

[AC] 500 [×] .17 [×] 61 [÷] 365 [=] ⇒ 14.205479

EXAMPLE 17

Find the ordinary interest using exact time for the loan in Example 15.

Here, the denominator of the time fraction is 360 because the problem calls for ordinary interest, and the numerator is 61 since this is the exact number of days from March 15 to May 15.

$I = PRT$
$P = \$500$
$R = 17\% = 0.17$
$T = \frac{61}{360}$

$I = \$(500)(0.17)\left(\frac{61}{360}\right) = \$14.40$ (to nearest cent)

Calculator Sequence

[AC] 500 [×] .17 [×] 61 [÷] 360 [=] ⇒ 14.402777

banker's rule: the method for calculating simple interest that uses a 360-day year (ordinary interest) and the exact time. This method yields a slightly higher amount of interest.

Note that the amount of interest varies in each case. The last method illustrated, *ordinary interest using exact time,* is most often used by bankers when lending money because it yields a slightly higher amount of interest. It is sometimes called the **banker's rule.** When bankers pay interest on savings accounts, however, they usually use a 365-day year.

Calculating Simple Interest by Table

Tables are available for finding ordinary and exact interest. These tables make it easy to calculate the interest on loans.

EXAMPLE 18

Find the exact interest on a loan of \$6,500 at 11.75% for 45 days.

Table 10-2 can be used to find the interest. Move down the "Rate/Day" column to 45 days; then move across to $11\frac{3}{4}\%$. The number 1.448630 is the interest on \$100 for 45 days. The interest on \$6,500 is

$\frac{\$6,500 \times 1.448630}{\$100} = 65 \times 1.448630 = \$94.16$ (to nearest cent)

To check this answer, use the formula $I = PRT$.

$I = PRT$

$= \$6,500 \times 0.1175 \times \left(\frac{45}{365}\right) = \$94.16$

Self-Check

9. Figure the due date using ordinary time and exact time for a loan made on October 15 for 120 days.
10. A loan made on March 10 is due September 10 of the *following year.* Find the ordinary time and exact time for the loan in a non–leap year and a leap year.

Table 10-2 Simple Interest Table (Exact Interest)

Rate / Day	Interest per \$100 $11\frac{1}{2}\%$	$11\frac{3}{4}\%$	12.00%	$12\frac{1}{4}\%$	$12\frac{1}{2}\%$	$12\frac{3}{4}\%$
1	0.031507	0.032192	0.032877	0.033562	0.034247	0.034932
2	0.063014	0.064384	0.065753	0.067123	0.068493	0.069863
3	0.094521	0.096575	0.098630	0.100685	0.102740	0.104795
4	0.126027	0.128767	0.131507	0.134247	0.136986	0.139726
5	0.157534	0.160959	0.164384	0.167808	0.171233	0.174658
6	0.189041	0.193151	0.197260	0.201370	0.205479	0.209589
7	0.220548	0.225342	0.230137	0.234932	0.239726	0.244521
8	0.252055	0.257534	0.263014	0.268493	0.273973	0.279452
9	0.283562	0.289726	0.295890	0.302055	0.308219	0.314384
10	0.315068	0.321918	0.328767	0.335616	0.342466	0.349315
11	0.346575	0.354110	0.361644	0.369178	0.376712	0.384247
12	0.378082	0.386301	0.394521	0.402740	0.410959	0.419178
13	0.409589	0.418493	0.427397	0.436301	0.445205	0.454110
14	0.441096	0.450685	0.460274	0.469863	0.479452	0.489041
15	0.472603	0.482877	0.493151	0.503425	0.513699	0.523973
16	0.504110	0.515068	0.526027	0.536986	0.547945	0.558904
17	0.535616	0.547260	0.558904	0.570548	0.582192	0.593836
18	0.567123	0.579452	0.591781	0.604110	0.616438	0.628767
19	0.598630	0.611644	0.624658	0.637671	0.650685	0.663699
20	0.630137	0.643836	0.567534	0.671233	0.684932	0.698630
21	0.661644	0.676027	0.690411	0.704795	0.719178	0.733562
22	0.693151	0.708219	0.723288	0.738356	0.753425	0.768493
23	0.724658	0.740411	0.756164	0.771918	0.787671	0.803425
24	0.756164	0.772603	0.789041	0.805479	0.821918	0.838356
25	0.787671	0.804795	0.821918	0.839041	0.856164	0.873288
26	0.819178	0.836986	0.854795	0.872603	0.890411	0.908219
27	0.850685	0.869178	0.887671	0.906164	0.924658	0.943151
28	0.882192	0.901370	0.920548	0.939726	0.958904	0.978082
29	0.913699	0.933562	0.953425	0.973288	0.993151	1.013014
30	0.945205	0.965753	0.986301	1.006849	1.027397	1.047945
31	0.976712	0.997945	1.019178	1.040411	1.061644	1.082877
32	1.008219	1.030137	1.052055	1.073973	1.095890	1.117808
33	1.039726	1.062329	1.084932	1.107534	1.130137	1.152740
34	1.071233	1.094521	1.117808	1.141096	1.164384	1.187671
35	1.102740	1.126712	1.150685	1.174658	1.198630	1.222603
36	1.134247	1.158904	1.183562	1.208219	1.232877	1.257534
37	1.165753	1.191096	1.216438	1.241781	1.267123	1.292466
38	1.197260	1.223288	1.249315	1.275342	1.301370	1.327397
39	1.228767	1.255479	1.282192	1.308904	1.385616	1.362329
40	1.260274	1.287671	1.315068	1.342466	1.369863	1.397260
41	1.291781	1.319863	1.347945	1.376027	1.404110	1.432192
42	1.323288	1.352055	1.380822	1.409589	1.438356	1.467123
43	1.354795	1.384247	1.413699	1.443151	1.472603	1.502055
44	1.386301	1.416438	1.446575	1.476712	1.506849	1.536986
45	1.417808	1.448630	1.479452	1.510274	1.541096	1.571918
46	1.449315	1.480822	1.512329	1.543836	1.575342	1.606849
47	1.480822	1.513014	1.545205	1.577397	1.609589	1.641781
48	1.512329	1.545205	1.578082	1.610959	1.643836	1.676712
49	1.543836	1.577397	1.610959	1.644521	1.678082	1.711644
50	1.575342	1.609589	1.643836	1.678082	1.712329	1.746575

For Questions 11–13, use the following information: A loan for $3,000 with an interest rate of 15% was made on June 15 and was due on August 15.

11. Use ordinary time to find the ordinary interest on the loan.

12. Find the exact interest using exact time.

13. Find the ordinary interest using exact time.

14. Use Table 10-2 to find the exact interest on a loan of $3,500 at $12\frac{1}{2}$% interest for 45 days.

Cash Discounts Versus Borrowing

Borrowing money to pay cash for large purchases is sometimes profitable when a cash discount is allowed on the purchases. Joann Jimanez purchased a computer and printer during a special promotion for $5,890, with cash terms of 3/10, n/90. She does not have the cash to pay the bill within 10 days but expects to receive a royalty check in the amount of $6,250 within the next 3 months and plans to use this money to pay for the equipment. She finds a bank that will loan her the money at 13% (using ordinary interest) for 80 days. Should she take advantage of the special promotion and cash discount?

Cash discount = $5,890 × 0.03 = $176.70
$5,890 − $176.70 = $5,713.30
90 days − 10 days = 80 days

$I = PRT$

$$I = \$5{,}713.30 \times 0.13 \times \frac{80}{360}$$

$= \$165.05$

Savings from borrowing:

$176.70	cash discount
− 165.05	interest on loan
$ 11.65	amount saved by borrowing funds to take advantage of the cash discount

Although $11.65 could be saved by borrowing the money, the time used to make the loan, cost of travel, and other hidden expenses may make it impractical to take advantage of the cash discount offer.

promissory note: a legal document or instrument in which the borrower promises to repay a loan.

Promissory Notes

payee: the person loaning the money.

maker: the person or company borrowing money.

term: the length of time for which money is borrowed or invested.

face value: the amount of money borrowed on a promissory note.

When a business or individual borrows money, it is customary for the borrower to sign a legal document promising to repay the loan. The document is called a **promissory note.** The note includes all necessary information about the loan. The **maker** is the person borrowing the money. The **payee** is the person loaning the money. The **term** of the note is the length of time for which the money is borrowed; the due date, or maturity date, is the date on which the loan is due to be repaid. The rate is the percent of interest charged. The principal, or **face value,** of the note is the amount borrowed. The *maturity value* is the sum of the principal plus the interest and is the total amount due when the loan is repaid. A sample promissory note is shown in Figure 10-2.

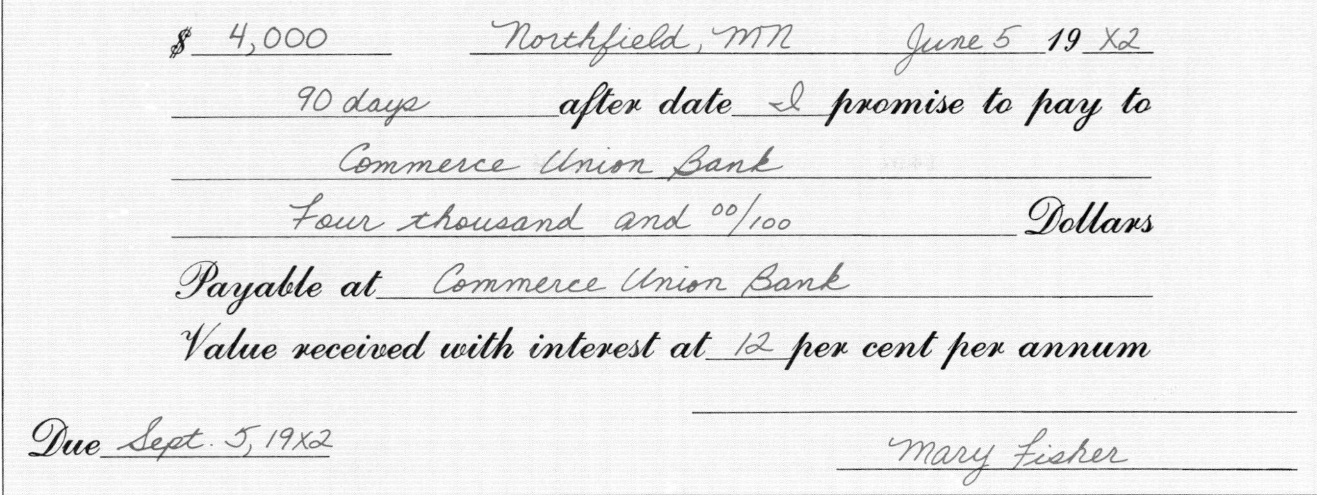

$ 4,000 Northfield, MN June 5 19 X2

90 days after date I promise to pay to

Commerce Union Bank

Four thousand and 00/100 Dollars

Payable at Commerce Union Bank

Value received with interest at 12 per cent per annum

Due Sept. 5, 19X2 Mary Fisher

Figure 10-2 A promissory note

Simple Discount Note

If money is borrowed from a bank, the bank often collects its fee, which is called a bank **discount,** at the time the loan is made. Thus, the maker receives the amount of the loan minus the bank discount.

discount: the interest or fee on a discounted note that is subtracted from the amount borrowed at the time the loan is made.

In the promissory note in Figure 10-2, the maker is Mary Fisher. The payee is Commerce Union Bank. The date of the loan is June 5, and the loan is due September 5. The amount of the loan is \$4,000. Since this is a simple discount note, in which the interest is deducted from the \$4,000 before the maker receives the loan, the note shows no interest to be paid. The interest has already been subtracted. The actual amount that Mary receives from the bank is called the **proceeds.** The method for calculating the proceeds, using the formula $I = PRT$, is shown in the box.

proceeds: the amount that the maker of a discounted note receives; face value − discount = proceeds.

Step by Step

Calculating Bank Discount and Proceeds on a Simple Discount Note

Step 1. Calculate bank discount using $I = PRT$ (I = bank discount).

Step 2. Calculate proceeds using the following formula:

Proceeds = face value − bank discount

EXAMPLE 19

Find the bank discount and proceeds on the promissory note shown in Figure 10-2. It is a loan to Mary Fisher of \$4,000 at 12% from June 5 to September 5.

$$\text{Bank discount} = P \times R \times T$$

$$\text{Bank discount} = \$4{,}000 \times 0.12 \times \frac{90}{360}$$

$$= \$120$$

$$\text{Proceeds} = \$4{,}000 - \$120$$

$$= \$3{,}880$$

The bank discount is \$120. To find the proceeds, the amount that Mary actually receives from the bank, subtract the bank discount from the face value of the note.

The bank discount is \$120.

The proceeds are \$3,880.

undiscounted note: a promissory note for which the interest is not collected when the note is made.

The difference between the simple interest note (which is also called an **undiscounted** promissory **note**) and the simple discount note is that with the simple discount note, the interest is figured on the maturity value, but the borrower has use of only the proceeds (maturity value − discount). Thus, if Bill borrows $5,000 with a discount of 18% or $900, he gets the use of only $4,100, but the bank charges interest figured on the full $5,000.

Here is a comparison of the simple interest versus simple discount notes:

	Simple Interest Note	Simple Discount Note
Face value	$5,000	$5,000
Interest	900	900
Amount available to borrower	5,000	4,100
Maturity value	5,900	5,000

Discounting a Note

discounted note: a promissory note for which the interest or fee is discounted or subtracted at the time the loan is made.

Many businesses accept simple interest and simple discount notes as payment for the sale of goods. If these businesses in turn need cash, they may sell such notes to a bank. Selling a note to a bank in return for cash is called discounting a note; the note is called a **discounted note.**

When the bank discounts a note, it gives the business owning the note the maturity value of the note minus a bank fee (called a bank discount), or the proceeds. The bank receives the full maturity value of the note from the maker when it comes due.

This process is handled the same way as a simple discount note. You have to find the discount period, which is the number of days the *bank* holds the note. The bank's discount is based on how long it holds the note. The following diagram shows how the discount period is figured:

Time of note

Jul. 14 → Sept. 12

Discount period

Aug. 3 → Sept. 12

There is a four-step procedure for calculating the amount of discount and proceeds for a discounted note.

Step by Step

Calculating Bank Discount and Proceeds for a Discounted Note

Step 1. Calculate the maturity value of the note.

Step 2. Calculate the discount period.

Step 3. Calculate the amount of bank discount ($I = PRT$).

Step 4. Calculate the proceeds (proceeds = maturity value − bank discount).

EXAMPLE 20

Holt Company delivers ski equipment to retailers in July but does not expect payment until mid-September, so the retailers agree to sign promissory notes for the equipment. These notes have a 10% interest rate using exact interest. Holt Company holds a promissory note for $8,000 that was made on July 14 and is due September 12. Holt needs cash, so they take the note to their bank. On August 3, the bank agrees to buy the note at a 12% discount rate using the banker's rule. Find the proceeds for the note. A table can be used to organize the facts:

Date of Note	Principal of Note	Interest Rate	Bank Discount Rate	Maturity Date
July 14	$8,000	10%	12%	Sept. 12

Step 1. Calculate the maturity value of the note.

September 12 = day 255
July 14 = day 195
60 days

First you have to calculate exact number of days from July 14 to Sept. 12. Use Table 10-1. There are 60 days.

$I = P \times R \times T$

$= \$8{,}000 \times 0.10 \times \frac{60}{365}$

$= \$131.51$ (rounded)

Use the interest equation to find exact interest.

The interest is $131.51.

Maturity value
= principal + interest
= $8,000 + $131.51
= $8,131.51

To find the maturity value, add the principal and the interest.
The maturity value is $8,131.51.

Step 2. Calculate the discount period.

Discount period
= number of days from August 3 to September 12

To calculate the number of days in the discount period you use Table 10-1 and subtract 215 from 255.

September 12 = day 255
August 3 = day 215
40 days

The discount period is 40 days.

Step. 3 Calculate the amount of bank discount.

$I = P \times R \times T$

Bank discount

$= \text{maturity value} \times \text{bank discount rate} \times \frac{\text{discount period}}{360 \text{ days}}$

$= \$8{,}131.51 \times 0.12 \times \frac{40}{360}$

$= \$108.42$

The amount of bank discount is $108.42.

Step 4. Calculate the proceeds.

Proceeds = maturity value − bank discount
= $8,131.51 − $108.42
= $8,023.09

The proceeds are $8,023.09.

TIPS & TRAPS

There is such a thing as a non-interest-bearing note. This simply means that you borrow a certain amount and pay that same amount back later. The note itself carries no interest amount on it, and the maturity value of the note is the same as the face value or principal.

What happens if a non-interest-bearing note is discounted? Use the information from Example 19.

Step 1. Calculate the maturity value of the note.

Maturity value = \$8,000 — In a non-interest-bearing note, the maturity value is the same as the principal.

Step 2. Calculate the discount period.

255 days − 215 days = 40 days — The discount period is 40 days.

Step 3. Calculate the amount of bank discount.

$$\text{Bank discount} = \$8{,}000 \times 0.12 \times \frac{40}{360}$$
$$= \$106.67$$

The bank discount is \$106.67

Step 4. Calculate proceeds

Proceeds = \$8,000 − \$106.67
= \$7,893.33

The proceeds are \$7,893.33

Self-Check

15. Use the simple interest formula to find the amount of interest paid on a \$2,500 note for 120 days if the bank charges 16% discount.
16. Find the amount of money the borrower would actually receive in the case described in Question 15.
17. Find the maturity value of the undiscounted promissory note shown here.

$ 3,000 Rockville, M.D Aug. 5, 19 X1

Nine Months after date I promise to pay to

City Bank

Three thousand and 00/100 Dollars

Payable at City Bank

Value received with interest at 16½ per cent per annum

Due May 5, 19X2 Phillip Estevez

18. A manufacturer holds an interest-bearing note of $5,000 that has an interest rate of 11%. The note was made on March 18 and is due November 13. The manufacturer sells the note to a bank on June 13 at a discount rate of 14%. Find the proceeds on the bank-discounted note.

Section Review

1. Time figured using 30 days per month is called what kind of time?

2. When the exact number of days in each month is used to figure time, it is called what kind of time?

Use the table to find the exact time from the first date to the second date for non–leap years unless leap year is indicated.

3. March 15 to July 10

4. April 12 to November 15

5. January 18 to October 6

6. November 12 to April 15 of the next year

7. January 5 to June 7

8. April 7, 1992, to August 15, 1992

9. January 12, 1991, to June 28, 1991

10. February 3, 1988, to August 12, 1988 (leap year)

11. January 27, 1996, to September 30, 1996 (leap year)

12. February 15, 1990, to June 15, 1991

If a loan is made on the given date, find the date it is due, using both ordinary time and exact time.

13. March 15 for 30 days

14. January 10 for 210 days

15. May 30 for 240 days

16. August 12 for 60 days

17. June 13 for 90 days

18. December 28 for 60 days

For each of the following problems, find (a) the ordinary interest using ordinary time, (b) the exact interest using exact time, and (c) the ordinary interest using exact time. Round answers to the nearest cent.

19. $5,000 at 17% for 90 days

20. $3,500 at 18% for 60 days

21. A loan of $4,225 at 8% made on March 5, and due on May 5 of the same year

22. A loan of \$1,200 at 10% made on October 15, and due on March 20 of the following year

23. A loan of \$500 at $17\frac{1}{2}\%$ made on February 3 and due on June 15 of the same year. (The year is not a leap year.)

Use the following note for Problems 24–30.

\$ 2,000 Greenville, MS Feb 10 19XX

Six months after date I promise to pay to

First State Bank

Two Thousand and 00/100 Dollars

Payable at First State Bank

Value received with interest at no per cent per annum

Due Aug. 10, 19XX Lida Jenkins

24. Who is the maker of the note shown here?

25. Who is the payee?

26. What is the face value of the note?

27. What is the due date?

28. If the bank charged 9%, find the discount on the note.

29. Find the proceeds of the note.

30. If the bank charged 14%, find the discount on the note. Find the proceeds of the note. Compare the proceeds at 14% interest with the proceeds at 9% (Problem 29).

Use Table 10-2.

31. Find the interest on a loan of $3,700 at $12\frac{1}{4}$% for 15 days.

32. Find the interest on a loan of $2,100 at $11\frac{1}{2}$% interest for 40 days.

33. Find the interest on a loan of $3,600 at 12.75% interest for 18 days.

34. MAK, Inc., accepted an interest-bearing note for $10,000 with 9% interest. The note was made on April 10 and was due December 6. MAK needed cash and took the note to First United Bank, which offered to buy the note at a discount rate of $12\frac{1}{2}$%. The transaction was made on July 7. How much cash did MAK receive for the note?

35. Allan Stojanovich can purchase an office desk for $1,500 with cash terms of 2/10, n/30. If he can borrow the money at 12% simple interest for 20 days, will he save money by taking advantage of the cash discount offered?

Summary

Topic	Page	What to Remember	Example
Simple interest formula	289	Interest = principal × rate × time ($I = PRT$) Always write the rate in decimal or fractional form to solve a problem, and write time as a whole or fractional part of a year.	The simple interest formula, in various forms, is used in the examples that follow.
Solving for interest	290	Interest = principal × rate × time	Milton borrowed $1,200 for 18 months at $14\frac{1}{2}\%$ interest. How much interest did he pay? I is unknown; $P = \$1,200$; $R = 14\frac{1}{2}\% = 0.145$; $T = \frac{18}{12}$ years $= 1.5$ years $I = PRT$ $= (\$1,200)(0.145)(1.5)$ $= \$261$
Maturity value	290–291	Maturity value = principal + interest	What is the maturity value of Milton's loan? $1,200 + $261 = $1,461
Solving for rate	293	$\text{Rate} = \frac{\text{interest}}{\text{principal} \times \text{time}}$ Remember to change the decimal value of R into a percent.	$6,000 was borrowed for $3\frac{1}{2}$ years, with $2,800 simple interest paid. What was the rate of interest? R is unknown; $I = \$2,800$; $P = \$6,000$; $T = 3.5$ years $R = \frac{2,800}{6,000(3.5)} = 13.3\%$
Solving for principal	294	$\text{Principal} = \frac{\text{interest}}{\text{rate} \times \text{time}}$	$675 interest charges are paid on an 18-month loan at 18% interest. Find the principal. P is unknown; $I = \$675$; $R = 18\% = 0.18$; $T = 18 \text{ months} = \frac{18}{12}$ $= 1.5$ years $P = \frac{675}{0.18(1.5)} = \$2,500$

Topic	Page	What to Remember	Example
Solving for time	294	$\text{Time} = \dfrac{\text{interest}}{\text{principal} \times \text{rate}}$	\$1,500 was borrowed at 16.5% interest. \$866.25 interest was paid. Find the duration (time) of the loan. $I = \$866.25$; $P = \$1{,}500$; $R = 16.5\% = 0.165$; T is unknown. $T = \dfrac{866.25}{(\$1{,}500)(0.165)}$ $= 3.5$ years
Finding ordinary time	300–302	In ordinary time, a month is considered to have 30 days.	Find the ordinary time of a loan made on October 1 and due the following May 1. October to May = 7 months 7 months × 30 days/month = 210 days
Finding exact time	300–302	Use Table 10-1 to find the numbers of the beginning and ending dates of the loan. If the loan spans more than one year, add the number of days of the loan in each year.	Find the exact time of a loan made on June 7 and due the following March 7. December 31 = day 365 June 7 = day 158 207 days (year 1) March 7 = + 66 days (year 2) 273 days The loan is made for 273 days in all.
Ordinary interest, ordinary time	300–302	$T = \dfrac{\text{number of months} \times 30\text{ days/ordinary month}}{360\text{ days in an ordinary year}}$	On May 15, Nora borrowed \$6,000 at 12.5% interest. The loan was due on November 15. Use ordinary time to find the ordinary interest due on the loan. $P = \$6{,}000$; $R = 12.5\% = 0.125$; $T = 6$ months $T = \dfrac{6\text{ months} \times 30\text{ days/month}}{360}$ $= \dfrac{180}{360}$ $I = PRT = (6{,}000)(0.125)\left(\dfrac{180}{360}\right)$ $= \$375$
Exact interest, exact time	303	$T = \dfrac{\text{exact number of days}}{365\text{ days in an exact year}}$ (Table 10-1)	Use ordinary interest and exact time to find the interest due on Nora's loan. To figure exact time: November 15 = day 319; May 15 = day 135; day 319 − day 135 = 184 days $P = \$6{,}000$; $R = 12.5\% = 0.125$; $T = \dfrac{184}{365}$ $I = PRT$ $= (6{,}000)(0.125)\left(\dfrac{184}{365}\right)$ $= \$378.08$

Topic	Page	What to Remember	Example
Ordinary interest, exact time (banker's rule)	304	$T = \dfrac{\text{exact number of days}}{\text{360 days in an ordinary year}}$ (Table 10-1)	Use ordinary interest and exact time to find the interest due on Nora's loan. To figure exact time: November 15 = day 319; May 15 = day 135 day 319 − day 135 = 184 days $T = \dfrac{\text{184 exact days}}{\text{360 days in an ordinary year}}$ $P = \$6{,}000$; $R = 12.5\% = 0.125$; $T = \dfrac{184}{360}$ $I = PRT = (6{,}000)(0.125)\left(\dfrac{184}{360}\right)$ $= \$383.33$
Proceeds of a discounted bank note	307–308	Discount (I) = PRT Proceeds = face value − discount (I)	The bank charged Daniel 16.5% discount on a bank note of \$1,500 for 120 days. Find the proceeds of the note. Discount (I) is unknown; $P = \$1{,}500$; $R = 16.5\% = 0.165$; $T = 120 \text{ days} = \dfrac{120}{360} \text{ year}$ Discount $= (1{,}500)(0.165)\left(\dfrac{120}{360}\right)$ $= \$82.50$ Proceeds $= \$1{,}500 - \$82.50$ $= \$1{,}417.50$
Maturity value of an undiscounted bank note	307–308	Maturity value = face value + interest	The bank charged Daniel 16.5% interest on an undiscounted bank note of \$1,500 for 120 days. Find the maturity value of the note. I is unknown; $P = \$1{,}500$; $R = 16.5\% = 0.165$; $T = 120 \text{ days} = \dfrac{120}{360} \text{ year}$ Interest $= (1{,}500)(0.165)\left(\dfrac{120}{360}\right)$ $= \$82.50$ Maturity value $= \$1{,}500 + \$82.50$ $= \$1{,}582.50$

Chapter Review

1. A promissory note has a face value of $5,000 and is discounted by the bank at the rate of 10%. If the note is made for 36 months, find the discount on the note.

2. Find the simple interest on $200 invested at 9% for 5 years.

3. How much money was borrowed at 8% for 6 months if the interest was $12?

4. A loan of $2,000 was made for 120 days. If the interest is $40 find the rate. Round to the nearest whole number percent.

5. Find the exact time from March 15 to September 28 of the same year.

6. Find the exact time from December 8 to May 12 of the following year.

7. Find the ordinary time from May 10 to August 30 of the same year.

8. Find the exact time from January 23, 1992 to April 10, 1992 (leap year).

9. Find the ordinary interest on a loan of $1,000 at 5% made on July 20 for 210 days. Use ordinary time.

10. A printer that originally cost $400 was purchased with a loan for 18 months at 14% simple interest. How much interest will the purchaser pay? What is the *total* cost of the printer?

11. An investment of $4,500 earns 8.5% simple interest. How much interest will be earned in 1 year?

12. A loan of $3,875 is repaid after $2\frac{1}{2}$ years. If the simple interest rate is 16%, how much interest is paid?

13. Find the exact interest on a loan of $2,300 at 9% if the loan is made on April 12 and repaid on September 19 of the same year.

14. How much money should be invested at 7.5% simple interest for 3 years to earn $580.05?

15. Angela Bowen invested $1,980 at $8\frac{3}{4}$% simple interest and earned $346.50 in interest. How long was the money invested?

16. Find the interest charged on a loan of $385 at a simple interest rate of 14.2% for 6 months.

17. A loan of $4,200 was made for 180 days. If the ordinary interest is $262.50, find the rate.

18. James Davis borrowed $5,000 venture capital. He plans to repay the loan in 18 months. How much interest must be paid if the loan rate is 9.25% simple interest?

Use the 6%, 60-day method.

19. Find the interest paid on a loan of $2,300 for 30 days at a simple interest rate of 12%.

20. Find the interest paid on a loan of $1,500 for 90 days at a simple interest rate of 8%.

21. Tonia Callahan can purchase a new stereo system for $2,500 with cash terms of 3/15, n/90. She can borrow the money to take advantage of the cash discount at 11% simple ordinary interest. Will she save money by borrowing to take advantage of the cash discount?

Use Table 10-2.

22. Find the interest on a loan of $2,400 at $11\frac{3}{4}$% interest for 34 days.

23. Find the interest on a loan of $1,450 at $12\frac{1}{2}$% interest for 30 days.

24. Find the interest on a loan of $5,200 at 12.25% interest for 24 days.

25. An interest-bearing note for $7,000 with 11% interest is made on April 12 and due September 30. The note is sold to a bank on June 15. The bank charges a discount rate of 14%. Find the proceeds received from the note on June 15.

26. Find the rate of interest for a loan of $8,000 for 3 years if the interest is $2,880.

27. Find the length of time $5,290 is invested if the interest is $264.50 and the money is invested at 10%.

Trial Test

1. Find the simple interest on $500 invested at 14% for three years.

2. How much money was borrowed at 17% for 6 months if the interest was $85?

3. A loan of $3,000 was made for 210 days. If ordinary interest is $350, find the rate.

4. A loan of $5,000 at 16% requires $1,200 interest. For how long is the money borrowed?

5. Find the exact time from February 13 to November 27 in a non-leap year.

6. Find the exact time from October 12 to March 28 of the following year (a leap year).

7. Find the exact time from January 28, 1996, to July 5, 1996.

8. Find the ordinary time from April 5 to December 20.

9. Find the simple interest on a loan of $20,000 at 21% interest for 2 years.

10. Use ordinary time to find the ordinary interest on a loan of $2,800 at 10% made on March 15 for 270 days.

11. Find the interest on a loan of $469 if the simple interest rate charged is 12% for 6 months.

12. An item with a cash price of $188 can be purchased with a 1-year loan at 10% simple interest. Find the total amount to be repaid.

13. An investment of $7,000 is made for 6 months at the rate of 19% simple interest. How much interest will the investor earn?

14. A copier that originally cost $300 was purchased with a loan for 12 months at 15% simple interest. What was the *total* cost of the copier?

15. Find the ordinary interest on a loan of $850 at 15%. The loan was made January 15 and was due March 15. Use ordinary time.

16. Find the exact interest in Problem 15. Use exact time in a non–leap year. Round to the nearest cent.

17. Find the duration of a loan of $3,000 if the loan required interest of $416.25 and was at a rate of $18\frac{1}{2}\%$ simple interest.

18. Find the simple interest on a loan of $165 if the interest rate is 16% over a 3-month period.

19. Find the rate of simple interest on a \$1,200 loan that requires the borrower to repay a total of \$1,440 after one year.

20. Find the rate of simple interest on a \$600 loan with total interest of \$40.50 if the loan is paid in 6 months.

21. A promissory note has a face value of \$5,000 and is discounted by the bank at the rate of $18\frac{1}{2}\%$. If the note is made for 180 days, find the discount of the note.

22. A promissory note with a face value of \$3,500 is discounted by the bank at the rate of $19\frac{1}{2}\%$. The term of the note is 6 months. Find the proceeds of the note.

23. Use the 6%, 60-day method to find the interest paid on a loan of \$1,600 for 90 days at a simple interest rate of 16%.

24. Jerry Brooks purchases office supplies totaling \$1,890. He can take advantage of cash terms of 2/10, n/30 if he obtains a short-term loan. If he can borrow the money at $10\frac{1}{2}\%$ simple ordinary interest, will he save money if he borrows to take advantage of the cash discount? How much will he save?

Use Table 10-2.

25. Find the interest on a loan of \$25,000 at $11\frac{3}{4}\%$ for 21 days.

26. Find the interest on a loan of \$1,510 at $12\frac{3}{4}\%$ interest for 27 days.

27. Find the interest on a loan of \$4,300 at 11.75% interest for 32 days.

Self-Check Solutions

1. $I = PRT$
$= \$2{,}400 \times 0.11 \times 1$
$= \$264$

2. $I = PRT$
$= \$800 \times 0.085 \times 2$
$= \$136$

3. $I = PRT$
$= \$1{,}400 \times 0.125 \times 3$
$= \$525$

Maturity value = \$1,400 + \$525 = \$1,925

4. 8 months $= \frac{8}{12}$ year
$= 0.6666666$, or 0.67 year

40 months $= \frac{40}{12}$ years
$= 3.333333$, or 3.33 years

5. $R = \frac{I}{PT}$ $\quad T = 30 \text{ months} = \frac{30}{12} \text{ years} = 2.5 \text{ years}$
$= \frac{\$360}{\$1{,}200 \times 2.5}$
$= \frac{360}{3{,}000}$
$= 0.12$, or 12%

6. $R = \frac{I}{PT}$ $\quad T = \frac{7}{12}$ year
$= \frac{\$53.96}{\$500 \times \frac{7}{12}}$ $\quad (\$500 \times \frac{7}{12} = \$291.6667)$
$= 0.185$, or 18.5%

7. $P = \frac{I}{RT}$
$= \frac{\$500}{0.09 \times 2}$
$= \frac{\$500}{0.18}$
$= \$2{,}777.78$

8. $T = \frac{I}{PR}$
$= \frac{\$360}{\$6{,}000 \times 0.12}$
$= \frac{360}{720}$
$= 0.5 = \frac{1}{2}$ year, or 6 months

9. Ordinary time: 120 days is $\frac{120}{30}$, or 4 months.

4 months from October 15 is February 15.
Exact time: October 15 = day 288
$\quad + 120$
$\quad 408$

$408 - 365 = 43$ days
The 43rd day is February 12.

10. *Non-leap year*

Ordinary time: March 10 to March 10 is 12 months, or 12 × 30 days = 360 days.

March 10 to September 10 is 6 months, or 6 × 30 days = 180 days.

360 days + 180 days = 540 days

Exact time: March 10 to March 10 of the following year is 1 year, or 365 days.

September 10 = day 253

March 10 = day 69

184 days

365 + 184 = 549 days

Leap year

366 + 184 = 550 days

11. Ordinary time = 2 months, or 2 × 30 = 60 days

$$I = \$3{,}000 \times 0.15 \times \frac{60}{360} = \$75$$

12. Exact time: August 15 = day 227

June 15 = day 166

61 days

$$I = \$3{,}000 \times 0.15 \times \frac{61}{365} = \$75.21$$

13. $I = \$3{,}000 \times 0.15 \times \frac{61}{360} = \$76.25$

14. $I = \$3{,}500 \times 1.541096 \div 100 = \$53.94$

15. $I = \$2{,}500 \times 0.16 \times \frac{120}{360} = \$133.33$

16. Proceeds = \$2,500 − \$133.33 = \$2,366.67

17. Calculate time: December 31 = day 365

August 5 = day 217

148 days

May 5 = day 125

273 days

$$I = \$3{,}000 \times 0.165 \times \frac{273}{365} = \$375.37$$

18. Maturity value of note: November 13 = day 317

March 18 = day 77

240 days

$$I = \$5{,}000 \times 0.11 \times \frac{240}{365} = \$361.64$$

Maturity value = \$5,000 + \$361.64 = \$5,361.64

Bank discount: November 13 = day 317

June 13 = day 164

153 days

$$I = \$5{,}361.64 \times 0.14 \times \frac{153}{360} = \$319.02$$

Proceeds = \$5,361.64 − \$319.02 = \$5,042.62

Compound Interest and Present Value 11

Learning Objectives

1. Understand and work with compound interest. (pp. 329–335)
2. Find the compound amount and future value of loans with and without a table. (pp. 329–334)
3. Find the present value of investments using compound interest with and without a table. (pp. 338–341)

In Chapter 10 you learned to calculate simple interest. You use simple interest to calculate the interest for a single period. With some loans or investments, the interest is added to the principal at the end of a specified time, and interest is then calculated on this principal plus interest for the next period. This process is called compounding interest. Compounding interest has several uses in the business world; the one with which you are probably familiar is used in a savings account, where you "earn interest on your interest."

Compound Interest and Future Value

In most loans made on a short-term basis, interest is computed by using the simple interest formula. If interest on a loan or investment is calculated more than once during the term of the loan or investment, this interest is added to the principal unless it is paid out. This sum (principal + interest) then becomes the principal for the next calculation of interest, and interest is charged or paid on this new amount.

This process of adding interest to the principal before interest is calculated for the next period is called *compounding interest.* This process of compounding interest is repeated as many times as there are **interest periods** in the term of the loan or investment. The total amount at the end of the loan or investment term is called the **compound total,** or **future value.** The difference between the original amount of the loan or investment and the compound total (or future value) is the **compound interest.** Note that when we calculate compound interest, whether for a loan or investment, none of the money borrowed or invested is repaid until the *end* of the term of the loan or investment.

The terms of a loan indicate how often and at what rate interest is compounded. To figure the interest, you use the same formula you used with simple interest, $I = P \times R \times T$. On a loan of \$500 at 12% for 6 years, you first multiply \$500 × 0.12 × 1 (for the first year) to get the first year's interest, \$60. This process is repeated, as shown in the accompanying box.

interest period: the length of time during which the interest on a loan or investment is compounded.

compound total: the total amount at the end of a loan or investment term (also called future value).

future value: the total amount at the end of a loan or investment term (also called compound amount, or compound total).

compound interest: the difference between the original amount of a loan or investment and the compound total (or future value).

Step by Step

Calculating Compound Total and Compound Interest

Step 1. Find the interest and add it to the principal; use this sum as the base to figure next year's interest.

Step 2. Repeat this for the number of years in the loan. The final figure is the compound total.

Step 3. Find the compound interest using this formula:

Compound interest = compound total − principal

EXAMPLE 1

A loan of $800 at 13% is made for 3 years, compounded annually. Find the compound amount and the amount of compound interest paid on the loan. Compare the compound interest with simple interest for the same period.

Find the compound amount

$800 × 0.13 = $104	Find the first year's interest.
$800 + $104 = $904	First year's interest + principal = second year's principal.
$904 × 0.13 = $117.52	Find the second year's interest.
$904 + $117.52 = $1,021.52	Second year's interest + second year's principal = third year's principal.
$1,021.52 × 0.13 = $132.7976	Find the third year's interest, rounded to the nearest cent.
$1,021.52 + $132.80 = $1,154.32	Third year's principal + third year's interest = compound total.

Find the amount of compound interest

$1,154.32	Compound total
− 800	Principal
$ 354.32	Compound interest

The compound interest is $354.32.

Comparing compound and simple interest

Use the simple interest formula to find the simple interest on $800 at 13% interest for 3 years.

$I = PRT$
$P = \$800;\ R = 13\% = 0.13;\ T = 3$
$I = \$800 \times 0.13 \times 3$
$I = \$312$

The simple interest is $312.

The compound interest is $42.32 more than the simple interest. This difference would be even greater if the interest were compounded more frequently.

TIPS & TRAPS

When compounding interest, be sure to add the interest to the *previous principal*. A common mistake is to add the interest to the *original principal*. We'll use the numbers from Example 1.

CORRECT	WRONG
$800 × 0.13 = $104	~~$800 × 0.13 = $104~~
$800 + $104 = $904	~~$800 + $104 = $904~~
$904 × 0.13 = $117.52	~~$904 × 0.13 = $117.52~~
$904 + $117.52 = $1,021.52	~~$800 + $117.52 = $917.52~~
$1,021.52 × 0.13 = $132.7976	~~$917.52 × 0.13 = $119.28~~
$1,021.52 + $132.80 = $1,154.32	~~$800 + $119.28 = $919.28~~

There is a shortcut for the method just shown. It is the following: For each year of the loan, multiply the new principal times 1 + the interest rate. The product is the next year's principal. Consider Example 1 again, a loan of $800 at 13% for 3 years, compounded annually.

Year 1: $800 × 1.13 = $904

Year 2: $904 × 1.13 = $1,021.52

Year 3: $1,021.52 × 1.13 = $1,154.3176, or $1,154.32

This eliminates the step of having to add the new interest to the old principal to find the new principal.

Using a Compound Interest Table

It is obvious from Example 1 that compounding interest for a large number of periods would be very time-consuming. This task is made simpler if you use a compound interest table, as shown in Table 11-1 on p. 332. The values listed in the table have been rounded.

The numbers in Table 11-1 show the compounded amount per dollar of principal, or the value of $1 at the end of the indicated period or number of years. Thus, the compound total for *each dollar* borrowed or invested at 6% interest compounded annually for 2 years would be $1.12360. The compound total (principal plus interest) for a 2-year loan of $300 at 6% interest compounded annually would be $300 × 1.12360 = $337.08 for the year.

Step by Step

Using a Compound Interest Table

Step 1. Look down the left column to find the correct number of periods or years; then look across that row to find the column for the correct interest rate. The number listed is the compound total for $1.

Step 2. Multiply the compound total for $1 times the amount of the loan in dollars:

Compound total = amount of loan × compound total for $1

Table 11-1 Compound Interest Table

Period	1%	$1\frac{1}{2}$%	2%	$2\frac{1}{2}$%	3%	4%	5%	6%	8%	10%	12%
	Rate per Period										
1	1.01000	1.01500	1.02000	1.02500	1.03000	1.04000	1.05000	1.06000	1.08000	1.10000	1.12000
2	1.02010	1.03023	1.04040	1.05063	1.06090	1.08160	1.10250	1.12360	1.16640	1.21000	1.25440
3	1.03030	1.04568	1.06121	1.07689	1.09273	1.12486	1.15763	1.19102	1.25971	1.33100	1.40493
4	1.04060	1.06136	1.08243	1.10381	1.12551	1.16986	1.21551	1.26248	1.36049	1.46410	1.57352
5	1.05101	1.07728	1.10408	1.13141	1.15927	1.21665	1.27628	1.33823	1.46933	1.61051	1.76234
6	1.06152	1.09344	1.12616	1.15969	1.19405	1.26532	1.34010	1.41852	1.58687	1.77156	1.97382
7	1.07214	1.10984	1.14869	1.18869	1.22987	1.31593	1.40710	1.50363	1.71382	1.94872	2.21068
8	1.08286	1.12649	1.17166	1.21840	1.26677	1.36857	1.47746	1.59385	1.85093	2.14359	2.47596
9	1.09369	1.14339	1.19509	1.24886	1.30477	1.42331	1.55133	1.68948	1.99900	2.35795	2.77308
10	1.10462	1.16054	1.21899	1.28008	1.34392	1.48024	1.62889	1.79085	2.15892	2.59374	3.10585
11	1.11567	1.17795	1.24337	1.31209	1.38423	1.53945	1.71034	1.89830	2.33164	2.85312	3.47855
12	1.12683	1.19562	1.26824	1.34489	1.42576	1.60103	1.79586	2.01220	2.51817	3.13843	3.89598
13	1.13809	1.21355	1.29361	1.37851	1.46853	1.66507	1.88565	2.13293	2.71962	3.45227	4.36349
14	1.14947	1.23176	1.31948	1.41297	1.51259	1.73168	1.97993	2.26090	2.93719	3.79750	4.88711
15	1.16097	1.25023	1.34587	1.44830	1.55797	1.80094	2.07893	2.39656	3.17217	4.17725	5.47357
16	1.17258	1.26899	1.37279	1.48451	1.60471	1.87298	2.18287	2.54035	3.42594	4.59497	6.13039
17	1.18430	1.28802	1.40024	1.52162	1.65285	1.94790	2.29202	2.69277	3.70002	5.05447	6.86604
18	1.19615	1.30734	1.42825	1.55966	1.70243	2.02582	2.40662	2.85434	3.99602	5.55992	7.68997
19	1.20811	1.32695	1.45681	1.59865	1.75351	2.10685	2.52695	3.02560	4.31570	6.11591	8.61276
20	1.22019	1.34686	1.48595	1.63862	1.80611	2.19112	2.65330	3.20714	4.66096	6.72750	9.64629
21	1.23239	1.36706	1.51567	1.67958	1.86029	2.27877	2.78596	3.39956	5.03383	7.40025	10.80385
22	1.24472	1.38756	1.54598	1.72157	1.91610	2.36992	2.92526	3.60354	5.43654	8.14027	12.10031
23	1.25716	1.40838	1.57690	1.76461	1.97359	2.46472	3.07152	3.81975	5.87146	8.95430	13.55235
24	1.26973	1.42950	1.60844	1.80873	2.03279	2.56330	3.22510	4.04893	6.34118	9.84973	15.17863
25	1.28243	1.45095	1.64061	1.85394	2.09378	2.66584	3.38635	4.29187	6.84848	10.83471	17.00006
26	1.29526	1.47271	1.67342	1.90029	2.15659	2.77247	3.55567	4.54938	7.39635	11.91818	19.04007
27	1.30821	1.49480	1.70689	1.94780	2.22129	2.88337	3.73346	4.82235	7.98806	13.10999	21.32488
28	1.32129	1.51722	1.74102	1.99650	2.28793	2.99870	3.92013	5.11169	8.62711	14.42099	23.88387
29	1.33450	1.53998	1.77584	2.04641	2.35657	3.11865	4.11614	5.41839	9.31727	15.86309	26.74993
30	1.34785	1.56308	1.81136	2.09757	2.42726	3.24340	4.32194	5.74349	10.06266	17.44940	29.95992

EXAMPLE 2

Use Table 11-1 to compute the compound interest on \$500 for 6 years compounded annually at 4%.

Find period 6 in the first column of the table and move across to the 4% column. This figure is 1.26532. This means that \$1 would be worth \$1.26532, compounded annually.

$\$500 \times 1.26532 = \$632.66$ — The loan is for \$500, so multiply \$500 by 1.26532 to find the compound amount.

Thus, the compound amount, or future value, is \$632.66.

$\$632.66 - \$500 = \$132.66$ — The compound amount minus the principal equals the compound interest.

Compounding for Periods of Less Than a Year

Sometimes loans or savings are compounded more than once a year. In such cases, you use the compound interest table in a three-step procedure.

Step by Step

Finding Compound Interest for Periods Less Than a Year

Step 1. Determine the number of interest periods by multiplying the number of years in the loan by the number of times compounding takes place each year.

Step 2. Find the interest rate per period by dividing the annual rate by the number of times compounding occurs per year.

Step 3. Use these two new figures to compute the compound interest, or use the table.

EXAMPLE 3

A loan of $300 at 8% is compounded *quarterly* (four times a year) for 3 years. Find the compound amount and the compound interest.

3 years × 4 periods = 12 periods	The loan is compounded four times a year for 3 years.
$\frac{8\%}{4} = 2\%$	Divide the annual rate of 8% by the number of periods per year to find the rate of interest for each period.
1.26824	Find 12 periods in the left-hand column of the table. Move across to the 2% column and find the compound amount per dollar of principal.
$300 × 1.26824 = $380.47	The amount of principal times the compound amount per dollar equals the total compound amount.

$380.47 is the compound amount, or future value.

$380.47 − 300 $ 80.47	The compound amount minus principal equals the total amount of compound interest.

The compound interest on the loan is $80.47.

(If the loan were compounded annually instead of quarterly for 3 years, the compound total would be $377.91 and the compound interest would be $77.91; if the interest on the loan were simple interest, at the end of 3 years the amount of interest would be $72.)

TIPS & TRAPS

There are many different types of compounding, and it helps to memorize the following:

Compounding annually	compounding 1 time each year
Compounding semiannually	compounding 2 times a year
Compounding quarterly	compounding 4 times a year
Compounding monthly	compounding 12 times a year
Compounding daily	compounding 365 times a year

Finding the Effective Rate

effective rate: the total interest for 1 year divided by the principal of a loan or investment.

You can see from Example 3 that a loan with an interest rate of 8%, compounded quarterly, carries higher interest charges than a loan with an interest rate of 8% compounded annually or a loan with a simple interest rate of 8%. When you evaluate the interest charges on a compound interest loan, you need to know the actual, or **effective, rate** of interest. You find this by dividing the total interest for the year by the principal of the loan.

EXAMPLE 4

Find the effective rate of interest for the loan of $300 at 8%, compounded quarterly, that was described in Example 3.

To find the *total interest* for the first year of the 3-year loan in Example 3, we must recalculate.

The number of periods in 1 year = 4

Rate per period is $\frac{8\%}{4} = 2\%$

1.08243 — Find period 4 in the left-hand column of the table. Move across to the 2% column.

$\$300 \times 1.08243 = \$324.729$ — The amount of principal times the compound amount per dollar equals the total compound amount.

$\$324.73 - \$300 = \$24.73$ — Compound amount − principal = interest. The compound interest for 1 year is $24.73.

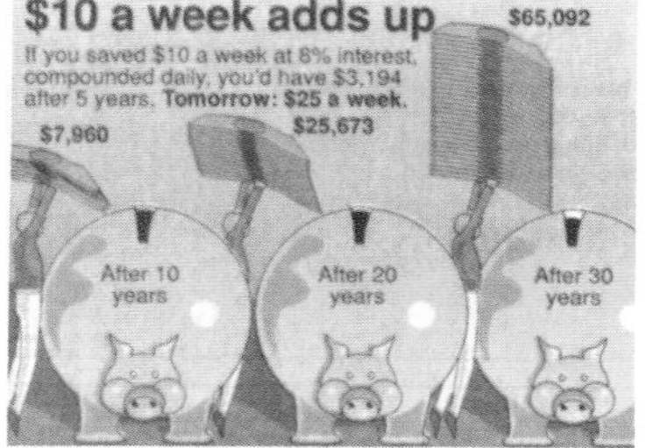

Source: USA TODAY research
By Julie Stacey, USA TODAY

$$\text{Effective rate} = \frac{\text{total compound interest for 1 year}}{\text{principal}}$$

$$= \frac{\$24.73}{\$300} = 0.0824, \text{ or } 8.24\%$$

Compounding Interest Daily

Some banks compound interest daily and others use continuous compounding to compute interest on savings accounts. There is very little difference in the interest earned on money using interest compounded daily and compounded continuously. The computer is generally used in calculating interest if either daily or continuous compounding is used.

Table 11-2 is part of a table that gives interest on $100 compounded daily using 365 days as a year. Notice that this table gives the *interest* on the principal rather than the *compound amount,* as is given in Table 11-1.

EXAMPLE 5

Find the interest compounded daily on $800 at 13% for 28 days.

1.002070 — Find 28 days in the left-hand column of the table. Move across to the 13% column and find the interest for $100.

$$\frac{\$800}{\$100} = 8 \times \$1.002070$$

$$= \$8.02$$

Table 11-2 Daily Compounding Per $100 (365-day Basis)

	Interest per $100								
Day	**12%**	**12.25%**	**12.5%**	**12.75%**	**13%**	**13.25%**	**13.5%**	**13.75%**	**14%**
1	0.032876	0.033561	0.034246	0.034931	0.035616	0.036301	0.036986	0.037671	0.038356
2	0.065764	0.067134	0.068504	0.069875	0.071245	0.072615	0.073986	0.075356	0.076727
3	0.098662	0.100718	0.102774	0.104831	0.106887	0.108943	0.110999	0.113056	0.115112
4	0.131571	0.134314	0.137056	0.139799	0.142541	0.145284	0.148027	0.150770	0.153512
5	0.164491	0.167920	0.171350	0.174779	0.178209	0.181638	0.185068	0.188498	0.191928
6	0.197422	0.201538	0.205655	0.209772	0.213889	0.218005	0.222123	0.226240	0.230357
7	0.230364	0.235168	0.239972	0.244776	0.249581	0.254386	0.259191	0.263996	0.268802
8	0.263316	0.268808	0.274301	0.279793	0.285286	0.290780	0.296273	0.301767	0.307261
9	0.296279	0.302460	0.308641	0.314823	0.321005	0.327187	0.333369	0.339552	0.345735
10	0.329253	0.336123	0.342994	0.349864	0.356735	0.363607	0.370479	0.377351	0.384224
11	0.362238	0.369798	0.377358	0.384918	0.392479	0.400040	0.407602	0.415164	0.422727
12	0.395234	0.403483	0.411733	0.419984	0.428235	0.436487	0.444739	0.452992	0.461246
13	0.428241	0.437181	0.446121	0.455062	0.464004	0.472947	0.481890	0.490834	0.499779
14	0.461258	0.470889	0.480520	0.490153	0.499786	0.509420	0.519054	0.528690	0.538327
15	0.494287	0.504609	0.514931	0.525255	0.535580	0.545906	0.556233	0.566561	0.576889
16	0.527326	0.538340	0.549354	0.560370	0.571387	0.582405	0.593425	0.604445	0.615467
17	0.560376	0.572082	0.583789	0.595498	0.607207	0.618918	0.630631	0.642344	0.654059
18	0.593437	0.605836	0.618236	0.630637	0.643040	0.655444	0.667850	0.680257	0.692666
19	0.626509	0.639601	0.652694	0.665789	0.678885	0.691984	0.705083	0.718185	0.731288
20	0.659591	0.673377	0.687164	0.700953	0.714744	0.728536	0.742330	0.756127	0.769925
21	0.692685	0.707164	0.721646	0.736129	0.750615	0.765102	0.779591	0.794083	0.808576
22	0.725789	0.740963	0.756140	0.771318	0.786498	0.801681	0.816866	0.832053	0.847242
23	0.758905	0.774774	0.790645	0.806519	0.822395	0.838274	0.854154	0.870038	0.885923
24	0.792031	0.808595	0.825162	0.841732	0.858304	0.874879	0.891457	0.908037	0.924619
25	0.825168	0.842428	0.859692	0.876958	0.894226	0.911498	0.928773	0.946050	0.963330
26	0.858316	0.876273	0.894233	0.912195	0.930161	0.948130	0.966102	0.984078	1.002056
27	0.891475	0.910129	0.928785	0.947446	0.966109	0.984776	1.003446	1.022120	1.040796
28	0.924645	0.943996	0.963350	0.982708	1.002070	1.021435	1.040804	1.060176	1.079552
29	0.957826	0.977874	0.997927	1.017983	1.038043	1.058107	1.078175	1.098246	1.118322
30	0.991017	1.011764	1.032515	1.053270	1.074029	1.094792	1.115560	1.136331	1.157107

Self-Check

1. A loan of $1,200 at 16% is made for 3 years, compounded annually. Find the compound amount and the amount of compound interest paid on the loan. Compare the compound interest with simple interest for the same period.
2. Use Table 11-1 to compute the compound interest on $2,000 for 4 years compounded annually at 8%.
3. A loan of $800 at 12% is compounded quarterly for 5 years. Find the compound amount and the compound interest.
4. Find the effective rate of interest for the loan described in Problem 3.
5. Find the interest compounded daily on $2,500 at $13\frac{1}{4}$% for 20 days.

Section Review

1. Calculate the compound interest on a loan of $1,000 at 8% compounded annually for 2 years.

2. Calculate the compound interest on a loan of $200 at 6% compounded annually for 4 years.

3. Calculate the compound interest on a 13% loan of $1,600 for 3 years if the interest is compounded annually.

4. Consult Table 11-1 to find the interest on a loan of $10,000 for 5 years at 4%, compounded semiannually.

5. How much more interest is paid on the loan in Problem 4 than if simple interest had been used?

6. Use Table 11-1 to find the compound interest on the following loans:

Principal	Term (years)	Rate of Compound Interest	Interest	Compounded
a. $2,000	3	3%	—	Annually
b. $3,500	4	10%	—	Semiannually
c. $ 800	2	6%	—	Quarterly

7. Use Table 11-1 to find the factor for compounding an amount for 25 periods at 8% per period.

8. Use Table 11-1 to find the compound amount on an investment of $8,000 compounded quarterly for 7 years at 8%.

9. An investment of $1,000 is made at the beginning of each year for 2 years, compounded semiannually at 10%. Find the compound amount and the compound interest at the end of the 2 years.

10. Calculate the compound interest on a loan of $5,000 for 2 years if the interest is compounded quarterly at 12%.

11. Calculate the compound interest on a loan of $5,000 for 2 years if the interest is compounded semiannually at 12%.

12. Find the effective interest rate for the loan described in Problem 10.

13. Find the effective interest rate for the loan described in Problem 11.

14. An investment of $2000 is made at the beginning of each year for 3 years. The investment is compounded annually at 8%. Find the compound amount and the compound interest at the end of 3 years.

15. Use Table 11-2 to find the amount of interest on $100 invested for 10 days at 13% compounded daily.

16. Use Table 11-2 to find the daily interest on an investment of $5,000 invested for 30 days at $13\frac{1}{2}$%.

17. Use Table 11-2 to find the compound interest and the compound amount of an investment of $2,000 if it is invested for 21 days at 13% compounded daily.

18. Use Table 11-1 to find the interest on an investment of $1,000 for 30 days if it is invested at 12% compounded monthly. Compare this interest to the interest earned on $1,000 for 30 days at 12% compounded daily.

19. Linda Boyd invests $2,000 at 8% compounded semiannually for 2 years and Inez Everett invests an equal amount at 8% compounded quarterly for 18 months. Use Table 11-1 to determine which investment yields the greatest interest.

20. What is the effective interest rate of each of the investments in Problem 19?

Present Value

In the first part of this chapter you learned how to calculate the future value (compound value) of an amount of money invested at the present time. Sometimes businesses and individuals need to know how much should be invested at the present time to yield a certain amount at some specified future date. For example, a business may wish to set aside a sum of money to repay a loan at some future date. Individuals may wish to set aside money now to pay for a child's college education or for a vacation. You can use the concepts of compound interest to figure the amount of money that must be set aside at present and compounded periodically to obtain a certain amount of money at some specific time in the future. The amount of money set aside at present is called **present value.**

present value: the amount of money needed at present to yield, or earn, a specified amount at a future date.

Present value can be found by dividing the maturity value by 1 + the interest rate expressed as a decimal. In other words, for a 6% interest rate, you would divide the maturity value by 1.06.

Step by Step

Calculating Present Value for an Amount Compounded Annually

Step 1. Express the interest rate as a decimal and add it to 1.

Step 2. The sum from Step 1 becomes the denominator in the following formula:

$$\text{Present value} = \frac{\text{maturity value}}{1 + \text{interest rate (a decimal)}}$$

EXAMPLE 6

Calculate the amount of money that should be set aside today to ensure a maturity value of $1,000 in 1 year if the interest rate is 8% and interest is compounded annually.

$1 + 0.08 = 1.08$ — Convert the interest rate to a decimal and add to 1.

$\frac{\$1{,}000}{1.08} = \$925.93$ — Divide the maturity value by 1.08 to get the present value.

An investment of $925.93 at 8% would have a value of $1,000 in 1 year.

Using a Present Value Table

If the interest in Example 6 had been compounded more than once a year, you would have to divide by 1.08 for each time the money was compounded. This would be very time-consuming if there were a large number of compounding periods. For this reason you can use a table showing the present value of $1 at different interest rates for different periods. You multiply the present value of $1 (from Table 11-3 on p. 340) by the desired maturity value to find how much money must be invested in the present to give us the desired future amount.

EXAMPLE 7

The Randles think they will need $20,000 in 10 years to send their child to college. How much must they invest at the present if they will receive 10% interest compounded annually?

0.38554

The money is to be compounded for 10 periods, so we find 10 (periods) in the left column of Table 11-3 and look under the 10% column to find the present value per dollar of future value.

$20,000 × 0.38554 = $7,710.80

Multiply the present value factor times the desired future value to find the amount that must be invested in the present.

The Randles should invest $7,710.80 today to have $20,000 in 10 years.

EXAMPLE 8

Use Table 11-3 to calculate the amount of money that must be invested now at 8%, compounded quarterly, to obtain $5,000 in 5 years.

5 years × 4 periods = 20 periods

Find the total number of periods.

$\frac{8\%}{4} = 2\%$ interest each period

Divide the annual rate of 8% by the number of periods per year to find the rate of interest for each period.

Table 11-3 Present Value Table

Period	1%	$1\frac{1}{2}$%	2%	$2\frac{1}{2}$%	3%	4%	5%	6%	8%	10%	12%
1	0.99010	0.98522	0.98039	0.97561	0.97087	0.96154	0.95238	0.94340	0.92593	0.90909	0.89286
2	0.98030	0.97066	0.96117	0.95181	0.94260	0.92456	0.90703	0.89000	0.85734	0.82645	0.79719
3	0.97059	0.95632	0.94232	0.92860	0.91514	0.88900	0.86384	0.83962	0.79383	0.75131	0.71178
4	0.96098	0.94218	0.92385	0.90595	0.88849	0.85480	0.82270	0.79209	0.73503	0.68301	0.63552
5	0.95147	0.92826	0.90573	0.88385	0.86261	0.82193	0.78353	0.74726	0.68058	0.62092	0.56743
6	0.94205	0.91454	0.88797	0.86230	0.83748	0.79031	0.74622	0.70496	0.63017	0.56447	0.50663
7	0.93272	0.90103	0.87056	0.84127	0.81309	0.75992	0.71068	0.66506	0.58349	0.51316	0.45235
8	0.92348	0.88771	0.85349	0.82075	0.78941	0.73069	0.67684	0.62741	0.54027	0.46651	0.40388
9	0.91434	0.87459	0.83676	0.80073	0.76642	0.70259	0.64461	0.59190	0.50025	0.42410	0.36061
10	0.90529	0.86167	0.82035	0.78120	0.74409	0.67556	0.61391	0.55839	0.46319	0.38554	0.32197
11	0.89632	0.84893	0.80426	0.76214	0.72242	0.64958	0.58468	0.52679	0.42888	0.35049	0.28748
12	0.88745	0.83639	0.78849	0.74356	0.70138	0.62460	0.55684	0.49697	0.39711	0.31863	0.25668
13	0.87866	0.82403	0.77303	0.72542	0.68095	0.60057	0.53032	0.46884	0.36770	0.28966	0.22917
14	0.86996	0.81185	0.75788	0.70773	0.66112	0.57748	0.50507	0.44230	0.34046	0.26333	0.20462
15	0.86135	0.79985	0.74301	0.69047	0.64186	0.55526	0.48102	0.41727	0.31524	0.23939	0.18270
16	0.85282	0.78803	0.72845	0.67362	0.62317	0.53391	0.45811	0.39365	0.29189	0.21763	0.16312
17	0.84438	0.77639	0.71416	0.65720	0.60502	0.51337	0.43630	0.37136	0.27027	0.19784	0.14564
18	0.83602	0.76491	0.70016	0.64117	0.58739	0.49363	0.41552	0.35034	0.25025	0.17986	0.13004
19	0.82774	0.75361	0.68643	0.62553	0.57029	0.47464	0.39573	0.33051	0.23171	0.16351	0.11611
20	0.81954	0.74247	0.67297	0.61027	0.55368	0.45639	0.37689	0.31180	0.21455	0.14864	0.10367
21	0.81143	0.73150	0.65978	0.59539	0.53755	0.43883	0.35894	0.29416	0.19866	0.13513	0.09256
22	0.80340	0.72069	0.64684	0.58086	0.52189	0.42196	0.34185	0.27751	0.18394	0.12285	0.08264
23	0.79544	0.71004	0.63416	0.56670	0.50669	0.40573	0.32557	0.26180	0.17032	0.11168	0.07379
24	0.78757	0.69954	0.62172	0.55288	0.49193	0.39012	0.31007	0.24698	0.15770	0.10153	0.06588
25	0.77977	0.68921	0.60953	0.53939	0.47761	0.37512	0.29530	0.23300	0.14602	0.09230	0.05882
26	0.77205	0.67902	0.59758	0.52623	0.46369	0.36069	0.28124	0.21981	0.13520	0.08391	0.05252
27	0.76440	0.66899	0.58586	0.51340	0.45019	0.34682	0.26785	0.20737	0.12519	0.07628	0.04689
28	0.75684	0.65910	0.57437	0.50088	0.43708	0.33348	0.25509	0.19563	0.11591	0.06934	0.04187
29	0.74934	0.64936	0.56311	0.48866	0.42435	0.32065	0.24295	0.18456	0.10733	0.06304	0.03738
30	0.74192	0.63976	0.55207	0.47674	0.41199	0.30832	0.23138	0.17411	0.09938	0.05731	0.03338

0.67297	Find 20 periods in Table 11-3 and look in the 2% column to find the present value per dollar of future value.
$5,000 × 0.67297 = $3,364.85	Multiply the number from the table by the future value to find the amount that must be invested in the present.

$3,364.85 invested now at 8%, compounded quarterly, will yield $5,000 in 5 years.

Self-Check

6. Compute the amount of money that should be set aside today to ensure a maturity value of $2,500 in 1 year if the interest rate is 11%, compounded annually.

7. Linda thinks she will need $2,000 in 3 years to make the down payment on a new car. How much must she invest today if she will receive 8% interest compounded annually?

8. Use Table 11-3 to calculate the amount of money that must be invested now at 6%, compounded quarterly, to obtain $1,500 in 3 years.

Real World Application

REAL ESTATE: IS THIS A GOOD DEAL?

One real estate sales technique is to encourage customers or clients to buy today, because the value of the property will only increase during the next few years. "Buy this lot today for $30,000. In two years, I project it will sell for $32,500." Let's see if this is a wise investment.

In two years the future value is projected to be $32,500. If the interest rate is 12%, compounded annually, what amount should you invest today to have the $32,500 in 2 years?

Using Table 11-3 in the text, the factor for 12% and 2 periods is 0.79719.

Present value = $32,500 × 0.79719 = $25,908.68

By investing only $25,908.68 today at 12% for 2 years, you will have the $32,500 needed to purchase the land. You have actually paid only $25,908.68 for the lot, a savings of $4,091.32. Of course, there are always problems with waiting to buy.

Application Questions

1. What are some of the problems with waiting to buy land?

2. What are some of the advantages of waiting?

3. Lots in a new subdivision sell for $15,600. If you invest your money today in an account earning 8% quarterly, how much will the lot actually cost you in a year assuming the price does not go up? How much do you save?

4. a. You have inherited $60,000 and plan to buy a home. If you invest the $60,000 today at 10% compounded annually, how much could you spend on the house in 1 year?

b. If you intend to spend $60,000 on a house in 1 year, how much of your inheritance should you invest today at 10% compounded annually? How much do you have left to spend on a car?

Section Review

In the following problems, find the amount of money that should be invested at the stated interest rate to yield the given amount (future value) after the indicated amount of time. Use Table 11-3.

1. $1,500 in 3 years at 10%, compounded annually

2. $2,000 in 5 years at 10%, compounded semiannually

3. $1,000 in 7 years at 8%, compounded quarterly

4. $3,500 in 12 years at 12%, compounded annually

5. $4,000 in 2 years at 12%, compounded quarterly

6. $10,000 in 7 years at 16%, compounded quarterly

7. $500 in 15 years at 8%, compounded semiannually

8. $800 in 4 years at 10%, compounded annually

9. $1,800 in 1 year at 12%, compounded monthly

10. $700 in 6 years at 8%, compounded quarterly

11. Myrna Lewis wished to have $4,000 in 4 years to tour Europe. How much must she invest today at 8% compounded quarterly to have the $4,000 in 4 years?

12. Louis Banks was offered $15,000 cash or $22,900 to be paid in two years for a resort cabin. If money can be invested in today's market for 12% compounded quarterly, which offer should Louis accept?

13. An art dealer offered a collector $8,000 cash for a painting. The collector could sell the painting to an individual for $11,000 to be paid in 18 months. On the current money market, investments bring 12%, compounded monthly. Which is the better deal for the collector?

14. If you were offered $700 today or $800 in 2 years, which would you accept if money can be invested at 12%, compounded monthly?

Summary

Topic	Page	What to Remember	Examples
Finding compound amount without using a table	329–330	The interest for each year is based on the sum of the previous year's principal and interest.	Find the compound amount on $500 at 7% compounded annually for 2 years. $500 × 0.07 = $35 interest for first year $500 + $35 = $535 principal for second year $535 × 0.07 = $37.45 interest for second year $535 + $37.45 = $572.45 compound amount, or future value
Finding compound interest using a table	331–332	Find the number of periods in the first column of the table and move across the column for the correct percent. Multiply the principal times the number in the table to find the compound amount or future value of the loan. Subtract the present value from the future value to find the compound interest.	Use Table 11-1 to find the compound interest on $800 at 8% compounded annually for 4 years. Find period 4 in the left-hand column of the table. Move across to the 8% column and find the compound amount per dollar of principal: 1.36049. $800 × 1.36049 = $1,088.39 compound amount $1,088.39 compound amount − 800 principal $288.39 compound interest

Topic	Page	What to Remember	Examples
Finding future value for periods less than a year	332–333	Years × periods/year = periods of loan Interest rate per period $= \frac{\text{annual rate}}{\text{periods per year}}$ Find the number of periods in the loan in the first column of Table 11-1. Move across to the column for the interest rate for each period and find the compound amount per dollar of principal. Multiply the value from the table times the principal to find the future value.	Find the compound amount (future value) of $2,000 at 12% compounded semiannually for 4 years. $4 \times 2 = 8$ periods $\frac{12\%}{2} = 6\%$ interest rate per period Find 8 periods in the left-hand column of Table 11-1 and move across to the 6% column: 1.59385. $2,000 × 1.59385 = $3,187.70 future value or compound amount
Finding the amount of compound interest	329–332	Amount of compound interest = compound amount or future value (use Table 11-1) − principal	Find the compound interest on $800 at 10% compounded annually for 4 years. Use the table value of 1.46410. $800 × 1.46410 = $1,171.28 compound amount or future value $1,171.28 − $800 = $371.28 compound interest
Finding the effective (actual) rate	334	Effective rate $= \frac{\text{total interest for 1 year}}{\text{principal}}$	Find the effective rate of interest on a loan of $3,000 at 8% compounded quarterly for 1 year. $3,000 × 1.08243 = $3,247.29 future value $3,247.29 − $3,000 = $247.29 interest for 1 year Effective rate $= \frac{\$247.29}{\$3,000} = 0.08243$, or 8.24%
Compounding interest daily using a table	334–335	Find the number of periods in the first column of Table 11-2 and move across to the column for the correct percent. Divide the principal by 100, then multiply the principal times the number in the table to find the compound daily interest for the loan or investment.	Find the interest on a $300 loan borrowed at 13% compounded daily for 21 days. Move down the left-hand column of Table 11-2 to 21 days; then move across to 13%. The table value is 0.750615. $\frac{\$300}{100} \times 0.750615 = \$2.25$ The interest on $300 is $2.25.

Topic	Page	What to Remember	Examples
Finding present value without using a table	339	Present value $= \dfrac{\text{desired future value}}{(1 + \text{decimal form of interest rate})}$	Find the amount of money that must be invested to produce \$4,000 in 1 year if the interest rate is 7% compounded annually. Present value $= \dfrac{\$4{,}000}{1 + 0.07}$ $= \dfrac{\$4{,}000}{1.07} = \$3{,}738.32$
Finding present value using a table	339–340	Years × periods/year = period of investment Interest rate per period $= \dfrac{\text{annual rate}}{\text{periods per year}}$ Find the number of periods of the investment in the first column of Table 11-3. Move across to the column for the interest rate for each period and find present value per dollar of future value. Multiply the value from the table times the future value to find the present value.	Find the amount of money that must be deposited to ensure \$3,000 at the end of 3 years if the investment earns 6% compounded semiannually. $3 \times 2 = 6$ periods $\dfrac{6\%}{2} = 3\%$ rate per period Find 6 in the left-hand column of Table 11-3 and move across to the 3% column: 0.83748. $\$3{,}000 \times 0.83748 = \$2{,}512.44$ The amount that must be invested now to have \$3,000 in 3 years is \$2,512.44.

1. Calculate the compound amount on a loan of $4,000 at 10% compounded annually for 2 years.

2. Use Table 11-1 to find the compound interest on the loan in Problem 1.

3. How much more interest is paid on the loan in Problem 1 than if simple interest had been used?

4. Use Table 11-1 to find the compound amount and the compound interest on a loan of $2,500 for 2 years if the loan is compounded semiannually at 12%.

5. Find the effective rate of interest on the loan in Problem 4.

6. Use Table 11-1 to find the compound amount and compound interest on a loan of $4,200 for 6 years at 8%, compounded quarterly.

7. Find the effective rate of interest on the loan in Problem 6.

8. Use Table 11-1 to find the factor for compounding an amount for 20 periods at 6%.

9. Use Table 11-1 to find the factor for compounding an amount at 12%, compounded monthly for 2 years.

10. Use Table 11-2 to find the amount of interest on an investment of $2,250 at 12.5% if it is compounded daily for 21 days.

11. Use Table 11-3 to find the factor needed to determine the present value of \$1 in 3 years at 12%, compounded annually.

12. Use Table 11-3 to find the factor needed to determine the present value of \$1 in 2 years at 12%, compounded semiannually.

13. Use Table 11-3 to find the factor for finding the present value of \$1 in 9 months at 8%, compounded quarterly.

14. Find the present value of an investment that will be worth \$5,000 in 2 years if the interest is 8%, compounded annually.

15. Find the present value of an investment that will be worth \$2,000 in 3 years if the interest is 16%, compounded semiannually.

16. Compute the amount of money that should be set aside today to ensure a maturity value of \$3,000 in 4 years if the interest rate is 20%, compounded quarterly.

17. How much money must be invested to make a \$3,500 down payment on house in 5 years if the investment will be compounded quarterly at an interest rate of 8%?

18. If you were offered \$1,000 today or \$1,300 in 1 year, which would you accept if money can be invested at 8%, compounded quarterly?

19. Jon Nichols wished to have \$5,000 in 5 years for a trip to Australia. How much must he invest today at 10% compounded semiannually to have the desired amount in 5 years?

20. Dawn Wilson's grandparents are investing for her college education. How much should they invest now to have \$12,000 in 15 years when she will enter college if money can be invested at 8%, compounded annually?

Trial Test

1. Calculate the compound interest on a loan of $2,000 at 7% compounded annually for 3 years.

2. Calculate the compound interest on a 14% loan of $3,000 for 4 years if interest is compounded annually.

3. Use Table 11-1 to find the interest on a loan of $5,000 for 6 years at 10% if interest is compounded semiannually.

4. Use Table 11-1 to find the compound amount on an investment of $12,000 for 7 years at 12%, compounded quarterly.

5. An investment of $1,500 is made at the beginning of each year for 2 years at 12%, compounded annually. Find the compound amount and the compound interest at the end of 2 years.

6. Use Table 11-1 to find the compound interest on a loan of $3,000 for 1 year at 12% if the interest is compounded quarterly.

7. Find the effective interest rate for the loan described in Problem 6.

8. Use Table 11-2 to find the daily interest on an investment of $2,000 invested at 14% for 28 days.

9. Use Table 11-1 and Table 11-2 to compare the interest on an investment of $3,000 that is invested at 12% compounded monthly and daily for the month of April (30 days).

In the following problems find the amount of money that should be invested today (present value) at the stated interest rate to yield the given amount after the indicated amount of time (future value).

10. $3,400 in 4 years at 8%, compounded annually

11. $5,000 in 8 years at 8%, compounded semiannually

12. $8,000 in 12 years at 12%, compounded annually

13. $6,000 in 6 years at 12%, compounded quarterly.

14. Jamie Juarez will need $12,000 in 10 years for her daughter's college education. Her parents are willing to invest the necessary funds. How much must be invested today at 8%, compounded semiannually, to have the necessary funds for college?

15. If you were offered $600 today or $680 in 1 year, which would you accept if money can be invested at 12%, compounded monthly?

16. Derek Anderson plans to buy a house in 4 years. He will make an $8,000 down payment on the property. How much should he invest today at 6%, compounded quarterly, to have the required amount in 4 years?

17. You have $2,000 to invest and have two options. Which of the two options will yield the greatest return on your investment?
Option 1: 8% compounded quarterly for 4 years
Option 2: $8\frac{1}{4}$% compounded annually for 4 years

18. If you invest $2,000 today at 8%, compounded quarterly, how much will you have after 3 years?

19. If you invest $1,000 today at 12%, compounded daily, how much will you have after 20 days?

20. One bank offers to use your money and pay you 12.25%, compounded annually. Another bank offers to pay you 12%, compounded quarterly. Which bank should you allow to use your money so that you will receive the greatest return? (*Hint.* Calculate the interest on a given amount of money, such as $100, for a given period of time, such as 1 year.)

Self-Check Solutions

1.

$$
\begin{aligned}
\$1,200 \times 0.16 &= \$192.00 \\
\$1,200 + \$192 &= \$1,392 \quad \text{(1st year)} \\
\$1,392 \times 0.16 &= \$222.72 \\
\$1,392 + \$222.72 &= \$1,614.72 \quad \text{(2nd year)} \\
\$1,614.72 \times 0.16 &= \$258.36 \quad \text{(rounded)} \\
\$1,614.72 + \$258.36 &= \$1,873.08 \quad \text{(3rd year)} \\
& \text{compound amount} \\
\text{Compound interest} &= \$1,873.08 - \$1,200 \\
&= \$673.08
\end{aligned}
$$

Shortcut

$$
\begin{aligned}
&\$1,200 \times 1.16 \\
&\quad = \$1,392 \\
&\$1,392 \times 1.16 \\
&\quad = \$1,614.72 \\
&\$1,614.72 \times 1.16 \\
&\quad = \$1,873.08
\end{aligned}
$$

Simple interest

$$
\begin{aligned}
&= \$1,200(0.16)(3) \\
&= \$576
\end{aligned}
$$

2. Find period 4 in the first column. Move across to the 8% column.

$$
\begin{aligned}
\text{Table value} &= 1.36049 \quad \text{(Table 11-1)} \\
\$2,000(1.36049) &= \$2,720.98 \quad \text{compound amount} \\
\$2,720.98 - \$2,000 &= \$720.98 \quad \text{compound interest}
\end{aligned}
$$

3. 5 years × 4 quarters per year = 20 periods

12% ÷ 4 quarters = 3% per period

$$
\begin{aligned}
\text{Table value} &= 1.80611 \\
\$800(1.80611) &= \$1,444.89 \quad \text{compound amount} \\
\$1,444.89 - \$800 &= \$644.89 \quad \text{compound interest}
\end{aligned}
$$

4. 1 year compounded quarterly = 4 periods at 3% per period

$$
\begin{aligned}
\text{Table value} &= 1.12551 \\
\$800(1.12551) &= \$900.41 \\
\$900.41 - \$800 &= \$100.41 \quad \text{compound interest for 1 year}
\end{aligned}
$$

$$\text{Effective rate} = \frac{\$100.41}{800} = 0.1255125 = 12.55\%$$

5. $13\frac{1}{4}\%$ for 20 days = table value 0.728536

$$\frac{\$2,500}{100} = 25$$

25(0.728536) = \$18.21 interest

6. $$\text{Present value} = \frac{\$2,500}{1 + 0.11} = \frac{\$2,500}{1.11} = \$2,252.25$$

7. 3 years = 3 periods at 8%, table amount = 0.79383

\$2,000(0.79383) = \$1,587.66 present amount to invest

8. 3 × 4 = 12 periods, 6% ÷ 4 = $1\frac{1}{2}\%$ per period, table amount = 0.83639

\$1,500(0.83639) = \$1,254.59 amount to invest

Consumer Credit 12

Learning Objectives

1. Calculate the cash price, total price, finance charge, and monthly payments for installment loans. (pp. 353–355)
2. Calculate the finance charge refund for an installment loan that is paid off before it is due using the rule of 78 and using a table. (pp. 355–358)
3. Figure the finance charges on a revolving charge account. (pp. 360–363)
4. Calculate the annual percentage rate for an installment loan. (pp. 365–371)

Many individuals and businesses make purchases for which they do not pay the full amount at the time of purchase. These purchases are paid for by paying a portion of the amount owed in regular payments. This type of loan or credit, by which many of us are able to purchase equipment, supplies, and other items we need in our businesses or personal lives, is called **consumer credit.**

consumer credit: a type of loan that is paid back through a number of regular payments over a period of time.

In the preceding chapters, we discussed the interest to be paid on loans that are paid in full on the date of maturity of the loan. But loans are often handled in other ways as well. Many times loans are made so that the maker (the borrower) pays a given amount in regular payments. This means that the borrower does not have use of the full amount of money borrowed for the full length of time it was borrowed; a certain portion of it has to be paid back with each regular payment. Loans with regular payments for a specified number of payments are called **installment loans.**

installment loan: a loan that is paid back through a specified number of payments.

There are two kinds of installment loans. Basic installment loans are loans in which the amount borrowed plus interest is repaid in a specified number of equal payments. **Open-end loans** are loans in which there is no fixed number of payments—the person keeps making payments until the amount is paid off, and the interest is computed on the unpaid balance at the end of each payment period. Credit card companies and retail stores most often use the open-end type of loan. Bank loans and loans for large purchases such as cars and appliances are examples of the basic installment loan.

open-end loans: loans in which there is no fixed number of payments—the borrower keeps making payments until the amount is paid off, and the interest is computed on the unpaid balance at the end of each payment period.

Installment Loans

The extra amount of money paid for an installment loan is not always called interest. *Finance charge* and *carrying charge* are terms most frequently used to mean interest. Some firms compute finance or carrying charges on the average daily balance of the account, whereas others use the adjusted balance, which changes with each payment. Other charges, such as insurance, credit-report fees, or loan fees, may be included in the cost of the loan. Under the *Truth-in-Lending Law, all* these charges must be totaled and included in the determination of the interest rate.

cash price: the cost of an item if one had paid the full amount at the time of the sale.

In determining the extra cost for buying on the installment plan we consider the **cash price** to be the cost of the item if we paid the full amount at the time of the sale. The **total price** is the total amount that must be paid

total price: the total amount that must be paid when the purchase is paid for over a given period of time.

finance charge (carrying charge): the difference between the total price and the cash price.

down payment: a partial payment made at the time of purchase.

when the purchase is paid for over a given period of time. The total price includes the cash price of the purchase plus all other charges for paying for the purchase over a given period of time. The **finance charge,** or **carrying charge,** is the difference between the total price and the cash price.

A **down payment** is a partial payment that is made at the time of purchase. To find the total cost of an item, multiply the amount of each payment by the number of payments of the loan and then add the down payment.

Step by Step

Finding the Total Price of an Installment Purchase

Total price
= number of payments × amount of payment + down payment

EXAMPLE 1

An item was purchased on the installment plan with a \$60 down payment and 12 payments of \$45.58. Find the total price of the item.

$$\begin{aligned}\text{Total price} &= \text{number of payments} \times \text{amount of payment} + \text{down payment}\\ &= 12 \times \$45.58 + \$60\\ &= \$546.96 + \$60\\ &= \$606.96\end{aligned}$$

The total price is \$606.96.

To find the amount of installment payment, divide the amount financed by the number of payments.

Step by Step

Finding the Amount of Installment Payment

Step 1. Find the amount financed:

Amount financed = installment price − down payment

Step 2. Find the amount of periodic (installment) payment:

$$\text{Installment payment} = \frac{\text{amount financed}}{\text{number of payments}}$$

EXAMPLE 2

A color television set sells for \$627 on the installment plan. (The finance charge is included in the installment price.) If the set is paid for in 12 equal payments with a \$75 down payment, compute the amount of each monthly payment.

$$\begin{aligned}\text{Amount financed} &= \text{installment price} - \text{down payment}\\ &= \$627 - \$75 = \$552\end{aligned}$$

$$\text{Monthly payment} = \frac{\text{amount financed}}{\text{number of payments}} = \frac{\$552}{12} = \$46$$

The amount financed is \$552, and the amount of each monthly payment is \$46.

Sometimes the finance charge is given as a percent of the cash price. In such a case, you use the simple interest formula ($I = PRT$), with the cash price being the principal, the percent interest charge being the rate per year, and the time being expressed in number of years.

EXAMPLE 3

An item with a \$4,000 cash price has a 12% annual finance charge. The item is to be paid for in 24 monthly installment payments. Find the amount of the finance charge, the total price, and the monthly payments.

First, recall that 24 months = 2 years.

$I = PRT$ — Compute the finance charge as simple interest.
$= \$4,000 \times 0.12 \times 2$
$= \$960$ — The finance charge is \$960.

Total price
$= \text{cash price} + \text{finance charge}$
$= \$4,000 + \$960$
$= \$4,960$ — The total price is \$4,960.

$$\text{Monthly payment} = \frac{\text{total cost}}{\text{number of monthly payments}}$$

$$= \frac{\$4,960}{24} = \$206.67 \quad \text{(rounded to the nearest cent)}$$

The finance charge is \$960, the total price is \$4,960, and the monthly payments are \$206.67.

Self-Check

1. Find the total price of a recliner bought on the installment plan with a \$100 down payment and 6 payments of \$108.20.
2. Find the amount of each monthly payment on a VCR that sells for \$929 on the installment plan, with 12 monthly payments and a down payment of \$100.
3. Find the amount financed if a \$125 down payment is made on a TV with a cash price of \$579.
4. A bedroom suite has a \$2,590 cash price. There is a 24% finance charge, and the suite will be paid for in 12 monthly payments. Find the amount of the monthly payments.

Paying Off a Loan Before It Is Due: The Rule of 78

If an installment loan is paid in full before the **date of maturity** (the date of the last payment), some of the interest is usually refunded or deducted from the total value of the loan. The amount of interest refunded is calculated by multiplying the total finance charge times the refund fraction, a fraction that shows what portion of the total finance charge has not been used at the time the loan is paid off.

date of maturity: the date of the last payment on an installment loan.

The refund fraction is the sum of the number of months remaining divided by the sum of the total number of months of the loan. Many lending institutions calculate this refund by using the **rule of 78,** which gets its

rule of 78: a method used to calculate the refund due when a loan is paid off early.

name from the fact that the *sum* of the numbers 1 through 12, representing the months in a 12-month loan, is 78 (1 + 2 + 3 + 4 + 5 + 6 + 7 + 8 + 9 + 10 + 11 + 12 = 78). For example, if a 12-month loan is paid off after 8 months (with 4 payments remaining), the refund fraction is

$$\frac{1 + 2 + 3 + 4}{1 + 2 + 3 + 4 + 5 + 6 + 7 + 8 + 9 + 10 + 11 + 12} = \frac{10}{78}$$

Step by Step

Finding the Finance Charge Refund for a Loan Paid Back Before It Is Due

Step 1. Find the refund fraction:

$$\text{Refund fraction} = \frac{\text{sum of the number of payments remaining}}{\text{sum of the total number of payments due}}$$

Step 2. Use the fraction from Step 1 to find the finance charge refund:

Finance charge refund = total finance charge × refund fraction

This same procedure, the rule of 78, is also used when refunds are made for unused portions of purchases paid for in advance, such as insurance premiums, installment purchases, etc.

EXAMPLE 4

A loan for 12 months with a finance charge of $117 is paid in full with four payments remaining. Find the amount of the finance charge (interest) refund.

Step 1. $\frac{1 + 2 + 3 + 4}{1 + 2 + 3 + 4 + 5 + 6 + 7 + 8 + 9 + 10 + 11 + 12} = \frac{10}{78}$

Four payments remain. Twelve payments in all were due.

Step 2. Refund = total finance charge

$$\times \frac{\text{sum of the number of payments remaining}}{\text{sum of the total number of payments due}}$$

$$\$117 \times \frac{10}{78} = \$15$$

The amount of refund is $15.

Calculator Sequence

[AC] 117 [×] 10 [÷] 78 [=] ⇒ 15

Finding the sum of the numbers of the months is not too difficult for a short-term loan, but it could be time-consuming for a loan of 24 or more months. Fortunately, there is a shortcut for finding the sum of a sequence of numbers. This shortcut can be used to find the sum of the number of payments remaining as well as the sum of the total number of payments.

Shortcut for Finding the Sum of the Number of Payments

Sum of the number of payments

$$= \frac{\text{number of payments} \times (\text{number of payments} + 1)}{2}$$

If a loan has 12 payments, then the sum of the number of payments is

$$\frac{12 \times (12 + 1)}{2} = \frac{12 \times 13}{2} = \frac{156}{2} = 78$$

If there are 5 payments left in a loan, the sum of the remaining number of payments is

$$\frac{5 \times (5 + 1)}{2} = \frac{5 \times 6}{2} = \frac{30}{2} = 15$$

EXAMPLE 5

A loan for 36 months, with a finance charge of $1276.50, is paid in full with 15 payments remaining. Find the amount of finance charge to be refunded.

$$\text{Refund fraction} = \frac{\text{sum of the number of payments remaining}}{\text{sum of the total number of payments due}}$$

$$= \frac{\frac{15 \times (15 + 1)}{2}}{\frac{36 \times (36 + 1)}{2}} = \frac{\frac{15 \times 16}{2}}{\frac{36 \times 37}{2}} = \frac{\frac{240}{2}}{\frac{1{,}332}{2}} = \frac{120}{666} = \frac{20}{111}$$

Finance charge refund = finance charge × refund fraction.

$$\text{Finance charge refund} = \$1{,}276.50 \times \frac{20}{111} = \$230$$

The refund is $230.

Calculator Sequence

Find the sum of the number of payments left to get the numerator of the refund fraction.

[AC] 15 [+] 1 [=] [×] 15 [÷] 2 [=] ⇒ 120

Find the sum of the total number of payments due to get the denominator of the refund fraction.

[AC] 36 [+] 1 [=] [×] 36 [÷] 2 [=] ⇒ 666

Multiply the total finance charge times the numerator of the refund fraction, then divide the result by the denominator of the refund fraction.

[AC] 1276.50 [×] 120 [=] [÷] 666 [=] ⇒ 229.9999 or $230

TIPS & TRAPS

Isn't there an easier way to find the refund fraction? Let's look at the fraction from Example 5 again:

$$\frac{\frac{15 \times (15 + 1)}{2}}{\frac{36 \times (36 + 1)}{2}}$$

Remembering what we covered in Chapter 2 on the division of fractions, we would first find the reciprocal of the divisor and then multiply the dividend by that reciprocal.

Step 1. Find the reciprocal of the divisor:

$$\text{Divisor: } \frac{36 \times (36 + 1)}{2} \qquad \text{Reciprocal: } \frac{2}{36 \times (36 + 1)}$$

Step 2. Multiply the dividend by the reciprocal of the divisor:

$$\frac{15 \times (15 + 1)}{\overset{}{\underset{1}{\cancel{2}}}} \times \frac{\overset{1}{\cancel{2}}}{36 \times (36 + 1)} = \frac{15 \times (15 + 1)}{36 \times (36 + 1)} = \frac{15 \times 16}{36 \times 37} = \frac{20}{111}$$

In Step 2, the two 2s will *always* divide out.

In general, if m represents the months remaining and n represents the total months, then

$$\frac{\frac{m \times (m + 1)}{2}}{\frac{n \times (n + 1)}{2}} = \frac{m \times (m + 1)}{n \times (n + 1)}$$

Real World Application

How much is the payoff on a loan if you decide to pay the remainder of a loan early? Once you have the finance charge refund, the amount of the payoff can easily be found. Simply multiply the number of remaining payments by the amount of each payment and subtract the finance charge refund. This amount is the payoff for your loan.

For example, suppose you have borrowed money that is being repaid at $45 a month for 12 months. What is the payoff after making 8 payments if the finance charge is $105?

Step 1. Find the finance charge refund.

$$12 - 8 = 4 \text{ payments remaining}$$

$$\frac{4 \times 5}{12 \times 13} \times \$105 = \$13.46$$

Step 2. Number of remaining payments × amount of payment − finance charge refund = payoff

$$4 \times \$45 - \$13.46 = \$166.54$$

Application Questions

1. Find the payoff on a 15-month loan with monthly payments of $103.50 if you decide to pay off the loan at the end of the tenth month. The finance charge is $215.55.

2. You have purchased a new stereo on the installment plan. The plan calls for 12 monthly payments of $45 and a $115 finance charge. After 9 months you decide to pay off the loan. How much is the payoff amount?

3. If you purchase a fishing boat for 18 monthly payments of $106 and an interest charge of $238, how much is the payoff after 10 payments?

Self-Check

5. Find the refund fraction on an 18-month loan if it is paid off with 8 months remaining.
6. Ted Davis made a loan for 18 months with a finance charge of $205. He paid the loan in full after 12 payments. How much finance charge refund should he get?
7. John Paszel made a loan for 48 months, but paid it in full after 28 months. Find the refund fraction he should use to calculate the amount of his refund.
8. If the finance charge on a loan made by Marjorie Young is $1,645 and the loan is to be paid in 48 monthly payments, find the finance charge refund if the loan is paid in full after 28 months.

Section Review

Use the rule of 78 to find the finance charge refund in each of the following.

	Finance Charge	Number of Monthly Payments	Remaining Payments	Finance Charge Refund
1.	$ 238	12	4	
2.	$1,076	18	6	
3.	$2,175	24	10	
4.	$ 476	12	5	
5.	$ 896	18	4	

Use the rule of 78 to solve the following problems.

6. The finance charges on a computer were $1,778. The loan for the computer was to be paid in 18 monthly payments. Find the finance charge refund if it is paid off in 8 months.

7. Find the refund fraction on a 48-month loan if it is paid off after 20 months.

8. Becky has a loan with $1,115 in finance charges, which she paid in full after 8 of the 18 monthly payments. What is her finance charge refund?

9. Find the refund due on a loan with charges of $657 if it is paid off after paying 7 of the 12 monthly payments.

10. Alice was charged $455 in finance charges on a loan for 15 months. Find the finance charge refund if she pays off the loan in full after 10 payments.

Open-End Credit

revolving charge accounts: open-end loans, in which borrowers keep making payments at a stated rate of interest until the loan is paid off.

Open-end loans used by retail stores and credit card companies are often called **revolving charge accounts.** With open-end loans, a person makes regular payments on the unpaid balance according to a stated rate of interest. The person continues making payments until there is no balance owed.

Meanwhile, the person may be getting additional credit before the initial amount is paid off. This occurs when the person makes additional purchases on a credit card while still paying off previous purchases in monthly payments. As a matter of fact, with some credit card holders, an account is never paid off—this is why it is called a revolving charge account. (Others pay the full amount owed at the end of each month and do not pay any finance charge.)

Finance charges on such accounts are figured according to the *unpaid balance method* or the *average daily balance method.*

Unpaid Balance Method

unpaid balance: the amount that has not been paid off at the end of the month.

When the amount owed on an account is not paid in full in any month, the company adds interest charges for the unpaid balance for that month. These interest, or finance, charges are calculated by multiplying the **unpaid balance** by the stated rate of interest:

$$\text{Interest} = \text{rate} \times \text{unpaid balance}$$

For example, if the unpaid balance on an account is $147 and the interest rate is $1\frac{1}{2}\%$, the interest is $\$147 \times 0.015 = \$2.21$ (rounded to the nearest cent).

In order to figure the correct interest for the following month, you must also take into account the purchases made during the month and the payment made the month before. The activity in a revolving charge account in any one month can be summed up as follows, to show the new unpaid balance:

$$\begin{matrix}\text{Previous} \\ \text{balance}\end{matrix} + \begin{matrix}\text{finance} \\ \text{charge}\end{matrix} + \begin{matrix}\text{purchases during} \\ \text{month}\end{matrix} - \text{payment} = \begin{matrix}\text{new} \\ \text{balance}\end{matrix}$$

The following procedure shows how to figure the finance charge and unpaid balance on an account.

Step by Step

Finding Finance Charge (Based on Unpaid Balance) and New Unpaid Balance

Step 1. Find the finance charge on the previous unpaid balance:

finance charge
= unpaid balance × rate per month charged by company

Step 2. Find the new unpaid balance:

$$\begin{matrix}\text{previous}\\ \text{balance}\end{matrix} + \begin{matrix}\text{finance}\\ \text{charge}\end{matrix} + \begin{matrix}\text{purchases or}\\ \text{cash advances}\\ \text{during month}\end{matrix} - \text{payment} = \begin{matrix}\text{new unpaid}\\ \text{balance}\end{matrix}$$

Example 6 shows how this works.

EXAMPLE 6

Rob Strong's charge account had an unpaid balance of $150 on September 1. During September Rob made purchases totaling $356.20 and a payment of $42.50. The bank charges 1.7% interest per month on any unpaid balance. Find the finance charge and the unpaid balance on October 1.

Step 1. Find the finance charge on the previous unpaid balance.

$$\begin{aligned}\text{Finance charge} &= \text{unpaid balance} \times \text{rate}\\ &= \$150 \times 0.017\\ &= \$2.55\end{aligned}$$

Step 2. Find the unpaid balance for October 1.

$$\begin{matrix}\text{Previous}\\ \text{balance}\end{matrix} + \begin{matrix}\text{finance}\\ \text{charge}\end{matrix} + \begin{matrix}\text{purchases}\\ \text{during month}\end{matrix} - \text{payment} = \begin{matrix}\text{new unpaid}\\ \text{balance}\end{matrix}$$

$$\$150 + \$2.55 + \$356.20 - \$42.50 = \$466.25$$

In October, Rob made a payment of $200 and made purchases of $50. Find the finance charge and unpaid balance on November 1.

Step 1. Find the finance charge.

$$\begin{aligned}\text{Finance charge} &= \text{unpaid balance} \times \text{rate}\\ &= \$466.25 \times 0.017 = \$7.93\end{aligned}$$

Step 2. Find the new unpaid balance.

$$\begin{matrix}\text{Previous}\\ \text{balance}\end{matrix} + \begin{matrix}\text{finance}\\ \text{charge}\end{matrix} + \begin{matrix}\text{purchases}\\ \text{during month}\end{matrix} - \text{payment} = \begin{matrix}\text{new unpaid balance}\\ \text{on November 1}\end{matrix}$$

$$\$466.25 + \$7.93 + \$50 - \$200 = \$324.18$$

By LeRoy Lottmann, USA TODAY

Average Daily Balance Method

More and more companies these days are determining the finance charge using the average daily balance method. In this method, the daily balances of the account are determined and then the sum of these balances is divided by the number of days in the billing cycle. The average daily balance is then multiplied by the interest rate to find the finance charge for the month.

Step by Step

Using Average Daily Balance and Finance Charge

Step 1. Find each daily balance:

Daily balance = previous balance + cash advances + purchases − payments

Step 2. Multiply each daily balance by the number of days it occurs to get a cumulative daily balance.

Step 3. Add together the cumulative daily balances for the billing cycle.

Step 4. Divide the total from Step 3 by the number of days in the billing cycle:

$$\text{average daily balance} = \frac{\text{sum of daily balances}}{\text{number of days in billing cycle}}$$

Step 5. Multiply the average daily balance times the interest rate per cycle to get the finance charge.

EXAMPLE 7

Use the following chart showing May activity in Karen Liu's charge account to determine the average daily balance and finance charge for the month (the bank's interest rate is 1.5% per month).

Date	Activity	Amount
May 1	Billing date	Previous balance $122.70
May 7	Payment	$ 25
May 10	Purchase—clothes	$ 12
May 13	Purchase—restaurant	$ 20
May 20	Cash advance	$ 50
May 23	Purchase—software	$100

In order to figure cumulative daily balances for each day of the billing cycle, determine each change in balance and the number of days of the cycle that show the same balance. Then multiply the balance times the number of days that it holds.

For example, the balance from May 1 to May 7 is the previous month's balance of $122.70, so you calculate as follows:

$$\$122.70 \times 7 = \$858.90$$

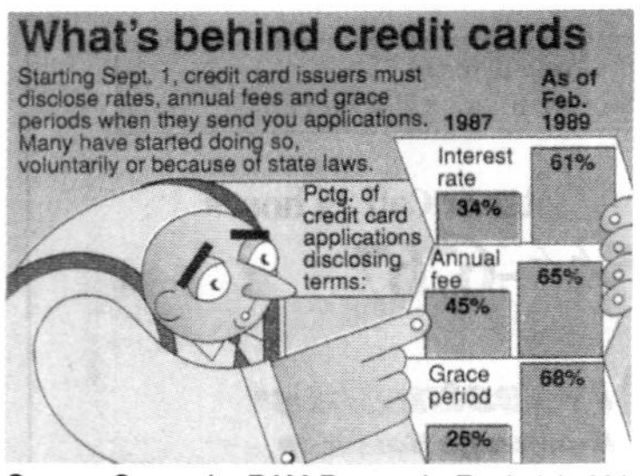

Source: Survey by RAM Research, Frederick, Md.
By Marcia Staimer, USA TODAY

On May 7 there is a payment of $25, which changes the balance:

$$\$122.70 - \$25 = \$97.70$$

The new balance of $97.70 holds until May 10 (3 days):

$$\$97.70 \times 3 = \$293.10$$

Continue doing this until you get to the end of the cycle. The following chart shows the results:

Date	Unpaid Balance	Number of Days	Total
May 1–May 7	$122.70	7	$ 858.90
May 8–May 10	97.70	3	293.10
May 11–May 13	109.70	3	329.10
May 14–May 20	129.70	7	907.90
May 21–May 23	179.70	3	539.10
May 24–May 31	279.70	8	2,237.60
31 days in cycle		31	$5,165.70

The average daily balance is then found by the formula:

$$\text{Average daily balance} = \frac{\text{sum of daily balances}}{\text{number of days in billing cycle}}$$

$$= \frac{\$5{,}165.70}{31} = \$166.64$$

The average daily balance is then multiplied by the bank's interest rate to figure the finance charge. In this example, the bank's interest rate is 1.5%:

$\$166.64 \times 0.015 = \$2.50$ finance charge for the cycle

The finance charge is $2.50.

Self-Check

9. What is the finance charge on an unpaid balance of $275.69 if the interest rate per month is 2.3%?
10. Find the new unpaid balance on an account with an interest rate of 1.6% per month if the previous unpaid balance was $176.95 and a payment of $45 was made.
11. Sam's charge account has a 1.8% interest rate per month on the average daily balance. Find the average daily balance if Sam has an unpaid balance on March 1 of $128.50; on March 6, a payment of $20; and on March 20, a purchase of $25.60. The billing cycle ends March 31.
12. Using Problem 11, find Sam's finance charge and unpaid balance on April 1.

Section Review

1. Find the interest on an unpaid balance of $265 with an interest rate of $1\frac{1}{2}\%$.

2. Find the finance charge on $371 if the interest charged is 1.4% of the unpaid balance.

3. Find the new unpaid balance on an account with a previous balance of $155, purchases of $47.38, a payment of $20, and an interest charge of 1.8%.

4. Find the interest rate charged on an account with an unpaid balance of $175 and finance charge of $3.50.

5. An item has been purchased on the installment plan with a down payment of $75 and 12 monthly payments of $55.50. Find the total price of the item.

6. Find the total price of a sofa that was bought on the installment plan with a down payment of $150 and 6 payments of $114.25.

7. Find the monthly payments on a TV that is sold for $849 on the installment plan with a $125 down payment and 3 monthly payments.

8. Find the amount financed if the cash price of a refrigerator is $1,249 and a down payment of $230 is made.

9. A stereo system has a $959 cash price. Find the monthly payments if 15 are to be made and a down payment of $100 is paid. There is a 15% finance charge.

10. What is the amount of the finance charge on $3,575 worth of furniture at 15% interest if no down payment is made and there are 24 monthly payments?

11. Find the cash price of a computer printer if the total price is $789 and the finance charge is $116.

12. If the installment price of patio furniture is $354 and there are to be 6 monthly payments, find the amount of each payment. There was no down payment.

13. A new desk for an office has a cash price of $1,500 and can be purchased on the installment plan with a 12.5% finance charge. The desk will be paid for in 12 monthly payments. Find the amount of the finance charge, the total price, and the amount of each monthly payment, if there was no down payment.

14. On June 1, the unpaid balance on a credit card was $174. During the month, purchases of $32, $14.50, and $28.75 are made. Using the unpaid balance method, find the unpaid balance on July 1 if the finance charge is 1.4% of the unpaid balance and a payment of $50 is made on June 15.

15. On January 1, the previous balance for Lynn's charge account was $569.80. On the following days, she made the purchases shown:

January 12	$38.50	jewelry
January 20	$44.56	clothing

On January 15, Lynn made a $50 payment. Using the average daily balance method, find the finance charge and unpaid balance on February 1 if the bank charges interest of 1.5% per month.

Annual Percentage Rates

In 1969, the federal government passed the Truth-in-Lending Law, which requires that a lending institution tell the borrower, in writing, what the actual annual rate of interest is. This interest rate tells the borrower what the true cost of the loan is.

For example, if you borrowed $1,500 for a year and paid an interest charge of $165, you would be paying an interest rate of 11%. But if you paid the money back in 12 monthly installments of $138.75 (($1,500 + $165) ÷ 12 = $138.75), you would not have the use of the $1,500 for a full year. Instead, you would be paying it back in 12 payments of $138.75 each. Thus you are losing the use of some of the money every month, but still paying interest as if you had use of the entire amount. This means that you are really paying more than 11% interest. The true **annual percentage rate (APR)**

annual percentage rate (APR): the actual annual rate of interest, which often differs from the stated rate because you do not have full use of the money for the whole period of the loan.

can be calculated one of two ways, by a formula or by using a government-issued table.

Using a Formula

constant ratio formula: method used to find the annual percentage rate when the loan covers a short period of time.

The **constant ratio formula** can be used to find the annual percentage rate on any loan that is paid back in equal monthly, quarterly, or weekly installments. This formula gives a close approximation of the actual interest if the time of the loan is short. On loans made for 10 years or more, this formula will not give a fair approximation of the actual interest rate.

Step by Step

Using the Constant Ratio Formula to Find the Annual Percentage Rate

Step 1. Set up the constant ratio formula as follows:

Annual percentage rate

$$= \frac{2 \times \text{number of payments in 1 year} \times \text{amount of interest paid}}{\text{amount of loan} \times (\text{number of payments made on the loan} + 1)}$$

a. when installments are made monthly, there are 12 payments a year; when installments are made quarterly, there are 4 payments a year; when installments are made weekly, there are 52 payments a year.

b. Amount of the loan = installment price − interest − down payment.

EXAMPLE 8

A loan of $600, borrowed for 3 years, required interest of $144. Find the annual percentage rate if the loan was repaid in monthly installments.

Number of payments in 1 year = 12
Amount of interest paid = $144
Amount of loan = $600
Number of payments on the loan = 3 years × 12 payments per year = 36
Annual percentage rate

$$= \frac{2 \times \text{number of payments in 1 year} \times \text{amount of interest paid}}{\text{amount of loan} \times (\text{number of payments made on the loan} + 1)}$$

$$= \frac{(2)\,(12)\,(144)}{(600)(36 + 1)} = 0.1556756, \quad \text{which rounds to 0.156, or 15.6\%}$$

The annual percentage rate is 15.6%.

Calculator Sequence

A continuous calculator sequence that uses the memory function of the calculator for this problem is

[AC] 36 [+] 1 [=] [×] 600 [=] [M+] [C/CE] 2 [×] 12 [×] 144 [÷] [MRC] [=] ⇒ 0.1556756

0.1556756 rounds to 0.156, or 15.6%.

EXAMPLE 9

A \$499 color television set sells for \$552 on the installment plan. If the set is paid for in 12 monthly payments with a \$60 down payment, compute the finance charge, monthly payment, and annual percentage rate.

$$\text{Finance charge (interest)} = \text{installment price} - \text{cash price}$$
$$= \$552 - \$499 = \$53$$

$$\text{Amount financed} = \text{installment price} - \text{down payment}$$
$$= \$552 - \$60 = \$492$$

$$\text{Monthly payment} = \frac{\text{amount financed}}{12} = \frac{\$492}{12} = \$41$$

Number of pay periods in 1 year = 12

Amount of interest paid (finance charge) = \$53

Amount of loan (installment price − interest − down payment) = \$439

Number of payments on the loan = 12 payments

Annual percentage

$$= \frac{2 \times \text{number of pay periods in 1 year} \times \text{amount of interest paid}}{\text{amount of loan} \times (\text{number of payments made on the loan} + 1)}$$

$$= \frac{2(12)(53)}{439(12 + 1)}$$

$$= 0.223 \quad \text{(rounded)}$$

$$= 22.3\%$$

The principal was obtained by subtracting the finance charge and the down payment from the installment price.

The annual percentage rate is 22.3%.

Using an APR Table

The federal government issues annual percentage rate tables, which are used to find exact APR rates (within $\frac{1}{4}$%, which is the federal standard). A portion of one of these tables is shown in Table 12-1; the following box tells how to use the table. Table 12-1 is based on monthly payments.

Step by Step

Calculating APR with a Table

Step 1. Multiply the finance charge by \$100 and divide by the amount financed:

$$\frac{\text{finance charge} \times \$100}{\text{amount financed}}$$

Step 2. Read down the left column of the table to the appropriate number of payments. Go across to find the number closest to that found in Step 1. Read up that column to find the annual percentage rate at the top of the column.

Table 12-1 Annual Percentage Rate Table for Monthly Payments (Finance Charge per $100 of Amount Financed)

Number of Payments	Annual percentage rate														
	10.00%	10.25%	10.50%	10.75%	11.00%	11.25%	11.50%	11.75%	12.00%	12.25%	12.50%	12.75%	13.00%	13.25%	13.50%	13.75
1	0.83	0.85	0.87	0.90	0.92	0.94	0.96	0.98	1.00	1.02	1.04	1.06	1.08	1.10	1.12	1.1
2	1.25	1.28	1.31	1.35	1.38	1.41	1.44	1.47	1.50	1.53	1.57	1.60	1.63	1.66	1.69	1.7
3	1.67	1.71	1.76	1.80	1.84	1.88	1.92	1.96	2.01	2.05	2.09	2.13	2.17	2.22	2.26	2.3
4	2.09	2.14	2.20	2.25	2.30	2.35	2.41	2.46	2.51	2.57	2.62	2.67	2.72	2.78	2.83	2.8
5	2.51	2.58	2.64	2.70	2.77	2.83	2.89	2.96	3.02	3.08	3.15	3.21	3.27	3.34	3.40	3.4
6	2.94	3.01	3.08	3.16	3.23	3.31	3.38	3.45	3.53	3.60	3.68	3.75	3.83	3.90	3.97	4.0
7	3.36	3.45	3.53	3.62	3.70	3.78	3.87	3.95	4.04	4.12	4.21	4.29	4.38	4.47	4.55	4.6
8	3.79	3.88	3.98	4.07	4.17	4.26	4.36	4.46	4.55	4.65	4.74	4.84	4.94	5.03	5.13	5.2
9	4.21	4.32	4.43	4.53	4.64	4.75	4.85	4.96	5.07	5.17	5.28	5.39	5.49	5.60	5.71	5.8
10	4.64	4.76	4.88	4.99	5.11	5.23	5.35	5.46	5.58	5.70	5.82	5.94	6.05	6.17	6.29	6.4
11	5.07	5.20	5.33	5.45	5.58	5.71	5.84	5.97	6.10	6.23	6.36	6.49	6.62	6.75	6.88	[illegible]
12	5.50	5.64	5.78	5.92	6.06	6.20	6.34	6.48	6.62	6.76	6.90	7.04	7.18	7.32	7.46	7.6
13	5.93	6.08	6.23	6.38	6.53	6.68	6.84	6.99	7.14	7.29	7.44	7.59	7.75	7.90	8.05	8.2
14	6.36	6.52	6.69	6.85	7.01	7.17	7.34	7.50	7.66	7.82	7.99	8.15	8.31	8.48	8.64	8.8
15	6.80	6.97	7.14	7.32	7.49	7.66	7.84	8.01	8.19	8.36	8.53	8.71	8.88	9.06	9.23	9.4
16	7.23	7.41	7.60	7.78	7.97	8.15	8.34	8.53	8.71	8.90	9.08	9.27	9.46	9.64	9.83	10.0
17	7.67	7.86	8.06	8.25	8.45	8.65	8.84	9.04	9.24	9.44	9.63	9.83	10.03	10.23	10.44	10.6
18	8.10	8.31	8.52	8.73	8.93	9.14	9.35	9.56	9.77	9.98	10.19	10.40	10.61	10.82	11.03	11.2
19	8.54	8.76	8.98	9.20	9.42	9.64	9.86	10.08	10.30	10.52	10.74	10.96	11.18	11.41	11.63	11.8
20	8.98	9.21	9.44	9.67	9.90	10.13	10.37	10.60	10.83	11.06	11.30	11.53	11.76	12.00	12.23	12.4
21	9.42	9.66	9.90	10.15	10.39	10.63	10.88	11.12	11.36	11.61	11.85	12.10	12.34	12.59	12.84	13.0
22	9.86	10.12	10.37	10.62	10.88	11.13	11.39	11.64	11.90	12.16	12.41	12.67	12.93	13.19	13.44	13.7
23	10.30	10.57	10.84	11.10	11.37	11.63	11.90	12.17	12.44	12.71	12.97	13.24	13.51	13.78	14.05	14.3
24	10.75	11.02	11.30	11.58	11.86	12.14	12.42	12.70	12.98	13.26	13.54	13.82	14.10	14.38	14.66	14.9
25	11.19	11.48	11.77	12.06	12.35	12.64	12.93	13.22	13.52	13.81	14.10	14.40	14.69	14.98	15.28	15.5
26	11.64	11.94	12.24	12.54	12.85	13.15	13.45	13.75	14.06	14.36	14.67	14.97	15.28	15.59	15.89	16.2
27	12.09	12.40	12.71	13.03	13.34	13.66	13.97	14.29	14.60	14.92	15.24	15.56	15.87	16.19	16.51	16.8
28	12.53	12.86	13.18	13.51	13.84	14.16	14.49	14.82	15.15	15.48	15.81	16.14	16.47	16.80	17.13	17.4
29	12.98	13.32	13.66	14.00	14.33	14.67	15.01	15.35	15.70	16.04	16.38	16.72	17.07	17.41	17.75	18.1
30	13.43	13.78	14.13	14.48	14.83	15.19	15.54	15.89	16.24	16.60	16.95	17.31	17.66	18.02	18.38	18.7
31	13.89	14.25	14.61	14.97	15.33	15.70	16.06	16.43	16.79	17.16	17.53	17.90	18.27	18.63	19.00	19.3
32	14.34	14.71	15.09	15.46	15.84	16.21	16.59	16.97	17.35	17.73	18.11	18.49	18.87	19.25	19.63	20.0
33	14.79	15.18	15.57	15.95	16.34	16.73	17.12	17.51	17.90	18.29	18.69	19.08	19.47	19.87	20.26	20.6
34	15.25	15.65	16.05	16.44	16.85	17.25	17.65	18.05	18.46	18.86	19.27	19.67	20.08	20.49	20.90	21.3
35	15.70	16.11	16.53	16.94	17.35	17.77	18.18	18.60	19.01	19.43	19.85	20.27	20.69	21.11	21.53	21.9
36	16.16	16.58	17.01	17.43	17.86	18.29	18.71	19.14	19.57	20.00	20.43	20.87	21.30	21.73	22.17	22.6
37	16.62	17.06	17.49	17.93	18.37	18.81	19.25	19.69	20.13	20.58	21.02	21.46	21.91	22.36	22.81	23.2
38	17.08	17.53	17.98	18.43	18.88	19.33	19.78	20.24	20.69	21.15	21.61	22.07	22.52	22.99	23.45	23.9
39	17.54	18.00	18.46	18.93	19.39	19.86	20.32	20.79	21.26	21.73	22.20	22.67	23.14	23.61	24.09	24.5
40	18.00	18.48	18.95	19.43	19.90	20.38	20.86	21.34	21.82	22.30	22.79	23.27	23.76	24.25	24.73	25.2
41	18.47	18.95	19.44	19.93	20.42	20.91	21.40	21.89	22.39	22.88	23.38	23.88	24.38	24.88	25.38	25.8
42	18.93	19.43	19.93	20.43	20.93	21.44	21.94	22.45	22.96	23.47	23.98	24.49	25.00	25.51	26.03	26.5
43	19.40	19.91	20.42	20.94	21.45	21.97	22.49	23.01	23.53	24.05	24.57	25.10	25.62	26.15	26.68	27.2
44	19.86	20.39	20.91	21.44	21.97	22.50	23.03	23.57	24.10	24.64	25.17	25.71	26.25	26.79	27.33	27.8
45	20.33	20.87	21.41	21.95	22.49	23.03	23.58	24.12	24.67	25.22	25.77	26.32	26.88	27.43	27.99	28.5
46	20.80	21.35	21.90	22.46	23.01	23.57	24.13	24.69	25.25	25.81	26.37	26.94	27.51	28.08	28.65	29.2
47	21.27	21.83	22.40	22.79	23.53	24.10	24.68	25.25	25.82	26.40	26.98	27.56	28.14	28.72	29.31	29.8
48	21.74	22.32	22.90	23.48	24.06	24.64	25.23	25.81	26.40	26.99	27.58	28.18	28.77	29.37	29.97	30.5
49	22.21	22.80	23.39	23.99	24.58	25.18	25.78	26.38	26.98	27.59	28.19	28.80	29.41	30.02	30.63	31.2
50	22.69	23.29	23.89	24.50	25.11	25.72	26.33	26.95	27.56	28.18	28.80	29.42	30.04	30.67	31.29	31.9
51	23.16	23.78	24.40	25.02	25.64	26.26	26.89	27.52	28.15	28.78	29.41	30.05	30.68	31.32	31.96	32.6
52	23.64	24.27	24.90	25.53	26.17	26.81	27.45	28.09	28.73	29.38	30.02	30.67	31.32	31.98	32.63	33.2
53	24.11	24.76	25.40	26.05	26.70	27.35	28.00	28.66	29.32	29.98	30.64	31.30	31.97	32.63	33.30	33.9
54	24.59	25.25	25.91	26.57	27.23	27.90	28.56	29.23	29.91	30.58	31.25	31.93	32.61	33.29	33.98	34.6
55	25.07	25.74	26.41	27.09	27.77	28.44	29.13	29.81	30.50	31.18	31.87	32.56	33.26	33.95	34.65	35.3
56	25.55	26.23	26.92	27.61	28.30	28.99	29.69	30.39	31.09	31.79	32.49	33.20	33.91	34.62	35.33	36.0
57	26.03	26.73	27.43	28.13	28.84	29.54	30.25	30.97	31.68	32.39	33.11	33.83	34.56	35.28	36.01	36.7
58	26.51	27.23	27.94	28.66	29.37	30.10	30.82	31.55	32.27	33.00	33.74	34.47	35.21	35.95	36.69	37.4
59	27.00	27.72	28.45	29.18	29.91	30.65	31.39	32.13	32.87	33.61	34.36	35.11	35.86	36.62	37.37	38.1
60	27.48	28.22	28.96	29.71	30.45	31.20	31.96	32.71	33.47	34.23	44.99	35.75	36.52	37.29	38.06	38.8

Table 12-1 (continued)

Number of Payments	Annual percentage rate 14.00%	14.25%	14.50%	14.75%	15.00%	15.25%	15.50%	15.75%	16.00%	16.25%	16.50%	16.75%	17.00%	17.25%	17.50%	17.75%
1	1.17	1.19	1.21	1.23	1.25	1.27	1.29	1.31	1.33	1.35	1.37	1.40	1.42	1.44	1.46	1.48
2	1.75	1.78	1.82	1.85	1.88	1.91	1.94	1.97	2.00	2.04	2.07	2.10	2.13	2.16	2.17	2.22
3	2.34	2.38	2.43	2.47	2.51	2.55	2.59	2.64	2.68	2.72	2.76	2.80	2.85	2.89	2.93	2.97
4	2.93	2.99	3.04	3.09	3.14	3.20	3.25	3.30	3.36	3.41	3.46	3.51	3.57	3.62	3.67	3.73
5	3.53	3.59	3.65	3.72	3.78	3.84	3.91	3.97	4.04	4.10	4.16	4.23	4.29	4.35	4.42	4.48
6	4.12	4.20	4.27	4.35	4.42	4.49	4.57	4.64	4.72	4.79	4.87	4.94	5.02	5.01	5.17	5.24
7	4.72	4.81	4.89	4.98	5.06	5.15	5.23	5.32	5.40	5.49	5.58	5.66	5.75	5.83	5.92	6.00
8	5.32	5.42	5.51	5.61	5.71	5.80	5.90	6.00	6.09	6.19	6.29	6.38	6.48	6.58	6.67	6.77
9	5.92	6.03	6.14	6.25	6.35	6.46	6.57	6.68	6.78	6.89	7.00	7.11	7.22	7.32	7.43	7.54
10	6.53	6.65	6.77	6.88	7.00	7.12	7.24	7.36	7.48	7.60	7.72	7.84	7.96	8.08	8.19	8.31
11	7.14	7.27	7.40	7.53	7.66	7.79	7.92	8.05	8.18	8.31	8.44	8.57	8.70	8.83	8.96	9.09
12	7.74	7.89	8.03	8.17	8.31	8.45	8.59	8.74	8.88	9.02	9.16	9.30	9.45	9.59	9.73	9.87
13	8.36	8.51	8.66	8.81	8.97	9.12	9.27	9.43	9.58	9.73	9.89	10.04	10.20	10.35	10.50	10.66
14	8.97	9.13	9.30	9.46	9.63	9.79	9.96	10.12	10.29	10.45	10.67	10.78	10.95	11.11	11.28	11.45
15	9.59	9.76	9.94	10.11	10.29	10.47	10.64	10.82	11.00	11.17	11.35	11.53	11.71	11.88	12.06	12.24
16	10.20	10.39	10.58	10.77	10.95	11.14	11.33	11.52	11.71	11.90	12.09	12.28	12.46	12.65	12.84	13.03
17	10.82	11.02	11.22	11.42	11.62	11.82	12.02	12.22	12.42	12.62	12.83	13.03	13.23	13.43	13.63	13.83
18	11.45	11.66	11.87	12.08	12.29	12.50	12.72	12.93	13.14	13.35	13.57	13.78	13.99	14.21	14.42	14.64
19	12.07	12.30	12.52	12.74	12.97	13.19	13.41	13.64	13.86	14.09	14.31	14.54	14.76	14.99	15.22	15.44
20	12.70	12.93	13.17	13.41	13.64	13.88	14.11	14.35	14.59	14.82	15.06	15.30	15.54	15.77	16.01	16.25
21	13.33	13.58	13.82	14.07	14.32	14.57	14.82	15.06	15.31	15.56	15.81	16.06	16.31	16.56	16.81	17.07
22	13.96	14.22	14.48	14.74	15.00	15.26	15.52	15.78	16.04	16.30	16.57	16.83	17.09	17.36	17.62	17.88
23	14.59	14.87	15.14	15.41	15.68	15.96	16.23	16.50	16.78	17.05	17.32	17.60	17.88	18.15	18.43	18.70
24	15.23	15.51	15.80	16.08	16.37	16.65	16.94	17.22	17.51	17.80	18.09	18.37	18.66	18.95	19.24	19.53
25	15.87	16.17	16.46	16.76	17.06	17.35	17.65	17.95	18.25	18.55	18.85	19.15	19.45	19.75	20.05	20.36
26	16.51	16.82	17.13	17.44	17.75	18.06	18.37	18.68	18.99	19.30	19.62	19.93	20.24	20.56	20.87	21.19
27	17.15	17.47	17.80	18.12	18.44	18.76	19.09	19.41	19.74	20.06	20.39	20.71	21.04	21.37	21.69	22.02
28	17.80	18.13	18.47	18.80	19.14	19.47	19.81	20.15	20.48	20.82	21.16	21.50	21.84	22.18	22.52	22.86
29	18.45	18.79	19.14	19.49	19.83	20.18	20.53	20.88	21.23	21.58	21.94	22.29	22.64	22.99	23.35	23.70
30	19.10	19.45	19.81	20.17	20.54	20.90	21.26	21.62	21.99	22.35	22.72	23.08	23.45	23.81	24.18	24.55
31	19.75	20.12	20.49	20.87	21.24	21.61	21.99	22.37	22.74	23.12	23.50	23.88	24.26	24.64	25.02	25.40
32	20.40	20.79	21.17	21.56	21.95	22.33	22.72	23.11	23.50	23.89	24.28	24.68	25.07	25.46	25.86	26.25
33	21.06	21.46	21.85	22.25	22.65	23.06	23.46	23.86	24.26	24.67	25.07	25.48	25.88	26.29	26.70	27.11
34	21.72	22.13	22.54	22.95	23.37	23.78	24.19	24.61	25.03	25.44	25.86	26.28	26.70	27.12	27.54	27.97
35	22.38	22.80	23.23	23.65	24.08	24.51	24.94	25.36	25.79	26.23	26.66	27.09	27.52	27.96	28.39	28.83
36	23.04	23.48	23.92	24.35	24.80	25.24	25.68	26.12	26.57	27.01	27.46	27.90	28.35	28.80	29.25	29.70
37	23.70	24.16	24.69	25.06	25.51	25.97	26.42	26.88	27.34	27.80	28.26	28.72	29.18	29.64	30.10	30.57
38	24.37	24.84	25.30	25.77	26.24	26.70	27.17	27.64	28.11	28.59	29.06	29.53	30.01	30.49	30.96	31.44
39	25.04	25.52	26.00	26.48	26.96	27.44	27.92	28.41	28.89	29.38	29.87	30.36	30.85	31.34	31.83	32.32
40	25.71	26.20	26.70	27.19	27.69	28.18	28.68	29.18	29.68	30.18	30.68	31.18	31.68	32.19	32.69	33.20
41	26.39	26.89	27.40	27.91	28.41	28.92	29.44	29.95	30.46	30.97	31.49	32.01	32.52	33.04	33.56	34.08
42	27.06	27.58	28.10	28.62	29.15	29.67	30.19	30.72	31.25	31.78	32.31	32.84	33.37	33.90	34.44	34.97
43	27.74	28.27	28.81	29.34	29.88	30.42	30.96	31.50	32.04	32.58	33.13	33.67	34.22	34.76	35.31	35.86
44	28.42	28.97	29.52	30.07	30.62	31.17	31.72	32.28	32.83	33.39	33.95	34.51	35.07	35.63	36.19	36.78
45	29.11	29.67	30.23	30.79	31.36	31.92	32.49	33.06	33.63	34.20	34.77	35.35	35.92	36.50	37.08	37.66
46	29.79	30.36	30.94	31.52	32.10	32.68	33.26	33.84	34.43	35.01	35.60	36.19	36.78	37.37	37.96	38.56
47	30.48	31.07	31.66	32.25	32.84	33.44	34.03	34.63	35.23	35.83	36.43	37.04	37.64	38.25	38.86	39.46
48	31.17	31.77	32.37	32.98	33.59	34.20	34.81	35.42	36.03	36.65	37.27	37.88	38.50	39.13	39.75	40.37
49	31.86	32.48	33.09	33.71	34.34	34.96	35.59	36.21	36.84	37.47	38.10	38.74	39.37	40.01	40.65	41.29
50	32.55	33.18	33.82	34.45	35.09	35.73	36.37	37.01	37.65	38.30	38.94	39.59	40.24	40.89	41.55	42.20
51	33.25	33.89	34.54	35.19	35.84	36.49	37.15	37.81	38.46	39.17	39.79	40.45	41.11	41.78	42.45	43.12
52	33.95	34.61	35.27	35.93	36.60	37.27	37.94	38.61	39.28	39.96	40.63	41.31	41.99	42.67	43.36	44.04
53	34.65	35.32	36.00	36.68	37.36	38.04	38.72	39.41	40.10	40.79	41.48	42.17	42.87	43.57	44.27	44.97
54	35.35	36.04	36.73	37.42	38.12	38.82	39.52	40.22	40.92	41.63	42.33	43.04	43.75	44.47	45.18	45.90
55	36.05	36.76	37.46	38.17	38.88	39.60	40.31	41.03	41.74	42.47	43.19	43.91	44.64	45.37	46.10	46.83
56	36.76	37.48	38.20	38.92	39.65	40.38	41.11	41.84	42.57	43.31	44.05	44.79	45.53	46.27	47.02	47.77
57	37.47	38.20	38.94	39.68	40.42	41.16	41.91	42.65	43.40	44.15	44.91	45.66	46.42	47.18	47.94	47.71
58	38.18	38.93	39.68	40.43	41.19	41.95	42.71	43.47	44.23	45.00	45.77	46.54	47.32	48.09	48.87	49.65
59	38.89	39.66	40.42	41.19	41.96	42.74	43.51	44.29	45.07	45.85	46.64	47.42	48.21	49.01	49.80	50.60
60	39.61	40.39	41.17	41.95	42.74	43.53	44.32	45.11	45.91	46.71	47.51	48.31	49.12	49.92	50.73	51.55

Table 12-1 (continued)

Number of Payments	Annual percentage rate															
	18.00%	18.25%	18.50%	18.75%	19.00%	19.25%	19.50%	19.75%	20.00%	20.25%	20.50%	20.75%	21.00%	21.25%	21.50%	21.75%
1	1.50	1.52	1.54	1.56	1.58	1.60	1.62	1.65	1.67	1.69	1.71	1.73	1.75	1.77	1.79	1.81
2	2.26	2.29	2.32	2.35	2.38	2.41	2.44	2.48	2.51	2.54	2.57	2.60	2.63	2.66	2.70	2.73
3	3.01	3.06	3.10	3.14	3.18	3.23	3.27	3.31	3.35	3.39	3.44	3.48	3.52	3.56	3.60	3.65
4	3.78	3.83	3.88	3.94	3.99	4.04	4.10	4.15	4.20	4.25	4.31	4.36	4.41	4.47	4.52	4.57
5	4.54	4.61	4.67	4.74	4.80	4.86	4.93	4.99	5.06	5.12	5.18	5.25	5.31	5.37	5.44	5.50
6	5.32	5.39	5.46	5.54	5.61	5.69	5.76	5.84	5.91	5.99	6.06	6.14	6.21	6.29	6.36	6.44
7	6.09	6.18	6.26	6.35	6.43	6.52	6.60	6.69	6.78	6.86	6.95	7.04	7.12	7.21	7.29	7.38
8	6.87	6.96	7.06	7.16	7.26	7.35	7.45	7.55	7.64	7.74	7.84	7.94	8.03	8.13	8.23	8.33
9	7.65	7.76	7.87	7.97	8.08	8.19	8.30	8.41	8.52	8.63	8.73	8.84	8.95	9.06	9.17	9.28
10	8.43	8.55	8.67	8.79	8.91	9.03	9.15	9.27	9.39	9.51	9.63	9.75	9.88	10.00	10.12	10.24
11	9.22	9.35	9.49	9.62	9.75	9.88	10.01	10.14	10.28	10.41	10.54	10.67	10.80	10.94	11.07	11.20
12	10.02	10.16	10.30	10.44	10.59	10.73	10.87	11.02	11.16	11.31	11.45	11.59	11.74	11.88	12.02	12.17
13	10.81	10.97	11.12	11.28	11.43	11.59	11.74	11.90	12.05	12.21	12.36	12.52	12.67	12.83	12.99	13.14
14	11.61	11.78	11.95	12.11	12.28	12.45	12.61	12.78	12.95	13.11	13.28	13.45	13.62	13.79	13.95	14.12
15	12.42	12.59	12.77	12.95	13.13	13.31	13.49	13.67	13.85	14.03	14.21	14.39	14.57	14.75	14.93	15.11
16	13.22	13.41	13.60	13.80	13.99	14.18	14.37	14.56	14.75	14.94	15.13	15.33	15.52	15.71	15.90	16.10
17	14.04	14.24	14.44	14.64	14.85	15.05	15.25	15.46	15.66	15.86	16.07	16.27	16.48	16.68	16.89	17.09
18	14.85	15.07	15.28	15.49	15.71	15.93	16.14	16.36	16.57	16.79	17.01	17.22	17.44	17.66	17.88	18.09
19	15.67	15.90	16.12	16.35	16.58	16.81	17.03	17.26	17.49	17.72	17.95	18.18	18.41	18.64	18.87	19.10
20	16.49	16.73	16.97	17.21	17.45	17.69	17.93	18.17	18.41	18.66	18.90	19.14	19.38	19.63	19.87	20.11
21	17.32	17.57	17.82	18.07	18.33	18.58	18.83	19.09	19.34	19.60	19.85	20.11	20.36	20.62	20.87	21.13
22	18.15	18.41	18.68	18.94	19.21	19.47	19.74	20.01	20.27	20.54	20.81	21.08	21.34	21.61	21.88	22.15
23	18.98	19.26	19.54	19.81	20.09	20.37	20.65	20.93	21.21	21.49	21.77	22.05	22.33	22.61	22.90	23.18
24	19.82	20.11	20.40	20.69	20.98	21.27	21.56	21.86	22.15	22.44	22.74	23.03	23.33	23.62	23.92	24.21
25	20.66	20.96	21.27	21.57	21.87	22.18	22.48	22.79	23.10	23.40	23.71	24.02	24.32	24.63	24.94	25.25
26	21.50	21.82	22.14	22.45	22.77	23.09	23.41	23.73	24.04	24.36	24.68	25.01	25.33	25.65	25.97	26.29
27	22.35	22.68	23.01	23.44	23.67	24.00	24.33	24.67	25.00	25.33	25.67	26.00	26.34	26.67	27.01	27.34
28	23.20	23.55	23.89	24.23	24.58	24.92	25.27	25.61	25.96	26.30	26.65	27.00	27.35	27.70	28.05	28.40
29	24.06	24.41	24.27	25.13	25.49	25.84	26.20	26.56	26.92	27.28	27.64	28.00	28.37	28.73	29.09	29.46
30	24.92	25.29	25.66	26.03	26.40	26.77	27.14	27.52	27.89	28.26	28.64	29.01	29.39	29.77	30.14	30.52
31	25.78	26.16	26.55	26.93	27.32	27.70	28.09	28.47	28.86	29.25	29.64	30.03	30.42	30.81	31.20	31.59
32	26.65	27.04	27.44	27.84	28.24	28.64	29.04	29.44	29.84	30.24	30.64	31.05	31.45	31.85	32.26	32.67
33	27.52	27.93	28.34	28.75	29.16	29.57	29.99	30.40	30.82	31.23	31.65	32.07	32.49	32.91	33.33	33.75
34	28.39	28.81	29.24	29.66	30.09	30.52	30.95	31.37	31.80	32.23	32.67	33.10	33.53	33.96	34.40	34.83
35	29.27	29.71	30.14	30.58	31.02	31.47	31.91	32.35	32.79	33.24	33.68	34.13	34.58	35.03	35.47	35.92
36	30.15	30.60	31.05	31.51	31.96	32.42	32.87	33.33	33.79	34.25	34.71	35.17	35.63	36.09	36.56	37.02
37	31.03	31.50	31.97	32.43	32.90	33.37	33.84	34.32	34.79	35.26	35.74	36.21	36.69	37.16	37.64	38.12
38	31.92	32.40	32.88	33.37	33.85	34.33	34.82	35.30	35.79	36.28	36.77	37.26	37.75	38.24	38.73	39.23
39	32.81	33.31	33.80	34.30	34.80	35.30	35.80	36.30	36.80	37.30	37.81	38.31	38.82	39.32	39.83	40.34
40	33.71	34.22	34.73	35.24	35.75	36.26	36.78	37.29	37.81	38.33	38.85	39.37	39.89	40.41	40.93	41.46
41	34.61	35.13	35.66	36.18	36.71	37.24	37.77	38.30	38.83	39.36	39.89	40.43	40.96	41.50	42.04	42.58
42	35.51	36.05	36.59	37.13	37.67	38.21	38.76	39.30	39.85	40.40	40.95	41.50	42.05	42.60	43.15	43.71
43	36.42	36.97	37.52	38.08	38.63	39.19	39.75	40.31	40.87	41.44	42.00	42.57	43.13	43.70	44.27	44.84
44	37.33	37.89	38.46	39.03	39.60	40.18	40.75	41.33	41.90	42.48	43.06	43.64	44.22	44.81	45.39	45.98
45	38.24	38.82	39.41	39.99	40.58	41.17	41.75	42.35	42.94	43.53	44.13	44.72	45.32	45.92	46.52	47.12
46	39.16	39.75	40.35	40.95	41.55	42.16	42.76	43.37	43.98	44.58	45.20	45.81	46.42	47.03	47.65	48.27
47	40.08	40.69	41.30	41.92	42.54	43.15	43.77	44.40	45.02	45.64	46.27	46.90	47.53	48.16	48.79	49.42
48	41.00	41.63	42.26	42.89	43.52	44.15	44.79	45.43	46.07	46.71	47.35	47.99	48.64	49.28	49.93	50.58
49	41.93	42.57	43.22	43.86	44.51	45.16	45.81	46.46	47.12	47.77	48.43	49.09	49.75	50.41	51.08	51.74
50	42.86	43.52	44.18	44.84	45.50	46.17	46.83	47.50	48.17	48.84	49.52	50.19	50.87	51.55	52.23	52.91
51	43.79	44.47	45.14	45.82	46.50	47.18	47.86	48.55	49.23	49.92	50.61	51.30	51.99	52.69	53.38	54.08
52	44.73	45.42	46.11	46.80	47.50	48.20	48.89	49.59	50.30	51.00	51.71	52.41	53.12	53.83	54.55	55.26
53	45.67	46.38	47.08	47.79	48.50	49.22	49.93	50.65	51.37	52.09	52.81	53.53	54.26	54.98	55.71	56.44
54	46.62	47.34	48.06	48.79	49.51	50.24	50.97	51.70	52.44	53.17	53.91	54.65	55.39	56.14	56.88	57.63
55	47.57	48.30	49.04	49.78	50.52	51.27	52.02	52.76	53.52	54.27	55.02	55.78	56.54	57.30	58.08	58.82
56	48.52	49.27	50.03	50.78	51.54	52.30	53.06	53.83	54.60	55.37	56.14	56.91	57.68	58.46	59.24	60.02
57	49.47	50.24	51.01	51.79	52.56	53.34	54.12	54.90	55.68	56.47	57.25	58.04	58.84	59.63	60.43	61.22
58	50.43	51.22	52.00	52.79	53.58	54.38	55.17	55.97	56.77	57.57	58.38	59.18	59.99	60.80	61.62	62.43
59	51.39	52.20	53.00	53.80	54.61	55.42	56.23	57.05	57.87	58.68	59.51	60.33	61.15	61.98	62.81	63.64
60	52.36	53.18	54.00	54.82	55.64	56.47	57.30	58.13	58.96	59.80	60.64	61.48	62.32	63.17	64.01	64.86

EXAMPLE 10

Lewis Strang bought a motorcycle for $3,000, which was financed at $140 per month for 24 months. There was no down payment. The total finance charge was $360. Find the annual percentage rate.

Step 1.

$$\frac{\text{finance charge} \times \$100}{\text{amount financed}} = \frac{\$360 \times \$100}{\$3{,}000} = \$12$$

Step 2. Read down the left column of the table to number 24, the number of payments to be made. Go across to find the number nearest to $12 (it is $12.14). Go up to the top of that column to find the annual percentage rate, which is 11.25%.

Self-Check

13. Use the constant ratio formula to find the annual percentage rate on a loan of $1,500 borrowed for 2 years with interest of $265. The loan is repaid in monthly payments.
14. A fishing boat is purchased for $5,600 and financed for 36 months. If the total finance charge is $1,025, find the annual percentage rate using Table 12-1.
15. An air compressor costs $780 and is financed with monthly payments for 12 months. The total finance charge is $90. Find the annual percentage rate using Table 12-1.

Section Review

Use the constant ratio formula to find the annual percentage rate for the following questions. Give the answers to the nearest tenth of a percent.

1. Find the annual percentage rate on a loan of $1,500 for 18 months if the loan requires $190 interest and is repaid monthly.

2. Find the annual percentage rate on a loan that is repaid weekly for 25 weeks if the amount of the loan is $300. The loan requires $20 interest.

3. Find the annual percentage rate on a loan of $3,820 if the monthly payment is $120 for 36 months.

4. Find the annual percentage rate on a loan of $700 with 12 monthly payments. The loan requires $101 interest.

5. A vacuum cleaner was purchased on the installment plan with 10 monthly payments of $10.50 each. If the cash price was $95, find the annual percentage rate.

Use Table 12-1 to find the annual percentage rate for the following.

6. A merchant charged $420 in cash for a dining-room set that could be bought for $50 down and $40.75 per month for 10 months. What is the annual percentage rate?

7. A man borrowed $500. He repaid the loan in 22 monthly payments of $26.30 each. Find the annual percentage rate.

8. An electric mixer was purchased on the installment plan for a down payment of $60 and 11 monthly payments of $11.05 each. The cash price was $170. Find the annual percentage rate.

9. A loan of $3,380 was paid back in 30 monthly payments with an interest charge of $620. Find the annual percentage rate to the nearest tenth percent.

10. A typewriter was purchased by paying $50 down and 24 monthly payments of $65 each. The cash price was $1,400. Find the annual percentage rate to the nearest tenth of a percent.

Summary

Topic	Page	What to Remember	Examples
Finding total price of an installment purchase	354	Total price = (number of payments × payment amount) + down payment	Find the total price of a computer that is paid for in 24 monthly payments of $113 if a down payment of $50 is made. (24 × $113) + $50 = $2,712 + $50 = $2,762
Finding finance charge and monthly payments	354	Finance charge = Cash price × rate of interest × time Total price = cash price + finance charge Monthly payment = $\frac{\text{total price}}{\text{number of monthly payments}}$	Find the amount ot finance charge on a computer if the cash price is $3,285 and 14% simple interest is used to calculate the total interest for 12 months. $3,825 × 0.14 × 1 = $459.90 Total price = $3,285 + $459.90 = $3,744.90 Monthly payment = $\frac{\$3,744.90}{12}$ = $312.08

Topic	Page	What to Remember	Examples
Finding the amount of monthly payments	354	Amount financed = installment price − down payment Monthly payment = $\frac{\text{amount financed}}{\text{number of payments}}$	A computer has an installment price of $2,187.25 when financed over 18 months. If a $100 down payment is made, find the monthly payment. $2,187.25 − $100 = $2,087.25 $\frac{\$2,087.25}{18} = \$115.96$
Finding finance charge refund	356	Finance charge refund = total finance charge × refund fraction Refund fraction = $\frac{\text{sum of the number of payments remaining}}{\text{sum of the total number of payments due}}$ Sum of number of payments due = $\frac{\text{(number of payments)(number of payments + 1)}}{2}$	Find the finance charge refund on a loan that has a total finance charge of $892 and was made for 24 months. The loan is paid in full with 10 months (payments) remaining. Sum of number of payments remaining = $\frac{10(11)}{2} = 55$ Sum of total number of payments due = $\frac{24(25)}{2} = 300$ Finance charge refund = $\$892 \times \frac{55}{300} = \$163.53$
Finding interest on a charge account	361	Interest = rate × unpaid balance Interest is usually charged only on previous month's balance, not on purchases or cash advances made during the month of the statement.	A charge account has an unpaid balance of $1,384.37 and the monthly interest rate is 1.75%. Find the interest. 0.0175 × $1,384.37 = $24.23
Finding APR with the constant ratio formula	366	Annual percentage rate = $\frac{\text{2(number pay periods per year)(amount interest)}}{\text{(loan amount)(number of payments made + 1)}}$	Find the annual percentage rate for a loan of $13,850 that is repaid in 42 monthly installments. The interest for the loan is $2,382.20. $\text{APR} = \frac{2(12)(\$2,382.20)}{\$13,850(43)}$ $= 0.096 = 9.6\%$
Finding APR using Table 12-1	367–368	Value = $\frac{\text{finance charge} \times \$100}{\text{amount financed}}$ Find number of payments and move across to closest value. Read up to final rate.	Find the annual percentage rate on a loan of $500 that is repaid in 36 monthly installments. The interest for the loan is $95. $\frac{95 \times 100}{500} = \$19$ Find 36 (months) in left column. Move across to 19.14 (nearest to 19). APR is at top of column, 11.75%.

Chapter Review

1. Find the finance charge on a credit card with an unpaid balance of $465 if the rate charged is 1.25%.

2. Find the new unpaid balance on an account with a previous balance of $263.50, purchases of $38.75, a payment of $35, and a finance charge of 1.5% of the unpaid balance.

3. Find the monthly rate of interest on an account with an unpaid balance of $126 and a finance charge of $2.65.

4. A television set has been purchased on the installment plan with a down payment of $120 and 6 monthly payments of $98.50. Find the total price of the television set.

5. Find the amount of each monthly payment on a water bed that is sold for $1,050 on the installment plan with a down payment of $200 and 10 monthly payments.

6. If the cash price of a refrigerator is $879 and a down payment of $150 is made, how much is to be financed?

7. What is the cash price of a chair if the total price is $679 and the finance charge is $102?

8. On August 1, the unpaid balance on a credit card is $206. During the month, purchases of $98.65 and a payment of $60 were made. Using the unpaid balance method and a finance charge of 1.5%, find the unpaid balance on September 1.

9. Use the activity chart to find the unpaid balance on November 1. The billing cycle ended on October 31. (Use the average daily balance method.)

Date	Activity	Amount
October 1	Billing date	Previous balance $426.40
October 7	Purchase	$41.60
October 10	Payment	$70
October 15	Purchase	$31.25
October 20	Purchase	$26.80

The bank charges 1.5% interest per month.

10. Find the refund fraction on a 36-month loan if it is paid off after 16 months.

11. The finance charges on a camera were $273. The loan was to be paid in 12 monthly payments. Find the finance charge refund if the loan is paid off in 5 months.

12. Use the constant ratio formula to find the annual percentage rate on a loan of $2,000 for 12 months with interest of $210. The loan is repaid monthly.

13. Use Table 12-1 to find the annual percentage rate on an $850 loan to be repaid in 30 monthly payments. The amount of interest is $129.

Trial Test

1. Find the finance charge on an item with a cash price of \$469 if the total price is \$503.

2. An item with a cash price of \$578 can be purchased on the installment plan in 15 monthly payments of \$46. Find the amount of finance charge.

3. A copier that originally cost \$300 was sold on the installment plan at \$28 per month for 12 months. Find the amount of finance charge.

4. Use Table 12-1 to find the annual percentage rate for the loan in Problem 3.

5. Use the constant ratio formula to find the actual rate of interest, to the nearest tenth percent, for the copier in Problem 3.

6. Use the constant ratio formula to find the actual rate of interest, to the nearest tenth percent, on a loan of \$3,000 at 9% for 3 years if the loan had interest of \$810 and was repaid monthly.

7. Find the interest on an unpaid balance of \$165 if the monthly interest rate is $1\frac{3}{4}\%$.

8. Find the yearly rate of interest on a loan if the monthly rate is 2%.

9. Find the amount of interest refunded on a 15-month loan with total interest of \$72 if the loan is paid in full with 6 months remaining.

10. Find the actual interest rate on a loan of $1,600 for 24 months if $200 interest is charged and the loan is repaid in monthly payments.

11. Find the actual interest rate on a loan that is repaid weekly for 26 weeks if the amount of the loan is $1,025. The interest charged is $60.

12. Office equipment was purchased on the installment plan with 12 monthly payments of $11.20 each. If the cash price was $120, find the annual percentage rate.

13. Find the new unpaid balance on an account with a previous balance of $205.60, purchases of $67.38, a payment of $40, and a finance charge of 1.75%.

14. A canoe has been purchased on the installment plan with a down payment of $75 and 10 monthly payments of $80 each. Find the total price of the canoe.

15. Find the amount of each of 12 monthly payments when the total price is $2,300 and a down payment of $400 is made.

16. How much is to be financed on a cash price of $729 if a down payment of $75 is made?

17. Find the refund fraction on a 4-year loan if it is paid off in 25 months.

18. The unpaid balance on a credit card is $288.93. During the month, purchases totaling $75.60 and one payment of $50 were made. Using the unpaid balance method and a finance rate of 1.9% per month, find the unpaid balance at the end of the cycle.

19. Use the following activity chart to find the unpaid balance based on the average daily balance and a finance rate of 1.75% per month. The billing cycle has 31 days.

Date	Activity	Amount
July 1	Billing date	Previous balance $441.05
July 4	Payment	$75
July 15	Purchase	$23.50
July 25	Purchase	$31.40

Self-Check Solutions

1. $6 \times \$108.20 + \$100 = \$749.20$

2. $\dfrac{\$929 - \$100}{12} = \dfrac{\$829}{12} = \$69.08$

3. $\$579 - \$125 = \$454$

4. $\$2{,}590 \times 24\% \times 1 = \$621.60$;
$\dfrac{\$2{,}590 + \$621.60}{12} = \$267.63$

5. $\dfrac{8(9)}{18(19)} = \dfrac{72}{342} = \dfrac{4}{19}$

6. $18 - 12 = 6$ months remaining
$\dfrac{6(7)}{18(19)} \times \$205 = \$25.18$

7. $48 - 28 = 20$ months remaining
$\dfrac{20(21)}{48(49)} = \dfrac{5}{28}$

8. $48 - 28 = 20$ months remaining
$\dfrac{20(21)}{48(49)} \times \$1{,}645 = \$293.75$

9. $\$275.69 \times 0.023 = \$6.34$

10. $\$176.95 \times 0.016 = \$2.83$
$\$176.95 + \$2.83 - \$45 = \$134.78$

11. March 1–6 $\quad 6 \times \$128.50 = \$\ 771.00$
$\$128.50 - \$20 = \$108.50$
March 7–20 $\quad 14 \times 108.50 = 1{,}519.00$
$\$108.50 + \$25.60 = \$134.10$
March 21–31 $\quad 11 \times 134.10 = \underline{1{,}475.10}$
$\$3{,}765.10$
$\$3{,}765.10 \div 31 = \$\ 121.45$

12. $\$121.45 \times 0.018 = \$2.19$;
$\$134.10 + \$2.19 = \$136.29$

13. $\dfrac{2 \times 12 \times 265}{1{,}500 \times (24 + 1)} = 17.0\%$

14. $\dfrac{\$1{,}025 \times 100}{\$5{,}600} = \$18.30$
Move down the left column to 36. Then move across to 18.29 (nearest to 18.30). The percent at the top of this column is 11.25%, which is the rate.

15. $\dfrac{\$90 \times 100}{\$780} = \$11.54$
Move down the left column to 12. Then move across to 11.59 (nearest to 11.54). The percent at the top of this column is 20.75%, which is the rate.

Depreciation 13

Learning Objectives

1. Understand depreciation, book value, and salvage value. (pp. 381–383)
2. Understand and use the straight-line method of depreciation. (pp. 382–383)
3. Explain and use the units-of-production method of depreciation. (pp. 385–386)
4. Use the sum-of-the-years'-digits method of depreciation. (pp. 389–391)
5. Understand and apply declining-balance methods of depreciation. (pp. 393–395)
6. Use ACRS and MACRS tables to depreciate equipment. (pp. 397–401)

Buildings, machinery, equipment, furniture, and other items bought for the operation of a business are included among the **assets** of that business. The dollar value of each asset is used in figuring the value and profitability of the business and in figuring the taxable income from the business. The expense of running a business, including the purchase of assets, can be deducted from the company's income before taxes are calculated, so it is important to have a way of keeping track of the value of assets.

assets: buildings, machinery, equipment, furniture, and other items bought for the operation of a business.

Some assets have a useful life of 1 year or less, and their costs can be deducted from the business's income in the year they are purchased. The costs of items that are expected to last more than a year can be prorated and deducted over a period of years, called the **estimated life,** or **useful life,** of the item. During this time period, the asset *depreciates,* or decreases in value. At the end of an asset's estimated life, it may still have a dollar value, called the **salvage value,** or **scrap value.** The amount an asset decreases in value from its original cost is called its **depreciation.**

estimated life (**useful life**): the number of years an asset is expected to be usable; for some assets the estimated life is calculated in units of production such as miles for vehicles or units of work for some machines.

salvage value (scrap value): the estimated dollar value of an asset at the end of the asset's estimated useful life.

depreciation: the amount an asset decreases in value from its original cost.

This chapter is concerned with determining the amount an asset has depreciated. This involves the question of how the estimated life of a piece of equipment is to be defined—in years? In miles driven, if it is a car? In items produced, if it is a machine? It also involves a question of what percentage of the original cost can be deducted each year. Some types of equipment may be used more heavily some years than others; some machines depreciate rapidly at first and slowly later; some machines may not wear out but may become outdated because a better model has been invented. All these factors must be considered in choosing the method of depreciation for a particular asset.

Six widely used depreciation methods are examined: straight-line, units-of-production, sum-of-the-years'-digits, declining-balance, the accelerated cost recovery system (ACRS), and the modified accelerated cost recovery system (MACRS). The Internal Revenue Service regulates which methods of depreciation are allowed for income tax purposes. In general, the same depreciation method must be used throughout the useful life of any particular asset.

straight-line depreciation: a method of depreciation in which the amount of depreciation of an asset is spread equally over the number of years of useful life of the asset.

The **straight-line depreciation** method is the most commonly used method of depreciation. It is easy to use because the depreciation is the same for each full year the equipment is used.

If you know the original cost of an asset, its estimated useful life, and its salvage value, you can find the yearly depreciation amount. Remember, in calculating depreciation, by whatever method, the cost of an asset means the *total cost,* including shipping and installation charges if the asset is a piece of equipment. The *depreciable value* is the cost minus the salvage value.

Step by Step

Straight-line Depreciation Method

$$\text{Yearly depreciation} = \frac{\text{cost of equipment} - \text{salvage value}}{\text{expected life (in years)}}$$

EXAMPLE 1

Use the straight-line method to find the yearly depreciation for a machine that has an expected useful life of 5 years if the machine cost \$27,300, its shipping costs totaled \$250, installation charges came to \$450, and its salvage value is \$1,000.

$$\text{Original cost} = \text{cost of asset} + \text{shipping} + \text{installation}$$
$$= \$27{,}300 + \$250 + \$450 = \$28{,}000$$

Salvage value = \$1,000

Expected life = 5 years

$$\text{Yearly depreciation} = \frac{\text{total cost of equipment} - \text{salvage value}}{\text{expected life (in years)}}$$
$$= \frac{(\$28{,}000 - \$1{,}000)}{5} = \frac{\$27{,}000}{5} = \$5{,}400$$

The depreciation is \$5,400 per year.

Calculator Sequence

[AC] 27300 [+] 250 [+] 450 [−] 1000 [=] [÷] 5 [=] ⇒ 5400

Table 13-1 Straight-Line Depreciation Method

Year	Original Cost	Depreciation	Accumulated Depreciation	Book Value
1	\$28,000	\$5,400	\$ 5,400	\$22,600
2		\$5,400	\$10,800	\$17,200
3		\$5,400	\$16,200	\$11,800
4		\$5,400	\$21,600	\$ 6,400
5		\$5,400	\$27,000	\$ 1,000

Once we have calculated the yearly depreciation, we can prepare a depreciation schedule. Using the figures from Example 1, Table 13-1 shows the original cost, the amount of depreciation taken each year, and the changing book value of the equipment. **Book value** is the original cost minus the *accumulated depreciation*, which is the total amount of depreciation taken as of a certain time. Every year the depreciation amount is subtracted from the previous year's book value, and the book value goes down.

book value: the original cost of an asset minus the accumulated depreciation.

TIPS & TRAPS

A common mistake in figuring straight-line depreciation is to divide the cost of the expected life without subtracting the salvage value of the asset. See what happens when this is done with Example 1:

$$\text{Yearly depreciation} = \frac{\text{total cost of equipment}}{\text{expected life (in years)}} = \frac{\$28{,}000}{5} = \$5{,}600$$

WRONG

$$\text{Yearly depreciation} = \frac{\text{total cost of equipment} - \text{salvage value}}{\text{expected life (in years)}}$$

$$= \frac{\$28{,}000 - \$1{,}000}{5} = \frac{\$27{,}000}{5} = \$5{,}400$$

CORRECT

Self-Check

1. Use the straight-line method to find the yearly depreciation for a van that cost $18,000, has an expected useful life of 3 years, and has a salvage value of $3,000.

Section Review

1. A company automobile has an original cost of $14,500 and a trade-in (salvage) value of $2,500 after 5 years. Find its depreciable value.

2. A computer system was purchased for $7,500. Shipping charges were $75 and installation charges were $50. What was the total cost of the computer system?

Use straight-line depreciation to figure the yearly depreciation on the following. Round answers to the nearest cent.

	Original Cost	Salvage Value	Expected Life
3.	$ 7,200	$ 300	3 years
4.	$ 6,000	$ 50	11 years
5.	$ 12,000	$ 2,500	5 years
6.	$ 50,000	$ 5,000	10 years
7.	$100,000	$10,000	20 years

8. A machine was purchased by the Wabash Company for $5,900. Its normal life expectancy is 4 years. If it can be traded in for $900 at the end of this time, determine the yearly depreciation by the straight-line method.

9. A stamping machine was purchased by Break Fast Glass Company for $8,595. Freight and installation costs were $405. If it will be worth $2,000 after 7 years, find the annual depreciation using the straight-line method.

10. Station WMAT spent $5,000 for a new television camera. This camera will be replaced in 5 years. If the scrap value will be $500, determine the annual depreciation by the straight-line method.

11. A dress factory paid $14,000 for an assembly-line system. If the used equipment will be worth $2,000 at the end of 15 years, find the annual depreciation by the straight-line method.

12. A computer was purchased by the Acme Management Corporation for $5,400. Its life expectancy is projected to be 4 years, and the salvage value will be $800. Make a straight-line depreciation table like Table 13-1 to show each year's depreciation, the accumulated depreciation, and the year-end book value.

Year	Original Cost	Annual Depreciation	Accumulated Depreciation	Book Value

Units-of-Production Method of Depreciation

The **units-of-production depreciation** method is used with machines and other types of equipment that are used heavily for a period of time and then sit idle for another period of time, sometimes months. For example, earth-moving equipment and farm equipment are often idle during the winter months. Instead of basing depreciation on the expected lifetime of a piece of equipment, this method takes into account how the equipment is used—for example, how many items it has produced, how many miles it has been driven, how many hours it has operated, or how many times it has performed some particular operation.

To use this method, you first figure how much the equipment depreciates with each unit produced or each mile driven and then multiply that amount by the number of units produced or miles driven.

units-of-production depreciation: a method of depreciation that is based on the expected number of units produced by an asset, such as miles driven for a vehicle or labels produced for a label machine; each year's depreciation is based on the number of units of work produced by the asset during the year.

Step by Step

The Units-of-Production Depreciation Method

$$\text{Unit depreciation} = \frac{\text{total cost} - \text{salvage value}}{\text{expected life (in units produced)}}$$

$$\text{Depreciation amount} = \text{unit depreciation} \times \text{units produced}$$

EXAMPLE 2

A label-making machine that costs $28,000 after shipping and installation is expected to print 50,000,000 labels during its useful life. If the salvage value of the machine is $1,000, find the unit depreciation for printing 2,125,000 labels.

$$\text{Unit depreciation} = \frac{\text{total cost} - \text{salvage value}}{\text{expected life (in number of units produced)}}$$

$$= \frac{\$28{,}000 - \$1{,}000}{50{,}000{,}000}$$

$$= \$0.00054 \text{ depreciation per unit produced}$$

$2{,}125{,}000 \times \$0.00054 = \$1{,}147.50$ Do not round the unit depreciation.

The depreciation is $1,147.50.

Calculator Sequence

[AC] 28000 [−] 1000 [=] [÷] 50,000,000 [×] 2,125,000 [=] ⇒ 1147.50

The depreciation of the label maker is recorded in a depreciation schedule like the one shown in Table 13-2. Note that the table shows the number of labels made each year and that the number differs from year to year. This pattern of use is typical of equipment that is depreciated by this method.

Table 13-2 Units-of-Production Depreciation Schedule

Year	Original Cost	Number of Labels Printed during Year	Annual Depreciation	Accumulated Depreciation	End-of-Year Book Value
1	$28,000	2,125,000	$1,147.50	$ 1,147.50	$26,852.50
2		11,830,000	6,388.20	7,535.70	20,464.30
3		12,765,000	6,893.10	14,428.80	13,571.20
4		12,210,000	6,593.40	21,022.20	6,977.80
5		11,070,000	5,977.80	27,000.00	1,000.00

Self-Check

2. A van that costs $18,000 is expected to be driven 75,000 miles during its useful life. If the salvage value of the van is $3,000, find the unit depreciation and the amount of depreciation after the van has been driven 56,000 miles.

Section Review

1. A microcomputer costs $2,500 and has an expected life of 25,000 hours. Find the unit depreciation for the computer if its salvage value is $400.

Find the unit and yearly depreciation for the following.

	Cost	Scrap Value	Expected Life	Hours Operated This Year
2.	$42,000	$2,000	80,000 hours	6,700 hours
3.	$25,000	$2,500	90,000 hours	7,000 hours
4.	$ 4,340	$ 340	16,000 hours	2,580 hours
5.	$19,000	$1,000	45,000 hours	8,000 hours
6.	$2,370	$ 420	7,800 hours	1,520 hours

7. SERV-U Computer Service Company bought a laser printer for $15,000. The machine is expected to operate for 28,000 hours, after which its trade-in value will be $1,000. Find the unit depreciation for the printer. The first year the machine was operated 4,160 hours. Find the depreciation for the year.

8. A bottle-making machine costs $12,000 and has a scrap value of $1,500. It is expected to make 1,500,000 bottles during its useful life. Find the depreciation when 1,000,000 bottles have been produced.

9. BEST Delivery Service purchased a delivery truck for $18,500 and expected to resell it for $2,000 after driving it 150,000 miles. Find the unit depreciation for the truck.

10. Make a depreciation table similar to Table 13-2 to show the number of miles driven during the year, annual depreciation, accumulated depreciation, and end-of-year book value if the truck of Exercise 9 is driven 28,580 miles the first year, 32,140 miles the second year, 29,760 miles the third year, 31,810 miles the fourth year, and 27,710 miles the fifth year.

Year	Original Cost	Number of Miles Driven during Year	Annual Depreciation	Accumulated Depreciation	End-of-Year Book Value

11. Find the unit depreciation for an air conditioning–heating unit that cost $7,800 and has a scrap value of $600 if it is expected to operate 40,000 hours.

12. If the unit in Exercise 11 operates 2,190 hours the first year, what is the depreciation for the year?

13. If the unit in Exercise 11 operates 4,599 hours the second year, what is the depreciation for the year?

14. We-Kare Child Care Center purchased a van for $21,500 and expects it to be driven 75,000 miles. If the resale value of the van is projected to be $6,500, find the unit depreciation for the van.

15. Employees of We-Kare Child Care Center drove the van (Exercise 14) 19,740 miles the first year. Find the depreciation for the year.

Sum-of-the-Years'-Digits Method of Depreciation

The straight-line depreciation method of depreciating an asset is the simplest way to depreciate it, but it is not always the best method of depreciation to use. Most equipment depreciates more during its first year of operation than during any other subsequent year. Most businesses want an immediate tax advantage and prefer to use a method that depreciates the largest amount possible during the first year or two. A method that does this is the **sum-of-the-years'-digits depreciation** method.

sum-of-the-years'-digits depreciation: a method of depreciating an asset by allowing the greatest depreciation during the first year and a decreasing amount of depreciation each year thereafter.

To compute depreciation by this method, first list, *in reverse order,* the number of years in the asset's expected life, For example, if a machine has an expected life of 5 years, you would list the digits

$$5, 4, 3, 2, 1$$

This list tells you how many remaining years of expected life the machine has each year. (Five years remain the first year; 4 years remain the second year; and so on.)

Then find the sum of these digits:

$$5 + 4 + 3 + 2 + 1 = 15$$

You can use a formula for finding the sum of the years' digits by using the formula $\frac{n(n + 1)}{2}$, where n is the number of expected years for the asset. The value of this formula will be the denominator of the depreciation rate fraction.

$$\frac{5(5 + 1)}{2} = \frac{5(6)}{2} = 15$$

Next, we make fractions by placing each digit over the number 15:

$$\frac{5}{15}, \frac{4}{15}, \frac{3}{15}, \frac{2}{15}, \frac{1}{15}$$

These fractions show the *rate of depreciation* for each year. The first-year rate is $\frac{5}{15}$, the second-year rate is $\frac{4}{15}$, and so on.

To find each year's depreciation, multiply the rate of depreciation for the year times the depreciable amount (the difference between the original cost and the salvage value of the asset).

Step by Step

Sum-of-the-Years'-Digits Method of Depreciation

Step 1. Find the depreciation rate fraction for the year in question.

$$\text{Depreciation rate fraction} = \frac{\text{number of useful years remaining}}{\frac{n(n + 1)}{2}}$$

Step 2. To find the amount of depreciation in a specific year, multiply the rate of depreciation for the year times the depreciable amount (difference between the original cost and the salvage value of the asset).

(Original cost − salvage value) × depreciation rate fraction

EXAMPLE 3

Find the depreciation for each of 5 years of expected life of a piece of equipment that costs $27,300 and has a shipping cost of $250, an installation cost of $450, and a salvage value of $1,000.

Step 1. Depreciation rate fraction

$$= \frac{\text{number of useful years remaining}}{\frac{n(n+1)}{2} = \frac{5(6)}{2} = 15}$$

Find the denominator of the depreciation rate fractions.

$$\frac{5}{15}, \frac{4}{15}, \frac{3}{15}, \frac{2}{15}, \frac{1}{15}$$

↑ ↑ ↑ ↑ ↑

Year 1 2 3 4 5

Write the depreciation rate fraction for each year.

Step 2. At this point, a depreciation table helps organize information and calculations (see Table 13-3). Find the depreciation amount for each year by multiplying the depreciation rate fraction times the depreciable amount (cost of the asset minus the salvage value).

Table 13-3 Sum-of-the-Years'-Digits Method of Depreciation

Year	Depreciation Rate Fraction	Cost Minus Salvage Value	Depreciation Amount	Accumulated Depreciation	Book Value
1	$\frac{5}{15}$	$27,000	$9,000	$ 9,000	$19,000
2	$\frac{4}{15}$	$27,000	$7,200	$16,200	$11,800
3	$\frac{3}{15}$	$27,000	$5,400	$21,600	$ 6,400
4	$\frac{2}{15}$	$27,000	$3,600	$25,200	$ 2,800
5	$\frac{1}{15}$	$27,000	$1,800	$27,000	$ 1,000

Calculator Solution

The calculator sequence for the first year's depreciation is:

[AC] 5 [÷] 15 [=] [×] 27000 [=] ⇒ 8999.991

Different calculators will give varying numbers of decimal places. If a basic calculator is used, the answer shown will appear in the display. This answer should be rounded to 9000. If a scientific calculator is used, the display will show 9000.

The calculator sequence for subsequent calculations will be:

[AC] (year's depreciation rate fraction) [×] 27000 [=] ⇒ year's depreciation

TIPS & TRAPS

A common mistake is to list the smallest fraction rather than the largest fraction for the first year's depreciation rate. In Example 3, the smallest fraction is $\frac{1}{15}$ and the largest is $\frac{5}{15}$. The confusion often occurs because the smallest fraction goes with the largest year—that is, year 5 uses $\frac{1}{15}$, and year 1 uses $\frac{5}{15}$.

Let's look at how to figure the depreciation amount for year 1 from Example 3 again, showing both the wrong and correct ways to do it:

Year 1	Year 1
~~$\frac{1}{15} \times \$27,000 = \$1,800$~~	$\frac{5}{15} \times \$27,000 = \$9,000$
WRONG	CORRECT

An easy way to check yourself on this is to remember that when using the sum-of-the-years'-digits method, the *first* year's depreciation should be the *largest*. This shows you that \$9,000 is correct and \$1,800 is wrong for the first year's depreciation amount.

Self-Check

3. Find the depreciation for each of the 3 years of expected life of a van that costs \$18,000 and has a salvage value of \$3,000.

Section Review

Find the sum of the digits (the denominator of the depreciation rate fraction) for assets depreciated for the following number of years.

1. 7 years

2. 12 years

3. 8 years

4. 2 years

5. 15 years

6. 20 years

7. 25 years

8. 40 years

9. Make a table to show the yearly depreciation of a machine that cost $4,200 and will be worth $750 at the end of 5 years.

Year	Depreciation Rate	Cost Minus Salvage Value	Depreciation Amount	Accumulated Depreciation	Book Value

10. Make a table to show the yearly depreciation of an asset that cost $21,500 and will be worth $5,000 at the end of 8 years.

Year	Depreciation Rate	Cost Minus Salvage Value	Depreciation Amount	Accumulated Depreciation	Book Value

Declining-Balance Method of Depreciation

Another way to calculate depreciation so that the depreciation is large in the early years of the asset's life and becomes smaller in the later years is the **declining-balance method.** Some assets can be depreciated at twice the straight-line rate, which is called the **double-declining-balance rate.** The Internal Revenue Service (IRS) places limitations on the use of the declining-balance method of depreciation, so you should consult the IRS or an accountant before choosing any depreciation method.

First, you must determine the **straight-line rate** of depreciation. To do this, write a fraction with a numerator of 1 and a denominator equal to the number of useful years of an asset. Write the decimal or percent equivalent of this fraction. The decimal equivalent is used in making calculations, and the percent equivalent is used to identify the *rate* of depreciation.

The double-declining rate is found by multiplying the straight-line rate by 2. If the decimal equivalent does not come out even, it should be expressed as a decimal number with six decimal places. The percent equivalent can be rounded to the nearest hundredth of a percent.

declining-balance depreciation: a method of depreciation that provides for large depreciation in the early years of the life of an asset; the beginning book value using this method is the cost of the asset rather than the difference in the cost and the scrap value as in other depreciation methods.

double-declining-balance depreciation: a method of declining-balance depreciation in which the rate of depreciation is twice the straight-line depreciation rate.

straight-line rate: when used with the declining-balance method of depreciation, the straight-line rate is a fraction with a numerator of 1 and a denominator equal to the number of useful years of an asset. This fraction is usually expressed as a decimal equivalent when making calculations and a percent equivalent when identifying the rate of depreciation.

Step by Step

Declining-Balance and Double-Declining Balance Methods of Depreciation

$$\text{Straight-line, declining-balance depreciation rate} = \frac{1}{\text{expected useful life (in years)}}$$

$$\text{Double-declining-balance depreciation rate} = \frac{1}{\text{expected useful life (in years)}} \times 2$$

EXAMPLE 4

An asset has a useful life of 6 years. Find (a) the straight-line rate expressed as a decimal and percent and (b) the double-declining rate expressed as a decimal and percent.

a. $\text{Straight-line rate} = \frac{1}{\text{expected useful life}} = \frac{1}{6}$

$\frac{1}{6} = 0.166667$ (decimal equivalent)

$= 16.67\%$ (percent equivalent)

b. $\text{Double-declining rate} = \frac{1}{\text{expected useful life}} \times 2 = \frac{1}{6} \times 2 = \frac{2}{6} = \frac{1}{3}$

$\frac{1}{3} = 0.333333$ (decimal equivalent)

$= 33.33\%$ (percent equivalent)

Using the Declining-Balance Method

After you find the rate of depreciation, multiply it times the beginning book value of the asset to find the depreciation for the first year. Note that the *beginning book value* is the cost of the asset. *Do not* subtract the salvage value from the original book value to find the depreciable amount in this method. At the end of the year, subtract the year's depreciation from the beginning book value to find the *new* book value for the beginning of the next year. This process continues for the number of years the asset is to be depreciated, or until the book value equals the salvage value. The ending balance for any given year *cannot* drop below the salvage value of the asset. If this occurs, the year's ending value is the salvage value, and the year's depreciation is adjusted. There will then be no further depreciation in future years.

Step by Step

Using the Declining Balance Method of Depreciation

Step 1. Find the declining rate. The decimal equivalent of the rate should be computed to six decimal places.

$$\frac{1}{\text{Expected useful life}}$$

$$\left(\text{or } \frac{1}{\text{expected useful life}} \times 2 \quad \text{for double-declining balance}\right)$$

Step 2. Find the depreciation amount:

Book value × declining rate = depreciation amount

Step 3. Find next year's book value:

Book value − depreciation amount = next year's book value

Step 4. Repeat steps 2 and 3 for the required number of years, or until book value is equal to or less than the salvage value.

EXAMPLE 5

A machine costing \$28,000 with an expected life of 5 years and a resale value of \$1,000 is depreciated by the declining-balance method at twice the straight-line rate. Determine the depreciation and the year-end book value for each of the 5 years.

Step 1. Double-declining rate $= \dfrac{1}{\text{expected useful life}} \times 2 = \dfrac{1}{5} \times 2 = \dfrac{2}{5}$

$$\frac{2}{5} = 0.4 = 40\%$$

Step 2. Initial book value × declining rate = depreciation amount (year 1)

$$\$28{,}000 \times 0.4 = \$11{,}200$$

Step 3. Initial book value − depreciation amount = book value (year 2)

$$\$28{,}000 - \$11{,}200 = \$16{,}800$$

Book value (year 2) × declining rate

= depreciation amount (year 2)

$$\$16{,}800 \times 0.4 = \$6{,}720$$

Book value (year 2) − depreciation amount = book value (year 3)

$16,800 − $6,720 = $10,080

Book value (year 3) × declining rate

= depreciation amount (year 3)

$10,080 × 0.4 = $4,032

Book value (year 3) − depreciation amount = book value (year 4)

$10,080 − $4,032 = $6,048

Book value (year 4) × declining rate

= depreciation amount (year 4)

$6,048 × 0.4 = $2,419.20

Book value (year 4) − depreciation amount = book value (year 5)

$6,048 − $2,419.20 = $3,628.80

Book value (year 5) × declining rate

= depreciation amount (year 5)

$3,628.80 × 0.4 = $1,451.52

Book value (year 5) − depreciation amount = book value (ending)

$3,628.80 − $1,451.52 = $2,177.28

The given information and calculations are most useful if they are organized into a depreciation schedule like the one shown in Table 13-4.

Table 13-4 Double-declining Balance Method of Depreciation

Year	Start-of-Year Book Value	Declining Rate	Depreciation Amount for Year	End-of-Year Book Value	Accumulated Depreciation
1	$28,000.00	0.4	$11,200.00	$16,800.00	$11,200.00
2	$16,800.00	0.4	$ 6,720.00	$10,080.00	$17,920.00
3	$10,080.00	0.4	$ 4,032.00	$ 6,048.00	$21,952.00
4	$ 6,048.00	0.4	$ 2,419.20	$ 3,628.80	$24,371.20
5	$ 3,628.80	0.4	$ 1,451.52	$ 2,177.28	$25,822.72

TIPS & TRAPS

Be sure to use the cost of the asset as the beginning book value when using the declining-balance method. A common error is to use cost − salvage value rather than just cost. Look what happens in Example 5 if this is done.

~~Cost − salvage value = $28,000 − $1,000 = $27,000~~

~~Depreciation for year 1 = $27,000 × 0.4 = $10,800~~

WRONG

Cost × declining rate = depreciation for year 1

$28,000 × 0.4 = $11,200

CORRECT

The error shown will cause the entire depreciation table to be incorrect, because each year's depreciation depends on the book value at the end of the previous year.

Self-Check

4. An asset has a useful life of 3 years. Find (a) the straight-line declining rate expressed as a decimal and percent and (b) the double-declining rate expressed as a decimal and percent.

5. A van costing $18,000 with an expected life of 4 years and a resale value of $1,000 is depreciated by the declining-balance method at twice the straight-line rate. Determine the depreciation and the year-end book value for each of the 4 years.

Section Review

Find the decimal equivalent expressed to six decimal places for (a) the straight-line declining rate and (b) the double-declining-rate for the following times.

1. 4 years

2. 11 years

3. 16 years

4. Carneal Enterprises purchased a tractor at a cost of $8,500. If the estimated life of the tractor is 8 years and the estimated scrap value is $1,500, prepare a declining-balance depreciation schedule using a straight-line rate.

Year	Start-of-Year Book Value	Declining Rate	Depreciation Amount for Year	End-of-Year Book Value	Accumulated Depreciation

5. Concon Corp. bought office equipment for $6,000. At the end of 3 years, its scrap value is $750. Using a double-declining rate, make a depreciation schedule. Note that an asset can *not* be depreciated below its scrap value.

Year	Start-of-Year Book Value	Declining Rate	Depreciation Amount for Year	End-of-Year Book Value	Accumulated Depreciation

6. Calculate the yearly depreciation for a machine costing $21,000 with an estimated life of 3 years and a resale value of $1,000. Make a depreciation schedule using the double-declining rate of depreciation.

Year	Start-of-Year Book Value	Declining Rate	Depreciation Amount for Year	End-of-Year Book Value	Accumulated Depreciation

Accelerated Cost-Recovery System

In 1981 the Internal Revenue Service (IRS) enacted the **accelerated cost-recovery system (ACRS)** for the depreciation of property placed in service after 1980. This method of depreciation, which is used only in figuring depreciation for federal income tax purposes, allows businesses to write off the cost of assets more quickly than in the past. (The other methods of depreciation are used for accounting purposes.) The faster depreciation was meant to encourage businesses to invest in more assets despite an economic slowdown at the time.

accelerated cost-recovery system (ACRS): a method of depreciation used for federal income tax purposes that allows businesses to write off the cost more quickly than traditional methods of depreciation.

Under ACRS, property is depreciated over a 3-year, 5-year, 10-year, 15-year, or 19-year recovery period, depending on the type of property. *Recovery period* is used in this system instead of estimated useful life. In most cases the recovery period allowed by ACRS is much shorter than the estimated useful life would have been. The IRS lists examples of types of property in each of the time categories to guide taxpayers. The following was taken from a recent IRS publication.

3-year property: Automobiles, tractor units for use over the road, light-duty trucks, and certain special manufacturing tools

5-year property: Most equipment, office furniture and fixtures

10-year property: Certain real property such as public utility property, theme park structures, and mobile homes

15-year real property: All real property placed in service before March 15, 1984, such as buildings not designated as 10-year property

19-year real property: All real property placed in service after March 15, 1984, such as buildings not designated as 10-year property

Calculating ACRS Deductions

The depreciation deduction for property placed in service under the ACRS is figured by multiplying the "unadjusted basis" (original cost) by a rate that is determined by the IRS. This rate varies from year to year during the recovery period. Table 13-5 shows the rates that were published in a recent IRS publication.

EXAMPLE 6

Find the depreciation deduction for each year for a piece of equipment that was purchased for $28,000 and placed in service under the ACRS method of depreciation as a 5-year property.

Depreciation amount (year 1) = 15% × cost
= 0.15 × $28,000 = $4,200

Depreciation amount (year 2) = 22% × cost
= 0.22 × $28,000 = $6,160

Depreciation amount (year 3) = 21% × cost
= 0.21 × $28,000 = $5,880

Depreciation amount (year 4) = 21% × cost
= 0.21 × $28,000 = $5,880

Depreciation amount (year 5) = 21% × cost
= 0.21 × $28,000 = $5,880

The sum of the depreciation amounts should equal the purchase price. $4,200 + $6,160 + $5,880 + $5,880 + $5,880 = $28,000

Table 13-5 Cost Recovery Percentages for ACRS

If the Recovery Year Is:	The Percentage for the Class of Property Is:			
	3-year	5-year	10-year	15-year
1	25	15	8	5
2	38	22	14	10
3	37	21	12	9
4		21	10	8
5		21	10	7
6			10	7
7			9	6
8			9	6
9			9	6
10			9	6
11				6
12				6
13				6
14				6
15				6

Calculator Sequence

Since the cost is used in the calculation of depreciation for each year, you can store the cost amount in the calculator's memory and enter the depreciation rate for each year.

[AC] 28000 [M+] [C/CE] Rate [×] [MR] ⇒

The solution to Example 6 is most useful if it is organized into a depreciation schedule like the one shown in Table 13-6 on p. 400.

Real World Application

THE TAX REFORM ACT OF 1986

Writers of the Tax Reform Act of 1986 had simplicity, fairness, and tax reduction as their goals. No one is sure yet whether any of those goals have been met. One thing that is certain is that many aspects of depreciation have become more complicated and others that were complicated have been simplified, for better or worse. Before using depreciation methods on any property, the best advice is to see an accountant. Your accountant should have information to help simplify the new laws. Depreciation of real estate has definitely changed!

Basically, 27.5-year property such as rental apartments and houses, and 31.5-year property, commercial property such as office buildings and industrial buildings, are depreciated by the straight-line method. Five- and seven-year assets include the equipment used in industry and businesses and may be depreciated by the double-declining balance method. From this information, can you guess what the lawmakers had in mind when writing the new tax laws?

The new tax laws are to encourage investors from "glutting" the market with more rental property and commercial property. The textiles industry and others are encouraged to invest in new technology and new equipment—automated manufacturing. To do this they are providing fewer tax breaks on real estate and more incentive to update equipment.

Application Questions

1. Before the 1986 Tax Reform Act, a commercial building purchased in June, 1985 for $300,000 could have been depreciated in several ways. The most common method used for this property was the accelerated 175% DB for an 18-year asset. For the first year, the depreciation would have been 5%, and 9% for the second recovery year.

a. Find the amount of depreciation on a $300,000 commercial building for the first recovery year.

b. Find the amount of depreciation on the same building for the second recovery year.

2. After the Tax Reform Act of 1986, the recovery percentages for commercial property are found on the 31.5-year assets, straight-line chart shown below. If a $300,000 commercial building is purchased in June, 1988, what is the percentage and the amount of depreciation for the first and the second recovery years? Compare these answers with the answers to Question 1.

Recovery Percentages for Nonresidential Real Property

Recovery Year	Month Placed in Service											
	1	2	3	4	5	6	7	8	9	10	11	12
2	3.04	2.78	2.51	2.25	1.98	1.72	1.46	1.19	0.93	0.66	0.40	0.13
2–31	3.17	3.17	3.17	3.17	3.17	3.17	3.17	3.17	3.17	3.17	3.17	3.17
32	1.86	2.12	2.39	2.65	2.92	3.17	3.17	3.17	3.17	3.17	3.17	3.17
33	0	0	0	0	0	0.01	0.27	0.54	0.80	1.07	1.33	1.60

Table 13-6 Table Showing Accelerated Cost Recovery System (ACRS) of Depreciation

Year	Start-of-Year Book Value	ACRS Rate	Depreciation Amount for Year	End-of-Year Book Value	Accumulated Depreciation
1	$28,000	15	$4,200	$23,800	$ 4,200
2	$23,800	22	$6,160	$17,640	$10,360
3	$17,640	21	$5,880	$11,760	$16,240
4	$11,760	21	$5,880	$ 5,880	$22,120
5	$ 5,880	21	$5,880		$28,000

Modified Accelerated Cost-Recovery System

modified accelerated cost-recovery system (MACRS): a method of depreciation of assets for tax purposes that is a modification of the ACRS method; it added two new classes of property, reclassified some types of property, and changed the depreciation rates in each category.

The Tax Reform Act of 1986 introduced some changes in the depreciation rates for property put in use after 1986 (but not affecting equipment in use before 1986). Under the **modified accelerated cost-recovery system (MACRS),** two new classes of property are added to the four described in the original ACRS, some equipment is put in a new category, and the depreciation rates change. IRS Publication 534 outlines all the options that may be used in figuring depreciation with MACRS. One option is to use a table of rates; several are provided by the IRS. MACRS rates when property is placed in service at midyear are shown in Table 13-7. Other tables are available for properties placed in service at other times during the year.

EXAMPLE 7

Find the depreciation deduction for each year for a piece of equipment that was purchased for $28,000 and placed in service at mid-year under the MACRS method of depreciation as a 5-year property.

Table 13-7 Depreciation Rates Using MACRS When Properties Are Placed in Service at Half-Year

Recovery Year	Recovery Period					
	3-year	5-year	7-year	10-year	15-year	20-year
1	33.33	20.00	14.29	10.00	5.00	3.750
2	44.45	32.00	24.49	18.00	9.50	7.219
3	14.81	19.20	17.49	14.40	8.55	6.677
4	7.41	11.52	12.49	11.52	7.70	6.177
5		11.52	8.93	9.22	6.93	5.713
6		5.76	8.92	7.37	6.23	5.285
7			8.93	6.55	5.90	4.888
8			4.46	6.55	5.90	4.522
9				6.56	5.91	4.462
10				6.55	5.90	4.461
11				3.28	5.91	4.462
12					5.90	4.461
13					5.91	4.462
14					5.90	4.461
15					5.91	4.462
16					2.95	4.461
17						4.462
18						4.461
19						4.462
20						4.461
21						2.231

Table 13-8 Table Showing Modified Accelerated Cost Recovery System (MACRS) of Depreciation

Year	Start-of-Year Book Value	MACRS Rate	Depreciation Amount for Year	End-of-Year Book Value	Accumulated Depreciation
1	$28,000.00	20.00	$5,600.00	$22,400.00	$ 5,600.00
2	$22,400.00	32.00	$8,960.00	$13,440.00	$14,560.00
3	$13,440.00	19.20	$5,376.00	$ 8,064.00	$19,936.00
4	$ 8,064.00	11.52	$3,225.60	$ 4,838.40	$23,161.60
5	$ 4,838.40	11.52	$3,225.60	$ 1,612.80	$26,387.20
6	$ 1,612.80	5.76	$1,612.80	$ 0	$28,000.00

$$\text{Depreciation amount (year 1)} = 20\% \times \text{cost} = 0.20 \times \$28{,}000 = \$5{,}600$$

$$\text{Depreciation amount (year 2)} = 32\% \times \text{cost} = 0.32 \times \$28{,}000 = \$8{,}960$$

$$\text{Depreciation amount (year 3)} = 19.2\% \times \text{cost} = 0.192 \times \$28{,}000 = \$5{,}376$$

$$\text{Depreciation amount (year 4)} = 11.52\% \times \text{cost} = 0.1152 \times \$28{,}000 = \$3{,}225.60$$

$$\text{Depreciation amount (year 5)} = 11.52\% \times \text{cost} = 0.1152 \times \$28{,}000 = \$3{,}225.60$$

$$\text{Depreciation amount (year 6)} = 5.76\% \times \text{cost} = 0.0576 \times \$28{,}000 = \$1{,}612.80$$

The sum of the depreciation amounts should equal the purchase price.
$5,600 + $8,960 + $5,376 + $3,225.60 + $3,225.60 + $1,612.80 = $28,000

These calculations are most useful if they are organized into a depreciation schedule like the one shown in Table 13-8.

Self-Check

6. Find the depreciation deduction for each year for a van that was purchased for $18,000 and placed in service at mid-year under the ACRS method of depreciation as a 3-year property.

7. Find the depreciation deduction for each year for a van that was purchased for $18,000 and placed in service at half-year under the MACRS method of depreciation as a 3-year property.

Section Review

Round answers to the nearest cent in each of the following problems.

1. Find the depreciation deduction for each year for an automobile that was purchased for $14,489 and placed in service under the ACRS method of depreciation as a 3-year property.

2. Find the depreciation deduction for each year for a truck purchased to make deliveries. The truck was purchased for $13,984 and placed in service under the ACRS method of depreciation as a 3-year property.

3. Find the depreciation deduction for each year for a computer that was purchased for $2,588 and placed in service under the ACRS method of depreciation as a 5-year property.

4. Find the depreciation for each year for office furniture that cost $4,879 and was placed in service under the ACRS method of depreciation as a 5-year property.

5. Find the depreciation for each year for a copy machine that cost $3,898 and was placed in service under the ACRS method of depreciation as a 5-year property.

6. Make a depreciation table like Table 13-6 for an office building that cost $78,800 and was placed in service in 19X2 under the ACRS method of depreciation as a 10-year property.

Year	Start-of-Year Book Value	ACRS Rate	Depreciation Amount for Year	End-of-Year Book Value	Accumulated Depreciation

7. Find the depreciation deduction for each year for a laser printer that cost $5,800 and was placed in service at mid-year under the MACRS method of depreciation as a 5-year property.

8. Find the depreciation deduction for each year for a fork lift that cost $27,400 and was placed in service at mid-year under the MACRS method of depreciation as a 10-year property.

9. Make a depreciation table like Table 13-8 for an asset that cost $3,270 and was placed in service at mid-year under the MACRS method of depreciation as a 3-year property.

Year	Start-of-Year Book Value	MACRS Rate	Depreciation Amount for Year	End-of-Year Book Value	Accumulated Depreciation

10. Make a depreciation table like Table 13-8 for an asset that cost $16,250 and was placed in service at mid-year under the MACRS method of depreciation as a 5-year property.

Year	Start-of-Year Book Value	MACRS Rate	Depreciation Amount for Year	End-of-Year Book Value	Accumulated Depreciation

Topic	Page	What to Remember	Examples
Straight-line depreciation	382–383	Yearly depreciation $= \dfrac{\text{cost of equipment} - \text{salvage value}}{\text{expected life (in years)}}$	Make a depreciation table showing the yearly depreciation of a property that cost \$3,700 and has a salvage value of \$400 at the end of 3 years. Use the straight-line method of depreciation.

Year	Original Cost	Depreciation	Accumulated Depreciation	Book Value
1	$3,700	$1,100	$1,100	$2,600
2		$1,100	$2,200	$1,500
3		$1,100	$3,300	$ 400

Topic	Page	What to Remember	Examples
Units-of-production depreciation	385–386	Unit depreciation $= \dfrac{\text{total cost} - \text{salvage value}}{\text{expected life (units produced)}}$ Depreciation amount = unit depreciation × units produced	Use units-of-production depreciation to make a depreciation table to show the yearly depreciation of a vehicle that cost \$18,900 and has a resale value of \$3,000 after 150,000 miles. The vehicle is driven 39,270 miles the first year, 37,960 miles the second year, 38,520 miles the third year, and 34,250 miles the fourth year. Unit depreciation $= \dfrac{18{,}900 - 3{,}000}{150{,}000} = 0.106$

Year	Original Cost	Number of Miles Driven	Annual Depreciation	Accumulated Depreciation	End-of-Year Book Value
1	$18,900	39,270	$4,162.62	$ 4,162.62	$14,737.38
2		37,960	$4,023.76	$ 8,186.38	$10,713.62
3		38,520	$4,083.12	$12,269.50	$ 6,630.50
4		34,250	$3,630.50	$15,900.00	$ 3,000.00

Topic	Page	What to Remember	Examples
Sum-of-the-years'-digits depreciation	389–390	$\dfrac{n(n+1)}{2}$ = denominator of rate fraction Depreciation rate fraction $= \dfrac{\text{number of useful years remaining}}{\frac{n(n+1)}{2}}$ Year's depreciation = (original cost − salvage value) × depreciation rate fraction for year	Make a depreciation table showing the yearly depreciation of a property that cost \$3,700 and has a salvage value of \$400 at the end of 3 years. Use the sum-of-the-years'-digits method. Cost − salvage value = \$3,700 − \$400 = \$3,300

Topic	Page	What to Remember	Examples

Year	Depreciation Rate Fraction	Cost Minus Salvage Value	Depreciation Amount	Accumulated Depreciation	Book Value
1	$\frac{3}{6}$	$3,300	$1,650	$1,650	$2,050
2	$\frac{2}{6}$	$3,300	$1,100	$2,750	$ 950
3	$\frac{1}{6}$	$3,300	$ 550	$3,300	$ 400

Declining balance depreciation (393–395)

Straight-line declining balance rate

$$= \frac{1}{\text{Expected life (in years)}}$$

Double declining balance rate

$$= \frac{1}{\text{Expected life (in years)}} \times 2$$

Use the double-declining balance method of depreciation to make a depreciation table for a property that cost $3,700 and has a salvage value of $400 after 3 years' use.

Double-declining rate =

$$\frac{1}{3} \times 2 = \frac{2}{3} = 0.666667$$

Year	Start-of-Year Book Value	Declining Rate	Depreciation for Year	End-of-Year Book Value	Accumulated Depreciation
1	$3,700	0.666667	$2,466.67	$1,233.33	$2,466.67
2	$1,233.33	0.666667	$ 822.22	$ 411.11	$3,288.89
3	$ 411.11	*	$ 11.11	$ 400.00	$3,300.00

*Remember, an asset *cannot* be depreciated below its salvage value. So the depreciation for year 3 is $411.11 − $400 = $11.11.

ACRS depreciation for income tax purposes (397–400)

A table published by the IRS is used to determine the percentage allowed for each year's depreciation for specified classes of property. The entire cost is used as a base for depreciating the property.

Use the ACRS method of depreciation to make a depreciation table for a property that cost $3,700 and has a salvage value of $400. The property is classed as a 3-year property for depreciation purposes.

Year	Start-of-Year Book Value	ACRS Rate	Depreciation Amount	End-of-Year Book Value	Accumulated Depreciation
1	$3,700	25	$ 925	$2,775	$ 925
2	$2,775	38	$1,406	$1,369	$2,331
3	$1,369	37	$1,369	$ 0*	$3,700

*Note that the entire cost of the property is depreciated under this method. The salvage value of $400 is handled in the accounting system as income when the property is sold.

MACRS method of depreciation (400–401)

Tables published by the IRS are used to determine the percentage allowed for each year's depreciation for specified classes of property. Different tables are available for properties that are put into service at different times during the year.

Use the MACRS method of depreciation to make a depreciation table for a property that cost $3,700, put in to service at mid-year, and is to be depreciated over a 3-year recovery period.

Topic	Page	What to Remember	Examples

Year	Start-of-Year Book Value	MACRS Rate	Depreciation Amount	End-of-Year Book Value	Accumulated Depreciation
1	$3,700	33.33	$1,233.21	$2,466.79	$1,233.21
2	$2,466.79	44.45	$1,644.65	$ 822.14	$2,877.86
3	$ 822.14	14.81	$ 547.97	$ 274.17	$3,425.83
4	$ 274.17	7.41	$ 274.17	$ 0	$3,700

Chapter Review

1. Find the depreciable value of an asset that originally cost $8,320 and has a scrap value of $700.

2. Find the total cost of a drill punch if it can be purchased for $2,375, delivery charges are $84, and installation charges are $75.

3. Find the annual straight-line depreciation of a cutting machine that cost $8,300 and has a scrap value of $500. The expected life of the machine is 8 years.

4. Make a depreciation schedule (table) to show the annual straight-line depreciation, accumulated depreciation, and book value for an asset that cost $5,000 and has a scrap value of $800. The useful life of the asset is 5 years.

Year	Original Cost	Depreciation	Accumulated Depreciation	Book Value

5. Find the unit depreciation for a machine that cost $14,000 and will have a salvage value of $2,000. The expected life of the machine is 25,000 hours.

6. Triple T Company purchased a refrigeration unit for $18,500. Its expected life is 50,000 hours, and it will have a salvage value of $800. Find the year's depreciation on the unit if it is used 5,000 hours during the year.

7. Find the sum-of-the-years' digits for (a) 9 years and (b) 11 years.

8. Make a depreciation schedule to show the depreciation rate, yearly depreciation, accumulated depreciation, and book value for an asset that cost $10,000 and has a scrap value of $1,000 after 5 years. Use the sum-of-the-years' digits method of depreciation.

Year	Depreciation Rate	Cost Minus Salvage Value	Depreciation Amount	Accumulated Depreciation	Book Value

9. An asset has a useful life of 15 years. Find (a) the straight-line rate and (b) double-declining rate of depreciation. Write the rates as decimals with six places and percents rounded to the nearest hundredth percent.

10. Use the double-declining balance method to make a depreciation schedule for a machine that cost $3,480 and has a salvage value of $400. The machine is expected to be used 5 years. Show the year, beginning book value, declining rate, amount of depreciation, ending book value, and accumulated depreciation in the table.

Year	Start-of-Year Book Value	Declining Rate	Depreciation Amount for Year	End-of-Year Book Value	Accumulated Depreciation

11. Use the ACRS table to find the seventh year's depreciation for a property that cost $32,800 and is depreciated over a 10-year period.

12. Use the ACRS table to find the tenth year's depreciation for a property that cost $54,800 and is depreciated over a 15-year period.

13. Use the ACRS method to make a depreciation table to show the yearly depreciation of a property that cost $18,500 if the recovery period is 3 years. Use the following heads in your table.

Year	Start-of-Year Book Value	ACRS Rate	Depreciation Amount for Year	End-of-Year Book Value	Accumulated Depreciation

14. Use the MACRS table to find the eighth year's depreciation for a property that cost $15,400 and was placed in service at mid-year with a 7-year recovery period.

15. Use the MACRS table to make a depreciation schedule for a property that cost $13,790 and was placed in service at mid-year with a 3-year recovery period. Use the following heads for your table.

Year	Start-of-Year Book Value	MACRS Rate	Depreciation Amount for Year	End-of-Year Book Value	Accumulated Depreciation

Trial Test

1. Find the sum-of-the-year's digits for a term of 7 years.

2. Find the depreciable value of an asset that cost $38,490 and had a scrap value of $4,800 if the straight-line method of depreciation is used.

3. The purchase price of a van was $13,500. It cost $1,350 to customize the van for special use and $50 for delivery. What is the beginning book value of the van for depreciation purposes?

4. Make a depreciation schedule (table) to show the annual straight-line depreciation, accumulated depreciation, and book value for furniture that cost $4,500 and has a scrap value of $700. The useful life of the asset is 5 years.

Year	Original Cost	Depreciation	Accumulated Depreciation	Book Value

5. A pizza delivery car was purchased for $9,580. The car is expected to be driven 125,000 miles before being sold for $500. What is the unit depreciation on the car (depreciation per mile)?

6. A machine that cost $58,000 and will sell for $8,000 is expected to be useful for 100,000 hours. Find the depreciation per hour for the machine. If the machine is used 6,500 hours the first year, find the depreciation for the year.

7. Find the sum-of-the-years' digits for (a) 24 years and (b) 27 years.

8. Use the sum-of-the-years' digits method to make a depreciation schedule showing the yearly depreciation for an asset that cost $7,500 and has a salvage value of $1,500. The asset is to be used for 3 years. Use the following heads on your table.

Year	Fraction	Cost Minus Salvage Value	Depreciation Amount	Accumulated Depreciation	Book Value

9. An asset has a useful life of 12 years. Find (a) the straight-line declining rate and (b) the double-declining rate of depreciation. Write the rates as decimals with six places and percents rounded to the nearest hundredth percent.

10. Use the double-declining balance method to make a depreciation schedule for a piece of equipment that cost $2,780 and has a salvage value of $300. The equipment is expected to be used 4 years. Show the year, beginning book value, declining rate, amount of depreciation, ending book value, and accumulated depreciation in the table.

Year	Start-of-Year Book Value	Declining Rate	Depreciation Amount for Year	End-of-Year Book Value	Accumulated Depreciation

11. Use the ACRS depreciation method to make a depreciation schedule for a car that cost $15,490 and, according to the ACRS rules, will be depreciated over 3 years. Show the year, start-of-year book value, ACRS depreciation rate, amount of depreciation, end-of-year book value, and accumulated depreciation in the table.

Year	Start-of-Year Book Value	ACRS Rate	Depreciation Amount for Year	End-of-Year Book Value	Accumulated Depreciation

12. Use the ACRS depreciation method to make a depreciation schedule for a desk that cost $1,488 and will be depreciated over 5 years. Show the year, start-of-year book value, ACRS depreciation rate, amount of depreciation, end-of-year book value, and accumulated depreciation in the table.

Year	Start-of-Year Book Value	ACRS Rate	Depreciation Amount for Year	End-of-Year Book Value	Accumulated Depreciation

13. Use the MACRS depreciation schedule to find the first year's depreciation on an asset that cost $8,580 if the asset is to be depreciated over a 3-year period.

14. Use MACRS depreciation to make a depreciation schedule for a vehicle that was placed in service at mid-year and cost $13,580. The vehicle is to be depreciated over a 3-year period.

Year	Start-of-Year Book Value	MACRS Rate	Depreciation Amount for Year	End-of-Year Book Value	Accumulated Depreciation

15. Use MACRS depreciation to find the depreciation for the fourth year for a property that cost $17,872. A recovery period of 7 years is used for tax purposes.

Self-Check Solutions

1. Yearly depreciation $= \dfrac{\text{cost of equipment} - \text{salvage value}}{\text{expected life (in years)}}$

$$= \frac{\$18{,}000 - \$3{,}000}{3} = \frac{15{,}000}{3}$$

$$= \$5{,}000$$

2. Unit depreciation $= \dfrac{\$18{,}000 - \$3{,}000}{75{,}000} = \$0.20\text{/mile}$

Depreciation after 56,000 miles $= \$0.20 \times 56{,}000 = \$11{,}200$

3. Denominator of depreciation fraction = 3 + 2 + 1 = 6

Depreciation rate fraction for each year = $\frac{3}{6}, \frac{2}{6}, \frac{1}{6}$

Original cost − salvage value = \$18,000 − \$3,000 = \$15,000

Depreciation amount (year 1) = \$15,000 × $\frac{3}{6}$ = \$7,500

(year 2) = \$15,000 × $\frac{2}{6}$ = \$5,000

(year 3) = \$15,000 × $\frac{1}{6}$ = \$2,500

4. a. $\frac{1}{3}$ = 33.33% or 0.333333

b. $\frac{1}{3} \times 2 = \frac{2}{3}$ = 66.67%, or 0.666667

5. Double-declining rate = $\frac{1}{4} \times 2 = \frac{2}{4} = \frac{1}{2}$, or 0.5

Year	Start-of-Year Book Value	Declining Rate	Depreciation Amount for Year	End-of-Year Book Value	Accumulated Depreciation
1	$18,000	0.5	$9,000	$9,000	$ 9,000
2	$ 9,000	0.5	$4,500	$4,500	$13,500
3	$ 4,500	0.5	$2,250	$2,250	$15,750
4	$ 2,250	0.5	$1,125	$1,125	$16,875

6. Depreciation amount (year 1) = 25% × cost = 0.25 × \$18,000 = \$4,500

Depreciation amount (year 2) = 38% × cost = 0.38 × \$18,000 = \$6,840

Depreciation amount (year 3) = 37% × cost = 0.37 × \$18,000 = \$6,660

7. Depreciation amount (year 1) = 33.33% × cost

= 0.3333 × \$18,000 = \$5,999.40

Depreciation amount (year 2) = 44.45% × cost

= 0.4445 × \$18,000 = \$8,001

Depreciation amount (year 3) = 14.81% × cost

= 0.1481 × \$18,000 = \$2,665.80

Depreciation amount (year 4) = 7.41% × cost

= 0.0741 × \$18,000 = \$1,333.80

14 Inventory, Overhead, and Turnover

Learning Objectives

1. Understand and use the specific identification inventory method to find the cost of goods available for sale, the cost of ending inventory, and the cost of goods sold. (pp. 416–418)
2. Understand and use the weighted-average inventory method to find the average unit cost, the cost of the ending inventory, and the cost of goods sold. (pp. 418–419)
3. Understand and use the FIFO (first-in, first-out) inventory method to find the cost of goods sold and the cost of ending inventory. (pp. 419–420)
4. Understand and use the LIFO (last-in, first-out) inventory method to find the cost of goods sold and the cost of ending inventory. (pp. 420–422)
5. Understand and use the retail inventory method to find the cost of goods sold and the cost of ending inventory. (pp. 422–423)
6. Calculate inventory turnover. (pp. 426–428)
7. Figure the distribution of overhead on the basis of total sales. (pp. 429–430)
8. Figure the distribution of overhead on the basis of floor space. (pp. 430–431)

Inventory

inventory: the value of merchandise that is available for sale on a certain date.

periodic inventory: a physical count of the merchandise on hand at the end of a specified time to determine the value of merchandise available for sale.

perpetual inventory: a record of the amount and value of merchandise available for sale at any given time. Inventory records for this type of inventory are kept on computer and are adjusted with the sale of each item.

Inventory represents the *value* of merchandise that is available for sale on a certain date. Inventory may be determined weekly, monthly, quarterly, semiannually, annually, or at any other specific interval of time. At the end of the specified time, a physical count is made of the merchandise on hand. This type of inventory is called **periodic inventory,** or physical inventory.

Many stores have computerized the inventory process, so that the inventory is adjusted with each sale. This means that a count of merchandise available can be obtained at any time. This continual inventory method is called **perpetual inventory.** Even with a perpetual inventory system, a physical count is made periodically to verify and adjust the inventory records. A discrepancy between the perpetual inventory and the actual inventory is sometimes a result of theft or loss due to damage.

Once a count of merchandise has been made, the merchandise is given a value according to various accounting methods. What makes this a time consuming process is that the cost of the goods purchased during a specific period may vary. For example, at one point in a month coffee may be purchased at \$2.79 a pound; the next time coffee is ordered, the cost may be \$2.93 a pound. This chapter discusses the methods used by accountants to determine how to assign a cost value to an inventory of merchandise.

The value of inventory is important for a number of reasons. Two of the financial statements covered in Chapter 15 need inventory figures, as do various tax documents.

In this chapter the five methods commonly used to assign a value to inventory—specific identification, average cost, first-in, first-out (FIFO), last-in, first-out (LIFO), and retail—are discussed.

The same basic example will be used for each of the four methods, so that you can see the different figures that each method produces. The basic information that we will use is shown in Table 14-1.

Throughout this discussion the same formula will be used, which shows how to find the cost of goods sold:

$$\text{Cost of goods sold} = \text{cost of goods available for sale} - \text{ending inventory}$$

Table 14-1 shows that the cost of goods available for sale is \$560. This figure will remain the same throughout the discussion; what will vary with each method is the cost of the ending inventory and, thus, the cost of goods sold.

Real World Application

A PERPETUAL INVENTORY SYSTEM IN A RETAIL STORE

Computerized perpetual inventory systems are quite common in retail stores, where it is important to have up-to-date information on the flow of goods in and out of the store.

The two features that are most important in such a system are bar codes on products and the use of hand-held scanners that read the codes and transmit the information to the computer.

The bar codes, which look like stripes on the label or price tag of a product, are called uniform product codes (UPC). Each product and sometimes each product size has its own code. When goods are purchased by the store from a wholesaler, data entry clerks enter the information on inventory records stored in the computer.

When goods are sold to customers, a checkout clerk passes the scanner over the bar code on each item. The computer then does several things—it prints a cash register receipt for the customer listing the items and the price of each; it removes the item sold from the inventory records; and it prepares a reorder of goods if the supply of goods on hand has fallen below a certain point.

The hand-held scanners also help in taking a physical count of inventory, which is done a certain number of times a year even in a perpetual inventory system.

Application Question

1. How would a perpetual inventory system in a retail store be affected by a large amount of shoplifting?

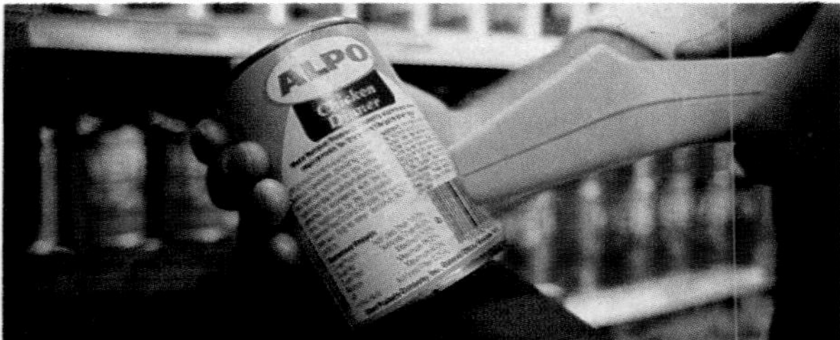

Table 14-1

Date of Purchase	Number of Units Purchased	Cost per Unit	Total Cost
Beginning inventory	29	$ 8	$232
January 15	18	7	126
February 4	9	10	90
March 3	+ 14	8	112
Goods available for sale	70		$560
Units sold	− 48		
Ending inventory	22		

Specific Identification Inventory Method

Many companies code their incoming merchandise with the purchase price or cost. Their inventory values are then based on the actual cost of each item available for sale. The **specific identification inventory method** is used when it is possible to identify the actual cost of the individual items bought—for example, an automobile dealer could use this method. The method is best for low-volume, high-cost items, such as automobiles or jewelry.

specific identification inventory method: incoming merchandise that is available for sale is coded with the actual cost so the inventory is based on the actual cost of the item.

Step by Step

Using the Specific Identification Inventory Method

Step 1. Find the cost of goods available for sale. This has already been done for you in Table 14-1; it is done by multiplying the number of units purchased by the cost per unit and then finding the total to get a total cost of goods available for sale.

Step 2. Find the cost of ending inventory. This is done by multiplying the number of units in ending inventory by the purchase price per unit. It is shown below in Example 1.

Step 3. Find the cost of goods sold:

Cost of goods sold
= cost of goods available for sale − cost of ending inventory

EXAMPLE 1

Step 1. Calculate the cost of goods available for sale from information in Table 14-1. This work has been done for you in the table, but it is shown again here.

Date of Purchase	Number of Units Purchased	Cost per Unit	Total Cost
Beginning inventory	29	$ 8	$232
January 15	18	7	126
February 4	9	10	90
March 3	14	8	112
Cost of goods available for sale			$560

Step 2. Find the cost of ending inventory. Use the following information.

Number of Units on Hand	Cost per Unit	Total Cost
10	$ 8	$ 80
5	7	35
3	10	30
4	8	32
Cost of ending inventory		$177

Step 3. Find the cost of goods sold.

$$\text{Cost of goods sold} = \text{cost of goods available for sale} - \text{ending inventory}$$
$$= \$560 - \$177$$
$$= \$383$$

The name of this method is derived from the fact that in each case, when figuring the cost of goods available for sale and the cost of ending inventory, an *exact price per unit* is available.

Weighted-Average Inventory Method

weighted-average inventory method: the total cost of goods available for sale is divided by the total number of units available for sale to obtain the average unit cost.

Another way to place a value on the ending inventory is the **weighted-average inventory method,** in which the total cost of goods available for sale is divided by the total number of units available for sale to get the average unit cost. This takes less time than figuring exact prices for each unit and is often used with goods that are similar in cost and the cost is relatively stable—for example, typewriter ribbons.

Step by Step

Using the Weighted-Average Inventory Method

Step 1. Find the average unit cost:

$$\text{Average unit cost} = \frac{\text{total cost of goods available for sale}}{\text{total number of units available for sale}}$$

Step 2. Find the cost of ending inventory by multiplying the number of units on hand by the average unit cost.

Step 3. Find the cost of goods sold (COGS) by one of two ways:
a. COGS = cost of goods available for sale − ending inventory
b. COGS = number of units sold × average price per unit

EXAMPLE 2

Step 1. Find the average unit cost using the information from Table 14-1 (repeated here).

Date of Purchase	Number of Units Purchased	Cost per Unit	Total Cost
Beginning inventory	29	$ 8	$232
January 15	18	7	126
February 4	9	10	90
March 3	+ 14	8	112
Goods available for sale	70		$560
Units sold	− 48		
Ending inventory	22		

$$\text{Average unit cost} = \frac{\text{total cost of goods available for sale}}{\text{total number of units available for sale}} = \frac{\$560}{70} = \$8$$

Step 2. Calculate cost of ending inventory.

Cost of ending inventory = number of units on hand × average unit cost

= 22 × $8

= $176

Step 3. Calculate cost of goods sold.

a. Cost of goods sold = Cost of goods available for sale − ending inventory

= $560 − $176

= $384

b. Cost of goods sold = number of units sold × average unit cost

= 48 × $8

= $384

Self-Check

1. Find the cost of the ending inventory from the following information.

Number of Units on Hand	Cost per Unit	Total Cost
43	$12	______
11	9	______
7	11	______
28	15	______

2. Find the average unit cost for the information shown in the table.

Date of Purchase	Number of Units Purchased	Cost per Unit	Total Cost
Beginning inventory	96	$12	______
April 12	23	9	______
May 8	15	11	______
June 2	37	15	______

3. Calculate the cost of the ending inventory and the cost of goods sold in Exercises 1 and 2 by using the weighted-average method.

FIFO: First-in, First-out Inventory Method

Many companies, especially those dealing in items that spoil or date quickly, use the FIFO method. In the **FIFO (first-in, first-out) inventory method,** the earliest items purchased (the first in) are assumed to be the first items sold (the first out). In this method, the ending inventory is made up of the most recently purchased goods. The cost of the goods available for sale will be relatively close to the current cost for purchasing additional items.

FIFO (first-in, first-out) inventory method: a method of determining the cost of the ending inventory in which each sale is assumed to be from the oldest item in the inventory; that is, the most recently purchased goods are the goods remaining in the ending inventory.

Step by Step

Using the FIFO Inventory Method

Step 1. Determine which items (at which prices) are in ending inventory.

Step 2. Multiply price per item by the number of items and add the sums to get a total cost of ending inventory.

Step 3. Find the cost of goods sold:

Cost of goods sold
= cost of goods available for sale − cost of ending inventory

EXAMPLE 3

Use the information from Table 14-1 (repeated here) to find the cost of goods sold using FIFO.

Date of Purchase	Number of Units Purchased	Cost per Unit	Total Cost
Beginning inventory	29	$ 8	$232
January 15	18	7	126
February 4	9	10	90
March 3	+ 14	8	112
Goods available for sale	70		$560
Units sold	− 48		
Ending inventory	22		

Step 1. Determine which items (at which prices) are in ending inventory.

Mar. 3	14 items	$ 8
Feb. 4	8 items	10
	22 items	

There are 22 items in ending inventory, and by this method they must be the most recently purchased items. Count back in the table from the most recently purchased until you have 22 items.

Step 2. Multiply the price per item times the number of items; then add the sums to get the cost of ending inventory.

Mar. 3	14 items	$ 8	$112
Feb. 4	8 items	10	80
	22 items		$192

Step 3. Find the cost of goods sold.

Cost of goods sold = cost of goods available for sale − ending inventory

= $560 − $192

= $368

LIFO (last-in, first-out) inventory method: a method of determining the cost of the ending inventory in which each sale is assumed to be from the goods most recently purchased; that is, the oldest goods are assumed to be the goods remaining in the ending inventory.

LIFO: Last-in, First-out Inventory Method

A fourth method for determining the cost of the ending inventory and the cost of goods sold is the **LIFO (last-in, first-out) inventory method.** In this method, the oldest goods are assumed to be the goods remaining in the ending inventory. The newest goods are sold first. That is, the last item in is the first item out (LIFO). The cost of the ending inventory will be figured on the cost of the oldest stock. Thus, the difference between the cost of the goods available for sale and the replacement costs for new goods could be significant. Also, the profit on goods sold would be less since the newer, higher priced goods were sold first.

Even though this method does not follow natural business practices of rotating stock to maintain freshness or quality, there are some economic advantages to using this method under certain conditions.

Step by Step

Using the LIFO Inventory Method

Step 1. Determine which items (at which prices) are in ending inventory.

Step 2. Multiply the price per item times the number of items; then add the sums to get the total cost of ending inventory.

Step 3. Find the cost of goods sold:

Cost of goods sold
= cost of goods available for sale − ending inventory

EXAMPLE 4

Use the information from Table 14-1, which is repeated here, to find the cost of goods sold using LIFO.

Date of Purchase	Number of Units Purchased	Cost per Unit	Total Cost
Beginning inventory	29	$ 8	$232
January 15	18	7	126
February 4	9	10	90
March 3	+ 14	8	112
Goods available for sale	70		$560
Units sold	− 48		
Ending inventory	22		

Step 1. Determine which items (at which prices) are in ending inventory.

Beginning inventory:
22 items $8

You know there are 22 items in ending inventory, and that with this method they were the first items purchased, so you count down from the top of the table until you have 22 items. In this case, they are all from beginning inventory.

Step 2. Multiply the price per item times the number of items; then add the sums to get the total cost of ending inventory.

Beginning inventory:
22 items $8 $176

In this case you do not have to add the sums, since all 22 items were from beginning inventory at $8 per item.

Step 3. Find the cost of goods sold.

$$\begin{aligned}\text{Cost of goods sold} &= \text{cost of goods available for sale} - \text{ending inventory}\\ &= \$560 - \$176\\ &= \$384\end{aligned}$$

The Retail Method of Estimating Inventory

retail inventory method: a method of determining inventory by comparing the cost of goods available for sale at cost and at retail.

Sometimes businesses do not have time to take monthly or periodic inventories. Instead, they estimate inventory cost rather than count goods individually. One method used to estimate inventory is called the **retail method.**

The retail method uses a ratio that compares the cost of goods available for sale at cost and at retail. This means a comparison of what it costs to buy the goods compared to what the goods will sell for. In order to use this method, you need to know the value of the beginning inventory at cost and at retail, the cost of net purchases at cost and at retail, and net sales at cost.

Step by Step

Using the Retail Method of Estimating Inventory

Step 1. Calculate the cost of goods available for sale at cost (using purchase price of goods).

Step 2. Calculate the cost of goods available for sale at retail.

Step 3. Find the ratio of goods at cost price to goods at retail price and convert it to a decimal equivalent (use six decimal places if the decimal does not terminate).

$$\text{Cost ratio} = \frac{\text{cost of goods available for sale at cost}}{\text{cost of goods available for sale at retail}}$$

Step 4. Find the ending inventory at retail.

$$\text{Ending inventory at retail} = \text{cost of goods available for sale at retail} - \text{net sales}$$

Step 5. Find ending inventory at cost and cost of goods sold.

$$\text{Ending inventory at cost} = \text{ending inventory at retail} \times \text{cost ratio}$$

$$\text{Cost of goods sold} = \text{net sales} \times \text{cost ratio}$$

EXAMPLE 5

The following table gives the information you need to find the ending inventory and cost of goods sold using the retail method. You also need to know that net sales for the period are $487.

Date of Purchase	Cost	Retail
Beginning inventory	$232	$331
January 15	126	180
February 4	90	129
March 3	112	160
Cost of goods available for sale	$560	$800

Steps 1 and 2 have been done for you in the table: The cost of goods available for sale at cost is $560; at retail, $800.

Step 3. Find the cost ratio.

$$\text{Cost ratio} = \frac{\text{cost of goods available for sale at cost}}{\text{cost of goods available for sale at retail}} = \frac{\$560}{\$800} = 0.7$$

Step 4. Find the ending inventory at retail.

Ending inventory at retail
= cost of goods available for sale at retail − net sales
= $800 − $487 = $313

Step 5. Find ending inventory at cost.

Ending inventory at cost = ending inventory at retail × cost ratio
= $313 × 0.7 = $219.10

Cost of goods sold = $487 × 0.7 = $340.90

Calculator Solution

The calculator can be used to:

1. Find the cost of goods available at retail and save in memory.

[AC] 331 [+] 180 [+] 129 [+] 160 [=] [M⁺] ⇒ 800

2. Find the cost of goods available at cost and leave in display.

[CE/C] 232 [+] 126 [+] 90 [+] 112 [=] ⇒ 560 (Do not clear.)

3. Find the cost ratio. Display still shows 560.

[÷] [MRC] [MRC] [=] [M⁺] ⇒ 0.7

(The first [MRC] recalls 800 from memory; the second [MRC] clears 800 from memory so that a new number can be stored there.) Now the cost ratio is in memory.

4. Find the ending inventory at retail.

[CE/C] 800 − 487 [=] ⇒ 313 (Do not clear.)

Clear display but do not clear memory.

5. Find ending inventory at cost. Display still shows 313.

[×] [MRC] [=] ⇒ 219.10

Find the cost of goods sold.

[CE/C] 487 [×] [MRC] [=] ⇒ 340.90

Comparison of Methods for Determining Inventory

Each of the different methods of figuring the value of inventory has advantages and disadvantages, depending on current economic conditions, tax regulations, and so on. However, it is important to know that once a business has selected a method, permission must be obtained from the Internal Revenue Service to change methods.

This section has shown the results of figuring the value of the same inventory by each of the five different methods. The five methods and the results obtained with each are compared in Table 14-2.

Table 14-2 Comparison of the five methods of figuring inventory

Method	Cost of Ending Inventory	Cost of Goods Sold	Comment
Specific identification	$154	$406	This method is the most accurate but most time-consuming.
Weighted	$176	$384	This method is less accurate than specific identification but takes less time.
			This method is perhaps the easiest to use when the economy is relatively stable. Radical changes in prices may result in a distorted inventory value.
FIFO	$192	$368	In this method the value of the remaining inventory is closely related to the current market price of the goods. During high inflation, this method produces the highest income.
LIFO	$176	$368	In this method the value of the remaining inventory may vary significantly from the current market price of the goods. During high inflation, this method produces lower income.
Retail	$219.10	$340.90	This method estimates the ending inventory based on the retail prices and the net sales. Since the information needed for using this method is easily accessible, this is one of the most efficient methods.

Self-Check

4. Find the cost of goods sold and the cost of the ending inventory using the LIFO method if 22 items are on hand.

Date of Purchase	Number of Units Purchased	Cost per Unit	Total Cost
Beginning inventory	96	$12	______
April 12	23	9	______
May 8	15	11	______
June 2	37	15	______

Assume the items on hand are the oldest items.

Section Review

1. Calculate the cost of goods available for sale from the following information.

Date of Purchase	Number of Units Purchased	Cost per Unit	Total Cost
Beginning inventory	42	$21	
August 20	35	18	
September 12	15	13	
October 2	28	21	
Cost of goods available for sale			

2. Find the cost of the ending inventory from the following information.

Number of Units on Hand	Cost per Unit	Total Cost
18	$21	
22	18	
9	13	
16	21	
Cost of ending inventory		

3. Find the cost of goods sold from Problems 1 and 2.

4. Find the average unit cost for the information shown in the table.

Date of Purchase	Number of Units Purchased	Cost per Unit	Total Cost
Beginning inventory	42	$21	
August 20	35	18	
September 12	15	13	
October 2	28	21	
Cost of goods available for sale			

5. Calculate the cost of the ending inventory and the cost of goods sold in Exercise 4 by using the weighted-average method.

6. Find the cost of goods sold and the cost of the ending inventory using the FIFO method if 48 items are on hand.

Date of Purchase	Number of Units Purchased	Cost per Unit	Total Cost
Beginning inventory	42	$21	
August 20	35	18	
September 12	15	13	
October 2	28	21	
Cost of goods available for sale			

7. Find the cost of goods sold and the cost of the ending inventory using the LIFO method if 52 items are on hand.

Date of Purchase	Number of Units Purchased	Cost per Unit	Total Cost
Beginning inventory	42	$21	
August 20	35	18	
September 12	15	13	
October 2	28	21	
Cost of goods available for sale			

8. Find the cost of goods sold and the cost of the ending inventory using the retail method if the net sales are $1,360.

Date of Purchase	Number of Units Purchased	Cost per Unit	Total Cost	Retail Price per Unit	Total Retail
Beginning inventory	42	$21		$26	
August 20	35	18		23	
September 12	15	13		16	
October 2	28	21		26	
Cost of goods available for sale					
Less net sales					
Ending inventory at retail					
Cost ratio (2,295 ÷ 2,865)					
Ending inventory at cost ($1,505 × 0.801047)					
Cost of goods sold					

Inventory Turnover

Most businesses must keep a careful watch over their *inventory turnover,* which is how often the inventory of merchandise is sold and replaced. This rate of inventory turnover varies greatly according to the type of business. A restaurant, for example, should have a high turnover but probably carries a small inventory of goods. A furniture company, on the other hand, would normally keep a large inventory but have a low turnover.

There are two ways to figure turnover rate: at cost or at retail. Cost means the price at which the company bought the merchandise; retail means the price at which the company sold the merchandise. To figure the turnover rate at cost, you divide the cost of goods sold by the average inventory at cost:

$$\text{Inventory turnover at cost} = \frac{\text{cost of goods sold}}{\text{average inventory at cost}}$$

To figure the turnover rate at retail, you divide the net sales by the average inventory at retail:

$$\text{Inventory turnover at retail} = \frac{\text{net sales}}{\text{average inventory at retail}}$$

Turnover can cover any period of time but is usually figured monthly, semiannually (twice a year), or yearly.

Step by Step

Calculating Inventory Turnover

Step 1. Find the average inventory:

$$\text{Average inventory} = \frac{\text{beginning inventory + ending inventory}}{2}$$

Step 2. Find the turnover rate:

a. Rate at cost:

$$\text{Turnover rate} = \frac{\text{cost of goods sold}}{\text{average inventory at cost}}$$

b. Rate at retail:

$$\text{Turnover rate} = \frac{\text{net sales}}{\text{average inventory at retail}}$$

EXAMPLE 6

A restaurant had net sales of $32,000 for the month of June. The inventory at the beginning of June was $7,000; the ending inventory was $9,000. Find the average inventory and turnover rate for the month of June.

First find the average inventory:

To find average inventory, add beginning inventory and ending inventory and divide by 2.

Average inventory

$$= \frac{\text{beginning inventory + ending inventory}}{2}$$

$$= \frac{\$7{,}000 + \$9{,}000}{2} = \frac{\$16{,}000}{2} = \$8{,}000$$

Then find turnover rate:

To find turnover rate, divide net sales by average inventory.

Turnover rate

$$= \frac{\text{net sales}}{\text{average inventory}}$$

Turnover rate

$$= \frac{\$32{,}000}{\$8{,}000} = 4 \text{ times}$$

The answer is 4; note that the rate is *not* a percent.

The turnover rate is 4 in the month of June.

By Bob Laird, USA TODAY

Knowing the turnover of a business can be useful in making future decisions and in analyzing business practices.

A low turnover rate may indicate the following:

1. Too much capital tied up in inventory.
2. Customer dissatisfaction with choice of merchandise, quality, or price.
3. Product obsolete or not properly marketed.

A high turnover rate may indicate the following:

1. Insufficient inventory that could result in a loss in sales because product is "out of stock."
2. Product is highly desirable.
3. Price may be significantly lower than the competition.

Section Review

1. Use the following inventories to find the average inventory: $2,596; $3,872.

Find the rate of stock turnover for the following. Round to the nearest tenth.

	Opening Inventory at Retail	Closing Inventory at Retail	Net Sales	Stock Turnover
2.	$ 8,920	$ 7,460	$19,270	
3.	$51,266	$42,780	$25,000	
	Opening Inventory at Cost	**Closing Inventory at Cost**	**Cost of Goods Sold**	
4.	$ 8,000	$10,000	$36,000	
5.	$26,108	$ 5,892	$73,600	

Overhead

A business encounters many expenses other than buying stock and equipment. Some of these expenses are salaries, rent, office supplies, taxes, insurance, and upkeep of equipment. These expenses, along with depreciation, are called **overhead.** It may be important for a company to know not only how much its total overhead expenses are but also to know the overhead expense of each department, so that it can reduce excessive overhead expenses of certain departments to increase profits. There are many methods of figuring overhead by department; two of the most widely used methods are according to net sales and according to total floor space. These two methods are described in detail. Other ways of figuring overhead are similar to these two and apply the same type of problem-solving approach.

overhead: expenses required for the operation of a business, such as salaries, rent, office supplies, taxes, insurance, and upkeep of equipment.

Overhead by Total Sales

Some companies divide their total overhead expenses on the basis of *total sales* for each department. To use this method, find a fraction for each department showing what part of the total sales were made by that department. Then multiply the total sales times each fraction to find the amount of overhead for each department.

Step by Step

Finding Overhead Based on Total Sales

Step 1. Add the sales amounts of individual departments to find the total sales amount.

Step 2. Find the sales fraction for each department and convert it to a decimal equivalent with six decimal places if the decimal does not terminate.

$$\text{Sales fraction} = \frac{\text{sales amount of each department}}{\text{total sales}}$$

Step 3. Figure the amount of overhead to be assigned to each department by multiplying each sales fraction times the total overhead.

EXAMPLE 7

A store's overhead expenses totaled $8,000 during one month. Find the amount of overhead for each department, based on total sales, if the store had the following monthly sales by department: cameras, $5,000; jewelry, $8,200; sporting goods, $6,700; silver, $9,200; and toys, $12,000.

Setting up and completing a table like the one shown here helps organize the information and calculations. List the sales of each department in the second column, and then find the total sales amount. In the third column, write the sales fraction for each department and its decimal equivalent. In the fourth column, multiply the decimal equivalent times the total overhead amount to find each department's overhead amount.

Department	Monthly Sales Amount	Sales Fraction and Decimal Equivalent	Amount of Overhead for Each Department
Cameras	\$ 5,000	$\frac{\$5,000}{\$41,100} = 0.121655$	$0.121655 \times \$8,000 = \$\ \ 973.24$
Jewelry	\$ 8,200	$\frac{\$8,200}{\$41,100} = 0.199513$	$0.199513 \times \$8,000 = \$1,596.10$
Sporting goods	\$ 6,700	$\frac{\$6,700}{\$41,100} = 0.163017$	$0.163017 \times \$8,000 = \$1,304.14$
Silver	\$ 9,200	$\frac{\$9,200}{\$41,100} = 0.223844$	$0.223844 \times \$8,000 = \$1,790.75$
Toys	\$12,000	$\frac{\$12,000}{\$41,100} = 0.291971$	$0.291971 \times \$8,000 = \$2,335.77$
Total	\$41,100	1.000000	\$8,000.00

Self-Check

5. A store's overhead expenses totaled \$6,000 during one month. Find the amount of overhead for each department, based on total sales, if the store had the following monthly sales by department: toys, \$4,000; appliances, \$6,600; children's clothing, \$6,800; books, \$4,600; and furniture, \$8,400.

Overhead by Unit Floor Space

Another way of distributing overhead is by unit floor space. Each department's overhead is determined by the number of square feet the department occupies. Basically this method is similar to the sales per department method. The floor space of each department is the numerator and the total floor space is the denominator of the floor-space fraction, which is converted to its decimal equivalent. Find the overhead for the department by multiplying the decimal equivalent of the floor-space fraction times the total overhead.

Step by Step

Finding Overhead Based on Floor Space

Step 1. Add the square feet of floor space in each department to find the total number of square feet of floor space.

Step 2. Find the floor-space fraction for each department and convert it to a decimal equivalent with six decimal places if the decimal does not terminate.

$$\text{Floor-space fraction} = \frac{\text{square feet of floor space in each department}}{\text{total square feet of floor space}}$$

Step 3. Figure the amount of overhead to be assigned to each department by multiplying each floor-space fraction times the total overhead.

EXAMPLE 8

A department store assigns overhead to its various departments according to the amount of floor space used by each department. The store's total overhead is $25,000. Find the amount of overhead for each department if each department occupies the following number of square feet: junior department, 3,000; women's wear, 4,000; men's wear, 3,500; children's wear, 3,000; china and silver, 2,500; housewares, 2,500; linens, 2,000; toys, 1,500; carpets, 3,500; and offices, 500. Round the *final* answers to the nearest cent if necessary.

Setting up and completing a table like the one shown here helps organize our information and calculations. List the square feet of floor space in each department in the second column, and then find the total number of square feet of floor space. In the third column, write the floor-space fraction for each department and its decimal equivalent. In the fourth column, multiply the decimal equivalent times the total overhead amount, to find each department's overhead amount.

Department	Department's Floor Space	Floor-Space Fraction and Decimal Equivalent	Amount of Overhead for Each Department
Junior department	3,000	$\frac{3,000}{26,000} = 0.115385$	0.115385 × $25,000 = $ 2,884.63
Women's wear	4,000	$\frac{4,000}{26,000} = 0.153846$	0.153846 × $25,000 = $ 3,846.15
Men's wear	3,500	$\frac{3,500}{26,000} = 0.134615$	0.134615 × $25,000 = $ 3,365.38
Children's wear	3,000	$\frac{3,000}{26,000} = 0.115385$	0.115385 × $25,000 = $ 2,884.63
China and silver	2,500	$\frac{2,500}{26,000} = 0.096154$	0.096154 × $25,000 = $ 2,403.85
Housewares	2,500	$\frac{2,500}{26,000} = 0.096154$	0.096154 × $25,000 = $ 2,403.85
Linens	2,000	$\frac{2,000}{26,000} = 0.076923$	0.076923 × $25,000 = $ 1,923.08
Toys	1,500	$\frac{1,500}{26,000} = 0.057692$	0.057692 × $25,000 = $ 1,442.30
Carpets	3,500	$\frac{3,500}{26,000} = 0.134615$	0.134615 × $25,000 = $ 3,365.38
Offices	500	$\frac{500}{26,000} = 0.019231$	0.019231 × $25,000 = $ 480.78
Total	26,000	1.000000	$25,000.00

TIPS & TRAPS

When a problem requires several calculations it is helpful if you can periodically check your work rather than only checking the final answer.

Interim Check

In Example 8, the total of the decimal equivalents of the sales fraction should total (or be very close to) 1.

Final Check

The sum of the amount of overhead for each department should equal the total overhead.

Self-Check

6. A discount clothing store assigns overhead to its various departments according to the amount of floor space used by each department. The store's total monthly overhead is $15,800. Find the amount of overhead for each department if each department occupies the following number of square feet: women's clothing, 2,000; men's clothing, 1,200; children's clothing, 2,500. Round *final* answers to the nearest cent if necessary.

Section Review

Find the overhead for each department by total sales for the following exercises.

1. The nuts and bolts department had $1,500 in sales for the month, the electrical department had $4,000, and the paint department had $2,300. The total overhead was $3,800.

2. Department 1 had $5,200 in sales for the month, Department 2 had $4,700, Department 3 had $6,520, Department 4 had $4,870, and Department 5 had $2,010. The total overhead was $10,000.

Find the overhead for each department by units of floor space for the following problem.

3. Department A has 5,000 square feet of floor space, Department B has 2,500, Department C has 4,300, and Department D has 2,700. The total overhead is $8,200.

Summary

Topic	Page	What to Remember	Example
Figuring the amount of inventory	416–424	All inventory methods provide some way of finding the value of goods available for sale, the value of the ending inventory, and the value of goods sold.	Each inventory method is illustrated following.
Specific identification method	416–418	Incoming merchandise is coded with the actual cost, and inventory is based on the actual cost of the item. Cost of goods sold = cost of goods available for sale − cost of ending inventory	Use the specific identification method to calculate the cost of goods available for sale and the cost of the ending inventory and the cost of goods sold. Calculate the cost of goods available for sale from the following information.

Date of Purchase	Number of Units Purchased	Cost per Unit	Total Cost
Beginning inventory	17	$10	$170
January 8	25	8	200
February 3	22	12	264
March 5	20	8	160
Cost of goods available for sale			$794

Topic	Page	What to Remember	Example

Find the cost of ending inventory from the following information.

Number of Units on Hand	Cost per Unit	Total Cost
12	$10	$120
19	8	152
11	12	132
16	8	128
Cost of ending inventory		$532

Find the cost of goods sold from the preceding information: Cost of goods sold = cost of goods available − cost of ending inventory = $794 − $532 = $262

Weighted-average method — Page 418–419

What to Remember:

Average unit cost

$$= \frac{\text{total cost of goods available for sale}}{\text{total number of units available for sale}}$$

Average cost of ending inventory

$$= \text{number of units on hand} \times \text{average unit cost}$$

Cost of goods sold

$$= \text{number of units sold} \times \text{average unit cost}$$

Example:

Find the average unit cost for the information shown in the table.

Date of Purchase	Number of Units Purchased	Cost per Unit	Total Cost
Beginning inventory	18	$18	$ 324
April 6	25	19	475
May 4	26	12	312
June 9	22	8	176
Cost of goods available for sale	91		$1,287

	Number of Units on Hand	Cost per Unit	Total Cost
	12	$18	$216
	18	19	342
	7	12	84
	13	8	104
Cost of ending inventory	50		$746

Calculate the cost of the ending inventory and the cost of goods sold in the example by using the weighted-average method.

Average unit cost

$$= \frac{\text{total cost of goods available for sale}}{\text{total number of units available for sale}}$$

$$= \frac{\$1,287}{91} = \$14.14$$

Average cost of ending inventory

$$= \text{number of units on hand} \times \text{average unit cost}$$

$$= 50 \times \$14.14 = \$707$$

Cost of goods sold

$$= \text{number of units sold} \times \text{average unit cost}$$

$$= (91 - 50) \times \$14.14 = \$579.74$$

Topic	Page	What to Remember	Example
FIFO: first-in, first-out method	419–420	Each sale is assumed to be from the oldest item in the inventory, and the first item in is considered to be the first item out. The ending inventory is made up of the most recently purchased goods.	Find the cost of goods sold and the cost of the ending inventory using the FIFO method if 465 items are on hand.

Date of Purchase	Number of Units Purchased	Cost per Unit	Total Cost
Beginning inventory	222	$10	$2,220
January 15	142	12	1,704
February 5	134	15	2,010
March 2	141	24	3,384
Cost of goods available for sale	639		$9,318

Date of Purchase	Number of Units on Hand	Cost per Unit	Total Cost
Beginning inventory	48	$10	$ 480
January 15	142	12	1,704
February 5	134	15	2,010
March 2	141	24	3,384
Cost of ending inventory	465		$7,578

Cost of goods sold = $9,318 − $7,578 = $1,740

Topic	Page	What to Remember	Example
LIFO: last-in, first-out method	420–422	Each sale is assumed to be from the newest item in the inventory, and the last item in is considered to be the first item out. The ending inventory is made up of the oldest goods.	Use the LIFO method to find the cost of goods sold and the cost of the ending inventory if 282 items are on hand.

Date of Purchase	Number of Units Purchased	Cost per Unit	Total Cost
Beginning inventory	111	$10	$1,110
April 12	343	12	4,116
May 8	191	9	1,719
June 10	106	24	2,544
Cost of goods available for sale	751		$9,489

Date of Purchase	Number of Units on Hand	Cost per Unit	Total Cost
Beginning inventory	111	$10	$1,110
April 12	171	12	2,052
Cost of ending inventory	282		$3,162

Cost of goods sold = $9,489 − $3,162 = $6,327

Topic	Page	What to Remember	Example
Retail method	422–423	Inventory is estimated using the ratio of the cost of goods available for sale at cost to the cost of goods available for sale at retail.	Use the retail method to find the cost of goods sold and the cost of the ending inventory. Calculate the cost of goods sold and the cost of the ending inventory from the following information. (see table below)

	Cost	Retail
Beginning inventory	$4,824	$6,030
Purchases	872	1,090
Cost of goods available for sale	$5,696	$7,120
Less net sales		2,464
Ending inventory at retail		$4,656

$$\text{Cost ratio} = \frac{\$5{,}696}{\$7{,}120} = 0.8$$

Ending inventory at cost = $4,656 × 0.8 = $3,724.80

Cost of goods sold = $5,696 − $3,724.80 = $1,971.20

Calculate turnover (426–428)

What to Remember:

$$\text{Average inventory} = \frac{\text{beginning inventory} + \text{ending inventory}}{2}$$

a. Turnover rate at retail

$$= \frac{\text{net sales}}{\text{average inventory at retail}}$$

b. Turnover rate at cost

$$= \frac{\text{cost of goods sold}}{\text{average inventory at cost}}$$

Example:

A store had net sales of $10,000 ($5,000 cost) with a beginning inventory of $5,000 ($2,500 cost) and an ending inventory of $6,000 ($3,000 cost).

a. Average inventory at retail

$$= \frac{\$5{,}000 + \$6{,}000}{2} = \$5{,}500$$

$$\text{Turnover at retail} = \frac{\$10{,}000}{\$5{,}500} = 1.818182$$

b. Average inventory at cost

$$= \frac{\$2{,}500 + \$3{,}000}{2} = \$2{,}750$$

$$\text{Turnover rate at cost} = \frac{\$5{,}000}{\$2{,}750} = 1.818182$$

Finding overhead based on sales (429–430)

What to Remember:

Find the total sales amount. Then find the sales fraction for each department and convert it to a decimal equivalent.

$$\text{Sales fraction} = \frac{\text{sales amount of each department}}{\text{total sales}}$$

Example:

Make a table to show the overhead by departments if overhead is assigned based on total sales and the store had the following monthly sales by department: paint, $5,000; lumber, $6,200; wall coverings, $3,200; plumbing, $3,200; and electrical, $1,500. Overhead expenses during the month are $1,780.

Topic	Page	What to Remember	Example
Finding overhead based on sales	429–430	Multiply each department's sales fraction times the total overhead to find the amount of overhead for each department.	

Department	Monthly Sales Amount	Sales Fraction and Decimal Equivalent	Amount of Overhead for Each Department
Paint	\$ 5,000	$\frac{\$5,000}{\$19,100} = 0.261780$	0.261780 × \$1,780 = \$ 465.97
Lumber	\$ 6,200	$\frac{\$6,200}{\$19,100} = 0.324607$	0.324607 × \$1,780 = \$ 577.80
Wall coverings	\$ 3,200	$\frac{\$3,200}{\$19,100} = 0.167539$	0.167539 × \$1,780 = \$ 298.22
Plumbing	\$ 3,200	$\frac{\$3,200}{\$19,100} = 0.167539$	0.167539 × \$1,780 = \$ 298.22
Electrical	\$ 1,500	$\frac{\$1,500}{\$19,100} = 0.078534$	0.078534 × \$1,780 = \$ 139.79
Total	\$19,100	0.999999	\$1,780.00

Topic	Page	What to Remember	Example
Finding overhead based on floor space	430–431	Add the square feet of floor space in each department to find the total number of square feet of floor space.	Make a table to show the overhead for a store that had \$25,000 in overhead expenses if overhead is calculated based on number of square feet in a department.

Find the floor-space fraction for each department and convert it to a decimal equivalent.

Floor-space fraction

$$= \frac{\text{square feet of floor space in department}}{\text{total square feet of floor space}}$$

Multiply each floor-space fraction times the total overhead to find the amount of overhead for each department.

Department	Number of Square Feet
1	5,100
2	4,120
3	1,200
4	2,500

Department	Floor Space	Floor-Space Fraction and Decimal Equivalent	Amount of Overhead for Department
1	5,100	$\frac{5,100}{12,920} = 0.394737$	0.394737 × \$25,000 = \$ 9,868.43
2	4,120	$\frac{4,120}{12,920} = 0.318885$	0.318885 × \$25,000 = \$ 7,972.13
3	1,200	$\frac{1,200}{12,920} = 0.092879$	0.092879 × \$25,000 = \$ 2,321.98
4	2,500	$\frac{2,500}{12,920} = 0.193498$	0.193498 × \$25,000 = \$ 4,837.45
	12,920	0.999999	\$24,999.99

Chapter Review

1. Calculate the cost of goods available for sale from the following information.

Date of Purchase	Number of Units Purchased	Cost per Unit	Total Cost
Beginning inventory	32	$12	
January 12	17	10	
February 5	12	14	
March 4	21	9	
Cost of goods available for sale			

2. Find the cost of the ending inventory from the following information.

	Number of Units on Hand	Cost per Unit	Total Cost
	21	$12	
	12	10	
	5	14	
	16	9	
Cost of ending inventory			

3. Find the cost of goods sold from Exercises 1 and 2.

4. Find the average unit cost for the information shown in the table.

Date of Purchase	Number of Units Purchased	Cost per Unit	Total Cost
Beginning inventory	32	$12	
January 12	17	10	
February 5	12	14	
March 4	21	9	
Cost of goods available for sale			

5. Calculate the cost of the ending inventory and the cost of goods sold in Exercise 4 by using the weighted-average method if 54 items remain in inventory.

6. Find the cost of goods sold and the cost of the ending inventory using the FIFO method if 545 items are on hand.

Date of Purchase	Number of Units Purchased	Cost per Unit	Total Cost
Beginning inventory	168	$15	
January 15	372	12	
February 5	218	8	
March 2	127	21	
Cost of goods sold			

Date of Purchase	Number of Units on Hand	Cost per Unit	Total Cost
Beginning inventory	0	$15	
January 15	200	12	
February 5	218	8	
March 2	127	21	
Cost of ending inventory			

7. Find the cost of goods sold and the cost of the ending inventory for the purchases in Exercise 6 using the LIFO method if 234 items are on hand.

Date of Purchase	Number of Units on Hand	Cost per Unit	Total Cost
Beginning inventory	168	$15	
January 15	66	12	
February 5	0	8	
March 2	0	21	
Cost of ending inventory			

8. Find the cost of goods sold and the cost of the ending inventory at cost using the retail method if the net sales were $7,020.

Date of Purchase	Number of Units Units Purchased	Cost per Unit	Total Cost	Retail per Unit	Total Retail
Beginning inventory	168	$15		$21	
January 15	372	12		17	
February 5	218	8		11	
March 2	127	21		30	
Cost of goods available for sale					
Less net sales					
Cost of ratio ($11,395 ÷ $16,060)					
Ending inventory at cost ($9,040 × 0.709527)					
Cost of goods sold					

9. Blaine's Department Store assigns overhead to its various departments according to the amount of floor space used by each department. The store's total overhead for a month is $18,000. Find the amount of overhead for each department if each department occupies the following number of square feet: floor coverings, 3,000; furniture, 2,800; lamps, 1,800; china and crystal, 800; accessories, 900; linens, 1,200; and wall coverings, 700.

10. Kothe's Kids Korner had overhead expenses totaling $9,300 during one month. Find the amount of overhead for each department, based on total sales, if the store had the following monthly sales by department: bicycles, $5,000; stuffed toys, $3,900; trains and accessories, $8,200; books, $4,800; and other toys, $12,500.

11. Find the rate of stock turnover for a business with net sales of $50,000 and an average inventory of $12,500.

Trial Test

1. Calculate the cost of goods available for sale from the following information.

Date of Purchase	Number of Units Purchased	Cost per Unit	Total Cost
Beginning inventory	26	$10	
March 12	32	13	
April 3	29	9	
May 5	25	12	
Cost of goods available for sale			

2. Find the cost of the ending inventory from the following information.

	Number of Units on Hand	Cost per Unit	Total Cost
	17	$10	
	12	13	
	15	9	
	25	12	
Cost of ending inventory			

3. Find the cost of goods sold from Exercises 1 and 2.

4. Find the average unit cost for the information shown in the table.

Date of Purchase	Number of Units Purchased	Cost per Unit	Total Cost
Beginning inventory	26	$10	
March 12	32	13	
April 3	29	9	
May 5	25	12	
Cost of goods available for sale			

5. Calculate the cost of ending inventory and the cost of goods sold in Exercise 4 by using the weighted-average method if there are 69 units on hand.

6. Use the information in Exercise 4 to construct a table to find the cost of goods sold and the cost of the ending inventory using the FIFO method if 32 items are on hand.

Date of Purchase	Number of Units on Hand	Cost per Unit	Total Cost
Beginning inventory	0	$10	
March 12	0	13	
April 3	7	9	
May 5	25	12	
Cost of ending inventory			

7. Use the information in Exercise 4 to construct a table to find the cost of goods sold and the cost of the ending inventory using the LIFO method if 82 items are on hand.

Date of Purchase	Number of Units on Hand	Cost per Unit	Total Cost
Beginning inventory	26	$10	
March 12	32	13	
April 3	24	9	
May 5	0	12	
Cost of ending inventory			

8. AMX Department Store's overhead expenses totaled $12,000 during one month. The sales by department for the month were: cameras, $12,000; toys, $14,000; hardware, $13,500; garden supplies, $8,400; sporting goods, $9,500; and clothing, $28,600. Find the total monthly sales for all departments.

9. Make a table to show the overhead assigned to each department if overhead is assigned based on number of square feet of office space for Office Supply World. The overhead expenses for a month totaled $9,000 and each department occupies the following number of square feet: furniture, 2,000; computer supplies, 1,600; consumable office supplies, 2,500; leather goods, 1,200; and administrative services, 800.

10. A restaurant had a beginning inventory of $13,900 and an ending inventory of $10,000. If the net sales for the inventory period were $47,800, find the turnover rate.

11. A retail parts business had an average inventory of $258,968 and a net sales of $756,893 for the same period. Find the rate of turnover.

12. A plant had an average inventory of $13,000 and net sales of $26,000 for the same period. Find the rate of turnover.

Self-Check Solutions

1.

Number of Units on Hand	Cost per Unit	Total Cost
43	12	$ 516
11	9	99
7	11	77
28	15	420
		$1,112

2.

Date of Purchase	Number of Units Purchased	Cost per Unit	Total Cost
Beginning inventory	96	$12	$1,152
April 12	23	9	207
May 8	15	11	165
June 2	37	15	555
	171		$2,079

$$\text{Average unit cost} = \frac{\text{total cost of goods available for sale}}{\text{total number of units available for sale}}$$

$$= \frac{\$2{,}079}{171} = \$12.16$$

3. Number of units on hand (ending inventory) = 43 + 11 + 7 + 28 = 89
Cost of ending inventory = 89 × $12.16 = $1,082.24
Cost of goods sold = cost of goods available for sale − ending inventory
= $2,079 − $1,082.24 = $996.76

4.

	Number of Units on Hand	Cost per Unit	Total Cost
Cost of ending inventory	22	12	$264

Cost of goods sold = $2,079 − $264
= $1,815

5.

Department	Monthly Sales Amount	Sales Fraction and Decimal Equivalent	Amount of Overhead for Each Deparment
Toys	$ 4,000	$\frac{\$4{,}000}{\$30{,}400} = 0.131579$	0.131579 × $6,000 = $ 789.47
Appliances	$ 6,600	$\frac{\$6{,}600}{\$30{,}400} = 0.217105$	0.217105 × $6,000 = $1,302.63
Children's clothing	$ 6,800	$\frac{\$6{,}800}{\$30{,}400} = 0.223684$	0.223684 × $6,000 = $1,342.10
Books	$ 4,600	$\frac{\$4{,}600}{\$30{,}400} = 0.151316$	0.151316 × $6,000 = $ 907.90
Furniture	$ 8,400	$\frac{\$8{,}400}{\$30{,}400} = 0.276316$	0.276316 × $6,000 = $1,657.90
Total	$30,400	1.000000	$6,000.00

6.

Department	Floor Space	Floor-Space Fraction and Decimal Equivalent	Amount of Overhead for Each Department
Women's clothing	2,000	$\frac{2{,}000}{5{,}700} = 0.350877$	0.350877 × \$15,800 = \$5,543.86
Men's clothing	1,200	$\frac{1{,}200}{5{,}700} = 0.210526$	0.210526 × \$15,800 = \$3,326.31
Children's clothing	2,500	$\frac{2{,}500}{5{,}700} = 0.438596$	0.438596 × \$15,800 = \$6,929.82
Total	5,700	0.999999	\$15,799.99

15 Financial Statements

Learning Objectives

1. Understand and prepare vertical and horizontal analyses of individual and comparative balance sheets. (pp. 447–455)
2. Understand and prepare vertical and horizontal analyses of individual and comparative income statements. (pp. 457–461)
3. Understand and calculate important financial ratios. (pp. 462–466)

The financial condition of a business must be monitored all the time. The owner of a business, investors, and creditors need to know the financial condition of the business before they can make decisions and plans. Lending institutions consider the overall financial health of a business before lending money. The stockholders of incorporated businesses expect to receive periodic reports on the financial condition of the corporation. Most companies or organizations hire an auditor once a year to determine this condition. Two financial statements, the balance sheet and the income statement, are normally prepared as part of this analysis. The *balance sheet* describes the condition of a business at some exact point in time, whereas the *income statement* shows how the business did over a period of time.

The Balance Sheet

The **balance sheet** is a type of financial statement that indicates the worth or financial condition of a business *as of a certain date.* It does not give any historical background about the company or make future projections but rather shows the status of the company on a given date. This financial statement provides useful information about a company, but it is rarely used as the only basis for making important business decisions.

balance sheet: a type of financial statement that indicates the worth or financial condition of a business as of a certain date.

The "balances" in a balance sheet involve the three elements of any business: assets, liabilities, and owner's equity. The balance sheet uses the basic accounting equation of business:

$$\text{Assets} = \text{liabilities} + \text{owner's equity:}$$

$$A = L + OE$$

Assets are what is owned by the business; *liabilities* are what are owed to creditors by the business; *owner's equity* is what the business is worth once the liabilities have been paid off.

Before showing how to prepare a balance sheet, some of the terms that will appear on it must be explained.

Assets

Assets are properties owned by the business. They include anything of monetary value and things that could be exchanged for cash or other prop-

assets: properties owned by the business including anything of monetary value and things that can be exchanged for cash or other property.

current assets: cash or assets that are normally turned into cash within a year.

plant and equipment: assets used in transacting business; more long term in nature than current assets.

erty. Some examples of assets are listed next. **Current assets** are assets that are normally turned into cash within a year. **Plant and equipment** are assets that are used in transacting business and are more long term in nature.

Current Assets	**Cash**	Money in the bank as well as cash on hand.
	Accounts receivable	Money that customers owe the business for merchandise or services they have received but not paid for.
	Notes receivable	Promissory notes owed the business.
	Merchandise inventory	Value of merchandise on hand.
Plant and equipment	**Business equipment**	Value of equipment (tools, display cases, machinery, and so on) that the business owns.
	Office furniture and equipment	Value of office furniture (desks, chairs, filing cabinets, and so on) and equipment (typewriters, computers, printers, calculators, postage meters, and the like).
	Office supplies	Value of supplies such as stationery, pens, file folders, and diskettes.
	Building	Value of the building, minus depreciation.
	Land	Value of the property and grounds on which the building stands.

Liabilities

liabilities: amounts that the business owes.

current liabilities: liabilities that have to be paid within a short period of time.

long-term liabilities: liabilities that are to be paid over a long period of time.

owner's equity: what the business is worth once liabilities have been paid off; that is, the difference in total assets and total liabilities.

Liabilities are amounts that the business owes. Some examples of liabilities are listed next. **Current liabilities** are those that must be paid shortly. **Long-term liabilities** are those that will be paid over a long period of time—a year or more.

Current liabilities	**Accounts payable**	Accounts for merchandise or services that the business owes.
	Notes payable	Promissory notes that the business owes.
	Wages payable	Salaries that a business owes its employees.
Long-term liabilities	**Mortgage payable**	The debt owed on the purchase price of the building and land.
	Owner's equity	Owner's equity is the amount of clear ownership or the owner's right to the properties. It is the difference between assets and liabilities. For instance, if a business has assets of $175,000 and liabilities of $100,000, the owner's equity is $175,000 − $100,000, or $75,000. Other words used to mean the same thing as owner's equity are *capital, proprietorship,* and *net worth.*

A balance sheet (see Figure 15-1) lists the assets, liabilities, and owner's equity of a business on a specific date. On that date, it answers the questions:

Figure 15-1 A Balance Sheet

Sanders' Department Stores Balance Sheet June 30, 19XX	
Assets	
Current assets:	
Cash	$ 5,281.83
Accounts receivable	2,402.13
Merchandise inventory	26,921.52
Total current assets	34,605.48
Plant and equipment:	
Building	148,352.00
Land	12,852.00
Equipment	46,520.00
Total plant and equipment	207,724.00
Total Assets	$242,329.48
Liabilities	
Current liabilities:	
Accounts payable	8,401.52
Notes payable	25,000.00
Total current liabilities	33,401.52
Long-term liabilities:	
Mortgage note payable	69,431.42
Total long-term liabilities	69,431.42
Total Liabilities	102,832.94
Owner's Equity	
J. Sanders, Capital	139,496.54
Total Liabilities and Owner's Equity	$242,329.48

How much does the business own? What are its assets?

How much does the business owe? What are its liabilities?

How much is the business worth? What is the value of its equity (what is its capital)?

Step by Step

Preparing a Balance Sheet

Step 1. At the top of the sheet, write the name of the company, the name of the statement (balance sheet), and the date. (This answers the questions who, what, and when.)

Step 2. List the assets and total them.

- **a.** First list and total current assets.
- **b.** Next list and total plant and equipment.
- **c.** Add the two subtotals to get total assets. Draw a double line under this figure to show that a total has been reached.

Step 3. List the liabilities and total them.

- **a.** First list and total current liabilities.
- **b.** Next list and total long-term liabilities.
- **c.** Add the two subtotals to get total liabilities. Do *not* draw a double line under this figure; it is only another subtotal.

Step 4. List the owner's equity figure.

Step 5. Add the figures for total liabilities and owner's equity. Draw a double line under this figure.

Step 6. Make sure that the figure for assets equals the figure for total liabilities and owner's equity.

Vertical Analysis of a Balance Sheet

vertical analysis: an analysis of a balance sheet that shows the relationship between each item on the balance sheet and the total assets.

A **vertical analysis** of a balance sheet shows the relationship of each item on the balance sheet to the *total assets*. This is done using the percentage formula. In this use of the percentage formula, each item on the balance sheet is the portion, the total assets are the base, and the percent of total assets is the rate. Use this version of the formula: $R = \frac{P}{B}$.

Step by Step

Preparing a Vertical Analysis of a Balance Sheet

Step 1. Divide each item listed on the balance sheet by the total assets.

Step 2. Convert the decimal to a percent and round the result to the nearest tenth percent.

EXAMPLE 1

Prepare a vertical analysis of the balance sheet for Murphy's Sporting Goods, shown in Figure 15-2.

Figure 15-2 Vertical Analysis of a Balance Sheet

Murphy's Sporting Goods
Balance Sheet
June 30, 19XX

Assets		**Percent of Total Assets**	
Current assets:			
Cash	$ 2,237.15	7.8%	
Accounts receivable	1,714.36	6.0%	
Merchandise inventory	17,396.15	60.7%	
Total current assets	21,347.66		74.5%
Plant and equipment:			
Equipment	7,291.77	25.5%	
Total plant and equipment	7,291.77		25.5%
Total Assets	28,639.43	100.0%	
Liabilities			
Current liabilities:			
Accounts payable	3,174.76	11.1%	
Wages payable	1,224.15	4.3%	
Total current liabilities	4,398.91		15.4%
Total Liabilities	4,398.91	15.4%	
Owner's Equity			
G. Murphy, Capital	24,240.52	84.6%	
Total Liabilities and Owner's Equity	$28,639.43	100.0%	

Cash: $\frac{\$2,237.15}{\$28,639.43} = 0.078114 = 7.8\%$ (nearest tenth of a percent)

Accounts receivable: $\frac{1,714.36}{28,639.43} = 0.059860 = 6.0\%$

Inventory: $\frac{17,396.15}{28,639.43} = 0.607420 = 60.7\%$

Equipment: $\frac{7,291.77}{28,639.43} = 0.254606 = 25.5\%$

Total assets: $\frac{28,639.43}{28,639.43} = 1 = 100\%$

Accounts payable: $\frac{3,174.76}{28,639.43} = 0.110852 = 11.1\%$

Wages payable: $\frac{1,224.15}{28,639.43} = 0.042743 = 4.3\%$

Total liabilities: $\frac{4,398.91}{28,639.43} = 0.153596 = 15.4\%$

Capital: $\frac{24,240.52}{28,639.43} = 0.846403 = 84.6\%$

Total liabilities and capital: $\frac{28,639.43}{28,639.43} = 1 = 100\%$

Note that the entries for total assets and for total liabilities and capital equal 100%. Other percents in assets and liabilities and capital should add up to 100%.

Calculator Solution

Since each item on the balance sheet is divided by the total assets, the memory of a calculator can be used to facilitate the calculation.

[AC] 28639.43 [M+] — Enter total assets into memory. Clear display. Do not clear memory.

Enter the first amount:

[CE/C] 2237.15 [÷] [MRC] [=] ⇒ 0.0781143

Enter second amount:

[CE/C] 1714.36 [÷] [MRC] [=] ⇒ 0.059860

Continue with each amount.

TIPS & TRAPS

Be careful to use the total assets as the base when figuring each percent. Look what happens to the percent for *Wages payable* in Figure 15-2 if the total liabilities is used for the base instead of total assets:

WRONG (crossed out):

$R = \frac{P}{B}$

$= \frac{1,224.15}{4,398.91} = 0.278284$, or 27.8%

CORRECT:

$R = \frac{P}{B}$

$= \frac{1,224.15}{28,639.43} = 0.042743$, or 4.3%

Real World Application

Before lending large amounts of money (usually over $5,000), bankers require a personal financial statement. The same is true before one signs a commercial lease. By law, the information provided must be true and updated periodically. Using your personal data, prepare the financial statement shown here. The section for contingent liabilities refers to one of the following:

a. money borrowed for a corporation owned totally by you.
b. loans signed by you with a first-time buyer of a car, for example.
c. loans you have signed as extra security for someone with an explainable blemish on his or her credit record.

ASSETS	In Even Dollars			LIABILITIES	In Even Dollars		
Cash on hand and in banks				Notes payable to banks—secured			
Marketable Securities				Notes payable to banks—unsecured			
Non-Marketable Securities				Due to brokers			
Securities held by broker in margin accounts				Amounts payable to others—secured			
Restricted or control stocks				Amounts payable to others—unsecured			
Partial Interest in Real Estate Equities				Accounts and bills due			
				Unpaid income tax			
Real Estate Owned				Other unpaid taxes and interest			
Loans Receivable				Real estate mortgages payable			
Automobiles and other personal property							
Cash value—life insurance				Other debts—itemize:			
Other assets—itemize:							
				TOTAL LIABILITIES			
				NET WORTH			
TOTAL ASSETS				TOTAL LIAB. AND NET WORTH			

Are all bad and doubtful assets excluded from this statement?__________ If no, explain:__________

Income taxes settled through what date? __________ Additional assessments $__________

ANNUAL SOURCES OF INCOME		PERSONAL INFORMATION
Salary, bonus & commissions	$	Do you have a will? If yes, name of executor.
Dividends		
Real estate income		
		Are you a partner or officer in any other venture?
TOTAL	$	Number Of Dependents

CONTINGENT LIABILITIES		GENERAL INFORMATION
Do you have any contingent liabilities?		Are any assets pledged?
If yes, give details:		Are you defendant in any suits
As endorser, co-maker or guarantor	$	or legal actions?
On leases or contracts	$	Personal bank accounts carried at:
Legal claims	$	
Other special debt	$	Have you ever taken bankruptcy? Explain:
Amount of contested income tax liens	$	

Comparative Balance Sheets

One way to use the information that one is presented with in a balance sheet is to compare it with the information from the balance sheet of another year or series of years. Such a comparison is shown in a **comparative balance sheet,** in which the figures for two years are shown side by side. This can be seen in Figure 15-3, in which we show the vertical analysis of the balance sheets for 2 years. Note that the most recent date is on the *left.*

comparative balance sheet: a report form that is used to compare information on two or more balance sheets.

Horizontal Analysis of a Balance Sheet

Another way to analyze information on a comparative balance sheet is to compare item by item in a **horizontal analysis.** This means that instead of figuring the relationship of each item to total assets, you compare the same item for two different years, find the percent of increase or decrease in the item, and show that as a percent.

horizontal analysis: an analysis of a comparative balance sheet or comparative income statement which compares entries on a horizontal line.

Adams Shoe Corporation
Comparative Balance Sheet
December 31, 19X8 and 19X9

			Increase or (Decrease)*		Percent of total assets	
	19X9	**19X8**	**Amount**	**Percent**	**19X9**	**19X8**
Assets						
Current assets:						
Cash	$ 2,184	$ 1,973	$ 211	10.7	9.2	8.7
Accounts receivable	4,308	2,118	2,190	103.4	18.1	9.4
Merchandise inventory	17,317	18,476	(1,159)	(6.3)	72.7	81.9
Total current assets	$23,809	$22,567	$ 1,242	5.5	100.0	100.0
Plant and equipment:						
Equipment						
Total plant and equipment						
Total Assets	$23,809	$22,567	$ 1,242	5.5	100.0	100.0
Liabilities						
Current liabilities:						
Accounts payable	$ 1,647	$ 2,317	$ (670)	(28.9)	6.9	10.3
Wages payable	894	684	210	30.7	3.8	3.0
Total current liabilities	2,541	3,001	(460)	1.8	10.7	13.3
Long-term liabilities:						
Mortgage note payable						
Total long-term liabilities						
Total Liabilities	$ 2,541	$ 3,001	$ (460)	1.8	10.7	13.3
Owner's Equity						
Charles Adams, Capital	$21,268	$19,566	$ 1,702	8.7	89.3	86.7
Total Liabilities and Owner's Equity	$23,809	$22,567	$ 1,242	5.5	100.0	100.0

* Numbers in parentheses are decreases.

Figure 15-3 Vertical Analysis of a Comparative Balance Sheet

In order to do this, you again use the percentage formula. Recall that to find a percent of increase or decrease, you use $R = \frac{P}{B}$.

Step by Step

Horizontal Analysis of a Comparative Balance Sheet

Step 1. Find the amount of increase or decrease for each horizontal line by subtracting the amount in the right column from the amount in the left column.

Step 2. Find the percent of increase or decrease by using $R = \frac{P}{B}$, where the amount of increase is the portion, the *earlier* year's item is the base, and the percent of increase or decrease is the rate.

Step 3. Round to the nearest tenth percent.

Prepare a horizontal analysis of the comparative balance sheet for Adams Shoe Corporation, shown in Figure 15-4.

Cash: \$2,184 − \$1,973 = \$211 (increase)
\$211 ÷ \$1,973 = 0.106943 = 10.7% (increase)

Accounts receivable: \$4,308 − \$2,118 = \$2,190 (increase)
\$2,190 ÷ \$2,118 = 1.033994 = 103.4% (increase)

Inventory: \$18,476 − \$17,317 = \$1,159 (decrease)
\$1,159 ÷ \$18,476 = 0.062730 = 6.3% (decrease)

Total Assets: \$23,809 − \$22,567 = \$1,242 (increase)
\$1,242 ÷ \$22,567 = 0.055036 = 5.5% (increase)

Adams Shoe Corporation
Comparative Balance Sheet
December 31, 19X0 and 19X1

			Increase or (Decrease)	
	19X1	**19X0**	**Amount**	**Percent**
Assets				
Cash	\$ 2,184	\$ 1,973	\$ 211	10.7
Accounts receivable	4,308	2,118	2,190	103.4
Inventory	17,317	18,476	(1,159)	(6.3)
Total Assets	\$23,809	\$22,567	\$ 1,242	5.5
Liabilities				
Accounts payable	\$ 1,647	\$ 2,317	\$ (670)	(28.9)
Salaries payable	894	684	210	30.7
Total Liabilities	\$ 2,541	\$ 3,001	\$ (460)	(15.3)
Owner's Equity				
Charles Adams, Capital	\$21,268	\$19,566	\$ 1,702	8.7
Total Liabilities and Owner's Equity	\$23,809	\$22,567	\$ 1,242	5.5

Figure 15-4 Horizontal Analysis of a Comparative Balance Sheet

Accounts payable: $2,317 − $1,647 = $670 (decrease)
$670 ÷ $2,317 = 0.289167 = 28.9% (decrease)

Salaries payable: $894 − $684 = $210 (increase)
$210 ÷ $684 = 0.307018 = 30.7 (increase)

Total Liabilities: $3,001 − $2,541 = $460 (decrease)
$460 ÷ $3,001 = 0.153282 = 15.3% (decrease)

Charles Adams, capital: $21,268 − $19,566 = $1,702 (increase)
$1,702 ÷ $19,566 = 0.086987 = 8.7% (increase)

Total Liabilities and Owner's Equity:
$23,809 − $22,567 = $1,242 (increase)
$1,242 ÷ $22,567 = 0.055036 = 5.5% (increase)

If the horizontal analysis has been made properly, the amount of change in the Total Assets line should equal the sum of the asset increases minus any asset decreases. The amount of change in the Liabilities line should equal the sum of the liabilities increases minus any liabilities decreases. The amount of change in the Total Liabilities and Owner's Equity line should equal the sum of the total liabilities and the capital increases (or difference if one amount is a decrease). The Total Liabilities and Owner's Equity amount and percent of change should equal the respective Total Assets entry.

Self-Check

1. Complete the horizontal analysis on the comparative balance sheet for Maddy's Muffins. (Use parentheses to indicate decreases.)

Maddy's Muffins
Comparative Balance Sheet
December 31, 19X8 and 19X9

			Increase or (Decrease)	
	19X9	**19X8**	**Amount**	**Percent**
Assets				
Current assets:				
Cash	$1,985	$1,762		
Accounts receivable	4,219	3,785		
Merchandise inventory	2,512	2,036		
Total Assets	$8,716	$7,583		
Liabilities				
Current liabilities:				
Accounts payable	$3,483	$3,631		
Wages payable	1,696	1,421		
Total Liabilities	$5,179	$5,052		
Owner's Equity				
Maddy Engman, Capital	$3,537	$2,541		
Total Liabilities and Owner's Equity	$8,716	$7,583		

TIPS & TRAPS

In a horizontal analysis of a balance sheet, percents of change do *not* add (or subtract for decreases) to give any meaningful information or to serve as a check of calculations. On the other hand, the percent of total assets on a vertical analysis of a balance sheet can be added (or subtracted for decreases) to check calculations. These percents also show how parts relate to a whole and can be displayed in a circle graph.

Source: Battalia and Assoc. Inc. executive search firm
By Juan Thomassie, USA TODAY

Section Review

1. Complete the following balance sheet for Cox Company.

Cox Company Balance Sheet March 31, 19XX	
Assets	
Current assets:	
Cash	$ 1,724.00
Office supplies	173.00
Accounts receivable	9,374.00
Total current assets	
Plant and equipment:	
Equipment	$12,187.00
Total plant and equipment	12,187.00
Total Assets	
Liabilities	
Current liabilities:	
Accounts payable	$2,174.00
Wages payable	674.00
Property taxes payable	250.00
Total current liabilities	
Total Liabilities	
Owner's Equity	
D. W. Cox, Capital	$20,360.00
Total Liabilities and Owner's Equity	

2. Complete the vertical analysis and horizontal analysis of the comparative balance sheet for Ajax Appliance Company. Express percents to the nearest tenth of a percent.

Ajax Appliance Company
Comparative Balance Sheet
December 31, 19X5 and 19X6

			Increase or (Decrease)		Percent of total assets	
	19X6	**19X5**	**Amount**	**Percent**	**19X6**	**19X5**
Assets						
Current assets:						
Cash	$ 2,374	$ 2,184				
Accounts receivable	5,374	4,286				
Merchandise inventory	15,589	16,107				
Total Assets						
Liabilities						
Current liabilities:						
Accounts payable	$ 7,384	$ 6,118				
Wages payable	1,024	964				
Total Liabilities						
Owner's Equity						
James Ajax, Capital	$14,929	$15,495				
Total Liabilities and Owner's Equity						

Income Statements

The other important financial statement is the **income statement.** This is a statement that shows the net income of a business *over a period of time.* (Remember, the balance sheet shows the financial condition of a business at a *given* time.)

income statement: a statement that shows the financial condition of a business over a period of time.

Again, there are some terms we need to know.

Total sales Earnings from the sale of goods or the performance of services.

Sales returns or allowances Refunds or adjustments for unsatisfactory merchandise or services.

Net sales The difference between the total sales and the sales returns or allowances.

Cost of goods sold Cost to the business for merchandise or goods sold.

Gross profit The difference between the net sales and the cost of goods sold.

Operating expenses The overhead or cost incurred in operating the business. Examples of operating expenses are utilities, rent, insurance, permits, taxes, and employees' salaries.

Net income, or **net profit**	The difference between the gross profit (gross margin) and the operating expenses.

Calculating the cost of goods sold is an important part of preparing an income statement. What you must determine is how much was paid out for the goods that were sold during the period covered by the income statement. To find out, you start with the cost of the beginning inventory (the goods on hand at the beginning of the period), add the purchases of goods made within the period, and subtract the cost of the ending inventory (the goods on hand at the end of the period). Calculating cost of goods sold uses the following formula:

Cost of goods sold = beginning inventory + purchases − ending inventory

Now that you know how to calculate cost of goods sold, you can go on to the three basic formulas that are used in preparing an income statement. The three figures that are needed in an income statement are *net sales, gross profit,* and *net income.* Everything else on the income statement goes to making up these figures, using the following three formulas.

Step by Step

Formulas Used in Preparing Income Statements

Net sales = total sales − sales returns and allowances
Gross profit = net sales − cost of goods sold
Net income = gross profit − operating expenses

EXAMPLE 3

CORNER GROCERY INCOME STATEMENT For month ending June 30, 19X5	
Net sales	$25,000
Cost of goods sold	18,750
Gross profit	$ 6,250
Operating expenses	3,750
Net income	$ 2,500

Study the income statement for the Corner Grocery. Note how the gross profit and net income are calculated. In this case, the cost of goods sold and net sales are given; next you will be asked to find these amounts.

Gross profit = net sales − cost of goods sold
= $25,000 − $18,750 = $6,250

Net income = gross profit − operating expenses
= $6,250 − $3,750 = $2,500

The following procedure lists the steps necessary to construct an income statement. The box describes the basic calculations involved; see Figure 15-5 for the income statement.

Step by Step

Preparing the Income Statement

Step 1. The first section of the income statement is concerned with net sales. Enter gross sales and *subtract* sales returns and allowances to get net sales.

Step 2. The next section of the income statement is concerned with cost of goods sold. Enter beginning inventory, *add* purchases, and *subtract* ending inventory to get cost of goods sold.

Step 3. The next section of the income statement is concerned with gross profit. *Subtract* cost of goods sold from net sales to get gross profit.

Step 4. The next section of the income statement is concerned with operating expenses. Enter all the expenses and *add* them to get total operating expenses.

Step 5. The final section of the income statement is concerned with net income. *Subtract* total expenses from gross profit to get net income.

Martha's Gift Shop
Income Statement
For the year ending December 31, 19X2

Revenue:		
Gross sales		$246,891
Sales returns and allowances	$ 7,835	
Net sales		$239,056
Cost of goods sold:		
Beginning inventory, January 1, 19X2	$ 8,247	
Purchases	148,542	
Ending inventory, December 31, 19X2	9,583	
Cost of goods sold		$147,206
Gross Profit from Sales		$ 91,850
Operating expenses:		
Salary	$ 18,500	
Insurance	5,700	
Utilities	1,900	
Maintenance	280	
Rent	6,000	
Depreciation	1,500	
Total operating expenses		$ 33,880
Net Income		$ 57,970

Figure 15-5 An Income Statement

Vertical Analysis of an Income Statement

As with the vertical analysis of the balance sheet, you use the percentage formula $R = \frac{P}{B}$, in which R is the *percent of net sales*, P is the item of the income statement under consideration, and B is net sales.

EXAMPLE 4

Figure 15-6 shows the vertical analysis of Martha's Gift Shop income statement. Each entry is divided by the net sales, the quotient is converted to a percent, and the percent is rounded to the nearest tenth of a percent.

Martha's Gift Shop Income Statement For the year ending December 31, 19X2		Percent of Net Sales
Revenue:		
Gross sales	$246,891	103.3%
Sales returns and allowances	7,835	3.3
Net sales	239,056	100.0
Cost of goods sold:		
Beginning inventory, January 1, 19X2	$ 8,247	3.4
Purchases	148,542	62.1
Ending inventory, December 31, 19X2	9,583	4.0
Cost of goods sold	147,206	61.6
Gross Profit from Sales	$ 91,850	38.4
Operating Expenses:		
Salary	$ 18,500	7.7
Insurance	5,700	2.4
Utilities	1,900	0.8
Maintenance	280	0.1
Rent	6,000	2.5
Depreciation	1,500	0.6
Total operating expenses	$ 33,880	14.2
Net Income	$ 57,970	24.2

Figure 15-6 Vertical Analysis of an Income Statement

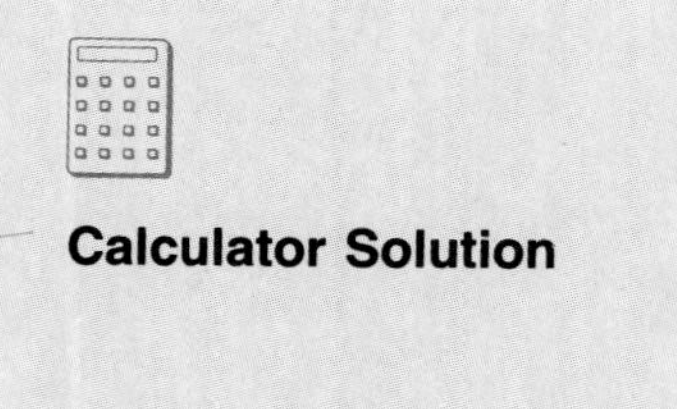

Calculator Solution

Enter the net sales into memory.

[AC] 239056 [M+]

Divide each entry by net sales.

[CE/C] 246891 [÷] [MRC] [=] ⇒ 1.0327747

[CE/C] 7835 [÷] [MRC] [=] ⇒ 0.0327747

Continue by dividing each item by the net sales which is stored in memory.

Comparative Income Statement

comparative income statement: a report form that is used to compare information on two or more income statements.

The information from more than one income statement can be compiled as a **comparative income statement.** As with the comparative balance sheet, we put the most recent information in the first column. Both vertical and horizontal analyses of a comparative income statement can be made, as shown in Figures 15-7 and 15-8.

Davis Company
Comparative Income Statement
For the years ending June 30, 19X2 and 19X3

	19X3	% of Net Sales	19X2	% of Net Sales
Net sales	$242,897	100.0	$239,528	100.0
Cost of goods sold	116,582	48.0	115,351	48.2
Gross profit	$126,315	52.0	$124,177	51.8
Operating expenses	38,725	15.9	37,982	15.9
Net income	$ 87,590	36.1	$ 86,195	36.0

Figure 15-7 Vertical Analysis of a Comparative Income Statement

Davis Company
Comparative Income Statement
For the years ending June 30, 19X2 and 19X3

			Increase (Decrease)	
	19X3	19X2	Amount	Percent
Net sales	$242,897	$239,528	3,369	1.4
Cost of goods sold	116,582	115,351	1,231	1.1
Gross profit	$126,315	$124,177	2,138	1.7
Operating expenses	38,725	37,982	743	2.0
Net income	$ 87,590	$ 86,195	1,395	1.6

Figure 15-8 Horizontal Analysis of a Comparative Income Statement

Self-Check

2. Complete the horizontal analysis of the comparative income statement for the Jones Grocery. Express percents to the nearest tenth of a percent.

Jones Grocery
Income Statement
For the years ending June 30, 19X8 and 19X9

			Increase (Decrease)	
	19X9	19X8	Amount	Percent
Net sales	$97,384	$92,196		
Cost of goods sold	82,157	72,894		
Gross profit				
Operating expenses	$ 4,783	$ 3,951		
Net income	$	$		

Section Review

1. Complete the following income statement and vertical analysis.

Marten's Family Store
Income Statement
For year ending December 31, 19X0

		Percent of Net Sales
Revenue:		
Gross sales	$238,923	
Sales returns and allowances	13,815	
Net sales		
Cost of goods sold:		
Beginning inventory, January 1, 19X0	$ 25,814	
Purchases	109,838	
Ending inventory, December 31, 19X0	23,423	
Cost of goods sold		
Gross Profit from Sales		
Operating expenses:		
Salary	$ 42,523	
Rent	8,640	
Utilities	1,484	
Insurance	2,842	
Fees	860	
Depreciation	1,920	
Miscellaneous	3,420	
Total operating expenses		
Net Income		

Financial Statement Ratios

financial ratio: shows how the parts of a business relate to one another.

Financial statements organize and summarize information about the financial condition of a business. This information is useful to owners, stockholders or investors, lending institutions, or prospective buyers. **Financial ratios** take the information from the financial statements and show how the parts of a business relate to one another. They give a number of ways to evaluate the condition of the business.

Current Ratio

working capital: current assets minus current liabilities.

It is important to know whether a business has enough assets to cover its liabilities. The **working capital** of a business is its current assets minus current liabilities. It does not tell much about the financial condition of the business, and it is difficult to compare the working capital of two businesses. Look at the information about Companies A and B:

2. Complete the following horizontal analysis of a comparative income statement.

Alonzo's Auto Parts
Comparative Income Statement
For years ending June 30, 19X8 and 19X9

	19X9	19X8	Increase (Decrease) Amount	Percent
Revenue:				
Gross sales	$291,707	$275,873		
Sales returns and allowances	5,895	6,821		
Net sales				
Cost of goods sold:				
Beginning inventory, July 1	$ 35,892	$ 32,587		
Purchases	157,213	146,999		
Ending inventory, June 30	32,516	30,013		
Cost of goods sold				
Gross Profit from Sales				
Operating expenses:				
Salary	$ 42,000	$ 40,000		
Insurance	3,800	3,800		
Utilities	1,986	2,097		
Rent	3,600	3,300		
Depreciation	4,000	4,500		
Total operating expenses				
Net Income				

	Company A	Company B
Current assets	$12,000	$615,000
Current liabilities	− 6,000	− 609,000
Working capital	$ 6,000	$ 6,000

(Working capital = current assets − current liabilities)

Both companies have the same working capital, but Company B *owes* almost as much as it *owns*. To compare these companies, we need to use ratios. A commonly used ratio in business is the **current ratio** (also called the **working capital ratio**), which tells how the current assets relate to the current liabilities.

current ratio (working capital ratio): a ratio which tells how the current assets relate to the current liabilities.

Step by Step

Current Ratio

$$\text{Current ratio} = \frac{\text{current assets}}{\text{current liabilities}}$$

Many lending companies consider a current ratio of 2 to 1 (2 : 1) to be the minimum acceptable current ratio for approving a loan to a business.

EXAMPLE 5

Find the current ratios for Companies A and B. Round to the nearest hundredth if necessary.

$$\text{Current ratio} = \frac{\text{current assets}}{\text{current liabilities}}$$

Company A:

$$\frac{\$12{,}000}{\$6{,}000} = 2$$

Current ratio for Company A is 2, or 2 to 1 (2 : 1).

Company B:

$$\frac{\$615{,}000}{\$609{,}000} = 1.009852 = 1.01$$

Current ratio for Company B is 1.01, or 1.01 to 1 (1.01 : 1).

Business ratios are normally expressed in decimal form. The decimal number is a numerator that is compared to a denominator of 1.

Acid-Test Ratio

acid-test ratio (quick ratio): a ratio used to determine the financial condition of a business; the ratio of quick current assets to current liabilities.

quick current assets: cash assets or assets that can be readily exchanged for cash, such as marketable securities and receivables.

marketable securities: current assets such as government bonds, which can be quickly turned into cash without loss.

Another ratio used to determine the financial condition of a business is the **acid-test ratio,** sometimes called the **quick ratio.** Instead of using the current assets of a business, the acid-test ratio uses only the **quick current assets,** those assets that can be readily exchanged for cash, **marketable securities,** accounts receivable, and notes receivable. Merchandise inventory is a current asset but it is not included, because a loss would probably occur if a business were to make a quick sale of all merchandise.

Step by Step

Acid-Test Ratio (Quick Ratio)

$$\text{Acid-test ratio} = \frac{\text{quick current assets}}{\text{current liabilities}}$$

EXAMPLE 6

Find the acid-test ratio if the balance sheet shows the following amounts:

Cash = $17,342
Marketable securities = $0
Receivables = $10,345
Current liabilities = $26,345

$$\text{Acid-test ratio} = \frac{\$17{,}342 + \$10{,}345}{\$26{,}345} = \frac{\$27{,}687}{\$26{,}345} = 1.05 \quad \text{(nearest hundredth)}$$

The acid-test ratio is 1.05 : 1.

Calculator Sequence

[AC] 17342 [+] 10345 [=] [÷] 26345 [=] ⇒ 1.0509394

If the acid-test ratio is 1 : 1, the business is in a satisfactory financial condition and has the ability to meet its obligations. If the ratio is *less* than 1 : 1 (such as 0.95 : 1), the business is in poor financial condition; and if the ratio is *more* than 1 : 1 (such as 1.05 : 1), the business is in good financial condition.

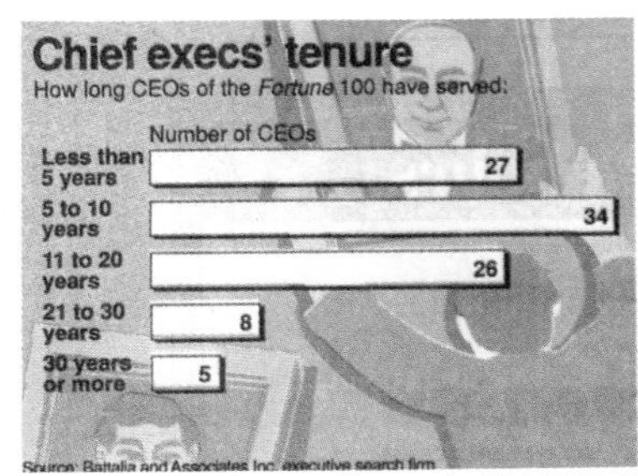

By Juan Thomassie, USA TODAY

Income Statement Ratios

On a comparative income statement, the horizontal analyses indicate the rate of change for the period, and the vertical analyses indicate what proportion or percent each entry is of the net sales at the beginning and at the end of the period. However, the mere statement of percentages is not enough. The analyst must use these percentages as *indicators,* interpret these indicators, and determine whether the various changes are favorable or unfavorable. This is done by the use of *income statement ratios.*

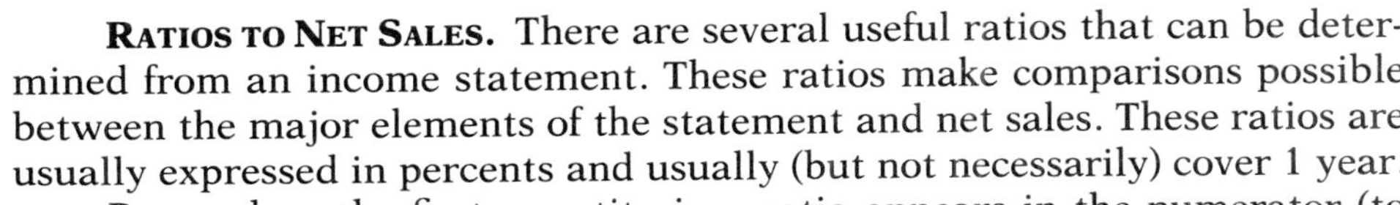

Ratios to Net Sales. There are several useful ratios that can be determined from an income statement. These ratios make comparisons possible between the major elements of the statement and net sales. These ratios are usually expressed in percents and usually (but not necessarily) cover 1 year.

Remember, the first quantity in a ratio appears in the numerator (to the left of the colon), and the second quantity appears in the denominator (to the right of the colon). Therefore, in each of the **ratios to net sales,** the denominator is the net sales. Using $R = \frac{P}{B}$, the rate (R) is the ratio, the portion (P) is the item considered, and the base (B) is always net sales.

ratios to net sales: ratios determined from an income statement that make comparisons possible between the major elements of the statement and new sales; these ratios (usually expressed in percents) usually cover a 1-year period.

Operating Ratio. The **operating ratio** indicates the amount of sales dollars that are used to pay for the cost of goods and administrative expenses. A ratio of less than 1 : 1 is desirable. The lower the operating ratio, the more income there is to meet financial obligations such as interest payments, dividends, etc.

operating ratio: the amount of sales dollars that are used to pay for the cost of goods and administrative expenses.

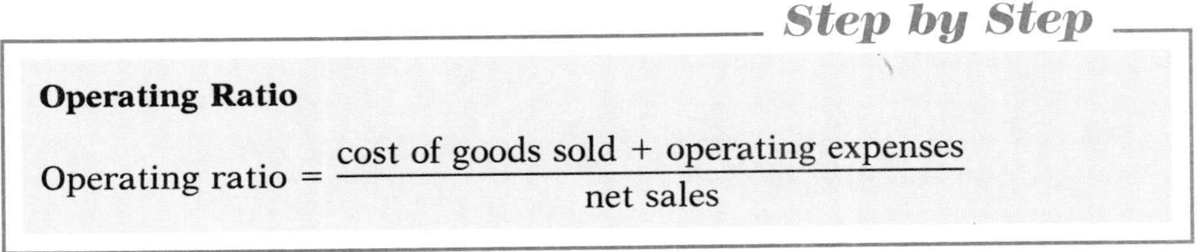

Step by Step

Operating Ratio

$$\text{Operating ratio} = \frac{\text{cost of goods sold} + \text{operating expenses}}{\text{net sales}}$$

Gross Profit Margin Ratio. The **gross profit margin ratio** shows the average spread between cost of goods sold and the selling price. The desirable gross profit margin ratio varies with the type of business. For example, a jewelry store might expect to have a ratio of 0.6 to 1, because there is a high rate of markup in jewelry. But an auto parts store may have a ratio of 0.25 to 1.

gross profit margin ratio: shows the average spread between cost of goods sold and the selling price.

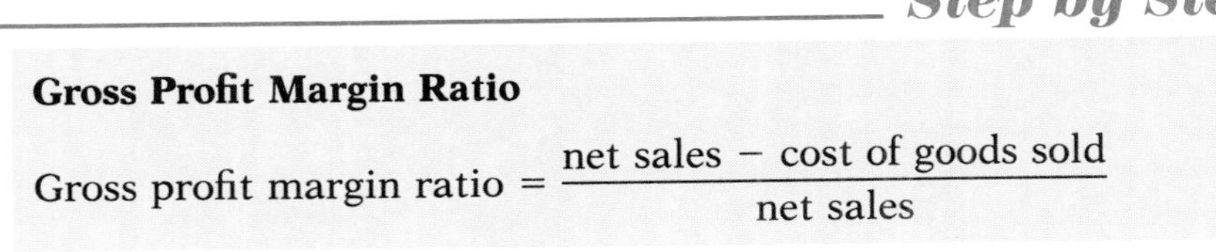

Step by Step

Gross Profit Margin Ratio

$$\text{Gross profit margin ratio} = \frac{\text{net sales} - \text{cost of goods sold}}{\text{net sales}}$$

To illustrate the calculation of these ratios, we will use a summary income statement for Martha's Gift Shop.

Martha's Gift Shop Income Statement For the year ending December 31, 19X2	
Net sales	$173,157
Cost of goods sold	
Beginning inventory	$ 37,376
Purchases	123,574
Goods available for sale	$160,950
Less: Ending inventory	34,579
Cost of goods sold	126,371
Gross profit	$ 46,786
Operating expenses	17,643
Net income	$ 29,143

EXAMPLE 7

Find the two ratios to net sales for Martha's Gift Shop. Express each answer as a percent rounded to the nearest tenth of a percent.

$$\text{Operating ratio} = \frac{\text{cost of goods sold} + \text{operating expenses}}{\text{net sales}}$$

$$= \frac{126{,}371 + 17{,}643}{173{,}157}$$

$$= 0.831696 \text{ or } 83.2\%$$

$$\text{Gross profit margin ratio} = \frac{\text{net sales} - \text{cost of goods sold}}{\text{net sales}}$$

$$= \frac{173{,}157 - 126{,}371}{173{,}157}$$

$$= 0.270194 \text{ or } 27.0\%$$

Self-Check

3. Find the current ratios for Companies X and Y. Round to the nearest hundredth if necessary.

	Company X	*Company Y*
Current assets	$28,000	$840,000
Current liabilities	− 7,000	− 819,000
Working capital	$21,000	$ 21,000

4. Find the acid-test ratio if the balance sheet shows the following amounts:

Cash = $32,981 Receivables = $12,045
Marketable securites = $0 Current liabilities = $22,178

Section Review

Find the current ratio for each of the following businesses. Round answers to the nearest hundredth.

	Current assets	Current liabilities
1.	$1,231,704	$784,184
2.	$32,194	$38,714
3.	$174,316	$125,342
4.	$724,987	$334,169

Find the acid-test ratio for each of these businesses. Express the answer to the nearest hundredth.

5. Stevens Gift Shop: cash, $2,345; accounts receivable, $5,450; government securities, $4,500; accounts payable, $6,748; notes payable, $7,457.

6. Central Office Supply: cash, $5,745; accounts receivable, $12,496; accounts payable, $10,475.

7. Find the operating ratio and gross profit margin ratio for the following income statement:

CORNER GROCERY INCOME STATEMENT For month ending June 30, 19X7	
Net sales	$25,000
Cost of goods sold	18,750
Gross profit	$ 6,250
Operating expenses	3,750
Net income	$ 2,500

Summary

Topic	Page	What to Remember	Examples
The basic accounting equation	447	Assets = liabilities + owner's equity	Assets = $50,000; liabilities = $10,000 $50,000 = $10,000 + owner's equity $40,000 = owner's equity
Preparing a balance sheet	449–451	Identify the company, the statement, and the date. List and total the assets. List and subtotal the liabilities. List the owner's equity and add it to the liabilities subtotal. Total assets equal total liabilities plus owner's equity.	*Assets* Cash $ 8,000 Accounts receivable 4,860 Inventory 19,823 Equipment 8,925 Total Assets $41,608 *Liabilities* Accounts payable $ 8,156 Wages payable 6,821 Total liabilities 7,489 Owner's Equity 19,142 Total Liabilities and Owner's Equity $41,608
Vertical analysis of a balance sheet	450	Find the total value of all assets. Divide the value of each item on the balance sheet by the total value of all assets, and change each resulting decimal number to a percent, rounded to the nearest tenth of a percent.	(see table below)
Horizontal analysis of a comparative balance sheet	454	Find the *amount* of increase or decrease for each horizontal line and then find the *percent* of increase or decrease for each horizontal line. Percent increase or decrease $= \frac{\text{amount of increase or decrease}}{\text{original amount}} \times 100$	(see tables below)
Net sales (on income statement)	457–460	Net sales = total sales − sales returns or allowances	Total sales = $85,700; sales returns = $4,892 Net sales = $85,700 − $4,892 = $80,808
Gross profit (on income statement)	457–460	Gross profit = net sales − cost of goods sold	Net sales = $48,831; cost of goods sold = $29,512 Gross profit = $48,831 − $29,512 = $19,319

Vertical analysis example:

Assets		*Percent of Total Assets*	
Cash	$18,211	12.7%	$18,211 ÷ $142,942
Accounts receivable	25,019	17.5%	$25,019 ÷ $142,942
Inventory	87,523	61.2%	$87,523 ÷ $142,942
Equipment	12,189	8.5%	$12,189 ÷ $142,942
Total Assets	$142,942	100.0%	$142,942 ÷ $142,942

Horizontal analysis example:

Assets	19X9	19X8
Cash	$ 28,134	$ 25,021
Accounts receivable	7,896	6,821
Inventory	89,087	69,598
Total Assets	$125,117	$101,440

	Increase or Decrease Amount	Percent
Cash	$ 3,113	12.4%
Accounts receivable	1,075	15.8%
Inventory	19,489	28.0%
Total Assets	$23,677	23.3%

Topic	Page	What to Remember	Examples
Net income (on income statement)	458–460	Net income (net profit) = gross profit − operating expenses	Gross profit = \$21,817; Operating expenses = \$3,846 Net income = \$21,817 − \$3,846 = \$17,971
Finding cost of goods sold	457–460	Goods available for sale = beginning inventory + purchases made Cost of goods sold = goods available for sale − ending inventory	Beginning inventory = \$16,592; purchases = \$146,983; ending inventory = \$18,096. Goods available for sale = \$16,592 + \$146,983 = \$163,575 Cost of goods sold = \$163,575 − \$18,096 = \$145,479
Vertical analysis of an income statement	459	Divide each amount on the income statement by the net sales amount. Express the quotient as a percent, rounded to the nearest tenth of a percent.	*Percent of Net Sales* Net sales \$38,000 100.0% Cost of goods sold 25,000 65.8% Gross profit 13,000 34.2% Operating expenses 7,000 18.4% Net income \$ 6,000 15.8%

Use the following information to calculate the indicated ratio. current assets, \$40,000; current liabilities, \$28,000; cash, \$15,892; marketable securities, \$10,000; receivables, \$7,486; cost of goods sold, \$146,800; net sales, \$179,500; gross profit, \$32,700; operating expenses, \$18,500; net income, \$14,200.

Topic	Page	What to Remember	Examples
Current ratio	462–463	$\text{Current ratio} = \dfrac{\text{current assets}}{\text{current liabilities}}$	$\dfrac{\$40{,}000}{\$28{,}000} = 1.42 \text{ to } 1$
Acid-test ratio (quick ratio)	464	Acid-test ratio $= \dfrac{\text{quick current assets}}{\text{current liabilities}}$ Quick current assets are cash, marketable securities, and receivables.	$\dfrac{\$15{,}892 + \$10{,}000 + \$7{,}486}{\$28{,}000} = 1.19 \text{ to } 1$
Operating ratio	465	Operating ratio $= \dfrac{\text{cost of goods sold} + \text{operating expenses}}{\text{net sales}}$	$\dfrac{\$146{,}800 + \$18{,}500}{\$179{,}500} = 0.921 \text{ or } 92.1\%$
Gross profit margin ratio	465	Gross profit margin ratio $= \dfrac{\text{net sales} - \text{cost of goods sold}}{\text{net sales}}$	$\dfrac{\$179{,}500 - \$146{,}800}{\$179{,}500} = 0.182 \text{ or } 18.2\%$

1. Complete the horizontal analysis on the comparative balance sheet for Kurt's Classy Cookies. (Use parentheses to indicate decreases.)

Kurt's Classy Cookies
Comparative Balance Sheet
December 31, 19X8 and 19X9

			Increase or Decrease	
	19X9	**19X8**	**Amount**	**Percent**
Assets				
Current assets:				
Cash	$ 3,462	$ 2,816		
Accounts receivable	1,586	1,821		
Merchandise inventory	4,216	4,073		
Total current assets				
Plant and equipment:				
Equipment	8,935	7,314		
Total plant and equipment				
Total Assets				
Liabilities				
Current liabilities:				
Accounts payable	6,215	3,816		
Salaries payable	396	1,203		
Total Current Liabilities				
Long-term liabilities:				
Mortgage note payable	724	707		
Total Long-Term Liabilities				
Total Liabilities				
Owner's Equity				
Kurt Johnson, Capital	$ 10,864	$ 10,298		
Total Liabilities and Owner's Equity				

2. Complete the income statement below.

Frank Cifaldi's Sport Shop Income Statement For the month ending June 30, 19X3	
Revenue:	
Gross sales	$49,943
Sales returns and allowances	2,087
Net sales	
Cost of goods sold:	
Beginning inventory, June 1, 19X3	14,812
Purchases	31,503
Ending inventory, June 30, 19X3	15,019
Cost of goods sold	
Gross Profit from Sales	
Operating expenses:	
Salary	1,307
Insurance	412
Utilities	183
Rent	290
Depreciation	400
Total operating expenses	
Net Income	

3. Complete the vertical analysis of the income statement below.

Frank Cifaldi's Sport Shop Income Statement For the year ending December 31, 19X3		
		Percent of Net Sales
Revenue:		
Gross sales	$289,521	
Sales returns and allowances	7,097	
Net sales		
Cost of goods sold:		
Beginning inventory, January 1, 19X3	9,572	
Purchases	117,097	
Ending inventory, December 31, 19X3	12,521	
Cost of goods sold		
Gross Profit from Sales		
Operating expenses:		
Salary	25,093	
Insurance	4,092	
Utilities	2,500	
Rent	4,200	
Depreciation	4,800	
Total operating expenses		
Net Income		

4. Complete the horizontal analysis of the comparative income statement below.

Ben's Fences
Comparative Income Statement
For years ending August 31, 19X2 and 19X3

	19X3	19X2	Increase or Decrease Amount	Percent
Revenue:				
Gross sales	$70,220	$59,786		
Sales returns and allowances	2,103	2,250		
Net sales	$68,117	$57,536		
Cost of goods sold:				
Beginning inventory	$12,521	$ 7,592		
Purchases	38,912	33,814		
Ending inventory	8,286	8,192		
Cost of goods sold	$43,147	$33,214		
Gross Profit from Sales	$24,970	$24,322		
Operating expenses:				
Salary	$13,500	$13,000		
Insurance	1,000	800		
Utilities	500	490		
Rent	1,200	1,200		
Depreciation	3,000	2,500		
Total operating expenses	$19,200	$17,990		
Net Income	$ 5,770	$ 6,332		

5. Find the current ratio for Kurt's Classy Cookies in Exercise 1.

6. Find the acid-test ratio for Kurt's Classy Cookies.

7. If you were a banker, would you approve a loan for Kurt's Classy Cookies?

8. Find the monthly operating ratio for Frank Cifaldi's Sport Shop.

9. Find the gross profit margin ratio for Frank Cifaldi's Sport Shop in Exercise 2.

Trial Test

1. Complete the horizontal analysis of the following comparative balance sheet. Express percents to the nearest tenth of a percent.

Morris Hardware Store
Comparative Balance Sheet
December 31, 19X6 and 19X7

	19X7	19X6	Increase or (Decrease) Amount	Increase or (Decrease) Percent
Assets				
Current assets:				
Cash	$ 7,318	$ 5,283		
Accounts receivable	3,147	3,008		
Merchandise inventory	63,594	60,187		
Total current assets	74,059	68,478		
Plant and equipment:				
Building	36,561	37,531		
Equipment	8,256	4,386		
Total plant and equipment				
Total Assets				
Liabilities				
Current liabilities:				
Accounts payable	5,174	4,563		
Wages payable	780	624		
Total current liabilities				
Long-term liabilities:				
Mortgage note payable	34,917	36,510		
Total long-term liabilities				
Total Liabilities				
Owner's Equity				
James Morris, Capital	$ 78,005	$ 68,698		
Total Liabilities and Owner's Equity				

2. Find the current ratio to the nearest hundredth for 19X7 on the Morris Hardware Store.

3. Find the acid-test ratio to the nearest hundredth for 19X7 on the Morris Hardware Store.

4. Find the current ratio to the nearest hundredth for 19X6 on the Morris Hardware Store.

5. Find the acid-test ratio to the nearest hundredth for 19X6 on the Morris Hardware Store.

6. Complete the horizontal analysis of the following comparative income statement.

The Jackson Company
Comparative Income Statement
For years ending December 31, 19X6 and 19X7

	19X7	19X6	Increase (Decrease) Amount	Increase (Decrease) Percent
Revenue:				
Gross sales	$219,827	$205,852		
Sales returns and allowances	8,512	7,983		
Net sales	211,315			
Cost of goods sold:				
Beginning inventory, January 1	42,816	40,512		
Purchases	97,523	94,812		
Ending inventory, December 31	43,182	42,521		
Cost of goods sold	97,157			
Gross Profit from Sales	114,158			
Operating expenses:				
Salary	28,940	27,000		
Insurance	800	750		
Utilities	1,700	1,580		
Rent	3,600	3,000		
Depreciation	2,000	2,400		
Total operating expenses	37,040			
Net Income	$ 77,118			

7. Find the operating ratio for the Jackson Company for 19X6 and 19X7.

8. Find the gross profit margin ratio for the Jackson Company for 19X7.

1.

Maddy's Muffins
Comparative Balance Sheet
December 31, 19X8 and 19X9

	19X9	19X8	Increase or Decrease Amount	Percent
Assets				
Current assets:				
Cash	$1,985	$1,762	$ 223	12.7
Accounts receivable	4,219	3,785	434	11.5
Merchandise inventory	2,512	2,036	476	23.4
Total current assets	8,716	7,583	1,133	14.9
Plant and equipment:				
Equipment				
Total plant and equipment				
Total Assets	8,716	7,583	1,133	14.9
Liabilities				
Current liabilities:				
Accounts payable	3,483	3,631	(148)	(4.1)
Wages payable	1,696	1,421	275	19.4
Total current liabilities	5,179	5,052	127	2.5
Long-term liabilities:				
Mortgage note payable				
Total long-term liabilities				
Total Liabilities	5,179	5,052	127	2.5
Owner's Equity				
Maddy Engman, Capital	3,537	2,541	996	39.2
Total Liabilities and Owner's Equity	$8,716	$7,593	$1,123	14.8

2.

Jones Grocery
Income Statement
For the years ending June 30, 19X8 and 19X9

	19X9	19X8	Increase (Decrease) Amount	Percent
Net sales	$97,384	$92,196	$ 5,188	5.6
Cost of goods sold	82,157	72,894	9,263	12.7
Gross profits	15,227	19,302	(4,075)	(21.1)
Operating expenses	4,783	3,951	832	21.1
Net income	$10,444	$15,351	(4,907)	(32.0)

3. $$\text{Current ratio (Company X)} = \frac{\text{current assets}}{\text{current liabilities}} = \frac{28{,}000}{7{,}000} = 4 \text{ or } 4:1.$$

$$\text{Current ratio (Company Y)} = \frac{840{,}000}{819{,}000} = 1.03 \text{ or } 1.03:1$$

4. $$\text{Acid-test ratio} = \frac{\text{quick current assets}}{\text{current liabilities}} = \frac{32{,}981 + 12{,}045}{22{,}178} = \frac{45{,}026}{22{,}178}$$

$$= 2.03 \text{ or } 2.03 \text{ to } 1$$

Insurance 16

Learning Objectives

1. Understand how fire insurance premiums are determined and calculate annual and monthly insurance premium amounts. (pp. 477–480)
2. Understand what factors determine motor vehicle insurance rates. (pp. 483–484)
3. Calculate the cost of motor vehicle insurance, using tables. (pp. 483–484)
4. Understand the differences between the various types of life insurance. (pp. 487–488)
5. Use tables to calculate the annual, monthly, quarterly, or semiannual premium for life insurance. (pp. 488–489)

Insurance is a form of protection against unexpected financial loss. Businesses and individuals need insurance to help bear the burden of a large financial loss. Insurance helps distribute the burden of financial loss among those who share the same type of risk. Many types of insurance are available, such as fire, life, homeowner's, health, accident, automobile, and others.

Before looking at specific types of insurance, important terms used in the insurance field need to be defined.

Insured (policyholder)	The individual, organization, or business that carries the insurance or financial protection against loss.
Insurer (underwriter)	The insurance company or carrier that assures payment for a specific loss according to contract provisions.
Policy	The contract between the insurer and the insured.
Premium	The amount paid by the insured for the protection provided by the policy.
Face value	The amount of insurance provided by the policy.
Beneficiary	The person to whom the proceeds of the policy are payable.

Fire Insurance

Fire insurance provides protection against fire losses or losses that may result directly from attempts to extinguish a fire, such as damage caused by water and chemical extinguishers, and damage to property by firefighters.

fire insurance: insurance that covers fire losses and losses that occur in trying to fight a fire, such as from water, from chemical extinguishers, and from firefighters.

Rates for fire insurance vary according to several factors, such as type of structure, location, nearness to the fire department, rating given by the fire department, water supply, and fire hazards. Most states have developed a system for classifying rates according to these factors; for example, a Class A building might be made of brick instead of wood. Or, the contents of the building might be resistant to fire damage, such as bags of cement, rather than fabric, which would be much more flammable (easily burned). Table 16-1 shows a sample classification system. The area ratings in the left column are based on how close the buildings are to a fire station and how easy access is to the building and its contents.

Table 16-1 Annual Fire Insurance Rates per $100

	Building Classification					
	Class A		Class B		Class C	
Area Rating	Building	Contents	Building	Contents	Building	Contents
1	$0.25	$0.32	$0.37	$0.48	$0.46	$0.51
2	$0.31	$0.45	$0.47	$0.57	$0.55	$0.76
3	$0.38	$0.48	$0.57	$0.63	$0.63	$0.80

As you can see from Table 16-1, insurance rates are expressed as an annual amount per $100 of coverage. To find the annual premium, divide the amount of coverage by $100 and multiply by the rate in the table. Do this for both building and contents.

Step by Step

Calculating the Annual Insurance Premium Amount

Step 1. Find the correct rate in the table for the building being insured, and use the following formula:

$$\text{Annual premium} = \frac{\text{amount of coverage}}{\$100} \times \text{rate}$$

Step 2. Find the correct rate in the table for contents of the building, and use same formula as in step 1.

EXAMPLE 1

A building is insured for $85,000 and the contents of the building are insured for $50,000. If it is a Class B building located in Area 2, find the annual premium for building and contents.

Step 1.

Annual premium for building

$$= \frac{\text{amount of coverage}}{\$100} \times \text{rate}$$

$$= \frac{\$85{,}000}{\$100} \times \$0.47 = \$399.50$$

Look up the amount of premium for a building that is classified as Class B in Area 2. The rate is $0.47. Multiply the rate times $85,000 divided by $100. The answer is $399.50.

Step 2.

Annual premium for contents

$$= \frac{\text{amount of coverage}}{\$100} \times \text{rate}$$

$$= \frac{\$50{,}000}{\$100} \times \$0.57 = \$285$$

Look up the amount of premium for contents classified as Class B in Area 2. The rate is $0.57. Multiply $0.57 times $50,000 divided by $100. The answer is $285.

The annual premium for the building is $399.50 and for its contents, the premium is $285.

Coinsurance

Because a fire rarely destroys a whole building or all its contents, many businesses take out policies that cover only a portion of the value of the building or its contents. They thus save money on premiums by having coverage of only 40% of their property's value, for example; if there were a fire, it might not destroy more than 40% of their property.

Insurance companies countered this with a plan that encouraged businesses to take out full insurance coverage. This plan, which is added to many fire insurance policies, is called a **coinsurance clause;** it means that the insured gets full protection (or compensation *up to* the face value of the policy) from the insurance company only if the property is insured for 80% of its replacement value. If the policy covers only 40% of the value, then the insured and the insurance company share the loss—the insured does not get full protection.

coinsurance clause: clause added to many fire insurance policies; says that insured gets full protection up to the face value of the policy from the company only if the property is insured for 80% of its value.

The following box shows how to figure how much the insurance company will pay if your policy has a coinsurance clause in it and you do not have full coverage.

Step by Step

Calculating Compensation with a Coinsurance Clause

Step 1. Determine how much insurance the coinsurance clause requires you to carry by multiplying 0.8 times the replacement value of your property.

Step 2. Use this formula to figure compensation:

$$\text{Compensation} = \text{amount of loss up to face value of insurance} \times \frac{\text{amount of insurance policy}}{\text{80\% of replacement value of property}}$$

EXAMPLE 2

Gregory Low owns a building valued at $200,000. He has a fire insurance policy with an 80% coinsurance clause, which has a face value of $130,000. There is a fire, and the building damage is figured to be $50,000. Find what the insurance company will pay as compensation.

Step 1. To find out if Gregory carries as much insurance as his coinsurance clause requires, multiply: 0.8 × $200,000 = $160,000. Gregory has a policy worth only $130,000, so he does not get full compensation.

Step 2. Use the formula to find the compensation:

$$\text{Compensation} = \$50{,}000 \times \frac{\$130{,}000}{\$160{,}000} = \$40{,}625$$

Gregory receives $40,625 compensation for his loss of $50,000.

If Gregory had carried a policy for 80% of the replacement value of his property, he would have gotten $\$50{,}000 \times \frac{160{,}000}{160{,}000} = \$50{,}000$ compensation for his loss.

TIPS & TRAPS

When calculating the amount of compensation an insurance company will pay if the policy has a coinsurance clause, the compensation for the amount of loss can be no more than the face value of the policy, regardless of the actual dollar value of the loss.

Terry McLean has insured his shop for 80% of the replacement value. The replacement value of the shop is $105,000. A fire causes $90,000 worth of damage to the property. How much compensation will Terry receive from the insurance company?

$0.8 \times \$105{,}000 = \$84{,}000$ face value of policy

WRONG	CORRECT
~~$\$90{,}000 \times \frac{\$84{,}000}{\$84{,}000} = \$90{,}000$~~	$\$84{,}000 \times \frac{\$84{,}000}{\$84{,}000} = \$84{,}000$

Compensation cannot exceed face value of policy.

Self-Check

1. Find the annual fire insurance premium on a Class A building located in Area 3 if the building is insured for $120,000 and its contents are insured for $75,000.
2. a. A Class C building and its contents are located in Area 1 and are insured for $150,000 and $68,000, respectively. Find the total annual insurance premium.
   b. If a 2% charge is added to the annual premium when payments are made semiannually, how much would semiannual payments be?
3. a. The market value of a building is $255,000. It has been insured for $204,000 in a fire insurance policy with an 80% coinsurance clause. What part of a loss due to fire will the insurance company pay?
   b. If a fire causes damages of $75,000, what is the amount of compensation?
4. A building valued at $295,000 is insured in a policy that contains an 80% coinsurance clause. The face value of the policy is $100,000. If the building is a total loss, what is the amount of compensation?

Section Review

Using Table 16-1, find the annual fire insurance premium for each of the following.

	Area Rating	Class	Building Coverage	Contents Coverage	Annual Premium Building	Annual Premium Contents
1.	3	A	$72,000	$26,000		
2.	1	C	$38,000	$21,000		
3.	2	B	$116,000	$41,700		
4.	2	A	$78,500	$32,300		
5.	3	C	$105,000	$63,500		

The following policies include an 80% coinsurance clause. A fire has caused the given amount of damage. Determine the amount to be paid by the insurance company.

	Value of Building	Face Value of Policy	Will the Owner Receive Full Compensation?	Amount of Damage	Amount Paid
6.	$105,600	$ 84,480		$17,000	
7.	$ 95,800	$ 72,300		$22,000	
8.	$131,300	$105,040		$65,000	
9.	$261,500	$115,500		$85,000	
10.	$ 76,400	$ 61,120		$65,000	

Use Table 16-1 when necessary to solve the following problems.

11. A sign company owns a Class A building in Area 2 valued at $95,000. The building is insured for $60,000 and the policy has an 80% coinsurance clause. How much will the owner of the sign company receive from his policy if a fire causes $38,000 in damages?

12. What part of the damages will Hampton Insurance Company pay on a building damaged by fire if the market value is $86,000 and it is insured for $68,800? The policy contains an 80% coinsurance clause.

13. Karla Jones insures her Class B building located in Area 3 for $60,000 and the contents for $35,000. Find the total annual insurance premium.

14. In Area 1, a Class C building is insured for $105,000 and its contents for $55,000. If no extra charge is added for semiannual payments, find the premium paid every 6 months.

15. The Country Store is valued at $73,500. To satisfy the 80% coinsurance clause of the policy, for how much should the owner insure the building?

16. a. John Long owns a building with a market value of $121,300. He has insured the building for $85,800. A fire has caused $52,370 in damages. How much will the insurance company pay as compensation, if his policy contains an 80% coinsurance clause?

b. If he had insured the building for 80% of its value, how much compensation would he receive?

17. Find the total annual premium for a Class A building in Area 1 if it is worth $85,000 and its contents are worth $23,200.

18. How much must the insured pay on a building worth $65,700 if it receives fire damages totaling $17,000? The building is insured for $50,000 and the fire insurance policy contains an 80% coinsurance clause.

19. a. The Greenwood Rental building is worth $86,900. The building is a Class A building in Area 3. What is the annual fire insurance premium on the building and its contents, which are valued at $32,000?

b. If the premium can be paid semiannually with a 2% annual charge added, what is the amount to be paid every 6 months?

20. Harry's Plumbing Company is in a building worth $75,000. Harry has insured the building for $50,000 with a policy containing an 80% coinsurance clause. Fire loss is found to be $37,500.

a. How much will the insurance company pay for the loss?

b. How much of the loss must he pay?

Motor Vehicle Insurance

Motor vehicle insurance is a major expense item for individuals and businesses because of the high risk of personal injury or death and damage to property. Insurance for motor vehicles may be purchased to protect the individual or business from several risks. These include liability for personal injury and property damage, damage or loss to the insured vehicle and its occupants caused by a collision, damage or loss to the insured vehicle caused by theft, fire, flooding, and other incidents that may not be related to a collision. These types of insurance generally fall into three types of insurance: liability, comprehensive, and collision.

Liability insurance protects the insured from losses incurred in a vehicle accident resulting in personal injury or property damage if the accident is the fault of the insured or his or her designated driver.

Comprehensive insurance protects the insured's vehicle for damage caused by fire, theft, vandalism, and other risks, such as falling debris, storm damage, or road hazards such as rocks.

Collision insurance protects the insured's vehicle for damage (both personal and property) caused by an automobile accident in which the driver of the insured vehicle is *not* at fault. This type of insurance is used when the driver of the vehicle that is at fault does not have insurance coverage.

Some states have **no-fault insurance** programs. In these states each person involved in an accident submits a claim for personal and property damages to his or her own insurance company if the amount is under a certain stated maximum. This does not mean the person cannot sue for additional compensation if the damage is above the stated maximum.

motor vehicle insurance: includes liability, comprehensive, and collision insurance for the owners of motor vehicles.

liability insurance: protects the owner of a vehicle if an accident causes personal injury or property damage and is the fault of the insured or the insured's designated driver.

comprehensive insurance: protects the insured's vehicle for damage caused by fire, theft, vandalism, and other risks that do not involve another vehicle.

collision insurance: covers the insured's vehicle for damage caused by an accident that is *not* the insured's fault.

no-fault insurance: program in a number of states that allows each person involved in an accident to submit a claim for damages to his or her own insurance company if the amount is under a certain stated maximum.

Determining the Cost of Automobile Insurance

Factors that affect the cost of automobile insurance include the location of the vehicle (large city, small town, rural area, etc.); the total distance traveled per year and the distance traveled to work each day; the types of use (pleasure, traveling to and from work, strictly business, etc.); the driving record and training of the insured driver(s); the academic grades of

Table 16-2 Annual Automobile Liability Insurance Premiums

Territory	Driver Class	Bodily Injury			Property Damage		
		20/40	50/100	100/300	5	10	25
1	A	$140	$155	$170	$132	$140	$143
	B	155	168	185	145	155	159
	C	163	177	198	152	163	168
2	A	167	178	189	158	167	177
	B	176	187	199	168	179	189
	C	198	210	225	196	208	218

drivers who are still in school; the age and sex of the insured driver(s); the type and age of the vehicle; and the amount of coverage desired.

Table 16-2 shows a hypothetical annual rate schedule for liability insurance. Notice that there are several columns of information. The *territory* refers to the type of area where the car is kept and driven. The *driver class* refers to such personal information about the driver as age, sex, or marital status. The 20/40 under the Bodily Injury heading means the insurance company will pay up to $20,000 for bodily injury of one individual in an accident and no more than a total of $40,000 per accident for bodily injury, regardless of the number of individuals injured in the accident. The 5 10 25 under the Property Damage heading indicates that the insurance company will pay up to $5,000, $10,000, and $25,000, respectively, for damage to the property of others. This may include other vehicles involved in the accident or property such as fences, buildings, and the like.

EXAMPLE 3

Use Table 16-2 to find the annual premium for an automobile liability insurance policy in which the insured lives in Territory 1, is Class A, and wishes to have 50/100/10 coverage.

The cost of 50/100 bodily injury coverage for Territory 1 and Class A is $155. The cost of $10,000 property damage insurance in this same category is $140. Therefore, the total cost of the insurance package is $155 + $140 = $295.

deductible amount: the insured must pay a certain amount before the insurance company will begin to pay.

Insurance tables for collision insurance are set up much the same way as Table 16-2. However, these policies usually include a *deductible clause,* which means the insured must pay a certain specified amount (the **deductible amount**) before the insurance company will begin to pay.

Self-Check

5. Find the annual premium for an automobile liability insurance policy if the insured lives in Territory 2 and is classified as a Class C driver. The policy contains 20/40/5 coverage.
6. Compare the annual premium on a 50/100/10 policy for a Class C driver in Territory 1 to a policy with the same coverage in Territory 2.
7. What are the monthly payments on an automobile liability insurance policy for a Class B driver in Territory 1 with 50/100/25 coverage?

8. How much will an automobile liability insurance policy pay an injured person with medical expenses of $8,362 if the insured has a policy with 20/40/5 coverage? How much must the insured pay the injured party?

Section Review

Use Table 16-2 to find the total annual premium for each of the following automobile liability insurance policies.

	Territory	Driver Class	Coverage	Total Annual Premium
1.	1	B	20/40/5	
2.	2	A	50/100/10	
3.	1	C	100/300/25	
4.	2	B	50/100/25	
5.	2	C	50/100/10	

Use Table 16-2 to solve the following problems.

6. a. Explain what an insurance policy with 50/100/25 coverage means.

b. If you live in Territory 1 and you are classified as a Class A driver, what would be the total cost of the annual premium for this policy?

7. If Louise Gonzales is a Class C driver and lives in Territory 1, what is her annual automobile liability insurance premium if she chooses $100,000 for bodily injury to one individual with $300,000 total bodily injury and $10,000 for property damage?

8. The company car for the Greenwood Rental Agency in Territory 2 for a Class C driver is insured with 50/100/25 coverage. What is the annual insurance premium?

9. If you have an accident that damages a fence, up to what amount would your automobile liability insurance policy pay if you have 20/40/10 coverage?

10. Larry Tremont has a collision insurance policy with a $200 deductible clause. If he hits a tree and causes $876 in damages to his car, how much must he pay and how much will the insurance company pay for his damages?

11. Sally Greenspan would like to buy a no-fault insurance policy for $20,000 and an uninsured motorist policy worth $25,000. The cost is $4.50 per $1,000 for the no-fault insurance and $3.50 per $1,000 for the uninsured motorist coverage. What is Sally's total annual coverage?

12. Fred Casey has an auto liability insurance policy with 20/40/10 coverage. He has an accident in which Sara Lovette, riding in another car, is injured. Her medical expenses totaled $36,243 and the damages to her car totaled $4,756. What is the total amount Fred's insurance will pay?

13. As a Class A driver in Territory 1, Laura Jansky is buying an auto liability insurance policy with 100/300/25 coverage. She would like to pay the premium quarterly. Her insurance agent has explained that a $3.50 charge is added to the quarterly payments.

a. How much would her quarterly payments be?

b. How much has she paid at the end of the year?

14. John Colding has auto liability insurance with 20/40/10 coverage. In an accident for which John is responsible, he injures a young couple. The husband has medical expenses of $23,268, and his wife's expenses are $21,764. Damage to their car totaled $2,769. How much will the insurer pay? How much will the insured pay?

15. Jeff Easley is a Class A driver living in Territory 1. He has auto liability insurance with 50/100/10 coverage. He is in an accident in which a young woman is injured and has medical expenses of $55,452. Her car has $5,678 in damages.

a. What is Jeff's annual premium?

b. How much will Jeff's insurance company pay the young woman for her medical expenses and the damages to her car?

Life insurance is a type of insurance that provides financial assistance to the surviving dependents of the insured person, in the event of the insured person's death. Several types of life insurance policies are available, some of which even function as savings reserves. In this section, we will look at four types of life insurance policies in common use: term, straight life, limited-payment, and endowment.

life insurance: a type of insurance that makes a payment to the surviving beneficiary of the insured person, in the event of his or her death.

Term Insurance

Term insurance is purchased for a certain period of time, such as 5, 10, or 20 years. For example, under a 10-year term policy, the insured pays premiums for 10 years or until he or she dies, whichever occurs first. If the insured dies during the 10-year period, the beneficiary of the policy would receive the face value of the policy. If the insured is still living at the end of the 10-year period, he or she will no longer be insured, and the policy has no cash value. The insured can then renew the policy, but at a higher rate than paid before. Term insurance is the least expensive type of life insurance, and most companies will allow policyholders to convert to other types of insurance without an additional physical examination.

term insurance: a type of life insurance that is purchased for a certain period of time, such as 5 or 10 years, and then must be renewed after that. Least expensive type of life insurance.

Straight-Life (Ordinary Life) Insurance

Under a **straight-life (ordinary life) insurance** policy, the insured agrees to pay premiums for his or her entire life. At the time of the insured's death, the beneficiary will receive the face value of the policy. This type of policy builds up a cash value. If the insured cancels the policy, he or she is entitled to a certain sum of money back, depending upon the amount that was paid in. The difference between term and straight-life insurance is that a straight-life policy has a cash value, whereas a term policy does not.

straight-life (ordinary life) insurance: a type of life insurance in which the insured agrees to pay premiums for his or her entire life. At the time of the insured's death, the beneficiary will receive the face value of the policy. Straight-life insurance policy builds up a cash value.

Limited-Payment Insurance

Limited-payment life insurance is another type of policy that provides permanent life protection. The difference between straight-life and limited-payment life is that the limited-payment policyholder pays premiums for a fixed period of time. After the fixed period of time (usually 20 or 30 years), the policyholder no longer makes payments but is insured for the rest of his or her life. Naturally this type of insurance is more expensive than straight-life insurance, since the policyholder pays premiums for a shorter period of time.

limited-payment insurance: a type of life insurance that provides permanent life protection, but the insured pays premiums for a fixed period of time, such as 20 years.

Endowment Insurance

endowment insurance: a type of life insurance that is really an insured savings plan. Premiums are paid for fixed period of time, and then the insured receives the cash value of the policy, which is equal to the face value, and the insurance expires.

The **endowment insurance** policy is the most expensive type of policy. Endowment insurance is really an insured savings plan. Premiums are paid for a fixed period of time; at the end of that time, the cash value is equal to the face value of the policy, and the insurance expires. The insured can re-

Table 16-3 Annual premium rates per $1,000 of life insurance

Age	5-year Term Male	5-year Term Female	Straight-life Male	Straight-life Female	20-year Life (Limited Payment) Male	20-year Life (Limited Payment) Female	20-year Endowment Male	20-year Endowment Female
20	4.43	4.32	10.91	10.03	18.34	17.04	20.61	20.19
30	4.88	4.68	14.97	13.53	23.82	21.96	27.68	26.98
40	7.32	6.17	21.88	19.41	31.91	29.45	41.07	39.75
50	14.03	11.57	33.68	27.44	43.97	39.78	72.24	70.15
60	29.40	23.25	54.50	46.93	63.96	56.70	—	—

ceive the money as a lump-sum payment or in monthly payments. If the insured dies before the end of the fixed period, the beneficiary receives the face value of the policy.

Table 16-3 shows typical rates for the four types of policies that have been discussed.

Step by Step

Calculating the Annual Premium

Step 1. Look up the annual premium rate in Table 16-3.

Step 2. Multiply the rate from Step 1 times the amount of coverage divided by $1,000:

$$\text{Annual premium} = \frac{\text{amount of coverage}}{\$1{,}000} \times \text{rate}$$

EXAMPLE 4

Find the annual premium of an insurance policy with a face value of $25,000 for a 30-year-old male for: (a) a 5-year term policy; (b) a straight-life policy; (c) a 20-year life policy, and (d) a 20-year endowment.

Annual premium

$$= \frac{\text{amount of coverage}}{\$1{,}000} \times \text{rate}$$

Multiply the rate per $1,000 of coverage times 25 to find the annual premium for each policy.

$$= \frac{\$25{,}000}{\$1{,}000} \times \text{rate} = 25 \times \text{rate}$$

Look in Table 16-3 to find the rate for each type of policy.

a. 5-year term policy: 25 × $4.88 = $122
b. Straight-life policy: 25 × $14.97 = $374.25
c. 20-year policy: 25 × $23.82 = $595.50
d. 20-year endowment: 25 × $27.68 = $692

Calculator Sequence

The calculator sequence is a simple multiplication application. The memory function can be used to store the number 25 so that it does not have to be reentered each time.

[AC] 25 [M+] [×] 4.88 [=] ⇒ 122

[CE/C] [MRC] [×] 14.97 [=] ⇒ 374.25

[CE/C] [MRC] [×] 23.82 [=] ⇒ 595.5

[CE/C] [MRC] [×] 27.68 [=] ⇒ 692

Since it is often inconvenient to make large annual payments, most companies allow payments to be made semiannually (twice a year), quarterly (every three months), or monthly for slightly higher rates than would apply on an annual basis. Table 16-4 shows some typical rates for periods of less than 1 year.

Table 16-4 Rates for Less than 1-year Period

Semiannual, 51% of annual prem.
Quarterly, 26% of annual prem.
Monthly, 8.75% of annual prem.

EXAMPLE 5

Use Tables 16-3 and 16-4 to find the (a) semiannual, (b) quarterly, and (c) monthly premiums for a \$30,000 straight-life policy on a 40-year-old female.

Annual premium

$$= \frac{\text{amount of coverage}}{\$1{,}000} \times \text{rate}$$

Multiply the rate per \$1,000 of coverage times 30 to find the annual premium. Find the correct rate in Table 16-3.

$$= \frac{\$30{,}000}{\$1{,}000} \times \text{rate}$$

$$= 30 \times \$19.41 = \$582.30$$

a. Semiannual premium:
$\$582.30 \times 51\%$
$= \$582.30 \times 0.51 = \$296.97$

Annual premium × semiannual rate = semiannual premium

b. Quarterly premium:
$\$582.30 \times 26\%$
$= \$582.30 \times 0.26 = \$151.40$

Annual premium × quarterly rate = quarterly premium

c. Monthly premium:
$\$582.30 \times 8.75\%$
$= \$582.30 \times 0.0875 = \$50.95$

Annual premium × monthly rate = monthly premium

Calculator Sequence

Again, the calculator sequence is a simple multiplication (after converting the percent to a decimal). The memory function can be used to store \$582.30.

[AC] 582.3 [M+] [×] .51 [=] ⇒ 296.973

[CE/C] [MRC] [×] .26 [=] ⇒ 151.398

[CE/C] [MRC] [×] 0.0875 [=] ⇒ 50.95125

Self-Check

Use Tables 16-3 and 16-4 to solve each of the following.

9. Find the annual premium for an insurance policy with a face value of \$45,000 for a 20-year-old female for each of the following policies:
   a. 5-year term
   b. Straight-life
   c. 20-year life
   d. 20-year endowment

10. What are the quarterly payments on a \$50,000 20-year life insurance policy for a 30-year-old male?

11. What are the monthly payments on a \$5,000 straight-life insurance policy for a 50-year-old male?

12. Compare a 5-year term policy for \$75,000 for a 40-year-old male to the same policy for a 40-year-old female. Make the same comparison for a 60-year-old male and female.

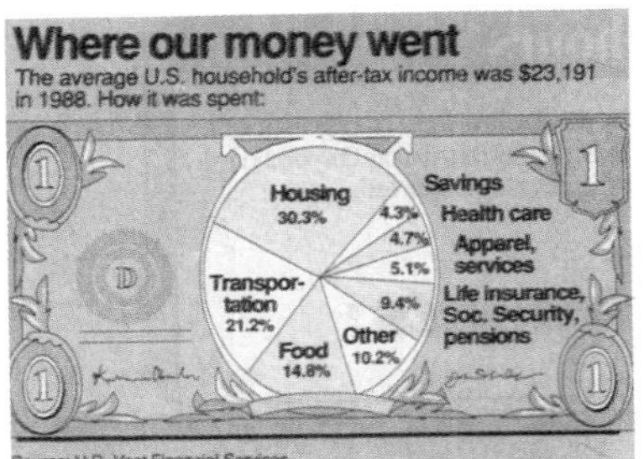

By John Sherlock, USA TODAY

Real World Application

REAL LIFE APPLICATION

A universal life insurance policy is a relatively new type of life insurance in which the company invests the cash value of your policy and gives you a certain percent of the returns on their investments. An annual report, similar to the portion shown below, shows the amount of cash value, the face value of the policy, and the interest earned. Locate the following amounts on the report.

Application Questions

1. How much are the death benefits of this policy?

2. How much are the monthly premiums?

3. What is the total cash value of the policy?

4. What is the total interest credited?

5. What is the guaranteed interest rate for the cash value accumulation?

DEATH BENEFIT—CURRENT OPTION 1 – LEVEL
BEG. OF YEAR: 60,000.00
END OF YEAR : 60,000.00
CURRENT SPECIFIED AMOUNT 60,000.00

SOC. SEC. NUMBER :
CASH VALUE
END OF PRIOR YEAR: 650.92
IMPAIRED BY LOANS : 0.00

SUMMARY OF ACTIVITY FOR POLICY YEAR ENDING 03/04/89

MONTH BEGIN	GROSS PREMIUM	LOADING	COST OF INSUR	EXPENSE CHARGES	INTEREST(4) CREDITED	PARTIAL WTHDRWL	LOAN(5) ACTIVITY	CASH VALUE
03/04	35.00	2.80	8.08	0.00	4.89	0.00	0.00	679.93
04/04	35.00	2.80	8.07	0.00	5.10	0.00	0.00	709.16
05/04	35.00	2.80	8.07	0.00	5.30	0.00	0.00	738.59
06/04	35.00	2.80	8.07	0.00	5.52	0.00	0.00	768.24
07/04	35.00	2.80	8.06	0.00	5.72	0.00	0.00	798.10
08/04	35.00	2.80	8.06	0.00	5.92	0.00	0.00	828.16
09/04	35.00	2.80	8.05	0.00	6.13	0.00	0.00	858.44
10/04	35.00	2.80	8.05	0.00	6.34	0.00	0.00	888.93
11/04	35.00	2.80	8.05	0.00	6.58	0.00	0.00	919.66
12/04	35.00	2.80	8.04	0.00	6.70	0.00	0.00	950.52
01/04	35.00	2.80	8.04	0.00	7.02	0.00	0.00	981.70
02/04	35.00	2.80	8.03	0.00	7.29	0.00	0.00	1013.16
TOT	420.00	33.60	(3) 96.67	0.00	(1) 72.51	(2) 0.00		

NEGATIVE VALUES INDICATE THAT PREMIUM WAS NOT PAID PRIOR TO THE CONTRACT'S ISSUE DATE OR MONTHLY ANNIVERSARY DATE. SUBSEQUENT PREMIUM PAYMENTS INCREASE THESE VALUES.

POLICY VALUES AS OF 03/04/89:
CASH VALUE: 1,013.16
UNPAID LOANS: 0.00
POLICY SURRENDER CHARGES: 0.00
POLICY SURRENDER VALUE: 1,013.16
(3)RIDER CHARGES INCLUDED: 0.00

(1)INTEREST CREDITED—
GUARANTEED PORTION: 34.32
EXCESS PORTION: 38.19
(2)PARTIAL WITHDRAWAL CHARGES
INCLUDED IN ABOVE: 0.00

(4)CURRENT ANNUAL INTEREST RATE SCHEDULE APPLICABLE TO CASH VALUE ACCUMULATION:

TYPE CASH VALUE ACCUMULATED	RATE
PRIMARY, UNIMPAIRED BY LOANS	9.000
IMPAIRED BY POLICY LOANS	4.500

(5)THE CURRENT LOAN INTEREST RATE IS 8.000% PAYABLE IN ARREARS.
THE DEATH BENEFIT IS REDUCED BY ANY OUTSTANDING LOAN BALANCE.

THE GUARANTEED INTEREST RATE FOR THE LIFE OF THE POLICY IS 4.500%
YOUR PLANNED PERIODIC PREMIUM IS 35.00 PAID MONTHLY.

Section Review

Use Table 16-3 to find the annual premium of each of the following life insurance policies.

	Sex	Age	Policy	Coverage	Annual Premium
1.	Male	20	5-year term	$30,000	
2.	Male	30	5-year term	$90,000	
3.	Female	20	Straight-life	$60,000	
4.	Male	50	Straight-life	$100,000	
5.	Female	40	20-year life	$100,000	

Use Tables 16-3 and 16-4 to find the following premiums.

	Sex	Age	Policy	Coverage	Annual	Payments Monthly	Payments Quarterly
6.	Female	60	Straight-life	$50,000			
7.	Male	20	Straight-life	$40,000			
8.	Male	30	Straight-life	$80,000			
9.	Female	50	20-year endowment	$30,000			
10.	Male	40	20-year life	$100,000			

Solve each of the following problems.

11. Explain the differences between term and straight-life insurance policies.

12. If Sam Molla has a 5-year term insurance policy with a value of $40,000 purchased at age 35, how much will his beneficiary receive if he dies at age 39? How much will the beneficiary receive if he dies at 41?

13. a. Find the annual premium paid by Sara Cushion, age 30, on a straight-life insurance policy for $25,000.

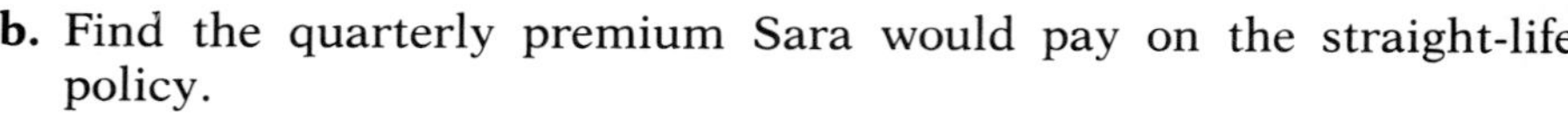

b. Find the quarterly premium Sara would pay on the straight-life policy.

14. Find the annual premium paid on a 20-year life insurance policy for $60,000 taken out at age 30 by a male. How much has he paid by age 45?

15. A straight-life policy purchased at age 60 by a male costs how much more per $1,000 than the same policy for a female age 60?

16. How much more would $50,000 in straight-life insurance cost in total annual premiums than $50,000 in 5-year term life insurance if both policies were purchased by a 20-year-old male?

17. How much more would be paid in monthly premiums than in annual premiums on a $50,000 straight-life term policy taken out at age 30 by a male?

18. Find the difference in monthly payments paid by a 40-year-old female on a 5-year term policy and a straight-life policy for $60,000.

19. How much are the quarterly payments paid by a husband, age 40, and his wife, age 30, if each has a 20-year life insurance policy for $70,000?

Other Types of Insurance

There are many different types of insurance. Insurance can be purchased for almost any risk an individual or business may encounter. *Liability* insurance protects the insured against injuries to people who are on the insured's property or use the insured's products. *Flood* and *earthquake* insurance protect the insured for losses due to flooding caused by extreme natural weather conditions and earthquakes. *Group life and health* insurance is designed to protect the employees of companies. Some companies pay the premiums for their employees; other companies make the policies available for employees to purchase. Premiums for group policies are generally lower than premiums for individual health and life insurance policies.

Many insurance companies offer a **comprehensive policy.** This type of insurance policy protects the insured for several risks. It is common, for example, to purchase fire, flood, and earthquake insurance in one comprehensive policy. The combined rate for a comprehensive policy is usually lower than if each type of protection were purchased in a separate policy.

comprehensive insurance policy: a policy protecting the insured from several risks, such as fire, flood, and earthquake. The combined rate for such a policy is usually lower than single rates for each type of protection.

Summary

Topic	Page	What to Remember	Example
Fire insurance	478	Annual premium per \$100 of coverage $= \frac{\text{amount of coverage}}{\$100} \times \text{rate}$ Annual premium per \$1,000 of coverage $= \frac{\text{amount of coverage}}{\$1{,}000} \times \text{rate}$	Use Table 16-1 to find the annual premium for building and contents if a building is insured for \$120,000 and its contents are insured for \$350,000. The building is a Class C building in Area 3. Annual premium for building: $\frac{\$120{,}000}{\$100} \times 0.63$ Annual premium for contents: $\frac{\$350{,}000}{\$100} \times 0.80 = \$2{,}800$ Total premium: \$756 + \$2,800 = \$3,556
Motor vehicle insurance	483–484	*Liability insurance*: covers the insured if responsible for an accident resulting in injury to another person or damage to another person's property. *Comprehensive insurance*: covers the insured's vehicle for damage or loss that was not caused in an accident involving another vehicle. *Collision insurance*: covers the insured for personal injury and property damage caused by an automobile accident in which the insured is not at fault.	Use Table 16-2 to find the annual premium for an automobile liability insurance policy in which the insured lives in Territory 2, in Class C, and wishes to have 20/40/10 coverage. The cost of 20/40 bodily injury coverage for Territory 2 and Class C is \$198. The cost of \$10,000 property damage is \$208. The total premium is \$198 + \$208 = \$406.

Topic	Page	What to Remember			Example
Life insurance	487–489	In the first 4 examples below, find the annual premium for a 40-year-old female for a policy with a face value of $50,000:			
Term insurance (least expensive)		Premium is paid for a fixed period of time or term	Coverage lasts for the term of the policy	If insured dies while premium is being paid, beneficiary receives face value	No cash value A 5-year policy: $\frac{\$50,000}{\$1,000} \times \$6.17 = \$308.50$
Straight-life (or ordinary life)		Premium is paid for entire life	Coverage lasts entire life	If insured dies while premium is being paid, beneficiary receives face value of policy	Policy has some cash value if canceled A straight-life policy: $\frac{\$50,000}{\$1,000} \times \$19.41 = \$970.50$
Limited-payment (more expensive than straight-life)		Premium is paid for a fixed period	Coverage lasts entire life	If insured dies while premium is being paid, beneficiary receives face value of policy	Cash value depends on the amount paid in A 20-year life policy: $\frac{\$50,000}{\$1,000} \times \$29.45$ $= \$1,472.50$
Endowment (most expensive)		Premium is paid for a fixed period	Coverage lasts for the term of the policy	If insured dies while premium is being paid, beneficiary receives face value	Cash value at end of term is face value A 20-year endowment policy: $\frac{\$50,000}{\$1,000} \times \$39.75$ $= \$1,987.50$
		$\text{Annual premium per } \$1,000 \text{ coverage} = \frac{\text{amount of coverage}}{\$1,000} \times \text{rate}$			
Premium periods of less than 1 year	489	$\text{Annual premium} \times \text{rate from Table 16-4} = \text{monthly, quarterly, or semiannual premium}$			Use Tables 16-3 and 16-4 to find the quarterly premium for a $50,000 straight-life policy on a 30-year-old male. Annual premium = $\frac{\$50,000}{\$1,000} \times \$14.97 = \$748.50$ Quarterly premium = $\$748.50 \times 0.26 = \$194.61$.

Chapter Review

Use Table 16-1 to find the annual fire insurance premium for building and contents.

	Area	Class	Building Coverage	Contents Coverage	Annual Premium
1.	2	B	$62,400	$23,000	
2.	3	A	$103,200	$46,200	

The following policies include an 80% coinsurance clause. A fire has caused the given amount of damage. Find the amount of compensation paid by the insurer.

	Market Value	Face Value	Amount of Damage	Amount of Compensation
3.	$78,250	$62,600	$15,300	
4.	$89,100	$60,000	$21,400	

Use Table 16-2 to find the annual premium for each of the following motor vehicle liability insurance policies.

	Territory	Driver Class	Coverage	Annual Premium
5.	1	A	20/40/5	
6.	2	C	50/100/25	

Use Table 16-3 to find the annual premium of each of the following life insurance policies.

	Sex	Age	Policy	Coverage	Annual Premium
7.	Male	30	Straight life	$80,000	
8.	Female	40	20-year life	$55,000	

Use Tables 16-1, 16-2, 16-3, or 16-4 to solve the following problems.

9. The market value of a building is $91,000. It has been insured for $60,000 in a policy with an 80% coinsurance clause. A fire has caused damages of $38,000. What is the amount of compensation paid by the insurer?

10. A $112,000 building has been declared a total loss in a recent fire. The owner had the building insured for $89,600 in a policy containing an 80% clause. How much of the loss will the insured pay?

11. Sam Rinola is classified as a Class A driver in Territory 1. Find his annual automobile liability insurance premium for a 50/100/10 policy.

12. Bonnie Lowe had an accident that injured a driver and did $3,250 in damages to his car. His medical expenses totaled $22,568. Bonnie's liability insurance coverage is 20/40/5. How much compensation will the driver of the other car receive from Bonnie's insurance company?

13. What are the semiannual premiums on a 100/300/10 policy for a Class A driver in Territory 2 if a 2% charge is added to the annual premium when it is paid semiannually?

14. Find the amount of the quarterly premiums on a $70,000, 20-year endowment life insurance policy for a 40-year-old female.

15. Ben Hoaster purchased a 5-year term life insurance policy at age 20. The policy had a face value of $40,000.
    a. If Ben dies at age 22, how much would his beneficiary receive?

    b. If Ben dies at age 26, how much would his beneficiary receive?

16. a. Meg is 20 years old. If she buys a $50,000 straight-life policy, what is the annual premium?

b. If she waits until age 30, how much will the annual premium be?

17. How much more would be paid in monthly premiums than in annual premiums for an $80,000 straight-life policy taken out at age 40 by a male?

18. If you have a collision insurance policy with a $200 deductible clause, how much of $1,648 in damages to your car will the policy cover?

19. What is the face value of a fire insurance policy covering 80% of a $115,000 building?

20. Compare the cost per year of a 20-year life insurance policy for $100,000 to a 20-year endowment policy for a 30-year-old male.

Trial Test

1. Find the annual premium on a $95,000 straight-life insurance policy for a 40-year-old male.

2. Find the annual premium on a 20/40/10 automobile liability insurance policy for a Class C driver in Territory 2.

3. Find the face value of a fire-protection policy on a building worth $87,500 if it is insured for 75% of its market value.

4. How much will a 50/100/10 automobile liability insurance policy pay for medical expenses of a couple injured in an accident if their total expenses were $53,768, but the expense of each was less than $50,000?

5. Find the monthly payments on a 20-year endowment policy for $75,000 for a 30-year-old male.

6. How much are the quarterly premiums on a 50/100/25 automobile liability insurance policy for a Class B driver in Territory 1 if a 2% charge is added to annual premiums that are paid quarterly?

7. How much more are the annual premiums of a Class A driver in Territory 2 than for a Class A driver in Territory 1 if both have 20/40/5 coverage?

8. A building and its contents are insured for $78,000 and $12,760, respectively. Find the total annual premium if the building is a Class C building in area 3.

9. Find the quarterly payments on a 20-year life insurance policy for $95,000 on a 40-year-old female.

10. If you have 20/40/10 automobile liability insurance and have an accident that injures the driver of the other car, how much must you pay for the $4,562 in damages to his car and $25,760 in medical expenses?

11. Explain the differences in term and straight-life insurance policies.

12. How much insurance do you need on a $68,500 building if you wish to satisfy the 80% coinsurance clause?

13. How much more would be paid by a 30-year-old male in monthly premiums than in annual premiums for a $60,000, 20-year life insurance policy?

14. Compare the cost per year of a 20-year life insurance policy for $70,000 to a 20-year endowment policy for a 20-year-old male.

15. If you have a collision insurance policy with a $250 deductible clause, how much of $675 damage to your car will the policy cover?

16. How much will a 5-year term policy pay to the beneficiary of a 26-year-old male if he purchased the $30,000 policy at age 20?

17. The market value of a building is $72,500. It has been insured for $50,000. What part of the damages will the policy cover?

18. A $67,200 building is insured for $40,000 by a fire insurance policy containing an 80% coinsurance clause. A fire causes $12,365 in damages. How much of the loss does the insured have to pay?

19. Find the semiannual premium for a 50/100/25 automobile liability insurance policy for a Class A driver in Territory 2 if there is no additional charge for semiannual payment.

20. Fire causes $18,700 in damages to a $98,000 building insured for $70,000. How much of the damages will the insurer pay?

Self-Check Solutions

1. $\dfrac{\$120{,}000}{100} \times 0.38 = \$456.00$

$\dfrac{\$75{,}000}{100} \times 0.48 = \$360.00$

$456 + $360 = $816.00 total annual premium

2. a. 0.80 × $255,000 = $204,000; since this is 80%, insurance company will pay all losses up to the face value of the policy, which is $204,000.

b. $75,000

3. a. $\dfrac{\$150{,}000}{100} \times 0.46 = \$690.00$

$\dfrac{\$68{,}000}{100} \times 0.51 = \$346.80$

$690 + $346.80 = $1,036.80 total annual premium

b. $1,036.80 × .02 = $20.74 charge;
($1,036.80 + $20.74) ÷ 2 = $1,057.54 ÷ 2 = $528.77 semiannual premium

4. 0.80 × $295,000 = $236,000

$\$295{,}000 \times \dfrac{\$100{,}000}{\$236{,}000} = \$125{,}000$ amount insurance company will pay

5. $198 + $196 = $394

6. Class C driver in Territory 1
$177 + $163 = $340

Class C driver in Territory 2
$210 + $208 = $418

Driver in Territory 2 is $78 more.

7. \$168 + \$159 = \$327 annual premium
\$327 ÷ 12 = \$27.25 monthly premium

8. \$8,362 for injuries; \$0

9. **a.** $\frac{\$45,000}{\$1,000} \times \$4.32 = \$194.40$

b. $\frac{\$45,000}{\$1,000} \times \$10.03 = \$451.35$

c. $\frac{\$45,000}{\$1,000} \times \$17.04 = \$766.80$

d. $\frac{\$45,000}{\$1,000} \times \$20.19 = \$908.55$

10. $\frac{\$50,000}{\$1,000} \times \$23.82 \times 0.26 = \$309.66$

11. $\frac{\$50,000}{\$1,000} \times \$33.68 \times 0.0875 = \$147.35$

12.

Age	Male	Female
40 years old	$\frac{\$75,000}{1,000} \times \$7.32 = \$549$	$\frac{\$75,000}{\$1,000} \times \$6.17 = \$462.75$
60 years old	$\frac{\$75,000}{\$1,000} \times \$29.40 = \$2,205$	$\frac{\$75,000}{\$1,000} \times \$23.25 = \$1,743.75$

Taxes 17

Learning Objectives

1. Find the amount of sales tax on a purchase with and without tax tables. (pp. 503–506)
2. Calculate the marked price from the total price of a purchase. (pp. 506–507)
3. Find the assessed value of a piece of property. (p. 509)
4. Understand and use the different ways of expressing tax rates. (pp. 509–510)
5. Use the formula for determining a community's tax rate. (pp. 511–512)
6. Understand personal income tax allowances, exemptions, and deductions, and use them to figure taxable income. (pp. 513–517)
7. Calculate the amount of personal income tax owed on taxable income using the tax table and tax rate schedules. (pp. 517–522)

Taxes affect everyone in one way or another. A **tax** is money collected by a government for its own support and for providing services to the taxpayers. Governments use tax money to pay the salaries of government officials and employees, to run and staff public schools, parks, and playgrounds, to provide police and fire protection, health services, and unemployment compensation, to build and maintain roads and highways, and to provide numerous other benefits.

tax: money collected by the government for its upkeep and to provide services to taxpayers.

Sales Tax

The sales tax is probably the first tax that most people encounter (45 states have sales taxes). At an early age children realize that an item in the store costs more money than the amount marked on the price tag. At the time of purchase, a store collects this extra amount, called a **sales tax,** and later pays it to the state. In some states, county or city governments charge a local sales tax in addition to the state sales tax. A third type of tax, called an **excise tax,** is charged by federal, state, or local governments on such goods as alcoholic beverages, tobacco, motor vehicles, furs, and jewelry, and on such services as telephone service and airline travel.

sales tax: an amount of money added to the price of an item, collected by the store when the item is sold and paid to the state or local government.

excise tax: a tax charged by federal, state, or local governments on certain items, such as alcoholic beverages, tobacco, cars, furs, jewelry, telephone service, and airline tickets.

Three basic ways of figuring the amount of sales tax are in common use. Many businesses use computerized cash registers that automatically figure sales tax. Some states assess tax by charging a certain number of cents for each whole dollar and some number of cents on amounts less than a dollar. In other states the sales tax is a specified percent of the selling price.

Not all items we might buy are taxed in all states. Many states charge no sales tax on food or medicine, and some states make other exceptions. New Jersey, for example, does not charge tax on clothing.

Using Tables to Figure Sales Tax

For convenience, many state or local governments distribute sales tax tables to businesses that request them. These tables allow employees to quickly determine the proper sales tax. Look at Table 17-1, on p. 504, which shows a small portion of a sales tax table.

Note that the *state* sales tax rate in Table 17-1 is 5.5%. There is also a local sales tax of 2.25%. This gives a combined tax rate of 7.75%.

Table 17-1 Sales Tax Table
Combining local tax (2¼%) and state tax (5½%) = total (7¾%)

Sales			Sales		
From	To	Tax	From	To	Tax
0.01 to	0.10	0.00	4.97	5.09	0.39
0.11	0.19	0.01	5.10	5.22	0.40
0.20	0.32	0.02	5.23	5.35	0.41
0.33	0.45	0.03	5.36	5.48	0.42
0.46	0.58	0.04	5.49	5.61	0.43
0.59	0.70	0.05	5.62	5.74	0.44
0.71	0.83	0.06	5.75	5.87	0.45
0.84	0.96	0.07	5.88	5.99	0.46
0.97	1.09	0.08	6.00	6.12	0.47
1.10	1.22	0.09	6.13	6.25	0.48
1.23	1.35	0.10	6.26	6.38	0.49
1.36	1.48	0.11	6.39	6.51	0.50
1.49	1.61	0.12	6.52	6.64	0.51
1.62	1.74	0.13	6.65	6.77	0.52
1.75	1.87	0.14	6.78	6.90	0.53
1.88	1.99	0.15	6.91	7.03	0.54
2.00	2.12	0.16	7.04	7.16	0.55
2.13	2.25	0.17	7.17	7.29	0.56
2.26	2.38	0.18	7.30	7.41	0.57
2.39	2.51	0.19	7.42	7.54	0.58
2.52	2.64	0.20	7.55	7.67	0.59
2.65	2.77	0.21	7.68	7.80	0.60
2.78	2.90	0.22	7.81	7.93	0.61
2.91	3.03	0.23	7.94	8.06	0.62
3.04	3.16	0.24	8.07	8.19	0.63
3.17	3.29	0.25	8.20	8.32	0.64
3.30	3.41	0.26	8.33	8.45	0.65
3.42	3.54	0.27	8.46	8.58	0.66
3.55	3.67	0.28	8.59	8.70	0.67
3.68	3.80	0.29	8.71	8.83	0.68
3.81	3.93	0.30	8.84	8.96	0.69
3.94	4.06	0.31	8.97	9.09	0.70
4.07	4.19	0.32	9.10	9.22	0.71
4.20	4.32	0.33	9.23	9.35	0.72
4.33	4.45	0.34	9.36	9.48	0.73
4.46	4.58	0.35	9.49	9.61	0.74
4.59	4.70	0.36	9.62	9.74	0.75
4.71	4.83	0.37	9.75	9.87	0.76
4.84	4.96	0.38	9.88	9.99	0.77

EXAMPLE 1

Find the sales tax on a purchase of $4.30 using the sales tax rate given in Table 17-1.

$4.30 falls within the interval $4.20–$4.32. The sales tax from the table is $0.33.

Table 17-1 shows the tax on purchases only up to $9.99. To find the tax on a purchase of more than $9.99, there are two different methods available.

The next section shows how to find tax without using a table. To use Table 17-1, however, you must add the taxes charged on two or more amounts that total the amount of the purchase.

EXAMPLE 2

Use Table 17-1 to find the sales tax for a purchase of $16.43.

Look in Table 17-1 to find two amounts which, when added together, equal $16.43.

$9.99 + $6.44 = $16.43	$9.99 and $6.44 are both in Table 17-1.
$0.77 + $0.50 $1.27	From Table 17-1, the tax on $9.99 is $0.77, and the tax on $6.44 is $0.50. Add the two amounts of tax to find the total tax due.

The tax on a purchase of $16.43 is $1.27.

Figuring Tax without Tables

Sales tax can be figured without the use of tables. Note that, except for the first interval shown in Table 17-1, the amount of tax can be found by simply taking the appropriate percent of the purchase and rounding to the nearest cent. From the table, note that tax on $0.58 is $0.04 and the tax on $0.59 is $0.05. To compare, find 7.75% of each of these amounts.

$0.58 × 0.0775 = $0.04495	$0.59 × 0.0775 = $0.045725
= $0.04	= $0.05
(Rounded to the nearest cent)	(Rounded to the nearest cent)

The calculated tax is the same as the amounts in the table. We can find the tax on any amount by multiplying the amount by 7.75%. With large amounts, multiplying by a percent is usually quicker than using the table, especially when a calculator is available. Remember to round the tax to the nearest cent.

EXAMPLE 3

Find the sales tax on $128.72 at 6%.

$128.72 × 0.06 $7.7232, which rounds to $7.72	Multiply the amount of the purchase by 6% = 0.06. Remember to change the percent to a decimal. Round the answer to nearest cent.

The sales tax is $7.72.

Since sales tax tables are not always readily available, it is convenient and practical to use percents to figure sales tax. In most states, except for the tax on purchases of less than $1, sales tax is figured by multiplying the purchase price by a percent of the purchase price. In recent years, the increasing popularity of straight percent sales tax rates has coincided with the growing availability of computerized cash registers.

In most areas, a sales tax is charged only on purchases made and delivered within the tax area. For instance, if an item is purchased in one state and delivered to another, the sales tax is not always charged. However, the state

Source: City & State magazine, for 1988
By Keith Carter, USA TODAY

to which large purchases are delivered may impose its sales tax. For instance, if an automobile is purchased in one state and delivered to another, the state into which it is delivered may require that sales tax be paid before the automobile can be registered.

Excise Tax

Some goods and services carry an additional *excise tax*, which is charged by the federal or local government on certain goods and services. Some excise taxes are fixed amounts and are the same regardless of the cost of the goods or services. An example of such a tax is a flat-rate tax charged for arriving at or departing from an international airport on a Saturday. More typically, the excise tax is simply a percent of the cost of the item or service being taxed. When you buy something that carries an excise tax, you must add the sales tax and the excise tax on the selling price to find the total tax.

EXAMPLE 4

A fashion designer bought a diamond tiara costing $8,500. The sales tax in her state is 5.5%, and the excise tax on jewelry is 10%. Find the total cost of the tiara.

$8,500 × 0.055 = $467.50
$8,500 ⟶ $850.00 + 850.00
$1,317.50

$8,500 + $1,317.50 = $9,817.50 total cost of tiara.

Change the sales tax percent to a decimal and multiply it times the cost of the tiara. Move the decimal point one place to the left to find the amount of the 10% excise tax. Add the two taxes to find the total tax owed.

Finding the Marked Price

marked price: the price of an item before sales tax is added.

total price: marked price plus sales tax.

Sometimes a bill gives a total of purchases and sales tax. The sales tax is not itemized, but you may want to know how much the sales tax was or what the marked price of the item was. The **marked price** is the price before tax is added. The **total price** is the marked price plus the sales tax.

Step by Step

Finding Marked Price

Step 1. Divide the total price by 1 + the sales tax rate written as a decimal:

$$\text{Marked price} = \frac{\text{total price}}{1 + \text{sales tax rate (as a decimal)}}$$

Step 2. Round the result to the nearest cent.

EXAMPLE 5

Find the marked price of a $23.83 total bill if there is a 5% sales tax charged.

Sales tax rate = 5% = 0.05 — Convert the sales tax rate to a decimal.

$$\frac{\$23.83}{1 + .05} = \frac{\$23.83}{1.05} = \$22.70$$

Divide the total price by 1 + the decimal. Round to the nearest cent.

TIPS & TRAPS

Remember, when you are calculating the marked price given the total price, you always divide the total price by the rate (1 + sales tax written as a decimal). Multiplying the total amount by the sales tax and subtracting the resulting amount from the total amount is *not* a correct method. Let's see what happens when we calculate a marked price *correctly* and *incorrectly*. Find the marked price if a purchase had a total cost of $26.78 and the sales tax rate is 5%.

$$\begin{array}{r} \$26.78 \\ \times \quad 0.05 \\ \hline 1.3390 \end{array} \qquad \begin{array}{r} \$26.78 \\ -\ \$\ 1.34 \\ \hline \$25.44 \end{array} \qquad \frac{\$26.78}{1.05} = \$25.50$$

WRONG (crossed out)   CORRECT

Real World Application

If you spend a night at a hotel in a small town in South Carolina, you will pay a 7% accommodations tax on the amount you pay for the room rental. You will also pay a 5% sales and use tax on the night's dinner at the restaurant.

You are planning to spend two nights at a hotel in South Carolina. The charge for the room is $52 per night. Your dinners cost $23.75 for the first night and $18.55 for the second night. Find the total bill, including all appropriate taxes.

$52 × 2 = $104 for 2 nights

$104 × 0.07 = $7.28 accommodations tax

$104 + 7.28 = $111.28 for the room

$18.55 × 0.05 = $0.93 sales and use tax

$18.55 + $0.93 = $19.48 for the first meal

$23.75 × 0.05 = $1.19 sales and use tax

$23.75 + $1.19 = $24.94 for the second meal

$111.28 + $19.48 + $24.94 = $155.70 total bill

Application Question

While on vacation in South Carolina, Russell spent 3 nights at an inn that charges $52 per night for a room. He charges the following meals to his account: $13.75, $24.50, $21.95. Find the appropriate taxes and the amount of his total bill.

Self-Check

1. Find the sales tax on a purchase of $12.36 using the sales tax rate given in Table 17-1.
2. Use Table 17-1 to find the sales tax for a purchase of $5.86.
3. Find the sales tax on an appliance costing $288.63 if the tax rate is 5.5%.
4. Figure the total tax on a ring that costs $2,860 in a state with a 6.5% sales tax and a 9% excise tax on jewelry.
5. What is the marked price if a total bill is $182.38 and the sales tax is 6%?

Section Review

Use Table 17-1 to find the sales tax on the following purchases.

1. $2.37
2. $3.72
3. $8.10
4. $12.93
5. $4.74
6. $11.04
7. $9.98
8. $29.95
9. $6.52
10. $5.47

Without using the table, calculate the sales tax or excise tax on the following purchases.

11. $237.42 at 6% sales tax
12. $523.85 at 5% sales tax
13. $1,294.26 at 4.5% excise tax
14. $482.12 at 6% sales tax
15. $675.93 at 5% sales tax
16. $2,998.97 at 4.5% sales tax

Find the marked price if each of the following represents a total bill at the indicated sales tax rate.

17. $27.45 at 5%
18. $139.53 at 6%
19. $347.28 at 4.5%
20. $53.92 at 5%
21. $87.26 at 3.5%

Property Tax

Most states allow cities and counties to collect money by charging a **property tax** on land, houses, buildings, and improvements and on such personal property as automobiles, jewelry, and furniture. Property tax is usually not paid on the **market value** (the expected selling price of the property), but on the **assessed value** of the property. The assessed value is a specified percent of the estimated market value of the property. This percent may vary according to the type of property and is set by the city or county that charges the tax. For example, in a particular city or county, farm property and single-family dwellings are assessed at 25% of the market value; businesses and multifamily dwellings (duplexes, apartments) are assessed at 40% of the market value. Utilities (power companies, telephone companies) are assessed at 50% of the market value.

property tax: a tax collected by cities and counties on land, houses, buildings, and improvements.

market value: the expected selling price of a piece of property.

assessed value: a percent of the estimated market value of a property. The percent is set by the city or county that charges the tax.

EXAMPLE 6

Find the assessed value of a farm with a market value of $175,000 if the assessed valuation is 25% of the market value.

$175,000 × 0.25 = $43,750	Find 25% of $175,000 (25% = 0.25).

Tax Rate Expressions

The city or county government, which imposes a property tax, might express the **property tax rate,** or the amount of tax that must be paid on a piece of property, in one of several different ways. The rate could be stated as a percent of the assessed value, as an amount of tax per $100 of assessed value, as an amount of tax per $1,000 of assessed value, or in mills. A **mill** is one thousandth ($\frac{1}{1000}$, or 0.001) of a dollar. Examples 7 through 10 show how to calculate the property tax on a home with an assessed value of $90,000 in a county that imposes an 11.08% tax when the tax is expressed in each of four different ways.

property tax rate: the rate of tax that must be paid on a piece of property; set by the city or county collecting the tax.

mill: one thousandth of a dollar ($0.001).

EXAMPLE 7

Find the tax on a home with an assessed valuation of $90,000 if the tax rate is 11.08% of the assessed value.

$90,000 × 0.1108 = $9,972	Change the rate to a decimal number and multiply it times the assessed value.

Calculator Sequence

[AC] 90000 [×] .1108 [=] ⇒ 9972

EXAMPLE 8

Find the tax on a home with an assessed value of $90,000 if the tax rate is $11.08 per $100 of assessed valuation.

$\frac{\$90{,}000}{\$100} = 900$	Divide the assessed value by $100 to find how many $100s are in the assessed value.
900 × $11.08 = $9,972	Multiply the number of $100s times the amount of tax owed per $100.

Calculator Sequence

[AC] 90000 [÷] 100 [×] 11.08 [=] ⇒ 9972

EXAMPLE 9

Find the tax on a home with an assessed valuation of \$90,000 if the tax rate is \$110.80 per \$1,000 of assessed valuation.

$\frac{\$90{,}000}{\$1{,}000} = 90$ — Divide the assessed value by \$1,000 to find how many \$1,000s are in the assessed value.

$90 \times \$110.80 = \$9{,}972$ — Multiply the number of \$1,000s times the amount of tax owed per \$1,000.

Calculator Sequence

[AC] 90000 [÷] 1000 [×] 110.80 [=] ⇒ 9972

The fourth way that a tax rate can be expressed is in mills. Recall that *percent* means *hundredths;* to change a percent to a decimal, divide by 100, or move the decimal point *two* places to the left. Similarly, *mills* means *thousandths* ($\frac{1}{10}$ of a cent or $\frac{1}{1000}$ of a dollar). To change mills to a decimal, divide by 1,000, or move the decimal point *three* places to the left.

If an area has a tax rate of 67 mills, you find the amount of tax by multiplying the assessed valuation by 0.067. Suppose the assessed valuation is \$57,000. The tax is

$$\$57{,}000 \times 0.067 = \$3{,}819$$

EXAMPLE 10

Find the tax on a home with an assessed valuation of \$90,000 if the tax rate is 110.80 mills.

110.80 mills ⟶ 110.80 = 0.1108 — Change the mills to a decimal number by moving the decimal point three places to the left.

$0.1108 \times \$90{,}000 = \$9{,}972$ — Multiply the decimal form of the number of mills times the assessed value to find the amount of tax owed.

Calculator Sequence

[AC] 110.80 [÷] 1000 [×] 90000 [=] ⇒ 9972

TIPS & TRAPS

Be sure to use the *assessed value* in calculating the amount of property tax. Let's look at what happens if you use the market value instead of the assessed value to calculate property tax.

Nancy Gordon's home has a market value of \$110,000 and an assessed value of \$44,280. Her town has a tax rate of \$173.60 per \$1,000 of assessed valuation. Find the tax owed.

Tax on market value:

$\$110{,}000 \times \frac{\$173.60}{\$1{,}000} = \$19{,}096$ (crossed out)

WRONG

Tax on assessed value:

$\$44{,}280 \times \frac{\$173.60}{\$1{,}000} = \$7{,}687.008$

CORRECT

Real World Application

Before purchasing investment property, an interested buyer can go to the tax assessor's office to find the amount of taxes to be paid on the property. Using a computer provided for this purpose, he or she can find the assessed value of the property and the tax rate, based on the location of the property. If the property is sold before the end of the year, the seller will pay the taxes only for the number of days he or she owns the land. This amount is called the seller's pro rata share of the taxes and can be found by dividing the total taxes by 365 days to get the taxes due per day and then multiplying by the number of days the land is owned during that year by the seller.

Dan is interested in buying a piece of investment property. The market value is $30,500 and the assessment rate is 18% of the market value. Dan found the city tax rate to be 92.7 mills and the county rate to be 138.4 mills. Dan buys the land on April 13. What is Dan's pro rata share of the property taxes?

$30,500 × 0.18 = $5.490	assessed value
$5,490 × 0.0927 = $508.92	city taxes per year
$5,490 × 0.1384 = $759.82	county taxes per year
$508.92 + $759.82 = $1,268.74	total taxes per year

The seller owns the land for 102 days from January 1 through April 12.

$1,268.74 ÷ 365 × 102 = $354.55
seller's pro rata share of the taxes

$1,268.74 − $354.55 = $914.19
Dan's pro rata share of the taxes

Application Question

Find the seller's pro rata share of the city and county taxes on property with a market value of $55,600. The property is assessed at 35% of the market value; city taxes are 107.6 mills, and county taxes are 95.8 mills. The closing date is June 23, the 174th day of the year.

Determining the Tax Rate

How does the city or county decide what the tax rate should be? The local government uses its estimated budget to determine how much money it will need in the year ahead. The government then divides that amount by the *total* assessed value of *all* the property in its area. This calculation tells how much tax must be collected for each dollar of assessed property value. The tax rate can be written as an amount per $100 or $1,000 of assessed value by dividing the tax rate by 100 or 1,000. Whenever you calculate the tax rate, if the division does not come out even, you round the decimal *up* to the next ten-thousandth.

Formula for determining the tax rate

$$\text{Tax rate per \$1 of assessed value} = \frac{\text{total expenses}}{\text{total assessed property value}}$$

$$\text{Tax rate per \$100 of assessed value} = \frac{\text{total expenses}}{\text{total assessed property value}} \times 100$$

$$\text{Tax rate per \$1,000 of assessed value} = \frac{\text{total expenses}}{\text{total assessed property value}} \times 1{,}000$$

EXAMPLE 11

Find the tax rate per $1,000 of assessed value if the total assessed property value in a community is $6,367,000 and the total expenses are $77,800.

$$\text{Tax rate per \$1,000 of assessed value} = \frac{\text{total expenses}}{\text{total assessed property value}} \times 1{,}000$$

$$= \frac{\$77{,}800}{\$6{,}367{,}000} \times 1{,}000 = 0.0122192 \times 1{,}000$$

$0.0122192 \times 1{,}000 = 12.2192$ which rounds up to 12.22

The tax rate per $1,000 is $12.22 per $1,000.

Calculator Sequence

[AC] 77800 [÷] 6367000 [×] 1000 [=] ⇒ 12.2192

12.2192 rounds *up* to 12.22.

Self-Check

By Marcy E. Mullins, USA TODAY

6. Find the assessed value of a store with a market value of $150,000 if the rate for assessed value is 35%.
7. What is the tax on a property with an assessed value of $88,500 if the tax is 4.5% of the assessed value?
8. Find the property tax on a vacant lot with an assessed value of $32,350 and a tax rate of $4.37 per $100 of assessed value.
9. Find the property tax on a home with an assessed value of $75,000 in a community with a tax rate of $12.75 per $1,000 of assessed value.
10. Calculate the property tax on a store with an assessed value of $150,250 if the tax rate is 58 mills.
11. Figure the tax rate per $100 assessed value for Mitchellville if the total assessed value of property in the town is $9,830,000 and the town's total expenses are $55,800.

Section Review

Find the assessed value of each property using the following rates:

Farm property or single-family dwellings: 25%
Commercial property or multiunit family dwellings: 40%
Utilities: 50%

1. Single-family dwelling with market value of $55,000

2. Apartment with market value of $235,000

3. Grocery store with market value of $115,000

4. Farm land with market value of $150,000

5. Power company with market value of $5,175,000

Find the tax on each assessed value at the indicated rate.

6. $37,000 at $1\frac{1}{2}\%$

7. $45,000 at $1\frac{3}{4}\%$

8. $12,500 at 2%

9. $575,000 at 1.8%

10. $85,000 at 2.5%

11. If the county tax rate is $3.74 per $100 of assessed value, find the tax on a property that is assessed at $35,000.

12. If the county tax rate is increased to $4.25 from $3.75 per $100 of assessed value, how much tax would have to be paid on the same $35,000? What is the amount of increase?

13. The tax rate for a city is $3.25 per $100 of assessed value. Find the tax on a property that is assessed at $125,000.

14. A home has a market value of $50,000 (assessed value = 25% of market value). Find the amount of county taxes to be paid on the home if the county tax rate is $4.00 per $100 of assessed value.

15. What is the city property tax on the house in Problem 14 if the city tax rate is $3.06 per $100 of assessed valuation?

16. Find the combined city and county tax for the property in Problems 14 and 15.

17. Find the combined city and county property tax on a business whose market value is $200,000 (assessed value = 40% of market value). The business is within the city and county whose tax rates are given in Problems 14 and 15.

Find the tax on each assessed value at the indicated rate.

18. $37,000 at $14.25 per $1,000 of assessed valuation

19. $150,000 at $15.50 per $1,000 of assessed valuation

20. $172,500 at $16.23 per $1,000 of assessed valuation

21. $32,250 at $13.78 per $1,000 of assessed valuation

22. $87,500 at $12.67 per $1,000 of assessed valuation

Change the following mill rates to decimals.

23. 34 mills

24. 63 mills

25. 51 mills

Find the tax on each property at the given assessed valuation and the indicated tax rate.

26. $12,500 at 65 mills

27. $23,275 at 55 mills

28. $52,575 at 71 mills

29. $28,750 at 64 mills

30. $32,500 at 67 mills

Complete the following table. (Express the tax levied on $1 of assessed valuation to the ten-thousandths place. Round up *any* remainder.)

Total Assessed Value	Total Expenses	Tax Rate Charged on: $1	$100	$1,000
31. $11,370,000	$ 386,450			
32. $87,460,000	$4,348,800			
33. $ 5,718,000	$ 374,740			

Income Taxes

The federal government collects a large portion of its revenue through individual **income taxes.** Income tax regulations are enacted by the Congress of the United States, and the tax laws are constantly changing. Because of these changes, no textbook can be current or comprehensive in a discussion of income tax. Although the laws and forms change from year to year, the *procedures* for computing income tax remain basically the same. In this section we introduce the terminology used and the principles of computing income tax. Each year an instruction booklet accompanies the current income tax forms. This booklet explains any recent changes in the tax laws, provides instructions for computing tax and filling out the forms, and contains various tax tables that are needed for filing an income tax return.

To figure the amount of income tax owed, you begin with a person's **gross income,** which is the money, goods, and property received during the year. From this you subtract any adjustments allowed, such as credit for employee expenses that are not reimbursed by the employer; this gives you the **adjusted gross income.** Next you arrive at the **taxable income,** which is the adjusted gross income minus exemptions and deductions. The taxable income is the amount that is used to figure the taxes owed.

Exemptions provide one of the ways of reducing taxable income. One personal exemption is allowed for the taxpayer, and additional exemptions are allowed for the taxpayer's spouse and other dependents. Other exemptions are allowed if the taxpayer or the spouse is over 65 or blind. The Tax Reform Act of 1986 increased the amount of money that can be subtracted for each personal exemption. The deduction for personal exemptions was $1,900 for 1987, $1,950 for 1988, and $2,000 for 1989. Beginning in 1988, the personal exemption was phased out for higher-income taxpayers.

income taxes: taxes paid on individual income to the federal government.

gross income: income from various sources, such as salary, investments, etc., before exemptions and deductions are subtracted.

adjusted gross income: gross income minus any allowable credits.

taxable income: adjusted gross income minus exemptions and deductions.

exemptions: an amount of money that each taxpayer is allowed to subtract from gross income. Each taxpayer is allowed one exemption for him or herself, and additional exemptions for the taxpayer's spouse and other dependents.

deductions: certain expenses that the taxpayer is allowed to subtract from his or her gross income. Includes such items as charitable contributions, excessive medical expenses, interest paid on certain loans, certain other taxes, etc.

itemized deductions: complete listing of all deductions claimed by the taxpayer when filing the regular 1040 form; used instead of standard deduction.

standard deduction: a taxpayer may choose to subtract a standard deduction from the gross income rather than itemize his or her various deductions. The amount of a standard deduction varies from year to year.

filing status: category of taxpayer—either single, married filing jointly, married filing separately, or head of household.

A taxpayer is allowed to take **deductions,** or to deduct certain expenses such as charitable contributions, interest paid on certain loans, certain taxes, losses, excessive medical expenses, and certain miscellaneous expenses, to name a few. Rather than listing these expenses (called **itemized deductions**), the taxpayer may choose to take the **standard deduction.** The amount that can be subtracted for a standard deduction changes from year to year, but in a recent year it was $5,000 for married taxpayers filing jointly (if both were under 65) or a qualifying widow (widower) with a dependent child; $2,500 for married taxpayers filing separately; $3,000 for single taxpayers; and $4,400 for taxpayers who were the head of a household. This standard deduction is automatically included in the tax tables and tax rate schedules used to compute income tax liability.

The amount of tax due on taxable income depends also on the **filing status** of the taxpayer. The taxpayer must select the filing status from five categories. The *single* category is for persons who have never married or who are legally separated, or who are divorced. A husband and wife filing a return together, even if only one had an income, are classified as *married filing jointly*. This filing status sometimes results in married persons paying less tax than single persons with a comparable income. When a husband and wife each file a separate return, they are classified as *married filing separately*, and this status usually results in a higher tax liability than the married filing jointly status.

The filing status *head of household* should be selected by individuals who provide a home for certain other persons.

Finding Taxable Income

Whether you choose to itemize deductions or use the standard deduction, you must determine your *taxable income* before you can compute the tax.

Step by Step

Finding Taxable Income

Taxable income = adjusted gross income − exemptions − deductions

EXAMPLE 12

Find the taxable income for a family of four (husband, wife, two children) if their total income is $27,754 and itemized deductions are $5,345.

No adjustments are indicated, so the adjusted gross income is the same as the gross income. Use $1,900 as the amount of each personal exemption: $1,900 × 4 = $7,600.

$$\begin{aligned}\text{Taxable income} &= \text{adjusted gross income} - \text{exemptions} - \text{deductions}\\ &= \$27{,}754 - \$7{,}600 - \$5{,}345\\ &= \$14{,}809\end{aligned}$$

Calculator Sequence

[AC] 27754 [−] 7600 [−] 5345 [=] ⇒ 14809

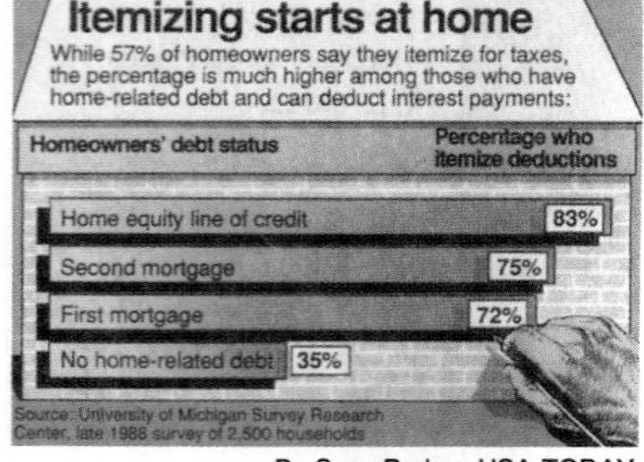

By Suzy Parker, USA TODAY

Self-Check

12. Find the taxable income for a family of 6 (husband, wife, 4 children) whose adjusted gross income is $43,873 and itemized deductions are $9,582.
13. Find the taxable income for a single person whose adjusted gross income is $28,932 and itemized deductions are $4,915.

Section Review

Use $1,900 for each allowed personal exemption in Problems 1–3.

1. Find the taxable income for a husband and wife whose adjusted gross income is $18,378 and personal deductions are $4,023.

2. Find the taxable income for a family of four (husband, wife, two children) if the wife is blind, the adjusted gross income is $34,728, and the itemized deductions are $7,246.

3. Find the taxable income for a family of three (husband, wife, one child) if their adjusted gross is $22,376 and itemized deductions are $4,375.

Use $2,000 for each exemption in Problems 4–6.

4. Find the taxable income for a single person whose adjusted gross is $14,312 and itemized deductions are $3,412.

5. Find the taxable income for a family of three (husband, wife, one child) if their gross income is $66,833 and itemized deductions are $12,583.

6. Find the taxable income for a husband and wife who have a gross income of $26,000 and are filing jointly. Their total itemized deductions are $3,589.

Using the Tax Table

The tax table is used to find the tax liability for taxable incomes of *less than* $50,000. To use the table you need to know your *taxable income* and your filing status, which is discussed in the preceding section. Table 17-2 (pp. 518–519) shows a portion of the tax table.

1988 Tax Table—*Continued*

If line 37 (taxable income) is— At least	But less than	And you are— Single	Married filing jointly *	Married filing separately	Head of a household
		Your tax is—			
14,000					
14,000	**14,050**	2,104	2,104	2,104	2,104
14,050	**14,100**	2,111	2,111	2,111	2,111
14,100	**14,150**	2,119	2,119	2,119	2,119
14,150	**14,200**	2,126	2,126	2,126	2,126
14,200	**14,250**	2,134	2,134	2,134	2,134
14,250	**14,300**	2,141	2,141	2,141	2,141
14,300	**14,350**	2,149	2,149	2,149	2,149
14,350	**14,400**	2,156	2,156	2,156	2,156
14,400	**14,450**	2,164	2,164	2,164	2,164
14,450	**14,500**	2,171	2,171	2,171	2,171
14,500	**14,550**	2,179	2,179	2,179	2,179
14,550	**14,600**	2,186	2,186	2,186	2,186
14,600	**14,650**	2,194	2,194	2,194	2,194
14,650	**14,700**	2,201	2,201	2,201	2,201
14,700	**14,750**	2,209	2,209	2,209	2,209
14,750	**14,800**	2,216	2,216	2,216	2,216
14,800	**14,850**	2,224	2,224	2,224	2,224
14,850	**14,900**	2,231	2,231	2,231	2,231
14,900	**14,950**	2,239	2,239	2,245	2,239
14,950	**15,000**	2,246	2,246	2,259	2,246
15,000					
15,000	**15,050**	2,254	2,254	2,273	2,254
15,050	**15,100**	2,261	2,261	2,287	2,261
15,100	**15,150**	2,269	2,269	2,301	2,269
15,150	**15,200**	2,276	2,276	2,315	2,276
15,200	**15,250**	2,284	2,284	2,329	2,284
15,250	**15,300**	2,291	2,291	2,343	2,291
15,300	**15,350**	2,299	2,299	2,357	2,299
15,350	**15,400**	2,306	2,306	2,371	2,306
15,400	**15,450**	2,314	2,314	2,385	2,314
15,450	**15,500**	2,321	2,321	2,399	2,321
15,500	**15,550**	2,329	2,329	2,413	2,329
15,550	**15,600**	2,336	2,336	2,427	2,336
15,600	**15,650**	2,344	2,344	2,441	2,344
15,650	**15,700**	2,351	2,351	2,455	2,351
15,700	**15,750**	2,359	2,359	2,469	2,359
15,750	**15,800**	2,366	2,366	2,483	2,366
15,800	**15,850**	2,374	2,374	2,497	2,374
15,850	**15,900**	2,381	2,381	2,511	2,381
15,900	**15,950**	2,389	2,389	2,525	2,389
15,950	**16,000**	2,396	2,396	2,539	2,396
16,000					
16,000	**16,050**	2,404	2,404	2,553	2,404
16,050	**16,100**	2,411	2,411	2,567	2,411
16,100	**16,150**	2,419	2,419	2,581	2,419
16,150	**16,200**	2,426	2,426	2,595	2,426
16,200	**16,250**	2,434	2,434	2,609	2,434
16,250	**16,300**	2,441	2,441	2,623	2,441
16,300	**16,350**	2,449	2,449	2,637	2,449
16,350	**16,400**	2,456	2,456	2,651	2,456
16,400	**16,450**	2,464	2,464	2,665	2,464
16,450	**16,500**	2,471	2,471	2,679	2,471
16,500	**16,550**	2,479	2,479	2,693	2,479
16,550	**16,600**	2,486	2,486	2,707	2,486
16,600	**16,650**	2,494	2,494	2,721	2,494
16,650	**16,700**	2,501	2,501	2,735	2,501
16,700	**16,750**	2,509	2,509	2,749	2,509
16,750	**16,800**	2,516	2,516	2,763	2,516
16,800	**16,850**	2,524	2,524	2,777	2,524
16,850	**16,900**	2,531	2,531	2,791	2,531
16,900	**16,950**	2,539	2,539	2,805	2,539
16,950	**17,000**	2,546	2,546	2,819	2,546

If line 37 (taxable income) is— At least	But less than	And you are— Single	Married filing jointly *	Married filing separately	Head of a household
		Your tax is—			
17,000					
17,000	**17,050**	2,554	2,554	2,833	2,554
17,050	**17,100**	2,561	2,561	2,847	2,561
17,100	**17,150**	2,569	2,569	2,861	2,569
17,150	**17,200**	2,576	2,576	2,875	2,576
17,200	**17,250**	2,584	2,584	2,889	2,584
17,250	**17,300**	2,591	2,591	2,903	2,591
17,300	**17,350**	2,599	2,599	2,917	2,599
17,350	**17,400**	2,606	2,606	2,931	2,606
17,400	**17,450**	2,614	2,614	2,945	2,614
17,450	**17,500**	2,621	2,621	2,959	2,621
17,500	**17,550**	2,629	2,629	2,973	2,629
17,550	**17,600**	2,636	2,636	2,987	2,636
17,600	**17,650**	2,644	2,644	3,001	2,644
17,650	**17,700**	2,651	2,651	3,015	2,651
17,700	**17,750**	2,659	2,659	3,029	2,659
17,750	**17,800**	2,666	2,666	3,043	2,666
17,800	**17,850**	2,674	2,674	3,057	2,674
17,850	**17,900**	2,685	2,681	3,071	2,681
17,900	**17,950**	2,699	2,689	3,085	2,689
17,950	**18,000**	2,713	2,696	3,099	2,696
18,000					
18,000	**18,050**	2,727	2,704	3,113	2,704
18,050	**18,100**	2,741	2,711	3,127	2,711
18,100	**18,150**	2,755	2,719	3,141	2,719
18,150	**18,200**	2,769	2,726	3,155	2,726
18,200	**18,250**	2,783	2,734	3,169	2,734
18,250	**18,300**	2,797	2,741	3,183	2,741
18,300	**18,350**	2,811	2,749	3,197	2,749
18,350	**18,400**	2,825	2,756	3,211	2,756
18,400	**18,450**	2,839	2,764	3,225	2,764
18,450	**18,500**	2,853	2,771	3,239	2,771
18,500	**18,550**	2,867	2,779	3,253	2,779
18,550	**18,600**	2,881	2,786	3,267	2,786
18,600	**18,650**	2,895	2,794	3,281	2,794
18,650	**18,700**	2,909	2,801	3,295	2,801
18,700	**18,750**	2,923	2,809	3,309	2,809
18,750	**18,800**	2,937	2,816	3,323	2,816
18,800	**18,850**	2,951	2,824	3,337	2,824
18,850	**18,900**	2,965	2,831	3,351	2,831
18,900	**18,950**	2,979	2,839	3,365	2,839
18,950	**19,000**	2,993	2,846	3,379	2,846
19,000					
19,000	**19,050**	3,007	2,854	3,393	2,854
19,050	**19,100**	3,021	2,861	3,407	2,861
19,100	**19,150**	3,035	2,869	3,421	2,869
19,150	**19,200**	3,049	2,876	3,435	2,876
19,200	**19,250**	3,063	2,884	3,449	2,884
19,250	**19,300**	3,077	2,891	3,463	2,891
19,300	**19,350**	3,091	2,899	3,477	2,899
19,350	**19,400**	3,105	2,906	3,491	2,906
19,400	**19,450**	3,119	2,914	3,505	2,914
19,450	**19,500**	3,133	2,921	3,519	2,921
19,500	**19,550**	3,147	2,929	3,533	2,929
19,550	**19,600**	3,161	2,936	3,547	2,936
19,600	**19,650**	3,175	2,944	3,561	2,944
19,650	**19,700**	3,189	2,951	3,575	2,951
19,700	**19,750**	3,203	2,959	3,589	2,959
19,750	**19,800**	3,217	2,966	3,603	2,966
19,800	**19,850**	3,231	2,974	3,617	2,974
19,850	**19,900**	3,245	2,981	3,631	2,981
19,900	**19,950**	3,259	2,989	3,645	2,989
19,950	**20,000**	3,273	2,996	3,659	2,996

If line 37 (taxable income) is— At least	But less than	And you are— Single	Married filing jointly *	Married filing separately	Head of a household
		Your tax is—			
20,000					
20,000	**20,050**	3,287	3,004	3,673	3,004
20,050	**20,100**	3,301	3,011	3,687	3,011
20,100	**20,150**	3,315	3,019	3,701	3,019
20,150	**20,200**	3,329	3,026	3,715	3,026
20,200	**20,250**	3,343	3,034	3,729	3,034
20,250	**20,300**	3,357	3,041	3,743	3,041
20,300	**20,350**	3,371	3,049	3,757	3,049
20,350	**20,400**	3,385	3,056	3,771	3,056
20,400	**20,450**	3,399	3,064	3,785	3,064
20,450	**20,500**	3,413	3,071	3,799	3,071
20,500	**20,550**	3,427	3,079	3,813	3,079
20,550	**20,600**	3,441	3,086	3,827	3,086
20,600	**20,650**	3,455	3,094	3,841	3,094
20,650	**20,700**	3,469	3,101	3,855	3,101
20,700	**20,750**	3,483	3,109	3,869	3,109
20,750	**20,800**	3,497	3,116	3,883	3,116
20,800	**20,850**	3,511	3,124	3,897	3,124
20,850	**20,900**	3,525	3,131	3,911	3,131
20,900	**20,950**	3,539	3,139	3,925	3,139
20,950	**21,000**	3,553	3,146	3,939	3,146
21,000					
21,000	**21,050**	3,567	3,154	3,953	3,154
21,050	**21,100**	3,581	3,161	3,967	3,161
21,100	**21,150**	3,595	3,169	3,981	3,169
21,150	**21,200**	3,609	3,176	3,995	3,176
21,200	**21,250**	3,623	3,184	4,009	3,184
21,250	**21,300**	3,637	3,191	4,023	3,191
21,300	**21,350**	3,651	3,199	4,037	3,199
21,350	**21,400**	3,665	3,206	4,051	3,206
21,400	**21,450**	3,679	3,214	4,065	3,214
21,450	**21,500**	3,693	3,221	4,079	3,221
21,500	**21,550**	3,707	3,229	4,093	3,229
21,550	**21,600**	3,721	3,236	4,107	3,236
21,600	**21,650**	3,735	3,244	4,121	3,244
21,650	**21,700**	3,749	3,251	4,135	3,251
21,700	**21,750**	3,763	3,259	4,149	3,259
21,750	**21,800**	3,777	3,266	4,163	3,266
21,800	**21,850**	3,791	3,274	4,177	3,274
21,850	**21,900**	3,805	3,281	4,191	3,281
21,900	**21,950**	3,819	3,289	4,205	3,289
21,950	**22,000**	3,833	3,296	4,219	3,296
22,000					
22,000	**22,050**	3,847	3,304	4,233	3,304
22,050	**22,100**	3,861	3,311	4,247	3,311
22,100	**22,150**	3,875	3,319	4,261	3,319
22,150	**22,200**	3,889	3,326	4,275	3,326
22,200	**22,250**	3,903	3,334	4,289	3,334
22,250	**22,300**	3,917	3,341	4,303	3,341
22,300	**22,350**	3,931	3,349	4,317	3,349
22,350	**22,400**	3,945	3,356	4,331	3,356
22,400	**22,450**	3,959	3,364	4,345	3,364
22,450	**22,500**	3,973	3,371	4,359	3,371
22,500	**22,550**	3,987	3,379	4,373	3,379
22,550	**22,600**	4,001	3,386	4,387	3,386
22,600	**22,650**	4,015	3,394	4,401	3,394
22,650	**22,700**	4,029	3,401	4,415	3,401
22,700	**22,750**	4,043	3,409	4,429	3,409
22,750	**22,800**	4,057	3,416	4,443	3,416
22,800	**22,850**	4,071	3,424	4,457	3,424
22,850	**22,900**	4,085	3,431	4,471	3,431
22,900	**22,950**	4,099	3,439	4,485	3,439
22,950	**23,000**	4,113	3,446	4,499	3,446

* This column must also be used by a qualifying widow(er).

Continued on next page

1988 Tax Table—*Continued*

If line 37 (taxable income) is— At least	But less than	And you are— Single	Married filing jointly *	Married filing sepa-rately	Head of a house-hold
		Your tax is—			
23,000					
23,000	**23,050**	4,127	3,454	4,513	3,454
23,050	**23,100**	4,141	3,461	4,527	3,461
23,100	**23,150**	4,155	3,469	4,541	3,469
23,150	**23,200**	4,169	3,476	4,555	3,476
23,200	**23,250**	4,183	3,484	4,569	3,484
23,250	**23,300**	4,197	3,491	4,583	3,491
23,300	**23,350**	4,211	3,499	4,597	3,499
23,350	**23,400**	4,225	3,506	4,611	3,506
23,400	**23,450**	4,239	3,514	4,625	3,514
23,450	**23,500**	4,253	3,521	4,639	3,521
23,500	**23,550**	4,267	3,529	4,653	3,529
23,550	**23,600**	4,281	3,536	4,667	3,536
23,600	**23,650**	4,295	3,544	4,681	3,544
23,650	**23,700**	4,309	3,551	4,695	3,551
23,700	**23,750**	4,323	3,559	4,709	3,559
23,750	**23,800**	4,337	3,566	4,723	3,566
23,800	**23,850**	4,351	3,574	4,737	3,574
23,850	**23,900**	4,365	3,581	4,751	3,581
23,900	**23,950**	4,379	3,589	4,765	3,592
23,950	**24,000**	4,393	3,596	4,779	3,606
24,000					
24,000	**24,050**	4,407	3,604	4,793	3,620
24,050	**24,100**	4,421	3,611	4,807	3,634
24,100	**24,150**	4,435	3,619	4,821	3,648
24,150	**24,200**	4,449	3,626	4,835	3,662
24,200	**24,250**	4,463	3,634	4,849	3,676
24,250	**24,300**	4,477	3,641	4,863	3,690
24,300	**24,350**	4,491	3,649	4,877	3,704
24,350	**24,400**	4,505	3,656	4,891	3,718
24,400	**24,450**	4,519	3,664	4,905	3,732
24,450	**24,500**	4,533	3,671	4,919	3,746
24,500	**24,550**	4,547	3,679	4,933	3,760
24,550	**24,600**	4,561	3,686	4,947	3,774
24,600	**24,650**	4,575	3,694	4,961	3,788
24,650	**24,700**	4,589	3,701	4,975	3,802
24,700	**24,750**	4,603	3,709	4,989	3,816
24,750	**24,800**	4,617	3,716	5,003	3,830
24,800	**24,850**	4,631	3,724	5,017	3,844
24,850	**24,900**	4,645	3,731	5,031	3,858
24,900	**24,950**	4,659	3,739	5,045	3,872
24,950	**25,000**	4,673	3,746	5,059	3,886
25,000					
25,000	**25,050**	4,687	3,754	5,073	3,900
25,050	**25,100**	4,701	3,761	5,087	3,914
25,100	**25,150**	4,715	3,769	5,101	3,928
25,150	**25,200**	4,729	3,776	5,115	3,942
25,200	**25,250**	4,743	3,784	5,129	3,956
25,250	**25,300**	4,757	3,791	5,143	3,970
25,300	**25,350**	4,771	3,799	5,157	3,984
25,350	**25,400**	4,785	3,806	5,171	3,998
25,400	**25,450**	4,799	3,814	5,185	4,012
25,450	**25,500**	4,813	3,821	5,199	4,026
25,500	**25,550**	4,827	3,829	5,213	4,040
25,550	**25,600**	4,841	3,836	5,227	4,054
25,600	**25,650**	4,855	3,844	5,241	4,068
25,650	**25,700**	4,869	3,851	5,255	4,082
25,700	**25,750**	4,883	3,859	5,269	4,096
25,750	**25,800**	4,897	3,866	5,283	4,110
25,800	**25,850**	4,911	3,874	5,297	4,124
25,850	**25,900**	4,925	3,881	5,311	4,138
25,900	**25,950**	4,939	3,889	5,325	4,152
25,950	**26,000**	4,953	3,896	5,339	4,166

If line 37 (taxable income) is— At least	But less than	And you are— Single	Married filing jointly *	Married filing sepa-rately	Head of a house-hold
		Your tax is—			
26,000					
26,000	**26,050**	4,967	3,904	5,353	4,180
26,050	**26,100**	4,981	3,911	5,367	4,194
26,100	**26,150**	4,995	3,919	5,381	4,208
26,150	**26,200**	5,009	3,926	5,395	4,222
26,200	**26,250**	5,023	3,934	5,409	4,236
26,250	**26,300**	5,037	3,941	5,423	4,250
26,300	**26,350**	5,051	3,949	5,437	4,264
26,350	**26,400**	5,065	3,956	5,451	4,278
26,400	**26,450**	5,079	3,964	5,465	4,292
26,450	**26,500**	5,093	3,971	5,479	4,306
26,500	**26,550**	5,107	3,979	5,493	4,320
26,550	**26,600**	5,121	3,986	5,507	4,334
26,600	**26,650**	5,135	3,994	5,521	4,348
26,650	**26,700**	5,149	4,001	5,535	4,362
26,700	**26,750**	5,163	4,009	5,549	4,376
26,750	**26,800**	5,177	4,016	5,563	4,390
26,800	**26,850**	5,191	4,024	5,577	4,404
26,850	**26,900**	5,205	4,031	5,591	4,418
26,900	**26,950**	5,219	4,039	5,605	4,432
26,950	**27,000**	5,233	4,046	5,619	4,446
27,000					
27,000	**27,050**	5,247	4,054	5,633	4,460
27,050	**27,100**	5,261	4,061	5,647	4,474
27,100	**27,150**	5,275	4,069	5,661	4,488
27,150	**27,200**	5,289	4,076	5,675	4,502
27,200	**27,250**	5,303	4,084	5,689	4,516
27,250	**27,300**	5,317	4,091	5,703	4,530
27,300	**27,350**	5,331	4,099	5,717	4,544
27,350	**27,400**	5,345	4,106	5,731	4,558
27,400	**27,450**	5,359	4,114	5,745	4,572
27,450	**27,500**	5,373	4,121	5,759	4,586
27,500	**27,550**	5,387	4,129	5,773	4,600
27,550	**27,600**	5,401	4,136	5,787	4,614
27,600	**27,650**	5,415	4,144	5,801	4,628
27,650	**27,700**	5,429	4,151	5,815	4,642
27,700	**27,750**	5,443	4,159	5,829	4,656
27,750	**27,800**	5,457	4,166	5,843	4,670
27,800	**27,850**	5,471	4,174	5,857	4,684
27,850	**27,900**	5,485	4,181	5,871	4,698
27,900	**27,950**	5,499	4,189	5,885	4,712
27,950	**28,000**	5,513	4,196	5,899	4,726
28,000					
28,000	**28,050**	5,527	4,204	5,913	4,740
28,050	**28,100**	5,541	4,211	5,927	4,754
28,100	**28,150**	5,555	4,219	5,941	4,768
28,150	**28,200**	5,569	4,226	5,955	4,782
28,200	**28,250**	5,583	4,234	5,969	4,796
28,250	**28,300**	5,597	4,241	5,983	4,810
28,300	**28,350**	5,611	4,249	5,997	4,824
28,350	**28,400**	5,625	4,256	6,011	4,838
28,400	**28,450**	5,639	4,264	6,025	4,852
28,450	**28,500**	5,653	4,271	6,039	4,866
28,500	**28,550**	5,667	4,279	6,053	4,880
28,550	**28,600**	5,681	4,286	6,067	4,894
28,600	**28,650**	5,695	4,294	6,081	4,908
28,650	**28,700**	5,709	4,301	6,095	4,922
28,700	**28,750**	5,723	4,309	6,109	4,936
28,750	**28,800**	5,737	4,316	6,123	4,950
28,800	**28,850**	5,751	4,324	6,137	4,964
28,850	**28,900**	5,765	4,331	6,151	4,978
28,900	**28,950**	5,779	4,339	6,165	4,992
28,950	**29,000**	5,793	4 346	6,179	5,006

If line 37 (taxable income) is— At least	But less than	And you are— Single	Married filing jointly *	Married filing sepa-rately	Head of a house-hold
		Your tax is—			
29,000					
29,000	**29,050**	5,807	4,354	6,193	5,020
29,050	**29,100**	5,821	4,361	6,207	5,034
29,100	**29,150**	5,835	4,369	6,221	5,048
29,150	**29,200**	5,849	4,376	6,235	5,062
29,200	**29,250**	5,863	4,384	6,249	5,076
29,250	**29,300**	5,877	4,391	6,263	5,090
29,300	**29,350**	5,891	4,399	6,277	5,104
29,350	**29,400**	5,905	4,406	6,291	5,118
29,400	**29,450**	5,919	4,414	6,305	5,132
29,450	**29,500**	5,933	4,421	6,319	5,146
29,500	**29,550**	5,947	4,429	6,333	5,160
29,550	**29,600**	5,961	4,436	6,347	5,174
29,600	**29,650**	5,975	4,444	6,361	5,188
29,650	**29,700**	5,989	4,451	6,375	5,202
29,700	**29,750**	6,003	4,459	6,389	5,216
29,750	**29,800**	6,017	4,470	6,403	5,230
29,800	**29,850**	6,031	4,484	6,417	5,244
29,850	**29,900**	6,045	4,498	6,431	5,258
29,900	**29,950**	6,059	4,512	6,445	5,272
29,950	**30,000**	6,073	4,526	6,459	5,286
30,000					
30,000	**30,050**	6,087	4,540	6,473	5,300
30,050	**30,100**	6,101	4,554	6,487	5,314
30,100	**30,150**	6,115	4,568	6,501	5,328
30,150	**30,200**	6,129	4,582	6,515	5,342
30,200	**30,250**	6,143	4,596	6,529	5,356
30,250	**30,300**	6,157	4,610	6,543	5,370
30,300	**30,350**	6,171	4,624	6,557	5,384
30,350	**30,400**	6,185	4,638	6,571	5,398
30,400	**30,450**	6,199	4,652	6,585	5,412
30,450	**30,500**	6,213	4,666	6,599	5,426
30,500	**30,550**	6,227	4,680	6,613	5,440
30,550	**30,600**	6,241	4,694	6,627	5,454
30,600	**30,650**	6,255	4,708	6,641	5,468
30,650	**30,700**	6,269	4,722	6,655	5,482
30,700	**30,750**	6,283	4,736	6,669	5,496
30,750	**30,800**	6,297	4,750	6,683	5,510
30,800	**30,850**	6,311	4,764	6,697	5,524
30,850	**30,900**	6,325	4,778	6,711	5,538
30,900	**30,950**	6,339	4,792	6,725	5,552
30,950	**31,000**	6,353	4,806	6,739	5,566
31,000					
31,000	**31,050**	6,367	4,820	6,753	5,580
31,050	**31,100**	6,381	4,834	6,767	5,594
31,100	**31,150**	6,395	4,848	6,781	5,608
31,150	**31,200**	6,409	4,862	6,795	5,622
31,200	**31,250**	6,423	4,876	6,809	5,636
31,250	**31,300**	6,437	4,890	6,823	5,650
31,300	**31,350**	6,451	4,904	6,837	5,664
31,350	**31,400**	6,465	4,918	6,851	5,678
31,400	**31,450**	6,479	4,932	6,865	5,692
31,450	**31,500**	6,493	4,946	6,879	5,706
31,500	**31,550**	6,507	4,960	6,893	5,720
31,550	**31,600**	6,521	4,974	6,907	5,734
31,600	**31,650**	6,535	4,988	6,921	5,748
31,650	**31,700**	6,549	5,002	6,935	5,762
31,700	**31,750**	6,563	5,016	6,949	5,776
31,750	**31,800**	6,577	5,030	6,963	5,790
31,800	**31,850**	6,591	5,044	6,977	5,804
31,850	**31,900**	6,605	5,058	6,991	5,818
31,900	**31,950**	6,619	5,072	7,005	5,832
31,950	**32,000**	6,633	5,086	7,019	5,846

* This column must also be used by a qualifying widow(er).

Continued on next page

Step by Step

Using the Tax Table to Figure Taxes

Step 1. Locate your taxable income under the column headed, "If line 37 (taxable income) is—".

Step 2. Go across to the column headed, "And you are—," which has the four categories of filing status listed under it. The tax you owe will appear under the appropriate category.

EXAMPLE 13

Find the tax owed by a married taxpayer filing separately on a taxable income of $19,478.

Since the taxable income of $19,478 is less than $50,000, the tax table in Table 17-2 is appropriate.

First, locate the income range in which $19,478 falls. Because $19,478 is at *least* $19,450 *but less than* $19,500, it falls within the range $19,450–$19,500.

Next, locate the tax for this taxable income range to the right in the column headed *married filing separately*. The tax is $3,519.

EXAMPLE 14

Find the tax owed by the same taxpayer in Example 13 if the taxpayer files jointly with his or her spouse.

For the taxable income range $19,450–$19,500, the tax for a taxpayer *married filing jointly* is $2,921.

From Examples 13 and 14 and from an inspection of Table 17-2, it is clear that a taxpayer's filing status (single, married filing jointly, married filing separately, head of household) significantly affects the amount of tax owed.

Using the Tax Rate Schedules

tax rate schedules: used to figure tax on taxable incomes of $50,000 or more.

The **tax rate schedules** are used to compute tax on taxable incomes of $50,000 *or more*. For the tax year 1988, there was a separate tax rate schedule for single taxpayers, heads of households, and married taxpayers (and certain qualifying widows and widowers).

The Tax Reform Act of 1986 changed the tax rate structure that had existed in the years before that. An individual's income is taxed at different rates depending on how much of his or her income falls into each of various income brackets. Table 17-3 shows the tax rates for 1988.

Step by Step

Using Tax Rate Schedules to Figure Tax Owed

Step 1. Locate the correct schedule according to filing status.

Step 2. Find the range in which the taxable income falls.

Step 3. Subtract the lower end of the range from the taxable income.

Step 4. Multiply the result from Step 3 by the indicated rate.

Step 5. Add the dollar amount indicated for the range to the result from Step 4.

EXAMPLE 15

Find the tax on a taxable income of $58,743 for a married taxpayer filing jointly using Table 17-3.

Step 1. The taxpayer would use Schedule Y-1.

Step 2. Schedule Y-1 shows that the taxable income falls in the range $29,750–$71,900.

Step 3. $58,743 − $29,750 = $29,993

Step 4. $29,993 × 0.28 = $8,398.04

Step 5. $8,398.04 + $4,462.50 = $12,860.54.

The tax is $12,860.54.

Table 17-3 Tax Rate Schedules

1988 Tax Rate Schedules

Caution: *Use ONLY if your taxable income (Form 1040, line 37) is $50,000 or more. If less, use the* ***Tax Table.***

Schedule X—Use if your filing status is **Single**

If the amount on Form 1040, line 37, is: Over—	But not over—	Enter on Form 1040, line 38	of the amount over—
$0	$17,850	.......15%	**$0**
17,850	43,150	**$2,677.50 + 28%**	**17,850**
43,150	89,560	**9,761.50 + 33%**	**43,150**
89,560	....	Use **Worksheet** below to figure your tax.	

Schedule Z—Use if your filing status is **Head of household**

If the amount on Form 1040, line 37, is: Over—	But not over—	Enter on Form 1040, line 38	of the amount over—
$0	$23,900	.......15%	**$0**
23,900	61,650	**$3,585 + 28%**	**23,900**
61,650	123,790	**14,155 + 33%**	**61,650**
123,790	....	Use **Worksheet** below to figure your tax.	

Schedule Y-1—Use if your filing status is **Married filing jointly or Qualifying widow(er)**

If the amount on Form 1040, line 37, is: Over—	But not over—	Enter on Form 1040, line 38	of the amount over—
$0	$29,750	.......15%	**$0**
29,750	71,900	**$4,462.50 + 28%**	**29,750**
71,900	149,250	**16,264.50 + 33%**	**71,900**
149,250	....	Use **Worksheet** below to figure your tax.	

Schedule Y-2—Use if your filing status is **Married filing separately**

If the amount on Form 1040, line 37, is: Over—	But not over—	Enter on Form 1040, line 38	of the amount over—
$0	$14,875	.......15%	**$0**
14,875	35,950	**$2,231.25 + 28%**	**14,875**
35,950	113,300	**8,132.25 + 33%**	**35,950**
113,300	....	Use **Worksheet** below to figure your tax.	

EXAMPLE 16

Find the tax owed on a taxable income of $67,587 for a married taxpayer filing separately. Use Table 17-3.

Step 1. The taxpayer is married filing separately, so use Schedule Y-2.

Step 2. The taxable income, $67,587, falls in the range $35,950–$113,300.

Step 3. $67,587 − $35,950 = $31,637

Step 4. $31,637 × 0.33 = $10,440.21

Step 5. $10,440.21 + $8,132.25 = $18,572.46.

The tax is $18,572.46.

Self-Check

14. Charles Baker is single and calculates his taxable income to be $30,175. How much tax does he owe? Use Table 17-2.

15. Tommy and Michelle Stark have a combined taxable income of $23,300. How much tax should they pay? Use Table 17-2.

16. Bradley Bishop is married and filing his tax jointly with his wife, Margaret. Their combined taxable income is $67,983. Use the tax rate schedules (Table 17-3) to calculate the tax they must pay.

17. Dr. Steven Katz is single and has a taxable income of $40,842. Use the tax rate schedules (Table 17-3) to calculate his income tax liability.

Section Review

Use Table 17-2 to find the tax owed by taxpayers with the following taxable incomes:

1. $19,730 (single person)

2. $19,312 (single person)

3. $14,069 (single person)

4. $26,500 (single person)

5. $16,980 (married, filing jointly)

6. $31,500 (married, filing jointly)

7. $28,450 (married, filing jointly)

8. $24,059 (married, filing jointly)

Use Table 17-2 to find the tax on the following taxable incomes.

9. $54,456 (married, filing jointly)

10. $72,478 (married, filing separately)

11. $51,200 (head of household)

12. $88,342 (single)

Summary

Topic	Page	What to Remember	Examples
Sales tax	503–505	Sales tax can be looked up in a table or computed by hand or on a calculator if given as a percentage.	Use the percentage method to find the sales tax on a $1,685 fax machine at 6.6%. $1,685 × 0.066 = $111.21

Topic	Page	What to Remember	Examples
Excise tax	506	An additional tax, usually a percentage of the purchase price, may be charged on certain goods and services.	Find the total cost of a \$1,436 diamond necklace if the sales tax is 7% and the excise tax is 11%. 7% sales tax: \$1,436 × 7% = \$1,436 × 0.07 = \$100.52 11% excise tax: \$1,436 × 11% = \$1,436 × 0.11 = \$157.96 Total cost: \$1,436 + \$100.52 + \$157.96 = \$1,694.48
Marked price	506–507	Marked price = $\frac{\text{total price}}{1 + \text{sales tax rate (as a decimal)}}$	Find the marked price on a total bill of \$142.01 if a 6% sales tax is charged. Marked price $= \frac{\$142.01}{1 + 0.06} = \frac{\$142.01}{1.06}$ = \$133.97
Property tax and assessed valuation	509	Property tax is based on the *assessed value,* not the *market value,* of property. Assessed value = a percent of market value	Find the assessed value of a home with a market value of \$106,000 if the assessed value is 30% of the market value. \$106,000 × 30% = \$106,000 × 0.3 = \$31,800
Four ways of expressing tax rate and figuring tax due	509–510	The tax rate is the number used to find how much tax is owed on property. The tax rate can be expressed in four different ways:	Find the tax on a farm with an assessed valuation of \$430,000 in each case.
		As a percent of the assessed valuation	The tax rate is 8.05% of the assessed value: \$430,000 × 8.05% = \$430,000 × 0.0805 = \$34,615
		As an amount due for each \$100 of assessed valuation	The tax rate is \$8.05 per \$100 of assessed value: $\frac{\$430,000}{\$100} \times 8.05 = \$34,615$
		As an amount due for each \$1,000 of assessed valuation	The tax rate is \$80.05 per \$1,000 of assessed value: $\frac{\$430,000}{\$1,000} \times \$80.50$ = \$34,615
		As a number of mills times the assessed valuation	The tax rate is $80\frac{1}{2}$ mills: $80\frac{1}{2}$ mills → 0.0805 \$430,000 × 0.0805 = \$34,615

Topic	Page	What to Remember	Examples
Determining the tax rate	511–512	Divide the local budget by the total assessed property value. Always round up. Tax rate can be expressed in several different ways. Tax rate per $1 of assessed value $= \frac{\text{total expenses}}{\text{total assessed property value}}$ Tax rate per $100 of assessed value $= \frac{\text{total expenses}}{\text{total assessed property value}} \times 100$ Tax rate per $1,000 of assessed value $= \frac{\text{total expenses}}{\text{total assessed property value}} \times 1{,}000$	Find the tax rate per $1, per $100, and per $1,000 if the total assessed property value in a town is $8,746,000 and its total expenses are $92,300. $\frac{\$92{,}300}{\$8{,}746{,}000} = 0.0105533$ $= \$0.0106$ per $1 $\frac{\$92{,}300}{\$8{,}746{,}000} \times 100$ $= 0.0105533 \times 100$ $= \$1.06$ per $100 $\frac{\$92{,}300}{\$8{,}746{,}000} \times 1{,}000$ $= 0.0105533 \times 1{,}000$ $= \$10.56$ per $1,000
Finding taxable income	516	Taxable income = adjusted gross income − deductions	Toni Wilson and her spouse earned $33,200 gross income and had itemized deductions of $8,700. They have a 7-year-old daughter. Find the taxable income, using $1,900 for each exemption. Taxable income $= \$33{,}200 - (3 \times \$1{,}900) - \$8{,}700$ $= 33{,}200 - \$5{,}700 - \$8{,}700$ $= \$18{,}800$
Computing tax with the tax tables	517–520	Find the amount of taxable income; then locate the bracket in Table 17-2 that includes this amount. Move across to the appropriate filing status column to find the tax due.	Use Table 17-2 to find Toni's tax if she and her husband file jointly. Find the range $18,800–$18,850. Move across to the tax in the column "Married, filing jointly," which is $2,824.
Computing tax with tax rate schedules	520–521	Select the appropriate schedule in Table 17-3 as determined by taxpayer filing status. Find the range that includes the taxable income. Subtract the lower end of the tax range from the taxable income and multiply this result by the indicated rate. Add the dollar amount given plus the calculated amount for total tax.	Susan Wilson has a taxable income of $53,897. Her filing status is single. Find the amount of tax she owes. Use Schedule X. The range is $43,150–$89,560. $\$53{,}897 - \$43{,}150 = \$10{,}747$ $\$10{,}747 \times 0.33 = \$3{,}546.51$ Tax $= \$9{,}761.50 + \$3{,}546.51$ $= \$13{,}308.01$

Chapter Review

Use the tax chart in Table 17-1 to determine the sales tax on the following amounts.

	From	To	Tax
1. $10.83			

2. $0.76

3. $0.38

4. $0.09

5. $12.40

6. $8.27

Find the sales tax on the following amounts at the indicated rates.

7. $15.83 at 6%

8. $38.17 at 5%

9. $132.40 at $6\frac{1}{2}\%$

10. $83.97 at 7%

11. $2.37 at $7\frac{1}{2}\%$

12. $4.98 at $6\frac{3}{4}\%$

13. A diamond ring costing $2,999 was purchased in a city where the combined city and state sales tax rate is $6\frac{1}{4}\%$ and the excise tax on luxury items, including fine jewelry, is 10%. What are the amount of sales tax, the amount of excise tax, and the total tax paid on the ring? What is the total cost of the ring?

Find the marked price on the items whose total prices and sales tax rates are given.

14. $243.87; 6%

15. $4.29; 7%

16. \$13.86; $5\frac{3}{4}\%$

17. \$89.37; $6\frac{1}{2}\%$

18. Carlo paid \$13.83 for an item, and the tax is \$0.90. What is the total cost of the item?

19. What is the total cost of a microwave oven if the marked price is \$499 and the tax rate is 5%?

20. What is the marked price of an item if the total price is \$15.98 and the tax is \$0.98? What is the sales tax rate?

Find the property tax on the following assessed values at the indicated rates.

21. \$15,800 at 1.9%

22. \$38,500 at $2\frac{1}{4}\%$

23. \$82,400 at \$3.13 per \$100 of assessed valuation

24. \$58,200 at \$4.28 per \$100 of assessed valuation

25. \$39,180 at \$12.57 per \$1,000 of assessed valuation

26. \$132,840 at \$14.12 per \$1,000 of assessed valuation

27. \$35,280 at 67 mills

28. \$148,420 at 42 mills

29. The city tax rate is \$3.46 per \$100 of assessed valuation. Find the city tax on a property that is assessed at \$142,000.

30. The county tax rate for the property in Problem 28 is \$2.83 per \$100 of assessed value. What is the county tax?

31. What is the combined city and county tax on the property in Problems 28 and 29?

32. What is the assessed value of a condominium with a market value of \$285,000? (Commercial property or multiunit family dwellings are assessed at 40% of market value.)

33. Find the tax rate for a county if the total assessed value of property in the county is \$27,842,000 and total expenses are \$915,000.

34. Abdullah Samardar had an adjusted gross income of \$42,896. Find his taxable income if his deductions total \$7,923 and he is married and has a daughter. (Use \$1,900 as the amount of each personal exemption.)

35. Find the taxable income for Dr. Gregory Maksi if he is single and has an adjusted gross income of \$64,817 and itemized deductions of \$15,783. (Use \$1,900 for each personal exemption.)

36. Geraldine Lewis is married and has a family taxable income of \$15,842. Use Table 17-2 to find the amount of tax owed by the Lewis family.

37. Brent Musterwood, who is single, has a taxable income of \$81,842. How much tax must he pay? (Use Table 17-3.)

38. Rosalyn Johnson, a single person, has a taxable income of \$17,852. If her employer withheld \$2,496 during the year, how much additional tax must she pay when she files her tax return?

39. Bill Luttrell, owner of Luttrell Heating and Air Conditioning Company, had a personal taxable income of \$82,500. If Bill is married and files jointly with his wife, Carolyn, their combined taxable income will be

$97,821. How much income tax must they pay to the federal government? (Use Table 17-3.)

40. If Bill and Carolyn Luttrell have already paid $18,927 in withholding taxes for the year, how much more should they pay when they file their income tax form?

Trial Test

Find the sales tax on purchases that have the following marked prices and sales tax rates.

1. \$15.17 at 5%

2. \$18.26 at $6\frac{1}{4}\%$

3. \$287.52 at $7\frac{3}{4}\%$

4. \$2.98 at 6.5%

What is the total price on items that have the following marked prices and sales tax rates?

5. \$187.21 at 6%

6. \$4.25 at 5.25%

Find the marked price on items that have the indicated total prices and tax rates.

7. \$18.84 at 7%

8. \$7.87 at 6.5%

9. \$52.63 at 5.25%

10. A telephone bill of \$84.15 is assessed state sales tax at the rate of 6% and excise tax at the rate of 10%. Find the total tax on the telephone bill.

11. Find the total telephone bill in Problem 10.

12. Find the assessed value of an apartment building (assessed at 40% of the market value) if the market value is \$485,298.

13. Find the tax on a utility property if the assessed value of the property is \$385,842 and the tax rate is 10.23%.

14. Find the tax on a business property if the assessed value of the property is \$176,297 and the tax rate is \$7.56 per \$100 of assessed value.

15. Find the tax on a home if the assessed value is \$24,375 and the tax rate is \$43.97 per \$1,000.

16. Convert 36 mills to a decimal.

17. Find the tax on a property with an assessed value of \$46,820 if the property tax rate is 87 mills.

18. A property has an assessed value of \$72,000. The city tax rate for this property is \$4.12 per \$100 of assessed valuation. Find the city tax on the property.

19. The property in Problem 18 is located in a county that has set a property tax rate of \$2.57 per \$100. What is the county tax on the property?

20. Find the tax rate per \$100 of assessed value that a county should set if the total assessed property value in the county is \$31,800,000 and the total expenses are \$957,300.

21. Use Table 17-3 to calculate the amount of tax owed by Sue Cowan if her taxable income is \$42,817 and her filing status is single.

22. Charles Wossum and his wife, Ruby, are filing their income tax jointly. Their combined taxable income is \$29,872. How much tax must they pay? Use Table 17-2.

23. Juanita and Robert Gray have a gross income of \$68,521 all of which is subject to income tax. They have two children and plan to file a joint income tax return. If each exemption is \$1,900 and they have itemized deductions of \$14,521, what is their taxable income?

Self-Check Solutions

1. $12.36

	From	*To*	*Tax*
1. $12.36	12.33	12.45	0.96

	From	*To*	*Tax*
2. $5.86	5.75	5.87	0.45

3. $288.63 × 0.055 = $15.87465 = $15.87 (rounded)

4. $2,860 × 0.065 = $185.90 Sales tax
   $2,860 × 0.09 = $257.40 Excise tax
   $185.90 + $257.40 = $443.30 Total tax

5. $182.38 ÷ 1.06 = $172.0566 = $172.06 (rounded)

6. $150,000 × 0.35 = $52,500

7. $88,500 × 0.045 = $3,982.50

8. $32,350 ÷ $100 × $4.37 = $1,413.695 = $1,413.70 (rounded)

9. $75,000 ÷ $1,000 × $12.75 = $956.25

10. $150,250 × $0.058 = $8,714.50

11. $55,800 ÷ $9,830,000 × $100 = $0.56765 = $0.57 (rounded)

12. Exemptions = $1,900 × 6 = $11,400
    Taxable income = $43,873 − $11,400 − $9,582 = $22,891

13. Exemption = $1,900 × 1 = $1,900
    Taxable income = $28,932 − $1,900 − $4,915 = $22,117

14. Locate the range that includes $30,175. $30,175 is in the range $30,150–$30,200. Look under the single column. The tax owed is $6,129.

15. Locate the range $23,300–$23,350. Look under the column "Married filing jointly." The tax owed is $3,499.

16. Use Schedule Y-1 since Bradley is filing jointly with his wife.
    The taxable income is in the range $29,750–$71,900.
    $67,983 − $29,750 = $38,233
    $38,233 × 0.28 = $10,705.24
    $10,705.24 + $4,462.50 = $15,167.74 (tax owed)

17. Use Schedule X, since Dr. Katz's filing status is "single."
    Taxable income is in the range $17,850–$43,150.
    $40,842 − $17,850 = $22,992
    $22,992 × 0.28 = $6,437.76
    $6,437.76 + $2,677.50 = $9,115.26

Stocks and Bonds 18

Learning Objectives

1. Understand the basics of stocks and bonds. (pp. 535–551)
2. Read and understand stock and bond listings. (pp. 535–551)
3. Calculate, for stocks: amount of dividends, distribution of dividends, current yield, PE ratio, return on investment. (pp. 535–543)
4. Calculate, for bonds: amount of interest, amount of accrued interest, current yield. (pp. 546–551)
5. For either stocks or bonds, calculate: commission, cost of a purchase, receipt from a sale, which of two investments has the greater gain or the greater yield. (pp. 535–551)

Stocks

You hear a lot about "stocks and bonds" in business news, but often listeners have unanswered questions: What exactly is a stock? How is it different from a bond? What do all those technical terms mean? How are those figures arrived at? This chapter presents some of the basic information and computations related to investments.

A business may need capital (cash) to operate or expand. For example, a business just starting up may seek individual persons willing to invest money in the company. The investor takes the risk of losing some or all of the investment if the business does poorly, in exchange for the opportunity to make a profit if the business does well. The same dynamics of risk versus potential gain underlie stock investments.

To raise money, a corporation can issue **stock.** Each **share** of stock is a part ownership in the company. There are two basic types of stock: **preferred stock** and **common stock.** Preferred stockholders receive certain preferential benefits over common stockholders. But common stockholders have voting rights in the company—one vote per share—that preferred stockholders do not have.

At the time the company issues (first sells) the stock, each share has a specific value, called the **face value,** or **par value.** A person buying shares of stock receives a certificate of ownership, a **stock certificate.**

After the stock is issued, people buy and sell their shares in the **stock market** for prices that vary from day to day and within a day. The price of a given company's shares are affected by supply and demand: When more people want to buy than want to sell, the price tends to rise; when more people want to sell than want to buy, the price tends to fall. Keep in mind that for each sale (called a **trade**), there is both a buyer and seller at a given price, but supply and demand exerts a pressure on the price to go up or down. Other factors affect prices, such as good news about a company's product, bad news of higher-than-expected business expenses, international events, or what people think the trend of the national economy or of the business will be.

The actual buying and selling is done by a person called a **stock broker,** who specializes in work in the stock market. Usually a person who wishes to buy or sell stock contacts a broker, and the broker's representative at the actual trading location (such as at the New York Stock Exchange on Wall Street in New York or at the American Stock Exchange in Chicago)

stock: a part ownership of a corporation; can be bought and sold.

share: one unit of stock.

preferred stock: a type of stock with preferential rights, such as a fixed dividend (compare with common stock).

common stock: a share of ownership in a company, with voting rights (compare to preferred stock).

face value (par value): for stocks, the amount at the time of issue; for bonds, usually $1,000.

stock certificate: the document showing information of ownership.

stock market: the buying or selling of stocks to the public; the location where such trades are made.

trade: a purchase or sale of stocks or bonds.

stock broker: a specialist in stock market trading and investments.

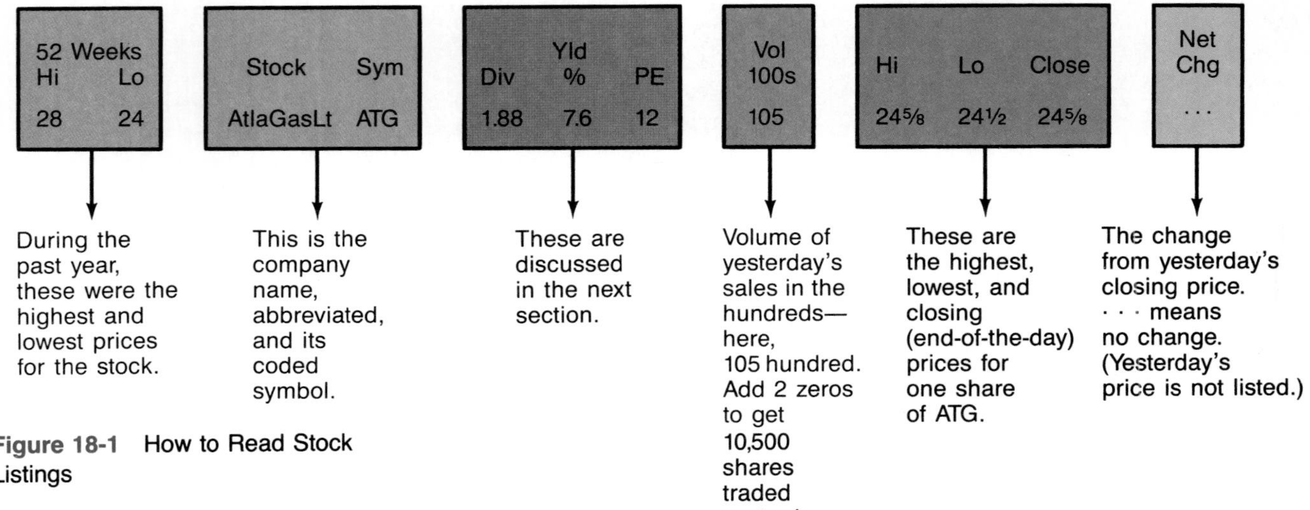

Figure 18-1 How to Read Stock Listings

commission: fee received by a stock broker for the services of buying and selling stocks.

performs the transaction. The broker receives a fee called a **commission** for the services of both buying and selling stocks.

The daily prices of stocks, along with other information about the companies, are reported in newspapers. Here we look at listings from the *Wall Street Journal* to see how to read stock listings. Stock prices are listed in dollars and fractions of a dollar such as eighths, fourths, and halves. Thus $\frac{1}{8}$ means \$0.125 ($12\frac{1}{2}$ cents), $\frac{1}{4}$ means \$0.25 (25 cents), $\frac{1}{2}$ means \$0.50, $\frac{3}{8}$ means \$0.375, and so forth. Positive and negative signs show the direction of change. Thus $+\frac{1}{8}$ is read "up one-eighth" and means the price of each share has increased by one-eighth of a dollar, or $\frac{1}{8}$ **point.** A point is \$1. Similarly, $-1\frac{3}{4}$ means the price of one share of stock has gone down by one and three-fourths points, or \$1.75.

point: in stock listings, a number representing \$1.

Reading Stock Listings

Figure 18-1 shows a sample of the type of stock listings reported in the *Wall Street Journal.* The heading of each column is explained.

Figure 18-2 gives a sample of stock quotations. The symbol "pf" following a stock name indicates it is a preferred stock; all others are common stock.

EXAMPLE 1

How many shares of Atlantic Richfield were traded today (Figure 18-2)?

2,676 hundred or 267,600 shares

What was the difference between the high price and low price of the day?

$$\begin{array}{r} \text{High } 91\frac{5}{8} \\ -\text{Low } 90\frac{5}{8} \\ \hline 1 \end{array}$$ point difference, or \$1 per share

What was the closing price yesterday?

Today's closing price is $91\frac{3}{8}$, which is up $1\frac{1}{8}$ from yesterday's close. Subtract $1\frac{1}{8}$ to get yesterday's closing price, $90\frac{1}{4}$.

Figure 18-2

52 Weeks Hi	Lo	Stock	Sym	Div	Yld %	PE	Vol 100s	Hi	Lo	Close	Net Chg
28	24	AtlaGasLt	ATG	1.88	7.6	12	105	24⅝	24½	24⅝	...
35	31⅞	AtlanEngy	ATE	2.76	8.5	9	100	32⅞	32⅝	32⅝	...
92¾	76⅛	AtlanRich	ARC	4.50	4.9	10	2676	91⅝	90⅝	91⅜	+1⅛
220	183	AtlanRich pf		2.80	1.3	...	2	218¾	218¾	218¾	+2
41	23¾	AtlasCp	AZ		...	...	32	28	27½	27⅝	– ⅜
17¼	14¾	ATMOS En	ATO	1.12	7.2	8	22	15⅝	15⅜	15⅝	+ ¼
8	4¼	AudioVideo	AVA		...	20	219	5½	5¼	5½	+ ⅛
14⅞	10½	Augat	AUG	.40	3.3	...	181	12¼	12	12¼	+ ¼
37¼	24⅞	Ausimont	AUS	.60	1.7	17	229	34⅝	34⅜	34⅜	...
44⅝	34⅝	AutoDataProc	AUD	.52	1.3	17	1541	38⅞	38⅜	38⅞	+ ¼
6¾	4¼	Avalon	AVL		...	...	52	6½	6⅜	6½	– ⅛
28¾	22¼	AVEMCO	AVE	.40	1.7	12	20	24	23¾	24	+ ⅛
26	19¾	AveryInt	AVY	.56	2.4	13	376	23¾	23¼	23¾	+ ¼
27⅞	19	Avnet	AVT	.50	2.2	16	717	22⅝	22¼	22⅝	+ ⅜
26⅝	18⅝	AvonPdts	AVP	1.00	4.0	...	2771	25¼	24¾	24⅞	...
26¼	19⅜	AvonPdts pf		2.00	7.9	...	401	25½	25¼	25⅜	+ ¼
s 16½	12⅝	Aydin	AYD		...	9	80	15¾	15⅜	15¾	+ ⅛
		-B-B-B-									
33⅛	29½	BellCda g	BCE	2.48	...	...	301	31¼	31⅛	31⅛	...
19	14⅜	BET	BEP	.82e	4.7	10	11	17⅜	17⅜	17⅜	+ ¼
9⅜	6	BMC	BMC		...	10	287	9⅛	8⅞	9	+ ⅛

Real World Application

Most stock market reports include a small section of explanatory notes at the bottom of the page. In some instances the explanation is as vague as the abbreviation. A few of the most common symbols and their meanings are given here.

"f—dealt in flat" means without interest.

"x—ex-dividend" means without the dividend.

"x—ex-rights" means without the rights. The seller keeps the right to subscribe to shares of stock within a given period of time and at a given price.

"ww—with warrants" A warrant gives the holder of the stock the opportunity to buy specific numbers of shares at a given price within a given time. The abbreviation "ex-warrants" means without warrants.

Many other symbols are listed in the explanatory footnotes, but these are the most common ones with meanings that are not as clear as others. Read the footnote section from the New York Stocks section shown here. Find examples of these notations in the section of this partial list of stocks.

FOOTNOTES:

Sales figures are unofficial. No PE unless stated in U.S. money. Stock market transactions are in 100-share lots unless preceded by a Z, which means the total is for the actual number of shares traded. Unless otherwise noted, rates of dividends annual reimbursements based on the last quarterly or semiannual declaration. Special or extra dividends or payments not designated as regular are identified as follows: a — also extra, or extras; b — annual rate plus stock dividend; c — liquidating dividend; d — indicates a new 52-week low; e — declared or paid in preceding 12 months; f — dealt in flat; g — dividends or earnings in Canadian money; i — declared or paid after stock dividend or split up; j — paid this year, dividend omitted, deferred or no action taken at last dividend meeting; k— declared or paid this year, an accumulative issue with dividends in arrears; n — new issue in the past 52 weeks; r — declared or paid in preceding 12 months plus stock dividend; s — split or stock dividend of 25 percent or more in the past 52 weeks; t — paid in stock in preceding 12 months, estimated cash value on ex-dividend or ex-distribution date; u — indicates a new 52-week high; x — ex-dividend or ex-rights; y — ex-dividend and sales in full; z — sales in full; wd — when distributed; wi — when issued; ww — with warrants; vi — in bankruptcy or receivership or being reorganized under the Bankruptcy Act, or securities assumed by such companies.

Stock	PE	Vol	Hi	Lo	Last	Chg
MiltnR .44	19	3572	u18⅝	15½	17⅝	+ 1⅞
MMM 2.60	**14**	**x21257**	**u75⅜**	**72⅞**	**73¾**	**— ⅜**
MinnPL 1.78	10	931	24⅞	24⅜	24¾	+ ⅜
Mitel	1	1389	2¾	2⅝	2¾	+ ⅛
Mobil 2.60	**11**	**36819**	**52⅜**	**50½**	**52⅛**	**+ ¾**
Mohasc	..	84	31¼	31	31	— ⅛
MonCa	13	1394	39⅞	38¾	39¼	+ ¼
Monrch .80	34	248	18⅞	18⅛	18¾	— ⅜
Monsan 3.40	12	12327	u106½	100¾	106½	+ 4½
MonPw 2.76	13	10337	u41¾	38⅛	40½	+ 2¼
Monted .33e	9	381	15	14½	14⅞	— ¼
MonSt 1.88	..	331	17⅞	17½	17¾	+ ⅛
MONY .72	17	787	8⅜	8	8¼	+ ¼
Moore .88	15	x3432	u31	30	30½	+ ⅛
Morgan 1.66	9	30712	u41	38¾	41	+ 2½
Morgn pf5e	..	43	57¼	56¼	56¼	.....
MorgGr	..	286	u 9¼	8⅞	9¼	+ ¼
MorKeg .20	24	114	9	8½	8¾	— ⅛
MorgnP	36	456	18¼	17¾	18	+ ⅜
MorgSt s.90	7	2524	66¾	62⅝	66¼	+ 3¼
MorKnd 1.48	..	1588	42	40⅞	41⅜	— ½
MtgRty 2	9	493	17	16¾	16⅞	+ ⅛
Morton .92	**19**	**x5651**	**47¼**	**46⅛**	**46⅜**	**.....**
Motel 61.22	193	2136	u14¼	13½	13½	— ½
Motorla .76	16	29551	54⅜	50½	54⅜	+ 1¾
MunHi n.32e	.	1032	10	9¾	9⅞	— ⅛
MunFd n.12e	..	963	11⅝	11¼	11½	+ ⅛
Munsng	..	942	3¾	3¼	3¾	+ ⅛
MurpO 1	25	2034	u38¾	37⅜	37¾	+ ⅛
MutOm 1.56e	..	88	14¼	14	14¼	+ ¼
MyerL	..	429	5	4¾	4⅞	— ⅛
Mylan .10	20	3803	10	9⅜	10	+ ¼
—N—						
NBB .92	10	234	16⅜	16⅛	16¼	— ¼
NBD 1.68	9	4937	u47⅜	46⅛	47⅜	+ ½
NBI	..	456	2¼	2	2	.....
NCH .72a	11	x71	43½	42½	43	+ ¼
NCNB 1	**15**	**x54054**	**u45⅛**	**41⅝**	**44¾**	**+ 3⅝**

Stock	PE	Vol	Hi	Lo	Last	Chg
PiedNG 1.60	**10**	**242**	**24⅜**	**24**	**24¼**	**— ⅛**
Pier1 .12	20	6569	14	13⅜	13¾	+ ¼
PilgRg .50e	..	650	u 9⅛	8⅞	9	.....
PilgPr .06	24	693	8⅜	7¾	7¾	— ⅜
PinWst 1.60	..	15491	13⅛	12½	13	.....
PionrEl .53e	26	2	48½	48½	48½	—1
PitnyBw 1.04	15	x5689	46⅞	45	45⅛	— ⅞
Pittstn .20	19	2473	21⅜	20	21¼	+ ½
PlcrD g.30	..	x15444	13⅛	12½	12¾	— ⅛
PlainsP .10e	29	797	34¾	33⅜	33⅞	— ⅞
Playboy	..	54	14⅝	14¼	14¼	— ⅜
Plesey 1.47e	14	1	43	43	43	.....
PogoPd	..	11534	u7¼	5¼	6¾	+ 1⅜
Polaroid .60	..	x21387	40⅛	38⅞	40⅛	+ 1⅜
PopeTal .60	8	1795	u24	22¾	23¾	+ ⅞
Portec	38	311	8⅛	7⅞	7⅞	— ¼
PortGC 1.96	11	5062	24⅛	23¼	24	+ ⅝
PorG pf2.60	..	13	27¼	26¾	27¼	+ ⅝
Potltch 1.04	8	1813	u35¾	34½	35⅝	+ ⅝
PotmEl 1.46	10	x47557	22	20⅝	21⅛	— ⅜
PotEl pf2.44	..	2	127	126	126	—1
PotEl pf3.37	..	334	41¼	41⅛	41¼	+ ¼
Premrk .84	13	5317	u39⅝	37	37½	—1⅞
Premr .48	18	394	29¼	29	29⅛	+ ⅛
Primrk	..	699	8½	8¼	8⅜	.....
PrimeC	..	22450	16⅝	15⅛	16½	+ 1¼
PrimeM .08	13	3865	31⅛	30½	30¾	.....
PrMLtd 2.04	16	193	14¾	14½	14⅝	+ ⅛
Primca .28	6	26220	22⅞	21⅜	22⅛	+ ⅞
ProctG 3.20	**15**	**17119**	**u103¾**	**101¼**	**102⅝**	**+ ½**
PrdRs .48	19	586	20½	20⅛	20½	+ ¼
ProgCp .44	8	5478	28⅝	27⅞	27⅞	.....
Proler 1.40	6	131	74⅝	73	74	— ½
ProsSt n1.44	..	668	9⅜	9	9⅜	+ ⅜
PruInt 1.02	..	3181	8⅞	8¾	8⅞	.....
PruRtC	3	276	1⅜	1¼	1¼	.....
PruRl .68	..	x398	6⅝	6¼	6½	+ ¼
PruStr 1.05a	..	5661	8½	8¼	8⅜	+ ⅛
PSvCol 2	12	6375	22¼	21⅝	21⅞	— ⅜
PSCol pf7.15	..	z10	69½	69½	69½	—1
PSCol pf2.10	..	31	21⅝	21⅜	21⅜	.....
PSIn pfB1.04	..	z5200	u13¾	13	13	— ½
PSIn pfC1.08	..	z330	13	12¾	12¾	—1
PSIn pfF8.52	..	z1020	87⅞	87½	87⅞	+ 1⅞

TIPS & TRAPS

Calculations are generally made using a calculator; therefore, you may want to memorize the decimal equivalents for eighths.

$\frac{1}{8} = 0.125$ $\frac{2}{8} = \frac{1}{4} = 0.25$ $\frac{3}{8} = 0.375$ $\frac{4}{8} = \frac{1}{2} = 0.5$

$\frac{5}{8} = 0.625$ $\frac{6}{8} = \frac{3}{4} = 0.75$ $\frac{7}{8} = 0.875$

Self-Check

Use information about the common stock for AudioVideo (Figure 18-2).

1. What was the closing price in dollars and cents?
2. During the last year, what was its high price? Its low price?
3. What is the difference between today's high price and low price?
4. What was yesterday's closing price?

		Yield	
	Div	%	PE
ATG	1.88	7.6	12

Figure 18-3

Calculating and Distributing Dividends

dividend: an amount of money paid per share of stock from profits.

Returning to the headings in Figure 18-1, look at the three columns repeated in Figure 18-3. After a company's earnings are computed for a given period, with its expenses subtracted, any extra earned money is *profit*. The board of directors can vote to reinvest some money into the business or can declare a dividend with some or all of the profits. A **dividend** is an amount of money per share to be distributed to the stockholders. The dividend can be expressed either as a percentage of the par value or face value or as a dollar amount. It is usually declared quarterly (every 3 months), but if business is poor or if the directors so decide, there may be no dividends at all. The number in the "Div" column in Figure 18-3 is the dollar amount of the last annual dividend received by an investor for each share of stock owned. Here the investor in ATG received $1.88 per share.

cumulative preferred stock: a type of stock that guarantees dividends each year even if the company does not pay a dividend.

dividends in arrears: dividends on cumulative preferred stock that have not been paid previously but that have priority when dividends are paid.

Preferred stockholders have first claim to a company's dividends; common stockholders receive dividends after the preferred stockholders have received theirs. Similarly, in case of bankruptcy, preferred stockholders must be paid before common stockholders.

Dividends on preferred stock are at a fixed rate. There are various types of preferred stock. *Convertible preferred stock* allows the stock to be exchanged for a certain number of shares of common stock later on. With *participating preferred stock,* the stockholder can receive additional dividends if the company does well. And with **cumulative preferred stock,** dividends are earned every year. If no dividends are paid one year, the amounts not paid are recorded. These **dividends in arrears** must be paid when money becomes available before other preferred or common stock dividends are paid.

Step by Step

Distributing Dividends from an Amount of Available Money

Step 1. First pay dividends in arrears. (Multiply the number of shares held by preferred stockholders by the rate.)

Step 2. Subtract the amount of dividends in arrears from the total amount. This is the subtotal.

Step 3. From this subtotal, pay the present year's preferred stockholders. (Multiply the number of preferred shares held by stockholders by the rate.)

Step 4. Subtract this payment from the subtotal.

Step 5. Divide the remaining amount by the number of common shares held by stockholders. This is the dividend per share for common stockholders.

EXAMPLE 2

Your company has issued 20,000 shares of cumulative preferred stock that will earn dividends at \$0.60 per share and 100,000 shares of common stock. Last year you paid no dividends; this year there is \$250,000 available for dividends. How are the dividends to be distributed to the preferred and common stockholders?

Preferred stockholders received no dividends last year so this year's dividends in arrears must be paid them:

$20{,}000 \times \$0.60 = \$12{,}000$

The remaining money ($\$250{,}000 - \$12{,}000 = \$238{,}000$) is distributed to the preferred and common stockholders for this year as follows:

To preferred stockholders: $20{,}000 \times \$0.60 = \$12{,}000$

Amount left for common stockholders ($\$238{,}000 - \$12{,}000 = \$226{,}000$) is divided among all the common stockholders.

To common stockholders: $\dfrac{\$226{,}000}{100{,}000} = \$2.26$ per share

Notice that the \$0.60 dividend per share for the preferred stock is a guaranteed but fixed rate, whereas the dividend per share of common stock has the potential to be higher (or lower) than that, but with no guarantee. Last year's common stock owners received no dividends, but this year they received more than did the preferred stockholders for 2 years. Since dividends are income to the stockholder, they are one measure of the desirability of owning a particular stock.

Self-Check

Your company has \$200,000 to distribute in dividends. There are 20,000 shares of preferred stock which earns dividends at \$0.50 per share and 80,000 shares of common stock.

5. How much money goes to preferred stockholders?

6. How much goes to common stockholders?

7. How much per share does a common stockholder receive in dividends?

Current Stock Yield

The second column in Figure 18-3 is "Yield %," sometimes called the current **yield** for the stock. It is a comparative measure of the dividend. It tells (as a percent) how great the dividend is compared to today's closing price for the stock.

yield: for stocks, current yield is annual earnings per share (dividends) divided by today's closing price; for bonds, current yield is annual earnings per bond (interest) divided by today's closing price.

Step by Step

Calculating Current Stock Yield

Step 1. Divide the annual dividend per share by today's closing price (expressed as a decimal):

$$\text{Current stock yield} = \frac{\text{annual dividend per share}}{\text{today's closing price}}$$

Step 2. Express the answer as a percent, rounded to the nearest tenth.

EXAMPLE 3

For Figure 18-2, Ausimont (AUS) has a \$0.60 dividend. Today's closing price is $34\frac{3}{8}$. Calculate the current stock yield.

$$\text{Current stock yield} = \frac{\$0.60}{\$34.375} = 0.01745$$

$$= 1.7\%$$

This matches the figure for AUS in the "Yield %" column.

Notice that because the numerator of the fraction is the amount of the dividend, if no dividend has been declared, there can be no yield. This is indicated by three dots in the yield column.

It might seem as if a large yield would always be more desirable than a small one, but if a company is putting its profits into redevelopment instead of dividends, there may be a small yield now. However, if the company becomes a stronger business, the stock price itself might rise. If an investor sold the stock at that later time, the return on the investment then could be high, even though the yield figure now is low.

Comparing Price to Earnings

price-earnings (PE) ratio: closing price per share of stock divided by the annual net income per share.

The third column in Figure 18-3, "PE," gives the **price-earnings (PE) ratio.** It is a measure of how much the stock is selling for, compared with its per share earnings. The figures used in the calculation are the current price per share (at the close of the business day) and the annual net income per share for the last four quarters. (The last figure is reported by the company and is found by dividing the company's total earnings by the number of shares outstanding.)

Step by Step

Calculating the PE Ratio

Step 1. Divide the closing price per share by the annual net income per share:

$$\text{PE ratio} = \frac{\text{closing price per share}}{\text{annual net income per share}}$$

Step 2. Round to the nearest whole number.

EXAMPLE 4

BRT Rlty Tr. (Figure 18-2) has a closing price of $15\frac{7}{8}$ and annual net income per share of \$2.48. What is the PE ratio?

$$\text{PE ratio} = \frac{15\frac{7}{8}}{2.48} = \frac{15.875}{2.48}$$

$$= 6.4012096$$

$$= 6$$

which matches the figure for BRT Rlty in the "PE" column.

The PE ratio can vary, usually between 3 and 50. A high value indicates a high price relative to a stock's earnings. This can happen if the price is too high (the stock is overpriced) or if earnings have been low, either as a result of poor business or if the company is not yet earning to its potential. A low value for the PE ratio shows a lower price compared to earnings. This can happen if the price is too low (the stock is undervalued) or if people feel the business' potential is poor. If a PE ratio is not given in the stock listings, the company probably has lost money during the past year.

Self-Check

8. The stock of a new company is selling for $24\frac{1}{2}$ and the company has annual income of \$1.75 per share. What is its PE ratio?

Consider the following three stocks:

		Yield	
	Div	%	PE
ATE	2.76	8.5	9
AVT	0.50	2.2	16
BRT	2.48	15.6	6

ATE had the highest dividend, BRT had the greatest yield, and AVT had the highest PE ratio. Thus these figures, by themselves and with no interpretation, would not tell us which investment was best. So a cautious investor often "follows the stock market" and seeks advice from knowledgeable persons in order to tell whether a particular company meets his or her investment needs.

Cost of Buying and Selling Stocks

For each purchase or sale of stock, the commission, an added cost of trading stock, must be considered in addition to the purchase or sale price. Brokers' commissions can vary; for example, *discount brokers* usually charge less because they do not give advice or provide background research about stocks but only handle buy-sell transactions. Also the number of shares traded affects the cost of the sale. A group of 100 shares or a multiple of 100 shares is called a *round lot;* a group less than 100 is called an *odd lot,* and there is an extra charge for trading it.

EXAMPLE 5

Your broker charges 2% of the stock price for trading round lots and an additional 1% on the odd-lot portion. You buy 250 shares of Avon Products (Figure 18-2) at 25. What is your total cost for the purchase?

Cost for 250 shares	$250 \times \$25 = \$6{,}250.00$
Commission on round lot	$0.02 \times 200 \times \$25 = \$\ \ 100.00$
Commission on odd-lot portion	$0.03 \times 50 \times \$25 = \$\ \ \ \ 37.50$

The cost of purchase of stock:

$\$6{,}250.00 + \$100.00 + \$37.50 = \$6{,}387.50$

EXAMPLE 6

After a year you sell the 250 shares of Avon Products for $32 per share. Your broker charges the same commission percentages for selling the stock. What are your total receipts from the sale?

Proceeds from 250 shares	$250 \times \$32 = \$8{,}000$
Commission on round lot	$0.02 \times 200 \times \$32 = \$\ \ 128$
Commission on odd-lot portion	$0.03 \times 50 \times \$32 = \$\ \ \ \ 48$

Total receipt from sale of stock:

$\$8{,}000 - \$128 - \$48 = \$7{,}824$

TIPS & TRAPS

Commission increases the cost of a purchase but decreases the profit from a sale. (Add the commission when figuring cost; subtract the commission when figuring profit.)

Return on Investment

return on investment (ROI): total gain on a purchase divided by the total cost of the purchase.

The **return on investment (ROI)** is a percent that measures the total amount of money received after all costs of commission have been subtracted and dividends have been added. It is expressed in relation to the cost of purchase as a percent to the nearest hundredth.

Step by Step

Calculating ROI (a gain is assumed)

Step 1. Find the net gain by subtracting the total cost of purchase from the total receipts of sale.

Step 2. Add the amount of annual dividends to the net gain to find the total gain.

Step 3. Divide total gain by cost of purchase:

$$\text{ROI} = \frac{\text{total gain}}{\text{cost of purchase}}$$

Step 4. Express the answer as a percent, rounded to the nearest hundredth.

EXAMPLE 7

What is the return on your investment in Avon Products stock? (See Examples 5 and 6.) Assume your dividends during the past year were $1 per share.

Step 1. Total receipt from purchase ($7,824) minus total cost of purchase of stock ($6,387.50) gives the net gain, $1,436.50.

Step 2. Adding dividends ($250 for all the shares) gives a total gain of $1,686.50.

Step 3. $\text{ROI} = \dfrac{\text{total gain}}{\text{cost of purchase}}$

$$= \frac{\$1{,}686.50}{\$6{,}387.50}$$

$$= 0.264031$$

Step 4. 0.264031 = 26.40% (rounded)

Obviously, a high ROI figure indicates a high gain compared to cost. An investor is usually seeking the maximum return on investment.

Self-Check

You buy 250 shares of XYZ stock at $4 per share. Your broker charges 2% of the stock price for round lots and an additional 1% for odd lots.

9. What was the commission on the round lot? On the odd lot?
10. What was your total cost for purchasing the stock?
11. If you sell these shares through the same broker for $5 per share, what will be the commission on the round lot? On the odd lot?
12. What are your total receipts from the sale?
13. Do you have a gain or a loss? How much?
14. You purchased 100 shares of stock at $5 per share and sold them for $7 per share. During that time you received $0.50 per share in dividends. What is your return on this investment? (Disregard commissions.)

Section Review

For Problems 1–4 and 10–14, refer to Figure 18-4, p. 546.

1. **a.** How many shares of Huffy stock (HUF) were traded?
   b. What is the difference between the high and low prices of the last 52 weeks?
   c. What is today's closing price?
   d. What was yesterday's closing price?

2. **a.** What was the dividend for one share of Huffy stock?
   b. What is the day's closing price for one share of Huffy stock?

   c. Using the information from (a) and (b), determine the current yield on Huffy stock. Round to the nearest hundredth percent.

Figure 18-4

	52 Weeks Hi	Lo	Stock	Sym	Div	Yld %	PE	Vol 100s	Hi	Lo	Close	Net Chg
↑	34⅛	21¼	Holiday	HIA		...	7	1266	34½	33½	34¼	+1¼
	63⅛	26⅞	HollyFarms	HFF	1.32	2.1	13	1598	61¾	61½	61¾	+ ¼
↑	37⅝	22⅞	HomeDepot	HD	.12	.3	25	2106	38¼	37½	37⅞	+ ¾
	14¾	10½	HomeGp	HME	.20	1.4	5	353	13⅞	13⅝	13⅞	+ ¼
	22½	20⅝	HomeIns pf		2.95	13.8	...	101	21⅜	21¼	21⅜	+ ⅛
	18½	7¼	HomeOwnrS&L	HFS		...	11	138	8⅞	8¾	8¾	– ⅛
↑	36⅝	21⅜	Homefed	HFD	.20	.5	7	1117	37	36⅛	37	+ ⅞
	16¾	12⅛	Homestake	HM	.20	1.5	8	1092	13¾	13½	13½	– ⅛
	6⅞	3½	HomestdFnl	HFL	.25	6.7	...	110	4	3¾	3¾	– ⅛
	6⅝	3½	HomestdFnlB	HFLB	.15	4.3	...	2	3½	3½	3½	...
s	37½	24⅞	HondaMotor	HMC		...	17	446	29	28¾	29	+ ½
	76⅝	56¾	Honeywell	HON	2.10	2.9	...	1503	72	70¾	71⅜	+ ¾
n	22⅛	18¼	HongKongTelcm	HKT	.42e	2.0	...	1828	20½	20⅜	20½	+ ¼
	9⅜	5½	HopperSol	HS		...	...	34	7½	7¼	7⅜	+ ⅛
	3⅛	1⅝	HorizonHlth	HHC		...	...	4	1¾	1¾	1¾	...
	16⅜	7⅞	HotelInvTr	HOT	1.00	11.6	78	60	8⅞	8⅝	8⅝	– ¼
	50¼	30⅝	HougtnMif	HTN	.66	1.4	27	405	46¾	46	46⅛	+ ⅛
	25	15¾	HouseFab	HF	.48	2.0	14	1275	25	24	24½	+ ⅛
	65½	51½	HouseInt	HI	2.14b	3.4	9	1288	63⅛	62⅝	63	+ ⅛
	55⅛	52	HouseInt wi			...	...	60	52¼	52¼	52¼	+ ¼
	126½	107	HouseInt pf		6.25	5.2	...	7	120⅞	120⅜	120⅞	–2⅜
	32½	26⅝	HoustnInd	HOU	2.96	10.6	8	1374	27⅞	27⅝	27⅞	+ ¼
	2¼	1⅛	HoustnOilR	RTH		...	...	35	1⅝	1⅝	1⅝	...
	14½	6	HowellCp	HWL		...	...	6	8	8	8	...
s	19¾	12⅛	Huffy	HUF	.32	1.8	33	97	17¾	17½	17⅝	...
s	19⅜	16½	HughsSply	HUG	.32	1.7	9	7	18½	18⅜	18⅜	...
↑	30	22½	Humana	HUM	.92	3.0	13	3353	30¼	29⅜	30¼	+ ⅞
	30	23¼	HuntMfg	HUN	.40	1.4	19	6	29⅜	29¼	29¼	...
↑	37⅛	20	Huntgint	HTD	.22e	.6	24	327	37⅝	36⅝	37¼	+ ½
n	12⅝	11⅜	Huntway	HWY	1.38	11.9	...	171	11⅝	11½	11⅝	...
	34⅛	25⅛	Hydraulic	THC	1.58	5.7	14	29	27⅞	27¾	27⅞	+ ⅛

3. a. How much money was received in dividends for one share of Honeywell stock? For 50 shares? For 100 shares?

   b. What is today's closing price for one share of Honeywell stock?

   c. What is the current yield on Honeywell stock? Round to the nearest hundredth percent.

4. a. Calculate the current yield for Homestd Fnl (HFL). (Does your answer in (a) match the "Yield %" figure?)

   b. Which of the two companies, Homestd Fnl or Honeywell, has the greater dividend per share?

   c. Which of the two companies, Homestd Fnl or Honeywell, has the greater yield?

5. Stock A pays $1 dividend and sells for $5 a share. Stock B pays $1 dividend and sells for $50 a share. Which stock will have the greater yield? Why?

6. You own 100 shares of preferred cumulative stock that pays dividends at $0.85 per share in a company that did not pay any dividends for the past two years. This year you expect to receive dividends in arrears.

a. How much will you receive for dividends in arrears?

b. How much will you receive for this year's dividends?
c. If you had owned 100 shares of common stock which will pay \$1.80 per share this year, how much would you have received in dividends from that investment for the three years?

7. Your company has 120,000 shares of preferred stock which pays dividends at \$0.25 per share, and 200,000 shares of common stock. This year \$500,000 is to be distributed. The preferred stockholders are also due to receive dividends in arrears for 1 year.
   a. What is the amount of the dividends in arrears?

   b. How much will go to the preferred stockholders for this year?

   c. How much money will be distributed in all to common stockholders?
   d. What is the dividend per share for the common stockholders?

8. A new company's stock is selling for $18\frac{1}{2}$ and has annual earnings of \$1.20 per share. What is its PE ratio?

9. Penny Stock Corp. stock is selling for $1\frac{1}{4}$ per share and has annual earnings of \$0.10 per share. What is its PE ratio?

For Problems 10–14, take the rate of commission to be 2% on the round lot and an additional 1% on the odd-lot portion.

10. You wish to purchase 150 shares of Holly Farms stock at $61\frac{3}{4}$.
    a. What is the broker's commission on the round lot? On the odd-lot portion?

    b. What is your cost of purchasing the stock, including commission?

11. You wish to purchase 120 shares of Hunt Mfg (HMN) at $29\frac{1}{4}$.
    a. What is the broker's commission on the entire purchase?

b. Including commission, what is your cost of purchasing the stock?

12. Later you sell the 120 shares of Hung Mfg stock (see Problem 11) for $31 per share.

a. What is the broker's commission on the entire sale?

b. What are your final receipts from the sale of the stock?

13. a. Compare your answer in Problem 11(b) with that in Problem 12(b). Do you have a net gain or a net loss? How much?

b. Assume that you received $0.40 per share in dividends last year. Use that information and your answer to part (a) to calculate the return on your investment in Hunt Mfg. Round to the nearest hundredth percent.

14. You own 100 shares of Humana stock, for which you paid $28\frac{1}{2}$. You received annual dividends of $0.92 per share. You are about to sell the same shares for $30\frac{1}{4}$. Calculate your ROI.

Bonds

bond: a legal promise to repay an amount of money at a fixed time, with annual interest, given by a corporation, municipality, or the federal government.

face value (par value): for stocks, the amount at the time of issue; for bonds, usually $1,000.

maturity date: the date on which a corporation will repay the face value of a bond.

After time passes, a corporation may need to raise more money than its initial offering of stock produced. It can then issue more stock, thereby creating more shares or ownership. However, the company management may be reluctant to do this because additional shares would lessen the ownership rights (dilute the rights) of the existing stockholders. To raise the needed money, the company may decide to borrow it for a short term from a bank, or for a longer term (5 years or more) from the public, by selling bonds. In exchange for money from the public, the company gives a **bond,** a promise to repay the money at a specific later date and in the meantime to pay interest annually.

A bond has a **face value (par value),** usually $1,000; a certain date of repayment **(maturity date);** and a certain fixed *rate of interest* per year.

Since a bond is an obligation of the company with a promise of future repayment, the public's judgment of the company's future will affect the sale of the bond. The amount of interest to be paid is another key feature that investors look at closely.

Not only do companies sell bonds, called **corporate bonds,** but state and local government sell *municipal bonds* and the federal government sells *treasury bonds.* Government bonds are often attractive to investors because the interest payments on them are exempt from federal income tax. This discussion deals only with corporate bonds, which come in various types. Among them are bonds in which the investor sends in a coupon at a specified time to receive interest (*coupon bonds*) or receives interest automatically by being listed with the corporation (*registered bonds*). Bonds can have a provision that allows them to be converted to stock (*convertible bonds*) or that allows the corporation to repurchase the bond before its maturity date (*recallable bonds*).

corporate bond: a bond issued by a corporation, as distinguished from a municipal or treasury bond.

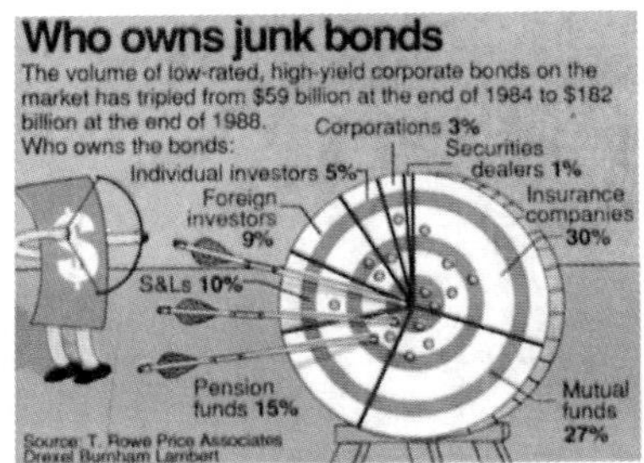

By Shelley Arps, USA TODAY

Since bonds are a legal debt of the corporation, if the company goes bankrupt, the bondholders' claims have priority over those of the stockholders. Bonds of businesses that are bankrupt or in financial difficulty, called *junk bonds,* can thus yield a high return (or be next to worthless) but are a risky and speculative investment.

Once bonds are issued, people buy and sell them at varying prices in the **bond market.** Here, as in the stock market, "market conditions" prevail: A given bond can sell for more than its face value (a **premium bond**) or less than its face value (a **discount bond**). A bond with high interest payments may be attractive to investors, so its price may rise, causing the bond to *sell at a premium.* Or, if interest payments are low, a bond price may tend to drop in order to attract investors, causing the bond to *sell at a discount.*

bond market: the buying or selling of bonds to the public; the location where such trades are made.

premium bond: a bond selling for more than its face value.

discount bond: a bond selling for less than its face value.

> **TIPS & TRAPS**
> Keep in mind that no matter what the market price of a bond, the corporation pays interest on the face value of $1,000 per bond.

Reading Bond Listings

Figure 18-5 shows how bonds are listed in the *Wall Street Journal,* with the headings of each column explained. This discussion assumes the face

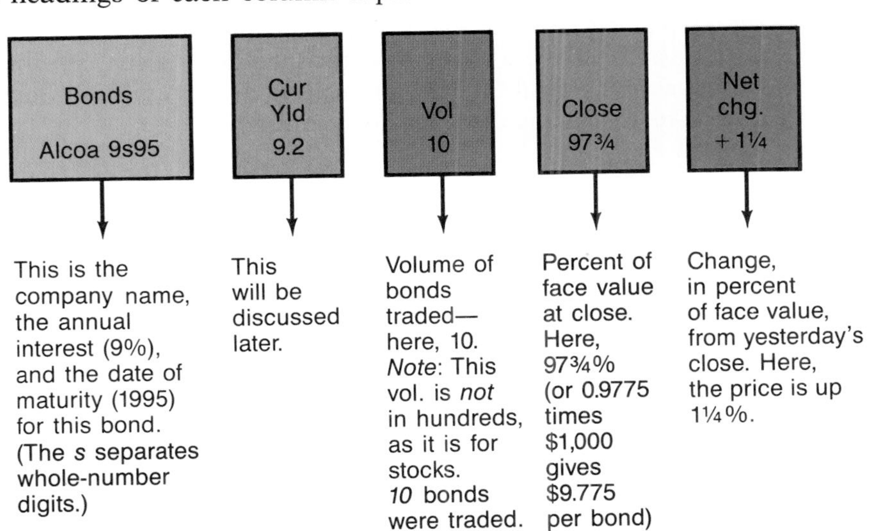

Figure 18-5 How to Read Bond Listings

Bonds	Cur Yld	Vol	Close	Net Chg.
Alcoa 9s95	9.2	.0	97¾	+ 1¼
AMAX 14¼90	13.8	10	103⅜	− 1
AMAX 14½94	12.6	35	115	+ ¾
AForP 5s30	9.7	2	51⅝	− ⅛
AAirl 4¼92	5.1	14	83	...
ABrnd 8⅝90	8.8	2	97¾	...
AmMed 9½01	cv	67	97¾	+ ¼
AmMed 8¼08	cv	16	66¾	+ ¾
ATT 6s00	8.0	29	75	+ ⅛
ATT 5⅛01	7.5	10	68	− ⅛
ATT 8¾00	9.5	474	92¼	+ ⅜
ATT 7s01	8.7	87	80½	+ ¼
ATT 7⅛03	8.9	27	79⅝	+ ½
ATT 8.80s05	9.7	63	91⅛	+ ⅛
ATT 8⅝s07	9.6	5	89½	+ ⅜
ATT 8⅝26	9.8	115	87⅞	+ ½
Amoco 6s98	7.1	62	85	+ 4½
Amoco 9.2s04	9.5	10	96⅜	+ 1½
Amoco 7⅞07	9.3	6	84½	...
AmocoCda 7⅜13	7.1	193	104½	+ ¼
AmocoCd na13½03	...	6	120	+ 5½
Andarko 5¾12	cv	10	97½	+ ½
Apch 8.5s06	8.5	24	99¾	+ 2
Apch 7½12	cv	35	86½	+ ½
ArizP 10⅝00	10.6	50	100½	+ ½
Atchsn 4s95	5.6	5	72	− ½
Atchn 4s95r	5.6	20	72	...
ARich 5⅝97	6.7	2	84	− ¼
ARch dc7s91	7.6	40	92¼	+ ⅜
ARch 10⅜95	10.1	10	102½	+ ½
ARch 9½96	9.7	10	98	+ ⅜
ARch 9⅞16	9.8	50	100½	...
AutDt 6½11	cv	50	108	− ½
Avnet 8s13	cv	9	83¾	...
BPNA 9¼01	9.7	20	95	− 1½
BRE 9½08	cv	35	99¾	+ ¼
BakrHgh 9½06	cv	10	93	− ½
Bally 6s98	cv	3	89½	+ ½
Bally 10s06	cv	20	92	+ ½

Figure 18-6

value of all bonds to be $1,000. It is important to notice that bond prices are given as a *percent of face value,* not in dollars (points), as for stock. Thus, in Figure 18-5, Alcoa's closing price is $97\frac{3}{4}\%$ of its face value. ($97\frac{3}{4}\%$ equals the decimal 0.9775. The face value is $1,000.) In dollars, the bond price is $977.50.

The number of bonds traded on any given day is much less than the number of stocks, so the "Vol." column in Figure 18-5 gives the *actual number* of bonds traded, not a number to be multiplied by 100, as for stocks. And, because there is less activity in the bond market, daily prices vary less, so the day's high, low, and closing prices tend to be the same. (In Figure 18-5 and subsequent figures, only closing prices are shown.) As with stocks, yesterday's closing price for bonds is not listed but can be easily calculated.

Step by Step

Calculating the Price of a Bond from a Bond Listing

Step 1. Find the price listed. It is expressed as a percent of $1,000.

Step 2. Change the percent to a decimal.

Step 3. Multiply this by $1,000.

Step 4. Express the answer in dollars and cents. This is the dollar price of one bond.

EXAMPLE 8

To calculate yesterday's bond price from today's listing of Alcoa (Figure 18-6), notice that the bond closed at $97\frac{3}{4}\%$ of its face value, which was up $1\frac{1}{4}\%$ from yesterday's close. So yesterday's listing must have been $1\frac{1}{4}\%$ less:

$97\frac{3}{4}\% - 1\frac{1}{4}\% = 96\frac{1}{2}\%$ (or a listing of $96\frac{1}{2}\%$)

$96\frac{1}{2}\% = 0.965$; $0.965 \times \$1{,}000 = \$965$ yesterday's bond price

Self-Check

15. What is the dollar price of a bond that is listed as $98\frac{1}{2}$?

16. From Figure 18-6, what was yesterday's closing bond price for BPNA?

A quick look at the closing price column in Figure 18-6 reveals no bond selling at exactly par value (100%). The discount bonds have a listing less than 100; the premium bonds have a listing greater than 100. (Alcoa is selling at a discount, whereas both AMAX bonds are selling at a premium.) Some of the symbols used in the listing are explained in Figure 18-7.

Figure 18-7

EXPLANATORY NOTES
(For New York and American Bonds)

Yield is current yield.

cv-Convertible bond. cf-Certificates. dc-Deep discount. ec-European currency units. f-Dealt in flat. il-Italian lire. kd-Danish kroner. m-Matured bonds, negotiability impaired by maturity. na-No accrual. r-Registered. rp-Reduced principal. st-Stamped. t-Floating rate. wd-When distributed. ww-With warrants. x-Ex interest. xw-Without warrants. zr-Zero coupon.

vj-In bankruptcy or receivership or being reorganized under the Bankruptcy Act, or securities assumed by such companies.

Cost of Buying and Selling Bonds

Broker's fees for trading bonds also vary, but for purposes of our discussion, let us consider the commission to be $5 for each bond traded.

Step by Step

Calculating the Net Receipt from a Sale of Bonds

Step 1. Multiply the price of one bond (in dollars) times the number of bonds. This gives you the gross receipt from the sale of bonds, before commission.

Step 2. Calculate the commission:

Commission = number of bonds × commission charge per bond

Step 3. Subtract the commission from the gross receipts:

Net receipts = gross receipts − commission

Bonds	Cur Yld	Vol	Close	Net Chg.
GlfRes 12½04	13.4	10	93	+ ½
Hallb 9¼00	9.6	5	95⅞	+ 1
Hawn 9s2000	9.7	5	93	+ ⅜
Heinz 7¼97	8.7	10	83¾	− 2¼
Hercul 8s10	cv	5	111	+ 1½
Holidy 10½94	11.2	220	93⅞	− ⅛
Holidy 11s99	11.9	228	92⅛	+ ⅛
HollyFar 6s17	cv	1	104½	...
HomFSD 6½11	cv	25	99	+ 1
HomeGp 14⅞98	14.3	35	104	+ ½
HousF 8.2s07	9.7	5	84⅝	...
Humn 8½09	cv	108	99½	...
vjHuntIR 9⅞04f	...	45	10	− ⅞
IBM Cr 8s90	8.2	1268	97½	...
IBM Cr 9⅝92	9.5	7	101⅝	+ 1⅞
ICN 12⅞98	14.5	99	88⅝	− ⅛
ITTF 11.85s99	11.8	20	100½	− 1⅜
IllBel 8¼16	9.7	5	84⅝	− ⅞

Figure 18-8

EXAMPLE 9

You sell three Heinz bonds at the day's closing price (see Figure 18-8). What will be your net receipt from the sale of the bonds (after deducting broker's fees)?

Step 1. The price of one bond, as listed, is $83\frac{3}{4}\%$ of face value. The price, in dollars, is $837.50 per bond.

Step 2. For three bonds, your receipts will be $2,512.50, before commission.

Step 3. For three bonds, commission is 3 × $5 = $15.

Step 4. Subtract $15 commission for the three bonds to get $2,497.50 as your net receipts from the sale.

Accrued Interest on Bonds

Returning to Example 9, which calculated the receipts from selling Heinz bonds, note that the computation shown did not take into account an important consideration: In actuality a person most often sells a bond *within an interest period* and the bond has already earned **(accrued)** interest up to that day. So the seller should receive that interest, and in fact it is customary for the buyer to pay for accrued interest at the time of the sale. The buyer will later recover that amount, along with the rest of the interest payment, at the next date that interest is paid by the corporation.

accrued interest: interest earned on bonds since the last annual interest payment.

Accrued interest is calculated by counting the number of days after the last interest payment up to the day before the bond trade. A year is taken as 360 days. The fraction of the counted days divided by 360, multiplied by the annual rate of interest due on the bonds and by the face value of the bonds, gives the accrued interest.

Step by Step

Calculating the Accrued Interest on Bonds

Step 1. Divide the number of days interest has been earned by 360 days.

Step 2. Multiply the fraction from Step 1 by the annual rate of interest and by the face value of the bonds:

$$\frac{\text{Number of days interest earned}}{360} \times \text{annual rate of interest} \times \text{face value of bonds} = \text{accrued interest on bonds}$$

EXAMPLE 10

What is the amount of accrued interest on three Heinz bonds for 26 days of accrued interest?

$$\text{Accrued interest} = \frac{26}{360} \times 0.0725 \times \$3{,}000$$

$$= \$15.71$$

The buyer will pay an additional $15.71 in accrued interest. Heinz, when it sends its next interest payment to the new owner, will effectively reimburse the new owner for that $15.71.

Self-Check

17. You sell two bonds listing at $80\frac{1}{2}$ and pay commission of $5 per bond. What is your net receipt from the sale?

18. What is the amount of accrued interest for 12 days on two bonds paying 9% yearly interest?

Current Bond Yield

yield: for stocks, current yield is annual earnings per share (dividends) divided by today's closing price; for bonds, current yield is annual earnings per bond (interest) divided by today's closing price.

An investor in bonds, like an investor in stocks, wants to know the **yield** of his or her investment. In Figure 18-5, the "Cur Yld" (current yield) column gives a measure of how profitable the investment is. *Current bond yield,* sometimes called *average annual yield,* compares annual earnings (interest) with the closing price of a bond. It is expressed as a percentage of face value.

Step by Step

Calculating Current Bond Yield

Step 1. Divide the annual interest per bond in dollars by the current price per bond in dollars:

$$\text{Current bond yield} = \frac{\text{annual interest per bond}}{\text{current price per bond}}$$

Step 2. Express the answer as a percent.

EXAMPLE 11

What is the current bond yield for Alcoa (Figure 18-5)?

Step 1. 9% interest gives 0.09 × $1,000, or $90, interest per bond. The current price is $97\frac{3}{4}$% of face value, which is $977.50 per bond. The current bond yield is

$$\frac{90}{977.50} = 0.092$$

Step 2. 0.092 = 9.2%, which matches the figure listed under "Cur Yld."

(If commission were to be included in this calculation, the yield would decrease.)

Interest is paid on the $1,000 face value of the bond. Although the stated interest rate for Alcoa is 9%, the current bond yield is higher, at 9.2%. This shows that a discounted bond has a higher yield than its stated interest rate, and a premium bond has a lower yield than its stated interest rate.

Since a bond matures at a fixed future date, we can consider not only its current yield but its long-term yield, called the *yield to maturity*. The details of calculating yield to maturity are not discussed, but it gives a somewhat more accurate measure of an investor's income than does the current annual yield.

Comparing Investments

Many times an investor wants to know which of two investments is performing better. The investor could compare the amount in dollars that would be received by each as of today if the stocks or bonds in question were to be sold. But since there may be quite different amounts invested in each, a better measure of comparative performance is the yield of each.

Step by Step

Comparing the Current Yield of Two Investments

Step 1. Find the current yield, as a percent, of the first stock or bond.

Step 2. Find the current yield, as a percent, of the second stock or bond.

Step 3. Compare the answers in Steps 1 and 2 to determine which is greater.

EXAMPLE 12

Which of the two AmMed bonds (Figure 18-6) is producing the greater yield?

Step 1. AmMed $9\frac{1}{2}01$ yield is $\frac{95}{977.50} = 9.7\%$.

Step 2. AmMed $8\frac{1}{4}08$ yield is $\frac{82.50}{667.50} = 12.4\%$.

Step 3. The second bond has the higher yield.

Self-Check

19. A bond pays 8% annual interest and is selling for 102% of face value. What is its current yield?

20. Which of the two Bally bonds (Figure 18-6) is producing the greater yield?

Section Review

For Problems 1–9 and 12, refer to Figure 18-8.

1. a. How many JCP $9\frac{5}{8}06$ bonds were traded today?
b. What is the annual interest for this bond?
c. What is the date of maturity of this bond?

2. a. What is the dollar price of a Holly Farms bond that is listed at $104\frac{1}{2}$?

b. What is the dollar price of a JCP bond listed at $93\frac{1}{8}$?

c. Which of these bonds is selling at a discount? At a premium?

3. a. Calculate yesterday's closing price for an InMin bond.

b. Calculate yesterday's closing price for a John Ct bond.

4. True or false? If false, explain why: In the *Wall Street Journal* listings, bond prices are given in points (dollars) and stock prices are given as a percent of face value.

For Problems 5–8, take the commission to be $5 per bond.

5. What is the cost of buying three InMin bonds at the closing price, including commission?

6. How much will it cost to purchase five John Ct bonds at the closing price? Include commission.

7. After paying commission, what will you receive from the sale of ten IBM $9\frac{3}{8}04$ bonds at $97\frac{3}{4}\%$?

8. What will be your receipts from the sale of two Holidy $10\frac{1}{2}94$ bonds? Assume you sell at $93\frac{7}{8}$ and that commission is deducted.

9. Your Holidy $10\frac{1}{2}94$ bonds have earned an additional 30 days of accrued interest when you sell them.
   a. What is the amount of accrued interest on one bond?

   b. What is the amount of accrued interest on two bonds?
   c. At the time of the sale, who receives this accrued interest?

10. Corporation X has a 9% bond.

a. How much annual interest does one bond pay (in dollars)?

b. If you own two bonds for 3 years, how much interest will you receive?

c. If you own two bonds for 3 years and 20 days, how much interest, including accrued interest, will you receive?

11. For a bond with annual interest of $12 and current price of 112, what is the current yield?

12. Which has the greater current yield, an IBM $10\frac{1}{4}95$ bond or a Holidy $10\frac{1}{2}94$ bond?

13. You have invested $1,000 in bond A with yearly interest of 10% and $1,000 in bond B with yearly interest of 8%. Today's closing price for bond A shows it is selling at a premium, 120% of face value, whereas bond B is selling at a discount, 80% of face value.

a. What is the current yield on bond A?

b. What is the current yield on bond B?

c. Which is the better investment?

14. You own bond C, which has a current price of 80 and annual interest of 6%, and bond D, which has a current price of 120 and annual interest of 10%. Which bond is the better investment? Why?

Summary

Topic	Page	What to Remember	Example
Reading stock prices	536–537	Stock prices are listed in dollars and fractions of a dollar—eighths, fourths, halves.	A stock is listed as having a closing price of $21\frac{3}{4}$, up $\frac{1}{4}$ from yesterday's close. What is the price today? What was it yesterday? $21.75 today; $21.50 yesterday
Reading stock volume	536–537	Add two zeros to the number listed in the "Vol." column to get the number of shares traded.	Stock A has 15 listed in the "Vol." column. How many shares were traded today? 1,500 shares traded today
Distribution of dividends	538–539	When dividends are distributed, dividends in arrears have first priority, then current dividends on preferred stock, then common stock dividends.	$500,000 is available for dividends, including $20,000 for dividends in arrears, and $20,000 for current preferred stock dividends. How much will be given for common stock dividends? $500,000 − $40,000 = $460,000
Amount of common stock dividend (dividend per share)	538–539	To find the amount of a common stock dividend, divide the total amount available for common stock dividends by the total number of shares of common stocks. This is the dividend per share.	$460,000 is available for common stock dividends. There are 300,000 shares of common stock. What is the dividend per share? $\frac{\$460{,}000}{300{,}000} = \$1.53$ per share
Stock commission	541–542	Commission is charged on both buying and selling stocks. Rates vary. There is usually a higher commission for odd lots (less than 100 shares) than for round lots (multiples of 100 shares).	Taking stock commission to be 2% of the stock price for round lots and an additional 1% for the odd-lot portion (throughout this Summary), what is the commission on the purchase of 350 shares of stock selling at 13 per share? Commission: on round lot: 0.02 × 300 × $13 = $78 on odd lot portion: 0.03 × 50 × $13 = $19.50 Total commission: $97.50
Cost of a stock purchase	542	Compute the cost of the stock and add commission to get the total cost of a purchase.	You purchase 350 shares of stock at $13 per share. Commission is $97.50. What is your total cost for the purchase?

Topic	Page	What to Remember	Example
			Cost of stock: 350 × $13 = $4,550 Commission $ 97.50 Cost of purchase; $4,647.50
Current stock yield	539–540	Divide annual dividends per share by today's closing price and express as a percent. This "yield %" is given in the stock listings. It is a measure of income compared to today's price.	Stock X has a \$0.75 dividend and a closing price of 25. What is its current yield? $\frac{.75}{25} = 3\%$
Price-earnings ratio (PE ratio)	540	Divide closing price per share by the amount of annual earnings (dividends) per share, and express as a whole number. The PE ratio is a measure of the company's performance; it compares the current price to earnings. Interpretations of the PE ratio may vary.	Stock Y has a closing price of $16\frac{7}{8}$ and an annual net income per share of \$1.50. What is the PE ratio? $\frac{16.875}{1.50} = 11.25$ PE ratio is 11. Price is "eleven times" earnings.
Receipt from a sale of stock	542	Compute receipt from stocks and subtract commission to get final receipt from the sale.	You sell 350 shares of stock at \$15 per share. What is your final receipt from the sale? From stocks: 350 × \$15 = \$5,250 Commission: 0.02 × 300 × 15 = 90 0.03 × 50 × 15 = 22.50 \$90 + \$22.50 = \$112.50 Final receipt from sale: \$5,250 − \$112.50 = \$5,137.50
Return on investment (ROI)	542	Find total gain (total receipt minus total cost plus dividends). Divide by total cost and express as a percent rounded to the nearest hundredth. The ROI figure is a measure of how much gain was "returned" to you, compared with the amount invested.	Assume your total gain from a stock is \$780 (that is, \$5,137.50 − \$4,647.50 + dividends of \$290). Assume that your total cost is \$4,647.50. What is the return on your investment? $\frac{\$780}{\$4{,}647.50} = 16.8\%$
Reading bond prices	547–548	Bond prices are listed as a percent of face value. 100% of face value is \$1,000.	A bond is listed as having a closing price of $80\frac{3}{8}$, up $\frac{1}{8}$ from yesterday's close. What is the price today? What was it yesterday? $80\frac{3}{8}\%$ of face value is 0.80375 × \$1,000 or \$803.75 per bond today. $80\frac{3}{8}\% - \frac{1}{8}\% = 80\frac{1}{4}\%$ or \$802.50 per bond yesterday.

Topic	Page	What to Remember	Example
Reading bond volume	548	Volume figure is the actual number of bonds traded.	Bond A has 15 listed in the "Volume" column. How many bonds were traded today? 15
Bond interest	549–550	Bonds pay annual interest. Interest is computed on face value, $1,000, regardless of the market price of the bond.	A bond listed as $6\frac{5}{8}$91 will pay how much interest annually? $6\frac{5}{8}\%$ of $1,000 is $66.25
Bond accrued interest	549–550	At the time of sale, a bond may have earned (accrued) some interest since its last annual interest payment. To compute the amount, find the number of days accrued, divide by 360, multiply by the annual interest rate, and multiply by the face value of the bond.	A bond earning 8% interest has accrued interest for 18 days. What is the amount of accrued interest? $\frac{18}{360} \times 0.08 \times \$1,000 = \$4$
Bond commission	548–549	Commission is charged on both buying and selling bonds. Rates vary.	Taking bond commission to be $5 per bond (throughout this Summary), what is the commission on the purchase of 5 bonds at $98\frac{1}{2}$ per bond? $5 \times \$5 = \$25$
Cost of a bond purchase	549	Compute cost of bonds and add commission to get the total cost of a purchase.	You purchase five bonds listed at $98\frac{1}{2}$. What is the total cost of the purchase? For one bond: $ 985 For five bonds: $4,925 Commission: $ 25 Total cost of purchase: $4,950
Current bond yield	550	Divide the annual interest per share by the current price (in dollars) per bond and express as a percent. The yield figure is given in the bond listings. It is a measure of income compared to the current price of the bond.	Bond B has 8% annual interest and a closing price of 102. What is the current bond yield? $\frac{80}{1,020} = 7.8\%$
Receipt from a bond sale	550	Compute the receipt from the bonds and subtract commission to get the final receipt from the sale.	You sell 10 bonds at 98. What is your final receipt from the sale? From bonds: $9,800 Commission: $ 50 Receipt from sale: $9,750

Chapter Review

1. A corporation's stock listing is as follows:

52 Weeks Hi	Lo	Stock	Sym	Div	Yield %	PE	Vol 100s	Hi	Lo	Close	Net Chg
$28\frac{3}{4}$	$22\frac{1}{4}$	AVEMCO	AVE	.40	1.7	12	20	24	$23\frac{3}{4}$	24	$+\frac{1}{4}$
(a)	(b)	(c)		(d)	(e)	(f)	(g)	(h)	(i)	(j)	(k)

a.–k. Explain the meaning of each entry.

Use the information from Problem 1 for Problem 2.

2. a. What is your cost to purchase 150 shares of AVEMCO at $23\frac{3}{4}$? (Disregard commission.)

b. If commission is 2% on the round lot and an additional 1% on the odd-lot portion, what is your total cost to purchase the shares, including commission?

c. Taking commission into account, if you later sold those 150 shares at 24, would you have a gain or loss? How much?

3. What is the cost of purchasing 250 shares of Huffy stock at $17\frac{5}{8}$? (Disregard commission.)

4. Good Food Corp. earned $3.50 per share last year and is selling at a closing price of $25\frac{1}{2}$. What is its PE ratio?

5. Use the following information about San Diego General stock:

Closing price, $37\frac{3}{8}$ PE ratio, 12

Annual dividends per share, $2.70 Today's volume, 35,700

Select the appropriate information and calculate the current stock yield (to the nearest tenth percent).

6. Sanchez Corp. pays \$1.60 on its 15,000 shares of cumulative preferred stock but has paid no dividends for last year. This year \$500,000 will be paid in dividends.

a. How much will be paid for dividends in arrears?

b. How much will be paid for this year's dividends for the 15,000 shares of preferred stock?

c. There are 75,000 shares of common stock. How much will be paid in all to common stockholders?

d. What is the dividend per share for common stockholders?

7. Atlantic Richfield common stock is listed with dividends of \$4.50; Atlantic Richfield preferred stock is listed with dividends of \$2.80. The common stock is selling at $91\frac{3}{8}$, the preferred, at $218\frac{3}{8}$. Which has the greater yield?

8. A corporation's bond listing is as follows:

Bonds	Cur Yld	Vol	Close	Net Chg
ARch $9\frac{7}{8}$16 (a)	9.8 (b)	50 (c)	$100\frac{1}{2}$ (d)	. . . (e)

a.–e. Explain the meaning of each entry.

Use the information from Exercise 8 for Exercise 9.

9. a. Taking commission at \$5 per bond, find your cost to purchase four bonds of ARch Corporation.

b. Is the bond selling at a premium or a discount?

10. Use the following information about an Epps Oil Corp. bond:

Earns $7\frac{5}{8}$ annual interest
Matures in 2001
Closing price is 94
Net change from yesterday is $+\frac{1}{8}$

Select the appropriate information and calculate the current bond yield.

11. You wish to purchase 8 bonds (Amoco $7\frac{7}{8}$07 bonds) at $84\frac{1}{2}$; they have earned 35 days of accrued interest.
a. What is the amount of accrued interest?

b. Is your cost of purchase increased or decreased by the amount of the accrued interest?
c. Taking into account commission at $5 per bond but not accrued interest, what is your cost of purchase?

12. Compare two bonds: Amoco $7\frac{7}{8}$07 at $84\frac{1}{2}$ and IPap $8\frac{1}{4}$91 at 97.
a. Which would pay more interest next year?

b. Which has the greater current bond yield?

c. Which would require more money to purchase?

13. You bought 5 AmBrnd $8\frac{5}{8}$90 bonds 2 years ago at 95. Today you sell them at $97\frac{3}{4}$.
a. What was your cost of purchase, disregarding commission?

b. What was your receipt from the sale, disregarding commission?

c. What is your return on your investment (ROI)? (Include interest.)

14. ATT has several bonds. You want to purchase five of the same bonds with the greatest current yield for $4,000 or less.

	Bonds	Cur Yield	Vol	Close
a.	ATT $5\frac{1}{8}$01	7.5	10	68
b.	ATT $8\frac{3}{4}$00	9.5	474	$92\frac{1}{4}$
c.	ATT $7\frac{1}{8}$03	8.9	27	$79\frac{5}{8}$
d.	ATT $8\frac{5}{8}$26	9.8	115	$87\frac{7}{8}$

Which one do you choose? Why?

15. As a stock brocker, you must advise your client on a sale. Your client owns 100 shares of Stock A, with total purchase cost of $2,000 and a potential sale receipt of $3,000; it has had annual dividends of $2 per share. She also owns 100 shares of Stock B, with a total purchase cost of $1,500, a potential sale receipt of $2,500, and annual dividends of $1.50 per share.

a. Calculate the return on investment (ROI) for each sale.

b. Which stock, if sold, would give the greater return on investment?

Trial Test

For Problems 1–15, consider the commission on stocks to be 2% on round lots and an additional 1% on the odd-lot portion; consider the bonds to be $1,000 and the commission on bonds to be $5 per bond.

Use the following stock listing for Problems 1–5.

52 Weeks Hi	Lo	Stock	Sym	Div	Yield %	PE	Vol 100s	Hi	Lo	Close	Net Chg
68	$50\frac{1}{8}$	MAPCO	MDA	1.00		11	763	$67\frac{1}{2}$	$66\frac{3}{4}$	$66\frac{3}{4}$	$-\frac{3}{4}$

1. a. What is the difference between today's high and low?

b. What is today's closing price, in dollars?

c. What was yesterday's closing price, in dollars?

d. How many shares were traded today?

2. Select the appropriate information to compute the current yield (not listed).

3. Last year you bought 120 shares of MAPCO at $50\frac{1}{2}$.
a. Calculate the commission on that purchase.

b. What was your total cost for the purchase?

4. Today you wish to sell your 120 shares of MAPCO at $66\frac{3}{4}$.
a. Calculate the commission on the sale.

b. What is your receipt from the sale of the stock?

5. Use your answers to Problems 3 and 4 and the dividend listed to calculate your return on this investment.

6. Your company has $200,000 to distribute in dividends to three groups:

A: One year's dividends in arrears for 5,000 shares of cumulative preferred stock ($0.40 per share)

B: The current year's dividends for those 5,000 shares of preferred stock

C: Dividends on 75,000 shares of common stock.

a. How much is distributed to group A?
b. How much is distributed to group B?
c. How much is distributed to group C?

d. What is the dividend per share of common stock?

7. Select the appropriate information and calculate the current stock yield of stock A and stock B.

52 Weeks				Yield		Vol			
Hi	Lo	Stock	Div	%	PE	100s	Hi	Lo	Close
$34\frac{3}{4}$	$27\frac{3}{4}$	A	1.68		9	415	$34\frac{3}{8}$	$34\frac{1}{8}$	$34\frac{1}{4}$
$65\frac{3}{4}$	$51\frac{1}{8}$	B	2.60		13	1467	$62\frac{7}{8}$	$62\frac{3}{8}$	$62\frac{5}{8}$

8. Stock C has annual earnings of $1.20 per share and a closing price of 48.
a. What is the PE ratio of stock C?

b. If earnings go up next year, but the price stays the same, will the PE ratio increase or decrease?

c. If earnings stay the same next year, but the price goes up, will the PE ratio increase or decrease?

Use the following bond listing for Problems 9–12.

Bond	Cur Yield	Vol	Close	Net Chg
Revln $11\frac{3}{4}$ 95	13.1	91	$89\frac{7}{8}$	$+\frac{3}{8}$

9. a. What is the date of maturity of the bond?
   b. What is the closing price of the bond, in dollars?
   c. What was yesterday's closing price, in dollars?

   d. Is the bond selling at a discount or at a premium?

10. a. How much interest was received last year on one Revln bond?

    b. If the bond has accrued interest for 90 days, how much interest has accrued?

11. Assume that 3 years ago you purchased five Revln bonds at 85.
    a. What was the commission on the purchase? $5 \times \$5 = \$25$
    b. What was your total cost of purchase?

12. Assume that you sell the five Revln bonds today at $89\frac{7}{8}$.
    a. What is the commission on the sale?
    b. What is your receipt from the sale?

    c. Disregard any accrued interest or annual interest. How much gain or loss do you have on these five bonds?

13. Compare the following two stocks.

    Common stock of Enron Cp (2.48 dividend; $41\frac{1}{2}$ closing price)
    Preferred stock of Enron Cp (10.50 dividend; $145\frac{1}{2}$ closing price)

    Which stock of Enron Cp has the greater yield, the common stock or the preferred stock?

14. Compare the following two bonds.

Mobil $7\frac{5}{8}91$ (closing price $94\frac{7}{8}$)
Mobil $8\frac{5}{8}94$ (closing price $95\frac{1}{8}$)

Which bond has the greater yield?

15. As a stock broker, you must advise your client on a purchase. Stock A is selling for 20 now. Next year an owner can reasonably expect to sell it for 22. Dividends have been steady at $1 per year.

Stock B is selling for 50 now. Next year an owner can reasonably expect to sell it for 55. Dividends have been steady at $1 per year.

a. Calculate the ROI for each investment. (Disregard commissions; assume the owner sells the stock in 1 year.)

b. Which stock, A or B, gives the higher return on investment?

Self-Check Solutions

1. $5.50

2. 8 points ($8); $4\frac{1}{4}$ points ($4.25)

3. $5\frac{1}{2} - 5\frac{1}{4} = \frac{1}{4}$ point ($0.25)

4. $5\frac{1}{2} - \frac{1}{8} = 5\frac{3}{8}$ pts ($5.375)

5. 20,000 × $0.50 = $10,000

6. $200,000 − $10,000 = $190,000

7. $\frac{190{,}000}{80{,}000} = \$2.38$ per share

8. PE ratio $= \frac{24.5}{1.75} = 14$

9. 0.02 × 200 × $4 = $16; 0.03 × 50 × $4 = $6

10. Cost of stock: $250 \times \$4 = \$1{,}000$; commission: $\$16 + \$6 = \$22$. Total cost: \$1,022

11. $0.02 \times 200 \times \$5 = \$20$; $0.03 \times 50 \times \$5 = \$7.50$

12. Received for stock: $250 \times \$5 = \$1{,}250$; commission: \$27.50. Total receipts: \$1,222.50

13. Gain; $\$1{,}222.50 - \$1{,}022 = \$200.50$

14.

Receipt from sale:	$100 \times \$7$	= \$700
Dividends:	$100 \times \$0.50$	= \$ 50
Total gain:		\$750
Cost of purchase:	$100 \times \$5$	= \$500

$$\text{Rate of return} = \frac{\$750}{\$500} = 0.15, \text{ or } 15\%$$

15. $98\frac{1}{2}\%$ of $\$1{,}000 = 0.985 \times \$1{,}000 = \$985$

16. Today's closing price is 95, down $1\frac{1}{2}$ from yesterday's closing price. So yesterday's price was $95 + 1\frac{1}{2}$, or $96\frac{1}{2}$ ($96\frac{1}{2}\%$ of face value).

17.

Receipt from bonds:	$2 \times \$805$	= \$1,610
Commission:	$2 \times \$5$	= \$ 10
Net receipts from sale:		\$1,600

18. $\frac{12}{360} \times 0.09 \times \$2{,}000 = \$6$

19. $$\text{Current yield} = \frac{\$80}{\$1{,}020} = 0.0784, \text{ or } 7.8\%$$

20. Bally 6% bond has yield: $\frac{\$60}{\$895} = 0.0670$, or 6.7%

Bally 10% bond has yield: $\frac{\$100}{\$920} = 0.1087$, or 10.9%

19

Tables, Graphs, and Statistics

Learning Objectives

1. Understand how to read and find information in a table. (pp. 567–570)
2. Read, interpret, and draw bar graphs, line graphs, and circle graphs. (pp. 571–576)
3. Understand and use the basic vocabulary and concepts of statistics. (pp. 578–582)

In the fast-paced world of business, we must be able to communicate information about numbers quickly and clearly. Tables, graphs, and statistics are used in corporate reports, newspapers, professional journals, nonfiction books, and on television to present numerical information in an organized manner.

A **table** shows one or more lists of numerical information grouped in some meaningful form. A table may be as simple as a list of entrance-test scores for students at a college over the past 5 years to show how scores have changed.

table: one or more lists of numerical information grouped in some meaningful form.

A **graph** is a symbolic or pictorial display of numerical information. It could be a circle divided into sections to show how tax dollars are used or it could be a line on a grid, tracing the number of people in a certain company over the past 10 years, or it could be bars that show how the spending habits of different age groups compare.

graph: a symbolic or pictorial display of numerical information.

A **statistic** is a number that describes numerical data. Statistics help us understand how individual pieces of information fit in with other, comparable pieces of information. Statistics may be represented in tables and graphs or used alone.

statistic: a number that describes numerical data.

Tables

Tables are used to display numerical information in a clear, readily understandable fashion. It is important to give a table a title that clearly indicates its purpose and to define what each column of numbers represents so that the information in the table can be used effectively.

In Examples 1 through 3, which discuss how to use information in a table, refer to Table 19-1. The Feel Good Fitness Club has offered monthly memberships since it opened in 1985. At the end of the fifth year, the membership office prepared Table 19-1, which shows how many members the club has had at the end of each month since it opened.

You can find some information in the table with only a quick inspection: The entries for March 1985 show that during the first month, 21 men and 8 women joined the club. The November 1988 entries show that between the end of October and the end of November 1988, the number of women exceeded the number of men for the first time.

You can compare pieces of information in a table with one another using addition, subtraction, or percent to find additional information.

Table 19-1 Monthly* Membership of the Feel Good Fitness Club, 1985–1989

	1985		1986		1987		1988		1989	
	Men	**Women**	**Men**	**Women**	**Men**	**Women**	**Men**	**Women**	**Men**	**Women**
January	82	29	101	66	129	105	148	147	169	173
February	84	32	108	70	135	115	148	151	176	179
March	21	8	87	33	108	74	138	117	151	154
April	29	12	88	39	110	76	141	125	153	155
May	35	14	89	43	111	78	140	126	154	156
June	38	15	89	44	109	79	135	125	152	158
July	49	15	86	44	107	78	132	125	150	156
August	53	17	86	45	107	77	133	127	148	155
September	59	20	88	47	109	79	135	132	151	159
October	65	23	91	51	113	86	138	137	157	163
November	71	25	95	58	118	92	140	142	159	165
December	79	28	98	61	127	101	143	144	166	172

*Number of members at the end of each month.

EXAMPLE 1

How many men joined the health club between the end of April and the end of May 1985?

$$\begin{array}{r} 35 \\ -\ 29 \\ \hline 6 \end{array}$$

35 (number of men at the end of May, 1985)
− 29 (number of men at the end of April, 1985)

Subtract the number of male club members in April 1985 from the number of male club members in May 1985.

Six men joined during May 1985.

Recall, from Chapter 2, that a ratio indicates division and can be thought of as a fraction. The *ratio* of one number to another is found by placing the first number in the numerator of a fraction that has the second number in the denominator. Reduce the ratio if possible.

EXAMPLE 2

Find the ratio of men to women in the club at the end of June 1988.

$\frac{135}{125}$ (the number of men) / (the number of women)

The numerator is the number of men in the club as of the end of June 1988; the denominator is the number of women.

$$\frac{135}{125} = \frac{27}{25}$$

The ratio of men to women was $\frac{27}{25}$ at the end of June 1988.

Calculator Sequence

[AC] 135 [÷] 125 [=] ⇒ 1.08   The ratio can also be written as 1.08.

EXAMPLE 3

What percent of new club members between March 1988 and March 1989 were women?

March 1989		March 1988
151	⟵ (number of men) ⟶	138
+ 154	← (number of women) ⟶	+ 117
305	⟵ (total members) ⟶	255

Find the total number of club members at the end of March 1988 and March 1989 by adding the number of male and female club members.

305	(total members, March 1989)
− 255	(total members, March 1988)
50	(total new members)

Subtract the total members in 1988 from the total members in 1989 to find total new members.

154	(number of women in March 1989)
− 117	(number of women in March 1988)
37	(number of new women members)

Subtract the number of women in 1988 from the number of women in 1989 to find total new women members.

$$\frac{37}{50} \times 100 = 74\%$$

Divide the number of new women members by the total number of new members and multiply by 100 to find the percent of new women club members.

74% of the new members between March 1988 and March 1989 were women.

TIPS & TRAPS
It is easy to select the wrong value from a table or to use the correct value in the wrong place in a problem. Plan the solution using words and labels for the table values. Then substitute the values from the table and make the calculations.

Self-Check

Refer to Table 19-1 to answer the following questions.

1. How many more women members than men members were there in October of 1989?
2. Find the ratio of men to women in the club as of the end of December 1988.
3. What percent of new club members between December 1988 and December 1989 were men?

Table 19-2 Class Enrollment by Period and Days of the Week for the Second Semester

Period	Mon.	Tues.	Wed.	Thur.	Fri.	Sat.
1. 7:00– 7:50 A.M.	277	374	259	340	207	0
2. 7:55– 8:45 A.M.	653	728	593	691	453	361
3. 8:50– 9:40 A.M.	908	863	824	798	604	361
4. 9:45–10:35 A.M.	962	782	849	795	561	361
5. 10:40–11:30 A.M.	914	858	795	927	510	361
6. 11:35–12:25 P.M.	711	773	375	816	527	182
7. 12:30– 1:20 P.M.	686	734	696	733	348	161
8. 1:25– 2:15 P.M.	638	647	659	627	349	85
9. 2:20– 3:10 P.M.	341	313	325	351	136	78
10. 3:15– 4:05 P.M.	110	149	151	160	45	0
11. 4:10– 5:00 P.M.	46	72	65	67	11	0
12. 5:05– 5:55 P.M.	37	91	68	48	0	0
13. 6:00– 6:50 P.M.	809	786	796	705	373	0
14. 6:55– 7:45 P.M.	809	786	796	705	373	0
15. 7:50– 8:40 P.M.	565	586	577	531	373	0
16. 8:45– 9:35 P.M.	727	706	817	758	373	0
17. 9:40–10:30 P.M.	702	706	817	758	27	0
18. 10:35–11:25 P.M.	76	70	46	98	0	0

Section Review

Use Table 19-2 to solve Exercises 1–10. A calculator may help.

1. How many students were enrolled in class on Wednesday during the fifth period?

2. How many students were enrolled in classes on Monday during the eleventh period?

3. What is the total class enrollment for the third period Monday through Friday?

4. What is the total class enrollment for the ninth period Monday through Friday?

5. How many more people are enrolled in third period Monday through Friday than in ninth period?

6. Find the total class enrollment by periods Monday through Friday.

Period	Students
1	______
2	______
3	______
4	______
5	______
6	______
7	______

Period	Students
8	_____
9	_____
10	_____
11	_____
12	_____
13	_____
14	_____
15	_____
16	_____
17	_____
18	_____

7. What period has the highest enrollment during the day (periods 1–12)?

8. What period has the highest enrollment at night (periods 13–18)?

9. If 1,768 day students were enrolled during the second semester, what percent of the students were enrolled in a fourth-period class on Monday? Round to the nearest tenth of a percent.

10. Complete Table 19-3, computing day enrollment (periods 1–12) and night enrollment (periods 13–18).

Table 19-3 Day and Night Class Enrollment Second Semester

	Periods	Mon.	Tues.	Wed.	Thurs.	Fri.	Sat.
Day	1–12						
Night	13–18						

Graphs

Graphs are used in business to give a quick and easy visual interpretation of information and to emphasize changes or trends in business. Statistical information usually makes a stronger impression if it can be presented visually. Graphs, like tables, must always have a *title* so that the reader will know what the facts being illustrated represent.

Bar Graphs

bar graph: a graph made with horizontal or vertical bars and used to compare several related values.

Bar graphs are often used *to compare several related values*. Vertical or horizontal bars may be used, and the height or length of each bar corresponds

By Aaron Hightower, USA TODAY

to a specific value. The bars taken together show how the different values relate to one another. It is important to label the axes (the horizontal and vertical sides) of a bar graph, so the person reading it will know the range of possible values and will be able to interpret the values represented by the bars.

Suppose you wish to graph the following data, which show that Hanson's Department Store had the given sales during January through June:

January	$37,534	April	$52,175
February	$43,284	May	$56,394
March	$58,107	June	$63,784

The lowest number is $37,534 and the highest number is $63,784. Therefore, your graph must show values from $30,000 to $70,000. To avoid using very large numbers, you can indicate on the graph that the numbers represent thousands of dollars. Therefore, 65 on the graph would represent $65,000. The bars can be either horizontal or vertical, but you must be sure to label the sides of the graph clearly. All the information needed to interpret the bars on the graph should be clearly stated. Remember, you must always title and label your graphs.

EXAMPLE 4

Draw a horizontal bar graph representing the sales from January through June for Hanson's department store.

You can answer certain questions simply by looking at Figure 19-1. For example, sales were the highest in June. Sales were the second highest in March. In April there was a decline in sales from the previous month.

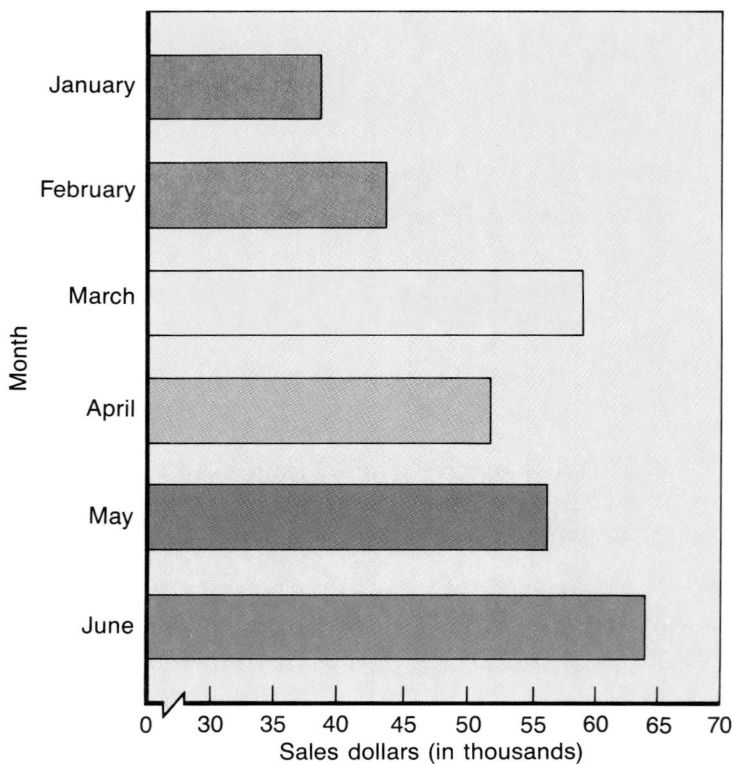

Figure 19-1 Hanson's Department Store Sales, January–June

Line Graphs

A **line graph** is used *to show trends*. Studying the trends shown on a line graph can help businesspeople predict future trends. A line graph of changes in some value helps you quickly determine whether the value is steadily increasing, steadily decreasing, or fluctuating—that is, sometimes increasing and sometimes decreasing. In a single line graph you are not comparing several items, as in a bar graph. You are looking at the *changes* in a particular value.

line graph: a graph made with a series of connected line segments used to show trends.

The information in Table 19-4 can be presented on a line graph as shown in Figure 19-2. The least and greatest values in the table are $1,237 and $1,984, respectively, so the graph may go from $1,000 to $2,000 in $100 intervals. The horizontal side of the graph will show the days of the week, and the vertical side will show the daily sales. Plot each day's sales by placing a dot directly above the appropriate day of the week across from the approximate value. For example, the sales for Monday totaled $1,567. Place the dot above Monday in the interval between $1,500 and $1,600. After each amount has been plotted, connect the dots with straight lines.

Table 19-4 Neighborhood Grocery Daily Sales for Week Beginning Monday, June 21

Monday	$1,567
Tuesday	$1,323
Wednesday	$1,237
Thursday	$1,435
Friday	$1,848
Saturday	$1,984

EXAMPLE 5

Draw a line graph to represent the data in Table 19-4.

Do not label every interval. This would crowd the side of the graph and make it harder to read. Remember the purpose of any graph is to give information that is quick and easy to understand and interpret.

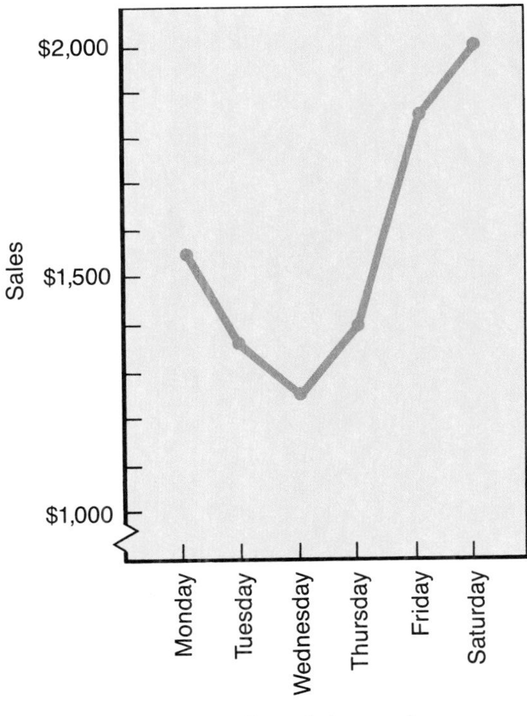

Figure 19-2 Neighborhood Grocery Daily Sales for Week Beginning Monday, June 21

Self-Check

4. Draw a bar graph comparing the quarterly sales of the Oxford Company: January–March, $280,000; April–June, $310,000; July–September, $250,000; October–December, $400,000.

Figure 19-3 Distribution of Family Monthly Take-home Pay of $1,600 for 2-year College Graduates

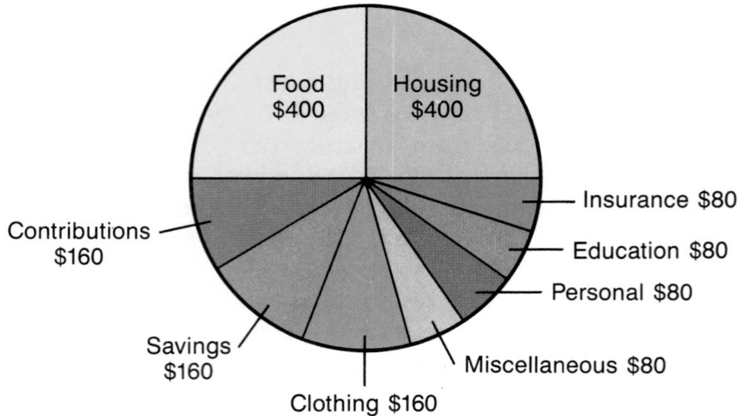

Circle Graphs

circle graph: a graph made by dividing a circle into proportionate parts to show how some whole quantity is being divided into parts.

A **circle graph** is a circle divided into two or more sections to give a visual picture of *how some whole quantity* (represented by the whole circle) *is being divided.* Each section represents a portion of the total amount being illustrated. Figure 19-3 shows a sample circle graph.

The circle graph shows visually how different portions of a family's total income is spent on nine categories of expenses: food, housing, contributions, savings, clothing, insurance, education, personal items, and miscellaneous items.

You can compute the percent of the take-home pay allowed for any of the nine categories of expenses. To do this, write a fraction with the part (category) as numerator and the whole (take-home pay) as denominator, divide to get a decimal equivalent, and then convert the decimal equivalent to a percent. Convert a decimal number to a percent by moving the decimal point two places to the right or by using the [%] key on your calculator.

EXAMPLE 6

Find the percent of total take-home pay spent for food in Figure 19-3.

$\$400 + \$400 + \$80 + \$80 + \$80 + \$80 + \$160 + \$160 + \$160 = \$1{,}600$ Add the amounts shown in each section of the graph to find the total take-home pay.

$\frac{\text{food}}{\text{take-home pay}} = \frac{400}{1{,}600} = \frac{4}{16} = \frac{1}{4}$ Divide the amount spent on food by the total take-home pay.

$\frac{1}{4} = 0.25 \quad 0.25 \times 100 = 25\%$ Convert $\frac{1}{4}$ to a percent.

25% of the family's take-home pay is spent on food.

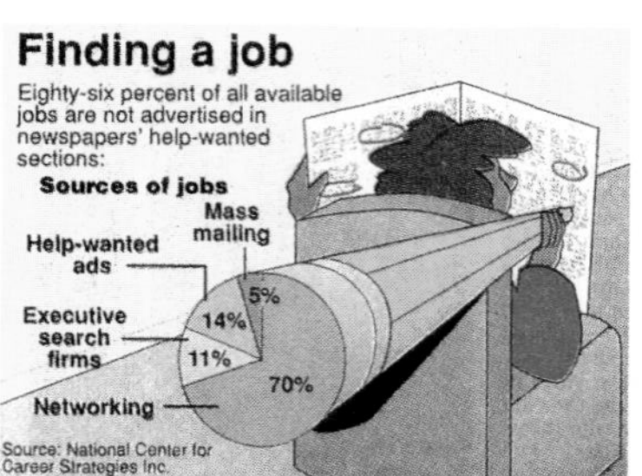

By Marcy E. Mullins, USA TODAY

Together food and housing account for half (50%) of the take-home pay spending, since the same amount is spent on housing as is spent on food ($2 \times 25\% = 50\%$).

You can extend your analysis using the circle graph in Figure 19-3. Suppose you want to know what percent of total take-home pay would be available for a family vacation if the savings and education expenses for 1 month were used for the vacation.

EXAMPLE 7

Compute the percent of take-home pay available for a vacation if the family's savings and education expenses for 1 month were used.

savings	$160	Add savings and education costs for one month.
education	+ 80	
	$240	

$$\begin{matrix}\text{(Part)} \rightarrow \\ \text{(Whole)} \rightarrow\end{matrix} \frac{240}{1{,}600} = \frac{3}{20} = 0.15$$

Write a fraction with the part as the numerator and the whole as the denominator. Multiply by 100 to write the decimal as a fraction.

$0.15 \times 100 = 15\%$

Calculator Sequence

The calculator sequence is

[AC] 160 [+] 80 [=] [÷] 1600 [%] [=] ⇒ 15

The answer is 15%.

A circle graph takes longer to construct than a bar or line graph because you must perform a number of calculations before you can actually draw the graph. A circle stands for 100% of whatever quantity the graph represents, and each "slice" of the circle stands for some part of the total quantity. To divide a circle into slices for a circle graph, you need to know what fraction of the whole quantity makes up each part. Once you know the fraction for each part, you can calculate how much of the circle goes into each part. Since the whole circle has 360° **(degrees)**, you multiply the fraction for each part times 360 to find out how many degrees each slice should have.

degree: $\frac{1}{360}$ of a complete circle. There are 360° in a circle.

EXAMPLE 8

Construct a circle graph showing the following amounts, which a certain business recorded as operating expenses:

	Amount	Fraction for each part of whole	× 360 =	Width of slice (in degrees)
Salary	$25,000	$\frac{25{,}000}{53{,}000} = \frac{25}{53}$	$= 0.47 \times 360 =$	170
Rent	8,500	$\frac{8{,}500}{53{,}000} = \frac{85}{530}$	$= 0.16 \times 360 =$	57
Depreciation	2,500	$\frac{2{,}500}{53{,}000} = \frac{25}{530}$	$= 0.05 \times 360 =$	17
Miscellaneous	2,000	$\frac{2{,}000}{53{,}000} = \frac{2}{53}$	$= 0.04 \times 360 =$	14
Taxes and insurance	10,000	$\frac{10{,}000}{53{,}000} = \frac{10}{53}$	$= 0.19 \times 360 =$	68
Utilities	2,000	$\frac{2{,}000}{53{,}000} = \frac{2}{53}$	$= 0.04 \times 360 =$	14
Advertising	3,000	$\frac{3{,}000}{53{,}000} = \frac{3}{53}$	$= 0.06 \times 360 =$	20
Total	$53,000			360

Use a compass to draw a circle. Then measure the sections of the circle with a protractor, using the calculations you just made.

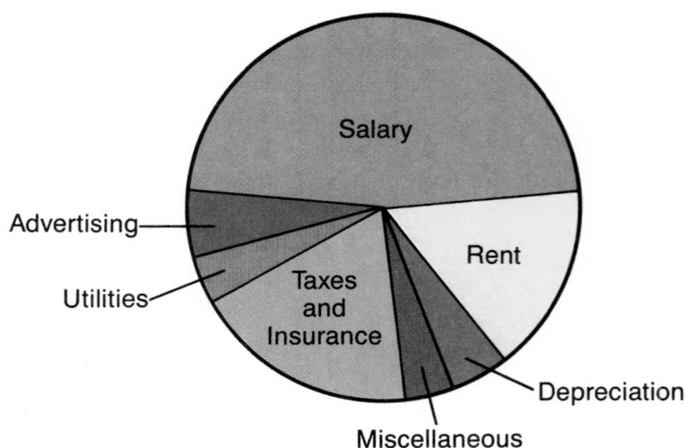

Self-Check

5. Use Figure 19-3 to find the percent of total take-home pay spent for clothing.
6. Use Figure 19-3 to compute the percent of take-home pay available for education if the family's education, savings, and miscellaneous expenses funds were used.

Section Review

Use the following data for Exercises 1–4. The Family Clothing Store recorded the following information concerning its 19X1 and 19X2 sales.

	19X1	19X2
Girls' clothing	$ 74,675	$ 81,534
Boys' clothing	$ 65,153	$ 68,324
Women's clothing	$125,115	$137,340
Men's clothing	$ 83,895	$ 96,315

1. What is the least value for 19X1 sales? For 19X2 sales?

2. What is the greatest value for 19X1 sales? For 19X2 sales?

3. If the values are given in thousands of dollars, which of the following interval sizes would be more appropriate to use in making a bar graph?
   a. $1,000 intervals ($60,000, $61,000, $62,000, . . .)
   b. $10,000 intervals ($60,000, $70,000, $80,000, . . .)

4. Draw a comparative bar graph to show both the 19X1 and 19X2 values.

Be sure to include a title, explanation of the scales, and any additional information needed.

Use the following information for Exercises 5–9. The temperatures were recorded at 2-hour intervals June 24.

12 A.M.	76°	8 A.M.	70°	2 P.M.	84°	8 P.M.	82°
2 A.M.	75°	10 A.M.	76°	4 P.M.	90°	10 P.M.	79°
4 A.M.	72°	12 P.M.	81°	6 P.M.	90°	12 A.M.	77°
6 A.M.	70°						

5. What is the least value?

6. What is the greatest value?

7. Which interval size is most appropriate when making a line graph? Why?
a. 1 **b.** 5 **c.** 50 **d.** 100

8. Draw a line graph representing the data. Be sure to include the title, explanation of the scales, and any additional information needed.

9. Which of the following terms would describe this line graph?
   a. Continually increasing   b. Continually decreasing
   c. Fluctuating

Table 19-5 Automobile Dealership's New and Repeat Business

Customer	Cars Sold
New	920
Repeat	278

Answer the following questions using the information in Table 19-5.

10. What was the total number of cars sold?

11. How many degrees should be used to represent the new business on the circle (to nearest whole degree)?

12. How many degrees should be used to represent the repeat business on the circle (to nearest whole degree)?

13. Construct a circle graph for this data. Label the parts of the graph as "New" and "Repeat." Be sure to include a title and any additional information needed.

Statistics

Statistics make numerical information more meaningful by helping you understand how individual pieces of information fit in with other, comparable pieces of information. Statistics may be represented in tables and graphs or used alone.

Look at Table 19-6, which shows prices of used automobiles sold on a particular weekend in Tireville. What do these prices mean?

Range

range: the smallest number subtracted from the largest number in a group of numbers.

The numbers show a **range** of used-automobile prices from a low of $1,850 to a high of $11,500. The range of a group of values (numbers) is found by subtracting the smallest number in the group from the largest number in the group. A small range indicates that the values in the group are very similar to one another, whereas a large range indicates that they are very different.

Table 19-6 Prices of Used Automobiles Sold in Tireville Over the Weekend of May 1–2

$1,850	$ 5,600
$2,300	$ 5,800
$2,750	$ 6,100
$4,600	$ 9,430
$4,800	$11,500
$5,200	

Step by Step

Finding the Range of a Group of Values

Range = largest value − smallest value

EXAMPLE 9

Find the range in the used automobile prices in Table 19-6.

range = largest value − smallest value
= $11,500 − $1,850
= $9,650

Inspection shows that the lowest price is $1,850 and the highest price is $11,500. Subtract to obtain the range.

The range is $9,650, which is quite large. This means that the lowest and highest prices in the group are very different.

Mean

You know from the range that the used car prices vary quite a bit. In this case you might want to consider the **mean** price. Mean is the statistical term for the ordinary arithmetic average. To find the mean, or arithmetic average, add the values in a group and divide the total by the number of items added.

mean: the sum of a set of values divided by the number of values in the set.

Step by Step

Finding the Mean of a Group of Values

Step 1. Add all the values.

Step 2. Divide the total by the number of values:

$$\text{Mean} = \frac{\text{sum of values}}{\text{number of values}}$$

EXAMPLE 10

Find the mean used car price for the prices in Table 19-6.

Add the prices of the 11 cars.

$ 1,850
2,300
2,750
4,600
4,800
5,200
5,600
5,800
6,100
9,430
+ 11,500
$59,930

$59,930 ÷ 11 = $5,448.1818 = $5,448 (rounded to the nearest whole number)	There are 11 prices listed, so find the mean by dividing the total by 11.

The mean price is $5,448.

On a calculator these calculations would, of course, be carried out continuously by adding all the prices and then dividing the total by 11.

Median

median: the middle number in a set of values that are arranged in order from smallest to largest.

Another kind of average is called the **median.** The median of a group of values is found by arranging the numbers in order from the largest to the smallest and selecting the number in the middle. If the group has an even number of values, so that no one value is exactly in the middle, find the average of the two numbers in the middle of the group.

Step by Step

Finding the Median of a Group of Values

Step 1. Arrange the values in the group from largest to smallest.

Step 2. Find the middle value.

- **a.** The median is the middle value if the group has an odd number of values.
- **b.** The median is the average of the two middle numbers if the group has an even number of values.

EXAMPLE 11

Find the median price of used cars in Table 19-6.

$11,500
9,430
6,100
5,800
5,600
5,200 ← Median price; there are 5 values above and 5 below it.
4,800
4,600
2,750
2,300
1,850

Arrange the numbers from the highest to the lowest. The median is the price in the middle of the list.

There are 11 prices. The median (middle) price is 6 from the top or 6 from the bottom. $5,200 is the median price of the used cars.

Mode

mode: the value that occurs most frequently in a group of values.

The third average considered is the **mode.** The mode is the value that occurs most frequently in a group of values. If no number occurs most frequently in a group, then there is no mode for that group of numbers. No used car price in Table 19-6 occurs more than once, so there is no mode for that group of used car prices.

Step by Step

Finding the Mode of a Group of Values

Step 1. Find the number that occurs most frequently.

EXAMPLE 12

Find the mode for this group of test grades in a mathematics class:

76, 83, 94, 76, 53, 18, 74, 76, 97, 83, 65, 77, 76, 81

The grade of 76 occurs four times. The grade of 83 occurs two times. All other grades occur once each. The grade of 76 occurs most frequently.

The mode is 76 for this group of test grades.

Putting Statistics to Work

Taken together, the mean, median, and mode describe the tendency of a group of numbers to cluster together in the center of the range of values. Sometimes it is useful to know all three of these measures, since each represents a different way of describing the numerical information. It is like looking at the same thing from three different points of view. The mean, median, and mode may each be called an "average."

To look at just one statistic for a set of numbers often distorts the total picture. It is advisable to find the range, mean, median, and mode and then analyze the results.

We may read that the average cost of a home in a certain area was $71,000 during the past 3 months. But is this "average" the mean, median, or mode? What is the range of prices? We need this kind of information to get a true picture of what a home might cost in that area. A real estate agent might provide this list of selling prices of houses over the past 3 months:

$170,000	$150,000	$50,000
$50,000	$50,000	$50,000
$49,000	$45,000	$25,000

What are the range, the mean, the median, and the mode? What do these numbers tell us about the cost of houses in this area? Example 13 provides the answers to these questions.

EXAMPLE 13

Find the range, mean, median, and mode for the home prices just listed.

Range = highest − lowest
= $170,000 − $25,000
= $145,000

Such a large range indicates extremes in prices, so that a mean price does not indicate what one can realistically expect to pay for a home in this area.

Mean = total ÷ number of items
= $639,000 ÷ 9
= $71,000

The large range, however, suggests that prices were not generally around $71,000 but were probably a mixture of much lower and much higher prices.

Median (middle amount): $50,000
Mode (most frequent amount): $50,000

Conclusion: Because of the large range (and extreme price differences that produced the large range), the median and the mode give a more realistic picture of what a home is likely to cost in this area.

Self-Check

7. Find the range of the following numbers: 3,850; 5,300; 8,550; 4,200; 5,350.
8. Find the mean of the following numbers: 3,850; 5,300; 8,550; 4,200; 5,350.
9. Find the median of the following numbers: 3,850; 5,300; 8,550; 4,200; 5,350.
10. Find the mode for the following numbers: 86, 94, 73, 94, 84, 86, 94.
11. Last Saturday, Autowonderland sold cars for the following prices: \$15,300, \$17,500, \$11,400, \$14,500, and \$13,500. Find the range, the mean, the median, and the mode for these numbers. What do these numbers tell us about the cost of cars sold last Saturday? Which statistic(s) would give the most realistic description of Autowonderland's prices on Saturday?

Section Review

Find the range, mean, median, and mode for the following. Round to nearest hundredth if necessary.

1. New car mileages
   17 mi/gal
   16 mi/gal
   25 mi/gal
   22 mi/gal
   30 mi/gal

2. Test scores
   61
   72
   63
   70
   93
   87

3. Sandwiches
   \$0.95
   \$1.65
   \$1.27
   \$1.97
   \$1.65
   \$1.15

4. Credit hours
   16
   12
   18
   15
   16
   12
   12

Summary

Topic	Page	What to Remember	Example
Tables	567–569	A *table* consists of one or more lists of numerical information grouped in some meaningful form.	Size of Graduating Class at Winston College, 19X5–19X9 (see table below)
How tables are used	567–569	We can compare pieces of information in a table with one another, using addition, subtraction, or percent, to find additional information.	How many more women than men graduated in 19X6? 149 − 111 = 38 more women than men graduated in 19X6. Men made up what percent of the graduating class in 19X9? $\frac{141}{316} = 45\%$
Bar graphs	571–572	A bar graph compares several related values. Vertical or horizontal bars may be used; the height or length of each bar corresponds to a certain value.	
Line graphs	573	A line graph shows changes in some value and helps us see whether the value is increasing, decreasing, or fluctuating.	
Circle graphs	574–575	A circle graph shows some whole quantity, represented by a whole circle divided into smaller parts, shown by different sized slices of the circle.	

Size of Graduating Class at Winston College, 19X5–19X9

	Men	Women	Total
19X5	130	128	258
19X6	111	149	260
19X7	125	171	296
19X8	135	168	303
19X9	141	175	316

Topic	Page	What to Remember	Example
Statistics	578–582	*Statistics* are numbers that describe numerical information and show how individual pieces of information fit in with other, comparable pieces of information.	We will use this information in the examples that follow: A survey of 7 computer stores in a large city showed that a certain printer was sold for the following prices: \$435, \$398, \$429, \$479, \$435, \$495, and \$435.
Finding the range of a group of values	578–579	Range = largest value − smallest value	Find the range of printer prices: \$495 − \$398 = \$97
Finding the mean of a group of values	579–580	Mean = sum of values ÷ number of values	Find the mean price of the printer: \$435 + \$398 + \$429 + \$479 + \$435 + \$495 + \$435 = \$3106 $\frac{\$3106}{7} = \$443.71$
Finding the median of a group of values	580	Arrange the values in the group from largest to smallest. If the group has an odd number of values, the median is the middle value; if the group has an even number of values, the median is the average of the two middle numbers.	Find the median price of the printer: \$495, \$479, \$435, \$435, \$435, \$429, \$398 The median price is \$435.
Finding the mode of a group of values	580–581	The mode is the number that occurs most frequently.	\$435 is the mode.

Chapter Review

Number of Automobiles Sold by Three Area Dealers

Dealer	Compact 19X1	Compact 19X2	Standard 19X1	Standard 19X2	Luxury 19X1	Luxury 19X2
Mid-City Autos	1,825	1,963	1,742	1,697	1,021	1,280
Ocean Front Autos	987	1,143	799	1,086	523	613
Bradshaw Autos	1,786	1,952	2,105	2,106	2,033	2,214
Total	4,598	5,058	4,646	4,889	3,577	4,107

1. How many standard cars were sold in 19X2?

2. Which dealer showed the largest decrease in standard car sales from 19X1 to 19X2?

3. Find the ratio of total compact car sales to total luxury car sales in 19X2.

4. Which dealer sold the most cars in 19X1?

5. Which dealer had the greatest *increase* in car sales from 19X1 to 19X2? How much was the increase?

6. What percent of total sales for 19X1 was made by Mid-City Autos?

7. The total number of compact cars sold in 19X2 is what percent of the total number of cars sold for 19X2?

Find the range, mean, median, and mode for the following. Round to the nearest hundredth if necessary.

8. Test scores
83
75
87
96
75
82
75
96

9. Days absent from work for the past 7 years
17
3
5
8
2
3
7

10. Business mileage
218
312
146
52
416
215
386
97
205

11. Expenses for a week
$ 84.21
$136.52
$127.83
$ 76.24
$136.52

	19X1	19X2
Textbooks	$852,986	$912,218
Clothing	$ 62,521	$ 73,812
Supplies	$136,482	$128,719

Use the marginal data in Problems 12–15. Campus Bookstore recorded the following information concerning its 19X1 and 19X2 sales.

12. What is the highest value for 19X1 sales? For 19X2 sales?

13. Which item showed a *decrease* from 19X1 to 19X2? How much was the decrease?

14. What was the percent of increase in textbook sales from 19X1 to 19X2?

15. What was the percent of decrease in supplies sales from 19X1 to 19X2?

Use the following information in Problems 16–18. The data are the number of fan belts sold each day during the past 3 weeks.

76, 82, 97, 83, 58, 92, 83, 46, 77, 82, 83, 93, 85, 81, 87

16. What is the least value?

17. What is the greatest value?

18. Which interval size is most appropriate for making a line graph? Why?
a. 1 b. 5 c. 50 d. 100

Solve the following problems using the information in the marginal table.

Suburban Auto Dealership's Car Sales

Type of Vehicle	Vehicles Sold
Compact car	230
Standard car	418
Luxury car	187
Sports car	52
Standard truck	697

19. What was the total number of vehicles sold?

20. In a circle graph, how many degrees are represented by *each* type of vehicle (to the nearest whole degree)?

21. Construct a circle graph for these data. Label each part of the graph with the appropriate type of vehicle. Be sure to include a title, explanation of the scales, and any additional information needed.

Trial Test

Use the following data for Problems 1–4.

42	86	92	15	32	67	48	19	87	63
15	19	21	17	53	27	21	15	82	15

1. What is the range?

2. What is the mean?

3. What is the median?

4. What is the mode?

Use the following data for Problems 5–8.

105	215	165	172	138
198	165	170	165	146
187	170	165	146	200

5. What is the range?

6. What is the mean?

7. What is the median?

8. What is the mode?

The following are costs of producing a piece of luggage at ACME Luggage Company: labor, $45; materials, $40; overhead, $35.

9. What is the total cost of producing a piece of luggage?

10. What percent of the total cost is attributed to labor?

11. What percent of the total cost is attributed to materials?

12. What percent of the total cost is attributed to overhead?

13. Compute the number of degrees needed for labor, materials, and overhead if a circle graph is to be constructed.

Katz Florist recorded sales for a 6-month period for fresh and silk flowers. The following sales were recorded.

	January	February	March	April	May	June
Fresh	$11,520	$22,873	$10,380	$12,562	$23,712	$15,816
Silk	$8,460	$14,952	$5,829	$10,621	$17,892	$7,583

14. What is the greatest value for fresh flowers? For silk flowers?

15. What is the least value for fresh flowers? For silk flowers?

16. What interval size would be most appropriate when making a bar graph? Why?
a. $100 **b.** $1,000 **c.** $5,000 **d.** $10,000

Use the following data to answer Problems 17–19. The total numbers of daisy-wheel printers sold in the years 1984 through 1989 by Smart Brothers Computer Store are as follows:

1984 983 1985 1,052 1986 1,117 1987 615 1988 213 1989 43

17. What is the least value? The greatest value?

18. Draw a line graph representing the data. Use an interval of 250. Be sure to include a title, explanation of the scales, and the like.

19. Which of the following terms would describe this line graph?
 a. Continually increasing
 b. Continually decreasing
 c. Fluctuating
 d. Increasing, then decreasing
 e. Decreasing, then increasing

Self-Check Solutions

1. $163 - 157 = 6$

2. $\frac{\text{Men}}{\text{Women}} = \frac{143}{144}$

3. Total club members on December 1988 = 143 + 144 = 287
Total club members on December 1989 = 166 + 172 = 338

New club members between December 1988 and 1989 = 338 − 287 = 51

New club members who are men for period December 1988 to 1989 = 166 − 143 = 23

Percent of new club members that are men $= \frac{P}{B} = \frac{23}{51} = 0.45 = 45\%$

4.

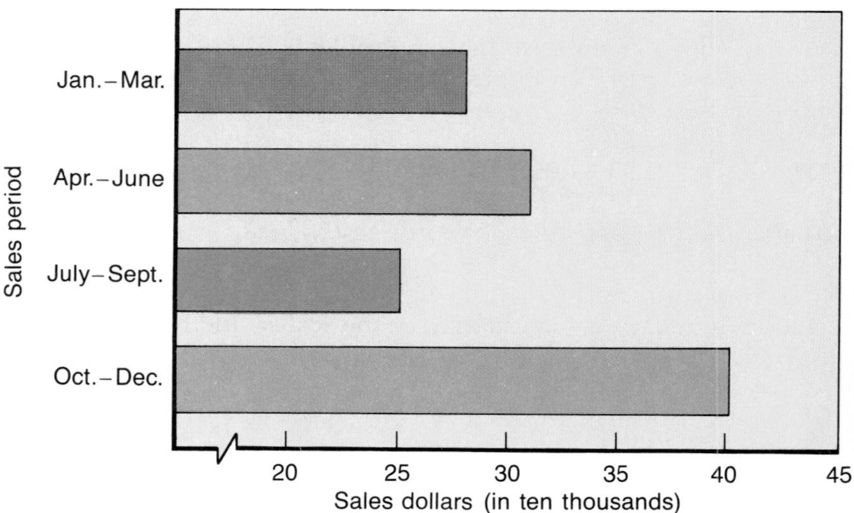

5. Percent of total take-home pay spent for clothing $= \frac{P}{B} = \frac{160}{1600} = 0.1 = 10\%$

6. Percent of total take-home pay spent for education (education, savings, and miscellaneous) $= \frac{P}{B} = \frac{320}{1600} = 0.2 = 20\%$

7. Range = 8,550 − 3,850 = 4,700

8. Mean $= (3{,}850 + 5{,}300 + 8{,}550 + 4{,}200 + 5{,}350) \div 5 = \dfrac{27{,}250}{5} = 5{,}450$

9. Arrange the numbers from least to greatest:

3,850 4,200 5,300 5,350 8,550

↑ middle number (5,300)

Median: 5,300

10. Arrange the numbers from least to greatest:

73, 84, 86, 86, 94, 94, 94

Mode: 94

11. Arrange the prices in order from least to greatest:

\$11,400 \$13,500 \$14,500 \$15,300 \$17,500

range = \$17,500 − \$11,400 = \$6,100
mean = (\$11,400 + \$13,500 + \$14,500 + \$15,300 + \$17,500) ÷ 5
= \$72,200 ÷ 5 = \$14,440

median = \$14,500
no mode

Since the mean and median are close but the range is large, we can use the mean and median to get a realistic picture of the cost of an automobile in this area.

CHAPTER 1

Section Review (pp. 6–7)

1. four thousand, two hundred nine **3.** three hundred one million, nine **5.** 400 **7.** 9,000 **9.** 830 **11.** 30,000 **13.** 28,000,000,000 **15.** 3,780,000 **17.** 5,180 **19.** 10,100,000 **21.** 400 **23.** 700,000

Section Review (pp. 9–13)

1. 20 **3.** 35 **5.** 28 **7.** 30,787 **9.** 1,832 **11.** 5,773 **13.** 44,014 **15.** 310,000 (estimate); 318,936 (exact) **17.** 22,000 (estimate); 21,335 (exact) **19.** 2,600 (estimate); 2,612 (exact) **21.** 230 items **23.** 469 dolls **25.** 671 points **27.** 541,679 **29.** 2,708,562 **31.** 3,988,906 **33.** 10,550,004 **35.** 200,000 (estimate); 182,902 (exact) **37.** 8,000 (estimate); 7,310 (exact) **39.** 75,000 (estimate); 74,385 (exact) **41.** 73 tickets

Section Review (pp. 19–22)

1. 4,952,385 **3.** 782,878 **5.** 41,772 **7.** 6,938,694 **9.** 861,900 **11.** 16,500 **13.** 48,000 **15.** 30,000 **17.** 47,220,000 **19.** 162,000 **21.** 210,000 (estimate); 254,626 (exact) **23.** 1,500,000 (estimate); 1,495,184 (exact) **25.** 120 ribbons **27.** 140 pieces **29.** 42 R3 **31.** 52 R2 **33.** 804 **35.** 420 R2 **37.** 600 (estimate); 505 R161 (exact) **39.** 119 countertops

Chapter Review (pp. 25–26)

1. thirty-four thousand, three hundred four **3.** 8,500 **5.** 2,500,000 **7.** 32 **9.** 1,682 **11.** 841 **13.** 112 **15.** 2,147 **17.** 2,688 **19.** 32,652 **21.** 56 **23.** 16 R5 **25.** $40,170 **27.** $9,216

Trial Test (pp. 27–28)

1. 1,242 **3.** 44,978 **5.** 785 **7.** 62 **9.** five hundred three **11.** 84,300 **13.** 80,000 **15.** 2,200 **17.** 45,000 **19.** 1,153 items

CHAPTER 2

Section Review (pp. 37–39)

1. 20 R4, or $20\frac{2}{3}$ **3.** 7 **5.** 8 R1, or $8\frac{1}{2}$ **7.** 12 R2, or $12\frac{2}{5}$ **9.** 14 R22, or $14\frac{22}{25}$ **11.** $\frac{35}{6}$ **13.** $\frac{13}{3}$ **15.** $\frac{100}{3}$ **17.** $\frac{5}{8}$ **19.** $\frac{5}{6}$ **21.** $\frac{7}{8}$ **23.** $\frac{3}{8}$ **25.** $\frac{3}{4}$ **27.** $\frac{2}{5}$ **29.** $\frac{7}{9}$ **31.** $\frac{5}{6}$ **33.** $\frac{3}{5}$ **35.** $\frac{2}{3}$ **37.** $\frac{13}{24}$ **39.** $\frac{54}{72}$ **41.** $\frac{10}{12}$ **43.** $\frac{10}{15}$ **45.** $\frac{63}{77}$ **47.** $\frac{117}{143}$ **49.** $\frac{1}{7}$

Section Review (pp. 44–50)

1. 48 **3.** 420 **5.** 1,008 **7.** $1\frac{3}{8}$ **9.** $1\frac{5}{8}$ **11.** $1\frac{29}{48}$ **13.** $2\frac{37}{144}$ **15.** $2\frac{4}{5}$ **17.** $20\frac{1}{2}$ **19.** 16 **21.** $9\frac{5}{12}$ **23.** $65\frac{1}{6}$ **25.** $56\frac{1}{24}$ **27.** $137\frac{59}{120}$ **29.** $22\frac{5}{8}$ feet **31.** $\frac{1}{2}$ **33.** $\frac{1}{2}$ **35.** $\frac{17}{30}$ **37.** $\frac{9}{14}$ **39.** $6\frac{1}{6}$ **41.** $2\frac{1}{4}$ **43.** $246\frac{13}{18}$ **45.** $36\frac{7}{9}$ **47.** $68\frac{7}{8}$ **49.** $91\frac{11}{12}$ **51.** $2\frac{3}{8}$ feet

Section Review (pp. 54–57)

1. $\frac{7}{32}$ **3.** $\frac{5}{18}$ **5.** $\frac{9}{20}$ **7.** $3\frac{1}{3}$ **9.** $2\frac{5}{8}$ **11.** $\frac{5}{9}$ **13.** $\frac{7}{18}$ **15.** $\frac{84}{125}$ **17.** $\frac{8}{49}$ **19.** $\frac{3}{41}$ **21.** $37\frac{1}{10}$ **23.** $74\frac{47}{48}$ **25.** $94\frac{2}{7}$ **27.** $48 **29.** $4,110 **31.** $\frac{8}{5}$ **33.** $\frac{4}{1}$, or 4 **35.** $\frac{4}{13}$ **37.** $\frac{5}{8}$ **39.** 3 **41.** $\frac{10}{21}$ **43.** $\frac{1}{20}$ **45.** $3\frac{3}{4}$ **47.** $\frac{4}{7}$ **49.** 32 pieces

Chapter Review (pp. 61–65)

1. $57\frac{2}{3}$ **3.** $\frac{1}{3}$ **5.** $\frac{4}{11}$ **7.** 360 **9.** $1\frac{7}{30}$ **11.** $1\frac{17}{24}$ **13.** $193\frac{53}{60}$ **15.** $\frac{7}{24}$ **17.** $\frac{19}{56}$ **19.** $\frac{7}{12}$ **21.** $119\frac{3}{4}$ **23.** $88\frac{1}{3}$ **25.** $\frac{2}{45}$ **27.** $\frac{4}{45}$ **29.** $42\frac{11}{18}$ **31.** $\frac{11}{3}$ **33.** $\frac{4}{9}$ **35.** 20 **37.** $1\frac{7}{15}$ **39.** $1\frac{13}{95}$ **41.** She processes 637 to 638 forms. **43.** 7 lengths

Trial Test (pp. 66–67)

1. $\frac{1}{6}$ **3.** $\frac{7}{16}$ **5.** $1\frac{19}{23}$ **7.** $44\frac{13}{15}$ **9.** $34\frac{1}{2}$ **11.** $2\frac{7}{8}$ **13.** $310\frac{5}{6}$ **15.** $47\frac{1}{5}$ **17.** $209\frac{3}{4}$ **19.** $107\frac{1}{2}$

CHAPTER 3

Section Review (pp. 73–74)

1. five tenths **3.** one hundred eight thousandths **5.** two hundred seventy-five hundred-thousandths **7.** seventeen and eight tenths **9.** one hundred twenty-eight and twenty-three hundredths **11.** five hundred and seven ten-thousandths **13.** eight and one-third hundredths **15.** eighty-three and one-third hundredths **17.** 0.135 **19.** 380 **21.** 1,700 **23.** $175

Section Review (pp. 77–78)

1. 1.246 **3.** 165.8312 **5.** $20.93 total cost **7.** 376.74 **9.** 57.4525 **11.** 135.6 **13.** 419.103 **15.** 325.74 **17.** 2.3068 **19.** 0.001474 **21.** $88.96 reduced **23.** $92.61

Section Review (pp. 82–85)

1. 193.41 **3.** 50.076 **5.** 21.2352 **7.** 275.8 **9.** 198.74 **11.** 27,300 **13.** 17,454 **15.** 370,000 **17.** $12,850 **19.** 0.15 **21.** 2.187, or 2.19 **23.** 8.572, or 8.57 **25.** 33.766, or 33.77 **27.** 1559.789, or 1,559.79 **29.** 60713.235, or 60,713.24 **31.** 8.572 **33.** 0.019874 **35.** 0.0018 **37.** 37.49298 **39.** 0.0178 **41.** $0.989 (gasoline not rounded to hundreds)

Section Review (pp. 88–89)

1. $\frac{3}{4}$ **3.** $\frac{16}{25}$ **5.** $\frac{11}{2}$ **7.** 0.6 **9.** $0.12\frac{4}{8}$, or $0.12\frac{1}{2}$ **11.** $0.44\frac{4}{9}$ **13.** 8.58 **15.** $21\frac{3}{5}$ **17.** 0.1390, or 0.139 **19.** 10

Chapter Review (pp. 92–94)

1. two hundred seventy-four and one thousand seven hundred fifty-nine ten-thousandths **3.** 175.375 **5.** 506.54 **7.** 70.285 **9.** 994.50 **11.** 0.0003525 **13.** 34.44 **15.** 1,734,980 **17.** 2.236, or 2.24 **19.** 174.895, or 174.90 **21.** 374.928 **23.** 357.8423 **25.** $\frac{2}{5}$ **27.** $5\frac{1}{8}$ **29.** $3\frac{41}{50}$ **31.** $0.42\frac{6}{7}$ **33.** 0.8 **35.** $0.54\frac{6}{11}$ **37.** $10\frac{26}{45}$ **39.** 10 **41.** 70 **43.** 3.0334, or 3.03 **45.** 40,714 or 41,000 **47.** $37 **49.** $234.40

Trial Test (pp. 95–96)

1. 30.5 **3.** 24.092 **5.** 224.857 **7.** 447.12 **9.** 89.82 **11.** 2,379.019 **13.** 179.24 **15.** 1.610, or 1.61 **17.** $\frac{17}{50}$ **19.** 1.76 = degree drop in temperature

CHAPTER 4

Section Review (pp. 104–106)

1. $296.83 **3.** deposit slip total: $894.96 **5.** ending balance: $4,278.24 **7.** ending balance: $933.71

Section Review (pp. 113–114)

1. **a.** four deposits **b.** $2.00 **c.** $238.00 **d.** five checks **e.** $4,782.96 **f.** $5,074.67 **g.** $29.36 **h.** 7/7

Chapter Review (pp. 117–119)

1. ending balance, check register: \$5,835.11; deposit slip total: \$1,967.96 **3.** adjusted statement and checkbook balance: \$461.57

Trial Test (pp. 120–121)

1. ending balance: \$2,432.09 **3.** adjusted statement and checkbook balance: \$1,589.10

CHAPTER 5

Section Review (pp. 130–131)

1. subtraction **3.** division **5.** multiplication and subtraction **7.** $N = 17$ **9.** $N = 7$ **11.** $A = 12$ **13.** $N = 4$ **15.** $A = 24$ **17.** $X = 7$

Section Review (pp. 136–142)

1. The number is 9. **3.** The number is 5. **5.** The amount of money spent on supplies is \$96. **7.** 416 fan belts should be ordered. **9.** The amount spent on groceries is \$57.50. **11.** Shaquita earns \$8.75 each hour. **13.** Molly earns \$272.32 for 37 hours of work. **15.** Wall paper for the kitchen will cost \$116.73. **17.** The total weight of the shipment is 830 pounds. **19.** Each shirt was reduced by \$3.02. **21.** There are 11 executive desks and 29 secretarial desks. **23.** There are 280 headlights purchased at a cost of \$3,906. There are 720 taillights purchased at a total cost of \$5,436.

Chapter Review (pp. 146–152)

1. subtraction **3.** multiplication **5.** $R = 5$ **7.** $M = 15$ **9.** $B = 36$ **11.** $A = 32$ **13.** The number is 36. **15.** The number is 8. **17.** The difference is \$23.61. **19.** The cost of the chair is \$110 and the cost of the desk is \$330. **21.** The smaller check is \$365 and the larger check is \$385. **23.** The new salary is \$245.76. **25.** 20 cases can be stacked. **27.** The weekly income is \$1,028. **29.** There were 26 large and 10 small cheesecakes ordered. The bakery took in \$364 on the large cheesecakes and \$80 on the small cheesecakes.

Trial Test (pp. 153–156)

1. addition **3.** multiplication **5.** $N = 11$ **7.** $A = 18$ **9.** $A = 5$ **11.** $N = 6$. **13.** The number is 26. **15.** The new salary is \$285. **17.** 130 containers are needed. **19.** 116 ceramic cups and 284 plastic cups were sold. The value of the ceramic cups was \$464. The value of the plastic cups was \$994.

CHAPTER 6

Section Review (pp. 164–165)

1. 23% **3.** 82% **5.** 3% **7.** 34% **9.** 60.1% **11.** 100% **13.** 300% **15.** 99% **17.** 20% **19.** 65% **21.** 340% **23.** 750% **25.** 81.1% **27.** 254% **29.** 39% **31.** 33.33% **33.** 3%

Section Review (pp. 168–170)

1. 0.98 **3.** 2.56 **5.** 0.917 **7.** 0.005 **9.** 0.06 **11.** $\frac{1}{10}$ **13.** $\frac{3}{50}$ **15.** $\frac{89}{100}$ **17.** $2\frac{1}{2}$ **19.** 2.74 **21.** 0.30 **23.** $\frac{9}{20}$ **25.** $2\frac{1}{4}$ **27.** $\frac{1}{8}$ **29.** **a.** 40% **b.** 0.4 **31.** **a.** $\frac{1}{2}$ **b.** 0.50 **33.** **a.** $\frac{7}{8}$ **b.** 0.875

Section Review (pp. 173–174)

1. $P = 81$ **3.** $P = 25$ **5.** $R = 25\%$ **7.** $R = 33\frac{1}{3}\%$ **9.** $B = 12{,}000$ **11.** $B = 200$ **13.** $P = 15.12$ **15.** $B = \$26{,}093.75$ **17.** $P = \$1{,}134.24$ **19.** $B = 305.88$ **21.** $R = 250\%$ **23.** $P = 51.44$

Section Review (pp. 180–183)

1. $P = 24$ **3.** $P = 8.1$ **5.** $B = 30$ **7.** $B = 180$ **9.** $R = 97\%$ **11.** $R = 2\%$ **13.** $R = 200\%$ **15.** $P = 32$ customers paid with credit cards **17.** $B = 2{,}270$ town's population **19.** $R = 74\%$ attended the meeting **21.** $R = 80\%$ of the questions were answered correctly **23.** $R = 19.29\%$ (approximately) of the restrooms can accommodate the disabled. **25.** $R = 26\%$. The amount spent is *not* within the budgeted 25%. **27.** $R = 9.5\%$ **29.** $R = 8.5\%$

Chapter Review (pp. 185–187)

1. % **3.** 70% **5.** 81.3% **7.** 33.33% **9.** 62.5% **11.** 750% **13.** 0.0067 (rounded) **15.** 0.08 **17.** 0.008 **19.** $2\frac{1}{4}$ **21.** $\frac{2}{3}$ **23.** $P = \$62.40$ **25.** $R = 37.5\%$ **27.** $P = 22$ **29.** $R = 20\%$ **31.** $B = \$99$ **33.** $P = 80$ **35.** $R = 6.8\%$

Trial Test (pp. 188–191)

1. 0.24 **3.** 0.09 **5.** 0.275 **7.** 0.005 **9.** 0.00125 **11.** 24% **13.** 60% **15.** $37\frac{1}{2}\%$ or 37.5% **17.** $\frac{7}{8}$ **19.** $\frac{1}{3}$ **21.** 21% **23.** $37\frac{1}{2}\%$ or 37.5% **25.** 77.78% (rounded) **27.** $P = 0.26$ **29.** $P = 113$ **31.** $R = 250\%$ **33.** 100% of 32 is 32. **35.** $B = 2{,}130$ **37.** $B = 113$ **39.** $P = \$2.52$ **41.** $R = 3\frac{1}{3}\%$ **43.** $R = 78\%$ **45.** $R = 10.34\%$ or 10% (rounded) **47.** $R = 60\%$ **49.** $B = \$15{,}333.33$ **51.** $R = 15\%$ raise

CHAPTER 7

Section Review (pp. 199–203)

1. \$425 **3.** \$480 **5.** \$1,076.40 **7.** Allen = \$483.14 Brown = \$206.26 Pick = \$316.02 Sayer = \$372.48 Lovet = \$228.80 **9.** \$200 **11.** \$216.45 (gross weekly earnings) **13.** \$486.15 **15.** \$910 **17.** \$400 **19.** \$800 **21.** \$7,800 **23.** \$1,191.20 **25.** \$334.64

Section Review (pp. 215–216)

1. \$1 **3.** \$23 **5.** \$33 **7.** \$7.55 (tax) **9.** \$158.58 **11.** The tax is \$6.68. **13.** Total tax is \$27.64. **15.** \$11.79 **17.** \$1,802.40 **19.** \$1,368.70

Employee	Withholding Tax	FICA	Total Deductions	Net Earnings
21. Abrams	\$0	\$10.89	\$32.83	\$112.17
23. Mason	\$0	\$12.39	\$12.39	\$152.61

25. \$108.23

Chapter Review (pp. 220–222)

1. \$771.83 **3.** \$477.92 **5.** \$236.80 **7.** \$566.12 **9.** \$294.60 **11.** total FICA tax: \$19.53 **13.** FICA tax: \$57.45 **15.** total deductions: \$130.36 **17.** \$378

Trial Test (pp. 223–225)

1. \$354 **3.** \$262.50 **5.** \$126 **7.** \$522 **9.** \$27.13 **11.** \$9 **13.** \$221.27 **15.** net earnings: \$166.23 **17.** net earnings: \$241.23 **19.** net earnings: \$194.35 **21.** \$378 **23.** \$0

CHAPTER 8

Section Review (pp. 232–233)

1. \$45 **3.** \$25.50 **5.** \$7.57 **7.** \$102.50 **9.** \$19.80 **11.** \$94.50 **13.** \$16.50 trade discount **15.** \$18 **17.** \$6.13 **19.** \$336.03 **21.** \$1.25; \$23.75 **23.** \$0.02; \$.87 **25.** \$357; \$1,743 **27.** 95%; \$399.95 **29.** 97%; \$699.54

Section Review (pp. 236–239)

1. 0.8 (0.9); 0.72; \$144 **3.** 0.8 (0.85) (0.9); 0.612; \$918 **5.** 0.85 (0.95); 0.8075; \$323 **7.** \$513 net price

9. $2,592 net price 11. 82%; 18% 13. 65.02%; 34.98% 15. 28% 17. 16.21% 19. 32% 21. $595 is better deal; net price $570. 23. table at $190 better deal; net price $169.10. 25. $260 better deal; net price $189.54.

Section Review (pp. 246–247)

1. 3% discount 3. Yes 5. $5.40 cash discount 7. $1.40 cash discount; $68.60 amount paid 9. a. $343 b. $346.50 c. $350 (no discount) 11. $637 amount paid 13. $24.78 cash discount $801.22 amount paid

Chapter Review (pp. 250–251)

1. receipt of goods; end of month 3. $188.50 net price 5. 0.648 net decimal equivalent 7. $490 amount due 9. $204.08 credited to account; $187.92 outstanding balance 11. $20 net price 13. $66.95 is better deal; net price $61.20. 15. total net price: $2,070 17. oven for $600 better deal; net price $480 19. $945 net price

Trial Test (pp. 252–254)

1. $110 trade discount 3. $29.24 net price 5. $250 chair is better deal; net price $200 7. 0.684 net decimal equivalent 9. receipt of goods 11. $1,080 net price 13. end of month 15. $2 cash discount 17. $392 amount due 19. $489.60 total net price 21. $618.56 credited to account; $276.44 outstanding balance

CHAPTER 9

Section Review (pp. 264–271)

1. 150%; $75 3. 200%; $41; $82 5. 58%; $52.48; $90.48 7. 85%; 100%; $45.33; $53.33 9. $6; $21 11. C = $36; R = 25% 13. markup = $39.80; markup % = 25.1% 15. cost (B) = $24; S = $36 17. C = $35.70; S = $51 19. markup % = 31.62%; markup amount = $18.50 21. C = $14; M = $21 23. $57; 56.14%; 35.96% 25. $0.44; 28.21%; 22% 27. $68.45; $95.83; 28.57% 29. $49.60; $74.40; 60% 31. $16.11; $2.84; 17.63% 33. $1.89; $10.88; 17.37%

Section Review (pp. 276–278)

1. amount of markdown = $38; markdown % = 10%
3. markdown = $24.99; markdown % = 28%
5. markdown = $50; sale price = $199.99
7. markdown = $19.75; sale price = $59.25
9. first reduction: markdown = $6.25, sale price = $25 second reduction: markdown = $7.50; sale price = $17.50
11. $0.54

Chapter Review (pp. 282–283)

1. $3 3. S = $496.25 5. $118.44 7. C = $75 9. C = $416.67 11. markdown % = 16.7% 13. $146.87

Trial Test (pp. 284–285)

1. $7.16 3. C = $15.50 (cost) 5. S = $22.68 7. $26.07 (discount) 9. S = $126.75 11. 25% (rounded) 13. S = $160 15. $48.74

CHAPTER 10

Section Review (pp. 296–300)

1. I = $120 3. I = $2,252.25 5. I = $144 7. I = $30,254.40; total amount to be repaid = $45,534.40 9. R = 15.5% 11. R = 12.5% 13. R = 15% 15. T = 3 years 17. $T = 1\frac{1}{2}$ years 19. T = 2 years 21. T = 9 months 23. P = $500 25. P = $1,000 27. P = $1,500 29. P = $900 31. $\frac{7}{12}$ year 33. $\frac{4}{3}$ or 1.3333 years 35. $\frac{1}{4}$ or 0.25 year 37. I = $1,050 39. I = $20 41. I = $12 43. I = $16

Section Review (pp. 311–316)

1. ordinary time 3. 117 days 5. 261 days 7. 153 days 9. 167 days 11. 247 days 13. Apr. 14 15. Jan. 25 17. Sept. 11 19. a. I = $212.50 b. I = $209.59 c. I = $212.50 21. a. I = $56.33 b. I = $56.49 c. I = $57.27 23. a. I = $32.08 b. I = $31.64 c. I = $32.08 25. First State Bank 27. August 10, 19XX 29. $1,909.50 31. I = $18.63 33. I = $22.64 35. Yes, he will save $20.20.

Chapter Review (pp. 319–322)

1. $1,500 3. $300 5. 197 days 7. 110 days 9. $29.17 11. $382.50 13. $90.74 15. 2 years 17. 12.5% 19. $23 21. Yes, she will save $63.89. 23. $14.90 25. $7,054.45 27. 6 months

Trial Test (pp. 323–325)

1. $210 3. 20% 5. 287 days 7. 159 days 9. $8,400 11. $28.14 13. $665 15. $21.25 17. 9 months 19. 20% 21. $462.50 23. $64 25. $169.01 27. $44.30

CHAPTER 11

Section Review (pp. 335–338)

1. $166.40 3. $708.64 5. $189.90 difference 7. 6.84848 9. $2,318.01 compound amount $318.01 compound interest 11. $1,312.40 compound interest 13. 12.36% 15. $0.36 17. $15.01 compound interest $2,015.01 compound amount 19. The 2-year investment yields the most interest ($339.72).

Section Review (pp. 342–343)

1. $1,126.97 3. $574.37 5. $3,157.64 7. $154.16 9. $1,597.41 11. $2,913.80 13. $11,000 in 18 months is better.

Chapter Review (pp. 346–347)

1. $4,840 3. $40 more 5. 12.36% effective rate 7. 8.24% effective rate 9. 1.26973 11. 0.71178 13. 0.94232 15. $1,260.34 17. $2,355.40 19. $3,069.55

Trial Test (pp. 348–350)

1. $450.09 compound interest 3. $3,979.30 compound interest 5. $3,561.60 compound amount $561.60 compound interest 7. 12.55% effective rate 9. $30 compounded monthly, $29.73 compounded daily. 11. $2,669.55 13. $2,951.58 15. $680 in 1 year is slightly better. 17. Option 2 yields the greater return by $0.68. 19. $1,006.60

CHAPTER 12

Section Review (pp. 359–360)

1. $30.51 3. $398.75 5. $52.40 7. $\frac{29}{84}$ 9. $126.35

Section Review (pp. 363–365)

1. $3.98 3. $185.17 5. $741 7. $241.33 9. $68 11. $673 13. Finance charge: $187.50 Total price: $1,687.50 Monthly payment: $140.63 15. $8.75 finance charge $611.70 unpaid balance

Section Review (pp. 371–373)

1. 16% 3. 8.5% 5. 29.1% 7. 15.75% 9. 13.50%

Chapter Review (pp. 375–376)

1. $5.81 **3.** 2.1% **5.** $85 **7.** $577 **9.** $462.60 unpaid balance on November 1 **11.** $98 **13.** 11.25%

Trial Test (pp. 377–379)

1. $34 **3.** $36 **5.** 22.2% **7.** $2.89 **9.** $12.60 **11.** 22.5% **13.** $236.58 **15.** $158.33 **17.** $\frac{23}{98}$

CHAPTER 13

Section Review (pp. 383–385)

1. $12,000 **3.** $2,300 **5.** $1,900 **7.** $4,500 **9.** $1,000 **11.** $800

Section Review (pp. 386–388)

1. $0.084 **3.** $0.25; $1,750 **5.** $0.40; $3,200 **7.** $0.50; $2,080 **9.** $0.11 **11.** $0.18 **13.** $827.82 **15.** $3,948

Section Review (pp. 391–392)

1. 28 **3.** 36 **5.** 120 **7.** 325 **9.** Year 1: $1,150; Year 2: $920; Year 3: $690; Year 4: $460; Year 5: $230

Section Review (pp. 396–397)

1. a. 0.25 **b.** 0.5 **3. a.** 0.0625 **b.** 0.125 **5.** Year 1: $6,000; 0.666667; $4,000; $2,000; $4,000. Year 2: $2,000; 0.666667; $1,250; $750; $5,250. Year 3: $750; 0.666667; $0; $750; $5,250.

Section Review (pp. 401–403)

1. $3,622.25; $5,505.82; $5,360.93 **3.** $388.20; $569.36; $543.48; $543.48; $543.48. **5.** $584.70, $857.56; $818.58; $818.58; $818.58. **7.** $1,160; $1,856; $1,113.60; $668.16; $668.16; $334.08 **9.** Year 1: $3,270; 33.33; $1,089.89; $2,180.11; $1,089.89 Year 2: $2,180.11; 44.45; $1,453.51; $726.60; $2,543.40 Year 3: $726.60; 14.81; $484.29; $242.31; $3,027.69 Year 4: $242.31; 7.41; $242.31; $0; $3,270.

Chapter Review (pp. 407–409)

1. $7,620 **3.** $975 **5.** $0.48 **7. a.** 45 **b.** 66 **9.** 6.67%, 13.33% **11.** $2,952 **13.** Year 1: $18,500; 25; $4,625; $13,875; $4,625 Year 2: $13,875; 38; $7,030; $6,845; $11,655 Year 3: $6,845; 37; $6,845; $0; $18,500
15. Year 1: $13,790; 33.33; $4,596.21; $9,193.79; $4,596.21
Year 2: $9,193.79; 44.45; $6,129.66; $3,064.13; $10,725.87
Year 3: $3,064.13; 14.81; $2,042.30; $1,021.83; $12,768.17
Year 4: $1,021.83; 7.41; $1,021.84; $0; $13,790.01

Trial Test (pp. 410–412)

1. 28 **3.** $14,900 **5.** $0.07264 **7. a.** 300 **b.** 378 **9. a.** 8.33% **b.** 16.67% **11.** Year 1: $15,490; 25; $3,872.50; $11,617.50; $3,872.50. Year 2: $11,617.50; 38; $5,886.20; $5,731.30; $9.758.70. Year 3: $5,731.30; 37; $5,731.30; $0; $15,490. **13.** $2,859.71 **15.** $2,232.21

CHAPTER 14

Section Review (pp. 424–426)

1. $2,295 **3.** $1,068 **5.** $1,243.45, ending inventory; $1,051.55, cost of goods sold **7.** $1,062, ending inventory; $1,233, cost of goods sold

Section Review (p. 428)

1. $3,234 **3.** 0.5 times **5.** 4.6 times

Section Review (pp. 432–433)

1. $730.77; $1,948.72; $1,120.51 **3.** $2,827.59; $1,413.79; $2,431.73; $1,526.90

Chapter Review (pp. 438–440)

1. $911 **3.** $325 **5.** $599.94, ending inventory; $311.06, cost of goods sold **7.** $3,312, ending inventory; $8,083, cost of goods sold **9.** $4,821.43, $4,500; $2,892.85; $1,285.72; $1,446.43; $1,928.57; $1,125 **11.** 4

Trial Test (pp. 441–443)

1. $1,237 **3.** $601 **5.** $761.76, ending inventory; $475.24, cost of goods sold **7.** $892, ending inventory; $345, cost of goods sold **9.** 4

CHAPTER 15

Section Review (p. 456)

1. $11,271, total current assets; $23,458, total assets; $3,098, total current liabilities; $3,098, total liabilities; $23,458, total liabilities and owner's equity

Section Review (p. 462)

1. $225,108, net sales; $112,229, cost of goods sold; $112,879, gross profit from sales; $61,689, total operating expenses; $51,190, net income. Percent of net sales column: 106.1%, 6.1%, 100%, 11.5%, 48.8%, 10.4%, 49.9%, 50.1%, 18.9%, 3.8%, 0.7%, 1.3%, 0.4%, 0.9%, 1.5%, 27.4%, 22.7%.

Section Review (p. 467)

1. 1.57 to 1 **3.** 1.39 to 1 **5.** 0.87 to 1 **7.** 0.9 or 90%, operating ratio; 0.25 or 25%, gross profit margin

Chapter Review (pp. 470–472)

1. 19X9 column: $9,264, total current assets; $8,935, total plant and equipment; $18,199, total assets; $6,611, total current liabilities; $7,335, total liabilities; $18,199, total liabilities and owner's equity. 19X8 column: $8,710, total current assets; $7,314, total plant and equipment; $16,024, total assets; $5,019, total current liabilities; $5,726, total liabilities; $16,024, total liabilities and owner's equity. Increase or decrease columns: $646, 22.9%; ($235, 12.9%); $143, 3.5%; $554, 6.4%; $1,621, 22.2%; $1,621, 22.2%; $2,175, 13.6%; $2,399, 62.9%; ($807, 67.1%); $1,592, 31.7%; $17, 2.4%; $1,609, 28.1%; $566, 5.5%; $2,175, 13.6%. **3.** $282,424, net sales; $114,148, cost of goods sold; $168,276, gross profit from sales; $40,685, total operating expenses; $127,591, net income. Percent of net sales column: 102.5%, 2.5%, 100%, 3.4%, 41.5%, 4.4%, 40.4%, 59.6%, 8.9%, 1.4%, 0.9% 1.5%, 1.7%, 14.4%, 45.2%. **5.** 2.56 to 1 **7.** Yes. **9.** 0.35 or 35%

Trial Test (pp. 473–474)

1. 19X7 column: $74,059, total current assets; $44,817, total plant and equip.; $118,876, total assets; $5,954, total current liabilities; $34,917, total long-term liabilities; $40,871, total liabilities; $118,876, total liabilities and owner's equity. 19X6 column: $68,478, total current assets; $41,917, total plant and equip.; $110,395, total assets; $5,187, total current liabilities; $36,510, total long-term liabilities; $41,697, total liabilities; $110,395, total liabilities and owner's equity. Increase or decrease columns: $2,035, 38.5%; $139, 4.6%; $3,407, 5.7%; $5,581, 8.2%; ($970, 2.6%); $3,870, 88.2%; $2,900, 6.9%; $8,481, 7.7%; $611, 13.4%; $156, 25.0%; $767, 14.8%; ($1,593, 4.4%); ($1,593, 4.4%); ($826, 2.0%); $9,307, 13.5%; $8,481, 7.7%. **3.** 1.76 to 1 **5.** 1.60 to 1 **7.** 0.64 or 64% for both 19X6 and 19X7

CHAPTER 16

Section Review (pp. 481–483)

1. $273.60, $124.80 **3.** $545.20, $237.69 **5.** $661.50, $508 **7.** $20,754.18 **9.** $46,928.78 **11.** $30,000 **13.** $562.50 **15.** $58,800 **17.** $286.74 **19. a.** $483.82 **b.** $246.75

Section Review (pp. 485–486)

1. $300 **3.** $366 **5.** $418 **7.** $361 **9.** $10,000 **11.** $177.50 **13. a.** $81.75 **b.** $327 **15. a.** $295 **b.** $50,000 medical expenses, $5,678 property damage

Section Review (pp. 491–492)

1. $132.90 **3.** $601.80 **5.** $2,945 **7.** $113.46 **9.** $547.17 **13. a.** $338.25 **b.** $87.95 **15.** $7.57 more per $1,000 **17.** $37.38 **19.** $980.43

Chapter Review (pp. 495–497)

1. $424.38 **3.** $15,300 **5.** $272 **7.** $1,197.60 **9.** $31,318.68 **11.** $295 **13.** $181.56 **15. a.** $40,000 **b.** $0 **17.** $87.52 **19.** $92,000

Trial Test (pp. 498–500)

1. $2,078.60 **3.** $65,625 **5.** $181.65 **7.** $53 more **9.** $727.42 **13.** $71.52 **15.** $425 **17.** 86% **19.** $177.50

CHAPTER 17

Section Review (p. 508)

1. $0.18 **3.** $0.63 **5.** $0.37 **7.** $0.77 **9.** $0.51 **11.** $14.25 **13.** $58.24 **15.** $33.80 **17.** $26.14 **19.** $332.33 **21.** $84.31

Section Review (pp. 512–515)

1. $13,750 **3.** $46,000 **5.** $2,587,500,000 **7.** $787.50 **9.** $10,350 **11.** $1,309 **13.** $4,062.50 **15.** $382.50 **17.** $5,648 **19.** $2,325 **21.** $444.41 **23.** $0.034 **25.** $0.051 **27.** $1,280.13 **29.** $1,840 **31.** $33.99 **33.** $49.73 **35.** $65.54

Section Review (p. 517)

1. $10,555 **3.** $12,301 **5.** $48,250

Section Review (pp. 522–523)

1. $3,203 **3.** $2,111 **5.** $2,546 **7.** $4,271 **9.** $11,301.18 **11.** $11,229

Chapter Review (pp. 526–529)

1. $0.84 **3.** $0.03 **5.** $0.96 **7.** $0.95 (rounded) **9.** $8.61 (rounded) **11.** $0.18 (rounded) **13.** $187.44 sales tax, $299.90 excise tax, $487.34 total tax, $3,486.34 total cost. **15.** $4.01 (rounded) **17.** $83.92 (rounded) **19.** $523.95 **21.** $300.20 **23.** $2,579.12 **25.** $492.49 (rounded) **27.** $2,363.76 **29.** $4,913.20 **31.** $8,931.80 **33.** $0.04 (rounded up) **35.** $47,134 **37.** $22,529.86 **39.** $24,800.43

Trial Test (pp. 530–532)

1. $0.76 (rounded) **3.** $22.28 (rounded) **5.** $198.44 **7.** $17.61 (rounded) **9.** $50 (rounded) **11.** $97.62 **13.** $39,471.64 (rounded) **15.** $1,071.77 (rounded) **17.** $4,073.34 **19.** $1,850.40 **21.** $6,991 **23.** $46,400

CHAPTER 18

Section Review (pp. 543–546)

1. a. 9,700 **b.** $7\frac{5}{8}$ points ($7.625) **c.** $17\frac{5}{8}$ **d.** no change, $17\frac{5}{8}$ **3. a.** $2.10, $105, $210 **b.** $71\frac{3}{8}$ ($71.375) **c.** 2.9% **5.** A. A's yield is ten times B's. **7. a.** $30,000 **b.** $30,000 **c.** $440,000 **d.** $2.20 per share **9.** 12.5, or 13 **11. a.** $76.05 **b.** $3,586.05 **13. a.** gain of $53.35 **b.** ROI = 2.8%

Section Review (pp. 551–553)

1. a. 10 **b.** $96.25 **c.** 2006 **3. a.** $280 **b.** $1,450 **5.** $892.50 **7.** $9,725 **9. a.** $8.75 **b.** $17.50 **c.** seller **11.** 10.7% **13. a.** $8\frac{1}{3}$% **b.** 10% **c.** Bond B

Chapter Review (pp. 557–560)

1. a. Last year's high price of $28\frac{3}{8}$ **b.** Last year's low price of $22\frac{1}{4}$ **c.** Stock name, AVEMCO **d.** $0.40 per share annual dividend **e.** Current stock yield, 1.7% **f.** Price-earning ratio, 12 **g.** 2,000 shares traded today **h.** Today's high price 24 ($24) **i.** Today's low price, $23\frac{3}{4}$ ($23.75) **j.** Today's closing price, 24 ($24) **k.** Today's closing price is up $\frac{1}{8}$ from yesterday's. **3.** $4,406.25 **5.** 7.2% **7.** common stock **9. a.** $4,040 **b.** premium **11. a.** $61.25 **b.** increased **c.** $6,800 **13. a.** $4,750 **b.** $4,887.50 **c.** 21% **15. a.** Stock A: 60%, Stock B: 76.6% **b.** Stock B.

Trial Test (pp. 561–564)

1. a. $\frac{3}{4}$ point or 0.75 **b.** $66.75 per share **c.** $67.125 per share **d.** 76,300 **3. a.** $131.30 **b.** $6,191.30 **5.** 28.5% **7.** Stock A: 4.9%; Stock B: 4.2% **9. a.** 1995 **b.** $898.75 per bond **c.** $895 **d.** yes; no **11. a.** $25 **b.** $4,275 **13.** preferred **15. a.** Stock A: 15%, Stock B: 12% **b.** Stock A

CHAPTER 19

Section Review (pp. 566–567)

1. 795 **3.** 3,997 **5.** 2,531 **7.** Period 5 **9.** 54.4%

Section Review (pp. 572–574)

1. 19X1: $65,153; 19X2: $68,324 **3.** (b) **5.** 70°; 90° **7.** (b) **9.** (c) **11.** 276°

Section Review (p. 578)

1. Range: 14, mean: 22, median: 22, no mode **3.** Range: 1.02, mean: 1.44, median: 1.46, mode: 1.65

Chapter Review (pp. 581–583)

1. 4,889 **3.** 1.23 **5.** Ocean Front Autos: 533 **7.** 36% **9.** Range: 15, mean: 6.4, median: 5, mode: 3 **11.** Range: $60.28, mean: $112.26, median: $127.83, mode: $136.52 **13.** $7,763 **15.** 5.7% **17.** 97 **19.** 1,584

Trial Test (pp. 584–586)

1. 77 **3.** 29.5 **5.** 110 **7.** 165 **9.** $120 **11.** 33.3% **13.** Labor: 135°, materials: 119.9°, overhead: 105.1° **15.** $5,829 **17.** Least: 43, greatest: 1,117 **19.** (d)

Index

Glossary terms are defined on the page on which they occur. Pages where glossary terms appear are indicated in the index by a **boldface** page number.